III

Lectures and Essays in Criticism

MATTHEW ARNOLD

LECTURES AND ESSAYS IN CRITICISM

Edited by R. H. Super
With the Assistance of Sister Thomas Marion Hoctor

ANN ARBOR   THE UNIVERSITY OF MICHIGAN PRESS

112816

Manufactured in the United States of America by
Vail-Ballou Press, Inc., Binghamton, New York

Editor's Preface

This third volume of Arnold's prose works contains the first series of *Essays in Criticism* (with the exception of "A Persian Passion Play," which will appear in a later volume), *On the Study of Celtic Literature*, and four critical essays of the period 1862–63 that Arnold did not reprint. One of these, the anonymous review of Willis's translation of Spinoza's *Tractatus Theologico-Politicus*, was first traced by the present editor from Arnold's quarterly accounts. (Another anonymous article on "The Illuminations," recently claimed for Arnold in *PMLA*, LXXVI, 622 [December, 1961] must be rejected both on external evidence and on grounds of style.) Except for his terminal lecture on "Culture and Its Enemies," all Arnold's surviving discourses from the Chair of Poetry at Oxford will be found either in the first volume or in the present one.

Shortly after my edition of Arnold was projected, and before any editorial work on the third volume was undertaken, Sister Thomas Marion Hoctor, acting on the thoughtful suggestion of her supervisor, Professor Robert A. Donovan of Cornell University, called my attention to an edition of *Essays in Criticism* which she had prepared as a doctoral dissertation and expressed the hope that it would facilitate my work. Though I have depended entirely on my own collation and have taken over none of her explanatory notes as they stand, and though she has no responsibility for any part of the present edition in its final form, I am with her consent acknowledging my respect for her painstakingly accurate work, my sense of the many weeks by which she shortened my labors, and my gratitude for her kindness by placing her name on the title page.

The principles upon which this volume is edited are those which governed the first and second volumes. The text is the latest which could have had Arnold's attention; for most of the volume this is the edition printed in Edinburgh for Macmillan and Company of New York in 1883. Variants in the language of earlier texts (if any) are recorded in the Textual Notes; variants in punctuation are generally ignored. Manifest misprints are corrected, but if there is any reasonable suspicion that they were errors of the author rather than the typesetter the fact of the correction is recorded. Notes at the bottom of the page are by Arnold himself, unless bracketed.

Fraser Neiman's edition of *Essays, Letters, and Reviews by Matthew Arnold* (Cambridge: Harvard University Press, 1960), which contains five of the items printed here, reached me after most of the present volume was completed; I have acknowledged my debt to him in several instances and expect to owe much more to his scholarship in future volumes. Another work which came into my hands too late to be helpful here was the dissertation by Charles T. Wilkins, *The English Reputation of Matthew Arnold, 1840–1877* (Ann Arbor: University Microfilms, 1959); Professor Wilkins has now generously given me copies he has assembled of the less accessible reviews of all Arnold's works, and I expect to place myself further in his debt also as this edition advances. His dissertation adds impressively to the list of known writings about Arnold and is an admirable bibliographical study. To two of my former seminar students, Donald E. Billiar and John C. Mathes, to Professors Roger L. Brooks of the Texas Technological College and S. M. B. Coulling of Washington and Lee University, and to my colleagues Professors Otto G. Graf, Leo F. McNamara, and Paul M. Spurlin, I owe thanks for most useful assistance in details.

The volume was prepared during a year's leave of absence from teaching made possible by a fellowship from the American Council of Learned Societies. The Horace H. Rackham School of Graduate Studies at The University of Michigan has provided funds for expenses incurred in its preparation and has advanced the cost of its publication. The editor is most grateful for the generous support of these two bodies.

Ann Arbor, Michigan

Contents

Essays in Criticism

First Series

"*Our antagonist is our helper. This amicable conflict with difficulty obliges us to an intimate acquaintance with our object, and compels us to consider it in all its relations. It will not suffer us to be superficial.*"

—BURKE.

Dante and Beatrice

Those critics who allegorize the *Divine Comedy*, who exaggerate, or, rather, who mistake the supersensual element in Dante's work, who reduce to nothing the sensible and human element, are hardly worth refuting. They know nothing of the necessary laws under which poetic genius works, of the inevitable conditions under which the creations of poetry are produced. But, in their turn, those other critics err hardly less widely, who exaggerate, or, rather, who mistake the human and real element in Dante's poem; who see, in such a passion as that of Dante for Beatrice, an affection belonging to the sphere of actual domestic life, fitted to sustain the wear and tear of our ordinary daily existence. Into the error of these second critics an accomplished recent translator of Dante, Mr. Theodore Martin, seems to me to have fallen. He has ever present to his mind, when he speaks of the Beatrice whom Dante adored, Wordsworth's picture of—

> The perfect woman, nobly planned
> To warm, to comfort, and command;
> And yet a spirit still, and bright
> With something of an angel light.

He is ever quoting these lines in connexion with Dante's Beatrice; ever assimilating to this picture Beatrice as Dante conceived her; ever attributing to Dante's passion a character identical with that of the affection which Wordsworth, in the poem from which these lines are taken, meant to portray. The affection here portrayed by Wordsworth is, I grant, a substantial human affection, inhabiting the domain of real life, at the same time that it is poetical and beautiful. But in order to give this

3

flesh-and-blood character to Dante's passion for Beatrice, what a task has Mr. Martin to perform! how much is he obliged to imagine! how much to shut his eyes to, or to disbelieve! Not perceiving that the vital impulse of Dante's soul is towards reverie and spiritual vision; that the task Dante sets himself is not the task of reconciling poetry and reality, of giving to each its due part, of supplementing the one by the other; but the task of sacrificing the world to the spirit, of making the spirit all in all, of effacing the world in presence of the spirit—Mr. Martin seeks to find a Dante admirable and complete in the life of the world as well as in the life of the spirit; and when he cannot find him, he invents him. Dante saw the world, and used in his poetry what he had seen; for he was a born artist. But he was essentially aloof from the world, and not complete in the life of the world; for he was a born spiritualist and solitary. Keeping in our minds this, his double character, we may seize the exact truth as to his relations with Beatrice, and steer a right course between the error of those who deliteralize them too much, on the one hand, and that of those who literalize them too much, on the other.

The *Divine Comedy*, I have already said, is no allegory, and Beatrice no mere personification of theology. Mr. Martin is quite right in saying that Beatrice is the Beatrice whom men turned round to gaze at in the streets of Florence; that she is no 'allegorical phantom,' no 'fiction purely ideal.' He is quite right in saying that Dante 'worships no phantoms,' that his passion for Beatrice was a real passion, and that his love-poetry does not deal 'in the attributes of celestial charms.' He was an artist—one of the greatest of artists; and art abhors what is vague, hollow, and impalpable.

Enough to make this fully manifest we have in the *Vita Nuova*. Dante there records how, a boy of ten, he first saw Beatrice, a girl of nine, dressed in crimson; how, a second time, he saw her, nine years later, passing along the street, dressed in white, between two ladies older than herself, and how she saluted him. He records how afterwards she once denied him her salutation; he records the profound impression which, at her father's death, the grief and beauty of Beatrice made on all those who visited her; he records his meeting with her at a party after her marriage, his emotion, and how some ladies present, observing his emotion, 'made a mock of him to that most gentle being;' he records her death, and how, a year afterwards, some gentlemen found him, on the anniversary of her death, 'sketching an angel on his tablets.' He tells us how, a little later, he had a vision of the dead Beatrice 'arrayed in the same crimson robe in which she had originally appeared to my eyes, and she seemed as youthful as on the day I saw her first.' He mentions how, one day, the sight of some pilgrims passing along a particular street in Florence brought to his mind the thought that perhaps these pilgrims, coming from a far country, had never even heard the name of her who filled his thoughts so entirely. And even in the *Divine Comedy*, composed many years afterwards, and treating of the glorified Beatrice only, one distinct trait of the earthly Beatrice is still preserved—her smile; the *santo riso* of the *Purgatory*, the *dolce riso* of the *Paradise*.

Yes, undoubtedly there was a real Beatrice, whom Dante had seen living and moving before him, and for whom he had felt a passion. This basis of fact and reality he took from the life of the outward world: this basis was indispensable to him, for he was an artist.

But this basis was enough for him as an artist: to have seen Beatrice two or three times, to have spoken to her two or three times, to have felt her beauty, her charm; to have had the emotion of her marriage, her death—this was enough. Art requires a basis of fact, but it also desires to treat this basis of fact with the utmost freedom; and this desire for the freest handling of its object is even thwarted when its object is too near, and too real. To have had his relations with Beatrice more positive, intimate, and prolonged, to have had an affection for her into which there entered more of the life of this world, would have even somewhat impeded, one may say, Dante's free use of these relations for the purpose of art. And the artist nature in him was in little danger of being thus impeded; for he was a born solitary.

Thus the conditions of art do not make it necessary that Dante's relations with Beatrice should have been more close

and real than the *Vita Nuova* represents them; and the conditions of Dante's own nature do not make it probable. Not
the less do such admirers of the poet as Mr. Martin—mis-
conceiving the essential characteristic of chivalrous passion
5   in general, and of Dante's divinization of Beatrice in particular,
misled by imagining this 'worship for woman,' as they call
it, to be something which it was not, something involving
modern relations in social life between the two sexes—insist
upon making out of Dante's adoration of Beatrice a substantial
10 modern love-story, and of arranging Dante's real life so as to
turn it into the proper sort of real life for a 'worshipper of
woman' to lead. The few real incidents of Dante's passion,
enumerated in the *Vita Nuova*, sufficient to give to his great
poem the basis which it required, are far too scanty to give to
15 such a love-story as this the basis which it requires; therefore
they must be developed and amplified. Beatrice was a living
woman, and Dante had seen her; but she must become

> The creature not too bright and good
> For human nature's daily food,

20 of Wordsworth's poem: she must become 'pure flesh and blood
—beautiful, yet substantial,' and 'moulded of that noble humanity wherewith Heaven blesses, not unfrequently, our common earth.' Dante had saluted Beatrice, had spoken to her;
but this is not enough: he has surely omitted to 'record par-
25 ticulars:' it is 'scarcely credible that he should not have found
an opportunity of directly declaring his attachment;' for 'in
position, education, and appearance he was a man worth any
woman,' and his face 'at that time of his life must have been
eminently engaging.' Therefore 'it seems strange that his love
30 should not have found its issue in marriage;' for 'he loved Beatrice as a man loves, and with the passion that naturally per-
severes to the possession of its mistress.'

However, his love did *not* find its issue in marriage. Beatrice
married Messer Simone dei Bardi, to whom, says Mr. Martin,
35 'her hand had been, perhaps lightly or to please her parents,
pledged, in ignorance of the deep and noble passion which
she had inspired in the young poet's heart.' But she certainly

could not 'have been insensible to his profound tenderness and
passion;' although whether 'she knew of it before her marriage,'
and whether 'she, either then or afterwards, gave it her countenance and approval, and returned it in any way, and in what
degree'—questions which, Mr. Martin says, 'naturally suggest
themselves'—are, he confesses, questions for solving which 'the
materials are most scanty and unsatisfactory.' 'Unquestion-
ably,' he adds, 'it startles and grieves us to find Beatrice taking
part with her friends' in laughing at Dante when he was overcome at first meeting her after her marriage. 'But there may,'
he thinks, 'have been causes for this—causes for which, in justice
to her, allowance must be made, even as we see that Dante made
it.' Then, again, as to Messer Simone dei Bardi's feelings about
this attachment of Dante to his wife. 'It is true,' says Mr. Martin, 'that we have no direct information on this point;' but
'the love of Dante was of an order too pure and noble to occasion distrust, even if the purity of Beatrice had not placed her
above suspicion;' but Dante 'did what only a great and manly
nature could have done—he triumphed over his pain; he uttered
no complaint; his regrets were buried within his own heart.'
'At the same time,' Mr. Martin thinks, 'it is contrary to human
nature that a love unfed by any tokens of favour should retain
all its original force; and without wrong either to Beatrice or
Dante, we may conclude that an understanding was come to
between them, which in some measure soothed his heart, if
it did not satisfy it.' And 'sooner or later, before Beatrice died,
we cannot doubt that there came a day when words passed
between them which helped to reconcile Dante to the doom
that severed her from his side during her all too brief sojourn
on earth, when the pent-up heart of the poet swept down the
barriers within which it had so long struggled, and he

> Caught up the whole of love, and utter'd it,
> Then bade adieu for ever,

if not to her, yet to all those words which it was no longer meet
should be spoken to another's wife.'

But Dante married, as well as Beatrice; and so Dante's married
life has to be *arranged* also. 'It is,' says Mr. Martin, 'only

those who have observed little of human nature, or of their own hearts, who will think that Dante's marriage with Gemma Donati argues against the depth or sincerity of his first love. Why should he not have sought the solace and the support of a generous woman's nature, who, knowing all the truth, was yet content with such affection as he was able to bring to a second love? Nor was that necessarily small. Ardent and affectionate as his nature was, the sympathies of such a woman must have elicited from him a satisfactory response; while, at the same time, without prejudice to the wife's claim on his regard, he might entertain his heavenward dream of the departed Beatrice.' The tradition is, however, that Dante did not live happily with his wife; and some have thought that he means to cast a disparaging reflection on his marriage in a passage of the *Purgatory*. I need not say that this sort of thing would never do for Mr. Martin's hero—that hero who can do nothing 'inconsistent with the purest respect to her who had been the wedded wife of another, on the one hand, or with his regard for the mother of his children, on the other.' Accordingly, 'are we to assume,' Mr. Martin cries, 'that the woman who gave herself to him in the full knowledge that she was not the bride of his imagination, was not regarded by him with the esteem which her devotion was calculated to inspire?' It is quite impossible. 'Dante was a true-hearted gentleman, and could never have spoken slightingly of her on whose breast he had found comfort amid many a sorrow, and who had borne to him a numerous progeny—the last a Beatrice.' Donna Gemma was a 'generous and devoted woman,' and she and Dante 'thoroughly understood each other.'

All this has, as applied to real personages, the grave defect of being entirely of Mr. Martin's own imagining. But it has a still graver defect, I think, as applied to Dante, in being so singularly inappropriate to its object. The grand, impracticable Solitary, with keen senses and ardent passions—for nature had made him an artist, and art must be, as Milton says, 'sensuous and impassioned'—but with an irresistible bent to the inward life, the life of imagination, vision, and ecstacy; with an inherent impatience of the outward life, the life of distraction, jostling,

mutual concession; this man 'of a humour which made him hard
to get on with,' says Petrarch; 'melancholy and pensive,' says
Boccaccio; 'by nature abstracted and taciturn, seldom speaking
unless he was questioned, and often so absorbed in his own
reflections that he did not hear the questions which were put
to him;' who could not live with the Florentines, who could
not live with Gemma Donati, who could not live with Can
Grande della Scala; this lover of Beatrice, but of Beatrice a
vision of his youth, hardly at all in contact with him in actual
life, vanished from him soon, with whom his imagination could
deal freely, whom he could divinize into a fit object for the
spiritual longing which filled him—this Dante is transformed,
in Mr. Martin's hands, into the hero of a sentimental, but strictly
virtuous, novel! To make out Dante to have been eminent for
a wise, complete conduct of his outward life, seems to me as
unimportant as it is impossible. I can quite believe the tradition
which represents him as not having lived happily with his wife,
and attributes her not having joined him in his exile to this
cause. I can even believe, without difficulty, an assertion of
Boccaccio which excites Mr. Martin's indignation, that Dante's
conduct, even in mature life, was at times exceedingly irregular.
We know how the followers of the spiritual life tend to be
antinomian in what belongs to the outward life: they do not
attach much importance to such irregularity themselves; it
is their fault, as complete men, that they do not; it is the fault
of the spiritual life, as a complete life, that it allows this tendency: by dint of despising the outward life, it loses the control
of this life, and of itself when in contact with it. My present
business, however, is not to praise or blame Dante's practical
conduct of his life, but to make clear his peculiar mental and
spiritual constitution. This, I say, disposed him to absorb himself
in the inner life, wholly to humble and efface before this the
outward life. We may see this in the passage of the *Purgatory*
where he makes Beatrice reprove him for his backslidings after
she, his visible symbol of spiritual perfection, had vanished
from his eyes.

'For a while'—she says of him to the 'pious substances,'
the angels—'for a while with my countenance I upheld him;

showing to him my youthful eyes, with me I led him, turned
towards the right way.

'Soon as I came on the threshold of my second age, and
changed my life, this man took himself from me and gave him-
5   self to others.

'When that I had mounted from flesh to spirit, and beauty
and spirit were increased unto me, I was to him less dear and
less acceptable.

'He turned his steps to go in a way not true, pursuing after
10   false images of good, which fulfil nothing of the promises
which they give.

'Neither availed it me that I obtained inspirations to be
granted me, whereby, both in dream and otherwise, I called
him back; so little heed paid he to them.

15   'So deep he fell, that, for his salvation all means came short,
except to show him the people of perdition.

'The high decree of God would be broken, could Lethe be
passed, and that so fair aliment tasted, without some scot paid
of repentance, which pours forth tears.'

20   Here, indeed, and in a somewhat similar passage of the next
canto, Mr. Martin thinks that the 'obvious allusion' is to certain moral shortcomings, occasional slips, of which (though he
treats Boccaccio's imputation as monstrous and incredible)
'Dante, with his strong and ardent passions, having, like meaner
25   men, to fight the perennial conflict between flesh and spirit,'
had sometimes, he supposes, been guilty. An Italian commentator gives at least as true an interpretation of these passages when
he says that 'in them Dante makes Beatrice, as the representative
of theology, lament that he should have left the study of
30   divinity—in which, by the grace of Heaven, he might have
attained admirable proficiency—to immerse himself in civil
affairs with the parties of Florence.' But the real truth is, that
all the life of the world, its pleasures, its business, its parties,
its politics, all is alike hollow and miserable to Dante in com-
35   parison with the inward life, the ecstacy of the divine vision;
every way which does not lead straight towards this is for
him a *via non vera;* every good thing but this is for him a
false image of good, fulfilling none of the promises which it

gives; for the excellency of the knowledge of this he counts
all things but loss. Beatrice leads him to this; herself symbolises
for him the ineffable beauty and purity for which he longs.
Even to Dante at twenty-one, when he yet sees the living
Beatrice with his eyes, she already symbolises this for him, she   5
is already not the 'creature not too bright and good' of Wordsworth, but a spirit far more than a woman; to Dante at twenty-
five composing the *Vita Nuova* she is still more a spirit; to
Dante at fifty, when his character has taken its bent, when
his genius is come to its perfection, when he is composing his   10
immortal poem, she is a spirit altogether.

Maurice de Guérin

I will not presume to say that I now know the French language well; but at a time when I knew it even less well than at present,—some fifteen years ago,—I remember pestering those about me with this sentence, the rhythm of which had lodged itself in my head, and which, with the strangest pronunciation possible, I kept perpetually declaiming: "*Les dieux jaloux ont enfoui quelque part les témoignages de la descendance des choses; mais au bord de quel Océan ont-ils roulé la pierre qui les couvre, ô Macarée!*"

These words come from a short composition called the *Centaur*, of which the author, Georges-Maurice de Guérin, died in the year 1839, at the age of twenty-eight, without having published anything. In 1840, Madame Sand brought out the *Centaur* in the *Revue des Deux Mondes*, with a short notice of its author, and a few extracts from his letters. A year or two afterwards she reprinted these at the end of a volume of her novels; and there it was that I fell in with them. I was so much struck with the *Centaur* that I waited anxiously to hear something more of its author, and of what he had left; but it was not till the other day—twenty years after the first publication of the *Centaur* in the *Revue des Deux Mondes*, that my anxiety was satisfied. At the end of 1860 appeared two volumes with the title *Maurice de Guérin, Reliquiæ*, containing the *Centaur*, several poems of Guérin, his journals, and a number of his letters, collected and edited by a devoted friend, M. Trebutien, and preceded by a notice of Guérin by the first of living critics, M. Sainte-Beuve.

The grand power of poetry is its interpretative power; by which I mean, not a power of drawing out in black and white

an explanation of the mystery of the universe, but the power
of so dealing with things as to awaken in us a wonderfully full,
new, and intimate sense of them, and of our relations with
them. When this sense is awakened in us, as to objects without
us, we feel ourselves to be in contact with the essential nature   5
of those objects, to be no longer bewildered and oppressed
by them, but to have their secret, and to be in harmony with
them; and this feeling calms and satisfies us as no other can.
Poetry, indeed, interprets in another way besides this; but one
of its two ways of interpreting, of exercising its highest power,   10
is by awakening this sense in us. I will not now inquire whether
this sense is illusive, whether it can be proved not to be illusive,
whether it does absolutely make us possess the real nature of
things; all I say is, that poetry can awaken it in us, and that
to awaken it is one of the highest powers of poetry. The in-   15
terpretations of science do not give us this intimate sense of
objects as the interpretations of poetry give it; they appeal to
a limited faculty, and not to the whole man. It is not Linnæus
or Cavendish or Cuvier who gives us the true sense of animals,
or water, or plants, who seizes their secret for us, who makes   20
us participate in their life; it is Shakspeare, with his

> "daffodils
> That come before the swallow dares, and take
> The winds of March with beauty;"

it is Wordsworth, with his   25
> "voice . . . heard
> In spring-time from the cuckoo-bird,
> Breaking the silence of the seas
> Among the farthest Hebrides;"

it is Keats, with his   30

> "moving waters at their priestlike task
> Of cold ablution round Earth's human shores;"

it is Chateaubriand, with his *"cîme indéterminée des forêts";*
it is Senancour, with his mountain birch-tree: *"Cette écorce
blanche, lisse et crevassée; cette tige agreste; ces branches qui*   35
*s'inclinent vers la terre; la mobilité des feuilles, et tout cet
abandon, simplicité de la nature, attitude des déserts."*

Eminent manifestations of this magical power of poetry are
very rare and very precious: the compositions of Guérin manifest it, I think, in singular eminence. Not his poems, strictly so
called,—his verse,—so much as his prose; his poems in general
5 take for their vehicle that favourite metre of French poetry,
the Alexandrine; and, in my judgment, I confess they have thus,
as compared with his prose, a great disadvantage to start with.
In prose, the character of the vehicle for the composer's
thoughts is not determined beforehand; every composer has to
10 make his own vehicle; and who has ever done this more admirably than the great prose-writers of France,—Pascal,
Bossuet, Fénelon, Voltaire? But in verse the composer has
(with comparatively narrow liberty of modification) to accept
his vehicle ready-made; it is therefore of vital importance to him
15 that he should find at his disposal a vehicle adequate to convey
the highest matters of poetry. We may even get a decisive test
of the poetical power of a language and nation by ascertaining
how far the principal poetical vehicle which they have employed, how far (in plainer words) the established national
20 metre for high poetry, is adequate or inadequate. It seems to
me that the established metre of this kind in France,—the Alexandrine,—is inadequate; that as a vehicle for high poetry it is
greatly inferior to the hexameter or to the iambics of Greece
(for example), or to the blank verse of England. Therefore the
25 man of genius who uses it is at a disadvantage as compared with
the man of genius who has for conveying his thoughts a more
adequate vehicle, metrical or not. Racine is at a disadvantage as
compared with Sophocles or Shakspeare, and he is likewise
at a disadvantage as compared with Bossuet.
30   The same may be said of our own poets of the eighteenth
century, a century which gave them as the main vehicle for
their high poetry a metre inadequate (as much as the French
Alexandrine, and nearly in the same way) for this poetry,—
the ten-syllable couplet. It is worth remarking, that the English
35 poet of the eighteenth century whose compositions wear best
and give one the most entire satisfaction,—Gray,—hardly uses
that couplet at all: this abstinence, however, limits Gray's

productions to a few short compositions, and (exquisite as these
are) he is a poetical nature repressed and without free issue.
For English poetical production on a great scale, for an English
poet deploying all the forces of his genius, the ten-syllable
couplet was, in the eighteenth century, the established, one   5
may almost say the inevitable, channel. Now this couplet, admirable (as Chaucer uses it) for story-telling not of the epic
pitch, and often admirable for a few lines even in poetry of
a very high pitch, is for continuous use in poetry of this latter
kind inadequate. Pope, in his *Essay on Man,* is thus at a dis-   10
advantage compared with Lucretius in his poem on Nature:
Lucretius has an adequate vehicle, Pope has not. Nay, though
Pope's genius for didactic poetry was not less than that of
Horace, while his satirical power was certainly greater, still
one's taste receives, I cannot but think, a certain satisfaction   15
when one reads the Epistles and Satires of Horace, which it fails
to receive when one reads the Satires and Epistles of Pope. Of
such avail is the superior adequacy of the vehicle used to com-
pensate even an inferiority of genius in the user! In the same
way Pope is at a disadvantage as compared with Addison. The   20
best of Addison's composition (the "Coverley Papers" in the
Spectator, for instance) wears better than the best of Pope's,
because Addison has in his prose an intrinsically better vehicle
for his genius than Pope in his couplet. But Bacon has no such
advantage over Shakspeare; nor has Milton, writing prose (for   25
no contemporary English prose-writer must be matched with
Milton except Milton himself), any such advantage over Milton
writing verse: indeed, the advantage here is all the other way.
    It is in the prose remains of Guérin,—his journals, his letters,
and the striking composition which I have already mentioned,   30
the *Centaur,*—that his extraordinary gift manifests itself. He has
a truly interpretative faculty; the most profound and delicate
sense of the life of Nature, and the most exquisite felicity in
finding expressions to render that sense. To all who love poetry,
Guérin deserves to be something more than a name; and I shall   35
try, in spite of the impossibility of doing justice to such a master
of expression by translations, to make English readers see for

themselves how gifted an organisation his was, and how few
artists have received from Nature a more magical faculty of
interpreting her.

In the winter of the year 1832 there was collected in Brit-
5   tany, around the well-known Abbé Lamennais, a singular
gathering. At a lonely place, La Chênaie, he had founded a
religious retreat, to which disciples, attracted by his powers
or by his reputation, repaired. Some came with the intention
of preparing themselves for the ecclesiastical profession; others
10 merely to profit by the society and discourse of so distinguished
a master. Among the inmates were men whose names have since
become known to all Europe,—Lacordaire and M. de Montalembert; there were others, who have acquired a reputation,
not European, indeed, but considerable,—the Abbé Gerbet, the
15 Abbé Rohrbacher; others, who have never quitted the shade of
private life. The winter of 1832 was a period of crisis in the
religious world of France: Lamennais's rupture with Rome, the
condemnation of his opinions by the Pope, and his revolt against
that condemnation, were imminent. Some of his followers, like
20 Lacordaire, had already resolved not to cross the Rubicon with
their leader, not to go into rebellion against Rome; they were
preparing to separate from him. The society of La Chênaie was
soon to dissolve; but, such as it is shown to us for a moment,
with its voluntary character, its simple and severe life in com-
25 mon, its mixture of lay and clerical members, the genius of its
chiefs, the sincerity of its disciples,—above all, its paramount
fervent interest in matters of spiritual and religious concern-
ment,—it offers a most instructive spectacle. It is not the spectacle we most of us think to find in France, the France we have
30 imagined from common English notions, from the streets of
Paris, from novels; it shows us how, wherever there is greatness
like that of France, there are, as its foundation, treasures of
fervour, pure-mindedness, and spirituality somewhere, whether
we know of them or not;—a store of that which Goethe calls
35 *Halt;*—since greatness can never be founded upon frivolity
and corruption.
   On the evening of the 18th of December in this year 1832,

M. de Lamennais was talking to those assembled in the sitting-room of La Chênaie of his recent journey to Italy. He talked with all his usual animation; "but," writes one of his hearers, a Breton gentleman, M. de Marzan, "I soon became inattentive and absent, being struck with the reserved attitude of a young stranger some twenty-two years old, pale in face, his black hair already thin over his temples, with a southern eye, in which brightness and melancholy were mingled. He kept himself somewhat aloof, seeming to avoid notice rather than to court it. All the old faces of friends which I found about me at this my re-entry into the circle of La Chênaie failed to occupy me so much as the sight of this stranger, looking on, listening, observing, and saying nothing."

The unknown was Maurice de Guérin. Of a noble but poor family, having lost his mother at six years old, he had been brought up by his father, a man saddened by his wife's death, and austerely religious, at the château of Le Cayla, in Languedoc. His childhood was not gay; he had not the society of other boys; and solitude, the sight of his father's gloom, and the habit of accompanying the curé of the parish on his rounds among the sick and dying, made him prematurely grave and familiar with sorrow. He went to school first at Toulouse, then at the Collège Stanislas at Paris, with a temperament almost as unfit as Shelley's for common school life. His youth was ardent, sensitive, agitated, and unhappy. In 1832 he procured admission to La Chênaie to brace his spirit by the teaching of Lamennais, and to decide whether his religious feelings would determine themselves into a distinct religious vocation. Strong and deep religious feelings he had, implanted in him by nature, developed in him by the circumstances of his childhood; but he had also (and here is the key to his character) that temperament which opposes itself to the fixedness of a religious vocation, or of any vocation of which fixedness is an essential attribute; a temperament mobile, inconstant, eager, thirsting for new impressions, abhorring rules, aspiring to a "renovation without end;" a temperament common enough among artists, but with which few artists, who have it to the same degree as Guérin, unite a seriousness and a sad intensity like his. After

leaving school, and before going to La Chênaie, he had been
at home at Le Cayla with his sister Eugénie (a wonderfully
gifted person, whose genius so competent a judge as M. Sainte-
Beuve is inclined to pronounce even superior to her brother's)
5   and his sister Eugénie's friends. With one of these friends he had
fallen in love,—a slight and transient fancy, but which had
already called his poetical powers into exercise; and his poems
and fragments, in a certain green note-book (*le Cahier Vert*)
which he long continued to make the depository of his
10   thoughts, and which became famous among his friends, he
brought with him to La Chênaie. There he found among the
younger members of the Society several who, like himself, had
a secret passion for poetry and literature; with these he became
intimate, and in his letters and journal we find him occupied,
15   now with a literary commerce established with these friends,
now with the fortunes, fast coming to a crisis, of the Society,
and now with that for the sake of which he came to La Chênaie,
—his religious progress and the state of his soul.

On Christmas-day, 1832, having been then three weeks at
20   La Chênaie, he writes thus of it to a friend of his family, M. de
Bayne:—

"La Chênaie is a sort of oasis in the midst of the steppes of
Brittany. In front of the château stretches a very large garden
cut in two by a terrace with a lime avenue, at the end of which
25   is a tiny chapel. I am extremely fond of this little oratory,
where one breathes a twofold peace,—the peace of solitude and
the peace of the Lord. When spring comes we shall walk to
prayers between two borders of flowers. On the east side, and
only a few yards from the château, sleeps a small mere between
30   two woods, where the birds in warm weather sing all day long;
and then,—right, left, on all sides,—woods, woods, everywhere
woods. It looks desolate just now that all is bare and the woods
are rust-colour, and under this Brittany sky, which is always
clouded and so low that it seems as if it were going to fall
35   on your head; but as soon as spring comes the sky raises itself
up, the woods come to life again, and everything will be
full of charm."

Of what La Chênaie will be when spring comes he has a
foretaste on the 3d of March.

"To-day" (he writes in his journal) "has enchanted me. For the first time for a long while the sun has shown himself in all his beauty. He has made the buds of the leaves and flowers swell, and he has waked up in me a thousand happy thoughts. The clouds assume more and more their light and graceful shapes, and are sketching, over the blue sky, the most charming fancies. The woods have not yet got their leaves, but they are taking an indescribable air of life and gaiety, which gives them quite a new physiognomy. Everything is getting ready for the great festival of Nature."

Storm and snow adjourn this festival a little longer. On the 11th of March he writes:—

"It has snowed all night. I have been to look at our primroses; each of them had its small load of snow, and was bowing its head under its burden. These pretty flowers, with their rich yellow colour, had a charming effect under their white hoods. I saw whole tufts of them roofed over by a single block of snow; all these laughing flowers thus shrouded and leaning one upon another, made one think of a group of young girls surprised by a shower, and sheltering under a white apron."

The burst of spring comes at last, though late. On the 5th of April we find Guérin "sitting in the sun to penetrate himself to the very marrow with the divine spring." On the 3d of May, "one can actually *see* the progress of the green; it has made a start from the garden to the shrubberies, it is getting the upper hand all along the mere; it leaps, one may say, from tree to tree, from thicket to thicket, in the fields and on the hill-sides; and I can see it already arrived at the forest edge and beginning to spread itself over the broad back of the forest. Soon it will have overrun everything as far as the eye can reach, and all those wide spaces between here and the horizon will be moving and sounding like one vast sea, a sea of emerald."

Finally, on the 16th of May, he writes to M. de Bayne that "the gloomy and bad days,—bad because they bring temptation by their gloom,—are, thanks to God and the spring, over; and I see approaching a long file of shining and happy days, to do me all the good in the world. This Brittany of ours," he continues, "gives one the idea of the grayest and most wrinkled old woman possible suddenly changed back by the touch of a

fairy's wand into a girl of twenty, and one of the loveliest in
the world; the fine weather has so decked and beautified the
dear old country." He felt, however, the cloudiness and cold of
the "dear old country" with all the sensitiveness of a child of
the South. "What a difference," he cries, "between the sky of
Brittany, even on the finest day, and the sky of our South!
Here the summer has, even on its highdays and holidays,
something mournful, overcast, and stinted about it. It is like
a miser who is making a show; there is a niggardliness in his
magnificence. Give me our Languedoc sky, so bountiful of
light, so blue, so largely vaulted!" And somewhat later, complaining of the short and dim sunlight of a February day in
Paris, "What a sunshine," he exclaims, "to gladden eyes accustomed to all the wealth of light of the South!—*aux larges et
libérales effusions de lumière du ciel du Midi.*"

In the long winter of La Chênaie his great resource was
literature. One has often heard that an educated Frenchman's
reading seldom goes much beyond French and Latin, and that
he makes the authors in these two languages his sole literary
standard. This may or may not be true of Frenchmen in general,
but there can be no question as to the width of the reading of
Guérin and his friends, and as to the range of their literary
sympathies. One of the circle, Hippolyte de La Morvonnais,—
a poet who published a volume of verse, and died in the prime
of life,—had a passionate admiration for Wordsworth, and had
even, it is said, made a pilgrimage to Rydal Mount to visit him;
and in Guérin's own reading I find, besides the French names
of Bernardin de St. Pierre, Chateaubriand, Lamartine, and Victor Hugo, the names of Homer, Dante, Shakspeare, Milton, and
Goethe; and he quotes both from Greek and from English
authors in the original. His literary tact is beautifully fine and
true. "Every poet," he writes to his sister, "has his own art of
poetry written on the ground of his own soul; there is no other.
Be constantly observing Nature in her smallest details, and then
write as the current of your thoughts guides you;—that is all."
But with all this freedom from the bondage of forms and rules,
Guérin marks with perfect precision the faults of the *free*
French literature of his time,—the *littérature facile,*—and judges

the romantic school and its prospects like a master: "that youthful literature which has put forth all its blossom prematurely,
and has left itself a helpless prey to the returning frost, stimulated as it has been by the burning sun of our century, by this
atmosphere charged with a perilous heat, which has over-   5
hastened every sort of development, and will most likely reduce
to a handful of grains the harvest of our age." And the popular
authors,—those "whose name appears once and disappears for
ever, whose books, unwelcome to all serious people, welcome
to the rest of the world, to novelty-hunters and novel-readers,   10
fill with vanity these vain souls, and then, falling from hands
heavy with the languor of satiety, drop for ever into the gulf
of oblivion;" and those, more noteworthy, "the writers of books
celebrated, and, as works of art, deserving celebrity, but which
have in them not one grain of that hidden manna, not one of   15
those sweet and wholesome thoughts which nourish the human
soul and refresh it when it is weary,"—these he treats with
such severity that he may in some sense be described, as he
describes himself, as "invoking with his whole heart a classical
restoration." He is best described, however, not as a partisan of 20
any school, but as an ardent seeker for that mode of expression
which is the most natural, happy, and true. He writes to his
sister Eugénie:—

"I want you to reform your system of composition; it is too
loose, too vague, too Lamartinian. Your verse is too sing-song;   25
it does not *talk* enough. Form for yourself a style of your own,
which shall be your real expression. Study the French language
by attentive reading, making it your care to remark constructions, turns of expression, delicacies of style, but without ever
adopting the manner of any master. In the works of these   30
masters we must learn our language, but we must use it each in
our own fashion." [1]

It was not, however, to perfect his literary judgment that
Guérin came to La Chênaie. The religious feeling, which was
as much a part of his essence as the passion for Nature and the 35

---

[1] Part of these extracts date from a time a little after Guérin's residence
at La Chênaie; but already, amidst the readings and conversations of
La Chênaie, his literary judgment was perfectly formed.

literary instinct, shows itself at moments jealous of these its
rivals, and alarmed at their predominance. Like all powerful
feelings, it wants to exclude every other feeling and to be absolute. One Friday in April, after he has been delighting himself
5   with the shapes of the clouds and the progress of the spring,
he suddenly bethinks himself that the day is Good Friday, and
exclaims in his diary:—

"My God, what is my soul about that it can thus go running
after such fugitive delights on Good Friday, on this day all
10   filled with thy death and our redemption? There is in me I
know not what damnable spirit, that awakens in me strong dis-
contents, and is for ever prompting me to rebel against the
holy exercises and the devout collectedness of soul which are
the meet preparation for these great solemnities of our faith.
15   Oh how well can I trace here the old leaven, from which I
have not yet perfectly cleared my soul!"

And again, in a letter to M. de Marzan: "Of what, my God,
are we made," he cries, "that a little verdure and a few trees
should be enough to rob us of our tranquillity and to distract us
20   from thy love?" And writing, three days after Easter Sunday,
in his journal, he records the reception at La Chênaie of a fervent neophyte, in words which seem to convey a covert blame
of his own want of fervency:—

"Three days have passed over our heads since the great
25   festival. One anniversary the less for us yet to spend of the
death and resurrection of our Saviour! Every year thus bears
away with it its solemn festivals; when will the everlasting
festival be here? I have been witness of a most touching sight;
François has brought us one of his friends whom he has gained
30   to the faith. This neophyte joined us in our exercises during the
Holy week, and on Easter day he received the communion with
us. François was in raptures. It is a truly good work which he
has thus done. François is quite young, hardly twenty years
old; M. de la M. is thirty, and is married. There is something
35   most touching and beautifully simple in M. de la M. letting
himself thus be brought to God by quite a young man; and to
see friendship, on François's side, thus doing the work of an
Apostle, is not less beautiful and touching."

Admiration for Lamennais worked in the same direction with this feeling. Lamennais never appreciated Guérin; his combative, rigid, despotic nature, of which the characteristic was energy, had no affinity with Guérin's elusive, undulating, impalpable nature, of which the characteristic was delicacy. He set little store by his new disciple, and could hardly bring himself to understand what others found so remarkable in him, his own genuine feeling towards him being one of indulgent compassion. But the intuition of Guérin, more discerning than the logic of his master, instinctively felt what there was commanding and tragic in Lamennais's character, different as this was from his own; and some of his notes are among the most interesting records of Lamennais which remain.

" 'Do you know what it is,' M. Féli [1] said to us on the evening of the day before yesterday, 'which makes man the most suffering of all creatures? It is that he has one foot in the finite and the other in the infinite, and that he is torn asunder, not by four horses, as in the horrible old times, but between two worlds.' Again he said to us as we heard the clock strike: 'If that clock knew that it was to be destroyed the next instant, it would still keep striking its hour until that instant arrived. My children, be as the clock; whatever may be going to happen to you, strike always your hour.' "

Another time Guérin writes:

"To-day M. Féli startled us. He was sitting behind the chapel, under the two Scotch firs; he took his stick and marked out a grave on the turf, and said to Élie, 'It is there I wish to be buried, but no tombstone! only a simple hillock of grass. Oh, how well I shall be there!' Élie thought he had a presentiment that his end was near. This is not the first time he has been visited by such a presentiment; when he was setting out for Rome, he said to those here: 'I do not expect ever to come back to you; you must do the good which I have failed to do.' He is impatient for death."

Overpowered by the ascendency of Lamennais, Guérin, in spite of his hesitations, in spite of his confession to himself

[1] The familiar name given to M. de Lamennais by his followers at La Chênaie.

that, "after a three weeks' close scrutiny of his soul, in the hope
of finding the pearl of a religious vocation hidden in some corner
of it," he had failed to find what he sought, took, at the end of
August 1833, a decisive step. He joined the religious order
which Lamennais had founded. But at this very moment the
deepening displeasure of Rome with Lamennais determined
the Bishop of Rennes to break up, in so far as it was a religious
congregation, the Society of La Chênaie, to transfer the novices
to Ploërmel, and to place them under other superintendence. In
September, Lamennais, "who had not yet ceased," writes M.
de Marzan, a fervent Catholic, "to be a Christian and a priest,
took leave of his beloved colony of La Chênaie, with the anguish
of a general who disbands his army down to the last recruit,
and withdraws annihilated from the field of battle." Guérin
went to Ploërmel. But here, in the seclusion of a real religious
house, he instantly perceived how alien to a spirit like his,—a
spirit which, as he himself says somewhere, "had need of the
open air, wanted to see the sun and the flowers,"—was the
constraint and monotony of a monastic life, when Lamennais's
genius was no longer present to enliven this life for him. On
the 27th of October he renounced the novitiate, believing himself a partisan of Lamennais in his quarrel with Rome, reproach-
ing the life he had left with demanding passive obedience instead
of trying "to put in practice the admirable alliance of order
with liberty, and of variety with unity," and declaring that,
for his part, he preferred taking the chances of a life of adventure to submitting himself to be *garrotté par un règlement,*
—tied hand and foot by a set of rules." In real truth, a life
of adventure, or rather a life free to wander at its own will,
was that to which his nature irresistibly impelled him.

    For a career of adventure, the inevitable field was Paris. But
before this career began, there came a stage, the smoothest,
perhaps, and the most happy in the short life of Guérin. M.
de La Morvonnais, one of his La Chênaie friends,—some years
older than Guérin, and married to a wife of singular sweetness
and charm,—had a house by the seaside at the mouth of one
of the beautiful rivers of Brittany, the Arguenon. He asked
Guérin, when he left Ploërmel, to come and stay with him at

this place, called Le Val de l'Arguenon, and Guérin spent the
winter of 1833–4 there. I grudge every word about Le Val
and its inmates which is not Guérin's own, so charming is the
picture he draws of them, so truly does his talent find itself
in its best vein as he draws it.   5

"How full of goodness" (he writes in his journal of the 7th
of December) "is Providence to me! For fear the sudden passage
from the mild and temperate air of a religious life to the torrid
clime of the world should be too trying for my soul, it has
conducted me, after I have left my sacred shelter, to a house   10
planted on the frontier between the two regions, where, without being in solitude, one is not yet in the world; a house whose
windows look on the one side towards the plain where the
tumult of men is rocking, on the other towards the wilderness
where the servants of God are chanting. I intend to write down   15
the record of my sojourn here, for the days here spent are full
of happiness, and I know that in the time to come I shall often
turn back to the story of these past felicities. A man, pious, and
a poet; a woman, whose spirit is in such perfect sympathy with
his that you would say they had but one being between them;   20
a child, called Marie like her mother, and who sends, like a star,
the first rays of her love and thought through the white cloud
of infancy; a simple life in an old-fashioned house; the ocean,
which comes morning and evening to bring us its harmonies;
and lastly, a wanderer who descends from Carmel and is going   25
on to Babylon, and who has laid down at this threshold his staff
and his sandals, to take his seat at the hospitable table;—here
is matter to make a biblical poem of, if I could only describe
things as I can feel them!"

Every line written by Guérin during this stay at Le Val is   30
worth quoting, but I have only room for one extract more:—

"Never" (he writes, a fortnight later, on the 20th of December), "never have I tasted so inwardly and deeply the happiness
of home-life. All the little details of this life, which in their
succession make up the day, are to me so many stages of a   35
continuous charm carried from one end of the day to the other.
The morning greeting, which in some sort renews the pleasure
of the first arrival, for the words with which one meets are

almost the same, and the separation at night, through the hours
of darkness and uncertainty, does not ill represent longer separa-
tions; then breakfast, during which you have the fresh enjoyment of having met together again; the stroll afterwards, when
5   we go out and bid Nature good-morning; the return and setting
to work in an old panelled chamber looking out on the sea,
inaccessible to all the stir of the house, a perfect sanctuary of
labour; dinner, to which we are called, not by a bell, which
reminds one too much of school or a great house, but by a
10   pleasant voice; the gaiety, the merriment, the talk flitting from
one subject to another and never dropping so long as the meal
lasts; the crackling fire of dry branches to which we draw our
chairs directly afterwards, the kind words that are spoken
round the warm flame which sings while we talk; and then, if it
15   is fine, the walk by the seaside, when the sea has for its visitors
a mother with her child in her arms, this child's father and a
stranger, each of these two last with a stick in his hand; the
rosy lips of the little girl, which keep talking at the same time
with the waves,—now and then tears shed by her and cries of
20   childish fright at the edge of the sea; our thoughts, the father's
and mine, as we stand and look at the mother and child smiling
at one another, or at the child in tears and the mother trying
to comfort it by her caresses and exhortations; the Ocean, going
on all the while rolling up his waves and noises; the dead
25   boughs which we go and cut, here and there, out of the copse-
wood, to make a quick and bright fire when we get home,—this
little taste of the woodman's calling which brings us closer to
Nature and makes us think of M. Féli's eager fondness for the
same work; the hours of study and poetical flow which carry us
30   to supper-time; this meal, which summons us by the same gentle
voice as its predecessor, and which is passed amid the same joys,
only less loud, because evening sobers everything, tones everything down; then our evening, ushered in by the blaze of a
cheerful fire, and which with its alternations of reading and
35   talking brings us at last to bed-time:—to all the charms of a
day so spent add the dreams which follow it, and your imagination will still fall far short of these home-joys in their delightful
reality."

I said the foregoing should be my last extract, but who could resist this picture of a January evening on the coast of Brittany?—

"All the sky is covered over with gray clouds just silvered at the edges. The sun, who departed a few minutes ago, has left behind him enough light to temper for awhile the black shadows, and to soften down, as it were, the approach of night. The winds are hushed, and the tranquil ocean sends up to me, when I go out on the doorstep to listen, only a melodious murmur, which dies away in the soul like a beautiful wave on the beach. The birds, the first to obey the nocturnal influence, make their way towards the woods, and you hear the rustle of their wings in the clouds. The copses which cover the whole hill-side of Le Val, which all the day-time are alive with the chirp of the wren, the laughing whistle of the woodpecker,[1] and the different notes of a multitude of birds, have no longer any sound in their paths and thickets, unless it be the prolonged high call of the blackbirds at play with one another and chasing one another, after all the other birds have their heads safe under their wings. The noise of man, always the last to be silent, dies gradually out over the face of the fields. The general murmur fades away, and one hears hardly a sound except what comes from the villages and hamlets, in which, up till far into the night, there are cries of children and barking of dogs. Silence wraps me round; everything seeks repose except this pen of mine, which perhaps disturbs the rest of some living atom asleep in a crease of my note-book, for it makes its light scratching as it puts down these idle thoughts. Let it stop, then! for all I write, have written, or shall write, will never be worth setting against the sleep of an atom."

On the 1st of February we find him in a lodging at Paris. "I enter the world" (such are the last words written in his journal at Le Val) "with a secret horror." His outward history for the next five years is soon told. He found himself in Paris, poor, fastidious, and with health which already, no doubt, felt the obscure presence of the malady of which he died—con-

---

[1] "The woodpecker *laughs*," says White of Selborne; and here is Guérin, in Brittany, confirming his testimony.

sumption. One of his Brittany acquaintances introduced him to editors, tried to engage him in the periodical literature of Paris; and so unmistakable was Guérin's talent that even his first essays were immediately accepted. But Guérin's genius was of a kind
5 which unfitted him to get his bread in this manner. At first he was pleased with the notion of living by his pen; "*je n'ai qu'à écrire*," he says to his sister,—"I have only got to write." But to a nature like his, endued with the passion for perfection, the necessity to produce, to produce constantly, to produce
10 whether in the vein or out of the vein, to produce something good or bad or middling, as it may happen, but at all events *something*,—is the most intolerable of tortures. To escape from it he betook himself to that common but most perfidious refuge of men of letters, that refuge to which Goldsmith and
15 poor Hartley Coleridge had betaken themselves before him,— the profession of teaching. In September 1834 he procured an engagement at the Collège Stanislas, where he had himself been educated. It was vacation-time, and all he had to do was to teach a small class composed of boys who did not go home for the
20 holidays,—in his own words, "scholars left like sick sheep in the fold, while the rest of the flock are frisking in the fields." After the vacation he was kept on at the college as a super- numerary. "The master of the fifth class has asked for a month's leave of absence; I am taking his place, and by this work I get
25 one hundred frances (£4). I have been looking about for pupils to give private lessons to, and I have found three or four. Schoolwork and private lessons together fill my day from half-past seven in the morning till half-past nine at night. The college dinner serves me for breakfast, and I go and dine in the
30 evening at twenty-four *sous*, as a young man beginning life should." To better his position in the hierarchy of public teachers it was necessary that he should take the degree of *agrégé ès lettres*, corresponding to our degree of Master of Arts; and to his heavy work in teaching, there was thus added
35 that of preparing for a severe examination. The drudgery of this life was very irksome to him, although less insupportable than the drudgery of the profession of letters; inasmuch as to a sensitive man like Guérin, to silence his genius is more tolerable

than to hackney it. Still the yoke wore him deeply, and he had
moments of bitter revolt; he continued, however, to bear it
with resolution, and on the whole with patience, for four years.
On the 15th of November 1838 he married a young Creole
lady of some fortune, Mademoiselle Caroline de Gervain,   5
"whom," to use his own words, "Destiny, who loves these
surprises, has wafted from the farthest Indies into my arms."
The marriage was happy, and it ensured to Guérin liberty and
leisure; but now "the blind Fury with the abhorred shears"
was hard at hand. Consumption declared itself in him: "I pass   10
my life," he writes, with his old playfulness and calm, to his
sister on the 8th of April 1839, "within my bed-curtains, and
wait patiently enough, thanks to Caro's [1] goodness, books, and
dreams, for the recovery which the sunshine is to bring with
it." In search of this sunshine he was taken to his native coun-   15
try, Languedoc, but in vain. He died at Le Cayla on the 19th
of July 1839.

The vicissitudes of his inward life during these five years
were more considerable. His opinions and tastes underwent
great, or what seem to be great, changes. He came to Paris the   20
ardent partisan of Lamennais: even in April 1834, after Rome
had finally condemned Lamennais,—"To-night there will go
forth from Paris," he writes, "with his face set to the west,
a man whose every step I would fain follow, and who returns
to the desert for which I sigh. M. Féli departs this evening   25
for La Chênaie." But in October 1835,—"I assure you," he
writes to his sister, "I am at last weaned from M. de Lamennais;
one does not remain a babe and suckling for ever; I am perfectly freed from his influence." There was a greater change
than this. In 1834 the main cause of Guérin's aversion to the   30
literature of the French romantic school, was that this literature, having had a religious origin, had ceased to be religious:
"it has forgotten," he says, "the house and the admonitions of
its Father." But his friend M. de Marzan tells us of a "deplorable
revolution" which, by 1836, had taken place in him. Guérin   35
had become intimate with the chiefs of this very literature; he
no longer went to church; "the bond of a common faith, in

[1] His wife.

which our friendship had its birth, existed between us no
longer." Then, again, "this interregnum was not destined to
last." Reconverted to his old faith by suffering and by the pious
efforts of his sister Eugénie, Guérin died a Catholic. His feelings about society underwent a like change. After "entering
the world with a secret horror," after congratulating himself
when he had been some months at Paris on being "disengaged
from the social tumult, out of the reach of those blows which,
when I live in the thick of the world, bruise me, irritate me, or
utterly crush me," M. Sainte-Beuve tells us of him, two years
afterwards, appearing in society "a man of the world, elegant,
even fashionable; a talker who could hold his own against the
most brilliant talkers of Paris."

In few natures, however, is there really such essential consistency as in Guérin's. He says of himself, in the very beginning of his journal: "I owe everything to poetry, for there
is no other name to give to the sum total of my thoughts; I
owe to it whatever I now have pure, lofty, and solid in my soul;
I owe to it all my consolations in the past; I shall probably owe
to it my future." Poetry, the poetical instinct, was indeed the
basis of his nature; but to say so thus absolutely is not quite
enough. One aspect of poetry fascinated Guérin's imagination
and held it prisoner. Poetry is the interpretress of the natural
world, and she is the interpretress of the moral world; it was
as the interpretress of the natural world that she had Guérin
for her mouthpiece. To make magically near and real the life
of Nature, and man's life only so far as it is a part of that
Nature, was his faculty; a faculty of naturalistic, not of moral
interpretation. This faculty always has for its basis a peculiar
temperament, an extraordinary delicacy of organisation and
susceptibility to impressions; in exercising it the poet is in a
great degree passive (Wordsworth thus speaks of a *wise pas-
siveness*); he aspires to be a sort of human Æolian harp, catching and rendering every rustle of Nature. To assist at the
evolution of the whole life of the world is his craving, and
intimately to feel it all:

>   . . . "the glow, the thrill of life,
>   Where, where do these abound?"

is what he asks: he resists being riveted and held stationary by
any single impression, but would be borne on for ever down
an enchanted stream. He goes into religion and out of religion,
into society and out of society, not from the motives which
impel men in general, but to feel what it is all like; he is thus   5
hardly a moral agent, and, like the passive and ineffectual
Uranus of Keats's poem, he may say:

> . . . . . . "I am but a voice;
> My life is but the life of winds and tides;
> No more than winds and tides can I avail."   10

He hovers over the tumult of life, but does not really put his
hand to it.

No one has expressed the aspirations of this temperament
better than Guérin himself. In the last year of his life he
writes:—   15

"I return, as you see, to my old brooding over the world of
Nature, that line which my thoughts irresistibly take; a sort of
passion which gives me enthusiasm, tears, bursts of joy, and an
eternal food for musing; and yet I am neither philosopher nor
naturalist, nor anything learned whatsoever. There is one word   20
which is the God of my imagination, the tyrant, I ought rather
to say, that fascinates it, lures it onward, gives it work to do
without ceasing, and will finally carry it I know not where; the
word *life*."

And in one place in his journal he says:—   25

"My imagination welcomes every dream, every impression,
without attaching itself to any, and goes on for ever seeking
something new."

And again in another:—

"The longer I live, and the clearer I discern between true   30
and false in society, the more does the inclination to live, not
as a savage or a misanthrope, but as a solitary man on the fron-
tiers of society, on the outskirts of the world, gain strength
and grow in me. The birds come and go and make nests around
our habitations, they are fellow-citizens of our farms and ham-   35
lets with us; but they take their flight in a heaven which is
boundless, but the hand of God alone gives and measures to

them their daily food, but they build their nests in the heart
of the thick bushes, or hang them in the height of the trees.
So would I, too, live, hovering round society, and having always at my back a field of liberty vast as the sky."

In the same spirit he longed for travel. "When one is a wanderer," he writes to his sister, "one feels that one fulfils the
true condition of humanity." And the last entry in his journal
is,—"The stream of travel is full of delight. Oh, who will set
me adrift on this Nile!"

Assuredly it is not in this temperament that the active virtues
have their rise. On the contrary, this temperament, considered
in itself alone, indisposes for the discharge of them. Something
morbid and excessive, as manifested in Guérin, it undoubtedly
has. In him, as in Keats, and as in another youth of genius,
whose name, but the other day unheard of, Lord Houghton
has so gracefully written in the history of English poetry,—
David Gray,—the temperament, the talent itself, is deeply influenced by their mysterious malady; the temperament is
devouring; it uses vital power too hard and too fast, paying
the penalty in long hours of unutterable exhaustion and in premature death. The intensity of Guérin's depression is described
to us by Guérin himself with the same incomparable touch
with which he describes happier feelings; far oftener than
any pleasurable sense of his gift he has "the sense profound,
near, immense, of my misery, of my inward poverty." And
again: "My inward misery gains upon me; I no longer dare look
within." And on another day of gloom he does look within, and
here is the terrible analysis:—

"Craving, unquiet, seeing only by glimpses, my spirit is
stricken by all those ills which are the sure fruit of a youth
doomed never to ripen into manhood. I grow old and wear
myself out in the most futile mental strainings, and make no
progress. My head seems dying, and when the wind blows I
fancy I feel it, as if I were a tree, blowing through a number
of withered branches in my top. Study is intolerable to me,
or rather it is quite out of my power. Mental work brings on,
not drowsiness, but an irritable and nervous disgust which
drives me out, I know not where, into the streets and public

places. The Spring, whose delights used to come every year
stealthily and mysteriously to charm me in my retreat, crushes
me this year under a weight of sudden hotness. I should be glad
of any event which delivered me from the situation in which
I am. If I were free I would embark for some distant country   5
where I could begin life anew."

Such is this temperament in the frequent hours when the
sense of its own weakness and isolation crushes it to the ground.
Certainly it was not for Guérin's happiness, or for Keats's, as
men count happiness, to be as they were. Still the very excess   10
and predominance of their temperament has given to the fruits
of their genius a unique brilliancy and flavour. I have said that
poetry interprets in two ways; it interprets by expressing with
magical felicity the physiognomy and movement of the outward world, and it interprets by expressing, with inspired con-   15
viction, the ideas and laws of the inward world of man's moral
and spiritual nature. In other words, poetry is interpretative
both by having *natural magic* in it, and by having *moral profundity*. In both ways it illuminates man; it gives him a satisfying sense of reality; it reconciles him with himself and the   20
universe. Thus Æschylus's "δράσαντι παθεῖν" and his "ἀνήριθμον
γέλασμα" are alike interpretative. Shakspeare interprets both
when he says,

> "Full many a glorious morning have I seen,
> Flatter the mountain-tops with sovran eye;"   25

and when he says,

> "There's a divinity that shapes our ends,
> Rough-hew them as we will."

These great poets unite in themselves the faculty of both kinds
of interpretation, the naturalistic and the moral. But it is ob-   30
servable that in the poets who unite both kinds, the latter (the
moral) usually ends by making itself the master. In Shakspeare
the two kinds seem wonderfully to balance one another; but
even in him the balance leans; his expression tends to become
too little sensuous and simple, too much intellectualised. The   35
same thing may be yet more strongly affirmed of Lucretius

and of Wordsworth. In Shelley there is not a balance of the two
gifts, nor even a co-existence of them, but there is a passionate
straining after them both, and this is what makes Shelley, as
a man, so interesting: I will not now inquire how much Shelley
achieves as a poet, but whatever he achieves, he in general fails
to achieve natural magic in his expression; in Mr. Palgrave's
charming *Treasury* may be seen a gallery of his failures.[1] But
in Keats and Guérin, in whom the faculty of naturalistic interpretation is overpoweringly predominant, the natural magic is
perfect; when they speak of the world they speak like Adam
naming by divine inspiration the creatures; their expression
corresponds with the thing's essential reality. Even between
Keats and Guérin, however, there is a distinction to be drawn.
Keats has, above all, a sense of what is pleasurable and open in
the life of Nature; for him she is the *Alma Parens:* his expression
has, therefore, more than Guérin's, something genial, outward,
and sensuous. Guérin has, above all, a sense of what there is
adorable and secret in the life of Nature; for him she is the
Magna Parens; his expression has, therefore, more than Keats's,
something mystic, inward, and profound.

So he lived like a man possessed; with his eye not on his
own career, not on the public, not on fame, but on the Isis whose
veil he had uplifted. He published nothing: "There is more
power and beauty," he writes, "in the well-kept secret of one's
self and one's thoughts, than in the display of a whole heaven
that one may have inside one." "My spirit," he answers the
friends who urge him to write, "is of the home-keeping order,
and has no fancy for adventure; literary adventure is above
all distasteful to it; for this, indeed (let me say so without the
least self-sufficiency), it has a contempt. The literary career
seems to me unreal, both in its own essence and in the rewards

[1] Compare, for example, his "Lines Written in the Euganean Hills,"
with Keats's "Ode to Autumn" (*Golden Treasury*, pp. 256, 284). The
latter piece *renders* Nature; the former *tries to render* her. I will not
deny, however, that Shelley has natural magic in his rhythm; what I deny
is, that he has it in his language. It always seems to me that the right
sphere for Shelley's genius was the sphere of music, not of poetry; the
medium of sounds he can master, but to master the more difficult medium
of words he has neither intellectual force enough nor sanity enough.

which one seeks from it, and therefore fatally marred by a secret absurdity." His acquaintances, and among them distinguished men of letters, full of admiration for the originality and delicacy of his talent, laughed at his self-depreciation, warmly assured him of his powers. He received their assurances with a mournful incredulity, which contrasts curiously with the self-assertion of poor David Gray, whom I just now mentioned. "It seems to me intolerable," he writes, "to appear to men other than one appears to God. My worst torture at this moment is the over-estimate which generous friends form of me. We are told that at the last judgment the secret of all consciences will be laid bare to the universe; would that mine were so this day, and that every passer-by could see me as I am!" "High above my head," he says at another time, "far, far away, I seem to hear the murmur of that world of thought and feeling to which I aspire so often, but where I can never attain. I think of those of my own age who have wings strong enough to reach it, but I think of them without jealousy, and as men on earth contemplate the elect and their felicity." And, criticising his own composition, "When I begin a subject, my self-conceit" (says this exquisite artist) "imagines I am doing wonders; and when I have finished, I see nothing but a wretched made-up imitation, composed of odds and ends of colour stolen from other people's palettes, and tastelessly mixed together on mine." Such was his *passion for perfection*, his disdain for all poetical work not perfectly adequate and felicitous. The magic of expression, to which by the force of this passion he won his way, will make the name of Maurice de Guérin remembered in literature.

I have already mentioned the *Centaur*, a sort of prose poem by Guérin, which Madame Sand published after his death. The idea of this composition came to him, M. Sainte-Beuve says, in the course of some visits which he made with his friend, M. Trebutien, a learned antiquarian, to the Museum of Antiquities in the Louvre. The free and wild life which the Greeks expressed by such creations as the Centaur had, as we might well expect, a strong charm for him; under the same inspiration he composed a *Bacchante*, which was meant by him to form

part of a prose poem on the adventures of Bacchus in India.
Real as was the affinity which Guérin's nature had for these
subjects, I doubt whether, in treating them, he would have
found the full and final employment of his talent. But the beauty
5   of his *Centaur* is extraordinary; in its whole conception and
expression this piece has in a wonderful degree that natural
magic of which I have said so much, and the rhythm has a charm
which bewitches even a foreigner. An old Centaur on his mountain is supposed to relate to Melampus, a human questioner,
10 the life of his youth. Untranslatable as the piece is, I shall conclude with some extracts from it:—

"THE CENTAUR.

"I had my birth in the caves of these mountains. Like the
stream of this valley, whose first drops trickle from some weep-
15 ing rock in a deep cavern, the first moment of my life fell in
the darkness of a remote abode, and without breaking the
silence. When our mothers draw near to the time of their delivery, they withdraw to the caverns, and in the depth of the
loneliest of them, in the thickest of its gloom, bring forth, with-
20 out uttering a plaint, a fruit silent as themselves. Their puissant
milk makes us surmount, without weakness or dubious struggle,
the first difficulties of life; and yet we leave our caverns later
than you your cradles. The reason is that we have a doctrine
that the early days of existence should be kept apart and en-
25 shrouded, as days filled with the presence of the gods. Nearly
the whole term of my growth was passed in the darkness where
I was born. The recesses of my dwelling ran so far under the
mountain that I should not have known on which side was the
exit, had not the winds, when they sometimes made their way
30 through the opening, sent fresh airs in, and a sudden trouble.
Sometimes, too, my mother came back to me, having about
her the odours of the valleys, or streaming from the waters
which were her haunt. Her returning thus, without a word said
of the valleys or the rivers, but with the emanations from them
35 hanging about her, troubled my spirit, and I moved up and down
restlessly in my darkness. 'What is it,' I cried, 'this outside world

whither my mother is borne, and what reigns there in it so
potent as to attract her so often?' ... At these moments my
own force began to make me unquiet. I felt in it a power which
could not remain idle; and betaking myself either to toss my
arms or to gallop backwards and forwards in the spacious dark-   5
ness of the cavern, I tried to make out from the blows which
I dealt in the empty space, or from the transport of my course
through it, in what direction my arms were meant to reach,
or my feet to bear me. Since that day, I have wound my arms
round the bust of Centaurs, and round the body of heroes, and   10
round the trunk of oaks; my hands have assayed the rocks, the
waters, plants without number, and the subtlest impressions of
the air,—for I uplift them in the dark and still nights to catch
the breaths of wind, and to draw signs whereby I may augur
my road; my feet,—look, O Melampus, how worn they are!   15
And yet, all benumbed as I am in this extremity of age, there
are days when, in broad sunlight, on the mountain-tops, I renew these gallopings of my youth in the cavern, and with the
same object, brandishing my arms and employing all the fleet-
ness which yet is left to me.   20

    .   .   .   .   .

   "O Melampus, thou who wouldst know the life of the
Centaurs, wherefore have the gods willed that thy steps should
lead thee to me, the oldest and most forlorn of them all? It is
long since I have ceased to practise any part of their life. I quit
no more this mountain summit, to which age has confined me.   25
The point of my arrows now serves me only to uproot some
tough-fibred plant; the tranquil lakes know me still, but the
rivers have forgotten me. I will tell thee a little of my youth;
but these recollections, issuing from a worn memory, come
like the drops of a niggardly libation poured from a damaged   30
urn. . . .
   "The course of my youth was rapid and full of agitation.
Movement was my life, and my steps knew no bound. . . . One
day when I was following the course of a valley seldom entered
by the Centaurs, I discovered a man making his way up the   35
stream-side on the opposite bank. He was the first whom my
eyes had lighted on: I despised him. 'Behold,' I cried, 'at the
utmost but the half of what I am! How short are his steps! and

his movement how full of labour! ... Doubtless he is a Centaur overthrown by the gods, and reduced by them to drag himself along thus.'

.   .   .   .   .

"Wandering along at my own will like the rivers, feeling
5 wherever I went the presence of Cybele, whether in the bed of
the valleys, or on the height of the mountains, I bounded whither
I would, like a blind and chainless life. But when Night, filled
with the charm of the gods, overtook me on the slopes of the
mountain, she guided me to the mouth of the caverns, and
10 there tranquillised me as she tranquillises the billows of the
sea.... Stretched across the threshold of my retreat, my flanks
hidden within the cave, and my head under the open sky, I
watched the spectacle of the dark.... The sea-gods, it is said,
quit during the hours of darkness their palaces under the deep;
15 they seat themselves on the promontories, and their eyes wander
over the expanse of the waves. Even so I kept watch, having
at my feet an expanse of life like the hushed sea.... My regards
had free range, and travelled to the most distant points. Like
sea-beaches which never lose their wetness, the line of moun-
20 tains to the west retained the imprint of gleams not perfectly
wiped out by the shadows. In that quarter still survived, in pale
clearness, mountain-summits naked and pure. There I beheld
at one time the god Pan descend, ever solitary; at another,
the choir of the mystic divinities; or I saw pass some mountain
25 nymph charm-struck by the night. Sometimes the eagles of
Mount Olympus traversed the upper sky, and were lost to view
among the far-off constellations, or in the shade of the dream-
ing forests....

"Thou pursuest after wisdom, O Melampus, which is the
30 science of the will of the gods; and thou roamest from people
to people like a mortal driven by the destinies.... In the times
when I kept my night-watches before the caverns, I have sometimes believed that I was about to surprise the thought of the
sleeping Cybele, and that the mother of the gods, betrayed by
35 her dreams, would let fall some of her secrets; but I have never
made out more than sounds which faded away in the murmur
of night, or words inarticulate as the bubbling of the rivers.

" 'O Macareus,' one day said the great Chiron to me, whose old age I tended; 'we are, both of us, Centaurs of the mountain; but how different are our lives! Of my days all the study is (thou seest it) the search for plants; thou, thou art like those mortals who have picked up on the waters or in the woods, and carried to their lips, some pieces of the reed-pipe thrown away by the god Pan. From that hour these mortals, having caught from their relics of the god a passion for wild life, or perhaps smitten with some secret madness, enter into the wilderness, plunge among the forests, follow the course of the streams, bury themselves in the heart of the mountains, restless, and haunted by an unknown purpose. The mares beloved of the winds in the farthest Scythia are not wilder than thou, nor more cast down at nightfall, when the North Wind has departed. Seekest thou to know the gods, O Macareus, and from what source men, animals, and the elements of the universal fire have their origin? But the aged Ocean, the father of all things, keeps locked within his own breast these secrets; and the nymphs, who stand around, sing as they weave their eternal dance before him, to cover any sound which might escape from his lips half-opened by slumber. The mortals, dear to the gods for their virtue, have received from their hands lyres to give delight to man, or the seeds of new plants to make him rich; but from their inexorable lips, nothing!'

. . . . .

"Such were the lessons which the old Chiron gave me. Waned to the very extremity of life, the Centaur yet nourished in his spirit the most lofty discourse.

. . . . .

"For me, O Melampus, I decline into my last days, calm as the setting of the constellations. I still retain enterprise enough to climb to the top of the rocks, and there I linger late, either gazing on the wild and restless clouds, or to see come up from the horizon the rainy Hyades, the Pleiades, or the great Orion; but I feel myself perishing and passing quickly away, like a snow-wreath floating on the stream; and soon shall I be mingled with the waters which flow in the vast bosom of Earth."

The Bishop and the Philosopher

"*Der Engländer ist eigentlich ohne Intelligenz,*" said Goethe; by
which he meant, not that the Englishman was stupid, but that
he occupied himself little with the *rationale* of things. He meant
that an Englishman held and uttered any given opinion as something isolated, without perceiving its relation to other ideas,
or its due place in the general world of thought; without, therefore, having any notion of its absolute value. He meant, in
short, that he was uncritical.

Heedless of what may be said about him, the Englishman
is generally content to pursue his own way, producing, indeed,
little in the sphere of criticism, but producing from time to
time in the sphere of pure creation masterpieces which attest
his intellectual power and extort admiration from his detractors.
Occasionally, however, he quits this safe course. Occasionally,
the uncritical spirit of our race determines to perform a great
public act of self-humiliation. Such an act it has recently accomplished. It has just sent forth as its scapegoat into the wilderness, amidst a titter from educated Europe, the Bishop of Natal.

The Bishop's book on the Pentateuch has been judged from
a theological point of view by members of his own profession;
and critics too, who were not members of that profession, have
judged it from the same point of view. From the theological
point of view I do not presume to judge it. But a work of this
kind has to justify itself before another tribunal besides an
ecclesiastical one; it is liable to be called up for judgment, not
only before a Court of Arches, but before the Republic of Letters. It is as a humble citizen of that republic that I wish to say
a few words about the Bishop of Natal's book. But what, it may
be asked, has literary criticism to do with books on religious

matters? That is what I will in the first instance try to show.

Literary criticism's most important function is to try books as to the influence which they are calculated to have upon the general culture of single nations or of the world at large. Of this culture literary criticism is the appointed guardian, and on this culture all literary works may be conceived as in some way or other operating. All these works have a special professional criticism to undergo: theological works that of theologians, historical works that of historians, philosophical works that of philosophers, and in this case each kind of work is tried by a separate standard. But they have also a general literary criticism to undergo, and this tries them all, as I have said, by one standard—their effect upon general culture. Every one is not a theologian, a historian, or a philosopher, but every one is interested in the advance of the general culture of his nation or of mankind. A criticism therefore which, abandoning a thousand special questions which may be raised about any book, tries it solely in respect of its influence upon this culture, brings it thereby within the sphere of every one's interest. This is why literary criticism has exercised so much power. The chief sources of intellectual influence in Europe, during the last century and a half, have been its three chief critics—Voltaire, Lessing, Goethe. The chief sources of intellectual influence in England, during the same period, have been its chief organs of criticism—Addison, Johnson, the first Edinburgh Reviewers.

Religious books come within the jurisdiction of literary criticism so far as they affect general culture. Undoubtedly they do affect this in the highest degree: they affect it whether they appeal to the reason, or to the heart and feelings only; whether they enlighten directly, or, by softening and purifying, prepare the way for enlightenment. So far as by any book on religious matters the raw are humanised or the cultivated are advanced to a yet higher culture, so far that book is a subject for literary criticism. But, undoubtedly, the direct promotion of culture by intellectual power is the main interest of literary criticism, not the indirect promotion of this culture by edification. As soon, therefore, as a religious work has satisfied it that it pursues no other end than edification, *and that it really*

does pursue this, literary criticism dismisses it without further question. Religious books, such as are sold daily all round us by thousands and tens of thousands, of no literary merit whatever, which do not pretend to enlighten intellectually, which only
5   profess to edify, and do in some way fulfil their profession, literary criticism thus dismisses with respect, without a syllable of disparaging remark. Even a work like that of M. Hengstenberg on the Pentateuch, which makes higher claims without fulfilling them, literary criticism may dismiss without censure,
10 because it is honestly written for purposes of edification. Over works, therefore, which treat of religious matters, literary criticism will only in certain cases linger long. One case is, when, through such works, though their object be solely or mainly general edification, there shines an ethereal light, the presence
15 of a gifted nature; for this entitles the "Imitation," the "Spiritual Works" of Fénelon, the "Pilgrim's Progress," the "Christian Year," to rank with the works which inform, not with those which edify simply; and it is with works which inform that the main business of literary criticism lies. And even over
20 works which cannot take this high rank, but which are yet freshened, as they pursue their aim of edification, with airs from the true poetical sky—such as the "Mother's Last Words" of Mrs. Sewell—literary criticism will be tempted to linger; it will, at least, salute them in passing, and say: "There, too, is
25 a breath of Arcadia!"

    This is one case; another is, when a work on religious matters entirely foregoes the task of edifying the uninstructed, and pursues solely that of informing the instructed, of raising the intellectual life of these to a yet higher stage. Such an attempt
30 to advance the highest culture of Europe, of course powerfully interests a criticism whose especial concern is with that culture. There is a third and last case. It is, when a work on religious matters is neither edifying nor informing; when it is neither good for the many nor yet for the few. A Hebrew moralist,
35 in the "Ethics of the Fathers," says: "Every dispute that is instituted for God's sake will in the end be established; but that which is not for God's sake will not be established." What may be considered as a dispute for God's sake? Literary crit-

icism regards a religious book, which tends to edify the multitude, as a dispute for God's sake; it regards a religious book
which tends to inform the instructed, as a dispute for God's
sake; but a religious book which tends neither to edify the multitude nor to inform the instructed, it refuses to regard as a   5
dispute for God's sake; it classes it, in the language of the
moralist just cited, not with the speaking of Hillel and Shammai, but with the gainsaying of Korah. It is bound, if the book
has notoriety enough to give it importance, to pass censure
on it.   10

According to these principles, literary criticism has to try
the book of the Bishop of Natal, which all England is now
reading. It has to try it in respect of the influence which it
is naturally calculated to exercise on the culture of England
or Europe; and it asks: "Does this book tend to advance that   15
culture, either by edifying the little-instructed, or by further
informing the much-instructed?"

Does it tend to edify the little-instructed—the great majority? Perhaps it will be said that this book professes not to edify
the little-instructed, but to enlighten them; and that a reli-   20
gious book which attempts to enlighten the little-instructed
by sweeping away their prejudices, attempts a good work and
is justifiable before criticism, exactly as much as a book which
attempts to enlighten on these matters the much-instructed.
No doubt, to say this is to say what seems quite in accordance   25
with modern notions; the *Times* tells us day after day how the
general public is the organ of all truth, and individual genius
the organ of all error; nay, we have got so far, it says, that the
superior men of former days, if they could live again now,
would abandon the futile business of running counter to the   30
opinions of the many, of persisting in opinions of their own:
they would sit at the feet of the general public, and learn from
its lips what they ought to say. And, no doubt, this doctrine
holds out, both for the superior man and the general public, a
prospect in a high degree tempting; the former is to get more   35
pudding than formerly, and the latter more praise. But it is a
doctrine which no criticism that has not a direct interest in
promulgating it can ever seriously entertain. The highly-

instructed few, and not the scantily-instructed many, will ever be the organ to the human race of knowledge and truth. Knowledge and truth, in the full sense of the words, are not attainable by the great mass of the human race at all. The great mass of the human race have to be softened and humanised through their heart and imagination, before any soil can be found in them where knowledge may strike living roots. Until the softening and humanising process is very far advanced, intellectual demonstrations are uninforming for them; and, if they impede the working of influences which advance this softening and humanising process, they are even noxious; they retard their development, they impair the culture of the world. All the great teachers, divine and human, who have ever appeared, have united in proclaiming this. "Remember the covenant of the Highest, and wink at ignorance," says the Son of Sirach. "Unto you," said Christ to a few disciples, "it is given to know the mysteries of the kingdom of heaven, but to them (the multitude) it is not given." "My words," said Pindar, "have a sound only for the wise." Plato interdicted the entry of his school of philosophy to all who had not first undergone the discipline of a severe science. "The vast majority," said Spinoza, "have neither capacity nor leisure to follow speculations." "The few (those who can have a saving knowledge) can never mean the many," says, in one of his noblest sermons, Dr. Newman. Old moral ideas leaven and humanise the multitude: new intellectual ideas filter slowly down to them from the thinking few; and only when they reach them in this manner do they adjust themselves to their practice without convulsing it. It was not by the intellectual truth of its propositions concerning purgatory, or prayer for the dead, or the human nature of the Virgin Mary, that the Reformation touched and advanced the multitude: it was by the moral truth of its protest against the sale of indulgences, and the scandalous lives of many of the clergy.

Human culture is not, therefore, advanced by a religious book conveying intellectual demonstrations to the many, unless they be conveyed in such a way as to edify them. Now, that the intellectual demonstrations of the Bishop of Natal's book are not in themselves of a nature to edify the general reader, that

is, to serve his religious feeling, the Bishop himself seems well aware. He expresses alarm and misgivings at what he is about, for this very reason, that he is conscious how, by shaking the belief of the many in the Inspiration of Scripture, he may be shaking their religious life—working, that is, not to their edi-   5
fication. He talks of "the sharp pang of that decisive stroke which is to sever their connexion with the ordinary view of the Mosaic story for ever." Again: "I tremble," he says, "at the results of my own inquiry—the momentous results" (he else-where calls them) "to which it leads." And again: "I cannot   10
but feel, that having thus been impelled to take an active part in showing the groundlessness of that notion of Scripture In-spiration which so many have long regarded as the very founda-tion of their faith and hope, a demand may be made upon me for something to supply the loss, for something *to fill up the*   15
aching void which will undoubtedly be felt at first." Even if he had not been himself conscious of the probable operation of his book, there were plenty of voices to tell him beforehand what it would be. He himself quotes these words of Mr. Cook: "One thing with the Englishman is fixed and certain;—a narra-   20
tive purporting to be one of positive facts, which is wholly, or in any considerable portion, untrue, can have no connexion with the Divine, and cannot have any beneficial influence on mankind" (*der Engländer ist eigentlich ohne Intelligenz*). He quotes Mr. Burgon as expressing the common belief of English   25
Christians when he says: "Every verse of the Bible, every word of it, every syllable of it, every letter of it, is the direct utter-ance of the Most High." And so, too, since the publication of the Bishop of Natal's book, a preacher in the Oxford University pulpit has declared, that if the historical credit of a single   30
verse of the Bible be shaken, all belief in the Bible is gone.

But indeed, without looking at all to these momentous results of his demonstrations, the Bishop would probably have no difficulty in admitting that these demonstrations can have in themselves nothing edifying. He is an excellent arithmetician,   35
and has published an admirable Manual of Arithmetic; and his book is really nothing but a series of problems in this his favourite science, the solution to each of which is to be the

reductio ad absurdum of that Book of the Pentateuch which
supplied its terms. The Bishop talks of the "multitude of
operatives" whose spiritual condition we must care for: he
allows that to the pious operative his proceedings must give a
5   terrible shock; but will the impious operative be softened or
converted by them? He cannot seriously think so; for softening and converting are positive processes, and his arithmetical
process is a purely negative one. It is even ruthlessly negative;
for it delights in nothing so much as in triumphing over at-
10 tempts which may be made to explain or attenuate the difficulties of the Bible narrative. Such an attempt Dr. Stanley has
made with respect to the history of the sojourn of the Israelites
in the wilderness; the quotations on this matter from Dr. Stanley's "Sinai and Palestine" are the refreshing spots of the Bishop
15 of Natal's volume, but he cites them only to refute them. In a
similar spirit he deals with M. Hengstenberg. M. Hengstenberg
is, in general, only too well contented to remain with his head
under water, raking about in the sand and mud of the letter
for the pearl which will never be found there; but occasion-
20 ally a mortal commentator must come up to breathe. M. Hengstenberg has hardly time to gasp out a rational explanation of
any passage, before the remorseless Bishop pushes him under
water again.

So we must look for the edifying part of the Bishop of
25 Natal's work elsewhere than in his arithmetical demonstrations. And I am bound to say, that such a part the Bishop does
attempt to supply. He feels, as I have said, that the work he
has been accomplishing is not in itself edifying to the common
English reader, that it will leave such a reader with an "aching
30 void" in his bosom; and this void he undoubtedly attempts to
fill. And how does he fill it? "I would venture to refer him,"
he says, "to my lately published Commentary on the Epistle
to the Romans . . . which I would humbly hope by God's mercy
may minister in some measure to the comfort and support of
35 troubled minds under present circumstances." He candidly
adds, however, that this Commentary was written "when I had
no idea whatever of holding my present views." So as a further
support he offers "the third and sixth chapters of Exodus"

(that Exodus on which he has just been inflicting such severe blows), "the noble words of Cicero preserved by Lactantius" in the eighth section of the sixth book of his "Divine Institutions," "the great truths revealed to the Sikh Gooroos," as these truths are set forth in Cunningham's "History of the Sikhs," pp. 355, 356, and lastly a Hindoo prayer, to be found in the *Journal of the Asiatic Society of Bengal*, vol. vi. pp. 484–487, 750–756, beginning "Whatever Rám willeth." And this is positively all. He finds the simple everyday Englishman going into church, he buries him and the sacred fabric under an avalanche of rule-of-three sums; and when the poor man crawls from under the ruins, bruised, bleeding, and bewildered, and begs for a little spiritual consolation, the Bishop "refers him" to his own Commentary on the Romans, two chapters of Exodus, a fragment of Cicero, a revelation to the Sikh Gooroos, and an invocation of Rám. This good Samaritan sets his battered brother on his own beast (the Commentary), and for oil and wine pours into his wounds the Hindoo prayer, the passage of Cicero, and the rest of it.

Literary criticism cannot accept this edification as sufficient. The Bishop of Natal must be considered to have failed to edify the little-instructed, to advance the lower culture of his nation. It is demanded of him, therefore, that he shall have informed the much-instructed, that he shall have advanced the higher culture of his nation or of Europe.

Literary criticism does not require him to edify this; it is enough if he informs it. We may dismiss the Commentary on the Romans and the truths revealed to the Sikh Gooroos from our consideration, for the Bishop himself has told us that it is the weak vessel, the little-instructed, whom he refers to these. There remain his arithmetical demonstrations. And, indeed, he himself seems to rely for his justification upon the informing influence which these are calculated to exercise upon the higher culture of his nation; for he speaks of the "more highly educated classes of society," and of the "intelligent operative" (that favourite character of modern disquisition)—those, that is, who have either read much or thought much—as the special objects of his solicitude. Now, on the higher culture of his

nation, what informing influence can the Bishop of Natal's
arithmetical demonstrations exercise? I have already said what
these are: they are a series of problems, the solution of each
of which is meant to be the *reductio ad absurdum* of that Book
5   of the Pentateuch which supplied its terms. This being so, it
must be said that the Bishop of Natal gives us a great deal
too many of them. For his purpose a smaller number of problems and a more stringent method of stating them would have
sufficed. It would then have been possible within the compass
10 of a single page to put all the information which the Bishop's
book aspires to convey to the mind of Europe. For example:
if we take the Book of Genesis, and the account of the family
of Judah there related—"*Allowing 20 as the marriageable age,
how many years are required for the production of 3 genera-*
15 *tions?*" The answer to that sum disposes (on the Bishop's plan)
of the Book of Genesis. Again, as to the account in the Book
of Exodus of the Israelites dwelling in tents—"*Allowing 10
persons for each tent (and a Zulu hut in Natal contains on
an average only 3½), how many tents would 2,000,000 per-*
20 *sons require?*" The parenthesis in that problem is hardly worthy
of such a master of arithmetical statement as Dr. Colenso; but,
with or without the parenthesis, the problem, when answered,
disposes of the Book of Exodus. Again, as to the account in
Leviticus of the provision made for the priests: "*If three
25 priests have to eat 264 pigeons a day, how many must each
priest eat?*" That disposes of Leviticus. Take Numbers, and
the total of first-borns there given, as compared with the
number of male adults: "*If, of 900,000 males, 22,273 are first-
borns, how many boys must there be in each family?*" That
30 disposes of Numbers. For Deuteronomy, take the number of
lambs slain at the Sanctuary, as compared with the space for
slaying them: "*In an area of 1,692 square yards, how many
lambs per minute can 150,000 persons kill in two hours?*"
Certainly not 1,250, the number required; and the Book of
35 Deuteronomy, therefore, shares the fate of its predecessors.
Omnes eodem cogimur.
  Even a giant need not waste his strength. The Bishop of
Natal has, indeed, other resources in his conflict with the

Pentateuch, if these are insufficient; he has the overcrowding
of the Tabernacle doorway, and the little difficulty about the
Danites; but he need not have troubled himself to produce
them. All he designed to do for the higher culture of his nation
has been done without them. It is useless to slay the slain.   5

Such are the Bishop of Natal's exploits in the field of biblical
criticism. The theological critic will regard them from his
own point of view; the literary critic asks only in what way can
they be informing to the higher culture of England or Europe?
This higher culture knew very well already that contradictions   10
were pointed out in the Pentateuch narrative; it had heard already all that the Bishop of Natal tells us as to the "impossibility of regarding the Mosaic story as a true narrative of actual
historical matters of fact;" of this impossibility, of which the
Bishop of Natal "had not the most distant idea" two years ago,   15
it had long since read expositions, if not so elaborate as his,
at least as convincing. That which the higher culture of Europe
wanted to know is,—*What then?* What follows from all this?
What change is it, if true, to produce in the relations of mankind to the Christian religion? If the old theory of Scripture   20
Inspiration is to be abandoned, what place is the Bible henceforth to hold among books? What is the new Christianity to be
like? How are Governments to deal with national Churches
founded to maintain a very different conception of Christianity?
It is these questions which the higher culture of Europe now   25
addresses to those who profess to enlighten it in the field of
free religious speculation, and it is intellectually informed
only so far as these questions are answered. It is these questions which freethinkers who really speak to the higher culture of their nation or of Europe—men such as Hegel was   30
in Germany, such as M. Renan now is in France—attempt to
answer; and therefore, unorthodox though such writers may
be, literary criticism listens to them with respectful interest.
And it is these questions which the Bishop of Natal never
touches with one of his fingers.   35

I will make what I mean yet clearer by a contrast. At this
very moment is announced [1] the first English translation of a

[1] The book has since been published.

foreign work which treats of the same matter as the Bishop of
Natal's work—the interpretation of Scripture—and, like the
Bishop of Natal's work, treats of it in an unorthodox way. I
mean a work signed by a great name—to most English read-
5   ers the name of a great heretic, and nothing more—the *Trac-*
tatus Theologico-Politicus of Spinoza. It is not so easy to give
a summary of this book as of the book of the Bishop of Natal.
Still, with the aim of showing how free religious speculation
may be conducted so as to be informing to the much-instructed,
10 even though it be not edifying to the little-instructed, I will
attempt the task.

The little-instructed Spinoza's work could not unsettle, for
it was inaccessible to them. It was written in Latin, the language of the instructed few—the language in which Coleridge
15 desired that all novel speculations about religion should be
written. Spinoza even expressly declares that he writes for
the instructed few only, and that his book is not designed for
the many—*reliquis hunc tractatum commendare non studeo.*
Not only the multitude, but all of a higher culture than the
20 multitude who yet share the passions of the multitude, he in-
treats not to read his book: they will only, he says, do harm
to others, and no good to themselves. So sincere was this
author's desire to be simply useful, his indifference to mere
notoriety, that when it was proposed to publish a Dutch trans-
25 lation of his work, and thus bring it within the reach of a
wider public, he requested that the project might be abandoned.
Such a publication could effect no benefit, he said, and it might
injure the cause which he had at heart.

He was moved to write, not by admiration at the magnitude
30 of his own sudden discoveries, not by desire for notoriety, not
by a transport of excitement, not because he "had launched his
bark on the flood and was carried along by the waters;" but
because, grave as was the task to be attempted, and slight as
was the hope of succeeding, the end seemed to him worth all
35 the labour and all the risk. "I fear that I have taken this work
in hand too late in the day; for matters are nearly come to that
pass that men are incapable, on these subjects, of having their
errors cleared away, so saturated with prejudices are their
minds. Still, I will persevere, and continue to make what

effort I can; for the case, after all, is not quite hopeless."
For the instructed few he was convinced that his work might
prove truly informing—*his hoc opus perquam utile fore con-
fido.*

Addressing these, he tells them how, struck with the contrast   5
between the precepts of Christianity and the common practice
of Christians, he had sought the cause of this contrast and
found it in their erroneous conception of their own religion.

[The rest of this paragraph, and the next eight paragraphs, were
transferred to "Spinoza and the Bible," below, pp. 161:9–169:36.]   10

Certainly it is not the doctrine of any of the old Churches
of Christendom; of the Church of Rome, or the Church of
Constantinople, or the Church of England. But Spinoza was
not a member, still less a minister, of any one of these Churches.
When he made a profession of faith widely different from   15
that of any of them, he had not vowed to minister the doctrine
of one of them "as that Church had received the same." When
he claimed for Churchmen the widest latitude of speculation
in religious matters, he was inviting Governments to construct
a new Church; he was not holding office in an old Church   20
under articles expressly promulgated to check "disputations,
altercations, or questions." The Bishop of Natal cries out, that
orders in the Church of England without full liberty of speculation are an intolerable yoke. But he is thus crying out for a
new Church of England, which is not that in which he has   25
voluntarily taken office. He forgets that the clergy of a Church
with formularies like those of the Church of England, exist
in virtue of their relinquishing in religious matters full liberty
of speculation. Liberal potentates of the English Church, who
so loudly sound the praises of freedom of inquiry, forget it   30
also. It may be time for the State to institute, as its national
clergy, a corporation enjoying the most absolute freedom of
inquiry; but that corporation will not be the present clergy
of the Church of England. Coleridge maintained that the whole
body of men of letters or science formed the true clergy of a   35
modern nation, and ought to participate in the endowments
of the National Church. That is a beautiful theory; but it has
not hitherto been cordially welcomed by the clergy of the

Church of England. It has not hitherto been put in practice
by the State. Is it to be put in practice for the future? To any
eminent layman of letters, who presents himself on the other
side the river with the exterminating Five Problems, the passage
of Cicero, and the prayer to Rám as his credentials, will the
gates of Lambeth fly open?

Literary criticism, however, must not blame the Bishop of
Natal because his personal position is false, nor praise Spinoza
because his personal position is sound. But, as it must deny to
the Bishop's book the right of existing, when it can justify its
existence neither by edifying the many nor informing the few,
it must concede that right to Spinoza's for the sake of its un-
questionably philosophic scope. Many and many are the propositions in Spinoza's work, which, brought by him to us out of
the sphere of his unaccepted philosophy, and presented with
all the calm inflexibility of his manner, are startling, repellent,
questionable. Criticism may take many and many objections
to the facts and arguments of his Treatise. But, by the whole
scope and drift of its argument, by the spirit in which the subject is throughout treated, his work undeniably becomes interesting and stimulating to the general culture of Europe. There
are alleged contradictions in Scripture; and the question
which the general culture of Europe, informed of this, asks
with real interest is, as I have said,—*What then?* To this question Spinoza returns an answer, and the Bishop of Natal returns
none. The Bishop of Natal keeps going round for ever within
the barren sphere of these contradictions themselves; he treats
them as if they were supremely interesting in themselves, as
if we had never heard of them before, and could never hear
enough of them now. Spinoza touches these verbal matters with
all possible brevity, and presses on to the more important. It
is enough for him to give us what is indispensably necessary
of them.

[The rest of this paragraph was transferred to "Spinoza and the
Bible," below, pp. 170:13–171:18.]

Thus Spinoza attempts to answer the crucial question, "*What
then?*" and by the attempt, successful or unsuccessful, he inter-

ests the higher culture of Europe. The Bishop of Natal does
not interest this, neither yet does he edify the unlearned. His
book, therefore, satisfies neither of the two conditions, one of
which literary criticism has a right to impose on all religious
books: *Edify the uninstructed*, it has a right to say to them,   5
or inform the instructed. Fulfilling neither of these conditions,
the Bishop of Natal's book cannot justify itself for existing.
When, in 1861, he heard for the first time that the old theory
of the verbal inspiration of Scripture was untenable, he should,
instead of proclaiming this news (if this was all he could pro-   10
claim) in an octavo volume, have remembered that excellent
saying of the Wise Man: "If thou hast heard a word, let it die
with thee; and be bold, it will not burst thee."

These two conditions, which the Bishop of Natal's book entirely fails to fulfil, another well-known religious book also—   15
that book which made so much noise two years ago, the
volume of *Essays and Reviews*—fails, it seems to me, to fulfil
satisfactorily. Treating religious subjects and written by clergymen, the compositions in that volume have in general, to the
eye of literary criticism, this great fault—that they tend neither   20
to edify the many, nor to inform the few. There is but one
of them—that by Mr. Pattison on the *Tendencies of Religious
Thought in England*—which offers to the higher culture of
Europe matter new and instructive. There are some of them
which make one, as one reads, instinctively recur to a saying   25
which was a great favourite—so that Hebrew moralist whom
I have already quoted tells us—with Judah Ben-Tamai: "The
impudent are for Gehinnan, and the modest for Paradise." But
even Dr. Temple's Essay on the *Education of the World*,
perfectly free from all faults of tone or taste, has this fault—   30
that while it offers nothing edifying to the uninstructed, it
offers to the instructed nothing which they could not have
found in a far more perfect shape in the works of Lessing. Mr.
Jowett's Essay, again, contains nothing which is not given, with
greater convincingness of statement and far greater fulness of   35
consequence in Spinoza's seventh chapter, which treats of the
Interpretation of Scripture. The doctrines of his Essay, as mere
doctrine, are neither milk for babes nor strong meat for men;

the weak among his readers will be troubled by them; the strong
would be more informed by seeing them handled as acquired
elements for further speculation by freer exponents of the
speculative thought of Europe, than by seeing them hesitatingly
5   exhibited as novelties. In spite of this, however, Mr. Jowett's
Essay has one quality which, at the tribunal of literary criticism,
is sufficient to justify it—a quality which communicates to all
works where it is present an indefinable charm, and which
is always, for the higher sort of minds, edifying;—it has *unction*.
10   From a clergyman's essay on a religious subject theological
criticism may have a right to demand more than this; literary
criticism has not. For a court of literature it is enough that
the somewhat pale stream of Mr. Jowett's speculation is gilded
by the heavenly alchemy of this glow.

15   [The next two paragraphs were transferred to "Spinoza and the
Bible," below, pp. 179:17–182:15.]

Still, the *Tractatus Theologico-Politicus* was deemed by
Spinoza himself a work not suitable to the general public, and
here is Mr. Trübner offering it to the general public in a trans-
20   lation! But a little reflection willl show that Mr. Trübner
is not therefore to be too hastily blamed. Times are changed
since Spinoza wrote; the reserve which he recommended
and practised is being repudiated by all the world. Speculation
is to be made popular, all reticence is to be abandoned, every
25   difficulty is to be canvassed publicly, every doubt is to be
proclaimed; information which, to have any value at all,
must have it as part of a series not yet complete, is to be flung
broadcast, in the crudest shape, amidst the undisciplined,
ignorant, passionate, captious multitude.

30   "Audax omnia perpeti
                 Gens humana ruit per vetitum nefas:"

and in that adventurous march the English branch of the race
of Japhet is, it seems, to be headed by its clergy in full canoni-
cals. If so it is to be, so be it. But, if this is to be so, the Editor
35   of the *Record* himself, instead of deprecating the diffusion of
Spinoza's writings, ought rather to welcome it. He would

prefer, of course, that we should all be even as he himself is; that we should all think the same thing as that which he himself thinks. This desire, although all might not consent to join in it, is legitimate and natural. But its realisation is impossible; heresy is here, it is pouring in on all sides of him. If we must have heresy, he himself will admit that we may as well have the informing along with the barren. The author of the *Tractatus Theologico-Politicus* is not more unorthodox than the author of the *Pentateuch Critically Examined*, and he is far more edifying. If the English clergy must err, let them learn from this outcast of Israel to err nobly! Along with the weak trifling of the Bishop of Natal, let it be lawful to cast into the huge caldron, out of which the new world is to be born, the strong thought of Spinoza!

Tractatus Theologico-Politicus *

Baruch Spinoza, the son of a small Jew trader whom religious persecution had driven from his native country, Portugal, was born at Amsterdam on the 24th of November, 1632. His talents were from his earliest boyhood remarked, and he was brought
5 up by the Jewish rabbins in all their learning. Dissatisfied with this learning, he turned from it to the study of philosophy, above all, the philosophy of Descartes, and made no secret of having abandoned the traditions of his Jewish masters. After vainly attempting to retain by bribes their promising disciple,
10 these masters tried to silence him by assassination. The attempt failed; but Spinoza long showed the cloak which had been pierced by the assassin's dagger. He was publicly excommunicated in the Portuguese synagogue at Amsterdam about the year 1660. He then changed his Hebrew name of Baruch for
15 the Latin name of Benedict, but he never was baptized or joined any religious communion. After a life of exemplary simplicity, moderation, and virtue, he died of consumption at the Hague, on the 21st of February, 1677, at the age of forty-four. His most celebrated work, his "Ethics," was published after his
20 death; the works which he published in his life-time were not numerous, the only one of great importance among them being the "Tractatus Theologico-Politicus," now translated into English for the first time.

Spinoza himself did not design this treatise for the general
25 public, but for the philosophic few. When it was proposed in

* Tractatus Theologico-Politicus: A Critical Inquiry into the History, Purpose, and Authenticity of the Hebrew Scriptures. By Benedict de Spinoza. From the Latin; with an Introduction and Notes by the Editor. London: Trübner & Co.

his life-time to bring out a Dutch translation of it, he expressed, in a letter which has been preserved, his objections to giving to such a work this kind of publicity. This is a point, however, on which an author cannot hope to have his own way. It is the fame of his book which, in the end, settles the question whether 5 it shall be translated or not; and the fame, if not of the "Tractatus Theologico-Politicus," at least of Spinoza, is such as to make one wonder that this book should not sooner have appeared in English. But, in truth, over Spinoza and his works there hangs a cloud—the cloud of a heterodoxy, bold, boundless, 10 uncompromising; so bold, so boundless, and so uncompromising that his enemies have not hesitated to give to it the terrible name of Atheism. This explains the long reserve of English translators and English publishers. Recent events, however, have powerfully called public attention to critical examinations 15 of Scripture, and at length an Englishman, bolder than the rest, takes a candle and invites his countrymen to follow him to the cavern of Spinoza, and see with their own eyes this famous Jew's "Critical Inquiry into the History, Purpose, and Authenticity of the Hebrew Scriptures." 20

He does well. Whatever Spinoza was, he was not an Atheist: "the more we know God, the more do we become masters of ourselves, and find in this knowledge our rest and our salvation." That is his doctrine from the first line of his works to the last. Unorthodox he is, but to that the Bishop of Natal has 25 accustomed us; and a public which devours the bishop's "Critical Inquiry" may as well read Spinoza's also. It will even find in the latter, if not so much arithmetic, at least a more interesting strain of criticism than in the former. "The religion of all the great churches of Christendom is a religion which is not 30 that of the Bible; it is a huge gloss put upon the Bible by generations of metaphysical theologians; the Bible, honestly and intelligently read, gives us a religion quite different and far simpler." Such is the thesis which Spinoza, with sincere earnestness, wonderful acuteness, and vast learning unfolds in his 35 treatise, and the thesis is undeniably an interesting one.

We therefore commend the English editor for his design of at last lighting us to Spinoza. But we are sorry to say that the

candle he takes with him is quite insufficient. In other words, he does not know the Latin language; and the best intentions will not enable a man who does not know that, to guide us to the knowledge of a book written in Latin. No man, it is said, is
5   aware of his own ignorance; so, for producing this most imperfect translation, its maker, perhaps, is not to be blamed; but he certainly does himself no credit by publishing it. It is remarkable how often work of this kind—the journeyman-work of literature, as it may be called, the work of translating, the
10 work of compiling, the work of dictionary-making—is ill done in this country. Probably the cause lies principally in that which is one of the distinctions we, as Britons, are so proud of —our want of a National Institute or Academy.

To be convinced that the English editor is incompetent to
15 translate a Latin book, one need not go beyond his version of Spinoza's preface and first chapter. We suppose it is indispensable to perform the ungrateful task of giving specimens of his mistakes. We shall do so with the utmost brevity consistent with making his incompetency clear to all fit judges.
20 In the fourteenth section of his preface, Spinoza says:—

"Miratus sæpe fui, quod homines, qui se Christianam religionem profiteri jactant, hoc est, amorem, gaudium, pacem, continentiam et erga omnes fidem, plus quam iniquo animo certarent et acerbissimum in invicem odium quotidiè exercerent, ita ut facilius ex his,
25 quam illis, fides uniuscujusque noscatur."

This the English editor renders as follows:—

"I have often wondered within myself that men who *boast of the great advantages they enjoy under the Christian dispensation—the peace, the joy they experience, the brotherly love they feel towards*
30 *all in its exercise*—should, nevertheless, contend with so much acrimony and show such intolerance and unappeasable hatred towards one another. *If faith had to be inferred from action rather than profession, it would be impossible to say to what sect or creed the majority of mankind belonged.*"

35 That is, to say the least, a very unsatisfactory style of translating; one is left in some doubt, however, whether the translator *cannot* or *will not* be accurate; whether he really cannot

seize the literal sense of the Latin words, or whether it is only his natural vagueness of mind and diffuseness of style which make him paraphrase his author thus loosely. But in the next extract he leaves us in no doubt. Spinoza, speaking of theologians who have, he asserts, foisted into the Christian religion the speculations of the Aristotelians and Platonists, says:—

"Fateor, eos nunquam satis mirari potuisse Scripturæ profundissima mysteria; attamen præter Aristotelicorum vel Platonicorum speculationes nihil docuisse video, atque his, ne gentiles sectari viderentur, Scripturam accommodaverunt. Non satis his fuit cum Græcis insanire, sed prophetas cum iisdem deliravisse voluerunt."

This the English editor turns into the following:—

"I confess, that *whilst with them I have never been able sufficiently to admire the unfathomed mysteries of Scripture, I have still found them giving utterance to nothing but Aristotelian and Platonic speculations,* artfully dressed up and cunningly accommodated to Holy Writ, lest the speakers should show themselves too plainly to belong to the sect of the Grecian heathens. *Nor was it enough for these men to discourse with the Greeks; they have further taken to raving with the Hebrew prophets.*"

This almost takes one's breath away, indeed; but it leaves one perfectly free from doubt as to its author's knowledge of Latin. No one who, in youth or age, had really learned the tongue of "the sect of the Latin heathens,"—no one who had ever walked for six months in the ways of *Grammar* and *Delectus,*—could possibly have imagined, however vague his mind or diffuse his style, that by saying, "I confess, that whilst with them I have never been able sufficiently to admire the unfathomable mysteries of Scripture," he was rendering, "Fateor eos nunquam satis mirari potuissc Scripturæ profundissima mysteria;" or that, "Nor was it enough for these men to discourse with the Greeks; they have further taken to raving with the Hebrew prophets," was a translation of "Non satis his fuit cum Græcis insanire, sed prophetas cum iisdem deliravisse voluerunt." And this in a passage really as clear as daylight, and of which neither the words nor the meaning contain the slightest difficulty. "I confess," says Spinoza, "they (the theologians)

have never been able sufficiently to profess their admiration
of the profound mysteries of Scripture, but I cannot see that
they have taught anything but speculations of the Aristotelians
and Platonists, and to these, that they might not seem to be followers of the heathen, they have accommodated Scripture.
They have not been content to go mad with the Greeks themselves; they will have it that the prophets have raved with them
also."

After this it is almost a waste of time to point out that "than
which I find nothing more reprehensible" is not the English
of "quo mihi quidem nihil magis ridiculum videtur;" or that
"plunged in wickedness and sin" is not the English of "illuvie
peccatorum inquinatos et sterquiliniis quasi immersos." It is
wearisome and useless to multiply instances of an inaccuracy
which shows itself in every page, and which is so astounding
as positively to make one rub one's eyes. The English editor is
apparently a man familiar with philosophical speculations and
capable enough of understanding Spinoza's thought when he
can get hold of it; but whether he gets hold of it or no is all a
chance, so ignorant is he of Latin. We turned to a passage in
the fourth chapter, where Spinoza's thought cannot be quite
rightly seized without attention and a clear head; we own we
were surprised to find how well our editor got on for a sentence or two; able to follow an intricate train of thought he
certainly is, but at any moment his ignorance of Latin may
throw him completely out. He can imagine that when Spinoza
says, "illa revelatio respectu solius Adami et propter solum
defectum ejus cognitionis lex fuit, Deusque quasi legislator aut
princeps (*that revelation in respect of Adam only and by reason only of his defect of knowledge was a law, and God as it
were a legislator and sovereign*)," he means, "the commandment in question is to be regarded as made in respect of Adam
alone; it was a law only by reason of his defect of apprehension, and God stood to him in the relation of a legislator or
prince to his people!" When Spinoza says that God told Adam
"bonum agere et quærere sub ratione boni, et non quatenus
contrarium est malo (*to do and seek good as such, and not as
the contrary of evil*)," his English editor can imagine that he

means, "God told Adam to do good and to proceed under the guidance of the good in itself, and not as it is the opposite of evil!" And when Spinoza comes to the very cardinal sentence of his whole treatise,—the sentence in which he declares what it is that revelation does really tell us which we could not have known without revelation,—when he says, "non possumus lumine naturali percipere quod simplex obedientia via ad salutem sit, sed sola revelatio docet, id ex singulari Dei gratiâ, quam ratione assequi non possumus, fieri (*by the light of nature alone we cannot make out that simple obedience is a way to salvation, but revelation alone teaches us that this is brought to pass by God's singular grace, which grace we with our reason cannot follow up*)," his translator makes him say, "we do not perceive by the light we bring with us into the world that simple obedience is the way of life, whilst revelation alone, by the singular grace of God, teaches this, which we could not learn by our reason."

In addition to his ignorance of Latin the English editor has a perplexed style, which makes him very unfit to be the translator of a book like Spinoza's treatise. Certainly it is hard to write well this noble but recalcitrant English language of ours; we are all privileged to write it somewhat badly, but this translator abuses all imaginable privilege of writing badly. In utter astonishment, we have sometimes fancied he must be a foreigner; but he cannot be a Frenchman, for his movement of mind is not in the least French; and no German (besides that a German is generally a painstaking man, who, if he has to translate a Latin book, duly learns his *Latin Grammar* first) could ever have thought that Schleiermacher, by "Opfert mit mir ehrerbietig den Manen des heiligen verstossenen Spinoza!" meant "Sacrifice with me a lock of hair to the manes of the pure and misunderstood Spinoza!" And besides his ignorance of Latin and his perplexed style, he has the fault (unpardonable in a translator) of putting himself a great deal too forward by notes and observations, and of even sacrificing his author's opinions to his own. For example, Spinoza has, at the end of his eighteenth chapter, some very curious remarks on the first English revolution and the death of Charles I., in which the

conduct of the popular party is severely criticised; these remarks his English editor has thought fit, as he himself informs
us in a note, to "condense and somewhat modify,"—*i.e.*, totally
to alter,—because they do not agree with his own notions, be-
5   cause, in his opinion, "there was no wanton bloodshed during
the great English revolution," and so on. What Spinoza's reader
wants to know is what Spinoza thought of the English revolution, not what his editor thinks.

      This, one would say, was enough; but in yet one other part
10 of an editor's true duty to his author does this translator fail.
It is the highest and most difficult part of an editor's duty,
certainly; but no man who cared for Spinoza should have
brought this treatise before the English public unless he could
discharge it. We mean the duty of skilfully introducing an
15 author around whose name there hangs, justly or unjustly,
a certain odium; of presenting him favourably, of removing
groundless prejudices against him, of conciliating the reader's
mind to him, of securing for him a good hearing. Spinoza's
English editor does the very contrary of all this. He presents
20 Spinoza to the English public by means of an introduction,
which is just calculated to set the English public still more
against him, an introduction filled with his own speculations
about religion; speculations which will certainly be unpalatable
to the general English reader, and which we assure that reader
25 (assuming for a moment the function which an author's editor
should himself discharge) are all of them the translator's thunder, not Spinoza's. We cannot, however, hope to do away with
the unfavourable bias with which many readers, after going
through this introduction, will approach Spinoza. The editor
30 has all the dreadful stock-in-trade of the regular British "advanced liberal" in religion and politics: "in this favoured land
we have long attained to a salutary conviction of the unmixed
advantages that accrue from the open discussion of political
and social questions;" "credulity and mystery have lost their
35 hold upon the educated mind of the nineteenth century, and
he who has made any progress in reasonable, as distinguished
from dogmatic, religion, finds no satisfaction for the aspirations of his spirit towards the infinite in ritual observance, in

parrot-like iteration of set formulæ, and in a mendacious prostration," &c.; "it is notorious that the zealous and perfectly
sincere professor—to say nothing of crimes of far deeper dye
perpetrated by the fanatic—the perfectly sincere professor, we
say, has occasionally proved the spoiler of the widow and the   5
orphan confided to his care; the forger of deeds that made innocent children beggars; the selfish sybarite, who consumed in
sensual indulgence the hard-won earnings of the labouring
poor;" "Spinoza had, indeed, a great contempt for the vul-
gar . . . . but in the course of two centuries the world has ad-   10
vanced in its notions of what constitutes real vulgarity and true
learning, and has decided that neither one nor other necessarily inheres in the possession, or in the want of Greek and
Latin." As to the last of these extracts, we say that no march
of intellect and civilization can ever make Latin and Greek   15
unnecessary possessions for people who translate Latin and
Greek books, whatever they may make them for the rest of the
world. As to all the other extracts, we say that there breathes
from them just that odour of Cato-street, which makes the
general British public choose rather to think wrong with the   20
late amiable Archbishop Howley, than to think right with their
new enlighteners.

If any one likes to buy this publication, of course he can buy
it; only let him be well assured that when he has got it he has
not got Spinoza's *Tractatus Theologico-Politicus*. If he is ab-   25
solutely bent on passing a little time over this work, for change
of air after the Bishop of Natal's *Critical Inquiry*, he may read
it in M. Saisset's French version. Let him bear in mind, however, that M. Saisset has a religion of his own in his writing-
table drawer, and that he cries down Spinoza's wares in order   30
to leave the market free for this ware of his own. Or he may
read it in the German version of M. Auerbach. Or (better
still) let him try and read it in the original Latin; Spinoza's
Latin is not classical Latin certainly, but it is very clear, mas-
sive, and characteristic; and, for all but scholars, far easier read-   35
ing than any classical Latin. If he knows neither Latin, French,
nor German, he must wait for a proper English translation. The
present English translation let no man buy.

We part from this book with sincere resentment. This publication is discreditable to all concerned in it; advantage has been taken of the curiosity which the Bishop of Natal's book has excited about Biblical criticism, to try and palm off upon
5   the British public an article which is, in the translator's own language, most "mendacious." And we have been compelled to perform a task which is revolting to us, and which is not the task we had thought to perform. We had thought to speak of a great thinker and his philosophy; and, instead of that, we
10 find ourselves with these hangman's hands. What right has any editor or publisher to force the peaceful haters of bloodshed to become butchers against their will, under penalty, if they hold back, of seeing a heinous literary sin committed; of seeing another great author lost sight of, or else seen all wrong, in the
15 hideous anarchy which is modern English literature?

Dr. Stanley's Lectures on the Jewish Church

Here is a book on religious matters, which, meant for all the world to read, fulfils the indispensable duty of edifying at the same time that it informs. Here is a clergyman, who, looking at the Bible, sees its contents in their right proportion, and gives to each matter its due prominence. Here is an inquirer, who, treating Scripture history with a perfectly free spirit,— falsifying nothing, sophisticating nothing—treats it so that his freedom leaves the sacred power of that history inviolate. Who that had been reproached with denying to an honest clergyman freedom to speak the truth, who that had been misrepresented as wishing to make religious truth the property of an aristocratic few, while to the multitude is thrown the sop of any convenient fiction, could desire a better opportunity than Dr. Stanley's book affords for showing what, in religious matters, is the true freedom of a religious speaker, and what the true demand and true right of his hearers?

His hearers are the many; those who prosecute the religious life, or those who need to prosecute it. All these come to him with certain demands in virtue of certain needs. There remain a few of mankind who do not come to him with these demands, or acknowledge these needs. Mr. Maurice (whom I name with gratitude and respect) says, in a remarkable letter, that I thus assert them to be without these needs. By no means: that is a matter which literary criticism does not try. But it sees that a very few of mankind aspire after a life which is not the life after which the vast majority aspire, and to help them to which the vast majority seek the aid of religion. It sees that the ideal life—the *summum bonum* for a born thinker, for a philosopher like Parmenides, or Spinoza, or Hegel—is an eternal series of

5

10

15

20

25

65

intellectual acts. It sees that this life treats all things, religion included, with entire freedom as subject-matter for thought, as elements in a vast movement of speculation. The few who live this life stand apart, and have an existence separate from that of the mass of mankind; they address an imaginary audience of their mates; the region which they inhabit is the laboratory wherein are fashioned the new intellectual ideas which, from time to time, take their place in the world. Are these few justified, in the sight of God, in so living? That is a question which literary criticism must not attempt to answer. But such is the worth of intellect, such the benefit which it procures for man, that criticism, itself the creation of intellect, cannot but recognise this purely intellectual life, when really followed, as justified so far as the jurisdiction of criticism extends, and even admirable. Those they regard as really following it, who show the power of mind to animate and carry forward the intellectual movement in which it consists. No doubt, many boast of living this life, of inhabiting this purely intellectual region, who cannot really breathe its air: they vainly profess themselves able to live by thought alone, and to dispense with religion: the life of the many, and not the life of the few, would have been the right one for them. They follow the life of the few at their own peril. No doubt the rich and the great, unsoftened by suffering, hardened by enjoyment, craving after novelty, imagining that they see a distinction in the freedom of mind with which the born thinker treats all things, and believing that all distinctions naturally belong to them, have in every age been prone to treat religion as something which the multitude wanted, but they themselves did not—to affect free-thinking as a kind of aristocratic privilege; while, in fact, for any real mental or moral life at all, their frivolity entirely disqualified them. They, too, profess the life of the few at their own peril. But the few do really remain, whose life, whose ideal, whose demand, is thought, and thought only: to the communications (however bold) of these few with one another through the ages, criticism assigns the right of passing freely.

But the world of the few—the world of speculative life—is not the world of the many, the world of religious life; the thoughts of the former cannot properly be transferred to the latter, cannot be called true in the latter, except on certain conditions. It is not for literary criticism to set forth adequately the religious life; yet what, even as criticism, it sees of this life, it may say. Religious life resides not in an incessant movement of ideas, but in a feeling which attaches itself to certain fixed objects. The religious life of Christendom has thus attached itself to the acts, and words, and death of Christ, as recorded in the Gospels and expounded in the Epistles of the New Testament; and to the main histories, the prophecies and the hymns of the Old Testament. In relation to these objects, it has adopted certain intellectual ideas; such are, ideas respecting the being of God, the laws of nature, the freedom of human will, the character of prophecy, the character of inspiration. But its essence, the essence of Christian life, consists in the ardour, the love, the self-renouncement, the ineffable aspiration with which it throws itself upon the objects of its attachment themselves, not in the intellectual ideas which it holds in relation to them. These ideas belong to another sphere, the sphere of speculative life, of intellect, of pure thought; transplanted into the sphere of religious life, they have no meaning in them, no vitality, no truth, unless they adjust themselves to the conditions of that life, unless they allow it to pursue its course freely. The moment this is forgotten, the moment in the sphere of the religious life undue prominence is given to the intellectual ideas which are here but accessories, the moment the first place is not given to the emotion which is here the principal, that moment the essence of the religious life is violated: confusion and falsehood are introduced into its sphere. And, if not only is undue prominence in this sphere given to intellectual ideas, but these ideas are so presented as in themselves violently to jar with the religious feeling, then the confusion is a thousand times worse confounded, the falsehood a thousand times more glaring.

"*The earth moves*," said Galileo, speaking as a philosopher in the sphere of pure thought, in which ideas have an absolute value; and he said the truth; he was a great thinker because he perceived this truth; he was a great man because he asserted

it in spite of persecution. It was the theologians, insisting upon
transplanting his idea into the world of theology, and placing
it in a false connexion there, who were guilty of folly. But if
Galileo himself, quitting the sphere of mathematics, coming
into the sphere of religion, had placed this thesis of his in juxtaposition with the Book of Joshua, had applied it so as to impair the value of the Book of Joshua for the religious life of
Christendom, to make that book regarded as a tissue of fictions,
for which no blame indeed attached to Joshua, because he
never meant it for anything else,—then Galileo would have
himself placed his idea in a false connexion, and would have
deserved censure: his *"the earth moves"* in spite of its absolute
truth, would have become a falsehood. Spinoza, again, speaking as a pure thinker to pure thinkers, not concerning himself
whether what he said impaired or confirmed the power and
virtue of the Bible for the actual religious life of Christendom, but pursuing a speculative demonstration, said: "The
Bible contains much that is mere history, and, like all history,
sometimes true, sometimes false." But we must bear in mind
that Spinoza did not promulgate this thesis in immediate connexion with the religious life of his times, but as a speculative
idea: he uttered it not as a religious teacher, but as an independent philosopher; and he left it, as Galileo left his, to filter
down gradually (if true) into the common thought of mankind, and to adjust itself, through other agency than his, to
their religious life. The Bishop of Natal does not speak as an
independent philosopher, as a pure thinker; if he did, and if
he spoke with power in this capacity, literary criticism would,
I have already said, have no right to condemn him. But he
speaks actually and avowedly, as by virtue of his office he was
almost inevitably constrained to speak, as a religious teacher
to the religious world. Well, then, any intellectual idea which,
speaking in this capacity, he promulgates, he is bound to place
in its right connexion with the religious life, he is bound to
make harmonise with that life, he is bound not to magnify
to the detriment of that life: else, in the sphere of that life, it is
false. He takes an intellectual idea, we will say, which is true;
the idea that Mr. Burgon's proposition, "Every letter of the

Bible is the direct utterance of the Most High," is false. And how does he apply this idea in connexion with the religious life? He gives to it the most excessive, the most exaggerated prominence; so much so, that hardly in one page out of twenty does he suffer his reader to recollect that the religious life exists out of connexion with this idea, that it is, in truth, wholly independent of it. And by way of adjusting this idea to the feeling of the religious reader of the Bible, he puts it thus:— "In writing the story of the Exodus from the ancient legends of his people, the Scripture writer may have had no more consciousness of doing wrong, or of practising historical deception, than Homer had, or any of the early Roman annalists." Theological criticism censures this language as unorthodox, irreverent: literary criticism censures it as *false*. Its employer precisely does what I have imagined Galileo doing: he misemploys a true idea so as to deprive it of all truth. It is a thousand times truer to say that the Book of Exodus is a sacred book, an inspired history, than to say that it is fiction, not culpable because no deception was intended, because its author worked in the same free poetic spirit as the creator of the Isle of Calypso and the Garden of Alcinous.

It is one of the hardest tasks in the world to make new intellectual ideas harmonise truly with the religious life, to place them in their right light for that life. The moments in which such a change is accomplished are epochs in religious history; the men through whose instrumentality it is accomplished are great religious reformers. The greatness of these men does not consist in their having these new ideas, in their originating them. The ideas are in the world; they come originally from the sphere of pure thought; they are put into circulation by the spirit of the time. The greatness of a religious reformer consists in his reconciling them with the religious life, in his starting this life upon a fresh period in company with them. No such religious reformer for the present age has yet shown himself. Till he appears, the true religious teacher is he who, not yet reconciling all things, at least esteems things still in their due order, and makes his hearers so esteem them; who, shutting his mind against no ideas brought by the spirit

of his time, sets these ideas, in the sphere of the religious life,
in their right prominence, and still puts that first which is
first; who, under the pressure of new thoughts, keeps the centre
of the religious life where it should be. The best distinction
5   of Dr. Stanley's lectures is that in them he shows himself such
a teacher. Others will praise them, and deservedly praise them,
for their eloquence, their varied information; for enabling us
to give such form and substance to our impressions from Bible
history. To me they seem admirable, chiefly by the clear per-
10 ception which they exhibit of a religious teacher's true business in dealing with the Bible. Dr. Stanley speaks of the Bible
to the religious world, and he speaks of it so as to maintain
the sense of the divine virtue of the Bible unimpaired, so as
to bring out this sense more fully. He speaks of the deliver-
15 ance of the Israelites out of the land of Egypt. He does not
dilate upon the difficulty of understanding how the Israelites
should have departed "harnessed;" but he points out how they
are "the only nation in ancient or modern times, which, throwing off the yoke of slavery, claims no merit, no victory of its
20 own: There is no Marathon, no Regillus, no Tours, no Mor-
garten. All is from above, nothing from themselves." He mentions the difficulty of "conceiving the migration of a whole
nation under such circumstances" as those of the Israelites, the
proposal "to reduce the numbers of the text from 600,000 to
25 600 armed men;" he mentions the difficulty of determining
the exact place of the passage of the Red Sea; but he quickly
"dismisses these considerations to fix the mind on the essential
features of this great deliverance"—on the Almighty, "through
the dark and terrible night, with the enemy pressing close
30 behind and the driving seas on either side, leading his people
like sheep by the hands of Moses and Aaron;" his people,
carrying with them from that night "the abiding impression
that this deliverance—the first and greatest in their history—
was effected not by their own power, but by the power of
35 God." He tells the reader how, "with regard to all the topographical details of the Israelite journey, we are still in the
condition of discoverers;" but, instead of impressing upon him
as an inference from this that the Bible narrative is a creation

such as the Iliad and Odyssey, he reminds him, with truth,
how "suspense as to the exact details of form and locality is
the most fitting approach for the consideration of the presence of Him who has made darkness his secret place, his pavil-
ion round about Him with dark water, and thick clouds to   5
cover them." Everywhere Dr. Stanley thus seeks to give its
due prominence to that for which the religious life really
values the Bible. If "the Jewish religion is characterised in an
eminent degree by the dimness of its conception of a future
life," Dr. Stanley does not find here, like Warburton, matter   10
for a baffling contrast between Jewish and pagan religion,
but he finds fresh proof of the grand edifying fact of Jewish
history, "the consciousness of the living, actual presence of
God himself—a truth, in the limited conceptions of this youthful nation, too vast to admit of any rival truth, however   15
precious." He speaks of the call of Samuel. What he finds to
dwell on in this call is not the exact nature of the voice that
called Samuel, on which Spinoza speculates so curiously; it is
the image of "childlike, devoted, continuous goodness," which
Samuel's childhood brings before us; the type which Samuel   20
offers "of holiness, of growth, of a new creation without con-
version." He speaks of the Prophets, and he avows that "the
Bible recognises 'revelation' and 'inspiration' outside the circle
of the chosen people;" but he makes it his business not to reduce, in virtue of this avowal, the greatness and significance of   25
Hebrew prophecy, but to set that greatness and significance
in clearer light than ever. To the greatness and significance of
what he calls "the negative side" of that prophecy—its attacks
on the falsehoods and superstitions which endeavoured to take
the place of God—he does due justice; but he reserves the   30
chief prominence for its "positive side—the assertion of the
spirituality, the morality of God, His justice, His goodness,
His love." Everywhere he keeps in mind the purpose for
which the religious life seeks the Bible—to be enlarged and
strengthened, not to be straitened and perplexed. He seizes   35
a truth of criticism when he says that the Bible narrative,
whatever inaccuracies of numbers the Oriental tendency to
amplification may have introduced into it, remains a "sub-

stantially historical" work—not a work like Homer's poems;
but to this proposition, which, merely so stated, is a truth of
criticism and nothing more, he assigns no undue prominence:
he knows that a mere truth of criticism is not, as such, a truth
5   for the religious life.

Dr. Stanley thus gives a lesson not only to the Bishop of
Natal, but to the Bishop of Natal's adversaries. Many of these
adversaries themselves exactly repeat the Bishop's error in this,
that they give a wholly undue prominence, in connexion with
10 the religious life, to certain intellectual propositions, on which
the essence and vitality of the religious life in no way depends. The Bishop devotes a volume to the exhibition of such
propositions, and he is censurable because, addressing the religious world, he exhibits his propositions so as to confuse the
15 religious life by them, not to strengthen it. He seems to have
so confused it in many of his hearers that they, like himself,
have forgotten in what it really consists. Puzzled by the
Bishop's sums, terrified at the conclusion he draws from them,
they, in their bewilderment, seek for safety in attacking the
20 sums themselves, instead of putting them on one side as irrelevant, and rejecting the conclusion deduced from them as
untrue. "Here is a Bishop," many of Dr. Stanley's brethren
are now crying in all parts of England—"here is a Bishop who
has learnt among the Zulus that only a certain number of
25 people can stand in a doorway at once, and that no man can
eat eighty-eight pigeons a day, and who tells us, as a consequence, that the Pentateuch is all fiction, which, however, the
author may very likely have composed without meaning to
do wrong, and as a work of poetry, like Homer's." "Well,"
30 one can imagine Dr. Stanley answering them, "you cannot
think that!" "No," they reply; "and yet the Bishop's sums
puzzle us, and we want them disproved. And powerful answers,
we know, are preparing. An adversary worthy of the Bishop
will soon appear,—

35   Exoriare aliquis nostris ex ossibus ultor!

He, when he comes, will make mincemeat of the Bishop's calculations. Those great truths, so necessary to our salvation,

which the Bishop assails, will at his hands receive all the strengthening they deserve. He will prove to demonstration that any number of persons can stand in the same doorway at once, and that one man can eat eighty-eight pigeons a day with ease." "Compose yourselves," says Dr. Stanley: "he cannot prove this." "What," cry his terrified interlocutors, "he cannot! In that case we may as well shut up our Bibles, and read Homer and the first books of Livy!" "Compose yourselves," says Dr. Stanley again: "it is not so. Even if the Bishop's sums are right, they do not prove that the Bible narrative is to be classed with the Iliad and the Legends of Rome. Even if you prove them wrong, your success does not bring you a step nearer to that which you go to the Bible to seek. Carry your achievements of this kind to the Statistical Society, to the Geographical Society, to the Ethnological Society. They have no vital interest for the religious reader of the Bible. The heart of the Bible is not there."

Just because Dr. Stanley has comprehended this, and, in a book addressed to the religious world makes us feel that he has comprehended it, his book is excellent and salutary. I praise it for the very reason for which some critics find fault with it—for not giving prominence, in speaking of the Bible, to matters with which the real virtue of the Bible is not bound up. "The book," a critic complains, "contains no solution of the difficulties which the history of the period traversed presents in the Bible. The oracle is dumb in the very places where many would wish it to speak. This must lessen Dr. Stanley's influence in the cause of Biblical science. The present time needs bold men, prepared to give utterance to their deepest thoughts." And which are a man's deepest thoughts I should like to know: his thoughts whether it was 215 years, or 430, or 1,000 that the Israelites sojourned in Egypt,—which question the critic complains of Dr. Stanley for saying that it is needless to discuss in detail,—or his thoughts on the moral lesson to be drawn from the story of the Israelites' deliverance? And which is the true science of the Bible—that which helps men to follow the cardinal injunction of the Bible, to be "transformed by the renewing of their mind, that they may prove what is that good, and acceptable, and perfect will of God"—or that which helps them to "settle the vexed question of the precise time when the Book of Deuteronomy assumed its present form"?—that which elaborates an octavo volume on the arithmetical difficulties of the Bible, with the conclusion that the Bible is as unhistorical as Homer's poetry, or that which makes us feel that "these difficulties melt away before the simple pathos and lofty spirit of the Bible itself"? Such critics as this critic of Dr. Stanley are those who commend the Bishop of Natal for "speaking the truth," who say that "liberals of every shade of opinion" are indignant with me for rebuking him. Ah! these liberals!—the power for good they have had, and lost: the power for good they will yet again have, and yet again lose! Eternal bondsmen of phrases and catchwords, will they never arrive at the heart of any matter, but always keep muttering round it their silly shibboleths like an incantation? There is truth of science and truth of religion: truth of science does not become truth of religion until it is made to harmonise with it. Applied as the laws of nature are applied in the "Essays and Reviews," applied as arithmetical calculations are applied in the Bishop of Natal's work, truths of science, even supposing them to be such, lose their truth, and the utterer of them is not a "fearless speaker of truth," but, at best, a blunderer. "Allowing two feet in width for each full-grown man, nine men could just have stood in front of the Tabernacle." "A priest could not have eaten, daily, eighty-eight pigeons for his own portion, 'in the most holy place.'" And as a conclusion from all this: "In writing the story of the Exodus from the ancient legends of his people, the Scripture-writer may have had no more consciousness of doing wrong, or of practising historical deception, than Homer had, or any of the early Roman annalists." Heaven and earth, what a gospel! Is it this which a "fearless speaker of truth" must "burst" if he cannot utter? Is this a message which it is woe to him if he does not preach?—this a testimony which he is straitened till he can deliver?

I am told that the Bishop of Natal explains to those who do not know it, that the Pentateuch is not to be read as an authentic history, but as a narrative full of divine instruction in morals and religion: I wish to lay aside all ridicule, into which literary criticism too readily falls, while I express my unfeigned conviction that in his own heart the Bishop of Natal honestly believes this, and that he originally meant to convey this to his readers. But I censure his book because it entirely fails to convey this. I censure it, because while it impresses strongly on the reader that "the Pentateuch is not to be read as an authentic narrative," it so entirely fails to make him feel that it is "a narrative full of divine instruction in morals and religion." I censure it, because, addressed to the religious world, it puts the non-essential part of the Bible so prominent, and the essential so much in the background, and, having established this false proportion, holds such language about the Bible in consequence of it, that, instead of serving the religious life, it confuses it. I do not blame the Bishop of Natal's doctrine for its novelty or heterodoxy—literary criticism takes no account of a doctrine's novelty or heterodoxy: I said expressly that Mr. Jowett's Essay was, for literary criticism, justified by its unction; I said that the Bishop of Natal's book was censurable, because, proclaiming what it did, *it proclaimed no more;* because, not taking rank as a book of pure speculation, inevitably taking rank as a religious book for the religious world, for the great majority of mankind, it treated its subject unedifyingly. Address what doctrine you like to the religious world, be as unorthodox as you will, literary criticism has no authority to blame you: only, if your doctrine is evidently not adapted to the needs of the religious life,—if, as you present it, it tends to confound that life rather than to strengthen it, literary criticism has the right to check you; for it at once perceives that your doctrine, as you present it, is false. Was it, nevertheless, your duty to put forth that doctrine, since you believed it to be true? The honoured authority of the Archbishop of Dublin is invoked to decide that it was. Which duty comes first for a man—the duty of proclaiming an inadequate idea, or the duty of making an inadequate idea adequate? But this difficult question we need not resolve: it is enough that, if it is a man's duty to announce even his inadequate ideas, it is the duty of criticism to tell him that they are inadequate.

But, again, it is said that the Bishop of Natal's book will, in the end, have a good effect, by loosening the superstitious attachment with which the mass of the English religious world clings to the letter of the Bible, and that it deserves from criticism indulgence on this ground. I cannot tell what may, in the end, be the effect of the Bishop of Natal's book upon the religious life of this country. Its natural immediate effect may be seen by any one who will take the trouble of looking at a newspaper called *Public Opinion*, in which the Bishop's book is the theme of a great continuous correspondence. There, week after week, the critical genius of our nation discovers itself in captivating nudity; and there, in the letters of a terrible athlete of Reason, who signs himself "Eagle-Eye," the natural immediate effect of the Bishop's book may be observed. Its natural ultimate effect would be, I think, to continue, in another form, the excessive care of the English religious world for that which is not of the real essence of the Bible: as this world has for years been prone to say, "We are the salt of the earth, because we believe that every syllable and letter of the Bible is the direct utterance of the Most High," so it would naturally, after imbibing the Bishop of Natal's influence, be inclined to say, "We are the salt of the earth, because we believe that the Pentateuch is unhistorical." Whether they believe the one or the other, what they should learn to say is: "We are unprofitable servants; the religious life is beyond." But, at all events, literary criticism, which is the guardian of literary truth, must judge books according to their intrinsic merit and proximate natural effect, not according to their possible utility and remote contingent effect. If the Bishop of Natal's demonstrations ever produce a salutary effect upon the religious life of England, it will be after some one else, or he himself, has supplied the now missing power of edification: for literary criticism his book, as it at present stands, must always remain a censurable production.

The situation of a clergyman, active-minded as well as pious, is, I freely admit, at the present moment one of great difficulty. Intellectual ideas are not the essence of the religious life; still the religious life connects itself, as I have said, with certain intellectual ideas, and all intellectual ideas follow a develop-

ment independent of the religious life. Goethe remarks somewhere how the *Zeit-Geist*, as he calls it, the Time-Spirit,
irresistibly changes the ideas current in the world. When he
was young, he says, the Time-Spirit had made every one disbelieve in the existence of a single Homer: when he was old, 5
it was bearing every one to a belief in it. Intellectual ideas,
which the majority of men take from the age in which they
live, are the dominion of this Time-Spirit; not moral and spiritual life, which is original in each individual. In the Articles of
the Church of England are exhibited the intellectual ideas 10
with which the religious life of that Church, at the time of the
Reformation, and almost to the present day, connected itself.
They are the intellectual ideas of the English Reformers and
of their time; they are liable to development and change.
Insensibly the Time-Spirit brings to men's minds a conscious- 15
ness that certain of these ideas have undergone such development, such change. For the laity, to whom the religious life of
their National Church is the great matter, and who owe to
that Church only the general adhesion of citizens to the Government under which they are born, this consciousness is not 20
irksome as it is for the clergy, who, as ministers of the Church,
undertake to become organs of the intellectual ideas of its
formularies. As this consciousness becomes more and more distinct, it becomes more and more irksome. One can almost fix
the last period in which a clergyman, very speculative by the 25
habit of his mind, or very sensible to the whispers of the Time-
Spirit, can sincerely feel himself free and at ease in his position
of a minister of the Church of England. The moment inevitably arrives when such a man feels himself in a false position. It is natural that he should try to defend his position, that 30
he should long prefer defending his position to confessing it
untenable, and demanding to have it changed. Still, in his own
heart, he cannot but be dissatisfied with it. It is not good for
him, not good for his usefulness, to be left in it. The sermons
of Tauler and Wesley were not preached by men hampered 35
by the consciousness of an unsound position. Even when a
clergyman, charged full with modern ideas, manages by a
miracle of address to go over the very ground most dangerous

to him without professional ruin, and even to exhibit unction
as he goes along, there is no reason to exult at the feat: he
would probably have exhibited more unction still if he had not
had to exhibit it upon the tight-rope. The time at last comes
5 for the State, the collective nation, to intervene. Some reconstruction of the English Church, a reconstruction hardly less
important than that which took place at the Reformation, is
fast becoming inevitable. It will be a delicate, a most difficult
task; and the reconstruction of the Protestant Churches of
10 Germany offers an example of what is to be avoided rather
than of what is to be followed.

Still, so divine, so indestructible is the power of Christianity
—so immense the power of transformation afforded to it by its
sublime maxim, "The letter killeth, but the spirit giveth life,"
15 that it will assuredly ever be able to adapt itself to new conditions, and, in connexion with intellectual ideas changed or developed, to enter upon successive stages of progress. It will
even survive the handling of "liberals of every shade of opinion." But it will not do this by losing its essence, by becoming
20 such a Christianity as these liberals imagine, the "Christianity
not Mysterious" of Toland; a Christianity consisting of half-a-
dozen intellectual propositions, and half-a-dozen moral rules
deduced from them. It will do it by retaining the religious
life in all its depth and fulness in connexion with new intel-
25 lectual ideas; and the latter will never have meaning for it until
they have been harmonised with the former, and the religious
teacher who presents the latter to it, without harmonising
them with the former, will never have fulfilled his mission. The
religious life existed in the Church of the Middle Ages, as it
30 exists in the Churches of Protestantism; nay, what monument
of that life have the Protestant Churches produced, which for
its most essential qualities, its tenderness, its spirituality, its
ineffable yearning, is comparable to the "Imitation." The critical ideas of the sixteenth century broke up the Church of the
35 Middle Ages, resting on the basis of a priesthood with supernatural power of interpreting the Bible. But Luther was a great
religious reformer, not because he made himself the organ of
these ideas, themselves negative, not because he shattered the

idol of a mediatory priesthood, but because he reconciled these ideas with the religious life, because he made the religious life feel that a positive and fruitful conclusion was to be drawn from them,—the conclusion that each man must "work out his own salvation with fear and trembling." Protestantism has formed the notion that every syllable and letter of the Bible is the direct utterance of the Most High. The critical ideas of our century are forcing Protestantism away from this proposition, untrue like the proposition that the Pope is infallible: but the religious reformer is not he who rivets our minds upon the untruth of this proposition, who bewilders the religious life by insisting on the intellectual blunder of which it has been guilty in entertaining it; he is the man who makes us feel the future which undoubtedly exists for the religious life in the absence of it.

Makes us all feel, not the multitude only. I am reproached with wishing to make free-thinking an aristocratic privilege, while a false religion is thrown to the multitude to keep it quiet; and in this country—where the multitude is in the first place, particularly averse to being called the multitude, and in the second, by its natural spirit of honesty, particularly averse to all underhand, selfish scheming—such an imputation is readily snatched up, and carries much odium with it. I will not seek to remove that odium by any flattery, by saying that I think we are all one enlightened public together. No, there *is* a multitude, a multitude made up out of all ranks: probably in no country—so much has our national life been carried on by means of parties, and so inevitably does party-spirit, in regarding all things, put the consideration of their intrinsic reason and truth second, and not first—is the multitude more unintelligent, more narrow-minded, and more passionate than in this. Perhaps in no country in the world is so much nonsense so firmly believed. But those on whose behalf I demand from a religious speaker edification are more than this multitude; and their cause and that of the multitude are one. They are all those who acknowledge the need of the religious life. The few whom literary criticism regards as exempt from all concern with edification, are far fewer than is commonly supposed.

Those whose life is all in thought, and to whom, therefore, literary criticism concedes the right of treating religion with absolute freedom, as pure matter for thought, are not a great class, but a few individuals. Let them think in peace, these sublime solitaries: they have a right to their liberty: Churches will never concede it to them; literary criticism will never deny it to them. From his austere isolation a born thinker like Spinoza cries with warning solemnity to the would-be thinker, what, from his austere isolation, a born artist like Michael Angelo cries to the would-be artist—"Canst thou drink of the cup that I drink of?" Those who persist in the thinker's life, are far fewer even than those who persist in the artist's. Of the educated minority, far the greatest number retain their demand upon the religious life. They share, indeed, the culture of their time, they are curious to know the new ideas of their time; their own culture is advanced, in so far as those ideas are novel, striking, and just. This course they follow, whether they feel or not (what is certainly true), that this satisfaction of their curiosity, this culture of theirs, is not without its dangers to the religious life. Thus they go on being informed, gathering intellectual ideas at their own peril, minding, as Marcus Aurelius reproached himself with too long minding, "life less than notion." But the moment they enter the sphere of religion, they too ask and need to be edified, not informed only. They inevitably, such is the law of the religious life, take the same attitude as the least-instructed. The religious voice that speaks to them must have the tone of the spiritual world: the intellectual ideas presented to them must be made to blend with the religious life.

The world may not see this, but cannot a clergyman see it? Cannot he see that, speaking to the religious life, he may honestly be silent about matters which he cannot yet use to edification, and of which, therefore, the religious life does not want to hear? Does he not see that he is even bound to take account of the circumstances of his hearers, and that information which is only fruitless to the religious life of some of his hearers, may be worse than fruitless, confounding, to the religious life of others of them? Certainly, Christianity has not two doctrines, one for the few, another for the many; but as certainly, Christ adapted His teaching to the different stages of growth in His hearers, and for all of them adapted it to the needs of the religious life. He came to preach moral and spiritual truths; and for His purpose moral genius was of more avail than intellectual genius, St. Peter than Solomon. But the speculative few who stood outside of his teaching were not the Pharisees and the Sadducees. The Pharisees were the narrow-minded, cruel-hearted religious professors of that day; the Sadducees were the "liberals of every shade of opinion." And who, then, were the thinking few of that time?—a student or two at Athens or Alexandria. That was the hour of the religious sense of the East: but the hour of the thought of the West, of Greek thought, was also to come. The religious sense had to ally itself with this, to make certain conditions with it, to be in certain ways inevitably modified by it. Now is the hour of the thought of the West. This thought has its apostles on every side, and we hear far more of its conquests than of the conquests of the religious sense. Still the religious life maintains its indefeasible claims, and in its own sphere inexorably refuses to be satisfied with the new thought, to admit it to be of any truth and significance, until it has harmonised it with itself, until it has imparted to it its own divine power of refreshing souls. Some day the religious life will have harmonised all the new thought with itself, will be able to use it freely: but it cannot use it yet. And who has not rejoiced to be able, between the old idea, tenable no longer, which once connected itself with certain religious words, and the new idea, which has not yet connected itself with them, to rest for awhile in the healing virtue and beauty of the words themselves? The old popular notion of perpetual special interventions of Providence in the concerns of man is weak and erroneous; yet who has yet found, to define Providence for the religious life, words so adequate as the words of Isaiah—"In all their affliction he was afflicted, and the angel of his presence saved them; and he bare them and carried them all the days of old?" The old popular notion of an incensed God appeased in His wrath against the helpless race of mankind by a bloody

sacrifice, is barbarous and false; but what intellectual definition
of the death of Christ has yet succeeded in placing it, for the
religious life, in so true an aspect as the sublime ejaculation
of the Litany: "O Lamb of God, that takest away the sins of
5   the world, have mercy upon us!"

And you are masters in Israel, and know not these things;
and you require a voice from the world of literature to tell
them to you! Those who ask nothing better than to remain
silent on such topics, who have to quit their own sphere to
10   speak of them, who cannot touch them without being reminded that they survive those who touched them with far
different power, you compel, in the mere interest of letters,
of intelligence, of general culture, to proclaim truths which
it was your function to have made familiar. And, when you
15   have thus forced the very stones to cry out, and the dumb to
speak, you call them singular because they know these truths,
and arrogant because they declare them!

Eugénie de Guérin

Who that had spoken of Maurice de Guérin could refrain
from speaking of his sister Eugénie, the most devoted of sisters,
one of the rarest and most beautiful of souls? "There is nothing
fixed, no duration, no vitality in the sentiments of women towards one another; their attachments are mere pretty knots   5
of ribbon, and no more. In all the friendships of women I observe this slightness of the tie. I know no instance to the contrary, even in history. Orestes and Pylades have no sisters." So
she herself speaks of the friendships of her own sex. But Electra
can attach herself to Orestes, if not to Chrysothemis. And to   10
her brother Maurice, Eugénie de Guérin was Pylades and Electra in one.

The name of Maurice de Guérin,—that young man so gifted,
so attractive, so careless of fame, and so early snatched away;
who died at twenty-nine; who, says his sister, "let what he did   15
be lost with a carelessness so unjust to himself, set no value
on any of his own productions, and departed hence without
reaping the rich harvest which seemed his due;" who, in spite
of his immaturity, in spite of his fragility, exercised such a
charm, "furnished to others so much of that which all live by,"   20
that some years after his death his sister found in a country-
house where he used to stay, in the journal of a young girl who
had not known him, but who heard her family speak of him,
his name, the date of his death, and these words, "*il était
leur vie*" (he was their life); whose talent, exquisite as that of   25
Keats, with much less of sunlight, abundance, inventiveness,
and facility in it than that of Keats, but with more of distinction and power, had "that winning, delicate, and beautifully

happy turn of expression" which is the stamp of the master,—
is beginning to be well known to all lovers of literature. This
establishment of Maurice's name was an object for which his
sister Eugénie passionately laboured. While he was alive, she
placed her whole joy in the flowering of this gifted nature;
when he was dead, she had no other thought than to make the
world know him as she knew him. She outlived him nine
years, and her cherished task for those years was to rescue the
fragments of her brother's composition, to collect them, to get
them published. In pursuing this task she had at first cheering
hopes of success; she had at last baffling and bitter disappointment. Her earthly business was at an end; she died. Ten years
afterwards, it was permitted to the love of a friend, M. Trebutien, to effect for Maurice's memory what the love of a sister
had failed to accomplish. But those who read, with delight and
admiration, the journal and letters of Maurice de Guérin,
could not but be attracted and touched by this sister Eugénie,
who met them at every page. She seemed hardly less gifted,
hardly less interesting, than Maurice himself. And presently
M. Trebutien did for the sister what he had done for the
brother. He published the journal of Mdlle. Eugénie de
Guérin, and a few (too few, alas!) of her letters.[1] The book
has made a profound impression in France; and the fame which
she sought only for her brother now crowns the sister also.

Parts of Mdlle. de Guérin's journal were several years ago
printed for private circulation, and a writer in the *National
Review* had the good fortune to fall in with them. The bees
of our English criticism do not often roam so far afield for
their honey, and this critic deserves thanks for having flitted
in his quest of blossom to foreign parts, and for having settled
upon a beautiful flower found there. He had the discernment
to see that Mdlle. de Guérin was well worth speaking of, and
he spoke of her with feeling and appreciation. But that, as I
have said, was several years ago; even a true and feeling
homage needs to be from time to time renewed, if the memory
of its object is to endure; and criticism must not lose the occa-

[1] A volume of these, also, has just been brought out by M. Trebutien.
One good book, at least, in the literature of the year 1865!

sion offered by Mdlle. de Guérin's journal being for the first time published to the world, of directing notice once more to this religious and beautiful character.

Eugénie de Guérin was born in 1805, at the château of Le Cayla, in Languedoc. Her family, though reduced in circumstances, was noble; and even when one is a saint one cannot quite forget that one comes of the stock of the Guarini of Italy, or that one counts among one's ancestors a Bishop of Senlis, who had the marshalling of the French order of battle on the day of Bouvines. Le Cayla was a solitary place, with its terrace looking down upon a stream-bed and valley; "one may pass days there without seeing any living thing but the sheep, without hearing any living thing but the birds." M. de Guérin, Eugénie's father, lost his wife when Eugénie was thirteen years old, and Maurice seven; he was left with four children,— Eugénie, Marie, Erembert, and Maurice,—of whom Eugénie was the eldest, and Maurice was the youngest. This youngest child, whose beauty and delicacy had made him the object of his mother's most anxious fondness, was commended by her in dying to the care of his sister Eugénie. Maurice at eleven years old went to school at Toulouse; then he went to the Collège Stanislas at Paris; then he became a member of the religious society which M. de Lamennais had formed at La Chênaie in Brittany; afterwards he lived chiefly at Paris, returning to Le Cayla, at the age of twenty-nine, to die. Distance, in those days, was a great obstacle to frequent meetings of the separated members of a French family of narrow means. Maurice de Guérin was seldom at Le Cayla after he had once quitted it, though his few visits to his home were long ones; but he passed five years,—the period of his sojourn in Brittany, and of his first settlement in Paris,—without coming home at all. In spite of the check from these absences, in spite of the more serious check from a temporary alteration in Maurice's religious feelings, the union between the brother and sister was wonderfully close and firm. For they were knit together, not only by the tie of blood and early attachment, but also by the tie of a common genius. "We were," says Eugénie, "two eyes looking out of one head." She, on her part, brought to her love for her brother the devotedness of a woman, the intensity of a recluse, almost the solicitude of a mother. Her home duties prevented her from following the wish, which often arose in her, to join a religious sisterhood. There is a trace,—just a trace,—of an early attachment to a cousin; but he died when she was twenty-four. After that, she lived for Maurice. It was for Maurice that, in addition to her constant correspondence with him by letter, she began in 1834 her journal, which was sent to him by portions as it was finished. After his death she tried to continue it, addressing it "to Maurice in heaven." But the effort was beyond her strength; gradually the entries become rarer and rarer; and on the last day of December 1840 the pen dropped from her hand: the journal ends.

Other sisters have loved their brothers, and it is not her affection for Maurice, admirable as this was, which alone could have made Eugénie de Guérin celebrated. I have said that both brother and sister had genius: M. Sainte-Beuve goes so far as to say that the sister's genius was equal, if not superior, to her brother's. No one has a more profound respect for M. Sainte-Beuve's critical judgments than I have; but it seems to me that this particular judgment needs to be a little explained and guarded. In Maurice's special talent, which was a talent for interpreting nature, for finding words which incomparably render the subtlest impressions which nature makes upon us, which bring the intimate life of nature wonderfully near to us, it seems to me that his sister was by no means his equal. She never, indeed, expresses herself without grace and intelligence; but her words, when she speaks of the life and appearances of nature, are in general but intellectual signs; they are not like her brother's—symbols equivalent with the thing symbolised. They bring the notion of the thing described to the mind, they do not bring the feeling of it to the imagination. Writing from the Nivernais, that region of vast woodlands in the centre of France: "It does one good," says Eugénie, "to be going about in the midst of this enchanting nature, with flowers, birds, and verdure all round one, under this large and blue sky of the Nivernais. How I love the gracious form of it, and those little white clouds here and there, like cushions of cotton, hung aloft

to rest the eye in this immensity!" It is pretty and graceful, but how different from the grave and pregnant strokes of
Maurice's pencil! "I have been along the Loire, and seen on
its banks the plains where nature is puissant and gay; I have
seen royal and antique dwellings, all marked by memories
which have their place in the mournful legend of humanity,—
Chambord, Blois, Amboise, Chenonceaux; then the towns on
the two banks of the river,—Orléans, Tours, Saumur, Nantes;
and at the end of it all, the Ocean rumbling. From there I passed
back into the interior of the country, as far as Bourges and
Nevers, a region of vast woodlands, in which murmurs of an
immense range and fulness" (*ce beau torrent de rumeurs,* as,
with an expression worthy of Wordsworth, he elsewhere calls
them) "prevail and never cease." Words whose charm is like
that of the sounds of the murmuring forest itself, and whose
reverberations, like theirs, die away in the infinite distance
of the soul.

Maurice's life was in the life of nature, and the passion for it
consumed him; it would have been strange if his accent had
not caught more of the soul of nature than Eugénie's accent,
whose life was elsewhere. "You will find in him," Maurice
says to his sister of a friend whom he was recommending to
her, "you will find in him that which you love, and which
suits you better than anything else,—*l'onction, l'effusion, la
mysticité.*" Unction, the pouring out of the soul, the rapture of
the mystic, were dear to Maurice also; but in him the bent of
his genius gave even to those a special direction of its own. In
Eugénie they took the direction most native and familiar to
them; their object was the religious life.

And yet, if one analyses this beautiful and most interesting
character quite to the bottom, it is not exactly as a saint that
Eugénie de Guérin is remarkable. The ideal saint is a nature
like Saint François de Sales or Fénelon; a nature of ineffable
sweetness and serenity, a nature in which struggle and revolt
is over, and the whole man (so far as is possible to human infirmity) swallowed up in love. Saint Theresa (it is Mdlle. de
Guérin herself who reminds us of it) endured twenty years of
unacceptance and of repulse in her prayers; yes, but the Saint

Theresa whom Christendom knows is Saint Theresa repulsed
no longer! it is Saint Theresa accepted, rejoicing in love, radiant
with ecstasy. Mdlle. de Guérin is not one of these saints arrived
at perfect sweetness and calm, steeped in ecstasy; there is some-
5 thing primitive, indomitable in her, which she governs, indeed,
but which chafes, which revolts. Somewhere in the depths of
that strong nature there is a struggle, an impatience, an in-
quietude, an ennui, which endures to the end, and which leaves
one, when one finally closes her journal, with an impression of
10 profound melancholy. "There are days," she writes to her
brother, "when one's nature rolls itself up, and becomes a
hedgehog. If I had you here at this moment, here close by me,
how I should prick you! how sharp and hard!" "Poor soul,
poor soul," she cries out to herself another day, "what is the
15 matter, what would you have? Where is that which will do you
good? Everything is green, everything is in bloom, all the air
has a breath of flowers. How beautiful it is! well, I will go out.
No, I should be alone, and all this beauty, when one is alone, is
worth nothing. What shall I do then? Read, write, pray, take
20 a basket of sand on my head like that hermit-saint, and walk
with it? Yes, work, work! keep busy the body which does mischief to the soul! I have been too little occupied to-day, and
that is bad for one, and it gives a certain ennui which I have in
me time to ferment."
25 *A certain ennui which I have in me:* her wound is there. In
vain she follows the counsel of Fénelon: "If God tires you, *tell
him that he tires you.*" No doubt she obtained great and frequent solace and restoration from prayer: "This morning I was
suffering; well, at present I am calm, and this I owe to faith,
30 simply to faith, to an act of faith. I can think of death and
eternity without trouble, without alarm. Over a deep of sorrow
there floats a divine calm, a suavity which is the work of God
only. In vain have I tried other things at a time like this: nothing human comforts the soul, nothing human upholds it:—

35   'A l'enfant il faut sa mère,
                 A mon âme il faut mon Dieu.'"

Still the ennui reappears, bringing with it hours of unutterable
forlornness, and making her cling to her one great earthly hap-

piness,—her affection for her brother,—with an intenseness, an
anxiety, a desperation in which there is something morbid, and
by which she is occasionally carried into an irritability, a jealousy which she herself is the first, indeed, to censure, which she
severely represses, but which nevertheless leaves a sense of pain.   5

Mdlle. de Guérin's admirers have compared her to Pascal,
and in some respects the comparison is just. But she cannot exactly be classed with Pascal, any more than with Saint François de Sales. Pascal is a man, and the inexhaustible power and
activity of his mind leave him no leisure for ennui. He has not   10
the sweetness and serenity of the perfect saint; he is, perhaps,
"der strenge, kranke Pascal—*the severe, morbid Pascal*,"—as
Goethe (and, strange to say, Goethe at twenty-three, an age
which usually feels Pascal's charm most profoundly) calls him.
But the stress and movement of the lifelong conflict waged in   15
him between his soul and his reason keep him full of fire, full
of agitation, and keep his reader, who witnesses this conflict,
animated and excited; the sense of forlornness and dejected
weariness which clings to Eugénie de Guérin does not belong
to Pascal. Eugénie de Guérin is a woman, and longs for a state   20
of firm happiness, for an affection in which she may repose.
The inward bliss of Saint Theresa or Fénelon would have satisfied her; denied this, she cannot rest satisfied with the triumphs
of self-abasement, with the sombre joy of trampling the pride
of life and of reason underfoot, of reducing all human hope   25
and joy to insignificance; she repeats the magnificent words of
Bossuet, words which both Catholicism and Protestantism have
uttered with indefatigable iteration: "On trouve au fond de
tout le vide et le néant—*at the bottom of everything one finds
emptiness and nothingness*," but she feels, as every one but   30
the true mystic must ever feel, their incurable sterility.

She resembles Pascal, however, by the clearness and firmness
of her intelligence, going straight and instinctively to the bottom of any matter she is dealing with, and expressing herself
about it with incomparable precision; never fumbling with   35
what she has to say, never imperfectly seizing or imperfectly
presenting her thought. And to this admirable precision she
joins a lightness of touch, a feminine ease and grace, a flowing
facility which are her own. "I do not say," writes her brother

Maurice, an excellent judge, "that I find in myself a dearth of
expression; but I have not this abundance of yours, this produc-
tiveness of soul which streams forth, which courses along without ever failing, and always with an infinite charm." And writ-
5   ing to her of some composition of hers, produced after her religious scruples had for a long time kept her from the exercise
of her talent: "You see, my dear Tortoise," he writes, "that
your talent is no illusion, since after a period, I know not how
long, of poetical inaction,—a trial to which any half-talent
10 would have succumbed,—it rears its head again more vigorous
than ever. It is really heart-breaking to see you repress and bind
down, with I know not what scruples, your spirit, which tends
with all the force of its nature to develop itself in this direction.
Others have made it a case of conscience for you to resist this
15 impulse, and I make it one for you to follow it." And she says
of herself, on one of her freer days: "It is the instinct of my
life to write, as it is the instinct of the fountain to flow." The
charm of her expression is not a sensuous and imaginative
charm like that of Maurice, but rather an intellectual charm;
20 it comes from the texture of the style rather than from its elements; it is not so much in the words as in the turn of the
phrase, in the happy cast and flow of the sentence. Recluse as
she was, she had a great correspondence: every one wished to
have letters from her; and no wonder.
25   To this strength of intelligence and talent of expression she
joined a great force of character. Religion had early possessed
itself of this force of character, and reinforced it: in the
shadow of the Cévennes, in the sharp and tonic nature of this
region of Southern France, which has seen the Albigensians,
30 which has seen the Camisards, Catholicism too is fervent and
intense. Eugénie de Guérin was brought up amidst strong religious influences, and they found in her a nature on which
they could lay firm hold. I have said that she was not a saint of
the order of Saint François de Sales or Fénelon; perhaps she had
35 too keen an intelligence to suffer her to be this, too forcible
and impetuous a character. But I did not mean to imply the
least doubt of the reality, the profoundness, of her religious
life. She was penetrated by the power of religion; religion was

the master-influence of her life; she derived immense consolations from religion, she earnestly strove to conform her whole
nature to it; if there was an element in her which religion could
not perfectly reach, perfectly transmute, she groaned over this
element in her, she chid it, she made it bow. Almost every   5
thought in her was brought into harmony with religion; and
what few thoughts were not thus brought into harmony were
brought into subjection.

Then she had her affection for her brother; and this, too,
though perhaps there might be in it something a little over-   10
eager, a little too absolute, a little too susceptible, was a pure,
a devoted affection. It was not only passionate, it was tender. It
was tender, pliant, and self-sacrificing to a degree that not in
one nature out of a thousand,—of natures with a mind and will
like hers,—is found attainable. She thus united extraordinary   15
power of intelligence, extraordinary force of character, and
extraordinary strength of affection; and all these under the control of a deep religious feeling.

This is what makes her so remarkable, so interesting. I shall
try and make her speak for herself, that she may show us the   20
characteristic sides of her rare nature with her own inimitable
touch.

It must be remembered that her journal is written for Maurice only; in her lifetime no eye but his ever saw it. "*Ceci n'est
pas pour le public,*" she writes; "*c'est de l'intime, c'est de l'âme,*   25
c'est pour un." "This is not for the public; it contains my inmost thoughts, my very soul; it is for *one*." And Maurice, this
one, was a kind of second self to her. "We see things with the
same eyes; what you find beautiful, I find beautiful; God has
made our souls of one piece." And this genuine confidence in   30
her brother's sympathy gives to the entries in her journal a
naturalness and simple freedom rare in such compositions. She
felt that he would understand her, and be interested in all that
she wrote.

One of the first pages of her journal relates an incident of   35
the home-life of Le Cayla, the smallest detail of which Maurice liked to hear; and in relating it she brings this simple life
before us. She is writing in November, 1834:—

"I am furious with the gray cat. The mischievous beast has made away with a little half-frozen pigeon, which I was trying to thaw by the side of the fire. The poor little thing was just beginning to come round; I meant to tame him; he would have grown fond of me; and there is my whole scheme eaten up by a cat! This event, and all the rest of to-day's history, has passed in the kitchen. Here I take up my abode all the morning and a part of the evening, ever since I am without Mimi.[1] I have to superintend the cook; sometimes papa comes down, and I read to him by the oven, or by the fireside, some bits out of the *Antiquities of the Anglo-Saxon Church*. This book struck Pierril[2] with astonishment. '*Que de mouts aqui dédins!* What a lot of words there are inside it!' This boy is a real original. One evening he asked me if the soul was immortal; then afterwards, what a philosopher was? We had got upon great questions, as you see. When I told him that a philosopher was a person who was wise and learned: 'Then, mademoiselle, you are a philosopher.' This was said with an air of simplicity and sincerity which might have made even Socrates take it as a compliment; but it made me laugh so much that my gravity as catechist was gone for that evening. A day or two ago Pierril left us, to his great sorrow: his time with us was up on Saint Brice's day. Now he goes about with his little dog, truffle-hunting. If he comes this way I shall go and ask him if he still thinks I look like a philosopher."

Her good sense and spirit made her discharge with alacrity her household tasks in this patriarchal life of Le Cayla, and treat them as the most natural thing in the world. She sometimes complains, to be sure, of burning her fingers at the kitchen-fire. But when a literary friend of her brother expresses enthusiasm about her and her poetical nature: "The poetess," she says, "whom this gentleman believes me to be, is an ideal being, infinitely removed from the life which is actually mine—a life of occupations, a life of household-business, which takes up all my time. How could I make it otherwise? I am sure I do not

[1] The familiar name of her sister Marie.
[2] A servant-boy at Le Cayla.

know; and, besides, my duty is in this sort of life, and I have no wish to escape from it."

Among these occupations of the patriarchal life of the châtelaine of Le Cayla intercourse with the poor fills a prominent place:—

"To-day," she writes on the 9th of December 1834, "I have been warming myself at every fireside in the village. It is a round which Mimi and I often make, and in which I take pleasure. To-day we have been seeing sick people, and holding forth on doses and sick-room drinks. 'Take this, do that;' and they attend to us just as if we were the doctor. We prescribed shoes for a little thing who was amiss from having gone barefoot; to the brother, who, with a bad headache, was lying quite flat, we prescribed a pillow; the pillow did him good, but I am afraid it will hardly cure him. He is at the beginning of a bad feverish cold: and these poor people live in the filth of their hovels like animals in their stable; the bad air poisons them. When I come home to Le Cayla I seem to be in a palace."

She had books, too; not in abundance, not for the fancying them; the list of her library is small, and it is enlarged slowly and with difficulty. The *Letters of Saint Theresa*, which she had long wished to get, she sees in the hands of a poor servant girl, before she can procure them for herself. "What then?" is her comment: "very likely she makes a better use of them than I could." But she has the *Imitation*, the *Spiritual Works* of Bossuet and Fénelon, the *Lives of the Saints*, Corneille, Racine, André Chénier, and Lamartine; Madame de Staël's book on Germany, and French translations of Shakspeare's plays, Ossian, the *Vicar of Wakefield*, Scott's *Old Mortality* and *Redgauntlet*, and the *Promessi Sposi* of Manzoni. Above all, she has her own mind; her meditations in the lonely fields, on the oak-grown hill-side of "The Seven Springs;" her meditations and writing in her own room, her *chambrette*, her *délicieux chez moi*, where every night, before she goes to bed, she opens the window to look out upon the sky,—the balmy moonlit sky of Languedoc. This life of reading, thinking, and writing was the life she liked best, the life that most truly suited her. "I find writ-

ing has become almost a necessity to me. Whence does it arise,
this impulse to give utterance to the voice of one's spirit, to
pour out my thoughts before God and one human being? I say
one human being, because I always imagine that you are present, that you see what I write. In the stillness of a life like
this my spirit is happy, and, as it were, dead to all that goes on
upstairs or downstairs, in the house or out of the house. But
this does not last long. 'Come, my poor spirit,' I then say to
myself, 'we must go back to the things of this world.' And
I take my spinning, or a book, or a saucepan, or I play with
Wolf or Trilby. Such a life as this I call heaven upon earth."

Tastes like these, joined with a talent like Mdlle. de Guérin's,
naturally inspire thoughts of literary composition. Such
thoughts she had, and perhaps she would have been happier if
she had followed them; but she never could satisfy herself that
to follow them was quite consistent with the religious life,
and her projects of composition were gradually relinquished:—

"Would to God that my thoughts, my spirit, had never taken
their flight beyond the narrow round in which it is my lot to
live! In spite of all that people say to the contrary, I feel that
I cannot go beyond my needlework and my spinning without
going too far: I feel it, I believe it: well, then, I will keep in
my proper sphere; however much I am tempted, my spirit shall
not be allowed to occupy itself with great matters until it occupies itself with them in Heaven."

And again:—

"My journal has been untouched for a long while. Do you
want to know why? It is because the time seems to me misspent
which I spend in writing it. We owe God an account of every
minute; and is it not a wrong use of our minutes to employ
them in writing a history of our transitory days?"

She overcomes her scruples, and goes on writing the journal;
but again and again they return to her. Her brother tells her
of the pleasure and comfort something she has written gives
to a friend of his in affliction. She answers:—

"It is from the Cross that those thoughts come, which your
friend finds so soothing, so unspeakably tender. None of them
come from me. I feel my own aridity; but I feel, too, that God,

when he will, can make an ocean flow upon this bed of sand. It is the same with so many simple souls, from which proceed the most admirable things; because they are in direct relation with God, without false science and without pride. And thus I am gradually losing my taste for books; I say to myself: 'What can they teach me which I shall not one day know in Heaven? let God be my master and my study here!' I try to make him so, and I find myself the better for it. I read little; I go out little; I plunge myself in the inward life. How infinite are the sayings, doings, feelings, events of that life! Oh, if you could but see them! But what avails it to make them known? God alone should be admitted to the sanctuary of the soul."

Beautifully as she says all this, one cannot, I think, read it without a sense of disquietude, without a presentiment that this ardent spirit is forcing itself from its natural bent, that the beatitude of the true mystic will never be its earthly portion. And yet how simple and charming is her picture of the life of religion which she chose as her ark of refuge, and in which she desired to place all her happiness:—

"Cloaks, clogs, umbrellas, all the apparatus of winter, went with us this morning to Andillac, where we have passed the whole day; some of it at the curé's house, the rest in church. How I like this life of a country Sunday, with its activity, its journeys to church, its liveliness! You find all your neighbours on the road; you have a curtsey from every woman you meet, and then, as you go along, such a talk about the poultry, the sheep and cows, the good man and the children! My great delight is to give a kiss to these children, and see them run away and hide their blushing faces in their mother's gown. They are alarmed at *las doumaïsélos*,[1] as at a being of another world. One of these little things said the other day to its grandmother, who was talking of coming to see us: '*Minino*, you mustn't go to that castle; there is a black hole there.' What is the reason that in all ages the noble's château has been an object of terror? Is it because of the horrors that were committed there in old times? I suppose so."

This vague horror of the château, still lingering in the mind

_____
[1] The young lady.

of the French peasant fifty years after he has stormed it, is
indeed curious, and is one of the thousand indications how unlike aristocracy on the Continent has been to aristocracy in
England. But this is one of the great matters with which Mdlle.
de Guérin would not have us occupied; let us pass to the subject of Christmas in Languedoc:—

"Christmas is come; the beautiful festival, the one I love
most, and which gives me the same joy as it gave the shep-
herds of Bethlehem. In real truth, one's whole soul sings with
joy at this beautiful coming of God upon earth,—a coming
which here is announced on all sides of us by music and by
our charming *nadalet*.[1] Nothing at Paris can give you a notion
of what Christmas is with us. You have not even the midnight-
mass. We all of us went to it, papa at our head, on the most
perfect night possible. Never was there a finer sky than ours
was that midnight;—so fine that papa kept perpetually throwing back the hood of his cloak, that he might look up at the
sky. The ground was white with hoar-frost, but we were not
cold; besides, the air, as we met it, was warmed by the bun-
dles of blazing torchwood which our servants carried in front
of us to light us on our way. It was delightful, I do assure you;
and I should like you to have seen us there on our road to
church, in those lanes with the bushes along their banks as
white as if they were in flower. The hoar-frost makes the most
lovely flowers. We saw a long spray so beautiful that we wanted
to take it with us as a garland for the communion-table, but it
melted in our hands: all flowers fade so soon! I was very sorry
about my garland; it was mournful to see it drip away, and
get smaller and smaller every minute."

The religious life is at bottom everywhere alike; but it is
curious to note the variousness of its setting and outward circumstance. Catholicism has these so different from Protestantism! and in Catholicism these accessories have, it cannot be
denied, a nobleness and amplitude which in Protestantism is
often wanting to them. In Catholicism they have, from the
antiquity of this form of religion, from its pretensions to uni-

[1] A peculiar peal rung at Christmas-time by the church bells of Languedoc.

versality, from its really widespread prevalence, from its sensuousness, something European, august, and imaginative: in
Protestantism they often have, from its inferiority in all these
respects, something provincial, mean, and prosaic. In revenge,
Protestantism has a future before it, a prospect of growth in   5
alliance with the vital movement of modern society; while
Catholicism appears to be bent on widening the breach between
itself and the modern spirit, to be fatally losing itself in the mul-
tiplication of dogmas, Mariolatry, and miracle-mongering. But
the style and circumstance of actual Catholicism is grander   10
than its present tendency, and the style and circumstance of
Protestantism is meaner than its tendency. While I was reading the journal of Mdlle. de Guérin there came into my hands
the memoir and poems of a young Englishwoman, Miss Emma
Tatham; and one could not but be struck with the singular   15
contrast which the two lives,—in their setting rather than in
their inherent quality,—present. Miss Tatham had not, certainly, Mdlle. de Guérin's talent, but she had a sincere vein of
poetic feeling, a genuine aptitude for composition. Both were
fervent Christians, and, so far, the two lives have a real re-   20
semblance; but, in the setting of them, what a difference! The
Frenchwoman is a Catholic in Languedoc; the Englishwoman
is a Protestant at Margate; Margate, that brick-and-mortar
image of English Protestantism, representing it in all its prose,
all its uncomeliness,—let me add, all its salubrity. Between the   25
external form and fashion of these two lives, between the
Catholic Mdlle. de Guérin's *nadalet* at the Languedoc Christmas, her chapel of moss at Easter-time, her daily reading of
the life of a saint, carrying her to the most diverse times,
places, and peoples,—her quoting, when she wants to fix her   30
mind upon the staunchness which the religious aspirant needs,
the words of Saint Macedonius to a hunter whom he met in
the mountains, "I pursue after God, as you pursue after game,"
—her quoting, when she wants to break a village girl of diso-
bedience to her mother, the story of the ten disobedient chil-   35
dren whom at Hippo Saint Augustine saw palsied;—between
all this and the bare, blank, narrowly English setting of Miss
Tatham's Protestantism, her "union in church-fellowship with

the worshippers at Hawley Square Chapel, Margate;" her "singing with soft, sweet voice, the animating lines—

> 'My Jesus to know, and feel His blood flow,
> 'Tis life everlasting, 'tis heaven below;' "

5 her "young female teachers belonging to the Sunday-school," and her "Mr. Thomas Rowe, a venerable class-leader,"—what a dissimilarity! In the ground of the two lives, a likeness; in all their circumstance, what unlikeness! An unlikeness, it will be said, in that which is non-essential and indifferent. Non-essen-
10 tial,—yes; indifferent,—no. The signal want of grace and charm in English Protestantism's setting of its religious life is not an indifferent matter; it is a real weakness. *This ought ye to have done, and not to have left the other undone.*

I have said that the present tendency of Catholicism,—the
15 Catholicism of the main body of the Catholic clergy and laity, —seems likely to exaggerate rather than to remove all that in this form of religion is most repugnant to reason; but this Catholicism was not that of Mdlle. de Guérin. The insufficiency of her Catholicism comes from a doctrine which Protestantism,
20 too, has adopted, although Protestantism, from its inherent element of freedom, may find it easier to escape from it; a doctrine with a certain attraction for all noble natures, but, in the modern world at any rate, incurably sterile,—the doctrine of the emptiness and nothingness of human life, of the superiority of
25 renouncement to activity, of quietism to energy; the doctrine which makes effort for things on this side of the grave a folly, and joy in things on this side of the grave a sin. But her Catholicism is remarkably free from the faults which Protestants commonly think inseparable from Catholicism; the relation to the
30 priest, the practice of confession, assume, when she speaks of them, an aspect which is not that under which Exeter Hall knows them, but which,—unless one is of the number of those who prefer regarding that by which men and nations die to regarding that by which they live,—one is glad to study. "*La*
35 *confession,*" she says twice in her journal, "*n'est qu'une expansion du repentir dans l'amour;*" and her weekly journey to the confessional in the little church of Cahuzac is her "*cher*

pèlerinage;" the little church is the place where she has "*laissé tant de misères.*"

"This morning," she writes one 28th of November, "I was up before daylight, dressed quickly, said my prayers, and started with Marie for Cahuzac. When we got there, the chapel was occupied, which I was not sorry for. I like not to be hurried, and to have time, before I go in, to lay bare my soul before God. This often takes me a long time, because my thoughts are apt to be flying about like these autumn leaves. At ten o'clock I was on my knees, listening to words the most salutary that were ever spoken; and I went away, feeling myself a better being. Every burden thrown off leaves us with a sense of lightness; and when the soul has laid down the load of its sins at God's feet, it feels as if it had wings. What an admirable thing is confession! What comfort, what light, what strength is given me every time after I have said, *I have sinned.*"

This blessing of confession is the greater, she says, "the more the heart of the priest to whom we confide our repentance is like that divine heart which 'has so loved us.' This is what attaches me to M. Bories." M. Bories was the curé of her parish, a man no longer young, and of whose loss, when he was about to leave them, she thus speaks:—

"What a grief for me! how much I lose in losing this faithful guide of my conscience, heart, and mind, of my whole self, which God has appointed to be in his charge, and which let itself be in his charge so gladly! He knew the resolves which God had put in my heart, and I had need of his help to follow them. Our new curé cannot supply his place: he is so young! and then he seems so inexperienced, so undecided! It needs firmness to pluck a soul out of the midst of the world, and to uphold it against the assaults of flesh and blood. It is Saturday, my day for going to Cahuzac; I am just going there, perhaps I shall come back more tranquil. God has always given me some good thing there, in that chapel where I have left behind me so many miseries."

Such is confession for her when the priest is worthy; and, when he is not worthy, she knows how to separate the man from the office:—

"To-day I am going to do something which I dislike; but I will do it, with God's help. Do not think I am on my way to the stake; it is only that I am going to confess to a priest in whom I have not confidence, but who is the only one here. In this act of religion the man must always be separated from the priest, and sometimes the man must be annihilated."

The same clear sense, the same freedom from superstition, shows itself in all her religious life. She tells us, to be sure, how once, when she was a little girl, she stained a new frock, and on praying, in her alarm, to an image of the Virgin which hung in her room, saw the stains vanish: even the austerest Protestant will not judge such Mariolatry as this very harshly. But, in general, the Virgin Mary fills in the religious parts of her journal no prominent place; it is Jesus, not Mary. "Oh, how well has Jesus said: 'Come unto me, all ye that labour and are heavy laden.' It is only there, only in the bosom of God, that we can rightly weep, rightly rid ourselves of our burden." And again: "The mystery of suffering makes one grasp the belief of something to be expiated, something to be won. I see it in Jesus Christ, the Man of Sorrow. *It was necessary that the Son of Man should suffer*. That is all we know in the troubles and calamities of life."

And who has ever spoken of justification more impressively and piously than Mdlle. de Guérin speaks of it, when, after reckoning the number of minutes she has lived, she exclaims:—

"My God, what have we done with all these minutes of ours, which thou, too, wilt one day reckon? Will there be any of them to count for eternal life? will there be many of them? will there be one of them? 'If thou, O Lord, wilt be extreme to mark what is done amiss, O Lord, who may abide it?' This close scrutiny of our time may well make us tremble, all of us who have advanced more than a few steps in life; for God will judge us otherwise than as he judges the lilies of the field. I have never been able to understand the security of those who place their whole reliance, in presenting themselves before God, upon a good conduct in the ordinary relations of human life. As if all our duties were confined within the narrow sphere of this world! To be a good parent, a good child, a good citi-

zen, a good brother or sister, is not enough to procure entrance into the kingdom of heaven. God demands other things
besides these kindly social virtues of him whom he means to
crown with an eternity of glory."

And, with this zeal for the spirit and power of religion, what
prudence in her counsels of religious practice; what discernment, what measure! She has been speaking of the charm of
the *Lives of the Saints*, and she goes on:—

"Notwithstanding this, the *Lives of the Saints* seem to me,
for a great many people, dangerous reading. I would not rec-
ommend them to a young girl, or even to some women who are
no longer young. What one reads has such power over one's
feelings; and these, even in seeking God, sometimes go astray.
Alas, we have seen it in poor C.'s case. What care one ought
to take with a young person; with what she reads, what she
writes, her society, her prayers,—all of them matters which
demand a mother's tender watchfulness! I remember many
things I did at fourteen, which my mother, had she lived,
would not have let me do. I would have done anything for
God's sake; I would have cast myself into an oven, and assuredly things like that are not God's will; He is not pleased
by the hurt one does to one's health through that ardent but
ill-regulated piety which, while it impairs the body, often leaves
many a fault flourishing. And, therefore, Saint François de
Sales used to say to the nuns who asked his leave to go
bare-foot: 'Change your brains and keep your shoes.'"

Meanwhile Maurice, in a five years' absence, and amid the
distractions of Paris, lost, or seemed to his sister to lose, something of his fondness for his home and its inmates: he certainly
lost his early religious habits and feelings. It is on this latter loss
that Mdlle. de Guérin's journal oftenest touches,—with infinite delicacy, but with infinite anguish:—

"Oh, the agony of being in fear for a soul's salvation, who can
describe it! That which caused our Saviour the keenest suffering, in the agony of his Passion, was not so much the thought
of the torments he was to endure, as the thought that these torments would be of no avail for a multitude of sinners; for all
those who set themselves against their redemption, or who do

not care for it. The mere anticipation of this obstinacy and
this heedlessness had power to make sorrowful, even unto death,
the divine Son of Man. And this feeling all Christian souls, according to the measure of faith and love granted them, more
5   or less share."

Maurice returned to Le Cayla in the summer of 1837, and
passed six months there. This meeting entirely restored the
union between him and his family. "These six months with
us," writes his sister, "he ill, and finding himself so loved by
10 us all, had entirely reattached him to us. Five years without
seeing us had perhaps made him a little lose sight of our affection for him; having found it again, he met it with all the
strength of his own. He had so firmly renewed, before he
left us, all family-ties, that nothing but death could have
15 broken them." The separation in religious matters between the
brother and sister gradually diminished, and before Maurice
died it had ceased. I have elsewhere spoken of Maurice's religious feeling and his character. It is probable that his diver-
gence from his sister in this sphere of religion was never so
20 wide as she feared, and that his reunion with her was never
so complete as she hoped. "His errors were passed," she says,
"his illusions were cleared away; by the call of his nature,
by original disposition, he had come back to sentiments of
order. I knew all, I followed each of his steps; out of the fiery
25 sphere of the passions (which held him but a little moment)
I saw him pass into the sphere of the Christian life. It was a
beautiful soul, the soul of Maurice." But the illness which had
caused his return to Le Cayla reappeared after he got back to
Paris in the winter of 1837–8. Again he seemed to recover;
30 and his marriage with a young Creole lady, Mdlle. Caroline de
Gervain, took place in the autumn of 1838. At the end of
September in that year Mdlle. de Guérin had joined her brother
in Paris; she was present at his marriage, and stayed with him
and his wife for some months afterwards. Her journal recom-
35 mences in April 1839. Zealously as she had promoted her brother's marriage, cordial as were her relations with her sister-in-
law, it is evident that a sense of loss, of loneliness, invades her,
and sometimes weighs her down. She writes in her journal on
the 3rd of May:—

"God knows when we shall see one another again! My own Maurice, must it be our lot to live apart, to find that this marriage which I had so much share in bringing about, which I hoped would keep us so much together, leaves us more asunder than ever? For the present and for the future, this troubles me more than I can say. My sympathies, my inclinations, carry me more towards you than towards any other member of our family. I have the misfortune to be fonder of you than of anything else in the world, and my heart had from of old built in you its happiness. Youth gone and life declining, I looked forward to quitting the scene with Maurice. At any time of life a great affection is a great happiness; the spirit comes to take refuge in it entirely. O delight and joy which will never be your sister's portion! Only in the direction of God shall I find an issue for my heart to love as it has the notion of loving, as it has the power of loving."

From such complainings, in which there is undoubtedly something morbid,—complainings which she herself blamed, to which she seldom gave way, but which, in presenting her character, it is not just to put wholly out of sight,—she was called by the news of an alarming return of her brother's illness. For some days the entries in the journal show her agony of apprehension. "He coughs, he coughs still! Those words keep echoing for ever in my ears, and pursue me wherever I go; I cannot look at the leaves on the trees without thinking that the winter will come, and then the consumptive die." She went to him, and brought him back by slow stages to Le Cayla, dying. He died on the 19th of July 1839.

Thenceforward the energy of life ebbed in her; but the main chords of her being, the chord of affection, the chord of religious longing, the chord of intelligence, the chord of sorrow, gave, so long as they answered to the touch at all, a deeper and finer sound than ever. Always she saw before her "that beloved pale face;" "that beautiful head, with all its different expressions, smiling, speaking, suffering, dying," regarded her always:—

"I have seen his coffin in the same room, in the same spot where I remember seeing, when I was a very little girl, his cradle, when I was brought home from Gaillac, where I was

then staying, for his christening. This christening was a grand
one, full of rejoicing, more than that of any of the rest of us;
specially marked. I enjoyed myself greatly, and went back to
Gaillac next day, charmed with my new little brother. Two
years afterwards I came home, and brought with me a frock
for him of my own making. I dressed him in the frock, and
took him out with me along by the warren at the north of the
house, and there he walked a few steps alone,—his first walking
alone,—and I ran with delight to tell my mother the news:
'Maurice, Maurice has begun to walk by himself!'—Recollections which, coming back to-day, break one's heart."

The shortness and suffering of her brother's life filled her
with an agony of pity. "Poor beloved soul, you have had
hardly any happiness here below; your life has been so short,
your repose so rare. O God, uphold me, establish my heart in
thy faith! Alas, I have too little of this supporting me! How
we have gazed at him and loved him, and kissed him,—his
wife, and we, his sisters; he lying lifeless in his bed, his head
on the pillow as if he were asleep! Then we followed him to
the churchyard, to the grave, to his last resting-place, and
prayed over him, and wept over him; and we are here again,
and I am writing to him again, as if he were staying away from
home, as if he were in Paris. My beloved one, can it be, shall
we never see one another again on earth?"

But in heaven?—and here, though love and hope finally
prevailed, the very passion of the sister's longing sometimes
inspired torturing inquietudes:—

"I am broken down with misery. I want to see him. Every
moment I pray to God to grant me this grace. Heaven, the
world of spirits, is it so far from us? O depth, O mystery of
the other life which separates us! I, who was so eagerly anxious
about him, who wanted so to know all that happened to him,—
wherever he may be now, it is over! I follow him into the
three abodes; I stop wistfully before the place of bliss, I pass
on to the place of suffering,—to the gulf of fire. My God, my
God, no! Not there let my brother be! not there! And he is
not: his soul, the soul of Maurice, among the lost ... horrible fear, no! But in purgatory, where the soul is cleansed

by suffering, where the failings of the heart are expiated, the doubtings of the spirit, the half-yieldings to evil? Perhaps my brother is there and suffers, and calls to us amidst his anguish of repentance, as he used to call to us amidst his bodily suffering: 'Help me, you who love me.' Yes, beloved one, by prayer. I will go and pray; prayer has been such a power to me, and I will pray to the end. Prayer! Oh! and prayer for the dead; it is the dew of purgatory."

Often, alas, the gracious dew would not fall; the air of her soul was parched; the arid wind, which was somewhere in the depths of her being, blew. She marks in her journal the 1st of May, "this return of the loveliest month in the year," only to keep up the old habit; even the month of May can no longer give her any pleasure: "*Tout est changé*—all is changed." She is crushed by "the misery which has nothing good in it, the tearless, dry misery, which bruises the heart like a hammer."

"I am dying to everything. I am dying of a slow moral agony, a condition of unutterable suffering. Lie there, my poor journal! be forgotten with all this world which is fading away from me. I will write here no more until I come to life again, until God re-awakens me out of this tomb in which my soul lies buried. Maurice, my beloved! it was not thus with me when I had *you!* The thought of Maurice could revive me from the most profound depression: to have him in the world was enough for me. With Maurice, to be buried alive would have not seemed dull to me."

And, as a burden to this funereal strain, the old *vide et néant* of Bossuet, profound, solemn, sterile:—

"So beautiful in the morning, and in the evening, *that!* how the thought disenchants one, and turns one from the world! I can understand that Spanish grandee who, after lifting up the winding-sheet of a beautiful queen, threw himself into the cloister and became a great saint. I would have all my friends at La Trappe, in the interest of their eternal welfare. Not that in the world one cannot be saved, not that there are not in the world duties to be discharged as sacred and as beautiful as there are in the cloister, but...."

And there she stops, and a day or two afterwards her journal comes to an end. A few fragments, a few letters carry us on a little later, but after the 22d of August 1845 there is nothing. To make known her brother's genius to the world was the one task she set herself after his death; in 1840 came Madame Sand's noble tribute to him in the *Revue des Deux Mondes;* then followed projects of raising a yet more enduring monument to his fame, by collecting and publishing his scattered compositions; these projects, I have already said, were baffled;—Mdlle. de Guérin's letter of the 22d of August 1845 relates to this disappointment. In silence, during nearly three years more, she faded away at Le Cayla. She died on the 31st of May 1848.

M. Trebutien has accomplished the pious task in which Mdlle. de Guérin was baffled, and has established Maurice's fame; by publishing this journal he has established Eugénie's also. She was very different from her brother; but she too, like him, had that in her which preserves a reputation. Her soul had the same characteristic quality as his talent,—*distinction.* Of this quality the world is impatient; it chafes against it, rails at it, insults it, hates it;—it ends by receiving its influence, and by undergoing its law. This quality at last inexorably corrects the world's blunders, and fixes the world's ideals. It procures that the popular poet shall not finally pass for a Pindar, nor the popular historian for a Tacitus, nor the popular preacher for a Bossuet. To the circle of spirits marked by this rare quality, Maurice and Eugénie de Guérin belong; they will take their place in the sky which these inhabit, and shine close to one another, *lucida sidera.*

Heinrich Heine

"I know not if I deserve that a laurel-wreath should one day be laid on my coffin. Poetry, dearly as I have loved it, has always been to me but a divine plaything. I have never attached any great value to poetical fame; and I trouble myself very little whether people praise my verses or blame them. But lay on my coffin a *sword*; for I was a brave soldier in the Liberation War of humanity." 5

Heine had his full share of love of fame, and cared quite as much as his brethren of the *genus irritabile* whether people praised his verses or blamed them. And he was very little of a 10 hero. Posterity will certainly decorate his tomb with the emblem of the laurel rather than with the emblem of the sword. Still, for his contemporaries, for us, for the Europe of the present century, he is significant chiefly for the reason which he himself in the words just quoted assigns. He is significant 15 because he was, if not pre-eminently a brave, yet a brilliant, a most effective soldier in the Liberation War of humanity.

To ascertain the master-current in the literature of an epoch, and to distinguish this from all minor currents, is one of the critic's highest functions; in discharging it he shows how far 20 he possesses the most indispensable quality of his office,— justness of spirit. The living writer who has done most to make England acquainted with German authors, a man of genius, but to whom precisely this one quality of justness of spirit is perhaps wanting,—I mean Mr. Carlyle,—seems to me 25 in the result of his labours on German literature to afford a proof how very necessary to the critic this quality is. Mr. Carlyle has spoken admirably of Goethe; but then Goethe stands before all men's eyes, the manifest centre of German literature; and from this central source many rivers flow. Which of these rivers is the main stream? which of the courses of spirit which we see active in Goethe is the course which will most influence the future, and attract and be continued by the most powerful of Goethe's successors?—that is the question. Mr. Carlyle attaches, it seems to me, far too much importance to the romantic school of Germany,—Tieck, Novalis, Jean Paul Richter,—and gives to these writers, really gifted as two, at any rate, of them are, an undue prominence. These writers, and others with aims and a general tendency the same as theirs, are not the real inheritors and continuators of Goethe's power; the current of their activity is not the main current of German literature after Goethe. Far more in Heine's works flows this main current; Heine, far more than Tieck or Jean Paul Richter, is the continuator of that which, in Goethe's varied activity, is the most powerful and vital; on Heine, of all German authors who survived Goethe, incomparably the largest portion of Goethe's mantle fell. I do not forget that when Mr. Carlyle was dealing with German literature, Heine, though he was clearly risen above the horizon, had not shone forth with all his strength; I do not forget, too, that after ten or twenty years many things may come out plain before the critic which before were hard to be discerned by him; and assuredly no one would dream of imputing it as a fault to Mr. Carlyle that twenty years ago he mistook the central current in German literature, overlooked the rising Heine, and attached undue importance to that romantic school which Heine was to destroy; one may rather note it as a misfortune, sent perhaps as a delicate chastisement to a critic, who,—man of genius as he is, and no one recognises his genius more admiringly than I do,—has, for the functions of the critic, a little too much of the self-will and eccentricity of a genuine son of Great Britain.

Heine is noteworthy, because he is the most important German successor and continuator of Goethe in Goethe's most important line of activity. And which of Goethe's lines of activity is this?—His line of activity as "a soldier in the war of liberation of humanity."

Heine himself would hardly have admitted this affiliation, though he was far too powerful-minded a man to decry, with some of the vulgar German liberals, Goethe's genius. "The wind of the Paris Revolution," he writes after the three days of 1830, "blew about the candles a little in the dark night of Germany, so that the red curtains of a German throne or two caught fire; but the old watchmen, who do the police of the German kingdoms, are already bringing out the fire engines, and will keep the candles closer snuffed for the future. Poor, fast-bound German people, lose not all heart in thy bonds! The fashionable coating of ice melts off from my heart, my soul quivers and my eyes burn, and that is a disadvantageous state of things for a writer, who should control his subject-matter and keep himself beautifully objective, as the artistic school would have us, and as Goethe has done; he has come to be eighty years old doing this, and minister, and in good condition:—poor German people! that is thy greatest man!"

But hear Goethe himself: "If I were to say what I had really been to the Germans in general, and to the young German poets in particular, I should say I had been their *liberator*."

Modern times find themselves with an immense system of institutions, established facts, accredited dogmas, customs, rules, which have come to them from times not modern. In this system their life has to be carried forward; yet they have a sense that this system is not of their own creation, that it by no means corresponds exactly with the wants of their actual life, that, for them, it is customary, not rational. The awakening of this sense is the awakening of the modern spirit. The modern spirit is now awake almost everywhere; the sense of want of correspondence between the forms of modern Europe and its spirit, between the new wine of the eighteenth and nineteenth centuries, and the old bottles of the eleventh and twelfth centuries, or even of the sixteenth and seventeenth, almost every one now perceives; it is no longer dangerous to affirm that this want of correspondence exists; people are even beginning to be shy of denying it. To remove this want of correspondence is beginning to be the settled endeavour of most persons of good sense. Dissolvents of the old European system of dominant ideas and facts we must all be, all of us who have any power of working; what we have to study is that we may not be acrid dissolvents of it.

And how did Goethe, that grand dissolvent in an age when there were fewer of them than at present, proceed in his task of dissolution, of liberation of the modern European from the old routine? He shall tell us himself. "Through me the German poets have become aware that, as man must live from within outwards, so the artist must work from within outwards, seeing that, make what contortions he will, he can only bring to light his own individuality. I can clearly mark where this influence of mine has made itself felt; there arises out of it a kind of poetry of nature, and only in this way is it possible to be original."

My voice shall never be joined to those which decry Goethe, and if it is said that the foregoing is a lame and impotent conclusion to Goethe's declaration that he had been the liberator of the Germans in general, and of the young German poets in particular, I say it is not. Goethe's profound, imperturbable naturalism is absolutely fatal to all routine thinking; he puts the standard, once for all, inside every man instead of outside him; when he is told, such a thing must be so, there is immense authority and custom in favour of its being so, it has been held to be so for a thousand years, he answers with Olympian politeness, "But *is* it so? is it so to *me?*" Nothing could be more really subversive of the foundations on which the old European order rested; and it may be remarked that no persons are so radically detached from this order, no persons so thoroughly modern, as those who have felt Goethe's influence most deeply. If it is said that Goethe professes to have in this way deeply influenced but a few persons, and those persons poets, one may answer that he could have taken no better way to secure, in the end, the ear of the world; for poetry is simply the most beautiful, impressive, and widely effective mode of saying things, and hence its importance. Nevertheless the process of liberation, as Goethe worked it, though sure, is undoubtedly slow; he came, as Heine says, to be eighty years old in thus working it, and at the end of that time the old

Middle-Age machine was still creaking on, the thirty German courts and their chamberlains subsisted in all their glory; Goethe himself was a minister, and the visible triumph of the modern spirit over prescription and routine seemed as far off as ever. It was the year 1830; the German sovereigns had passed the preceding fifteen years in breaking the promises of freedom they had made to their subjects when they wanted their help in the final struggle with Napoleon. Great events were happening in France; the revolution, defeated in 1815, had arisen from its defeat, and was wresting from its adversaries the power. Heinrich Heine, a young man of genius, born at Hamburg, and with all the culture of Germany, but by race a Jew; with warm sympathies for France, whose revolution had given to his race the rights of citizenship, and whose rule had been, as is well known, popular in the Rhine provinces, where he passed his youth; with a passionate admiration for the great French Emperor, with a passionate contempt for the sovereigns who had overthrown him, for their agents, and for their policy,— Heinrich Heine was in 1830 in no humour for any such gradual process of liberation from the old order of things as that which Goethe had followed. His counsel was for open war. Taking that terrible modern weapon, the pen, in his hand, he passed the remainder of his life in one fierce battle. What was that battle? the reader will ask. It was a life and death battle with Philistinism.

Philistinism!—we have not the expression in English. Perhaps we have not the word because we have so much of the thing. At Soli, I imagine, they did not talk of solecisms; and here, at the very headquarters of Goliath, nobody talks of Philistinism. The French have adopted the term *épicier* (grocer), to designate the sort of being whom the Germans designate by the term Philistine; but the French term,—besides that it casts a slur upon a respectable class, composed of living and susceptible members, while the original Philistines are dead and buried long ago,—is really, I think, in itself much less apt and expressive than the German term. Efforts have been made to obtain in English some term equivalent to *Philister* or *épicier;* Mr. Carlyle has made several such efforts: "respect-

ability with its thousand gigs," he says;—well, the occupant
of every one of these gigs is, Mr. Carlyle means, a Philistine.
However, the word *respectable* is far too valuable a word to
be thus perverted from its proper meaning; if the English are
5   ever to have a word for the thing we are speaking of,—and
so prodigious are the changes which the modern spirit is introducing, that even we English shall perhaps one day come
to want such a word,—I think we had much better take the
term *Philistine* itself.

10   *Philistine* must have originally meant, in the mind of those
who invented the nickname, a strong, dogged, unenlightened
opponent of the chosen people, of the children of the light. The
party of change, the would-be remodellers of the old traditional European order, the invokers of reason against custom,
15   the representatives of the modern spirit in every sphere where
it is applicable, regarded themselves, with the robust self-confidence natural to reformers, as a chosen people, as children
of the light. They regarded their adversaries as humdrum people, slaves to routine, enemies to light; stupid and oppressive,
20   but at the same time very strong. This explains the love
which Heine, that Paladin of the modern spirit, has for France;
it explains the preference which he gives to France over Germany: "the French," he says, "are the chosen people of the
new religion, its first gospels and dogmas have been drawn up
25   in their language; Paris is the new Jerusalem, and the Rhine is
the Jordan which divides the consecrated land of freedom from
the land of the Philistines." He means that the French, as a
people, have shown more accessibility to ideas than any other
people; that prescription and routine have had less hold upon
30   them than upon any other people; that they have shown most
readiness to move and to alter at the bidding (real or supposed) of reason. This explains, too, the detestation which
Heine had for the English: "I might settle in England," he
says, in his exile, "if it were not that I should find there two
35   things, coal-smoke and Englishmen; I cannot abide either."
What he hated in the English was the "ächt britische Be-
schränktheit," as he calls it,—the *genuine British narrowness*. In
truth, the English, profoundly as they have modified the old

Middle-Age order, great as is the liberty which they have secured for themselves, have in all their changes proceeded, to use a familiar expression, by the rule of thumb; what was intolerably inconvenient to them they have suppressed, and as they have suppressed it, not because it was irrational, but because it was practically inconvenient, they have seldom in suppressing it appealed to reason, but always, if possible, to some precedent, or form, or letter, which served as a convenient instrument for their purpose, and which saved them from the necessity of recurring to general principles. They have thus become, in a certain sense, of all people the most inaccessible to ideas and the most impatient of them; inaccessible to them, because of their want of familiarity with them; and impatient of them because they have got on so well without them, that they despise those who, not having got on as well as themselves, still make a fuss for what they themselves have done so well without. But there has certainly followed from hence, in this country, somewhat of a general depression of pure intelligence: Philistia has come to be thought by us the true Land of Promise, and it is anything but that; the born lover of ideas, the born hater of commonplaces, must feel in this country, that the sky over his head is of brass and iron. The enthusiast for the idea, for reason, values reason, the idea, in and for themselves; he values them, irrespectively of the practical conveniences which their triumph may obtain for him; and the man who regards the possession of these practical conveniences as something sufficient in itself, something which compensates for the absence or surrender of the idea, of reason, is, in his eyes, a Philistine. This is why Heine so often and so mercilessly attacks the liberals; much as he hates conservatism he hates Philistinism even more, and whoever attacks conservatism itself ignobly, not as a child of light, not in the name of the idea, is a Philistine. Our Cobbett is thus for him, much as he disliked our clergy and aristocracy whom Cobbett attacked, a Philistine with six fingers on every hand and on every foot six toes, four-and-twenty in number: a Philistine, the staff of whose spear is like a weaver's beam. Thus he speaks of him:—

"While I translate Cobbett's words, the man himself comes

bodily before my mind's eye, as I saw him at that uproarious dinner at the Crown and Anchor Tavern, with his scolding red face and his radical laugh, in which venomous hate mingles with a mocking exultation at his enemies' surely approaching downfall. He is a chained cur, who falls with equal fury on every one whom he does not know, often bites the best friend of the house in his calves, barks incessantly, and just because of this incessantness of his barking cannot get listened to, even when he barks at a real thief. Therefore the distinguished thieves who plunder England do not think it necessary to throw the growling Cobbett a bone to stop his mouth. This makes the dog furiously savage, and he shows all his hungry teeth. Poor old Cobbett! England's dog! I have no love for thee, for every vulgar nature my soul abhors; but thou touchest me to the inmost soul with pity, as I see how thou strainest in vain to break loose and to get at those thieves, who make off with their booty before thy very eyes, and mock at thy fruitless springs and thine impotent howling."

There is balm in Philistia as well as in Gilead. A chosen circle of children of the modern spirit, perfectly emancipated from prejudice and commonplace, regarding the ideal side of things in all its efforts for change, passionately despising half-measures and condescension to human folly and obstinacy, —with a bewildered, timid, torpid multitude behind,—conducts a country to the government of Herr von Bismarck. A nation regarding the practical side of things in its efforts for change, attacking not what is irrational, but what is pressingly inconvenient, and attacking this as one body, "moving altogether if it move at all," and treating children of light like the very harshest of stepmothers, comes to the prosperity and liberty of modern England. For all that, however, Philistia (let me say it again) is not the true promised land, as we English commonly imagine it to be; and our excessive neglect of the idea, and consequent inaptitude for it, threatens us, at a moment when the idea is beginning to exercise a real power in human society, with serious future inconvenience, and, in the meanwhile, cuts us off from the sympathy of other nations, which feel its power more than we do.

But, in 1830, Heine very soon found that the fire-engines of
the German governments were too much for his direct efforts
at incendiarism. "What demon drove me," he cries, "to write
my *Reisebilder*, to edit a newspaper, to plague myself with our
time and its interests, to try and shake the poor German   5
Hodge out of his thousand years' sleep in his hole? What good
did I get by it? Hodge opened his eyes, only to shut them
again immediately; he yawned, only to begin snoring again
the next minute louder than ever; he stretched his stiff ungainly
limbs, only to sink down again directly afterwards, and lie like   10
a dead man in the old bed of his accustomed habits. I must
have rest; but where am I to find a resting-place? In Germany
I can no longer stay."

This is Heine's jesting account of his own efforts to rouse
Germany: now for his pathetic account of them; it is be-   15
cause he unites so much wit with so much pathos that he is
so effective a writer:—

"The Emperor Charles the Fifth sate in sore straits, in the
Tyrol, encompassed by his enemies. All his knights and courtiers
had forsaken him; not one came to his help. I know not if he   20
had at that time the cheese face with which Holbein has painted
him for us. But I am sure that under lip of his, with its contempt for mankind, stuck out even more than it does in his
portraits. How could he but contemn the tribe which in the
sunshine of his prosperity had fawned on him so devotedly,   25
and now, in his dark distress, left him all alone? Then suddenly
his door opened, and there came in a man in disguise, and, as
he threw back his cloak, the Kaiser recognised in him his
faithful Conrad von der Rosen, the court jester. This man
brought him comfort and counsel, and he was the court jester!   30

"O German fatherland! dear German people! I am thy Conrad von der Rosen. The man whose proper business was to
amuse thee, and who in good times should have catered only
for thy mirth, makes his way into thy prison in time of need;
here, under my cloak, I bring thee thy sceptre and crown; dost   35
thou not recognise me, my Kaiser? If I cannot free thee, I
will at least comfort thee, and thou shalt at least have one
with thee who will prattle with thee about thy sorest affliction,

and whisper courage to thee, and love thee, and whose best joke and best blood shall be at thy service. For thou, my people, art the true Kaiser, the true lord of the land; thy will is sovereign, and more legitimate far than that purple *Tel est notre plaisir*, which invokes a divine right with no better warrant than the anointings of shaven and shorn jugglers; thy will, my people, is the sole rightful source of power. Though now thou liest down in thy bonds, yet in the end will thy rightful cause prevail; the day of deliverance is at hand, a new time is beginning. My Kaiser, the night is over, and out there glows the ruddy dawn.

" 'Conrad von der Rosen, my fool, thou art mistaken; perhaps thou takest a headsman's gleaming axe for the sun, and the red of dawn is only blood.'

" 'No, my Kaiser, it is the sun, though it is rising in the west; these six thousand years it has always risen in the east; it is high time there should come a change.'

" 'Conrad von der Rosen, my fool, thou hast lost the bells out of thy red cap, and it has now such an odd look, that red cap of thine!'

" 'Ah, my Kaiser, thy distress has made me shake my head so hard and fierce, that the fool's bells have dropped off my cap; the cap is none the worse for that.'

" 'Conrad von der Rosen, my fool, what is that noise of breaking and cracking outside there?'

" 'Hush! that is the saw and the carpenter's axe, and soon the doors of thy prison will be burst open, and thou wilt be free, my Kaiser!'

" 'Am I then really Kaiser? Ah, I forgot, it is the fool who tells me so!'

" 'Oh, sigh not, my dear master, the air of thy prison makes thee so desponding! when once thou hast got thy rights again, thou wilt feel once more the bold imperial blood in thy veins, and thou wilt be proud like a Kaiser, and violent, and gracious, and unjust, and smiling, and ungrateful, as princes are.'

" 'Conrad von der Rosen, my fool, when I am free, what wilt thou do then?'

" 'I will then sew new bells on to my cap.'

" 'And how shall I recompense thy fidelity?'

" 'Ah, dear master, by not leaving me to die in a ditch!' "

I wish to mark Heine's place in modern European literature, the scope of his activity, and his value. I cannot attempt to give here a detailed account of his life, or a description of his separate works. In May 1831 he went over his Jordan, the Rhine, and fixed himself in his new Jerusalem, Paris. There, thenceforward, he lived, going in general to some French watering-place in the summer, but making only one or two short visits to Germany during the rest of his life. His works, in verse and prose, succeeded each other without stopping; a collected edition of them, filling seven closely-printed octavo volumes, has been published in America;[1] in the collected editions of few people's works is there so little to skip. Those who wish for a single good specimen of him should read his first important work, the work which made his reputation, the *Reisebilder*, or "Travelling Sketches:" prose and verse, wit and seriousness, are mingled in it, and the mingling of these is characteristic of Heine, and is nowhere to be seen practised more naturally and happily than in his *Reisebilder*. In 1847 his health, which till then had always been perfectly good, gave way. He had a kind of paralytic stroke. His malady proved to be a softening of the spinal marrow: it was incurable; it made rapid progress. In May 1848, not a year after his first attack, he went out of doors for the last time; but his disease took more than eight years to kill him. For nearly eight years he lay helpless on a couch, with the use of his limbs gone, wasted almost to the proportions of a child, wasted so that a woman could carry him about; the sight of one eye lost, that of the other greatly dimmed, and requiring, that it might be exercised, to have the palsied eyelid lifted and held up by the finger; all this, and, besides this, suffering at short intervals paroxysms of nervous agony. I have said he was not pre-eminently brave; but in the astonishing force of spirit with which he retained his activity of mind, even his gaiety, amid all his suffering, and went on composing with undiminished fire to the last, he was truly brave. Nothing could clog that aërial lightness. "Pouvez-vous siffler?"

[1] A complete edition has at last appeared in Germany.

his doctor asked him one day, when he was almost at his last gasp;—"siffler," as every one knows, has the double meaning of *to whistle* and *to hiss:*—"Hélas! non," was his whispered answer; "pas même une comédie de M. Scribe!" M. Scribe is, or was, the favourite dramatist of the French Philistine. "My nerves," he said to some one who asked him about them in 1855, the year of the Great Exhibition in Paris, "my nerves are of that quite singularly remarkable miserableness of nature, that I am convinced they would get at the Exhibition the grand medal for pain and misery." He read all the medical books which treated of his complaint. "But," said he to some one who found him thus engaged, "what good this reading is to do me I don't know, except that it will qualify me to give lectures in heaven on the ignorance of doctors on earth about diseases of the spinal marrow." What a matter of grim seriousness are our own ailments to most of us! yet with this gaiety Heine treated his to the end. That end, so long in coming, came at last. Heine died on the 17th of February 1856, at the age of fifty-eight. By his will he forbade that his remains should be transported to Germany. He lies buried in the cemetery of Montmartre, at Paris.

His direct political action was null, and this is neither to be wondered at nor regretted; direct political action is not the true function of literature, and Heine was a born man of letters. Even in his favourite France the turn taken by public affairs was not at all what he wished, though he read French politics by no means as we in England, most of us, read them. He thought things were tending there to the triumph of communism; and to a champion of the idea like Heine, what there is gross and narrow in communism was very repulsive. "It is all of no use," he cried on his death-bed, "the future belongs to our enemies, the Communists, and Louis Napoleon is their John the Baptist." "And yet,"—he added with all his old love for that remarkable entity, so full of attraction for him, so profoundly unknown in England, the French people,—"do not believe that God lets all this go forward merely as a grand comedy. Even though the Communists deny him to-day, he knows better than they do, that a time will come when they will learn to believe in him." After 1831, his hopes of soon upsetting the German Governments had died away, and his propagandism took another, a more truly literary, character. It took the character of an intrepid application of the modern spirit to literature. To the ideas with which the burning questions of modern life filled him, he made all his subject-matter minister. He touched all the great points in the career of the human race, and here he but followed the tendency of the wide culture of Germany; but he touched them with a wand which brought them all under a light where the modern eye cares most to see them, and here he gave a lesson to the culture of Germany,—so wide, so impartial, that it is apt to become slack and powerless, and to lose itself in its materials for want of a strong central idea round which to group all its other ideas. So the mystic and romantic school of Germany lost itself in the Middle Ages, was overpowered by their influence, came to ruin by its vain dreams of renewing them. Heine, with a far profounder sense of the mystic and romantic charm of the Middle Age than Görres, or Brentano, or Arnim, Heine the chief romantic poet of Germany, is yet also much more than a romantic poet; he is a great modern poet, he is not conquered by the Middle Age, he has a talisman by which he can feel,—along with but above the power of the fascinating Middle Age itself,—the power of modern ideas.

A French critic of Heine thinks he has said enough in saying that Heine proclaimed in German countries, with beat of drum, the ideas of 1789, and that at the cheerful noise of his drum the ghosts of the Middle Age took to flight. But this is rather too French an account of the matter. Germany, that vast mine of ideas, had no need to import ideas, as such, from any foreign country; and if Heine had carried ideas, as such, from France into Germany, he would but have been carrying coals to Newcastle. But that for which France, far less meditative than Germany, is eminent, is the prompt, ardent, and practical application of an idea, when she seizes it, in all departments of human activity which admit it. And that in which Germany most fails, and by failing in which she appears so helpless and impotent, is just the practical application of her innumerable

ideas. "When Candide," says Heine himself, "came to Eldorado,
he saw in the streets a number of boys who were playing with
gold-nuggets instead of marbles. This degree of luxury made
him imagine that they must be the king's children, and he was
not a little astonished when he found that in Eldorado gold-nuggets are of no more value than marbles are with us, and that the
schoolboys play with them. A similar thing happened to a friend
of mine, a foreigner, when he came to Germany and first read
German books. He was perfectly astounded at the wealth of
ideas which he found in them; but he soon remarked that ideas
in Germany are as plentiful as gold-nuggets in Eldorado, and
that those writers whom he had taken for intellectual princes,
were in reality only common schoolboys." Heine was, as he
calls himself, a "Child of the French Revolution," an "Initiator,"
because he vigorously assured the Germans that ideas were
not counters or marbles, to be played with for their own sake;
because he exhibited in literature modern ideas applied with
the utmost freedom, clearness, and originality. And therefore
he declared that the great task of his life had been the endeavour to establish a cordial relation between France and Germany. It is because he thus operates a junction between the
French spirit, and German ideas and German culture, that he
founds something new, opens a fresh period, and deserves the
attention of criticism far more than the German poets his contemporaries, who merely continue an old period till it expires.
It may be predicted that in the literature of other countries,
too, the French spirit is destined to make its influence felt,—
as an element, in alliance with the native spirit, of novelty and
movement,—as it has made its influence felt in German literature; fifty years hence a critic will be demonstrating to our
grandchildren how this phenomenon has come to pass.

We in England, in our great burst of literature during the
first thirty years of the present century, had no manifestation
of the modern spirit, as this spirit manifests itself in Goethe's
works or Heine's. And the reason is not far to seek. We had
neither the German wealth of ideas, nor the French enthusiasm
for applying ideas. There reigned in the mass of the nation that
inveterate inaccessibility to ideas, that Philistinism,—to use

the German nickname,—which reacts even on the individual genius that is exempt from it. In our greatest literary epoch, that of the Elizabethan age, English society at large was accessible to ideas, was permeated by them, was vivified by them, to a degree which has never been reached in England since. Hence the unique greatness in English literature of Shakspeare and his contemporaries. They were powerfully upheld by the intellectual life of their nation; they applied freely in literature the then modern ideas,—the ideas of the Renascence and the Reformation. A few years afterwards the great English middle class, the kernel of the nation, the class whose intelligent sympathy had upheld a Shakspeare, entered the prison of Puritanism, and had the key turned on its spirit there for two hundred years. *He enlargeth a nation*, says Job, *and straiteneth it again*.

In the literary movement of the beginning of the nineteenth century the signal attempt to apply freely the modern spirit was made in England by two members of the aristocratic class, Byron and Shelley. Aristocracies are, as such, naturally impenetrable by ideas; but their individual members have a high courage and a turn for breaking bounds; and a man of genius, who is the born child of the idea, happening to be born in the aristocratic ranks, chafes against the obstacles which prevent him from freely developing it. But Byron and Shelley did not succeed in their attempt freely to apply the modern spirit in English literature; they could not succeed in it; the resistance to baffle them, the want of intelligent sympathy to guide and uphold them, were too great. Their literary creation, compared with the literary creation of Shakspeare and Spenser, compared with the literary creation of Goethe and Heine, is a failure. The best literary creation of that time in England proceeded from men who did not make the same bold attempt as Byron and Shelley. What, in fact, was the career of the chief English men of letters, their contemporaries? The greatest of them, Wordsworth, retired (in Middle-Age phrase) into a monastery. I mean, he plunged himself in the inward life, he voluntarily cut himself off from the modern spirit. Coleridge took to opium. Scott became the historiographer-royal of feudalism. Keats passionately gave himself up to a sensuous genius, to his faculty for interpreting nature; and he died of consumption at twenty-five. Wordsworth, Scott, and Keats have left admirable works; far more solid and complete works than those which Byron and Shelley have left. But their works have this defect,—they do not belong to that which is the main current of the literature of modern epochs, they do not apply modern ideas to life; they constitute, therefore, *minor currents*, and all other literary work of our day, however popular, which has the same defect, also constitutes but a minor current. Byron and Shelley will long be remembered, long after the inadequacy of their actual work is clearly recognised, for their passionate, their Titanic effort to flow in the main stream of modern literature; their names will be greater than their writings; *stat magni nominis umbra.*

Heine's literary good fortune was superior to that of Byron and Shelley. His theatre of operations was Germany, whose Philistinism does not consist in her want of ideas, or in her inaccessibility to ideas, for she teems with them and loves them, but, as I have said, in her feeble and hesitating application of modern ideas to life. Heine's intense modernism, his absolute freedom, his utter rejection of stock classicism and stock romanticism, his bringing all things under the point of view of the nineteenth century, were understood and laid to heart by Germany, through virtue of her immense, tolerant intellectualism, much as there was in all Heine said to affront and wound Germany. The wit and ardent modern spirit of France Heine joined to the culture, the sentiment, the thought of Germany. This is what makes him so remarkable; his wonderful clearness, lightness, and freedom, united with such power of feeling, and width of range. Is there anywhere keener wit than in his story of the French abbé who was his tutor, and who wanted to get from him that *la religion* is French for *der Glaube:* "Six times did he ask me the question: 'Henry, what is *der Glaube* in French?' and six times, and each time with a greater burst of tears, did I answer him—'It is *le crédit*.' And at the seventh time, his face purple with rage, the infuriated questioner screamed out: 'It is *la religion;*' and a rain of cuffs descended upon me, and all the other boys burst out laughing. Since that day I have never been able to hear *la religion* mentioned, without feeling a tremor run through my back, and my cheeks grow red with shame." Or in that comment on the fate of Professor Saalfeld, who had been addicted to writing furious pamphlets against Napoleon, and who was a professor at Göttingen, a great seat, according to Heine, of pedantry and Philistinism: "It is curious," says Heine, "the three greatest adversaries of Napoleon have all of them ended miserably. Castlereagh cut his own throat; Louis the Eighteenth rotted upon his throne; and Professor Saalfeld is still a professor at Göttingen." It is impossible to go beyond that.

What wit, again, in that saying which every one has heard: "The Englishman loves liberty like his lawful wife, the Frenchman loves her like his mistress, the German loves her like his old grandmother." But the turn Heine gives to this incomparable saying is not so well known; and it is by that turn he shows himself the born poet he is,—full of delicacy and tenderness, of inexhaustible resource, infinitely new and striking:—

"And yet, after all, no one can ever tell how things may turn out. The grumpy Englishman, in an ill-temper with his wife, is capable of some day putting a rope round her neck, and taking her to be sold at Smithfield. The inconstant Frenchman may become unfaithful to his adored mistress, and be seen fluttering about the Palais Royal after another. *But the German will never quite abandon his old grandmother;* he will always keep for her a nook by the chimney-corner, where she can tell her fairy stories to the listening children."

Is it possible to touch more delicately and happily both the weakness and the strength of Germany;—pedantic, simple, enslaved, free, ridiculous, admirable Germany?

And Heine's verse,—his *Lieder?* Oh, the comfort, after dealing with French people of genius, irresistibly impelled to try and express themselves in verse, launching out into a deep which destiny has sown with so many rocks for them,—the comfort of coming to a man of genius, who finds in verse his freest and most perfect expression, whose voyage over the deep of poetry destiny makes smooth! After the rhythm, to

us, at any rate, with the German paste in our composition, so
deeply unsatisfying, of—

> "Ah! que me dites-vous, et que vous dit mon âme?
> Que dit le ciel à l'aube et la flamme à la flamme?"

5   what a blessing to arrive at rhythms like—

> "Take, oh, take those lips away,
> That so sweetly were forsworn—"

or—

> "Siehst sehr sterbeblässlich aus,
10   Doch getrost! du bist zu Haus—"

in which one's soul can take pleasure! The magic of Heine's
poetical form is incomparable; he chiefly uses a form of old
German popular poetry, a ballad-form which has more rapidity
and grace than any ballad-form of ours; he employs this form
15   with the most exquisite lightness and ease, and yet it has at the
same time the inborn fulness, pathos, and old-world charm of
all true forms of popular poetry. Thus in Heine's poetry, too,
one perpetually blends the impression of French modernism
and clearness, with that of German sentiment and fulness; and
20   to give this blended impression is, as I have said, Heine's great
characteristic. To feel it, one must read him; he gives it in his
form as well as in his contents, and by translation I can only
reproduce it so far as his contents give it. But even the contents
of many of his poems are capable of giving a certain sense of
25   it. Here, for instance, is a poem in which he makes his profession of faith to an innocent beautiful soul, a sort of Gretchen,
the child of some simple mining people having their hut among
the pines at the foot of the Hartz Mountains, who reproaches
him with not holding the old articles of the Christian creed:—
30   "Ah, my child, while I was yet a little boy, while I yet sate
upon my mother's knee, I believed in God the Father, who
rules up there in Heaven, good and great;

"Who created the beautiful earth, and the beautiful men
and women thereon; who ordained for sun, moon, and stars
35   their courses.

"When I got bigger, my child, I comprehended yet a great

deal more than this, and comprehended, and grew intelligent; and I believe on the Son also;

"On the beloved Son, who loved us, and revealed love to us; and, for his reward, as always happens, was crucified by the people.

"Now, when I am grown up, have read much, have travelled much, my heart swells within me, and with my whole heart I believe on the Holy Ghost.

"The greatest miracles were of his working, and still greater miracles doth he even now work; he burst in sunder the oppressor's stronghold, and he burst in sunder the bondsman's yoke.

"He heals old death-wounds, and renews the old right; all mankind are one race of noble equals before him.

"He chases away the evil clouds and the dark cobwebs of the brain, which have spoilt love and joy for us, which day and night have loured on us.

"A thousand knights, well harnessed, has the Holy Ghost chosen out to fulfil his will, and he has put courage into their souls.

"Their good swords flash, their bright banners wave; what, thou wouldst give much, my child, to look upon such gallant knights?

"Well, on me, my child, look! kiss me, and look boldly upon me! one of those knights of the Holy Ghost am I."

One has only to turn over the pages of his *Romancero*,— a collection of poems written in the first years of his illness, with his whole power and charm still in them, and not, like his latest poems of all, painfully touched by the air of his *Matratzengruft*, his "mattress-grave,"—to see Heine's width of range; the most varied figures succeed one another,— Rhampsinitus, Edith with the Swan Neck, Charles the First, Marie Antoinette, King David, a heroine of *Mabille*, Melisanda of Tripoli, Richard Cœur de Lion, Pedro the Cruel, Firdusi, Cortes, Dr. Döllinger;—but never does Heine attempt to be *hübsch objectiv*, "beautifully objective," to become in spirit an old Egyptian, or an old Hebrew, or a Middle-Age knight, or a Spanish adventurer, or an English royalist; he always re-

mains Heinrich Heine, a son of the nineteenth century. To give
a notion of his tone, I will quote a few stanzas at the end of the
Spanish Atridæ, in which he describes, in the character of a
visitor at the court of Henry of Transtamare at Segovia,
Henry's treatment of the children of his brother, Pedro the
Cruel. Don Diego Albuquerque, his neighbour, strolls after
dinner through the castle with him:

"In the cloister-passage, which leads to the kennels where
are kept the king's hounds, that with their growling and yelp-
ing let you know a long way off where they are,

"There I saw, built into the wall, and with a strong iron
grating for its outer face, a cell like a cage.

"Two human figures sate therein, two young boys; chained
by the leg, they crouched in the dirty straw.

"Hardly twelve years old seemed the one, the other not
much older; their faces fair and noble, but pale and wan with
sickness.

"They were all in rags, almost naked; and their lean bodies
showed wounds, the marks of ill-usage; both of them shivered
with fever.

"They looked up at me out of the depth of their misery;
'Who,' I cried in horror to Don Diego, 'are these pictures of
wretchedness?'

"Don Diego seemed embarrassed; he looked round to see
that no one was listening; then he gave a deep sigh; and at last,
putting on the easy tone of a man of the world, he said:

" 'These are a pair of king's sons, who were early left or-
phans; the name of their father was King Pedro, the name of
their mother, Maria de Padilla.

" 'After the great battle of Navarette, when Henry of
Transtamare had relieved his brother, King Pedro, of the troublesome burden of the crown,

" 'And likewise of that still more troublesome burden, which
is called life, then Don Henry's victorious magnanimity had to
deal with his brother's children.

" 'He has adopted them, as an uncle should; and he has given
them free quarters in his own castle.

" 'The room which he has assigned to them is certainly

rather small, but then it is cool in summer, and not intolerably cold in winter.

" 'Their fare is rye-bread, which tastes as sweet as if the goddess Ceres had baked it express for her beloved Proserpine.

" 'Not unfrequently, too, he sends a scullion to them with garbanzos, and then the young gentlemen know that it is Sunday in Spain.

" 'But it is not Sunday every day, and garbanzos do not come every day; and the master of the hounds gives them the treat of his whip.

" 'For the master of the hounds, who has under his superintendence the kennels and the pack, and the nephews' cage also,

" 'Is the unfortunate husband of that lemon-faced woman with the white ruff, whom we remarked to-day at dinner.

" 'And she scolds so sharp, that often her husband snatches his whip, and rushes down here, and gives it to the dogs and to the poor little boys.

" 'But his majesty has expressed his disapproval of such proceedings, and has given orders that for the future his nephews are to be treated differently from the dogs.

" 'He has determined no longer to entrust the disciplining of his nephews to a mercenary stranger, but to carry it out with his own hands.'

"Don Diego stopped abruptly; for the seneschal of the castle joined us, and politely expressed his hope that we had dined to our satisfaction."

Observe how the irony of the whole of that, finishing with the grim innuendo of the last stanza but one, is at once truly masterly and truly modern.

No account of Heine is complete which does not notice the Jewish element in him. His race he treated with the same freedom with which he treated everything else, but he derived a great force from it, and no one knew this better than he himself. He has excellently pointed out how in the sixteenth century there was a double renascence,—a Hellenic renascence and a Hebrew renascence,—and how both have been great powers ever since. He himself had in him both the spirit of Greece and the spirit of Judæa; both these spirits reach the infinite, which is the true goal of all poetry and all art,—the Greek spirit by beauty, the Hebrew spirit by sublimity. By his perfection of literary form, by his love of clearness, by his love of beauty, Heine is Greek; by his intensity, by his untamableness, by his "longing which cannot be uttered," he is Hebrew. Yet what Hebrew ever treated the things of the Hebrews like this?—

"There lives at Hamburg, in a one-roomed lodging in the Baker's Broad Walk, a man whose name is Moses Lump; all the week he goes about in wind and rain, with his pack on his back, to earn his few shillings; but when on Friday evening he comes home, he finds the candlestick with seven candles lighted, and the table covered with a fair white cloth, and he puts away from him his pack and his cares, and he sits down to table with his squinting wife and yet more squinting daughter, and eats fish with them, fish which has been dressed in beautiful white garlic sauce, sings therewith the grandest psalms of King David, rejoices with his whole heart over the deliverance of the children of Israel out of Egypt, rejoices, too, that all the wicked ones who have done the children of Israel hurt, have ended by taking themselves off; that King Pharaoh, Nebuchadnezzar, Haman, Antiochus, Titus, and all such people, are well dead, while he, Moses Lump, is yet alive, and eating fish with wife and daughter; and I can tell you, Doctor, the fish is delicate and the man is happy, he has no call to torment himself about culture, he sits contented in his religion and in his green bedgown, like Diogenes in his tub, he contemplates with satisfaction his candles, which he on no account will snuff for himself; and I can tell you, if the candles burn a little dim, and the snuffers-woman, whose business it is to snuff them, is not at hand, and Rothschild the Great were at that moment to come in, with all his brokers, bill discounters, agents, and chief clerks, with whom he conquers the world, and Rothschild were to say: 'Moses Lump, ask of me what favour you will, and it shall be granted you;'—Doctor, I am convinced, Moses Lump would quietly answer: 'Snuff me those candles!' and Rothschild the Great would exclaim with admiration: 'If I were not Rothschild, I would be Moses Lump.' "

There Heine shows us his own people by its comic side; in

the poem of the *Princess Sabbath* he shows it to us by a more serious side. The Princess Sabbath, "the *tranquil Princess,* pearl and flower of all beauty, fair as the Queen of Sheba, Solomon's bosom friend, that blue-stocking from Ethiopia, who wanted to shine by her *esprit,* and with her wise riddles made herself in the long run a bore" (with Heine the sarcastic turn is never far off), this princess has for her betrothed a prince whom sorcery has transformed into an animal of lower race, the Prince Israel.

"A dog with the desires of a dog, he wallows all the week long in the filth and refuse of life, amidst the jeers of the boys in the street.

"But every Friday evening, at the twilight hour, suddenly the magic passes off, and the dog becomes once more a human being.

"A man with the feelings of a man, with head and heart raised aloft, in festal garb, in almost clean garb, he enters the halls of his Father.

" 'Hail, beloved halls of my royal Father! Ye tents of Jacob, I kiss with my lips your holy door-posts!' "

Still more he shows us this serious side in his beautiful poem on Jehuda ben Halevy, a poet belonging to "the great golden age of the Arabian, Old-Spanish, Jewish school of poets," a contemporary of the troubadours:—

"He, too,—the hero whom we sing,—Jehuda ben Halevy, too, had his lady-love; but she was of a special sort.

"She was no Laura, whose eyes, mortal stars, in the cathedral on Good Friday kindled that world-renowned flame.

"She was no châtelaine, who in the blooming glory of her youth presided at tourneys, and awarded the victor's crown.

"No casuistess in the Gay Science was she, no lady *doctrinaire,* who delivered her oracles in the judgment-chamber of a Court of Love.

"She, whom the Rabbi loved, was a woe-begone poor darling, a mourning picture of desolation ... and her name was Jerusalem."

Jehuda ben Halevy, like the Crusaders, makes his pilgrimage to Jerusalem; and there, amid the ruins, sings a song of Sion which has become famous among his people:—

"That lay of pearled tears is the wide-famed Lament, which

is sung in all the scattered tents of Jacob throughout the world,

"On the ninth day of the month which is called Ab, on the anniversary of Jerusalem's destruction by Titus Vespasianus.

"Yes, that is the song of Sion, which Jehuda ben Halevy sang
5 with his dying breath amid the holy ruins of Jerusalem.

"Barefoot, and in penitential weeds, he sate there upon the fragment of a fallen column; down to his breast fell,

"Like a gray forest, his hair; and cast a weird shadow on the face which looked out through it,—his troubled pale face, with
10 the spiritual eyes.

"So he sate and sang, like unto a seer out of the foretime to look upon; Jeremiah, the Ancient, seemed to have risen out of his grave.

"But a bold Saracen came riding that way, aloft on his barb,
15 lolling in his saddle, and brandishing a naked javelin;

"Into the breast of the poor singer he plunged his deadly shaft, and shot away like a winged shadow.

"Quietly flowed the Rabbi's life-blood, quietly he sang his song to an end; and his last dying sigh was Jerusalem!"

20   But, most of all, Heine shows us this side in a strange poem describing a public dispute, before King Pedro and his Court, between a Jewish and a Christian champion, on the merits of their respective faiths. In the strain of the Jew all the fierceness of the old Hebrew genius, all its rigid defiant Monotheism, ap-
25   pear:—

"Our God has not died like a poor innocent lamb for mankind; he is no gushing philanthropist, no declaimer.

"Our God is not love, caressing is not his line; but he is a God of thunder, and he is a God of revenge.

30   "The lightnings of his wrath strike inexorably every sinner, and the sins of the fathers are often visited upon their remote posterity.

"Our God, he is alive, and in his hall of heaven he goes on existing away, throughout all the eternities.

35   "Our God, too, is a God in robust health, no myth, pale and thin as sacrificial wafers, or as shadows by Cocytus.

"Our God is strong. In his hand he upholds sun, moon, and stars; thrones break, nations reel to and fro, when he knits his forehead.

"Our God loves music, the voice of the harp and the song of feasting; but the sound of church-bells he hates, as he hates the grunting of pigs."

Nor must Heine's sweetest note be unheard,—his plaintive note, his note of melancholy. Here is a strain which came from him as he lay, in the winter night, on his "mattress-grave" at Paris, and let his thoughts wander home to Germany, "the great child, entertaining herself with her Christmas-tree." "Thou tookest,"—he cries to the German exile,—

"Thou tookest thy flight towards sunshine and happiness; naked and poor returnest thou back. German truth, German shirts,—one gets them worn to tatters in foreign parts.

"Deadly pale are thy looks, but take comfort, thou art at home! one lies warm in German earth, warm as by the old pleasant fireside.

"Many a one, alas, became crippled, and could get home no more! longingly he stretches out his arms; God have mercy upon him!"

God have mercy upon him! for what remain of the days of the years of his life are few and evil. "Can it be that I still actually exist? My body is so shrunk that there is hardly anything of me left but my voice, and my bed makes me think of the melodious grave of the enchanter Merlin, which is in the forest of Broceliand in Brittany, under high oaks whose tops shine like green flames to heaven. Ah, I envy thee those trees, brother Merlin, and their fresh waving! for over my mattress-grave here in Paris no green leaves rustle; and early and late I hear nothing but the rattle of carriages, hammering, scolding, and the jingle of the piano. A grave without rest, death without the privileges of the departed, who have no longer any need to spend money, or to write letters, or to compose books. What a melancholy situation!"

He died, and has left a blemished name; with his crying faults,—his intemperate susceptibility, his unscrupulousness in passion, his inconceivable attacks on his enemies, his still more inconceivable attacks on his friends, his want of generosity, his sensuality, his incessant mocking,—how could it be otherwise? Not only was he not one of Mr. Carlyle's "respectable" people, he was profoundly *dis*respectable; and not even the merit of not

being a Philistine can make up for a man's being that. To his intellectual deliverance there was an addition of something else
wanting, and that something else was something immense; the
old-fashioned, laborious, eternally needful moral deliverance.
5   Goethe says that he was deficient in *love;* to me his weakness
seems to be not so much a deficiency in love as a deficiency in
self-respect, in true dignity of character. But on this negative
side of one's criticism of a man of great genius, I for my part,
when I have once clearly marked that this negative side is and
10 must be there, have no pleasure in dwelling. I prefer to say of
Heine something positive. He is not an adequate interpreter
of the modern world. He is only a brilliant soldier in the Liberation War of humanity. But, such as he is, he is (and posterity
too, I am quite sure, will say this), in the European poetry of
15 that quarter of a century which follows the death of Goethe,
incomparably the most important figure.

What a spendthrift, one is tempted to cry, is Nature! With
what prodigality, in the march of generations, she employs
human power, content to gather almost always little result
20 from it, sometimes none! Look at Byron, that Byron whom
the present generation of Englishmen are forgetting; Byron,
the greatest natural force, the greatest elementary power, I
cannot but think, which has appeared in our literature since
Shakspeare. And what became of this wonderful production
25 of nature? He shattered himself, he inevitably shattered himself to pieces against the huge, black, cloud-topped, interminable precipice of British Philistinism. But Byron, it may be said,
was eminent only by his genius, only by his inborn force and
fire; he had not the intellectual equipment of a supreme modern
30 poet; except for his genius he was an ordinary nineteenth-
century English gentleman, with little culture and with no
ideas. Well, then, look at Heine. Heine had all the culture of
Germany; in his head fermented all the ideas of modern Europe. And what have we got from Heine? A half-result, for
35 want of moral balance, and of nobleness of soul and character.
That is what I say; there is so much power, so many seem able
to run well, so many give promise of running well;—so few
reach the goal, so few are chosen. *Many are called, few chosen.*

Marcus Aurelius

Mr. Mill says, in his book on Liberty, that "Christian morality is in great part merely a protest against paganism; its ideal is negative rather than positive, passive rather than active." He says that, in certain most important respects, "it falls far below the best morality of the ancients." Now, the object of systems of morality is to take possession of human life, to save it from being abandoned to passion or allowed to drift at hazard, to give it happiness by establishing it in the practice of virtue; and this object they seek to attain by prescribing to human life fixed principles of action, fixed rules of conduct. In its uninspired as well as in its inspired moments, in its days of languor and gloom as well as in its days of sunshine and energy, human life has thus always a clue to follow, and may always be making way towards its goal. Christian morality has not failed to supply to human life aids of this sort. It has supplied them far more abundantly than many of its critics imagine. The most exquisite document, after those of the New Testament, of all the documents the Christian spirit has ever inspired,—the *Imitation*,— by no means contains the whole of Christian morality; nay, the disparagers of this morality would think themselves sure of triumphing if one agreed to look for it in the *Imitation* only. But even the *Imitation* is full of passages like these: "Vita sine proposito languida et vaga est;"—"Omni die renovare debemus propositum nostrum, dicentes: nunc hodiè perfectè incipiamus, quia nihil est quod hactenus fecimus;"—"Secundum propositum nostrum est cursus profectûs nostri;"—"Raro etiam unum vitium perfectè vincimus, et ad *quotidianum* profectum non accendimur;"—"Semper aliquid certi proponendum est;"—"Tibi ipsi violentiam frequenter fac:" (*A life without a purpose is a*

languid, drifting thing;—Every day we ought to renew our
purpose, saying to ourselves: This day let us make a sound be-
ginning, for what we have hitherto done is nought;—Our im-
provement is in proportion to our purpose;—We hardly ever
5   *manage to get completely rid even of one fault, and do not set*
our hearts on daily *improvement;—Always place a definite pur-*
pose before thee;—Get the habit of mastering thine inclination.)
These are moral precepts, and moral precepts of the best kind.
As rules to hold possession of our conduct, and to keep us in
10   the right course through outward troubles and inward perplexity, they are equal to the best ever furnished by the great
masters of morals—Epictetus or Marcus Aurelius.

But moral rules, apprehended as ideas first, and then rigorously followed as laws, are, and must be, for the sage only. The
15   mass of mankind have neither force of intellect enough to ap-
prehend them clearly as ideas, nor force of character enough
to follow them strictly as laws. The mass of mankind can be
carried along a course full of hardship for the natural man, can
be borne over the thousand impediments of the narrow way,
20   only by the tide of a joyful and bounding emotion. It is impossible to rise from reading Epictetus or Marcus Aurelius without
a sense of constraint and melancholy, without feeling that the
burden laid upon man is well-nigh greater than he can bear.
Honour to the sages who have felt this, and yet have borne it!
25   Yet, even for the sage, this sense of labour and sorrow in his
march towards the goal constitutes a relative inferiority; the
noblest souls of whatever creed, the pagan Empedocles as well
as the Christian Paul, have insisted on the necessity of an inspiration, a joyful emotion, to make moral action perfect; an ob-
30   scure indication of this necessity is the one drop of truth in the
ocean of verbiage with which the controversy on justification
by faith has flooded the world. But, for the ordinary man, this
sense of labour and sorrow constitutes an absolute disqualifica-
tion; it paralyses him; under the weight of it, he cannot make
35   way towards the goal at all. The paramount virtue of religion
is, that it has *lighted up* morality; that it has supplied the emotion and inspiration needful for carrying the sage along the narrow way perfectly, for carrying the ordinary man along it at

all. Even the religions with most dross in them have had something of this virtue; but the Christian religion manifests it with unexampled splendour. "Lead me, Zeus and Destiny!" says the prayer of Epictetus, "whithersoever I am appointed to go; I will follow without wavering; even though I turn coward and shrink, I shall have to follow all the same." The fortitude of that is for the strong, for the few; even for them the spiritual atmosphere with which it surrounds them is bleak and gray. But, "Let thy loving spirit lead me forth into the land of righteousness;"—"The Lord shall be unto thee an everlasting light, and thy God thy glory;"—"Unto you that fear my name shall the sun of righteousness arise with healing in his wings," says the Old Testament; "Born, not of blood, nor of the will of the flesh, nor of the will of man, but of God;"—"Except a man be born again, he cannot see the kingdom of God;"— "Whatsoever is born of God, overcometh the world," says the New. The ray of sunshine is there, the glow of a divine warmth;—the austerity of the sage melts away under it, the paralysis of the weak is healed; he who is vivified by it renews his strength; "all things are possible to him;" "he is a new creature."

Epictetus says: "Every matter has two handles, one of which will bear taking hold of, the other not. If thy brother sin against thee, lay not hold of the matter by this, that he sins against thee; for by this handle the matter will not bear taking hold of. But rather lay hold of it by this, that he is thy brother, thy born mate; and thou wilt take hold of it by what will bear handling." Jesus, being asked whether a man is bound to forgive his brother as often as seven times, answers: "I say not unto thee, until seven times, but until seventy times seven." Epictetus here suggests to the reason grounds for forgiveness of injuries which Jesus does not; but it is vain to say that Epictetus is on that account a better moralist than Jesus, if the warmth, the emotion, of Jesus's answer fires his hearer to the practice of forgiveness of injuries, while the thought in Epictetus's leaves him cold. So with Christian morality in general: its distinction is not that it propounds the maxim, "Thou shalt love God and thy neighbour," with more development, closer reasoning, truer

sincerity, than other moral systems; it is that it propounds this
maxim with an inspiration which wonderfully catches the
hearer and makes him act upon it. It is because Mr. Mill has attained to the perception of truths of this nature, that he is,—
5   instead of being, like the school from which he proceeds,
doomed to sterility,—a writer of distinguished mark and influence, a writer deserving all attention and respect; it is (I
must be pardoned for saying) because he is not sufficiently
leavened with them, that he falls just short of being a great
10 writer.

That which gives to the moral writings of the Emperor
Marcus Aurelius their peculiar character and charm, is their
being suffused and softened by something of this very sentiment whence Christian morality draws its best power. Mr.
15 Long has recently published in a convenient form a translation
of these writings, and has thus enabled English readers to judge
Marcus Aurelius for themselves; he has rendered his countrymen a real service by so doing. Mr. Long's reputation as a
scholar is a sufficient guarantee of the general fidelity and ac-
20 curacy of his translation; on these matters, besides, I am hardly
entitled to speak, and my praise is of no value. But that for
which I and the rest of the unlearned may venture to praise
Mr. Long is this; that he treats Marcus Aurelius's writings, as
he treats all the other remains of Greek and Roman antiquity
25 which he touches, not as a dead and dry matter of learning,
but as documents with a side of modern applicability and living
interest, and valuable mainly so far as this side in them can be
made clear; that as in his notes on Plutarch's Roman Lives he
deals with the modern epoch of Cæsar and Cicero, not as food
30 for schoolboys, but as food for men, and men engaged in the
current of contemporary life and action, so in his remarks and
essays on Marcus Aurelius he treats this truly modern striver
and thinker not as a Classical Dictionary hero, but as a present
source from which to draw "example of life, and instruction
35 of manners." Why may not a son of Dr. Arnold say, what
might naturally here be said by any other critic, that in this
lively and fruitful way of considering the men and affairs of
ancient Greece and Rome, Mr. Long resembles Dr. Arnold?

One or two little complaints, however, I have against Mr. Long, and I will get them off my mind at once. In the first place, why could he not have found gentler and juster terms to describe the translation of his predecessor, Jeremy Collier, —the redoubtable enemy of stage plays,—than these: "a most coarse and vulgar copy of the original?" As a matter of taste, a translator should deal leniently with his predecessor; but putting that out of the question, Mr. Long's language is a great deal too hard. Most English people who knew Marcus Aurelius before Mr. Long appeared as his introducer, knew him through Jeremy Collier. And the acquaintance of a man like Marcus Aurelius is such an imperishable benefit, that one can never lose a peculiar sense of obligation towards the man who confers it. Apart from this claim upon one's tenderness, however, Jeremy Collier's version deserves respect for its genuine spirit and vigour, the spirit and vigour of the age of Dryden. Jeremy Collier too, like Mr. Long, regarded in Marcus Aurelius the living moralist, and not the dead classic; and his warmth of feeling gave to his style an impetuosity and rhythm which from Mr. Long's style (I do not blame it on that account) are absent. Let us place the two side by side. The impressive opening of Marcus Aurelius's fifth book, Mr. Long translates thus:—

"In the morning when thou risest unwillingly, let this thought be present: I am rising to the work of a human being. Why then am I dissatisfied if I am going to do the things for which I exist and for which I was brought into the world? Or have I been made for this, to lie in the bed-clothes and keep myself warm?—But this is more pleasant.—Dost thou exist then to take thy pleasure, and not at all for action or exertion?"

Jeremy Collier has:—

"When you find an unwillingness to rise early in the morning, make this short speech to yourself: 'I am getting up now to do the business of a man; and am I out of humour for going about that which I was made for, and for the sake of which I was sent into the world? Was I then designed for nothing but to doze and batten beneath the counterpane? I thought action had been the end of your being.'"

In another striking passage, again, Mr. Long has:—

"No longer wonder at hazard; for neither wilt thou read thy own memoirs, nor the acts of the ancient Romans and Hellenes, and the selections from books which thou wast reserving for thy old age. Hasten then to the end which thou hast before thee, and, throwing away idle hopes, come to thine own aid, if thou carest at all for thyself, while it is in thy power."

Here his despised predecessor has:—

"Don't go too far in your books and overgrasp yourself. Alas, you have no time left to peruse your diary, to read over the Greek and Roman history: come, don't flatter and deceive yourself; look to the main chance, to the end and design of reading, and mind life more than notion: I say, if you have a kindness for your person, drive at the practice and help yourself, for that is in your own power."

It seems to me that here for style and force Jeremy Collier can (to say the least) perfectly stand comparison with Mr. Long. Jeremy Collier's real defect as a translator is not his coarseness and vulgarity, but his imperfect acquaintance with Greek; this is a serious defect, a fatal one; it rendered a translation like Mr. Long's necessary. Jeremy Collier's work will now be forgotten, and Mr. Long stands master of the field; but he may be content, at any rate, to leave his predecessor's grave unharmed, even if he will not throw upon it, in passing, a handful of kindly earth.

Another complaint I have against Mr. Long is, that he is not quite idiomatic and simple enough. It is a little formal, at least, if not pedantic, to say *Ethic* and *Dialectic,* instead of *Ethics* and *Dialectics,* and to say "*Hellenes* and Romans" instead of "*Greeks* and Romans." And why, too,—the name of Antoninus being preoccupied by Antoninus Pius,—will Mr. Long call his author Marcus *Antoninus* instead of Marcus *Aurelius?* Small as these matters appear, they are important when one has to deal with the general public, and not with a small circle of scholars; and it is the general public that the translator of a short masterpiece on morals, such as is the book of Marcus Aurelius, should have in view; his aim should be to make Marcus Aurelius's work as popular as the *Imitation,* and Marcus Aurelius's name as familiar as Socrates's. In rendering or naming him, therefore, punctilious accuracy of phrase is not so much to be sought as accessibility and currency; everything which may best enable the Emperor and his precepts *volitare per ora virûm*. It is essential to render him in language perfectly plain and unprofessional, and to call him by the name by which he is best and most distinctly known. The translators of the Bible talk of *pence* and not *denarii*, and the admirers of Voltaire do not celebrate him under the name of Arouet.

But, after these trifling complaints are made, one must end, as one began, in unfeigned gratitude to Mr. Long for his excellent and substantial reproduction in English of an invaluable work. In general the substantiality, soundness, and precision of Mr. Long's rendering are (I will venture, after all, to give my opinion about them) as conspicuous as the living spirit with which he treats antiquity; and these qualities are particularly desirable in the translator of a work like that of Marcus Aurelius, of which the language is often corrupt, almost always hard and obscure. Any one who wants to appreciate Mr. Long's merits as a translator may read, in the original and in Mr. Long's translation, the seventh chapter of the tenth book; he will see how, through all the dubiousness and involved manner of the Greek, Mr. Long has firmly seized upon the clear thought which is certainly at the bottom of that troubled wording, and, in distinctly rendering this thought, has at the same time thrown round its expression a characteristic shade of painfulness and difficulty which just suits it. And Marcus Aurelius's book is one which, when it is rendered so accurately as Mr. Long renders it, even those who know Greek tolerably well may choose to read rather in the translation than in the original. For not only are the contents here incomparably more valuable than the external form, but this form, the Greek of a Roman, is not exactly one of those styles which have a physiognomy, which are an essential part of their author, which stamp an indelible impression of him on the reader's mind. An old Lyons commentator finds, indeed, in Marcus Aurelius's Greek, something characteristic, something specially firm and imperial; but I think an ordinary mortal will hardly find this: he will find crabbed Greek, without any great charm of distinct

physiognomy. The Greek of Thucydides and Plato has this charm, and he who reads them in a translation, however accurate, loses it, and loses much in losing it; but the Greek of Marcus Aurelius, like the Greek of the New Testament, and
5   even more than the Greek of the New Testament, is wanting in it. If one could be assured that the English Testament were made perfectly accurate, one might be almost content never to open a Greek Testament again; and, Mr. Long's version of Marcus Aurelius being what it is, an Englishman who reads to
10   live, and does not live to read, may henceforth let the Greek original repose upon its shelf.

The man whose thoughts Mr. Long has thus faithfully reproduced, is perhaps the most beautiful figure in history. He is one of those consoling and hope-inspiring marks, which stand
15   for ever to remind our weak and easily discouraged race how high human goodness and perseverance have once been carried, and may be carried again. The interest of mankind is peculiarly attracted by examples of signal goodness in high places; for that testimony to the worth of goodness is the most striking which
20   is borne by those to whom all the means of pleasure and self-indulgence lay open, by those who had at their command the kingdoms of the world and the glory of them. Marcus Aurelius was the ruler of the grandest of empires; and he was one of the best of men. Besides him, history presents one or two other
25   sovereigns eminent for their goodness, such as Saint Louis or Alfred. But Marcus Aurelius has, for us moderns, this great superiority in interest over Saint Louis or Alfred, that he lived and acted in a state of society modern by its essential characteristics, in an epoch akin to our own, in a brilliant centre of
30   civilisation. Trajan talks of "our enlightened age" just as glibly as the *Times* talks of it. Marcus Aurelius thus becomes for us a man like ourselves, a man in all things tempted as we are. Saint Louis inhabits an atmosphere of mediæval Catholicism, which the man of the nineteenth century may admire, indeed,
35   may even passionately wish to inhabit, but which, strive as he will, he cannot really inhabit. Alfred belongs to a state of society (I say it with all deference to the *Saturday Review* critic who keeps such jealous watch over the honour of our Saxon

ancestors) half barbarous. Neither Alfred nor Saint Louis can
be morally and intellectually as near to us as Marcus Aurelius.

The record of the outward life of this admirable man has in
it little of striking incident. He was born at Rome on the 26th
of April, in the year 121 of the Christian era. He was nephew
and son-in-law to his predecessor on the throne, Antoninus
Pius. When Antoninus died, he was forty years old, but from
the time of his earliest manhood he had assisted in administering public affairs. Then, after his uncle's death in 161, for
nineteen years he reigned as emperor. The barbarians were
pressing on the Roman frontier, and a great part of Marcus
Aurelius's nineteen years of reign was passed in campaigning.
His absences from Rome were numerous and long. We hear
of him in Asia Minor, Syria, Egypt, Greece; but, above all, in
the countries on the Danube, where the war with the barbarians
was going on,—in Austria, Moravia, Hungary. In these countries much of his Journal seems to have been written; parts of it
are dated from them; and there, a few weeks before his fifty-
ninth birthday, he fell sick and died.[1] The record of him on
which his fame chiefly rests is the record of his inward life,—
his *Journal,* or *Commentaries,* or *Meditations,* or *Thoughts,* for
by all these names has the work been called. Perhaps the most
interesting of the records of his outward life is that which the
first book of this work supplies, where he gives an account of
his education, recites the names of those to whom he is indebted
for it, and enumerates his obligations to each of them. It is a
refreshing and consoling picture, a priceless treasure for those,
who, sick of the "wild and dreamlike trade of blood and guile,"
which seems to be nearly the whole of what history has to offer
to our view, seek eagerly for that substratum of right thinking
and well-doing which in all ages must surely have somewhere
existed, for without it the continued life of humanity would
have been impossible. "From my mother I learnt piety and
beneficence, and abstinence not only from evil deeds but even
from evil thoughts; and further, simplicity in my way of living, far removed from the habits of the rich." Let us remember that, the next time we are reading the sixth satire of Juvenal.

[1] He died on the 17th of March, A.D. 180.

"From my tutor I learnt" (hear it, ye tutors of princes!) "endurance of labour, and to want little, and to work with my own
hands, and not to meddle with other people's affairs, and not to
be ready to listen to slander." The vices and foibles of the Greek
sophist or rhetorician—the *Græculus esuriens*—are in everybody's mind; but he who reads Marcus Aurelius's account of his
Greek teachers and masters, will understand how it is that, in
spite of the vices and foibles of individual *Græculi*, the education of the human race owes to Greece a debt which can never
be overrated. The vague and colourless praise of history leaves
on the mind hardly any impression of Antoninus Pius: it is only
from the private memoranda of his nephew that we learn what
a disciplined, hard-working, gentle, wise, virtuous man he was;
a man who, perhaps, interests mankind less than his immortal
nephew only because he has left in writing no record of his
inner life,—*caret quia vate sacro.*

Of the outward life and circumstances of Marcus Aurelius,
beyond these notices which he has himself supplied, there are
few of much interest and importance. There is the fine anecdote
of his speech when he heard of the assassination of the revolted
Avidius Cassius, against whom he was marching; *he was sorry,*
he said, *to be deprived of the pleasure of pardoning him.* And
there are one or two more anecdotes of him which show the
same spirit. But the great record for the outward life of a man
who has left such a record of his lofty inward aspirations as
that which Marcus Aurelius has left, is the clear consenting
voice of all his contemporaries,—high and low, friend and
enemy, pagan and Christian,—in praise of his sincerity, justice,
and goodness. The world's charity does not err on the side of
excess, and here was a man occupying the most conspicuous
station in the world, and professing the highest possible standard
of conduct;—yet the world was obliged to declare that he
walked worthily of his profession. Long after his death, his bust
was to be seen in the houses of private men through the wide
Roman empire. It may be the vulgar part of human nature
which busies itself with the semblance and doings of living
sovereigns, it is its nobler part which busies itself with those of
the dead; these busts of Marcus Aurelius, in the homes of Gaul,

Britain, and Italy, bear witness, not to the inmates' frivolous curiosity about princes and palaces, but to their reverential memory of the passage of a great man upon the earth.

Two things, however, before one turns from the outward to the inward life of Marcus Aurelius, force themselves upon one's notice, and demand a word of comment; he persecuted the Christians, and he had for his son the vicious and brutal Commodus. The persecution at Lyons, in which Attalus and Pothinus suffered, the persecution at Smyrna, in which Polycarp suffered, took place in his reign. Of his humanity, of his tolerance, of his horror of cruelty and violence, of his wish to refrain from severe measures against the Christians, of his anxiety to temper the severity of these measures when they appeared to him indispensable, there is no doubt: but, on the one hand, it is certain that the letter, attributed to him, directing that no Christian should be punished for being a Christian, is spurious; it is almost certain that his alleged answer to the authorities of Lyons, in which he directs that Christians persisting in their profession shall be dealt with according to law, is genuine. Mr. Long seems inclined to try and throw doubt over the persecution at Lyons, by pointing out that the letter of the Lyons Christians relating it, alleges it to have been attended by miraculous and incredible incidents. "A man," he says, "can only act consistently by accepting all this letter or rejecting it all, and we cannot blame him for either." But it is contrary to all experience to say that because a fact is related with incorrect additions and embellishments, therefore it probably never happened at all; or that it is not, in general, easy for an impartial mind to distinguish between the fact and the embellishments. I cannot doubt that the Lyons persecution took place, and that the punishment of Christians for being Christians was sanctioned by Marcus Aurelius. But then I must add that nine modern readers out of ten, when they read this, will, I believe, have a perfectly false notion of what the moral action of Marcus Aurelius, in sanctioning that punishment, really was. They imagine Trajan, or Antoninus Pius, or Marcus Aurelius, fresh from the perusal of the Gospel, fully aware of the spirit and holiness of the Christian saints, ordering their extermination because he loved darkness rather than light. Far from this, the Christianity which these emperors aimed at repressing was, in their conception of it, something philosophically contemptible, politically subversive, and morally abominable. As men, they sincerely regarded it much as well-conditioned people, with us, regard Mormonism; as rulers, they regarded it much as Liberal statesmen, with us, regard the Jesuits. A kind of Mormonism, constituted as a vast secret society, with obscure aims of political and social subversion, was what Antoninus Pius and Marcus Aurelius believed themselves to be repressing when they punished Christians. The early Christian apologists again and again declare to us under what odious imputations the Christians lay, how general was the belief that these imputations were well-grounded, how sincere was the horror which the belief inspired. The multitude, convinced that the Christians were atheists who ate human flesh and thought incest no crime, displayed against them a fury so passionate as to embarrass and alarm their rulers. The severe expressions of Tacitus, *exitiabilis superstitio—odio humani generis convicti*, show how deeply the prejudices of the multitude imbued the educated class also. One asks oneself with astonishment how a doctrine so benign as that of Jesus Christ can have incurred misrepresentation so monstrous. The inner and moving cause of the misrepresentation lay, no doubt, in this,—that Christianity was a new spirit in the Roman world, destined to act in that world as its dissolvent; and it was inevitable that Christianity in the Roman world, like democracy in the modern world, like every new spirit with a similar mission assigned to it, should at its first appearance occasion an instinctive shrinking and repugnance in the world which it was to dissolve. The outer and palpable causes of the misrepresentation were, for the Roman public at large, the confounding of the Christians with the Jews, that isolated, fierce, and stubborn race, whose stubbornness, fierceness, and isolation, real as they were, the fancy of a civilised Roman yet further exaggerated; the atmosphere of mystery and novelty which surrounded the Christian rites; the very simplicity of Christian theism. For the Roman statesman, the cause of mistake lay in that character of secret assemblages which the meetings of the Christian community wore, under a State-system as jealous of unauthorised associations as is the State-system of modern France.

A Roman of Marcus Aurelius's time and position could not well see the Christians except through the mist of these prejudices. Seen through such a mist, the Christians appeared with a thousand faults not their own; but it has not been sufficiently remarked that faults really their own many of them assuredly appeared with besides, faults especially likely to strike such an observer as Marcus Aurelius, and to confirm him in the prejudices of his race, station, and rearing. We look back upon Christianity after it has proved what a future it bore within it, and for us the sole representatives of its early struggles are the pure and devoted spirits through whom it proved this; Marcus Aurelius saw it with its future yet unshown, and with the tares among its professed progeny not less conspicuous than the wheat. Who can doubt that among the professing Christians of the second century, as among the professing Christians of the nineteenth, there was plenty of folly, plenty of rabid nonsense, plenty of gross fanaticism? who will even venture to affirm that, separated in great measure from the intellect and civilisation of the world for one or two centuries, Christianity, wonderful as have been its fruits, had the development perfectly worthy of its inestimable germ? Who will venture to affirm that, by the alliance of Christianity with the virtue and intelligence of men like the Antonines,—of the best product of Greek and Roman civilisation, while Greek and Roman civilisation had yet life and power,—Christianity and the world, as well as the Antonines themselves, would not have been gainers? That alliance was not to be. The Antonines lived and died with an utter misconception of Christianity; Christianity grew up in the Catacombs, not on the Palatine. And Marcus Aurelius incurs no moral reproach by having authorised the punishment of the Christians; he does not thereby become in the least what we mean by a *persecutor*. One may concede that it was impossible for him to see Christianity as it really was;—as impossible as for even the moderate and sensible Fleury to see the Antonines as they really were;— one may concede that the point of view from which Christianity appeared something anti-civil and anti-social, which the

State had the faculty to judge and the duty to suppress, was inevitably his. Still, however, it remains true that this sage, who made perfection his aim and reason his law, did Christianity an immense injustice and rested in an idea of State-attributes which was illusive. And this is, in truth, characteristic of Marcus Aurelius, that he is blameless, yet, in a certain sense, unfortunate; in his character, beautiful as it is, there is something melancholy, circumscribed, and ineffectual.

For of his having such a son as Commodus, too, one must say that he is not to be blamed on that account, but that he is unfortunate. Disposition and temperament are inexplicable things; there are natures on which the best education and example are thrown away; excellent fathers may have, without any fault of theirs, incurably vicious sons. It is to be remembered, also, that Commodus was left, at the perilous age of nineteen, master of the world; while his father, at that age, was but beginning a twenty years' apprenticeship to wisdom, labour, and self-command, under the sheltering teachership of his uncle Antoninus. Commodus was a prince apt to be led by favourites; and if the story is true which says that he left, all through his reign, the Christians untroubled, and ascribes this lenity to the influence of his mistress Marcia, it shows that he could be led to good as well as to evil. But for such a nature to be left at a critical age with absolute power, and wholly without good counsel and direction, was the more fatal. Still one cannot help wishing that the example of Marcus Aurelius could have availed more with his own only son. One cannot but think that with such virtue as his there should go, too, the ardour which removes mountains, and that the ardour which removes mountains might have even won Commodus. The word *ineffectual* again rises to one's mind; Marcus Aurelius saved his own soul by his righteousness, and he could do no more. Happy they who can do this! but still happier, who can do more!

Yet, when one passes from his outward to his inward life, when one turns over the pages of his *Meditations*,—entries jotted down from day to day, amid the business of the city or the fatigues of the camp, for his own guidance and support, meant for no eye but his own, without the slightest attempt at style, with no care, even, for correct writing, not to be surpassed for naturalness and sincerity,—all disposition to carp and cavil dies away, and one is overpowered by the charm of a character of such purity, delicacy, and virtue. He fails neither in small things nor in great; he keeps watch over himself both that the great springs of action may be right in him, and that the minute details of action may be right also. How admirable in a hard-tasked ruler, and a ruler, too, with a passion for thinking and reading, is such a memorandum as the following:—

"Not frequently nor without necessity to say to any one, or to write in a letter, that I have no leisure; nor continually to excuse the neglect of duties required by our relation to those with whom we live, by alleging urgent occupation."

And, when that ruler is a Roman emperor, what an "idea" is this to be written down and meditated by him:—

"The idea of a polity in which there is the same law for all, a polity administered with regard to equal rights and equal freedom of speech, and the idea of a kingly government which respects most of all the freedom of the governed."

And, for all men who "drive at practice," what practical rules may not one accumulate out of these *Meditations:*—

"The greatest part of what we say or do being unnecessary, if a man takes this away, he will have more leisure and less uneasiness. Accordingly, on every occasion a man should ask himself: 'Is this one of the unnecessary things?' Now a man should take away not only unnecessary acts, but also unnecessary thoughts, for thus superfluous acts will not follow after."

And again:—

"We ought to check in the series of our thoughts everything that is without a purpose and useless, but most of all the over curious feeling and the malignant; and a man should use himself to think of those things only about which if one should suddenly ask, 'What hast thou now in thy thoughts?' with perfect openness thou mightest immediately answer, 'This or That;' so that from thy words it should be plain that everything in thee is simple and benevolent, and such as befits a social animal, and one that cares not for thoughts about sensual enjoyments, or any rivalry or envy and suspicion, or anything

else for which thou wouldst blush if thou shouldst say thou
hadst it in thy mind."

So, with a stringent practicalness worthy of Franklin, he
discourses on his favourite text, *Let nothing be done without*
a purpose. But it is when he enters the region where Franklin
cannot follow him, when he utters his thoughts on the ground-
motives of human action, that he is most interesting; that he
becomes the unique, the incomparable Marcus Aurelius. Christianity uses language very liable to be misunderstood when it
seems to tell men to do good, not, certainly, from the vulgar
motives of worldly interest, or vanity, or love of human praise,
but "that their Father which seeth in secret may reward them
openly." The motives of reward and punishment have come,
from the misconception of language of this kind, to be strangely
overpressed by many Christian moralists, to the deterioration
and disfigurement of Christianity. Marcus Aurelius says, truly
and nobly:—

"One man, when he has done a service to another, is ready
to set it down to his account as a favour conferred. Another
is not ready to do this, but still in his own mind he thinks of
the man as his debtor, and he knows what he has done. A third
in a manner does not even know what he has done, *but he is*
like a vine which has produced grapes, and seeks for nothing
more after it has once produced its proper fruit. As a horse
when he has run, a dog when he has caught the game, a bee
when it has made its honey, so a man when he has done a good
act, does not call out for others to come and see, but he goes
on to another act, as a vine goes on to produce again the grapes
in season. Must a man, then, be one of these, who in a manner
act thus without observing it? Yes."

And again:—

"What more dost thou want when thou hast done a man
a service? Art thou not content that thou hast done something
conformable to thy nature, and dost thou seek to be paid for
it, *just if the eye demanded a recompense for seeing, or the*
feet for walking?"

Christianity, in order to match morality of this strain, has to correct its apparent offers of external reward, and to say: *The kingdom of God is within you.*

I have said that it is by its accent of emotion that the morality of Marcus Aurelius acquires a special character, and reminds one of Christian morality. The sentences of Seneca are stimulating to the intellect; the sentences of Epictetus are fortifying to the character; the sentences of Marcus Aurelius find their way to the soul. I have said that religious emotion has the power to *light up* morality: the emotion of Marcus Aurelius does not quite light up his morality, but it suffuses it; it has not power to melt the clouds of effort and austerity quite away, but it shines through them and glorifies them; it is a spirit, not so much of gladness and elation, as of gentleness and sweetness; a delicate and tender sentiment, which is less than joy and more than resignation. He says that in his youth he learned from Maximus, one of his teachers, "cheerfulness in all circumstances as well as in illness; *and a just admixture in the moral character of sweetness and dignity:*" and it is this very admixture of sweetness with his dignity which makes him so beautiful a moralist. It enables him to carry even into his observation of nature a delicate penetration, a sympathetic tenderness, worthy of Wordsworth; the spirit of such a remark as the following has hardly a parallel, so far as my knowledge goes, in the whole range of Greek and Roman literature:—

"Figs, when they are quite ripe, gape open; and in the ripe olives the very circumstance of their being near to rottenness adds a peculiar beauty to the fruit. And the ears of corn bending down, and the lion's eyebrows, and the foam which flows from the mouth of wild boars, and many other things,—though they are far from being beautiful, in a certain sense,—still, because they come in the course of nature, have a beauty in them, and they please the mind; so that if a man should have a feeling and a deeper insight with respect to the things which are produced in the universe, there is hardly anything which comes in the course of nature which will not seem to him to be in a manner disposed so as to give pleasure."

But it is when his strain passes to directly moral subjects

that his delicacy and sweetness lend to it the greatest charm. Let those who can feel the beauty of spiritual refinement read this, the reflection of an emperor who prized mental superiority highly:—

5   "Thou sayest, 'Men cannot admire the sharpness of thy wits.' Be it so; but there are many other things of which thou canst not say, 'I am not formed for them by nature.' Show those qualities, then, which are altogether in thy power,—sincerity, gravity, endurance of labour, aversion to pleasure, contentment

10   with thy portion and with few things, benevolence, frankness, no love of superfluity, freedom from trifling, magnanimity. Dost thou not see how many qualities thou art at once able to exhibit, as to which there is no excuse of natural incapacity and unfitness, and yet thou still remainest voluntarily below the

15   mark? Or art thou compelled, through being defectively furnished by nature, to murmur, and to be mean, and to flatter, and to find fault with thy poor body, and to try to please men, and to make great display, and to be so restless in thy mind? No, indeed; but thou mightest have been delivered from these

20   things long ago. Only, if in truth thou canst be charged with being rather slow and dull of comprehension, thou must exert thyself about this also, not neglecting nor yet taking pleasure in thy dulness."

The same sweetness enables him to fix his mind, when he

25   sees the isolation and moral death caused by sin, not on the cheerless thought of the misery of this condition, but on the inspiriting thought that man is blest with the power to escape from it:—

"Suppose that thou hast detached thyself from the natural

30   unity,—for thou wast made by nature a part, but now thou hast cut thyself off,—yet here is this beautiful provision, that it is in thy power again to unite thyself. God has allowed this to no other part,—after it has been separated and cut asunder, to come together again. But consider the goodness with which

35   he has privileged man; for he has put it in his power, when he has been separated, to return and to be united and to resume his place."

It enables him to control even the passion for retreat and

solitude, so strong in a soul like his, to which the world could offer no abiding city:—

"Men seek retreats for themselves, houses in the country, seashores, and mountains; and thou, too, art wont to desire such things very much. But this is altogether a mark of the most common sort of men, for it is in thy power whenever thou shall choose to retire into thyself. For nowhere either with more quiet or more freedom from trouble does a man retire than into his own soul, particularly when he has within him such thoughts that by looking into them he is immediately in perfect tranquillity. Constantly, then, give to thyself this retreat, and renew thyself; and let thy principles be brief and fundamental, which, as soon as thou shalt recur to them, will be sufficient to cleanse the soul completely, and to send thee back free from all discontent with the things to which thou returnest."

Against this feeling of discontent and weariness, so natural to the great for whom there seems nothing left to desire or to strive after, but so enfeebling to them, so deteriorating, Marcus Aurelius never ceased to struggle. With resolute thankfulness he kept in remembrance the blessings of his lot; the true blessings of it, not the false:—

"I have to thank Heaven that I was subjected to a ruler and a father (Antoninus Pius) who was able to take away all pride from me, and to bring me to the knowledge that it is possible for a man to live in a palace without either guards, or embroidered dresses, or any show of this kind; but that it is in such a man's power to bring himself very near to the fashion of a private person, without being for this reason either meaner in thought or more remiss in action with respect to the things which must be done for public interest. . . . I have to be thankful that my children have not been stupid nor deformed in body; that I did not make more proficiency in rhetoric, poetry, and the other studies, by which I should perhaps have been completely engrossed, if I had seen that I was making great progress in them; . . . that I knew Apollonius, Rusticus, Maximus; . . . that I received clear and frequent impressions about living according to nature, and what kind of a life that is, so that, so far as depended on Heaven, and its gifts, help, and inspiration, nothing hindered me from forthwith living according to nature, though I still fall short of it through my own fault, and through not observing the admonitions of Heaven, and, I may almost say, its direct instructions; that my body has held out so long in such a kind of life as mine; that though it was my mother's lot to die young, she spent the last years of her life with me; that whenever I wished to help any man in his need, I was never told that I had not the means of doing it; that, when I had an inclination to philosophy, I did not fall into the hands of a sophist."

And, as he dwelt with gratitude on these helps and blessings vouchsafed to him, his mind (so, at least, it seems to me) would sometimes revert with awe to the perils and temptations of the lonely height where he stood, to the lives of Tiberius, Caligula, Nero, Domitian, in their hideous blackness and ruin; and then he wrote down for himself such a warning entry as this, significant and terrible in its abruptness:—

"A black character, a womanish character, a stubborn character, bestial, childish, animal, stupid, counterfeit, scurrilous, fraudulent, tyrannical!"

Or this:—

"About what am I now employing my soul? On every occasion I must ask myself this question, and enquire, What have I now in this part of me which they call the ruling principle, and whose soul have I now?—that of a child, or of a young man, or of a weak woman, or of a tyrant, or of one of the lower animals in the service of man, or of a wild beast?"

The character he wished to attain he knew well, and beautifully he has marked it, and marked, too, his sense of shortcoming:—

"When thou hast assumed these names,—good, modest, true, rational, equal-minded, magnanimous,—take care that thou dost not change these names; and, if thou shouldst lose them, quickly return to them. If thou maintainest thyself in possession of these names without desiring that others should call thee by them, thou wilt be another being, and wilt enter on another life. For to continue to be such as thou hast hitherto been, and to be torn in pieces and defiled in such a life, is the character of a very stupid man, and one overfond of his life, and like those half-devoured fighters with wild beasts, who though covered with wounds and gore still entreat to be kept to the following day, though they will be exposed in the same state to the same claws and bites. Therefore fix thyself in the possession of these few names: and if thou art able to abide in them, abide as if thou wast removed to the Happy Islands."

For all his sweetness and serenity, however, man's point of life "between two infinities" (of that expression Marcus Aurelius is the real owner) was to him anything but a Happy Island, and the performances on it he saw through no veils of illusion. Nothing is in general more gloomy and monotonous than declamations on the hollowness and transitoriness of human life and grandeur: but here, too, the great charm of Marcus Aurelius, his emotion, comes in to relieve the monotony and to break through the gloom; and even on this eternally used topic he is imaginative, fresh, and striking:—

"Consider, for example, the times of Vespasian. Thou wilt see all these things, people marrying, bringing up children, sick, dying, warring, feasting, trafficking, cultivating the ground, flattering, obstinately arrogant, suspecting, plotting, wishing for somebody to die, grumbling about the present, loving, heaping up treasure, desiring to be consuls or kings. Well then, that life of these people no longer exists at all. Again, go to the times of Trajan. All is again the same. Their life too is gone. But chiefly thou shouldst think of those whom thou hast thyself known distracting themselves about idle things, neglecting to do what was in accordance with their proper constitution, and to hold firmly to this and to be content with it."

Again:—

"The things which are much valued in life are empty, and rotten, and trifling; and people are like little dogs biting one another, and little children quarrelling, crying, and then straightway laughing. But fidelity, and modesty, and justice, and truth, are fled

'Up to Olympus from the wide-spread earth.'

What then is there which still detains thee here?"

And once more:—

"Look down from above on the countless herds of men, and their countless solemnities, and the infinitely varied voyagings in storms and calms, and the differences among those who are born, who live together, and die. And consider too the life lived by others in olden time, and the life now lived among barbarous nations, and how many know not even thy name, and how many will soon forget it, and how they who perhaps now are praising thee will very soon blame thee, and that neither a posthumous name is of any value, nor reputation, nor anything else."

He recognised, indeed, that (to use his own words) "the prime principle in man's constitution is the social;" and he laboured sincerely to make not only his acts towards his fellow-men, but his thoughts also, suitable to this conviction:—

"When thou wishest to delight thyself, think of the virtues of those who live with thee; for instance, the activity of one, and the modesty of another, and the liberality of a third, and some other good quality of a fourth."

Still, it is hard for a pure and thoughtful man to live in a state of rapture at the spectacle afforded to him by his fellow-creatures; above all it is hard, when such a man is placed as Marcus Aurelius was placed, and has had the meanness and perversity of his fellow-creatures thrust, in no common measure, upon his notice,—has had, time after time, to experience how "within ten days thou wilt seem a god to those to whom thou art now a beast and an ape." His true strain of thought as to his relations with his fellow-men is rather the following. He has been enumerating the higher consolations which may support a man at the approach of death, and he goes on:—

"But if thou requirest also a vulgar kind of comfort which shall reach thy heart, thou wilt be made best reconciled to death by observing the objects from which thou art going to be removed, and the morals of those with whom thy soul will no longer be mingled. For it is no way right to be offended with men, but it is thy duty to care for them and to bear with them gently; and yet to remember that thy departure will not be from men who have the same principles as thyself. For this is the only thing, if there be any, which could draw us the contrary way and attach us to life, to be permitted to live with those who have the same principles as ourselves. But now thou seest how great is the distress caused by the difference of those who live together, so that thou mayest say: 'Come quick, O death, lest perchance I too should forget myself.' "

O faithless and perverse generation! how long shall I be with you? how long shall I suffer you? Sometimes this strain rises even to passion:—

"Short is the little which remains to thee of life. Live as on a mountain. Let men see, let them know, a real man, who lives as he was meant to live. If they cannot endure him, let them kill him. For that is better than to live as men do."

It is remarkable how little of a merely local and temporary character, how little of those *scoriæ* which a reader has to clear away before he gets to the precious ore, how little that even admits of doubt or question, the morality of Marcus Aurelius exhibits. Perhaps as to one point we must make an exception. Marcus Aurelius is fond of urging as a motive for man's cheerful acquiescence in whatever befalls him, that "whatever happens to every man *is for the interest of the universal;*" that the whole contains nothing *which is not for its advantage;* that everything which happens to a man is to be accepted, "even if it seems disagreeable, *because it leads to the health of the universe.*" And the whole course of the universe, he adds, has a providential reference to man's welfare: *"all other things have been made for the sake of rational beings."* Religion has in all ages freely used this language, and it is not religion which will object to Marcus Aurelius's use of it; but science can hardly accept as severely accurate this employment of the terms *interest* and *advantage.* To a sound nature and a clear reason the proposition that things happen "for the interest of the universal," as men conceive of interest, may seem to have no meaning at all, and the proposition that "all things have been made for the sake of rational beings" may seem to be false. Yet even to this language, not irresistibly

cogent when it is thus absolutely used, Marcus Aurelius gives a turn which makes it true and useful, when he says: "The ruling part of man can make a material for itself out of that which opposes it, as fire lays hold of what falls into it, and
5   rises higher by means of this very material;"—when he says: "What else are all things except exercises for the reason? Persevere then until thou shalt have made these things thine own, as the stomach which is strengthened makes all things its own, as the blazing fire makes flame and brightness out of everything
10 that is thrown into it;"—when he says: "Thou wilt not cease to be miserable till thy mind is in such a condition, that, what luxury is to those who enjoy pleasure, such shall be to thee, in every matter which presents itself, the doing of the things which are conformable to man's constitution; for a man ought
15 to consider as an enjoyment everything which it is in his power to do according to his own nature,—and it is in his power everywhere." In this sense it is, indeed, most true that "all things have been made for the sake of rational beings;" that "all things work together for good."
20   In general, however, the action Marcus Aurelius prescribes is action which every sound nature must recognise as right, and the motives he assigns are motives which every clear reason must recognise as valid. And so he remains the especial friend and comforter of all clear-headed and scrupulous, yet pure-
25 hearted and upward striving men, in those ages most especially that walk by sight, not by faith, but yet have no open vision. He cannot give such souls, perhaps, all they yearn for, but he gives them much; and what he gives them, they can receive.
        Yet no, it is not for what he thus gives them that such souls
30 love him most! it is rather because of the emotion which lends to his voice so touching an accent, it is because he too yearns as they do for something unattained by him. What an affinity for Christianity had this persecutor of the Christians! The effusion of Christianity, its relieving tears, its happy self-
35 sacrifice, were the very element, one feels, for which his soul longed; they were near him, they brushed him, he touched them, he passed them by. One feels, too, that the Marcus Aurelius one reads must still have remained, even had Chris-

tianity been fully known to him, in a great measure himself;
he would have been no Justin;—but how would Christianity
have affected him? in what measure would it have changed him?
Granted that he might have found, like the *Alogi* of modern
times, in the most beautiful of the Gospels, the Gospel which
has leavened Christendom most powerfully, the Gospel of St.
John, too much Greek metaphysics, too much *gnosis;* granted
that this Gospel might have looked too like what he knew
already to be a total surprise to him: what, then, would he
have said to the Sermon on the Mount, to the twenty-sixth
chapter of St. Matthew? What would have become of his
notions of the *exitiabilis superstitio*, of the "obstinacy of the
Christians"? Vain question! yet the greatest charm of Marcus
Aurelius is that he makes us ask it. We see him wise, just,
self-governed, tender, thankful, blameless; yet, with all this,
agitated, stretching out his arms for something beyond,—
tendentemque manus ripæ ulterioris amore.

Spinoza and the Bible

"By the sentence of the angels, by the decree of the saints, we anathematise, cut off, curse, and execrate Baruch Spinoza, in the presence of these sacred books with the six hundred and thirteen precepts which are written therein, with the anathema
5   wherewith Joshua anathematised Jericho; with the cursing wherewith Elisha cursed the children; and with all the cursings which are written in the Book of the Law: cursed be he by day, and cursed by night; cursed when he lieth down, and cursed when he riseth up; cursed when he goeth out, and cursed
10 when he cometh in; the Lord pardon him never; the wrath and fury of the Lord burn upon this man, and bring upon him all the curses which are written in the Book of the Law. The Lord blot out his name under heaven. The Lord set him apart for destruction from all the tribes of Israel, with all the
15 curses of the firmament which are written in the Book of this Law.... There shall no man speak to him, no man write to him, no man show him any kindness, no man stay under the same roof with him, no man come nigh him."

   With these amenities, the current compliments of theological
20 parting, the Jews of the Portuguese synagogue at Amsterdam took in 1656 (and not in 1660, as has till now been commonly supposed) their leave of their erring brother, Baruch or Benedict Spinoza. They remained children of Israel, and he became a child of modern Europe.

25   That was in 1656, and Spinoza died in 1677, at the early age of forty-four. Glory had not found him out. His short life —a life of unbroken diligence, kindliness, and purity—was passed in seclusion. But in spite of that seclusion, in spite of the shortness of his career, in spite of the hostility of the

dispensers of renown in the 18th century,—of Voltaire's disparagement and Bayle's detraction,—in spite of the repellent form which he has given to his principal work, in spite of the exterior semblance of a rigid dogmatism alien to the most essential tendencies of modern philosophy, in spite, finally, of the immense weight of disfavour cast upon him by the long-repeated charge of atheism, Spinoza's name has silently risen in importance, the man and his work have attracted a steadily increasing notice, and bid fair to become soon what they deserve to become,—in the history of modern philosophy the central point of interest. An avowed translation of one of his works, —his *Tractatus Theologico-Politicus*,—has at last made its appearance in English. It is the principal work which Spinoza published in his lifetime; his book on ethics, the work on which his fame rests, is posthumous.

The English translator has not done his task well. Of the character of his version there can, I am afraid, be no doubt; one such passage as the following is decisive:—

"I confess that, *while with them* (the theologians) *I have never been able sufficiently to admire the unfathomed mysteries of Scripture, I have still found them giving utterance to nothing but Aristotelian and Platonic speculations*, artfully dressed up and cunningly accommodated to Holy Writ, lest the speakers should show themselves too plainly to belong to the sect of the Grecian heathens. *Nor was it enough for these men to discourse with the Greeks; they have further taken to raving with the Hebrew prophets*."

This professes to be a translation of these words of Spinoza: "Fateor, eos nunquam satis mirari potuisse Scripturæ profundissima mysteria; attamen præter Aristotelicorum vel Platonicorum speculationes nihil docuisse video, atque his, ne gentiles sectari viderentur, Scripturam accommodaverunt. Non satis his fuit cum Graecis insanire, sed prophetas cum iisdem deliravisse voluerunt." After one such specimen of a translator's force, the experienced reader has a sort of instinct that he may as well close the book at once, with a smile or a sigh, according as he happens to be a follower of the weeping or of the laughing philosopher. If, in spite of this instinct, he persists in going on with the English version of the *Tractatus Theologico-Politicus*, he will find many more such specimens. It is not, however, my intention to fill my space with these, or with strictures upon their author. I prefer to remark, that he renders a service to literary history by pointing out, in his preface, how "to Bayle may be traced the disfavour in which the name of Spinoza was so long held;" that, in his observations on the system of the Church of England, he shows a laudable freedom from the prejudices of ordinary English Liberals of that advanced school to which he clearly belongs; and lastly, that, though he manifests little familiarity with Latin, he seems to have considerable familiarity with philosophy, and to be well able to follow and comprehend speculative reasoning. Let me advise him to unite his forces with those of some one who has that accurate knowledge of Latin which he himself has not, and then, perhaps, of that union a really good translation of Spinoza will be the result. And, having given him this advice, let me again turn, for a little, to the *Tractatus Theologico-Politicus* itself.

This work, as I have already said, is a work on the interpretation of Scripture,—it treats of the Bible. What was it exactly which Spinoza thought about the Bible and its inspiration? That will be, at the present moment, the central point of interest for the English readers of his Treatise. Now, it is to be observed, that just on this very point the Treatise, interesting and remarkable as it is, will fail to satisfy the reader. It is important to seize this notion quite firmly, and not to quit hold of it while one is reading Spinoza's work. The scope of that work is this. Spinoza sees that the life and practice of Christian nations professing the religion of the Bible, are not the due fruits of the religion of the Bible; he sees only hatred, bitterness, and strife, where he might have expected to see love, joy, and peace in believing; and he asks himself the reason of this. The reason is, he says, that these people misunderstand their Bible. Well, then, is his conclusion, I will write a *Tractatus Theologico-Politicus*. I will show these people, that, taking the Bible for granted, taking it to be all which it asserts itself to be, taking it to have all the authority which it claims, it is not what they imagine it to be, it does not say what they

imagine it to say. I will show them what it really does say,
and I will show them that they will do well to accept this real
teaching of the Bible, instead of the phantom with which they
have so long been cheated. I will show their governments that
they will do well to remodel the national churches, to make   5
of them institutions informed with the spirit of the true Bible,
instead of institutions informed with the spirit of this false
phantom.

The comments of men, Spinoza said, had been foisted into
the Christian religion; the pure teaching of God had been lost   10
sight of. He determined, therefore, to go again to the Bible,
to read it over and over with a perfectly unprejudiced mind,
and to accept nothing as its teaching which it did not clearly
teach. He began by constructing a method, or set of conditions
indispensable for the adequate interpretation of Scripture.   15
These conditions are such, he points out, that a perfectly adequate interpretation of Scripture is now impossible. For example, to understand any prophet thoroughly, we ought to know
the life, character, and pursuits of that prophet, under what circumstances his book was composed, and in what state and   20
through what hands it has come down to us; and, in general,
most of this we cannot now know. Still, the main sense of the
Books of Scripture may be clearly seized by us. Himself a Jew
with all the learning of his nation, and a man of the highest
natural powers, Spinoza had in the difficult task of seizing this   25
sense every aid which special knowledge or pre-eminent
faculties could supply.

In what then, he asks, does Scripture, interpreted by its
own aid, and not by the aid of Rabbinical traditions or Greek
philosophy, allege its own divinity to consist? In a revelation   30
given by God to the prophets. Now all knowledge is a divine
revelation; but prophecy, as represented in Scripture, is one
of which the laws of human nature, considered in themselves
alone, cannot be the cause. Therefore nothing must be asserted
about it, except what is clearly declared by the prophets them-   35
selves; for they are our only source of knowledge on a matter
which does not fall within the scope of our ordinary knowing
faculties. But ignorant people, not knowing the Hebrew genius

and phraseology, and not attending to the circumstances of the speaker, often imagine the prophets to assert things which they do not.

The prophets clearly declare themselves to have received the revelation of God through the means of words and images;—not, as Christ, through immediate communication of the mind with the mind of God. Therefore the prophets excelled other men by the power and vividness of their representing and imagining faculty, not by the perfection of their mind. This is why they perceived almost everything through figures, and express themselves so variously, and so improperly, concerning the nature of God. Moses imagined that God could be seen, and attributed to him the passions of anger and jealousy; Micaiah imagined him sitting on a throne, with the host of heaven on his right and left hand; Daniel as an old man, with a white garment and white hair; Ezekiel as a fire; the disciples of Christ thought they saw the Spirit of God in the form of a dove; the apostles in the form of fiery tongues.

Whence, then, could the prophets be certain of the truth of a revelation which they received through the imagination, and not by a mental process?—for only an idea can carry the sense of its own certainty along with it, not an imagination. To make them certain of the truth of what was revealed to them, a reasoning process came in; they had to rely on the testimony of a sign; and (above all) on the testimony of their own conscience, that they were good men, and spoke for God's sake. Either testimony was incomplete without the other. Even the good prophet needed for his message the confirmation of a sign; but the bad prophet, the utterer of an immoral doctrine, had no certainty for his doctrine, no truth in it, even though he confirmed it by a sign. The testimony of a good conscience was, therefore, the prophet's grand source of certitude. Even this, however, was only a moral certitude, not a mathematical; for no man can be perfectly sure of his own goodness.

The power of imagining, the power of feeling what goodness is, and the habit of practising goodness, were therefore the sole essential qualifications of a true prophet. But for the purpose of the message, the revelation, which God designed him to

convey, these qualifications were enough. The sum and substance of this revelation was simply: *Believe in God, and lead a
good life.* To be the organ of this revelation, did not make a
man more learned; it left his scientific knowledge as it found
it. This explains the contradictory and speculatively false   5
opinions about God, and the laws of nature, which the
patriarchs, the prophets, the apostles entertained. Abraham
and the patriarchs knew God only as *El Sadai,* the power which
gives to every man that which suffices him; Moses knew him
as *Jehovah,* a self-existent being, but imagined him with the   10
passions of a man. Samuel imagined that God could not repent
of his sentences; Jeremiah, that he could. Joshua, on a day of
great victory, the ground being white with hail, seeing the
daylight last longer than usual, and imaginatively seizing this
as a special sign of the help divinely promised to him, declared 15
that the sun was standing still. To be obeyers of God themselves, and inspired leaders of others to obedience and good life,
did not make Abraham and Moses metaphysicians, or Joshua
a natural philosopher. His revelation no more changed the
speculative opinions of each prophet, than it changed his tem-   20
perament or style. The wrathful Elisha required the natural
sedative of music, before he could be the messenger of good
fortune to Jehoram. The high-bred Isaiah and Nahum have
the style proper to their condition, and the rustic Ezekiel and
Amos the style proper to theirs. We are not therefore bound to 25
pay heed to the speculative opinions of this or that prophet,
for in uttering these he spoke as a mere man: only in exhorting
his hearers to obey God and lead a good life was he the organ
of a divine revelation.

   To know and love God is the highest blessedness of man,   30
and of all men alike; to this all mankind are called, and not any
one nation in particular. The divine law, properly so named, is
the method of life for attaining this height of human blessedness: this law is universal, written in the heart, and one for
all mankind. Human law is the method of life for attaining and 35
preserving temporal security and prosperity: this law is dictated
by a lawgiver, and every nation has its own. In the case of the
Jews, this law was dictated, by revelation, through the prophets;

its fundamental precept was to obey God and to keep his commandments, and it is therefore, in a secondary sense, called divine; but it was, nevertheless, framed in respect of temporal things only. Even the truly moral and divine precept of this
5 law, to practise for God's sake justice and mercy towards one's neighbour, meant for the Hebrew of the Old Testament his Hebrew neighbour only, and had respect to the concord and stability of the Hebrew commonwealth. The Jews were to obey God and to keep his commandments, that they might continue
10 long in the land given to them, and that it might be well with them there. Their election was a temporal one, and lasted only so long as their State. It is now over; and the only election the Jews now have is that of the *pious*, the *remnant*, which takes place, and has always taken place, in every other nation also.
15 Scripture itself teaches that there is a universal divine law, that this is common to all nations alike, and is the law which truly confers eternal blessedness. Solomon, the wisest of the Jews, knew this law, as the few wisest men in all nations have ever known it; but for the mass of the Jews, as for the mass of
20 mankind everywhere, this law was hidden, and they had no notion of its moral action, its *vera vita* which conducts to eternal blessedness, except so far as this action was enjoined upon them by the prescriptions of their temporal law. When the ruin of their State brought with it the ruin of their temporal
25 law, they would have lost altogether their only clue to eternal blessedness.

Christ came when that fabric of the Jewish State, for the sake of which the Jewish law existed, was about to fall; and he proclaimed the universal divine law. A certain moral action is
30 prescribed by this law, as a certain moral action was prescribed by the Jewish law: but he who truly conceives the universal divine law conceives God's decrees adequately as eternal truths, and for him moral action has liberty and self-knowledge; while the prophets of the Jewish law inadequately conceived God's
35 decrees as mere rules and commands, and for them moral action had no liberty and no self-knowledge. Christ, who beheld the decrees of God as God himself beholds them,— as eternal truths, —proclaimed the love of God and the love of our neighbour as

commands, only because of the ignorance of the multitude: to those to whom it was "given to know the mysteries of the kingdom of God," he announced them, as he himself perceived them, as eternal truths. And the apostles, like Christ, spoke to many of their hearers "as unto carnal not spiritual;" presented to them, that is, the love of God and their neighbour as a divine command authenticated by the life and death of Christ, not as an eternal idea of reason carrying its own warrant along with it. The presentation of it as this latter their hearers "were not able to bear." The apostles, moreover, though they preached and confirmed their doctrine by signs as prophets, wrote their Epistles, not as prophets, but as doctors and reasoners. The essentials of their doctrine, indeed, they took not from reason, but, like the prophets, from fact and revelation; they preached belief in God and goodness of life as a catholic religion existing by virtue of the passion of Christ, as the prophets had preached belief in God and goodness of life as a national religion existing by virtue of the Mosaic covenant: but while the prophets announced their message in a form purely dogmatical, the apostles developed theirs with the forms of reasoning and argumentation, according to each apostle's ability and way of thinking, and as they might best commend their message to their hearers; and for their reasonings they themselves claim no divine authority, submitting them to the judgment of their hearers. Thus each apostle built essential religion on a non-essential foundation of his own, and, as St. Paul says, avoided building on the foundations of another apostle, which might be quite different from his own. Hence the discrepancies between the doctrine of one apostle and another,—between that of St. Paul, for example, and that of St. James; but these discrepancies are in the non-essentials not given to them by revelation, and not in essentials. Human churches, seizing these discrepant non-essentials as essentials, one maintaining one of them, another another, have filled the world with unprofitable disputes, have "turned the Church into an academy, and religion into a science, or rather a wrangling," and have fallen into endless schism.

What, then, are the essentials of religion according both to

the Old and to the New Testament? Very few and very simple.
The precept to love God and our neighbour. The precepts of
the first chapter of Isaiah: "Wash you, make you clean; put
away the evil of your doings from before mine eyes; cease to
5   do evil; learn to do well; seek judgment; relieve the oppressed;
judge the fatherless; plead for the widow." The precepts of
the Sermon on the Mount, which add to the foregoing the
injunction that we should cease to do evil and learn to do well,
not to our brethren and fellow-citizens only, but to all man-
10   kind. It is by following these precepts that belief in God is
to be shown: if we believe in him, we shall keep his commandment; and this is his commandment, that we love one another.
It is because it contains these precepts that the Bible is properly
called the Word of God, in spite of its containing much that is
15   mere history, and, like all history, sometimes true, sometimes
false; in spite of its containing much that is mere reasoning,
and, like all reasoning, sometimes sound, sometimes hollow.
These precepts are also the precepts of the universal divine
law written in our hearts; and it is only by this that the divinity
20   of Scripture is established;—by its containing, namely, precepts
identical with those of this inly-written and self-proving law.
This law was in the world, as St. John says, before the doctrine
of Moses or the doctrine of Christ. And what need was there,
then, for these doctrines? Because the world at large "knew
25   not" this original divine law, in which precepts are ideas, and
the belief in God the knowledge and contemplation of him.
Reason gives us this law, reason tells us that it leads to eternal
blessedness, and that those who follow it have no need of any
other. But reason could not have told us that the moral action
30   of the universal divine law,—followed not from a sense of
its intrinsic goodness, truth, and necessity, but simply in proof
of obedience (for both the Old and New Testament are but
one long discipline of obedience), simply because it is so commanded by Moses in virtue of the covenant, simply because
35   it is so commanded by Christ in virtue of his life and passion,—
can lead to eternal blessedness, which means, for reason, eternal
knowledge. Reason could not have told us this, and this is what
the Bible tells us. This is that "thing which had been kept secret

since the foundation of the world." It is thus that by means of the foolishness of the world God confounds the wise, and with things that are not brings to nought things that are. Of the truth of the promise thus made to obedience without knowledge, we can have no mathematical certainty; for we can have a mathematical certainty only of things deduced by reason from elements which she in herself possesses. But we can have a moral certainty of it; a certainty such as the prophets had themselves, arising out of the goodness and pureness of those to whom this revelation has been made, and rendered possible for us by its contradicting no principles of reason. It is a great comfort to believe it; because "as it is only the very small minority who can pursue a virtuous life by the sole guidance of reason, we should, unless we had this testimony of Scripture, be in doubt respecting the salvation of nearly the whole human race."

It follows from this that philosophy has her own independent sphere, and theology hers, and that neither has the right to invade and try to subdue the other. Theology demands perfect obedience, philosophy perfect knowledge: the obedience demanded by theology and the knowledge demanded by philosophy are alike saving. As speculative opinions about God, theology requires only such as are indispensable to the reality of this obedience; the belief that God is, that he is a rewarder of them that seek him, and that the proof of seeking him is a good life. These are the fundamentals of faith, and they are so clear and simple that none of the inaccuracies provable in the Bible narrative the least affect them, and they have indubitably come to us uncorrupted. He who holds them may make, as the patriarchs and prophets did, other speculations about God most erroneous, and yet their faith is complete and saving. Nay, beyond these fundamentals, speculative opinions are pious or impious, not as they are true or false, but as they confirm or shake the believer in the practice of obedience. The truest speculative opinion about the nature of God is impious if it makes its holder rebellious; the falsest speculative opinion is pious if it makes him obedient. Governments should never render themselves the tools of ecclesiastical ambition by pro-

mulgating as fundamentals of the national Church's faith more
than these, and should concede the fullest liberty of speculation.

But the multitude, which respects only what astonishes,
terrifies, and overwhelms it, by no means takes this simple view
5   of its own religion. To the multitude, religion seems imposing
only when it is subversive of reason, confirmed by miracles,
conveyed in documents materially sacred and infallible, and
dooming to damnation all without its pale. But this religion of
the multitude is not the religion which a true interpretation of
10 Scripture finds in Scripture. Reason tells us that a miracle,—
understanding by a miracle a breach of the laws of nature,—is
impossible, and that to think it possible is to dishonour God;
for the laws of nature are the laws of God, and to say that
God violates the laws of nature is to say that he violates his
15 own nature. Reason sees, too, that miracles can never attain
their professed object,—that of bringing us to a higher knowledge of God; since our knowledge of God is raised only by
perfecting and clearing our conceptions, and the alleged design
of miracles is to baffle them. But neither does Scripture any-
20 where assert, as a general truth, that miracles are possible.
Indeed, it asserts the contrary; for Jeremiah declares that Nature follows an invariable order. Scripture, however, like
Nature herself, does not lay down speculative propositions
(*Scriptura definitiones non tradit, ut nec etiam natura*). It
25 relates matters in such an order and with such phraseology as
a speaker (often not perfectly instructed himself) who wanted
to impress his hearers with a lively sense of God's greatness
and goodness would naturally employ; as Moses, for instance,
relates to the Israelites the passage of the Red Sea without any
30 mention of the east wind which attended it, and which is
brought accidentally to our knowledge in another place. So
that to know exactly what Scripture means in the relation of
each seeming miracle, we ought to know (besides the tropes
and phrases of the Hebrew language) the circumstances, and
35 also,—since every one is swayed in his manner of presenting
facts by his own preconceived opinions, and we have seen what
those of the prophets were,—the preconceived opinions of each
speaker. But this mode of interpreting Scripture is fatal to the

vulgar notion of its verbal inspiration, of a sanctity and absolute truth in all the words and sentences of which it is composed. This vulgar notion is, indeed, a palpable error. It is
demonstrable from the internal testimony of the Scriptures
themselves, that the books from the first of the Pentateuch to   5
the last of Kings were put together, after the first destruction
of Jerusalem, by a compiler (probably Ezra) who designed to
relate the history of the Jewish people from its origin to that
destruction; it is demonstrable, moreover, that the compiler
did not put his last hand to the work, but left it with its ex-   10
tracts from various and conflicting sources sometimes un-
reconciled, left it with errors of text and unsettled readings.
The prophetic books are mere fragments of the prophets, collected by the Rabbins where they could find them, and inserted
in the Canon according to their discretion. They, at first,   15
proposed to admit neither the Book of Proverbs nor the Book
of Ecclesiastes into the Canon, and only admitted them because
there were found in them passages which commended the law
of Moses. Ezekiel also they had determined to exclude; but one
of their number remodelled him, so as to procure his admission.   20
The Books of Ezra, Nehemiah, Esther, and Daniel are the work
of a single author, and were not written till after Judas Mac-
cabeus had restored the worship of the Temple. The Book of
Psalms was collected and arranged at the same time. Before
this time, there was no Canon of the sacred writings, and the   25
great synagogue, by which the Canon was fixed, was first
convened after the Macedonian conquest of Asia. Of that synagogue none of the prophets were members; the learned men
who composed it were guided by their own fallible judgment.
In like manner the uninspired judgment of human councils   30
determined the Canon of the New Testament.

Such, reduced to the briefest and plainest terms possible,
stripped of the developments and proofs with which he delivers
it, and divested of the metaphysical language in which much
of it is clothed by him, is the doctrine of Spinoza's treatise on   35
the interpretation of Scripture. By the whole scope and drift of
its argument, by the spirit in which the subject is throughout

treated, his work undeniably is most interesting and stimulating to the general culture of Europe. There are errors and contradictions in Scripture; and the question which the general culture of Europe, well aware of this, asks with real interest is: What then? What follows from all this? What change is it, if true, to produce in the relations of mankind to the Christian religion? If the old theory of Scripture inspiration is to be abandoned, what place is the Bible henceforth to hold among books? What is the new Christianity to be like? How are governments to deal with National Churches founded to maintain a very different conception of Christianity? Spinoza addresses himself to these questions. All secondary points of criticism he touches with the utmost possible brevity. He points out that Moses could never have written: "And the Canaanite was then in the land," because the Canaanite was in the land still at the death of Moses. He points out that Moses could never have written: "There arose not a prophet since in Israel like unto Moses." He points out how such a passage as, "These are the kings that reigned in Edom *before there reigned any king over the children of Israel*," clearly indicates an author writing not before the times of the Kings. He points out how the account of Og's iron bedstead: "Only Og the king of Bashan remained of the remnant of giants; behold, his bedstead was a bedstead of iron; is it not in Rabbath of the children of Ammon?"—probably indicates an author writing after David had taken Rabbath, and found there "abundance of spoil," amongst it this iron bedstead, the gigantic relic of another age. He points out how the language of this passage, and of such a passage as that in the Book of Samuel: "Beforetime in Israel, when a man went to inquire of God, thus he spake: Come and let us go to the seer; for he that is now called prophet was aforetime called seer"—is certainly the language of a writer describing the events of a long-past age, and not the language of a contemporary. But he devotes to all this no more space than is absolutely necessary. He apologises for delaying over such matters so long: *non est cur circa hæc diu detinear—nolo tædiosâ lectione lectorem detinere.* For him the interesting question is, not whether the fanatical devotee of the letter is to continue, for a longer or for a shorter time, to believe that Moses sate in the land of Moab writing the description of his own death, but what he is to believe when he does not believe this. Is he to take for the guidance of his life a great gloss put upon the Bible by theologians, who, "not content with going mad themselves with Plato and Aristotle, want to make Christ and the prophets go mad with them too,"—or the Bible itself? Is he to be presented by his national church with metaphysical formularies for his creed, or with the real fundamentals of Christianity? If with the former, religion will never produce its due fruits. A few elect will still be saved; but the vast majority of mankind will remain without grace and without good works, hateful and hating one another. Therefore he calls urgently upon governments to make the national church what it should be. This is the conclusion of the whole matter for him; a fervent appeal to the State, to save us from the untoward generation of metaphysical Article-makers. And therefore, anticipating Mr. Gladstone, he called his book *The Church in its Relations with the State*.

Such is really the scope of Spinoza's work. He pursues a great object, and pursues it with signal ability. But it is important to observe that he nowhere distinctly gives his own opinion about the Bible's fundamental character. He takes the Bible as it stands, as he might take the phenomena of nature, and he discusses it as he finds it. Revelation differs from natural knowledge, he says, not by being more divine or more certain than natural knowledge, but by being conveyed in a different way; it differs from it because it is a knowledge "of which the laws of human nature considered in themselves alone cannot be the cause." What is really its cause, he says, we need not here inquire (*verum nec nobis jam opus est propheticæ cognitionis causam scire*), for we take Scripture, which contains this revelation, as it stands, and do not ask how it arose (*documentorum causas nihil curamus*).

Proceeding on this principle, Spinoza leaves the attentive reader somewhat baffled and disappointed, clear as is his way of treating his subject, and remarkable as are the conclusions with which he presents us. He starts, we feel, from what is to him a hypothesis, and we want to know what he really thinks

about this hypothesis. His greatest novelties are all within limits
fixed for him by this hypothesis. He says that the voice which
called Samuel was an imaginary voice; he says that the waters
of the Red Sea retreated before a strong wind; he says that the
5 Shunammite's son was revived by the natural heat of Elisha's
body; he says that the rainbow which was made a sign to Noah
appeared in the ordinary course of nature. Scripture itself,
rightly interpreted, says, he affirms, all this. But he asserts that
the divine voice which uttered the commandments on Mount
10 Sinai was a real voice, *vera vox.* He says, indeed, that this voice
could not really give to the Israelites that proof which they
imagined it gave to them of the existence of God, and that God
on Sinai was dealing with the Israelites only according to their
imperfect knowledge. Still he asserts the divine voice to have
15 been a real one; and for this reason, that we do violence to
Scripture if we do not admit it to have been a real one (*nisi
Scripturæ vim inferre velimus, omnino concedendum est,
Israëlitas veram vocem audivisse*). The attentive reader wants
to know what Spinoza himself thought about this *vera vox* and
20 its possibility; he is much more interested in knowing this than
in knowing what Spinoza considered Scripture to affirm about
the matter.

The feeling of perplexity thus caused is not diminished by the
language of the chapter on miracles. In this chapter Spinoza
25 broadly affirms a miracle to be an impossibility. But he himself
contrasts the method of demonstration *à priori,* by which he
claims to have established this proposition, with the method
which he has pursued in treating of prophetic revelation. "This
revelation," he says, "is a matter out of human reach, and there-
30 fore I was bound to take it as I found it." *Monere volo, me aliâ
prorsus methodo circa miracula processisse, quam circa pro-
phetiam . . . quod etiam consulto feci, quia de prophetiâ,
quandoquidem ipsa captum humanum superat et quæstio mere
theologica est, nihil affirmare, neque etiam scire poteram in quo
35 ipsa potissimum constiterit, nisi ex fundamentis revelatis.* The
reader feels that Spinoza, proceeding on a hypothesis, has presented him with the assertion of a miracle, and afterwards, proceeding *à priori,* has presented him with the assertion that a

miracle is impossible. He feels that Spinoza does not adequately
reconcile these two assertions by declaring that any event really
miraculous, if found recorded in Scripture, must be "a spurious
addition made to Scripture by sacrilegious men." Is, then, he
asks, the *vera vox* of Mount Sinai in Spinoza's opinion a spurious 5
addition made to Scripture by sacrilegious men; or, if not, how
is it not miraculous?

Spinoza, in his own mind, regarded the Bible as a vast collection of miscellaneous documents, many of them quite dis-
parate and not at all to be harmonised with others; documents 10
of unequal value and of varying applicability, some of them
conveying ideas salutary for one time, others for another. But
in the *Tractatus Theologico-Politicus* he by no means always
deals in this free spirit with the Bible. Sometimes he chooses to
deal with it in the spirit of the veriest worshipper of the 15
letter; sometimes he chooses to treat the Bible as if all its parts
were (so to speak) equipollent; to snatch an isolated text which
suits his purpose, without caring whether it is annulled by the
context, by the general drift of Scripture, or by other passages
of more weight and authority. The great critic thus becomes 20
voluntarily as uncritical as Exeter Hall. The epicurean
Solomon, whose *Ecclesiastes* the Hebrew doctors, even after
they had received it into the canon, forbade the young and
weak-minded among their community to read, Spinoza quotes
as of the same authority with the severe Moses; he uses 25
promiscuously, as documents of identical force, without dis-
criminating between their essentially different character, the
softened cosmopolitan teaching of the prophets of the captivity
and the rigid national teaching of the instructors of Israel's
youth. He is capable of extracting, from a chance expression of 30
Jeremiah, the assertion of a speculative idea which Jeremiah
certainly never entertained, and from which he would have
recoiled in dismay,—the idea, namely, that miracles are impossible; just as the ordinary Englishman can extract from
God's words to Noah, *Be fruitful and multiply*, an exhortation 35
to himself to have a large family. Spinoza, I repeat, knew
perfectly well what this verbal mode of dealing with the Bible
was worth: but he sometimes uses it because of the hypothesis

from which he set out; because of his having agreed "to take Scripture as it stands, and not to ask how it arose."

No doubt the sagacity of Spinoza's rules for Biblical interpretation, the power of his analysis of the contents of the Bible, the interest of his reflections on Jewish history, are, in spite of this, very great, and have an absolute worth of their own, independent of the silence or ambiguity of their author upon a point of cardinal importance. Few candid people will read his rules of interpretation without exclaiming that they are the very dictates of good sense, that they have always believed in them; and without adding, after a moment's reflection, that they have passed their lives in violating them. And what can be more interesting, than to find that perhaps the main cause of the decay of the Jewish polity was one of which from our English Bible, which entirely mistranslates the 26th verse of the 20th chapter of Ezekiel, we hear nothing,—the perpetual reproach of impurity and rejection cast upon the mass of the Hebrew nation by the exclusive priesthood of the tribe of Levi? What can be more suggestive, after Mr. Mill and Dr. Stanley have been telling us how great an element of strength to the Hebrew nation was the institution of prophets, than to hear from the ablest of Hebrews how this institution seems to him to have been to his nation one of her main elements of weakness? No intelligent man can read the *Tractatus Theologico-Politicus* without being profoundly instructed by it: but neither can he read it without feeling that, as a speculative work, it is, to use a French military expression, *in the air;* that, in a certain sense, it is in want of a base and in want of supports; that this base and these supports are, at any rate, not to be found in the work itself, and, if they exist, must be sought for in other works of the author.

The genuine speculative opinions of Spinoza, which the *Tractatus Theologico-Politicus* but imperfectly reveals, may in his Ethics and in his Letters be found set forth clearly. It is, however, the business of criticism to deal with every independent work as with an independent whole, and, instead of establishing between the *Tractatus Theologico-Politicus* and the Ethics of Spinoza a relation which Spinoza himself has not established, to seize, in dealing with the *Tractatus Theologico-Politicus,* the important fact that this work has its source, not in the axioms and definitions of the Ethics, but in a hypothesis. The Ethics are not yet translated into English, and I have not here to speak of them. Then will be the right time for criticism to try and seize the special character and tendencies of that remarkable work, when it is dealing with it directly. The criticism of the Ethics is far too serious a task to be undertaken incidentally, and merely as a supplement to the criticism of the *Tractatus Theologico-Politicus.* Nevertheless, on certain governing ideas of Spinoza, which receive their systematic expression, indeed, in the Ethics, and on which the *Tractatus Theologico-Politicus* is not formally based, but which are yet never absent from Spinoza's mind in the composition of any work, which breathe through all his works, and fill them with a peculiar effect and power, I have a word or two to say.

A philosopher's real power over mankind resides not in his metaphysical formulas, but in the spirit and tendencies which have led him to adopt those formulas. Spinoza's critic, therefore, has rather to bring to light that spirit and those tendencies of his author, than to exhibit his metaphysical formulas. Propositions about substance pass by mankind at large like the idle wind, which mankind at large regards not; it will not even listen to a word about these propositions, unless it first learns what their author was driving at with them, and finds that this object of his is one with which it sympathises, one, at any rate, which commands its attention. And mankind is so far right that this object of the author is really, as has been said, that which is most important, that which sets all his work in motion, that which is the secret of his attraction for other minds, which, by different ways, pursue the same object.

Mr. Maurice, seeking for the cause of Goethe's great admiration for Spinoza, thinks that he finds it in Spinoza's Hebrew genius. "He spoke of God," says Mr. Maurice, "as an actual being, to those who had fancied him a name in a book. The child of the circumcision had a message for Lessing and Goethe which the pagan schools of philosophy could not bring." This seems to me, I confess, fanciful. An intensity and impressiveness,

which came to him from his Hebrew nature, Spinoza no doubt
has; but the two things which are most remarkable about him,
and by which, as I think, he chiefly impressed Goethe, seem to
me not to come to him from his Hebrew nature at all,—I mean
his denial of final causes, and his stoicism, a stoicism not passive,
but active. For a mind like Goethe's,—a mind profoundly impartial and passionately aspiring after the science, not of men
only, but of universal nature,—the popular philosophy which
explains all things by reference to man, and regards universal
nature as existing for the sake of man, and even of certain classes
of men, was utterly repulsive. Unchecked, this philosophy
would gladly maintain that the donkey exists in order that
the invalid Christian may have donkey's milk before breakfast;
and such views of nature as this were exactly what Goethe's
whole soul abhorred. Creation, he thought, should be made of
sterner stuff; he desired to rest the donkey's existence on larger
grounds. More than any philosopher who has ever lived,
Spinoza satisfied him here. The full exposition of the counter-
doctrine to the popular doctrine of final causes is to be found
in the Ethics; but this denial of final causes was so essential an
element of all Spinoza's thinking that we shall, as has been said
already, find it in the work with which we are here concerned,
the *Tractatus Theologico-Politicus*, and, indeed, permeating
that work and all his works. From the *Tractatus Theologico-
Politicus* one may take as good a general statement of this
denial as any which is to be found in the Ethics:—

"Deus naturam dirigit, prout ejus leges universales, non autem
prout humanæ naturæ particulares leges exigunt, adeoque Deus
non solius humani generis, sed totius naturæ rationem habet.
(*God directs nature, according as the universal laws of nature,
but not according as the particular laws of human nature require; and so God has regard, not of the human race only, but
of entire nature.*)"

And, as a pendant to this denial by Spinoza of final causes,
comes his stoicism:—

"Non studemus, ut natura nobis, sed contra ut nos naturæ
pareamus. (*Our desire is not that nature may obey us, but,
on the contrary, that we may obey nature.*)"

Here is the second source of his attractiveness for Goethe;
and Goethe is but the eminent representative of a whole order
of minds whose admiration has made Spinoza's fame. Spinoza
first impresses Goethe and any man like Goethe, and then he
composes him; first he fills and satisfies his imagination by the   5
width and grandeur of his view of nature, and then he fortifies
and stills his mobile, straining, passionate, poetic temperament
by the moral lesson he draws from his view of nature. And a
moral lesson not of mere resigned acquiescence, not of melancholy quietism, but of joyful activity within the limits of man's   10
true sphere:—

"Ipsa hominis essentia est conatus quo unusquisque suum
esse conservare conatur.... Virtus hominis est ipsa hominis
essentia, quatenus a solo conatu suum esse conservandi definitur.
... Felicitas in eo consistit quod homo suum esse conservare   15
potest.... Lætitia est hominis transitio ad majorem perfectio-
nem ... Tristitia est hominis transitio ad minorem perfec-
tionem. (*Man's very essence is the effort wherewith each man
strives to maintain his own being.... Man's virtue is this very
essence, so far as it is defined by this single effort to maintain*   20
*his own being.... Happiness consists in a man's being able to
maintain his own being.... Joy is man's passage to a greater
perfection.... Sorrow is man's passage to a lesser perfection.*)"

It seems to me that by neither of these, his grand characteristic doctrines, is Spinoza truly Hebrew or truly Christian.   25
His denial of final causes is essentially alien to the spirit of the
Old Testament, and his cheerful and self-sufficing stoicism is
essentially alien to the spirit of the New. The doctrine that
"God directs nature, not according as the particular laws of
human nature, but according as the universal laws of nature re-   30
quire," is at utter variance with that Hebrew mode of representing God's dealings, which makes the locusts visit Egypt to pun-
ish Pharaoh's hardness of heart, and the falling dew avert itself
from the fleece of Gideon. The doctrine that "all sorrow is a
passage to a lesser perfection" is at utter variance with the Chris- 35
tian recognition of the blessedness of sorrow, working "repentance to salvation not to be repented of;" of sorrow, which, in
Dante's words, "remarries us to God."

Spinoza's repeated and earnest assertions that the love of God is man's *summum bonum* do not remove the fundamental diversity between his doctrine and the Hebrew and Christian doctrines. By the love of God he does not mean the same thing which the Hebrew and Christian religions mean by the love of God. He makes the love of God to consist in the knowledge of God; and, as we know God only through his manifestation of himself in the laws of all nature, it is by knowing these laws that we love God, and the more we know them the more we love him. This may be true, but this is not what the Christian means by the love of God. Spinoza's ideal is the intellectual life; the Christian's ideal is the religious life. Between the two conditions there is all the difference which there is between the being in love, and the following, with delighted comprehension, a reasoning of Plato. For Spinoza, undoubtedly, the crown of the intellectual life is a transport, as for the saint the crown of the religious life is a transport; but the two transports are not the same.

This is true; yet it is true, also, that by thus crowning the intellectual life with a sacred transport, by thus retaining in philosophy, amid the discontented murmurs of all the army of atheism, the name of God, Spinoza maintains a profound affinity with that which is truest in religion, and inspires an indestructible interest. One of his admirers, M. Van Vloten, has recently published at Amsterdam a supplementary volume to Spinoza's works, containing the interesting document of Spinoza's sentence of excommunication, from which I have already quoted, and containing, besides, several lately found works alleged to be Spinoza's, which seem to me to be of doubtful authenticity, and, even if authentic, of no great importance. M. Van Vloten (who, let me be permitted to say in passing, writes a Latin which would make one think that the art of writing Latin must be now a lost art in the country of Lipsius) is very anxious that Spinoza's unscientific retention of the name of God should not afflict his readers with any doubts as to his perfect scientific orthodoxy:—

"It is a great mistake," he cries, "to disparage Spinoza as merely one of the dogmatists before Kant. By keeping the name of God, while he did away with his person and character, he has done himself an injustice. Those who look to the bottom of things will see that, long ago as he lived, he had even then reached the point to which the post-Hegelian philosophy and the study of natural science has only just brought our own 5 times. Leibnitz expressed his apprehension lest those who did away with final causes should do away with God at the same time. But it is in his having done away with final causes, *and with God along with them*, that Spinoza's true merit consists."

Now it must be remarked that to use Spinoza's denial of final 10 causes in order to identify him with the Coryphæi of atheism, is to make a false use of Spinoza's denial of final causes, just as to use his assertion of the all-importance of loving God to identify him with the saints would be to make a false use of his assertion of the all-importance of loving God. He is no 15 more to be identified with the post-Hegelian philosophers than he is to be identified with St. Augustine. Unction, indeed, Spinoza's writings have not; that name does not precisely fit any quality which they exhibit. And yet, so all-important in the sphere of religious thought is the power of edification, that in 20 this sphere a great fame like Spinoza's can never be founded without it. A court of literature can never be very severe to Voltaire: with that inimitable wit and clear sense of his, he cannot write a page in which the fullest head may not find something suggestive: still, because, handling religious ideas, 25 he yet, with all his wit and clear sense, handles them wholly without the power of edification, his fame as a great man is equivocal. Strauss has treated the question of Scripture miracles with an acuteness and fulness which even to the most informed minds is instructive; but because he treats it almost wholly 30 without the power of edification, his fame as a serious thinker is equivocal. But in Spinoza there is not a trace either of Voltaire's passion for mockery or of Strauss's passion for demolition. His whole soul was filled with desire of the love and knowledge of God, and of that only. Philosophy always pro- 35 claims herself on the way to the *summum bonum;* but too often on the road she seems to forget her destination, and suffers her hearers to forget it also. Spinoza never forgets his destination:

"The love of God is man's highest happiness and blessedness, and the final end and aim of all human actions;"—"The supreme reward for keeping God's Word is that Word itself—namely, to know him and with free will and pure and constant heart
5   love him:" these sentences are the keynote to all he produced, and were the inspiration of all his labours. This is why he turns so sternly upon the worshippers of the letter,—the editors of the *Masora*, the editor of the *Record*,—because their doctrine imperils our love and knowledge of God. "What!" he cries,
10 "our knowledge of God to depend upon these perishable things, which Moses can dash to the ground and break to pieces like the first tables of stone, or of which the originals can be lost like the original book of the Covenant, like the original book of the Law of God, like the book of the Wars of God! ...
15 which can come to us confused, imperfect, mis-written by copyists, tampered with by doctors! And you accuse others of impiety! It is you who are impious, to believe that God would commit the treasure of the true record of himself to any substance less enduring than the heart!"
20   And Spinoza's life was not unworthy of this elevated strain. A philosopher who professed that knowledge was its own reward, a devotee who professed that the love of God was its own reward, this philosopher and this devotee believed in what he said. Spinoza led a life the most spotless, perhaps, to be found
25 among the lives of philosophers; he lived simple, studious, even-tempered, kind; declining honours, declining riches, declining notoriety. He was poor, and his admirer Simon de Vries sent him two thousand florins;—he refused them. The same friend left him his fortune;—he returned it to the heir. He was asked
30 to dedicate one of his works to the magnificent patron of letters in his century, Louis the Fourteenth;—he declined. His great work, his Ethics, published after his death, he gave injunctions to his friends to publish anonymously, for fear he should give his name to a school. Truth, he thought, should
35 bear no man's name. And finally,—"Unless," he said, "I had known that my writings would in the end advance the cause of true religion, I would have suppressed them,—*tacuissem*." It was in this spirit that he lived; and this spirit gives to all he

writes not exactly unction,—I have already said so,—but a kind of sacred solemnity. Not of the same order as the saints, he yet follows the same service: *Doubtless thou art our Father, though Abraham be ignorant of us, and Israel acknowledge us not.*   5

Therefore he has been, in a certain sphere, edifying, and has inspired in many powerful minds an interest and an admiration such as no other philosopher has inspired since Plato. The lonely precursor of German philosophy, he still shines when the light of his successors is fading away; they had celebrity, Spinoza   10
has fame. Not because his peculiar system of philosophy has had more adherents than theirs; on the contrary, it has had fewer. But schools of philosophy arise and fall; their bands of adherents inevitably dwindle; no master can long persuade a large body of disciples that they give to themselves just the same ac-   15
count of the world as he does; it is only the very young and the very enthusiastic who can think themselves sure that they possess the whole mind of Plato, or Spinoza, or Hegel, at all. The very mature and the very sober can even hardly believe that these philosophers possessed it themselves enough to put   20
it all into their works, and to let us know entirely how the world seemed to them. What a remarkable philosopher really does for human thought, is to throw into circulation a certain number of new and striking ideas and expressions, and to stimulate with them the thought and imagination of his century or   25
of after-times. So Spinoza has made his distinction between adequate and inadequate ideas a current notion for educated Europe. So Hegel seized a single pregnant sentence of Heracleitus, and cast it, with a thousand striking applications, into the world of modern thought. But to do this is only enough   30
to make a philosopher noteworthy; it is not enough to make him great. To be great, he must have something in him which can influence character, which is edifying; he must, in short, have a noble and lofty character himself, a character,—to recur to that much-criticised expression of mine,—*in the grand*   35
style. This is what Spinoza had; and because he had it, he stands out from the multitude of philosophers, and has been able to inspire in powerful minds a feeling which the most remarkable

philosophers, without this grandiose character, could not inspire. "There is no possible view of life but Spinoza's," said
Lessing. Goethe has told us how he was calmed and edified by
him in his youth, and how he again went to him for support in
5   his maturity. Heine, the man (in spite of his faults) of truest
genius that Germany has produced since Goethe,—a man with
faults, as I have said, immense faults, the greatest of them being
that he could reverence so little,—reverenced Spinoza. Hegel's
influence ran off him like water: "I have seen Hegel," he cries,
10 "seated with his doleful air of a hatching hen upon his unhappy
eggs, and I have heard his dismal clucking.—How easily one
can cheat oneself into thinking that one understands everything, when one has learnt only how to construct dialectical
formulas!" But of Spinoza, Heine said: "His life was a copy of
15 the life of his divine kinsman, Jesus Christ."

And therefore, when M. Van Vloten violently presses the
parallel with the post-Hegelians, one feels that the parallel with
St. Augustine is the far truer one. Compared with the soldier
of irreligion M. Van Vloten would have him to be, Spinoza is
20 religious. "It is true," one may say to the wise and devout Christian, "Spinoza's conception of beatitude is not yours, and cannot satisfy you, but whose conception of beatitude would you
accept as satisfying? Not even that of the devoutest of your
fellow-Christians. Fra Angelico, the sweetest and most inspired
25 of devout souls, has given us, in his great picture of the Last
Judgment, his conception of beatitude. The elect are going
round in a ring on long grass under laden fruit-trees; two of
them, more restless than the others, are flying up a battle-
mented street,—a street blank with all the ennui of the Middle
30 Ages. Across a gulf is visible, for the delectation of the saints,
a blazing caldron in which Beelzebub is sousing the damned.
This is hardly more your conception of beatitude than Spinoza's is. But 'in my Father's house are many mansions;' only,
to reach any one of these mansions, there are needed the wings
35 of a genuine sacred transport, of an 'immortal longing.' " These
wings Spinoza had; and, because he had them, his own language
about himself, about his aspirations and his course, are true:
his foot is in the *vera vita*, his eye on the beatific vision.

Joubert

Why should we ever treat of any dead authors but the famous ones? Mainly for this reason: because, from these famous personages, home or foreign, whom we all know so well, and of whom so much has been said, the amount of stimulus which they contain for us has been in a great measure disengaged; people have formed their opinion about them, and do not readily change it. One may write of them afresh, combat received opinions about them, even interest one's readers in so doing; but the interest one's readers receive has to do, in general, rather with the treatment than with the subject; they are susceptible of a lively impression rather of the course of the discussion itself,—its turns, vivacity, and novelty,—than of the genius of the author who is the occasion of it. And yet what is really precious and inspiring, in all that we get from literature, except this sense of an immediate contact with genius itself, and the stimulus towards what is true and excellent which we derive from it? Now in literature, besides the eminent men of genius who have had their deserts in the way of fame, besides the eminent men of ability who have often had far more than their deserts in the way of fame, there are a certain number of personages who have been real men of genius,—by which I mean, that they have had a genuine gift for what is true and excellent, and are therefore capable of emitting a life-giving stimulus,—but who, for some reason or other, in most cases for very valid reasons, have remained obscure, nay, beyond a narrow circle in their own country, unknown. It is salutary from time to time to come across a genius of this kind, and to extract his honey. Often he has more of it for us, as I have already said, than greater men; for, though it is by no

means true that from what is new to us there is most to be
learnt, it is yet indisputably true that from what is new to us
we in general learn most.

Of a genius of this kind, Joseph Joubert, I am now going to
speak. His name is, I believe, almost unknown in England; and
even in France, his native country, it is not famous. M. Sainte-
Beuve has given of him one of his incomparable portraits; but,
—besides that even M. Sainte-Beuve's writings are far less
known amongst us than they deserve to be,—every country has
its own point of view from which a remarkable author may
most profitably be seen and studied.

Joseph Joubert was born (and his date should be remarked)
in 1754, at Montignac, a little town in Périgord. His father was
a doctor with small means and a large family; and Joseph, the
eldest, had his own way to make in the world. He was for
eight years, as pupil first, and afterwards as an assistant-master,
in the public school of Toulouse, then managed by the Jesuits,
who seem to have left in him a most favourable opinion, not
only of their tact and address, but of their really good qualities
as teachers and directors. Compelled by the weakness of his
health to give up, at twenty-two, the profession of teaching,
he passed two important years of his life in hard study, at home
at Montignac; and came in 1778 to try his fortune in the literary
world of Paris, then perhaps the most tempting field which has
ever yet presented itself to a young man of letters. He knew
Diderot, D'Alembert, Marmontel, Laharpe; he became intimate
with one of the celebrities of the next literary generation, then,
like himself, a young man,—Chateaubriand's friend, the future
Grand Master of the University, Fontanes. But, even then, it
began to be remarked of him, that M. Joubert "*s'inquiétait de
perfection bien plus que de gloire*—cared far more about perfecting himself than about making himself a reputation." His
severity of morals may perhaps have been rendered easier to
him by the delicacy of his health; but the delicacy of his health
will not by itself account for his changeless preference of being
to seeming, knowing to showing, studying to publishing; for
what terrible public performers have some invalids been! This
preference he retained all through his life, and it is by this that

he is characterised. "He has chosen," Chateaubriand (adopting Epicurus's famous words) said of him, "*to hide his life.*" Of a life which its owner was bent on hiding there can be but little to tell. Yet the only two public incidents of Joubert's life, slight as they are, do all concerned in them so much credit that they deserve mention. In 1790 the Constituent Assembly made the office of justice of the peace elective throughout France. The people of Montignac retained such an impression of the character of their young townsman,—one of Plutarch's men of virtue, as he had lived amongst them, simple, studious, severe, —that, though he had left them for years, they elected him in his absence without his knowing anything about it. The appointment little suited Joubert's wishes or tastes; but at such a moment he thought it wrong to decline it. He held it for two years, the legal term, discharging its duties with a firmness and integrity which were long remembered; and then, when he went out of office, his fellow-townsmen re-elected him. But Joubert thought that he had now accomplished his duty towards them, and he went back to the retirement which he loved. That seems to me a little episode of the great French Revolution worth remembering. The sage who was asked by the king, why sages were seen at the doors of kings, but not kings at the doors of sages, replied, that it was because sages knew what was good for them, and kings did not. But at Montignac the king—for in 1790 the people in France was king with a vengeance—knew what was good for him, and came to the door of the sage.

The other incident was this. When Napoleon, in 1809, reorganised the public instruction of France, founded the University, and made M. de Fontanes its Grand Master, Fontanes had to submit to the Emperor a list of persons to form the council or governing body of the new University. Third on his list, after two distinguished names, Fontanes placed the unknown name of Joubert. "This name," he said in his accompanying memorandum to the Emperor, "is not known as the two first are; and yet this is the nomination to which I attach most importance. I have known M. Joubert all my life. His character and intelligence are of the very highest order. I shall

rejoice if your Majesty will accept my guarantee for him."
Napoleon trusted his Grand Master, and Joubert became a
councillor of the University. It is something that a man, elevated to the highest posts of State, should not forget his obscure friends; or that, if he remembers and places them, he
should regard in placing them their merit rather than their obscurity. It is more, in the eyes of those whom the necessities,
real or supposed, of a political system have long familiarised
with such cynical disregard of fitness in the distribution of
office, to see a minister and his master alike zealous, in giving
away places, to give them to the best men to be found.

Between 1792 and 1809 Joubert had married. His life was
passed between Villeneuve-sur-Yonne, where his wife's family
lived,—a pretty little Burgundian town, by which the Lyons
railroad now passes,—and Paris. Here, in a house in the Rue
St.-Honoré, in a room very high up, and admitting plenty of
the light which he so loved,—a room from which he saw, in
his own words, "a great deal of sky and very little earth,"—
among the treasures of a library collected with infinite pains,
taste, and skill, from which every book he thought ill of was
rigidly excluded,—he never would possess either a complete
Voltaire or a complete Rousseau,—the happiest hours of his
life were passed. In the circle of one of those women who leave
a sort of perfume in literary history, and who have the gift of
inspiring successive generations of readers with an indescribable
regret not to have known them,—Pauline de Montmorin, Madame de Beaumont,—he had become intimate with nearly all
which at that time, in the Paris world of letters or of society,
was most attractive and promising. Amongst his acquaintances
one only misses the names of Madame de Staël and Benjamin
Constant. Neither of them was to his taste, and with Madame
de Staël he always refused to become acquainted; he thought
she had more vehemence than truth, and more heat than light.

Years went on, and his friends became conspicuous authors
or statesmen; but Joubert remained in the shade. His constitution was of such fragility that how he lived so long, or accomplished so much as he did, is a wonder: his soul had, for its basis
of operations, hardly any body at all: both from his stomach

and from his chest he seems to have had constant suffering, though he lived by rule, and was as abstemious as a Hindoo. Often, after overwork in thinking, reading, or talking, he remained for days together in a state of utter prostration,—condemned to absolute silence and inaction; too happy if the agitation of his mind would become quiet also, and let him have the repose of which he stood in so much need. With this weakness of health, these repeated suspensions of energy, he was incapable of the prolonged contention of spirit necessary for the creation of great works. But he read and thought immensely; he was an unwearied note-taker, a charming letter-writer; above all, an excellent and delightful talker. The gaiety and amenity of his natural disposition were inexhaustible; and his spirit, too, was of astonishing elasticity; he seemed to hold on to life by a single thread only, but that single thread was very tenacious. More and more, as his soul and knowledge ripened more and more, his friends pressed to his room in the Rue St.-Honoré; often he received them in bed, for he seldom rose before three o'clock in the afternoon; and at his bedroom-door, on his bad days, Madame Joubert stood sentry, trying, not always with success, to keep back the thirsty comers from the fountain which was forbidden to flow. Fontanes did nothing in the University without consulting him, and Joubert's ideas and pen were always at his friend's service.

When he was in the country, at Villeneuve, the young priests of his neighbourhood used to resort to him, in order to profit by his library and by his conversation. He, like our Coleridge, was particularly qualified to attract men of this kind and to benefit them: retaining perfect independence of mind, he was religious; he was a religious philosopher. As age came on, his infirmities became more and more overwhelming; some of his friends, too, died; others became so immersed in politics, that Joubert, who hated politics, saw them seldomer than of old; but the moroseness of age and infirmity never touched him, and he never quarrelled with a friend or lost one. From these miseries he was preserved by that quality in him of which I have already spoken; a quality which is best expressed by a word, not of common use in English,—alas, we have too little in our national character of the quality which this word expresses,—his inborn, his constant amenity. He lived till the year 1824. On the 4th of May in that year he died, at the age of seventy. A day or two after his death M. de Chateaubriand inserted in the *Journal des Débats* a short notice of him, perfect for its feeling, grace, and propriety. *On ne vit dans la mémoire du monde*, he says and says truly, *que par des travaux pour le monde*,—"a man can live in the world's memory only by what he has done for the world." But Chateaubriand used the privilege which his great name gave him to assert, delicately but firmly, Joubert's real and rare merits, and to tell the world what manner of man had just left it.

Joubert's papers were accumulated in boxes and drawers. He had not meant them for publication; it was very difficult to sort them and to prepare them for it. Madame Joubert, his widow, had a scruple about giving them a publicity which her husband, she felt, would never have permitted. But, as her own end approached, the natural desire to leave of so remarkable a spirit some enduring memorial, some memorial to outlast the admiring recollection of the living who were so fast passing away, made her yield to the entreaties of his friends, and allow the printing, but for private circulation only, of a volume of his fragments. Chateaubriand edited it; it appeared in 1838, fourteen years after Joubert's death. The volume attracted the attention of those who were best fitted to appreciate it, and profoundly impressed them. M. Sainte-Beuve gave of it, in the *Revue des Deux Mondes*, the admirable notice of which I have already spoken; and so much curiosity was excited about Joubert, that the collection of his fragments, enlarged by many additions, was at last published for the benefit of the world in general. It has since been twice reprinted. The first or preliminary chapter has some fancifulness and affectation in it; the reader should begin with the second.

I have likened Joubert to Coleridge; and indeed the points of resemblance between the two men are numerous. Both of them great and celebrated talkers, Joubert attracting pilgrims to his upper chamber in the Rue St.-Honoré, as Coleridge attracted pilgrims to Mr. Gillman's at Highgate; both of them

desultory and incomplete writers,—here they had an outward
likeness with one another. Both of them passionately devoted
to reading in a class of books, and to thinking on a class of subjects, out of the beaten line of the reading and thought of their
day; both of them ardent students and critics of old literature, 5
poetry, and the metaphysics of religion; both of them curious
explorers of words, and of the latent significance hidden under
the popular use of them; both of them, in a certain sense, conservative in religion and politics, by antipathy to the narrow
and shallow foolishness of vulgar modern liberalism;—here 10
they had their inward and real likeness. But that in which the
essence of their likeness consisted is this,—that they both had
from nature an ardent impulse for seeking the genuine truth
on all matters they thought about, and a gift for finding it and
recognising it when it was found. To have the impulse for seek- 15
ing this truth is much rarer than most people think; to have
the gift for finding it is, I need not say, very rare indeed. By
this they have a spiritual relationship of the closest kind with
one another, and they become, each of them, a source of stimulus and progress for all of us. 20

Coleridge had less delicacy and penetration than Joubert, but
more richness and power; his production, though far inferior
to what his nature at first seemed to promise, was abundant
and varied. Yet in all his production how much is there to dissatisfy us! How many reserves must be made in praising either 25
his poetry, or his criticism, or his philosophy! How little either
of his poetry, or of his criticism, or of his philosophy, can we
expect permanently to stand! But that which will stand of
Coleridge is this: the stimulus of his continual effort,—not a
moral effort, for he had no morals,—but of his continual in- 30
stinctive effort, crowned often with rich success, to get at and
to lay bare the real truth of his matter in hand, whether that
matter were literary, or philosophical, or political, or religious;
and this in a country where at that moment such an effort was
almost unknown; where the most powerful minds threw them- 35
selves upon poetry, which conveys truth, indeed, but conveys
it indirectly; and where ordinary minds were so habituated
to do without thinking altogether, to regard considerations of

established routine and practical convenience as paramount, that any attempt to introduce within the domain of these the disturbing element of thought, they were prompt to resent as an outrage. Coleridge's great usefulness lay in his supplying in
5 England, for many years and under critical circumstances, by the spectacle of this effort of his, a stimulus to all minds capable of profiting by it, in the generation which grew up around him. His action will still be felt as long as the need for it continues. When, with the cessation of the need, the action too
10 has ceased, Coleridge's memory, in spite of the disesteem—nay, repugnance—which his character may and must inspire, will yet for ever remain invested with that interest and gratitude which invests the memory of founders.

M. de Rémusat, indeed, reproaches Coleridge with his *juge-*
15 *ments saugrenus;* the criticism of a gifted truth-finder ought not to be *saugrenu,* so on this reproach we must pause for a moment. *Saugrenu* is a rather vulgar French word, but, like many other vulgar words, very expressive; used as an epithet for a judgment, it means something like *impudently absurd.*
20 The literary judgments of one nation about another are very apt to be *saugrenus.* It is certainly true, as M. Sainte-Beuve remarks in answer to Goethe's complaint against the French that they have undervalued Du Bartas, that as to the estimate of its own authors every nation is the best judge; the *positive*
25 estimate of them, be it understood, not, of course, the estimate of them in comparison with the authors of other nations. Therefore a foreigner's judgments about the intrinsic merit of a nation's authors will generally, when at complete variance with that nation's own, be wrong; but there is a permissible
30 wrongness in these matters, and to that permissible wrongness there is a limit. When that limit is exceeded, the wrong judgment becomes more than wrong, it becomes *saugrenu,* or impudently absurd. For instance, the high estimate which the French have of Racine is probably in great measure deserved;
35 or, to take a yet stronger case, even the high estimate which Joubert had of the Abbé Delille is probably in great measure deserved; but the common disparaging judgment passed on Racine by English readers is not *saugrenu,* still less is that passed

by them on the Abbé Delille *saugrenu*, because the beauty of
Racine, and of Delille too, so far as Delille's beauty goes, is
eminently in their language, and this is a beauty which a foreigner cannot perfectly seize;—this beauty of diction, *apicibus
verborum ligata*, as M. Sainte-Beuve, quoting Quintilian, says
of Chateaubriand's. As to Chateaubriand himself, again, the
common English judgment, which stamps him as a mere shallow rhetorician, all froth and vanity, is certainly wrong; one
may even wonder that we English should judge Chateaubriand
so wrongly, for his power goes far beyond beauty of diction;
it is a power, as well, of passion and sentiment, and this sort of
power the English can perfectly well appreciate. One production of Chateaubriand's, *René*, is akin to the most popular productions of Byron,—to the *Childe Harold* or *Manfred*,—in
spirit, equal to them in power, superior to them in form. But
this work, I hardly know why, is almost unread in England.
And only consider this criticism of Chateaubriand's on the true
pathetic: "It is a dangerous mistake, sanctioned, like so many
other dangerous mistakes, by Voltaire, to suppose that the
best works of imagination are those which draw most tears.
One could name this or that melodrama, which no one would
like to own having written, and which yet harrows the feelings
far more than the *Æneid*. The true tears are those which are
called forth by the *beauty* of poetry; there must be as much
admiration in them as sorrow. They are the tears which come
to our eyes when Priam says to Achilles, ἔτλην δ’, οἷ’ οὔπω . . .—
'And I have endured,—the like whereof no soul upon the
earth hath yet endured,—to carry to my lips the hand of him
who slew my child;' or when Joseph cries out: 'I am Joseph
your brother, whom ye sold into Egypt.' " Who does not feel
that the man who wrote that was no shallow rhetorician, but
a born man of genius, with the true instinct of genius for what
is really admirable? Nay, take these words of Chateaubriand,
an old man of eighty, dying, amidst the noise and bustle of the
ignoble revolution of February 1848: "Mon Dieu, mon Dieu,
quand donc, quand donc serai-je délivré de tout ce monde, ce
bruit; quand donc, quand donc cela finira-t-il?" Who, with any
ear, does not feel that those are not the accents of a trumpery

rhetorician, but of a rich and puissant nature,—the cry of the
dying lion? I repeat it, Chateaubriand is most ignorantly under-
rated in England; and we English are capable of rating him far
more correctly if we knew him better. Still Chateaubriand has
5   such real and great faults, he falls so decidedly beneath the
rank of the truly greatest authors, that the depreciatory judgment passed on him in England, though ignorant and wrong,
can hardly be said to transgress the limits of permissible ignorance; it is not a *jugement saugrenu*. But when a critic denies
10 genius to a literature which has produced Bossuet and Molière,
he passes the bounds; and Coleridge's judgments on French literature and the French genius are undoubtedly, as M. de Rémusat calls them, *saugrenus*.

And yet, such is the impetuosity of our poor human nature,
15 such its proneness to rush to a decision with imperfect knowledge, that his having delivered a *saugrenu* judgment or two in
his life by no means proves a man not to have had, in comparison with his fellow-men in general, a remarkable gift for truth,
or disqualifies him for being, by virtue of that gift, a source of
20 vital stimulus for us. Joubert had far less smoke and turbid
vehemence in him than Coleridge; he had also a far keener sense
of what was absurd. But Joubert can write to M. Molé (the
M. Molé who was afterwards Louis Philippe's well-known
minister): "As to your Milton, whom the merit of the Abbé
25 Delille" (the Abbé Delille translated *Paradise Lost*) "makes me
admire, and with whom I have nevertheless still plenty of fault
to find, why, I should like to know, are you scandalised that
I have not enabled myself to read him? I don't understand the
language in which he writes, and I don't much care to. If he is
30 a poet one cannot put up with, even in the prose of the younger
Racine, am I to blame for that? If by force you mean beauty
manifesting itself with power, I maintain that the Abbé Delille
has more force than Milton." That, to be sure, is a petulant
outburst in a private letter; it is not, like Coleridge's, a delib-
35 erate proposition in a printed philosophical essay. But is it possible to imagine a more perfect specimen of a *saugrenu* judgment? It is even worse than Coleridge's, because it is *saugrenu*
with reasons. That, however, does not prevent Joubert from

having been really a man of extraordinary ardour in the search
for truth, and of extraordinary fineness in the perception of it;
and so was Coleridge.

Joubert had around him in France an atmosphere of literary,
philosophical, and religious opinion as alien to him as that in
England was to Coleridge. This is what makes Joubert, too, so
remarkable, and it is on this account that I begged the reader to
remark his date. He was born in 1754; he died in 1824. He was
thus in the fulness of his powers at the beginning of the present
century, at the epoch of Napoleon's consulate. The French
criticism of that day—the criticism of Laharpe's successors, of
Geoffroy and his colleagues in the *Journal des Débats*—had a
dryness very unlike the telling vivacity of the early Edinburgh
reviewers, their contemporaries, but a fundamental narrowness,
a want of genuine insight, much on a par with theirs. Joubert,
like Coleridge, has no respect for the dominant oracle; he treats
his Geoffroy with about as little deference as Coleridge treats
his Jeffrey. "Geoffroy," he says of an article in the *Journal des
Débats* criticising Chateaubriand's *Génie du Christianisme*—
"Geoffroy in this article begins by holding out his paw prettily
enough; but he ends by a volley of kicks, which lets the whole
world see but too clearly the four iron shoes of the four-footed
animal." There is, however, in France a sympathy with intellectual activity for its own sake, and for the sake of its inherent
pleasurableness and beauty, keener than any which exists in
England; and Joubert had more effect in Paris,—though his
conversation was his only weapon, and Coleridge wielded besides his conversation his pen,—than Coleridge had or could
have in London. I mean, a more immediate, appreciable effect;
an effect not only upon the young and enthusiastic, to whom the
future belongs, but upon formed and important personages to
whom the present belongs, and who are actually moving society. He owed this partly to his real advantages over Coleridge.
If he had, as I have already said, less power and richness than
his English parallel, he had more tact and penetration. He was
more *possible* than Coleridge; his doctrine was more intelligible
than Coleridge's, more receivable. And yet with Joubert, the
striving after a consummate and attractive clearness of expres-

sion came from no mere frivolous dislike of labour and inability
for going deep, but was a part of his native love of truth and perfection. The delight of his life he found in truth, and in the satisfaction which the enjoying of truth gives to the spirit; and he
thought the truth was never really and worthily said, so long as
the least cloud, clumsiness, and repulsiveness hung about the expression of it.

Some of his best passages are those in which he upholds this
doctrine. Even metaphysics he would not allow to remain difficult and abstract: so long as they spoke a professional jargon,
the language of the schools, he maintained,—and who shall gain-
say him?—that metaphysics were imperfect; or, at any rate, had
not yet reached their ideal perfection.

"The true science of metaphysics," he says, "consists not in
rendering abstract that which is sensible, but in rendering sensible that which is abstract; apparent that which is hidden; imaginable, if so it may be, that which is only intelligible; and
intelligible, finally, that which an ordinary attention fails to
seize."

And therefore:—

"Distrust, in books on metaphysics, words which have not
been able to get currency in the world, and are only calculated
to form a special language."

Nor would he suffer common words to be employed in a
special sense by the schools:—

"Which is the best, if one wants to be useful and to be really
understood, to get one's words in the world, or to get them in
the schools? I maintain that the good plan is to employ words
in their popular sense rather than in their philosophical sense;
and the better plan still, to employ them in their natural sense
rather than in their popular sense. By their natural sense, I
mean the popular and universal acceptation of them brought
to that which in this is essential and invariable. To prove a
thing by definition proves nothing, if the definition is purely
philosophical; for such definitions only bind him who makes
them. To prove a thing by definition, when the definition expresses the necessary, inevitable, and clear idea which the world
at large attaches to the object, is, on the contrary, all in all;

because then what one does is simply to show people what they do really think, in spite of themselves and without knowing it. The rule that one is free to give to words what sense one will, and that the only thing needful is to be agreed upon the sense one gives them, is very well for the mere purposes of argumentation, and may be allowed in the schools where this sort of fencing is to be practised; but in the sphere of the true-born and noble science of metaphysics, and in the genuine world of literature, it is good for nothing. One must never quit sight of realities, and one must employ one's expressions simply as media, —as glasses, through which one's thoughts can be best made evident. I know, by my own experience, how hard this rule is to follow; but I judge of its importance by the failure of every system of metaphysics. Not one of them has succeeded; for the simple reason, that in every one ciphers have been constantly used instead of values, artificial ideas instead of native ideas, jargon instead of idiom."

I do not know whether the metaphysician will ever adopt Joubert's rules; but I am sure that the man of letters, whenever he has to speak of metaphysics, will do well to adopt them. He, at any rate, must remember:—

"It is by means of familiar words that style takes hold of the reader and gets possession of him. It is by means of these that great thoughts get currency and pass for true metal, like gold and silver which have had a recognised stamp put upon them. They beget confidence in the man who, in order to make his thoughts more clearly perceived, uses them; for people feel that such an employment of the language of common human life betokens a man who knows that life and its concerns, and who keeps himself in contact with them. Besides, these words make a style frank and easy. They show that an author has long made the thought or the feeling expressed his mental food; that he has so assimilated them and familiarised them, that the most common expressions suffice him in order to express ideas which have become every-day ideas to him by the length of time they have been in his mind. And lastly, what one says in such words looks more true; for, of all the words in use, none are so clear as those which we call common words; and clearness is so

eminently one of the characteristics of truth, that often it even
passes for truth itself."

These are not, in Joubert, mere counsels of rhetoric; they
come from his accurate sense of perfection, from his having
5   clearly seized the fine and just idea that beauty and light are
properties of truth, and that truth is incompletely exhibited if
it is exhibited without beauty and light:—

"Be profound with clear terms and not with obscure terms.
What is difficult will at last become easy; but as one goes deep
10 into things, one must still keep a charm, and one must carry
into these dark depths of thought, into which speculation has
only recently penetrated, the pure and antique clearness of
centuries less learned than ours, but with more light in them."

And elsewhere he speaks of those "spirits, lovers of light,
15 who, when they have an idea to put forth, brood long over it
first, and wait patiently till it *shines,* as Buffon enjoined, when
he defined genius to be the aptitude for patience; spirits who
know by experience that the driest matter and the dullest words
hide within them the germ and spark of some brightness, like
20 those fairy nuts in which were found diamonds if one broke
the shell and was the right person; spirits who maintain that,
to see and exhibit things in beauty, is to see and show things as
in their essence they really are, and not as they exist for the eye
of the careless, who do not look beyond the outside; spirits hard
25 to satisfy, because of a keen-sightedness in them, which makes
them discern but too clearly both the models to be followed
and those to be shunned; spirits active though meditative, who
cannot rest except in solid truths, and whom only beauty can
make happy; spirits far less concerned for glory than for per-
30 fection, who, because their art is long and life is short, often
die without leaving a monument, having had their own inward sense of life and fruitfulness for their best reward."

No doubt there is something a little too ethereal in all this,
something which reminds one of Joubert's physical want of
35 body and substance; no doubt, if a man wishes to be a great
author, it is to consider too curiously, to consider as Joubert
did; it is a mistake to spend so much of one's time in setting up
one's ideal standard of perfection, and in contemplating it.

Joubert himself knew this very well: "I cannot build a house for my ideas," said he; "I have tried to do without words, and words take their revenge on me by their difficulty." "If there is a man upon earth tormented by the cursed desire to get a whole book into a page, a whole page into a phrase, and this phrase into one word,—that man is myself." "I can sow, but I cannot build." Joubert, however, makes no claim to be a great author; by renouncing all ambition to be this, by not trying to fit his ideas into a house, by making no compromise with words in spite of their difficulty, by being quite single-minded in his pursuit of perfection, perhaps he is enabled to get closer to the truth of the objects of his study, and to be of more service to us by setting before us ideals, than if he had composed a celebrated work. I doubt whether, in an elaborate work on the philosophy of religion, he would have got his ideas about religion to *shine*, to use his own expression, as they shine when he utters them in perfect freedom. Penetration in these matters is valueless without soul, and soul is valueless without penetration; both of these are delicate qualities, and, even in those who have them, easily lost; the charm of Joubert is, that he has and keeps both. Let us try and show that he does.

"One should be fearful of being wrong in poetry when one thinks differently from the poets, and in religion when one thinks differently from the saints.

"There is a great difference between taking for idols Mahomet or Luther, and bowing down before Rousseau and Voltaire. People at any rate imagined they were obeying God when they followed Mahomet, and the Scriptures when they hearkened to Luther. And perhaps one ought not too much to disparage that inclination which leads mankind to put into the hands of those whom it thinks the friends of God the direction and government of its heart and mind. It is the subjection to irreligious spirits which alone is fatal, and, in the fullest sense of the word, depraving.

"May I say it? It is not hard to know God, provided one will not force oneself to define him.

"Do not bring into the domain of reasoning that which belongs to our innermost feeling. State truths of sentiment, and

do not try to prove them. There is a danger in such proofs; for in arguing it is necessary to treat that which is in question as something problematic: now that which we accustom ourselves to treat as problematic ends by appearing to us as really doubt-
5 ful. In things that are visible and palpable, never prove what is believed already; in things that are certain and mysterious,—mysterious by their greatness and by their nature,—make people believe them, and do not prove them; in things that are matters of practice and duty, command, and do not explain. 'Fear
10 God,' has made many men pious; the proofs of the existence of God have made many men atheists. From the defence springs the attack; the advocate begets in his hearer a wish to pick holes; and men are almost always led on, from the desire to contradict the doctor, to the desire to contradict the doctrine.
15 Make truth lovely, and do not try to arm her; mankind will then be far less inclined to contend with her.

"Why is even a bad preacher almost always heard by the pious with pleasure? *Because he talks to them about what they love.* But you who have to expound religion to the children
20 of this world, you who have to speak to them of that which they once loved perhaps, or which they would be glad to love, —remember that they do not love it yet, and to make them love it take heed to speak with power.

"You may do what you like, mankind will believe no one
25 but God; and he only can persuade mankind who believes that God has spoken to him. No one can give faith unless he has faith; the persuaded persuade, as the indulgent disarm.

"The only happy people in the world are the good man, the sage, and the saint; but the saint is happier than either of the
30 others, so much is man by his nature formed for sanctity."

The same delicacy and penetration which he here shows in speaking of the inward essence of religion, Joubert shows also in speaking of its outward form, and of its manifestation in the world:—
35 "Piety is not a religion, though it is the soul of all religions. A man has not a religion simply by having pious inclinations, any more than he has a country simply by having philanthropy.

A man has not a country until he is a citizen in a state, until he undertakes to follow and uphold certain laws, to obey certain magistrates, and to adopt certain ways of living and acting.

"Religion is neither a theology nor a theosophy; it is more than all this; it is a discipline, a law, a yoke, an indissoluble engagement."

Who, again, has ever shown with more truth and beauty the good and imposing side of the wealth and splendour of the Catholic Church, than Joubert in the following passage?—

"The pomps and magnificence with which the Church is reproached are in truth the result and the proof of her incomparable excellence. From whence, let me ask, have come this power of hers and these excessive riches, except from the enchantment into which she threw all the world? Ravished with her beauty, millions of men from age to age kept loading her with gifts, bequests, cessions. She had the talent of making herself loved, and the talent of making men happy. It is that which wrought prodigies for her; it is from thence that she drew her power."

"She had the talent of making herself *feared*,"—one should add that too, in order to be perfectly just; but Joubert, because he is a true child of light, can see that the wonderful success of the Catholic Church must have been due really to her good rather than to her bad qualities; to her making herself loved rather than to her making herself feared.

How striking and suggestive, again, is this remark on the Old and New Testaments:—

"The Old Testament teaches the knowledge of good and evil; the Gospel, on the other hand, seems written for the predestinated; it is the book of innocence. The one is made for earth, the other seems made for heaven. According as the one or the other of these books takes hold of a nation, what may be called the *religious humours* of nations differ."

So the British and North American Puritans are the children of the Old Testament, as Joachim of Flora and St. Francis are the children of the New. And does not the following maxim exactly fit the Church of England, of which Joubert certainly never thought when he was writing it?—"The austere sects excite the most enthusiasm at first; but the temperate sects have always been the most durable."

And these remarks on the Jansenists and Jesuits, interesting in themselves, are still more interesting because they touch matters we cannot well know at first-hand, and which Joubert, an impartial observer, had had the means of studying closely. We are apt to think of the Jansenists as having failed by reason of their merits; Joubert shows us how far their failure was due to their defects:—

"We ought to lay stress upon what is clear in Scripture, and to pass quickly over what is obscure; to light up what in Scripture is troubled, by what is serene in it; what puzzles and checks the reason, by what satisfies the reason. The Jansenists have done just the reverse. They lay stress upon what is uncertain, obscure, afflicting, and they pass lightly over all the rest; they eclipse the luminous and consoling truths of Scripture, by putting between us and them its opaque and dismal truths. For example, 'Many are called;' there is a clear truth: 'Few are chosen;' there is an obscure truth. 'We are children of wrath;' there is a sombre, cloudy, terrifying truth: 'We are all the children of God;' 'I came not to call the righteous, but sinners to repentance;' there are truths which are full of clearness, mildness, serenity, light. The Jansenists trouble our cheerfulness, and shed no cheering ray on our trouble. They are not, however, to be condemned for what they say, because what they say is true; but they are to be condemned for what they fail to say, for that is true too,—truer, even, than the other; that is, its truth is easier for us to seize, fuller, rounder, and more complete. Theology, as the Jansenists exhibit her, has but the half of her disk."

Again:—

"The Jansenists erect 'grace' into a kind of fourth person of the Trinity. They are, without thinking or intending it, Quaternitarians. St. Paul and St. Augustine, too exclusively studied, have done all the mischief. Instead of 'grace,' say help, succour, a divine influence, a dew of heaven; then one can come to a right understanding. The word 'grace' is a sort of talisman, all the baneful spell of which can be broken by translating it. The trick of personifying words is a fatal source of mischief in theology."

Once more:—

"The Jansenists tell men to love God; the Jesuits make men love him. The doctrine of these last is full of loosenesses, or, if you will, of errors; still,—singular as it may seem, it is undeniable,—they are the better directors of souls.

"The Jansenists have carried into religion more thought than the Jesuits, and they go deeper; they are faster bound with its sacred bonds. They have in their way of thinking an austerity which incessantly constrains the will to keep the path of duty; all the habits of their understanding, in short, are more Christian. But they seem to love God without affection, and solely from reason, from duty, from justice. The Jesuits, on the other hand, seem to love him from pure inclination; out of admiration, gratitude, tenderness; for the pleasure of loving him, in short. In their books of devotion you find joy, because with the Jesuits nature and religion go hand in hand. In the books of the Jansenists there is a sadness and a moral constraint, because with the Jansenists religion is for ever trying to put nature in bonds."

The Jesuits have suffered, and deservedly suffered, plenty of discredit from what Joubert gently calls their "loosenesses;" let them have the merit of their amiability.

The most characteristic thoughts one can quote from any writer are always his thoughts on matters like these; but the maxims of Joubert on purely literary subjects also have the same purged and subtle delicacy; they show the same sedulousness in him to preserve perfectly true the balance of his soul. Let me begin with this, which contains a truth too many people fail to perceive:—

"Ignorance, which in matters of morals extenuates the crime, is itself, in matters of literature, a crime of the first order."

And here is another sentence, worthy of Goethe, to clear the air at one's entrance into the region of literature:—

"With the fever of the senses, the delirium of the passions, the weakness of the spirit; with the storms of the passing time

and with the great scourges of human life,—hunger, thirst, dishonour, diseases, and death,—authors may as long as they like
go on making novels which shall harrow our hearts; but the soul
says all the while, 'You hurt me.' "

5   And again:—
"Fiction has no business to exist unless it is more beautiful
than reality. Certainly the monstrosities of fiction may be found
in the booksellers' shops; you buy them there for a certain
number of francs, and you talk of them for a certain number of
10   days; but they have no place in literature, because in literature
the one aim of art is the beautiful. Once lose sight of that, and
you have the mere frightful reality."

That is just the right criticism to pass on these "monstrosities:" *they have no place in literature,* and those who produce
15   them are not really men of letters. One would think that this
was enough to deter from such production any man of genuine
ambition. But most of us, alas! are what we must be, not what
we ought to be,—not even what we know we ought to be.

The following, of which the first part reminds one of Words-
20   worth's sonnet, "If thou indeed derive thy light from heaven,"
excellently defines the true salutary function of literature, and
the limits of this function:—
"Whether one is an eagle or an ant, in the intellectual world,
seems to me not to matter much; the essential thing is to have
25   one's place marked there, one's station assigned, and to belong decidedly to a regular and wholesome order. A small
talent, if it keeps within its limits and rightly fulfils its task,
may reach the goal just as well as a greater one. To accustom
mankind to pleasures which depend neither upon the bodily
30   appetites nor upon money, by giving them a taste for the
things of the mind, seems to me, in fact, the one proper fruit
which nature has meant our literary productions to have.
When they have other fruits, it is by accident, and, in general,
not for good. Books which absorb our attention to such a degree
35   that they rob us of all fancy for other books, are absolutely
pernicious. In this way they only bring fresh crotchets and
sects into the world; they multiply the great variety of weights,

rules, and measures already existing; they are morally and politically a nuisance."

Who can read these words and not think of the limiting
effect exercised by certain works in certain spheres and for
certain periods; exercised even by the works of men of genius 5
or virtue,—by the works of Rousseau, the works of Wesley,
the works of Swedenborg? And what is it which makes the
Bible so admirable a book, to be the one book of those who
can have only one, but the miscellaneous character of the contents of the Bible?

Joubert was all his life a passionate lover of Plato; I hope 10
other lovers of Plato will forgive me for saying that their adored
object has never been more truly described than he is here:—

"Plato shows us nothing, but he brings brightness with him;
he puts light into our eyes, and fills us with a clearness by 15
which all objects afterwards become illuminated. He teaches
us nothing; but he prepares us, fashions us, and makes us ready
to know all. Somehow or other, the habit of reading him aug-
ments in us the capacity for discerning and entertaining whatever fine truths may afterwards present themselves. Like 20
mountain-air, it sharpens our organs, and gives us an appetite
for wholesome food."

"Plato loses himself in the void" (he says again); "but one
sees the play of his wings, one hears their rustle." And the conclusion is: "It is good to breathe his air, but not to live upon 25
him."

As a pendant to the criticism on Plato, this on the French
moralist Nicole is excellent:—

"Nicole is a Pascal without style. It is not what he says which
is sublime, but what he thinks; he rises, not by the natural ele- 30
vation of his own spirit, but by that of his doctrines. One must
not look to the form in him, but to the matter, which is exquisite. He ought to be read with a direct view of practice."

English people have hardly ears to hear the praises of Bossuet, and the Bossuet of Joubert is Bossuet at his very best; but 35
this is a far truer Bossuet than the "declaimer" Bossuet of Lord
Macaulay, himself a born rhetorician, if ever there was one:—

"Bossuet employs all our idioms, as Homer employed all the dialects. The language of kings, of statesmen, and of warriors; the language of the people and of the student, of the country and of the schools, of the sanctuary and of the courts
5 of law; the old and the new, the trivial and the stately, the quiet and the resounding,—he turns all to his use; and out of all this he makes a style, simple, grave, majestic. His ideas are, like his words, varied,—common and sublime together. Times and doctrines in all their multitude were ever before his spirit, as things
10 and words in all their multitude were ever before it. He is not so much a man as a human nature, with the temperance of a saint, the justice of a bishop, the prudence of a doctor, and the might of a great spirit."

After this on Bossuet, I must quote a criticism on Racine, to
15 show that Joubert did not indiscriminately worship all the French gods of the grand century:—

"Those who find Racine enough for them are poor souls and poor wits; they are souls and wits which have never got beyond the callow and boarding-school stage. Admirable, as no doubt
20 he is, for his skill in having made poetical the most humdrum sentiments and the most middling sort of passions, he can yet stand us in stead of nobody but himself. He is a superior writer; and, in literature, that at once puts a man on a pinnacle. But he is not an inimitable writer."

25 And again: "The talent of Racine is in his works, but Racine himself is not there. That is why he himself became disgusted with them." "Of Racine, as of the ancients, the genius lay in taste. His elegance is perfect, but it is not supreme, like that of Virgil." And, indeed, there is something *supreme* in an elegance
30 which exercises such a fascination as Virgil's does; which makes one return to his poems again and again, long after one thinks one has done with them; which makes them one of those books that, to use Joubert's words, "lure the reader back to them, as the proverb says good wine lures back the wine-bibber." And
35 the highest praise Joubert can at last find for Racine is this, that he is the Virgil of the ignorant;—"*Racine est le Virgile des ignorants.*"

Of Boileau, too, Joubert says: "Boileau is a powerful poet,

but only in the world of half poetry." How true is that of Pope also! And he adds: "Neither Boileau's poetry nor Racine's flows from the fountain-head." No Englishman, controverting the exaggerated French estimate of these poets, could desire to use fitter words.

I will end with some remarks on Voltaire and Rousseau, remarks in which Joubert eminently shows his prime merit as a critic,—the soundness and completeness of his judgments. I mean that he has the faculty of judging with all the powers of his mind and soul at work together in due combination; and how rare is this faculty! how seldom is it exercised towards writers who so powerfully as Voltaire and Rousseau stimulate and call into activity a single side in us!

"Voltaire's wits came to their maturity twenty years sooner than the wits of other men, and remained in full vigour thirty years longer. The charm which our style in general gets from our ideas, his ideas get from his style. Voltaire is sometimes afflicted, sometimes strongly moved; but serious he never is. His very graces have an effrontery about them. He had correctness of judgment, liveliness of imagination, nimble wits, quick taste, and a moral sense in ruins. He is the most debauched of spirits, and the worst of him is that one gets debauched along with him. If he had been a wise man, and had had the self-discipline of wisdom, beyond a doubt half his wit would have been gone; it needed an atmosphere of *licence* in order to play freely. Those people who read him every day, create for themselves, by an invincible law, the necessity of liking him. But those people who, having given up reading him, gaze steadily down upon the influences which his spirit has shed abroad, find themselves in simple justice and duty compelled to detest him. It is impossible to be satisfied with him, and impossible not to be fascinated by him."

The literary sense in us is apt to rebel against so severe a judgment on such a charmer of the literary sense as Voltaire, and perhaps we English are not very liable to catch Voltaire's vices, while of some of his merits we have signal need; still, as the real definitive judgment on Voltaire, Joubert's is undoubtedly the true one. It is nearly identical with that of

Goethe. Joubert's sentence on Rousseau is in some respects
more favourable:—

"That weight in the speaker (*auctoritas*) which the ancients
talk of, is to be found in Bossuet more than in any other French
author; Pascal, too, has it, and La Bruyère; even Rousseau has
something of it, but Voltaire not a particle. I can understand
how a Rousseau—I mean a Rousseau cured of his faults—might
at the present day do much good, and may even come to be
greatly wanted; but under no circumstances can a Voltaire
be of any use."

The peculiar power of Rousseau's style has never been better
hit off than in the following passage:—

"Rousseau imparted, if I may so speak, *bowels of feeling* to
the words he used (*donna des entrailles à tous les mots*), and
poured into them such a charm, sweetness so penetrating, energy so puissant, that his writings have an effect upon the soul
something like that of those illicit pleasures which steal away
our taste and intoxicate our reason."

The final judgment, however, is severe, and justly severe:—

"Life without actions; life entirely resolved into affections
and half-sensual thoughts; do-nothingness setting up for a virtue; cowardliness with voluptuousness; fierce pride with nullity
underneath it; the strutting phrase of the most sensual of vaga-
bonds, who has made his system of philosophy and can give it
eloquently forth: there is Rousseau! A piety in which there is
no religion; a severity which brings corruption with it; a dogmatism which serves to ruin all authority: there is Rousseau's
philosophy! To all tender, ardent, and elevated natures, I say:
Only Rousseau can detach you from religion, and only true religion can cure you of Rousseau."

I must yet find room, before I end, for one at least of Joubert's sayings on political matters; here, too, the whole man
shows himself; and here, too, the affinity with Coleridge is
very remarkable. How true, how true in France especially, is
this remark on the contrasting direction taken by the aspirations
of the community in ancient and in modern states:—

"The ancients were attached to their country by three things,
—their temples, their tombs, and their forefathers. The two

great bonds which united them to their government were the bonds of habit and antiquity. With the moderns, hope and the love of novelty have produced a total change. The ancients said *our forefathers*, we say *posterity:* we do not, like them, love our *patria*, that is to say, the country and the laws of our fathers, rather we love the laws and the country of our children; the charm we are most sensible to is the charm of the future, and not the charm of the past."

And how keen and true is this criticism on the changed sense of the word "liberty":—

"A great many words have changed their meaning. The word *liberty*, for example, had at bottom among the ancients the same meaning as the word *dominion*. *I would be free* meant, in the mouth of the ancient, *I would take part in governing or administering the State;* in the mouth of a modern it means, *I would be independent*. The word *liberty* has with us a moral sense; with them its sense was purely political."

Joubert had lived through the French Revolution, and to the modern cry for liberty he was prone to answer:—

"Let your cry be for free souls rather even than for free men. Moral liberty is the one vitally important liberty, the one liberty which is indispensable; the other liberty is good and salutary only so far as it favours this. Subordination is in itself a better thing than independence. The one implies order and arrangement; the other implies only self-sufficiency with isolation. The one means harmony, the other a single tone; the one is the whole, the other is but the part."

"Liberty! liberty!" he cries again; "in all things let us have *justice*, and then we shall have enough liberty."

Let us have justice, and then we shall have enough liberty! The wise man will never refuse to echo those words; but then, such is the imperfection of human governments, that almost always, in order to get justice, one has first to secure liberty.

I do not hold up Joubert as a very astonishing and powerful genius, but rather as a delightful and edifying genius. I have not cared to exhibit him as a sayer of brilliant epigrammatic things, such things as "Notre vie est du vent tissu .... les dettes abrégent la vie .... celui qui a de l'imagination sans érudition

a des ailes et n'a pas de pieds (*Our life is woven wind . . . . debts
take from life . . . . the man of imagination without learning
has wings and no feet*)," though for such sayings he is famous.
In the first place, the French language is in itself so favourable a
vehicle for such sayings, that the making them in it has the less
merit; at least half the merit ought to go, not to the maker of the
saying, but to the French language. In the second place, the
peculiar beauty of Joubert is not there; it is not in what is exclusively intellectual,—it is in the union of *soul* with intellect,
and in the delightful, satisfying result which this union pro-
duces. "Vivre, c'est penser et sentir son âme . . . . le bonheur
est de sentir son âme bonne . . . . toute vérité nue et crue n'a
pas assez passé par l'âme . . . . les hommes ne sont justes qu'envers
ceux qu'ils aiment (*The essence of life lies in thinking and being
conscious of one's soul . . . . happiness is the sense of one's soul
being good . . . . if a truth is nude and crude, that is a proof it
has not been steeped long enough in the soul . . . . man cannot
even be just to his neighbour, unless he loves him*);" it is much
rather in sayings like these that Joubert's best and innermost
nature manifests itself. He is the most prepossessing and convincing of witnesses to the good of loving light. Because he
sincerely loved light, and did not prefer to it any little private
darkness of his own, he found light; his eye was single, and
therefore his whole body was full of light. And because he was
full of light, he was also full of happiness. In spite of his infirmities, in spite of his sufferings, in spite of his obscurity, he was
the happiest man alive; his life was as charming as his thoughts.
For certainly it is natural that the love of light, which is already,
in some measure, the possession of light, should irradiate and
beatify the whole life of him who has it. There is something
unnatural and shocking where, as in the case of Coleridge, it
does not. Joubert pains us by no such contradiction; "the same
penetration of spirit which made him such delightful company
to his friends, served also to make him perfect in his own personal life, by enabling him always to perceive and do what was
right;" he loved and sought light till he became so habituated
to it, so accustomed to the joyful testimony of a good conscience, that, to use his own words, "he could no longer exist

without this, and was obliged to live without reproach if he would live without misery."

Joubert was not famous while he lived, and he will not be famous now that he is dead. But, before we pity him for this, let us be sure what we mean, in literature, by *famous*. There are the famous men of genius in literature,—the Homers, Dantes, Shakspeares: of them we need not speak; their praise is for ever and ever. Then there are the famous men of ability in literature: their praise is in their own generation. And what makes this difference? The work of the two orders of men is at the bottom the same,—*a criticism of life*. The end and aim of all literature, if one considers it attentively, is, in truth, nothing but that. But the criticism which the men of genius pass upon human life is permanently acceptable to mankind; the criticism which the men of ability pass upon human life is transitorily acceptable. Between Shakspeare's criticism of human life and Scribe's the difference is there;—the one is permanently acceptable, the other transitorily. Whence then, I repeat, this difference? It is that the acceptableness of Shakspeare's criticism depends upon its inherent truth: the acceptableness of Scribe's upon its suiting itself, by its subject-matter, ideas, mode of treatment, to the taste of the generation that hears it. But the taste and ideas of one generation are not those of the next. This next generation in its turn arrives;—first its sharpshooters, its quick-witted, audacious light troops; then the elephantine main body. The imposing array of its predecessor it confidently assails, riddles it with bullets, passes over its body. It goes hard then with many once popular reputations, with many authorities once oracular. Only two kinds of authors are safe in the general havoc. The first kind are the great abounding fountains of truth, whose criticism of life is a source of illumination and joy to the whole human race for ever,— the Homers, the Shakspeares. These are the sacred personages, whom all civilised warfare respects. The second are those whom the out-skirmishers of the new generation, its forerunners,— quick-witted soldiers, as I have said, the select of the army,— recognise, though the bulk of their comrades behind might not, as of the same family and character with the sacred per-

sonages, exercising like them an immortal function, and like
them inspiring a permanent interest. They snatch them up,
and set them in a place of shelter, where the on-coming multitude may not overwhelm them. These are the Jouberts. They
5 will never, like the Shakspeares, command the homage of the
multitude; but they are safe; the multitude will not trample
them down. Except these two kinds, no author is safe. Let us
consider, for example, Joubert's famous contemporary, Lord
Jeffrey. All his vivacity and accomplishment avail him nothing;
10 of the true critic he had in an eminent degree no quality, except
one,—curiosity. Curiosity he had, but he had no gift for truth;
he cannot illuminate and rejoice us; no intelligent out-skir-
misher of the new generation cares about him, cares to put him
in safety; at this moment we are all passing over his body. Let
15 us consider a greater than Jeffrey, a critic whose reputation
still stands firm,—will stand, many people think, for ever,—
the great apostle of the Philistines, Lord Macaulay. Lord Macaulay was, as I have already said, a born rhetorician; a splendid rhetorician doubtless, and, beyond that, an *English* rhet-
20 orician also, an *honest* rhetorician; still, beyond the apparent
rhetorical truth of things he never could penetrate; for their
vital truth, for what the French call the *vraie vérité*, he had
absolutely no organ; therefore his reputation, brilliant as it
is, is not secure. Rhetoric so good as his excites and gives
25 pleasure; but by pleasure alone you cannot permanently bind
men's spirits to you. Truth illuminates and gives joy, and it is
by the bond of joy, not of pleasure, that men's spirits are in-
dissolubly held. As Lord Macaulay's own generation dies out,
as a new generation arrives, without those ideas and tendencies
30 of its predecessor which Lord Macaulay so deeply shared and
so happily satisfied, will he give the same pleasure? and, if he
ceases to give this, has he enough of light in him to make him
last? Pleasure the new generation will get from its own novel
ideas and tendencies; but light is another and a rarer thing,
35 and must be treasured wherever it can be found. Will Macaulay be saved, in the sweep and pressure of time, for his light's
sake, as Johnson has already been saved by two generations,
Joubert by one? I think it very doubtful. But for a spirit of any

delicacy and dignity, what a fate, if he could foresee it! to be
an oracle for one generation, and then of little or no account
for ever. How far better, to pass with scant notice through
one's own generation, but to be singled out and preserved by
the very iconoclasts of the next, then in their turn by those   5
of the next, and so, like the lamp of life itself, to be handed
on from one generation to another in safety! This is Joubert's
lot, and it is a very enviable one. The new men of the new
generations, while they let the dust deepen on a thousand
Laharpes, will say of him: "He lived in the Philistine's day, in   10
a place and time when almost every idea current in literature
had the mark of Dagon upon it, and not the mark of the
children of light. Nay, the children of light were as yet
hardly so much as heard of: the Canaanite was then in the land.
Still, there were even then a few, who, nourished on some secret   15
tradition, or illumined, perhaps, by a divine inspiration, kept
aloof from the reigning superstitions, never bowed the knee to
the gods of Canaan; and one of these few was called *Joubert*."

Pagan and Mediæval Religious Sentiment

I read the other day in the *Dublin Review:*—"We Catholics are apt to be cowed and scared by the lordly oppression of public opinion, and not to bear ourselves as men in the face of the anti-Catholic society of England. It is good to have an
5 habitual consciousness that the public opinion of Catholic Europe looks upon Protestant England with a mixture of impatience and compassion, which more than balances the arrogance of the English people towards the Catholic Church in these countries."
10 The Holy Catholic Church, Apostolic and Roman, can take very good care of herself, and I am not going to defend her against the scorns of Exeter Hall. Catholicism is not a great visible force in this country, and the mass of mankind will always treat lightly even things the most venerable, if they do not
15 present themselves as visible forces before its eyes. In Catholic countries, as the *Dublin Review* itself says with triumph, they make very little account of the greatness of Exeter Hall. The majority has eyes only for the things of the majority, and in England the immense majority is Protestant. And yet, in spite
20 of all the shocks which the feeling of a good Catholic, like the writer in the *Dublin Review,* has in this Protestant country inevitably to undergo, in spite of the contemptuous insensibility to the grandeur of Rome which he finds so general and so hard to bear, how much has he to console him, how many
25 acts of homage to the greatness of his religion may he see if he has his eyes open! I will tell him of one of them. Let him go in London to that delightful spot, that Happy Island in Bloomsbury, the reading-room of the British Museum. Let him visit its sacred quarter, the region where its theological books are

placed. I am almost afraid to say what he will find there, for
fear Mr. Spurgeon, like a second Caliph Omar, should give
the library to the flames. He will find an immense Catholic
work, the collection of the Abbé Migne, lording it over that
whole region, reducing to insignificance the feeble Protestant   5
forces which hang upon its skirts. Protestantism is duly represented, indeed: the librarian knows his business too well to
suffer it to be otherwise; all the varieties of Protestantism are
there; there is the Library of Anglo-Catholic Theology,
learned, decorous, exemplary, but a little uninteresting; there   10
are the works of Calvin, rigid, militant, menacing; there are
the works of Dr. Chalmers, the Scotch thistle valiantly doing
duty as the rose of Sharon, but keeping something very Scotch
about it all the time; there are the works of Dr. Channing, the
last word of religious philosophy in a land where every one has   15
some culture, and where superiorities are discountenanced,—
the flower of moral and intelligent mediocrity. But how are all
these divided against one another, and how, though they were
all united, are they dwarfed by the Catholic Leviathan, their
neighbour! Majestic in its blue and gold unity, this fills shelf   20
after shelf and compartment after compartment, its right mount-
ing up into heaven among the white folios of the *Acta Sanctorum*, its left plunging down into hell among the yellow octa-
vos of the *Law Digest*. Everything is there, in that immense
Patrologiæ Cursus Completus, in that *Encyclopédie Théolo-*   25
gique, that *Nouvelle Encyclopédie Théologique*, that *Troisième
Encyclopédie Théologique;* religion, philosophy, history, biography, arts, sciences, bibliography, gossip. The work embraces
the whole range of human interests; like one of the great Middle-
Age Cathedrals, it is in itself a study for a life. Like the net in   30
Scripture, it drags everything to land, bad and good, lay and
ecclesiastical, sacred and profane, so that it be but matter of
human concern. Wide-embracing as the power whose product
it is! a power, for history at any rate, eminently *the Church;*
not, perhaps, the Church of the future, but indisputably the   35
Church of the past and, in the past, the Church of the multitude.

   This is why the man of imagination—nay, and the philosopher too, in spite of her propensity to burn him—will always

have a weakness for the Catholic Church; because of the rich
treasures of human life which have been stored within her
pale. The mention of other religious bodies, or of their leaders,
at once calls up in our mind the thought of men of a definite
type as their adherents; the mention of Catholicism suggests no
such special following. Anglicanism suggests the English epis-
copate; Calvin's name suggests Dr. Candlish; Chalmers's, the
Duke of Argyll; Channing's, Boston society; but Catholicism
suggests,—what shall I say?—all the pell-mell of the men and
women of Shakspeare's plays. This abundance the Abbé Migne's
collection faithfully reflects. People talk of this or that work
which they would choose, if they were to pass their life with
only one; for my part I think I would choose the Abbé Migne's
collection. *Quicquid agunt homines,*—everything, as I have
said, is there. Do not seek in it splendour of form, perfection
of editing; its paper is common, its type ugly, its editing indifferent, its printing careless. The greatest and most baffling
crowd of misprints I ever met with in my life occurs in a very
important page of the introduction to the *Dictionnaire des
Apocryphes.* But this is just what you have in the world,—
quantity rather than quality. Do not seek in it impartiality,
the critical spirit; in reading it you must do the criticism for
yourself; it loves criticism as little as the world loves it. Like
the world, it chooses to have things all its own way, to abuse
its adversary, to back its own notion through thick and thin,
to put forward all the *pros* for its own notion, to suppress all
the *contras;* it does just all that the world does, and all that the
critical spirit shrinks from. Open the *Dictionnaire des Erreurs
Sociales:* "The religious persecutions of Henry the Eighth's and
Edward the Sixth's time abated a little in the reign of Mary, to
break out again with new fury in the reign of Elizabeth." There
is a summary of the history of religious persecution under the
Tudors! But how unreasonable to reproach the Abbé Migne's
work with wanting a criticism, which, by the very nature of
things, it cannot have, and not rather to be grateful to it
for its abundance, its variety, its infinite suggestiveness, its
happy adoption, in many a delicate circumstance, of the urbane

tone and temper of the man of the world, instead of the acrid
tone and temper of the fanatic!

Still, in spite of their fascinations, the contents of this collection sometimes rouse the critical spirit within one. It happened
that lately, after I had been thinking much of Marcus Aurelius   5
and his times, I took down the *Dictionnaire des Origines du
Christianisme*, to see what it had to say about paganism and
pagans. I found much what I expected. I read the article, *Révé-
lation Évangélique, sa Nécessité*. There I found what a sink of
iniquity was the whole pagan world; how one Roman fed his   10
oysters on his slaves, how another put a slave to death that a
curious friend might see what dying was like; how Galen's
mother tore and bit her waiting-women when she was in a passion with them. I found this account of the religion of paganism:
"Paganism invented a mob of divinities with the most hateful   15
character, and attributed to them the most monstrous and abominable crimes. It personified in them drunkenness, incest, kid-
napping, adultery, sensuality, knavery, cruelty, and rage." And
I found that from this religion there followed such practice as
was to be expected: "What must naturally have been the state   20
of morals under the influence of such a religion, which penetrated with its own spirit the public life, the family life, and the
individual life of antiquity?"

The colours in this picture are laid on very thick, and I for
my part cannot believe that any human societies, with a religion   25
and practice such as those just described, could ever have endured as the societies of Greece and Rome endured, still less
have done what the societies of Greece and Rome did. We are
not brought far by descriptions of the vices of great cities, or
even of individuals driven mad by unbounded means of self-   30
indulgence. Feudal and aristocratic life in Christendom has produced horrors of selfishness and cruelty not surpassed by the
grandee of pagan Rome; and then, again, in antiquity there is
Marcus Aurelius's mother to set against Galen's. Eminent examples of vice and virtue in individuals prove little as to the   35
state of societies. What, under the first emperors, was the condition of the Roman poor upon the Aventine compared with

that of our poor in Spitalfields and Bethnal Green? What, in comfort, morals, and happiness, were the rural population of the Sabine country under Augustus's rule, compared with the rural population of Hertfordshire and Buckinghamshire under
5   the rule of Queen Victoria?

But these great questions are not now for me. Without trying to answer them, I ask myself, when I read such declamation as the foregoing, if I can find anything that will give me a near, distinct sense of the real difference in spirit and sentiment be-
10 tween paganism and Christianity, and of the natural effect of this difference upon people in general. I take a representative religious poem of paganism,—of the paganism which all the world has in its mind when it speaks of paganism. To be a representative poem, it must be one for popular use, one that the
15 multitude listens to. Such a religious poem may be found at the end of one of the best and happiest of Theocritus's idylls, the fifteenth. In order that the reader may the better go along with me in the line of thought I am following, I will translate it; and, that he may see the medium in which religious poetry
20 of this sort is found existing, the society out of which it grows, the people who form it and are formed by it, I will translate the whole, or nearly the whole, of the idyll (it is not long) in which the poem occurs.

The idyll is dramatic. Somewhere about two hundred and
25 eighty years before the Christian era, a couple of Syracusan women, staying at Alexandria, agreed on the occasion of a great religious solemnity,—the feast of Adonis,—to go together to the palace of King Ptolemy Philadelphus, to see the image of Adonis, which the queen Arsinoe, Ptolemy's wife, had had
30 decorated with peculiar magnificence. A hymn, by a celebrated performer, was to be recited over the image. The names of the two women are Gorgo and Praxinoe; their maids, who are mentioned in the poem, are called Eunoe and Eutychis. Gorgo comes by appointment to Praxinoe's house to fetch her, and
35 there the dialogue begins:—

Gorgo.—Is Praxinoe at home?

Praxinoe.—My dear Gorgo, at last! Yes, here I am. Eunoe, find a chair,—get a cushion for it.

Gorgo.—It will do beautifully as it is.

Praxinoe.—Do sit down.

Gorgo.—Oh, this gad-about spirit! I could hardly get to you, Praxinoe, through all the crowd and all the carriages. Nothing but heavy boots, nothing but men in uniform. And what a journey it is! My dear child, you really live *too* far off.

Praxinoe.—It is all that insane husband of mine. He has chosen to come out here to the end of the world, and take a hole of a place,—for a house it is not,—on purpose that you and I might not be neighbours. He is always just the same;—anything to quarrel with one! anything for spite!

Gorgo.—My dear, don't talk so of your husband before the little fellow. Just see how astonished he looks at you. Never mind, Zopyrio, my pet, she is not talking about papa.

Praxinoe.—Good heavens! the child does really understand.

Gorgo.—Pretty papa!

Praxinoe.—That pretty papa of his the other day (though I told him beforehand to mind what he was about), when I sent him to a shop to buy soap and rouge, brought me home salt instead;—stupid, great, big, interminable animal!

Gorgo.—Mine is just the fellow to him. . . . But never mind now, get on your things and let us be off to the palace to see the Adonis. I hear the Queen's decorations are something splendid.

Praxinoe.—In grand people's houses everything is grand. What things you have seen in Alexandria! What a deal you will have to tell to anybody who has never been here!

Gorgo.—Come, we ought to be going.

Praxinoe. Every day is holiday to people who have nothing to do. Eunoe, pick up your work; and take care, lazy girl, how you leave it lying about again; the cats find it just the bed they like. Come, stir yourself, fetch me some water, quick! I wanted the water first, and the girl brings me the soap. Never mind; give it me. Not all that, extravagant! Now pour out the water; —stupid! why don't you take care of my dress? That will do. I have got my hands washed as it pleased God. Where is the key of the large wardrobe? Bring it here;—quick!

Gorgo.—Praxinoe, you can't think how well that dress, made full, as you have got it, suits you. Tell me, how much did it cost?—the dress by itself, I mean.

Praxinoe.—Don't talk of it, Gorgo: more than eight guineas of good hard money. And about the work on it I have almost
5   worn my life out.

Gorgo.—Well, you couldn't have done better.

Praxinoe.—Thank you. Bring me my shawl, and put my hat properly on my head;—properly. No, child (*to her little boy*), I am not going to take you; there's a bogy on horseback, who
10   bites. Cry as much as you like; I'm not going to have you lamed for life. Now we'll start. Nurse, take the little one and amuse him; call the dog in, and shut the street-door. (*They go out.*) Good heavens! what a crowd of people! How on earth are we ever to get through all this? They are like ants:
15   you can't count them. My dearest Gorgo, what will become of us? here are the royal Horse Guards. My good man, don't ride over me! Look at that bay horse rearing bolt upright; what a vicious one! Eunoe, you mad girl, do take care!—that horse will certainly be the death of the man on his back. How glad
20   I am now, that I left the child safe at home!

Gorgo.—All right, Praxinoe, we are safe behind them; and they have gone on to where they are stationed.

Praxinoe.—Well, yes, I begin to revive again. From the time I was a little girl I have had more horror of horses and snakes
25   than of anything in the world. Let us get on; here's a great crowd coming this way upon us.

Gorgo (*to an old woman*).—Mother, are you from the palace?

Old Woman.—Yes, my dears.

30   *Gorgo.*—Has one a tolerable chance of getting there?

Old Woman.—My pretty young lady, the Greeks got to Troy by dint of trying hard; trying will do anything in this world.

Gorgo.—The old creature has delivered herself of an oracle
35   and departed.

Praxinoe.—Women can tell you everything about everything, Jupiter's marriage with Juno not excepted.

Gorgo.—Look, Praxinoe, what a squeeze at the palace gates!

Praxinoe.—Tremendous! Take hold of me, Gorgo; and you, Eunoe, take hold of Eutychis!—tight hold, or you'll be lost. Here we go in all together. Hold tight to us, Eunoe! Oh, dear! oh, dear! Gorgo, there's my scarf torn right in two. For heaven's sake, my good man, as you hope to be saved, take care of my dress!

Stranger.—I'll do what I can, but it doesn't depend upon me.

Praxinoe.—What heaps of people! They push like a drove of pigs.

Stranger.—Don't be frightened, ma'am, we are all right.

Praxinoe.—May you be all right, my dear sir, to the last day you live, for the care you have taken of us! What a kind, considerate man! There is Eunoe jammed in a squeeze. Push, you goose, push! Capital! We are all of us the right side of the door, as the bridegroom said when he had locked himself in with the bride.

Gorgo.—Praxinoe, come this way. Do but look at that work, how delicate it is!—how exquisite! Why, they might wear it in heaven.

Praxinoe.—Heavenly patroness of needlewomen, what hands were hired to do that work? Who designed those beautiful patterns? They seem to stand up and move about, as if they were real;—as if they were living things, and not needlework. Well, man is a wonderful creature! And look, look, how charming he lies there on his silver couch, with just a soft down on his cheeks, that beloved Adonis,—Adonis, whom one loves even though he is dead!

Another Stranger.—You wretched women, do stop your incessant chatter! Like turtles, you go on for ever. They are enough to kill one with their broad lingo,—nothing but *a, a, a.*

Gorgo.—Lord, where does the man come from? What is it to you if we *are* chatterboxes? Order about your own servants! Do you give orders to Syracusan women? If you want to know, we came originally from Corinth, as Bellerophon did; we speak Peloponnesian. I suppose Dorian women may be allowed to have a Dorian accent.

Praxinoe.—Oh, honey-sweet Proserpine, let us have no more masters than the one we've got! We don't the least care for *you;* pray don't trouble yourself for nothing.

Gorgo.—Be quiet, Praxinoe! That first-rate singer, the Argive
5 woman's daughter, is going to sing the *Adonis* hymn. She is the same who was chosen to sing the dirge last year. We are sure to have something first-rate from *her*. She is going through her airs and graces ready to begin.—

So far the dialogue; and, as it stands in the original, it can
10 hardly be praised too highly. It is a page torn fresh out of the book of human life. What freedom! What animation! What gaiety! What naturalness! It is said that Theocritus, in compos-ing this poem, borrowed from a work of Sophron, a poet of an earlier and better time; but, even if this is so, the form is still
15 Theocritus's own, and how excellent is that form, how mas-terly! And this in a Greek poem of the decadence!—for Theoc-ritus's poetry, after all, is poetry of the decadence. When such is Greek poetry of the decadence, what must be Greek poetry of the prime?
20 Then the singer begins her hymn:—

"Mistress, who lovest the haunts of Golgi, and Idalium, and high-peaked Eryx, Aphrodite that playest with gold! how have the delicate-footed Hours, after twelve months, brought thy Adonis back to thee from the ever-flowing Acheron! Tardiest
25 of the immortals are the boon Hours, but all mankind wait their approach with longing, for they ever bring something with them. O Cypris, Dione's child! thou didst change—so is the story among men—Berenice from mortal to immortal, by dropping ambrosia into her fair bosom; and in gratitude to thee
30 for this, O thou of many names and many temples! Berenice's daughter, Arsinoe, lovely Helen's living counterpart, makes much of Adonis with all manner of braveries.

"All fruits that the tree bears are laid before him, all treas-ures of the garden in silver baskets, and alabaster boxes, gold-
35 inlaid, of Syrian ointment; and all confectionery that cunning women make on their kneading-tray, kneading up every sort of flowers with white meal, and all that they make of sweet honey and delicate oil, and all winged and creeping things

are here set before him. And there are built for him green bow-
ers with wealth of tender anise, and little boy-loves flutter about
over them, like young nightingales trying their new wings on
the tree, from bough to bough. Oh, the ebony, the gold, the
eagle of white ivory that bears aloft his cup-bearer to Cronos-   5
born Zeus! And up there, see! a second couch strewn for
lovely Adonis, scarlet coverlets softer than sleep itself (so Mil-
etus and the Samian wool-grower will say); Cypris has hers,
and the rosy-armed Adonis has his, that eighteen or nineteen-
year-old bridegroom. His kisses will not wound, the hair on   10
his lip is yet light.

"Now, Cypris, good-night, we leave thee with thy bridegroom; but to-morrow morning, with the earliest dew, we will
one and all bear him forth to where the waves splash upon the
sea-strand, and letting loose our locks, and letting fall our   15
robes, with bosoms bare, we will set up this, our melodious
strain:

" 'Beloved Adonis, alone of the demigods (so men say) thou
art permitted to visit both us and Acheron! This lot had neither
Agamemnon, nor the mighty moon-struck hero Ajax, nor Hec-   20
tor the first-born of Hecuba's twenty children, nor Patroclus,
nor Pyrrhus who came home from Troy, nor those yet earlier
Lapithæ and the sons of Deucalion, nor the Pelasgians, the root
of Argos and of Pelops' isle. Be gracious to us now, loved
Adonis, and be favourable to us for the year to come! Dear to   25
us hast thou been at this coming, dear to us shalt thou be when
thou comest again.' "

The poem concludes with a characteristic speech from
Gorgo:—

"Praxinoe, certainly women are wonderful things. That   30
lucky woman to know all that! and luckier still to have such a
splendid voice! And now we must see about getting home.
My husband has not had his dinner. That man is all vinegar,
and nothing else; and if you keep him waiting for his dinner,
he's dangerous to go near. Adieu, precious Adonis, and may   35
you find us all well when you come next year!"

So, with the hymn still in her ears, says the incorrigible
Gorgo.

But what a hymn that is! Of religious emotion, in our acceptation of the words, and of the comfort springing from religious emotion, not a particle. And yet many elements of religious emotion are contained in the beautiful story of Adonis.
5   Symbolically treated, as the thoughtful man might treat it, as the Greek mysteries undoubtedly treated it, this story was capable of a noble and touching application, and could lead the soul to elevating and consoling thoughts. Adonis was the sun in his summer and in his winter course, in his time of triumph
10 and his time of defeat; but in his time of triumph still moving towards his defeat, in his time of defeat still returning towards his triumph. Thus he became an emblem of the power of life and the bloom of beauty, the power of human life and the bloom of human beauty, hastening inevitably to diminution and
15 decay, yet in that very decay finding

"Hope, and a renovation without end."

But nothing of this appears in the story as prepared for popular religious use, as presented to the multitude in a popular religious ceremony. Its treatment is not devoid of a certain grace and
20 beauty, but it has nothing whatever that is elevating, nothing that is consoling, nothing that is in our sense of the word religious. The religious ceremonies of Christendom, even on occasion of the most joyful and mundane matters, present the multitude with strains of profoundly religious character, such
25 as the *Kyrie eleison* and the *Te Deum*. But this Greek hymn to Adonis adapts itself exactly to the tone and temper of a gay and pleasure-loving multitude,—of light-hearted people, like Gorgo and Praxinoe, whose moral nature is much of the same calibre as that of Phillina in Goethe's *Wilhelm Meister*, people who
30 seem never made to be serious, never made to be sick or sorry. And, if they happen to be sick or sorry, what will they do then? But that we have no right to ask. Phillina, within the enchanted bounds of Goethe's novel, Gorgo and Praxinoe, within the enchanted bounds of Theocritus's poem, never will be sick and
35 sorry, never can be sick and sorry. The ideal, cheerful, sensuous, pagan life is not sick or sorry. No; yet its natural end is in the sort of life which Pompeii and Herculaneum bring so

vividly before us,—a life which by no means in itself suggests
the thought of horror and misery, which even, in many ways,
gratifies the senses and the understanding; but by the very
intensity and unremittingness of its appeal to the senses and the
understanding, by its stimulating a single side of us too abso-   5
lutely, ends by fatiguing and revolting us; ends by leaving us
with a sense of confinement, of oppression,—with a desire for
an utter change, for clouds, storms, effusion, and relief.

In the beginning of the thirteenth century, when the clouds
and storms had come, when the gay sensuous pagan life was   10
gone, when men were not living by the senses and understanding, when they were looking for the speedy coming of
Antichrist, there appeared in Italy, to the north of Rome, in
the beautiful Umbrian country at the foot of the Apennines,
a figure of the most magical power and charm, St. Francis.   15
His century is, I think, the most interesting in the history of
Christianity after its primitive age, more interesting than even
the century of the Reformation; and one of the chief figures,
perhaps the very chief, to which this interest attaches itself, is
St. Francis. And why? Because of the profound popular in-   20
stinct which enabled him, more than any man since the primitive age, to fit religion for popular use. He brought religion to
the people. He founded the most popular body of ministers
of religion that has ever existed in the Church. He transformed
monachism by uprooting the stationary monk, delivering him   25
from the bondage of property, and sending him, as a mendicant
friar, to be a stranger and sojourner, not in the wilderness, but
in the most crowded haunts of men, to console them and to do
them good. This popular instinct of his is at the bottom of his
famous marriage with poverty. Poverty and suffering are the   30
condition of the people, the multitude, the immense majority
of mankind; and it was towards this *people* that his soul yearned.
"He listens," it was said of him, "to those to whom God himself
will not listen."

So in return, as no other man he was listened to. When an   35
Umbrian town or village heard of his approach, the whole population went out in joyful procession to meet him, with green
boughs, flags, music, and songs of gladness. The master, who

began with two disciples, could in his own lifetime (and he died
at forty-four) collect to keep Whitsuntide with him, in presence of an immense multitude, five thousand of his Minorites.
And thus he found fulfilment to his prophetic cry: "I hear in
5   my ears the sound of the tongues of all the nations who shall
come unto us; Frenchmen, Spaniards, Germans, Englishmen.
The Lord will make of us a great people, even unto the ends of
the earth."

Prose could not satisfy this ardent soul, and he made poetry.
10   Latin was too learned for this simple, popular nature, and he
composed in his mother tongue, in Italian. The beginnings of
the mundane poetry of the Italians are in Sicily, at the court
of kings; the beginnings of their religious poetry are in Umbria,
with St. Francis. His are the humble upper waters of a mighty
15   stream; at the beginning of the thirteenth century it is St. Francis, at the end, Dante. Now it happens that St. Francis, too,
like the Alexandrian songstress, has his hymn for the sun, for
Adonis. *Canticle of the Sun, Canticle of the Creatures,*—the
poem goes by both names. Like the Alexandrian hymn, it is
20   designed for popular use, but not for use by King Ptolemy's
people; artless in language, irregular in rhythm, it matches with
the childlike genius that produced it, and the simple natures
that loved and repeated it:—

"O most high, almighty, good Lord God, to thee belong
25   praise, glory, honour, and all blessing!

"Praised be my Lord God with all his creatures; and specially
our brother the sun, who brings us the day, and who brings us
the light; fair is he, and shining with a very great splendour:
O Lord, he signifies to us thee!

30   "Praised be my Lord for our sister the moon, and for the
stars, the which he has set clear and lovely in heaven.

"Praised be my Lord for our brother the wind, and for air
and cloud, calms and all weather, by the which thou upholdest
in life all creatures.

35   "Praised be my Lord for our sister water, who is very serv-
iceable unto us, and humble, and precious, and clean.

"Praised be my Lord for our brother fire, through whom

thou givest us light in the darkness; and he is bright, and pleasant, and very mighty, and strong.

"Praised be my Lord for our mother the earth, the which doth sustain us and keep us, and bringeth forth divers fruits, and flowers of many colours, and grass.

"Praised be my Lord for all those who pardon one another for his love's sake, and who endure weakness and tribulation; blessed are they who peaceably shall endure, for thou, O most Highest, shalt give them a crown!

"Praised be my Lord for our sister, the death of the body, from whom no man escapeth. Woe to him who dieth in mortal sin! Blessed are they who are found walking by thy most holy will, for the second death shall have no power to do them harm.

"Praise ye, and bless ye the Lord, and give thanks unto him, and serve him with great humility."

It is natural that man should take pleasure in his senses. But it is natural, also, that he should take refuge in his heart and imagination from his misery. And when one thinks what human life is for the vast majority of mankind, how little of a feast for their senses it can possibly be, one understands the charm for them of a refuge offered in the heart and imagination. Above all, when one thinks what human life was in the Middle Ages, one understands the charm of such a refuge.

Now, the poetry of Theocritus's hymn is poetry treating the world according to the demand of the senses; the poetry of St. Francis's hymn is poetry treating the world according to the demand of the heart and imagination. The first takes the world by its outward, sensible side; the second by its inward, symbolical side. The first admits as much of the world as is pleasure-giving; the second admits the whole world, rough and smooth, painful and pleasure-giving, all alike, but all transfigured by the power of a spiritual emotion, all brought under a law of super-sensual love, having its seat in the soul. It can thus even say: "Praised be my Lord for *our sister, the death of the body*."

But these very words are, perhaps, an indication that we are touching upon an extreme. When we see Pompeii, we can put our finger upon the pagan sentiment in its extreme. And when

we read of Monte Alverno and the *stigmata;* when we read of
the repulsive, because self-caused, sufferings of the end of St.
Francis's life; when we find him even saying, "I have sinned
against my brother the ass," meaning by these words that he
5   had been too hard upon his own body; when we find him assailed, even himself, by the doubt "whether he who had destroyed himself by the severity of his penances could find
mercy in eternity," we can put our finger on the mediæval
Christian sentiment in its extreme. Human nature is neither all
10 senses and understanding, nor all heart and imagination. Pompeii was a sign that for humanity at large the measure of sen-
sualism had been overpassed; St. Francis's doubt was a sign that
for humanity at large the measure of spiritualism had been overpassed. Humanity, in its violent rebound from one extreme,
15 had swung from Pompeii to Monte Alverno; but it was sure
not to stay there.

The Renascence is, in part, a return towards the pagan spirit,
in the special sense in which I have been using the word pagan;
a return towards the life of the senses and the understanding.
20 The Reformation, on the other hand, is the very opposite to
this; in Luther there is nothing Greek or pagan; vehemently as
he attacked the adoration of St. Francis, Luther had himself
something of St. Francis in him; he was a thousand times more
akin to St. Francis than to Theocritus or to Voltaire. The Ref-
25 ormation—I do not mean the inferior piece given under that
name, by Henry the Eighth and a second-rate company, in this
island, but the real Reformation, the German Reformation,
Luther's Reformation—was a reaction of the moral and spiritual
sense against the carnal and pagan sense; it was a religious re-
30 vival like St. Francis's, but this time against the Church of
Rome, not within her; for the carnal and pagan sense had now,
in the government of the Church of Rome herself, its prime
representative. But the grand reaction against the rule of the
heart and imagination, the strong return towards the rule of
35 the senses and understanding, is in the eighteenth century. And
this reaction has had no more brilliant champion than a man
of the nineteenth, of whom I have already spoken; a man who

could feel not only the pleasurableness but the poetry of the
life of the senses (and the life of the senses has its deep poetry);
a man who, in his very last poem, divided the whole world into
"barbarians and Greeks,"—Heinrich Heine. No man has reproached the Monte Alverno extreme in sentiment, the Chris-   5
tian extreme, the heart and imagination subjugating the senses
and understanding, more bitterly than Heine; no man has extolled the Pompeii extreme, the pagan extreme, more raptur-
ously.

"All through the Middle Age these sufferings, this fever, this   10
over-tension lasted; and we moderns still feel in all our limbs
the pain and weakness from them. Even those of us who are
cured have still to live with a hospital-atmosphere all around
us, and find ourselves as wretched in it as a strong man among
the sick. Some day or other, when humanity shall have got   15
quite well again, when the body and soul shall have made
their peace together, the factitious quarrel which Christianity has cooked up between them will appear something
hardly comprehensible. The fairer and happier generations,
offspring of unfettered unions, that will rise up and bloom   20
in the atmosphere of a religion of pleasure, will smile sadly
when they think of their poor ancestors, whose life was passed
in melancholy abstinence from the joys of this beautiful earth,
and who faded away into spectres, from the mortal compres-
sion which they put upon the warm and glowing emotions of   25
sense. Yes, with assurance I say it, our descendants will be
fairer and happier than we are; for I am a believer in progress,
and I hold God to be a kind being who has intended man to be
happy."

That is Heine's sentiment, in the prime of life, in the glow   30
of activity, amid the brilliant whirl of Paris. I will no more
blame it than I blamed the sentiment of the Greek hymn to
Adonis. I wish to decide nothing as of my own authority; the
great art of criticism is to get oneself out of the way and to let
humanity decide. Well, the sentiment of the "religion of pleas-   35
ure" has much that is natural in it; humanity will gladly accept it if it can live by it; to live by it one must never be sick

or sorry, and the old, ideal, limited, pagan world never, I have said, *was* sick or sorry, never at least shows itself to us sick or sorry:—

> "What pipes and timbrels! what wild ecstasy!"

5   For our imagination, Gorgo and Praxinoe cross the human stage chattering in their blithe Doric,—*like turtles*, as the cross stranger said,—and keep gaily chattering on till they disappear. But in the new, real, immense, post-pagan world,—in the barbarian world,—the shock of accident is unceasing, the se-
10 renity of existence is perpetually troubled, not even a Greek like Heine can get across the mortal stage without bitter calamity. How does the sentiment of the "religion of pleasure" serve then? does it help, does it console? Can a man live by it? Heine again shall answer; Heine just twenty years older,
15 stricken with incurable disease, waiting for death:—

  "The great pot stands smoking before me, but I have no spoon to help myself. What does it profit me that my health is drunk at banquets out of gold cups and in the most exquisite wines, if I myself, while these ovations are going on, lonely and
20 cut off from the pleasures of the world, can only just wet my lips with barley-water? What good does it do me that all the roses of Shiraz open their leaves and burn for me with passionate tenderness? Alas! Shiraz is some two thousand leagues from the Rue d'Amsterdam, where in the solitude of my sick cham-
25 ber all the perfume I smell is that of hot towels. Alas! the mockery of God is heavy upon me! The great author of the universe, the Aristophanes of Heaven, has determined to make the petty earthly author, the so-called Aristophanes of Germany, feel to his heart's core what pitiful needle-pricks his
30 cleverest sarcasms have been, compared with the thunderbolts which his divine humour can launch against feeble mortals! ...

  "In the year 1340, says the Chronicle of Limburg, all over Germany everybody was strumming and humming certain songs more lovely and delightful than any which had ever yet
35 been known in German countries; and all people, old and young, the women particularly, were perfectly mad about them, so that from morning till night you heard nothing else.

Only, the Chronicle adds, the author of these songs happened to be a young clerk, afflicted with leprosy, and living apart from all the world in a desolate place. The excellent reader does not require to be told how horrible a complaint was leprosy in the Middle Ages, and how the poor wretches who had this incurable plague were banished from society, and had to keep at a distance from every human being. Like living corpses, in a gray gown reaching down to the feet, and with the hood brought over their face, they went about, carrying in their hands an enormous rattle, called Saint Lazarus's rattle. With this rattle they gave notice of their approach, that every one might have time to get out of their way. This poor clerk, then, whose poetical gift the Limburg Chronicle extols, was a leper, and he sate moping in the dismal deserts of his misery, whilst all Germany, gay and tuneful, was praising his songs.

"Sometimes, in my sombre visions of the night, I imagine that I see before me the poor leprosy-stricken clerk of the Limburg Chronicle, and from under his gray hood his distressed eyes look out upon me in a fixed and strange fashion; but the next instant he disappears, and I hear dying away in the distance, like the echo of a dream, the dull creak of Saint Lazarus's rattle."

We have come a long way from Theocritus there; the expression of that has nothing of the clear, positive, happy, pagan character; it has much more the character of one of the indeterminate grotesques of the suffering Middle Age. Profoundness and power it has, though at the same time it is not truly poetical; it is not natural enough for that, there is too much waywardness in it, too much bravado. But as a condition of sentiment to be popular,—to be a comfort for the mass of mankind, under the pressure of calamity, to live by,—what a manifest failure is this last word of the religion of pleasure! One man in many millions, a Heine, may console himself, and keep himself erect in suffering, by a colossal irony of this sort, by covering himself and the universe with the red fire of this sinister mockery; but the many millions cannot,—cannot if they would. That is where the sentiment of a religion of sorrow has such a vast advantage over the sentiment of a religion of pleas-

ure; in its power to be a general, popular, religious sentiment, a stay for the mass of mankind, whose lives are full of hardship. It really succeeds in conveying far more joy, far more of what the mass of mankind are so much without, than its rival. I do
5   not mean joy in prospect only, but joy in possession, actual enjoyment of the world. Mediæval Christianity is reproached with its gloom and austerities; it assigns the material world, says Heine, to the devil. But yet what a fulness of delight does St. Francis manage to draw from this material world itself, and
10   from its commonest and most universally enjoyed elements, —sun, air, earth, water, plants! His hymn expresses a far more cordial sense of happiness, even in the material world, than the hymn of Theocritus. It is this which made the fortune of Christianity,—its gladness, not its sorrow; not its assigning the
15   spiritual world to Christ, and the material world to the devil, but its drawing from the spiritual world a source of joy so abundant that it ran over upon the material world and transfigured it.

     I have said a great deal of harm of paganism; and, taking
20   paganism to mean a state of things which it is commonly taken to mean, and which did really exist, no more harm than it well deserved. Yet I must not end without reminding the reader, that before this state of things appeared, there was an epoch in Greek life,—in pagan life,—of the highest possible beauty and
25   value. That epoch by itself goes far towards making Greece the Greece we mean when we speak of Greece,—a country hardly less important to mankind than Judæa. The poetry of later paganism lived by the senses and understanding; the poetry of mediæval Christianity lived by the heart and imagina-
30   tion. But the main element of the modern spirit's life is neither the senses and understanding, nor the heart and imagination; it is the imaginative reason. And there is a century in Greek life, —the century preceding the Peloponnesian war, from about the year 530 to the year 430 B.C.,—in which poetry made, it
35   seems to me, the noblest, the most successful effort she has ever made as the priestess of the imaginative reason, of the element by which the modern spirit, if it would live right, has chiefly to live. Of this effort, of which the four great names are

Simonides, Pindar, Æschylus, Sophocles, I must not now attempt more than the bare mention; but it is right, it is necessary, after all I have said, to indicate it. No doubt that effort was imperfect. Perhaps everything, take it at what point in its existence you will, carries within itself the fatal law of its own ulterior development. Perhaps, even of the life of Pindar's time, Pompeii was the inevitable bourne. Perhaps the life of their beautiful Greece could not afford to its poets all that fulness of varied experience, all that power of emotion, which

> "... the heavy and the weary weight
> Of all this unintelligible world"

affords the poet of after-times. Perhaps in Sophocles the thinking-power a little overbalances the religious sense, as in Dante the religious sense overbalances the thinking-power. The present has to make its own poetry, and not even Sophocles and his compeers, any more than Dante and Shakspeare, are enough for it. That I will not dispute; nor will I set up the Greek poets, from Pindar to Sophocles, as objects of blind worship. But no other poets so well show to the poetry of the present the way it must take; no other poets have lived so much by the imaginative reason; no other poets have made their work so well balanced; no other poets, who have so well satisfied the thinking-power, have so well satisfied the religious sense:—

"Oh! that my lot may lead me in the path of holy innocence of word and deed, the path which august laws ordain, laws that in the highest empyrean had their birth, of which Heaven is the father alone, neither did the race of mortal men beget them, nor shall oblivion ever put them to sleep. The power of God is mighty in them, and groweth not old."

Let St. Francis,—nay, or Luther either,—beat that!

The Literary Influence of Academies

It is impossible to put down a book like the history of the
French Academy, by Pellisson and D'Olivet, which M. Charles
Livet has lately re-edited, without being led to reflect upon the
absence, in our own country, of any institution like the French
5   Academy, upon the probable causes of this absence, and upon
its results. A thousand voices will be ready to tell us that this
absence is a signal mark of our national superiority; that it is
in great part owing to this absence that the exhilarating words
of Lord Macaulay, lately given to the world by his very clever
10 nephew, Mr. Trevelyan, are so profoundly true: "It may safely
be said that the literature now extant in the English language
is of far greater value than all the literature which three hundred years ago was extant in all the languages of the world together." I daresay this is so; only, remembering Spinoza's
15 maxim that the two great banes of humanity are self-conceit
and the laziness coming from self-conceit, I think it may do us
good, instead of resting in our pre-eminence with perfect security, to look a little more closely why this is so, and whether
it is so without any limitations.
20   But first of all I must give a very few words to the outward
history of the French Academy. About the year 1629, seven
or eight persons in Paris, fond of literature, formed themselves into a sort of little club to meet at one another's houses
and discuss literary matters. Their meetings got talked of, and
25 Cardinal Richelieu, then minister and all-powerful, heard of
them. He himself had a noble passion for letters, and for all
fine culture; he was interested by what he heard of the nascent
society. Himself a man in the grand style, if ever man was, he
had the insight to perceive what a potent instrument of the

grand style was here to his hand. It was the beginning of a great century for France, the seventeenth; men's minds were working, the French language was forming. Richelieu sent to ask the members of the new society whether they would be willing to become a body with a public character, holding regular meetings. Not without a little hesitation,—for apparently they found themselves very well as they were, and these seven or eight gentlemen of a social and literary turn were not perfectly at their ease as to what the great and terrible minister could want with them,—they consented. The favours of a man like Richelieu are not easily refused, whether they are honestly meant or no; but this favour of Richelieu's was meant quite honestly. The Parliament, however, had its doubts of this. The Parliament had none of Richelieu's enthusiasm about letters and culture; it was jealous of the apparition of a new public body in the State; above all, of a body called into existence by Richelieu. The King's letters-patent, establishing and authorising the new society, were granted early in 1635; but, by the old constitution of France, these letters-patent required the verification of the Parliament. It was two years and a half—towards the autumn of 1637—before the Parliament would give it; and it then gave it only after pressing solicitations, and earnest assurances of the innocent intentions of the young Academy. Jocose people said that this society, with its mission to purify and embellish the language, filled with terror a body of lawyers like the French Parliament, the stronghold of barbarous jargon and of chicane.

This improvement of the language was in truth the declared grand aim for the operations of the Academy. Its statutes of foundation, approved by Richelieu before the royal edict establishing it was issued, say expressly: "The Academy's principal function shall be to work with all the care and all the diligence possible at giving sure rules to our language, and rendering it pure, eloquent, and capable of treating the arts and sciences." This zeal for making a nation's great instrument of thought,—its language,—correct and worthy, is undoubtedly a sign full of promise,—a weighty earnest of future power. It is said that Richelieu had it in his mind that French should suc-

ceed Latin in its general ascendency, as Latin had succeeded
Greek; if it was so, even this wish has to some extent been fulfilled. But, at any rate, the *ethical* influences of style in language,
—its close relations, so often pointed out, with character,—
5   are most important. Richelieu, a man of high culture, and, at
the same time, of great character, felt them profoundly; and
that he should have sought to regularise, strengthen, and perpetuate them by an institution for perfecting language, is alone
a striking proof of his governing spirit and of his genius.

10   This was not all he had in his mind, however. The new
Academy, now enlarged to a body of forty members, and
meant to contain all the chief literary men of France, was to
be a *literary tribunal*. The works of its members were to be
brought before it previous to publication, were to be criticised
15   by it, and finally, if it saw fit, to be published with its declared
approbation. The works of other writers, not members of the
Academy, might also, at the request of these writers themselves, be passed under the Academy's review. Besides this, in
essays and discussions the Academy examined and judged works
20   already published, whether by living or dead authors, and literary matters in general. The celebrated opinion on Corneille's
Cid, delivered in 1637 by the Academy at Richelieu's urgent
request, when this poem, which strongly occupied public attention, had been attacked by M. de Scudéry, shows how fully
25   Richelieu designed his new creation to do duty as a supreme
court of literature, and how early it in fact began to exercise
this function. One [1] who had known Richelieu declared, after
the Cardinal's death, that he had projected a yet greater institution than the Academy, a sort of grand European college
30   of art, science, and literature, a Prytaneum, where the chief
authors of all Europe should be gathered together in one central home, there to live in security, leisure, and honour;—that
was a dream which will not bear to be pulled about too roughly.
But the project of forming a high court of letters for France
35   was no dream; Richelieu in great measure fulfilled it. This is
what the Academy, by its idea, really is; this is what it has
always tended to become; this is what it has, from time to time,

[1] La Mesnardière.

really been; by being, or tending to be this, far more than even by what it has done for the language, it is of such importance in France. To give the law, the tone to literature, and that tone a high one, is its business. "Richelieu meant it," says M. Sainte-Beuve, "to be a *haut jury*,"—a jury the most choice and authoritative that could be found on all important literary matters in question before the public; to be, as it in fact became in the latter half of the eighteenth century, "a sovereign organ of opinion." "The duty of the Academy is," says M. Renan, *"maintenir la délicatesse de l'esprit français"*—to keep the fine quality of the French spirit unimpaired; it represents a kind of *"maîtrise en fait de bon ton"*—the authority of a recognised master in matters of tone and taste. "All ages," says M. Renan again, "have had their inferior literature; but the great danger of our time is that this inferior literature tends more and more to get the upper place. No one has the same advantage as the Academy for fighting against this mischief;" the Academy, which, as he says elsewhere, has even special facilities for "creating a form of intellectual culture *which shall impose itself on all around.*" M. Sainte-Beuve and M. Renan are, both of them, very keen-sighted critics; and they show it signally by seizing and putting so prominently forward this character of the French Academy.

Such an effort to set up a recognised authority, imposing on us a high standard in matters of intellect and taste, has many enemies in human nature. We all of us like to go our own way, and not to be forced out of the atmosphere of commonplace habitual to most of us;—*"was uns alle bändigt,"* says Goethe, *"das Gemeine."* We like to be suffered to lie comfortably in the old straw of our habits, especially of our intellectual habits, even though this straw may not be very clean and fine. But if the effort to limit this freedom of our lower nature finds, as it does and must find, enemies in human nature, it finds also auxiliaries in it. Out of the four great parts, says Cicero, of the *honestum*, or good, which forms the matter on which *officium*, or human duty, finds employment, one is the fixing of a *modus* and an *ordo*, a measure and an order, to fashion and wholesomely constrain our action, in order to lift it above the level

it keeps if left to itself, and to bring it nearer to perfection.
Man alone of living creatures, he says, goes feeling after *"quid
sit* ordo, *quid sit quod* deceat, *in factis dictisque qui* modus
—the discovery of an *order*, a law of *good taste*, a *measure*
for his words and actions." Other creatures submissively follow
the law of their nature; man alone has an impulse leading him
to set up some other law to control the bent of his nature.

This holds good, of course, as to moral matters, as well as
intellectual matters: and it is of moral matters that we are generally thinking when we affirm it. But it holds good as to intellectual matters too. Now, probably, M. Sainte-Beuve had
not these words of Cicero in his mind when he made, about the
French nation, the assertion I am going to quote; but, for all
that, the assertion leans for support, one may say, upon the
truth conveyed in those words of Cicero, and wonderfully
illustrates and confirms them. "In France," says M. Sainte-
Beuve, "the first consideration for us is not whether we are
amused and pleased by a work of art or mind, nor is it whether
we are touched by it. What we seek above all to learn is,
whether *we were right* in being amused with it, and in applaud-
ing it, and in being moved by it." Those are very remarkable
words, and they are, I believe, in the main quite true. A Frenchman has, to a considerable degree, what one may call a conscience in intellectual matters; he has an active belief that
there is a right and a wrong in them, that he is bound to honour
and obey the right, that he is disgraced by cleaving to the
wrong. All the world has, or professes to have, this conscience
in moral matters. The word *conscience* has become almost confined, in popular use, to the moral sphere, because this lively
susceptibility of feeling is, in the moral sphere, so far more
common than in the intellectual sphere; the livelier, in the
moral sphere, this susceptibility is, the greater becomes a man's
readiness to admit a high standard of action, an ideal authorita-
tively correcting his everyday moral habits; here, such willing
admission of authority is due to sensitiveness of conscience.
And a like deference to a standard higher than one's own habitual standard in intellectual matters, a like respectful recognition of a superior ideal, is caused, in the intellectual sphere,

by sensitiveness of intelligence. Those whose intelligence is quickest, openest, most sensitive, are readiest with this deference; those whose intelligence is less delicate and sensitive are less disposed to it. Well, now we are on the road to see why the French have their Academy and we have nothing of the kind.

What are the essential characteristics of the spirit of our nation? Not, certainly, an open and clear mind, not a quick and flexible intelligence. Our greatest admirers would not claim for us that we have these in a pre-eminent degree; they might say that we had more of them than our detractors gave us credit for; but they would not assert them to be our essential characteristics. They would rather allege, as our chief spiritual characteristics, energy and honesty; and, if we are judged favourably and positively, not invidiously and negatively, our chief characteristics are, no doubt, these:—energy and honesty, not an open and clear mind, not a quick and flexible intelligence. Openness of mind and flexibility of intelligence were very signal characteristics of the Athenian people in ancient times; everybody will feel that. Openness of mind and flexibility of intelligence are remarkable characteristics of the French people in modern times; at any rate, they strikingly characterise them as compared with us; I think everybody, or almost everybody, will feel that. I will not now ask what more the Athenian or the French spirit has than this, nor what shortcomings either of them may have as a set-off against this; all I want now to point out is that they have this, and that we have it in a much lesser degree.

Let me remark, however, that not only in the moral sphere, but also in the intellectual and spiritual sphere, energy and honesty are most important and fruitful qualities; that, for instance, of what we call genius energy is the most essential part. So, by assigning to a nation energy and honesty as its chief spiritual characteristics,—by refusing to it, as at all eminent characteristics, openness of mind and flexibility of intelligence,—we do not by any means, as some people might at first suppose, relegate its importance and its power of manifesting itself with effect from the intellectual to the moral sphere. We only indicate its probable special line of successful ac-

tivity in the intellectual sphere, and, it is true, certain imper-
fections and failings to which, in this sphere, it will always be
subject. Genius is mainly an affair of energy, and poetry is
mainly an affair of genius; therefore, a nation whose spirit is
5   characterised by energy may well be eminent in poetry;—and
we have Shakspeare. Again, the highest reach of science is, one
may say, an inventive power, a faculty of divination, akin to
the highest power exercised in poetry; therefore, a nation
whose spirit is characterised by energy may well be eminent
10   in science;—and we have Newton. Shakspeare and Newton:
in the intellectual sphere there can be no higher names. And
what that energy, which is the life of genius, above everything demands and insists upon, is freedom; entire independence
of all authority, prescription, and routine,—the fullest room to
15   expand as it will. Therefore, a nation whose chief spiritual
characteristic is energy, will not be very apt to set up, in intellectual matters, a fixed standard, an authority, like an academy. By this it certainly escapes certain real inconveniences
and dangers, and it can, at the same time, as we have seen, reach
20   undeniably splendid heights in poetry and science. On the other
hand, some of the requisites of intellectual work are specially
the affair of quickness of mind and flexibility of intelligence.
The form, the method of evolution, the precision, the proportions, the relations of the parts to the whole, in an intellectual
25   work, depend mainly upon them. And these are the elements
of an intellectual work which are really most communicable
from it, which can most be learned and adopted from it, which
have, therefore, the greatest effect upon the intellectual performance of others. Even in poetry, these requisites are very
30   important; and the poetry of a nation, not eminent for the
gifts on which they depend, will, more or less, suffer by this
shortcoming. In poetry, however, they are, after all, secondary,
and energy is the first thing; but in prose they are of first-rate
importance. In its prose literature, therefore, and in the routine
35   of intellectual work generally, a nation with no particular gifts
for these will not be so successful. These are what, as I have
said, can to a certain degree be learned and appropriated, while
the free activity of genius cannot. Academies consecrate and

maintain them, and, therefore, a nation with an eminent turn
for them naturally establishes academies. So far as routine and
authority tend to embarrass energy and inventive genius, academies may be said to be obstructive to energy and inventive
genius, and, to this extent, to the human spirit's general advance.   5
But then this evil is so much compensated by the propagation,
on a large scale, of the mental aptitudes and demands which an
open mind and a flexible intelligence naturally engender,
genius itself, in the long run, so greatly finds its account in
this propagation, and bodies like the French Academy have   10
such power for promoting it, that the general advance of the
human spirit is perhaps, on the whole, rather furthered than
impeded by their existence.

How much greater is our nation in poetry than prose! how
much better, in general, do the productions of its spirit show in   15
the qualities of genius than in the qualities of intelligence! One
may constantly remark this in the work of individuals; how
much more striking, in general, does any Englishman,—of some
vigour of mind, but by no means a poet,—seem in his verse than
in his prose! His verse partly suffers from his not being really a   20
poet, partly, no doubt, from the very same defects which impair
his prose, and he cannot express himself with thorough success
in it. But how much more powerful a personage does he appear
in it, by dint of feeling, and of originality and movement of
ideas, than when he is writing prose! With a Frenchman of like   25
stamp, it is just the reverse: set him to write poetry, he is limited,
artificial, and impotent; set him to write prose, he is free, natural,
and effective. The power of French literature is in its prose-
writers, the power of English literature is in its poets. Nay, many
of the celebrated French poets depend wholly for their fame   30
upon the qualities of intelligence which they exhibit,—qualities
which are the distinctive support of prose; many of the celebrated English prose-writers depend wholly for their fame upon
the qualities of genius and imagination which they exhibit,—
qualities which are the distinctive support of poetry. But, as I   35
have said, the qualities of genius are less transferable than the
qualities of intelligence; less can be immediately learned and appropriated from their product; they are less direct and stringent

intellectual agencies, though they may be more beautiful and divine. Shakspeare and our great Elizabethan group were certainly more gifted writers than Corneille and his group; but what was the sequel to this great literature, this literature of genius, as we may call it, stretching from Marlow to Milton? What did it lead up to in English literature? To our provincial and second-rate literature of the eighteenth century. What, on the other hand, was the sequel to the literature of the French "great century," to this literature of intelligence, as, by comparison with our Elizabethan literature, we may call it; what did it lead up to? To the French literature of the eighteenth century, one of the most powerful and pervasive intellectual agencies that have ever existed,—the greatest European force of the eighteenth century. In science, again, we had Newton, a genius of the very highest order, a type of genius in science, if ever there was one. On the continent, as a sort of counterpart to Newton, there was Leibnitz; a man, it seems to me (though on these matters I speak under correction), of much less creative energy of genius, much less power of divination than Newton, but rather a man of admirable intelligence, a type of intelligence in science, if ever there was one. Well, and what did they each directly lead up to in science? What was the intellectual generation that sprang from each of them? I only repeat what the men of science have themselves pointed out. The man of genius was continued by the English analysts of the eighteenth century, comparatively powerless and obscure followers of the renowned master. The man of intelligence was continued by successors like Bernouilli, Euler, Lagrange, and Laplace, the greatest names in modern mathematics.

What I want the reader to see is, that the question as to the utility of academies to the intellectual life of a nation is not settled when we say, for instance: "Oh, we have never had an academy, and yet we have, confessedly, a very great literature." It still remains to be asked: "What sort of a great literature? a literature great in the special qualities of genius, or great in the special qualities of intelligence?" If in the former, it is by no means sure that either our literature, or the general intellectual life of our nation, has got already, without academies, all that academies can give. Both the one and the other may very well be somewhat wanting in those qualities of intelligence out of a lively sense for which a body like the French Academy, as I have said, springs, and which such a body does a great deal to spread and confirm. Our literature, in spite of the genius mani- fested in it, may fall short in form, method, precision, propor- tions, arrangement,—all of them, I have said, things where in- telligence proper comes in. It may be comparatively weak in prose, that branch of literature where intelligence proper is, so to speak, all in all. In this branch it may show many grave faults to which the want of a quick, flexible intelligence, and of the strict standard which such an intelligence tends to impose, makes it liable; it may be full of hap-hazard, crudeness, provin- cialism, eccentricity, violence, blundering. It may be a less stringent and effective intellectual agency, both upon our own nation and upon the world at large, than other literatures which show less genius, perhaps, but more intelligence.

The right conclusion certainly is that we should try, so far as we can, to make up our shortcomings; and that to this end, instead of always fixing our thoughts upon the points in which our literature, and our intellectual life generally, are strong, we should, from time to time, fix them upon those in which they are weak, and so learn to perceive clearly what we have to amend. What is our second great spiritual characteristic,— our honesty,—good for, if it is not good for this? But it will, —I am sure it will,—more and more, as time goes on, be found good for this.

Well, then, an institution like the French Academy,—an in- stitution owing its existence to a national bent towards the things of the mind, towards culture, towards clearness, correct- ness, and propriety in thinking and speaking, and, in its turn, promoting this bent,—sets standards in a number of directions, and creates, in all these directions, a force of educated opinion, checking and rebuking those who fall below these standards, or who set them at nought. Educated opinion exists here as in France; but in France the Academy serves as a sort of centre and rallying-point to it, and gives it a force which it has not got here. Why is all the *journeyman-work* of literature, as I

may call it, so much worse done here than it is in France? I do
not wish to hurt any one's feelings; but surely this is so. Think
of the difference between our books of reference and those of
the French, between our biographical dictionaries (to take a
5   striking instance) and theirs; think of the difference between
the translations of the classics turned out for Mr. Bohn's library and those turned out for M. Nisard's collection! As a
general rule, hardly any one amongst us, who knows French
and German well, would use an English book of reference
10 when he could get a French or German one; or would look at
an English prose translation of an ancient author when he could
get a French or German one. It is not that there do not exist
in England, as in France, a number of people perfectly well
able to discern what is good, in these things, from what is bad,
15 and preferring what is good; but they are isolated, they form
no powerful body of opinion, they are not strong enough to
set a standard, up to which even the journeyman-work of literature must be brought, if it is to be vendible. Ignorance and
charlatanism in work of this kind are always trying to pass off
20 their wares as excellent, and to cry down criticism as the voice
of an insignificant, over-fastidious minority; they easily persuade the multitude that this is so when the minority is scattered
about as it is here; not so easily when it is banded together as
in the French Academy. So, again, with freaks in dealing with
25 language; certainly all such freaks tend to impair the power
and beauty of language; and how far more common they are
with us than with the French! To take a very familiar instance.
Every one has noticed the way in which the *Times* chooses to
spell the word "diocese;" it always spells it diocess,[1] deriving
30 it, I suppose, from *Zeus* and *census*. The *Journal des Débats*
might just as well write "diocess" instead of "diocèse," but imagine the *Journal des Débats* doing so! Imagine an educated
Frenchman indulging himself in an orthographical antic of this
sort, in face of the grave respect with which the Academy and
35 its dictionary invest the French language! Some people will
say these are little things; they are not; they are of bad ex-

[1] The *Times* has now (1868) abandoned this spelling and adopted the
ordinary one.

ample. They tend to spread the baneful notion that there is
no such thing as a high, correct standard in intellectual matters;
that every one may as well take his own way; they are at variance with the severe discipline necessary for all real culture;
they confirm us in habits of wilfulness and eccentricity, which   5
hurt our minds, and damage our credit with serious people. The
late Mr. Donaldson was certainly a man of great ability, and I,
who am not an Orientalist, do not pretend to judge his *Jashar:*
but let the reader observe the form which a foreign Oriental-
ist's judgment of it naturally takes. M. Renan calls it a *tentative*   10
malheureuse, a failure, in short; this it may be, or it may not be;
I am no judge. But he goes on: "It is astonishing that a recent
article" (in a French periodical, he means) "should have
brought forward as the last word of German exegesis a work
like this, composed by a doctor of the University of Cambridge,   15
and universally condemned by German critics." You see what
he means to imply: an extravagance of this sort could never
have come from Germany, where there is a great force of
critical opinion controlling a learned man's vagaries, and keeping him straight; it comes from the native home of intellectual   20
eccentricity of all kinds,[1]—from England, from a doctor of the
University of Cambridge;—and I daresay he would not expect
much better things from a doctor of the University of Oxford.
Again, after speaking of what Germany and France have done
for the history of Mahomet: "America and England," M.   25
Renan goes on, "have also occupied themselves with Mahomet." He mentions Washington Irving's *Life of Mahomet,*
which does not, he says, evince much of an historical sense, a
sentiment historique fort élevé; "but," he proceeds, "this book
shows a real progress, when one thinks that in 1829 Mr. Charles   30
Forster published two thick volumes, which enchanted the
English *réverends,* to make out that Mahomet was the little
horn of the he-goat that figures in the eighth chapter of Daniel,
and that the Pope was the great horn. Mr. Forster founded on

[1] A critic declares I am wrong in saying that M. Renan's language im-   35
plies this. I still think that there is a shade, a *nuance* of expression, in M.
Renan's language, which does imply this; but, I confess, the only person
who can really settle such a question is M. Renan himself.

this ingenious parallel a whole philosophy of history, according
to which the Pope represented the Western corruption of
Christianity, and Mahomet the Eastern; thence the striking
resemblances between Mahometanism and Popery." And in a
note M. Renan adds: "This is the same Mr. Charles Forster who
is the author of a mystification about the Sinaitic inscriptions,
in which he declares he finds the primitive language." As much
as to say: "It is an Englishman, be surprised at no extravagance."
If these innuendoes had no ground, and were made in hatred
and malice, they would not be worth a moment's attention; but
they come from a grave Orientalist, on his own subject, and
they point to a real fact;—the absence, in this country, of any
force of educated literary and scientific opinion, making aberrations like those of the author of *The One Primeval Language*
out of the question. Not only the author of such aberrations,
often a very clever man, suffers by the want of check, by the
not being kept straight, and spends force in vain on a false road,
which, under better discipline, he might have used with profit
on a true one; but all his adherents, both "reverends" and others,
suffer too, and the general rate of information and judgment is
is in this way kept low.

In a production which we have all been reading lately, a
production stamped throughout with a literary quality very
rare in this country, and of which I shall have a word to say
presently—*urbanity;* in this production, the work of a man
never to be named by any son of Oxford without sympathy, a
man who alone in Oxford of his generation, alone of many
generations, conveyed to us in his genius that same charm, that
same ineffable sentiment which this exquisite place itself conveys,—I mean Dr. Newman,—an expression is frequently used
which is more common in theological than in literary language,
but which seems to me fitted to be of general service; the *note*
of so and so, the note of catholicity, the note of antiquity, the
note of sanctity, and so on. Adopting this expressive word, I
say that in the bulk of the intellectual work of a nation which
has no centre, no intellectual metropolis like an academy, like
M. Sainte-Beuve's "sovereign organ of opinion," like M.

Renan's "recognised authority in matters of tone and taste,"
—there is observable a *note of provinciality*. Now to get rid
of provinciality is a certain stage of culture; a stage the positive result of which we must not make of too much importance,
but which is, nevertheless, indispensable, for it brings us on to   5
the platform where alone the best and highest intellectual work
can be said fairly to begin. Work done after men have reached
this platform is *classical;* and that is the only work which, in
the long run, can stand. All the *scoriæ* in the work of men of
great genius who have not lived on this platform are due to   10
their not having lived on it. Genius raises them to it by moments, and the portions of their work which are immortal are
done at these moments; but more of it would have been immortal if they had not reached this platform at moments only, if
they had had the culture which makes men live there.   15

The less a literature has felt the influence of a supposed
centre of correct information, correct judgment, correct taste,
the more we shall find in it this note of provinciality. I have
shown the note of provinciality as caused by remoteness from
a centre of correct information. Of course the note of provin-   20
ciality from the want of a centre of correct taste is still more
visible, and it is also still more common. For here great—even
the greatest—powers of mind most fail a man. Great powers
of mind will make him inform himself thoroughly, great powers of mind will make him think profoundly, even with igno-   25
rance and platitude all round him; but not even great powers
of mind will keep his taste and style perfectly sound and sure,
if he is left too much to himself, with no "sovereign organ of
opinion" in these matters near him. Even men like Jeremy
Taylor and Burke suffer here. Take this passage from Taylor's   30
funeral sermon on Lady Carbery:—

"So have I seen a river, deep and smooth, passing with a still
foot and a sober face, and paying to the *fiscus,* the great exchequer of the sea, a tribute large and full; and hard by it a little
brook, skipping and making a noise upon its unequal and   35
neighbour bottom; and after all its talking and bragged motion, it paid to its common audit no more than the revenues of

a little cloud or a contemptible vessel: so have I sometimes compared the issues of her religion to the solemnities and famed
outsides of another's piety."

That passage has been much admired, and, indeed, the genius
5 in it is undeniable. I should say, for my part, that genius, the
ruling divinity of poetry, had been too busy in it, and intelligence, the ruling divinity of prose, not busy enough. But can
any one, with the best models of style in his head, help feeling
the note of provinciality there, the want of simplicity, the want
10 of measure, the want of just the qualities that make prose
classical? If he does not feel what I mean, let him place beside
the passage of Taylor this passage from the Panegyric of St.
Paul, by Taylor's contemporary, Bossuet:—

"Il ira, cet ignorant dans l'art de bien dire, avec cette locu-
15 tion rude, avec cette phrase qui sent l'étranger, il ira en cette
Grèce polie, la mère des philosophes et des orateurs; et malgré
la résistance du monde, il y établira plus d'Eglises que Platon
n'y a gagné de disciples par cette éloquence qu'on a crue
divine."

20 There we have prose without the note of provinciality—
classical prose, prose of the centre.

Or take Burke, our greatest English prose-writer, as I think;
take expressions like this:—

"Blindfold themselves, like bulls that shut their eyes when
25 they push, they drive, by the point of their bayonets, their
slaves, blindfolded, indeed, no worse than their lords, to take
their fictions for currencies, and to swallow down paper pills
by thirty-four millions sterling at a dose."

Or this:—

30 "They used it" (the royal name) "as a sort of navel-string,
to nourish their unnatural offspring from the bowels of royalty
itself. Now that the monster can purvey for its own subsistence,
it will only carry the mark about it, as a token of its having
torn the womb it came from."

35 Or this:—

"Without one natural pang, he" (Rousseau) "casts away, as a
sort of offal and excrement, the spawn of his disgustful amours,
and sends his children to the hospital of foundlings."

Or this:—

"I confess I never liked this continual talk of resistance and revolution, or the practice of making the extreme medicine of the constitution its daily bread. It renders the habit of society dangerously valetudinary; it is taking periodical doses of mercury sublimate, and swallowing down repeated provocatives of cantharides to our love of liberty."

I say that is extravagant prose; prose too much suffered to indulge its caprices; prose at too great a distance from the centre of good taste; prose, in short, with the note of provinciality. People may reply, it is rich and imaginative; yes, that is just it, it is *Asiatic* prose, as the ancient critics would have said; prose somewhat barbarously rich and overloaded. But the true prose is Attic prose.

Well, but Addison's prose is Attic prose. Where, then, it may be asked, is the note of provinciality in Addison? I answer, in the commonplace of his ideas.[1] This is a matter worth remarking. Addison claims to take leading rank as a moralist. To do that, you must have ideas of the first order on your subject— the best ideas, at any rate, attainable in your time—as well as be able to express them in a perfectly sound and sure style. Else you show your distance from the centre of ideas by your matter; you are provincial by your matter, though you may not be provincial by your style. It is comparatively a small matter to express oneself well, if one will be content with not expressing much, with expressing only trite ideas; the problem

---

[1] A critic says this is paradoxical, and urges that many second-rate French academicians have uttered the most commonplace ideas possible. I agree that many second-rate French academicians have uttered the most commonplace ideas possible; but Addison is not a second-rate man. He is a man of the order, I will not say of Pascal, but at any rate of La Bruyère and Vauvenargues; why does he not equal them? I say because of the medium in which he finds himself, the atmosphere in which he lives and works; an atmosphere which tells unfavourably, or rather *tends* to tell unfavourably (for that is the truer way of putting it) either upon style or else upon ideas; tends to make even a man of great ability either a Mr. Carlyle or else a Lord Macaulay.

It is to be observed, however, that Lord Macaulay's style has in its turn suffered by his failure in ideas, and this cannot be said of Addison's.

is to express new and profound ideas in a perfectly sound and
classical style. He is the true classic, in every age, who does that.
Now Addison has not, on his subject of morals, the force of
ideas of the moralists of the first class—the classical moralists;
he has not the best ideas attainable in or about his time, and
which were, so to speak, in the air then, to be seized by the
finest spirits; he is not to be compared for power, searchingness,
or delicacy of thought to Pascal or La Bruyère or Vauvenargues;
he is rather on a level, in this respect, with a man like Marmontel. Therefore, I say, he has the note of provinciality as a
moralist; he is provincial by his matter, though not by his style.

To illustrate what I mean by an example. Addison, writing
as a moralist on fixedness in religious faith, says:—

"Those who delight in reading books of controversy do
very seldom arrive at a fixed and settled habit of faith. The
doubt which was laid revives again, and shows itself in new
difficulties; and that generally for this reason,—because the
mind, which is perpetually tossed in controversies and disputes,
is apt to forget the reasons which had once set it at rest, and to
be disquieted with any former perplexity when it appears in a
new shape, or is started by a different hand."

It may be said, that is classical English, perfect in lucidity,
measure, and propriety. I make no objection; but, in my turn,
I say that the idea expressed is perfectly trite and barren, and
that it is a note of provinciality in Addison, in a man whom a
nation puts forward as one of its great moralists, to have no profounder and more striking idea to produce on this great subject. Compare, on the same subject, these words of a moralist
really of the first order, really at the centre by his ideas,—
Joubert:—

"L'expérience de beaucoup d'opinions donne à l'esprit beaucoup de flexibilité et l'affermit dans celles qu'il croit les meil-
leures."

With what a flash of light that touches the subject! how it sets
us thinking! what a genuine contribution to moral science it is!

In short, where there is no centre like an academy, if you
have genius and powerful ideas, you are apt not to have the

best style going; if you have precision of style and not genius, you are apt not to have the best ideas going.

The provincial spirit, again, exaggerates the value of its ideas for want of a high standard at hand by which to try them. Or rather, for want of such a standard, it gives one idea too much prominence at the expense of others; it orders its ideas amiss; it is hurried away by fancies; it likes and dislikes too passionately, too exclusively. Its admiration weeps hysterical tears, and its disapprobation foams at the mouth. So we get the *eruptive* and the *aggressive* manner in literature; the former prevails most in our criticism, the latter in our newspapers. For, not having the lucidity of a large and centrally placed intelligence, the provincial spirit has not its graciousness; it does not persuade, it makes war; it has not urbanity, the tone of the city, of the centre, the tone which always aims at a spiritual and intellectual effect, and not excluding the use of banter, never disjoins banter itself from politeness, from felicity. But the provincial tone is more violent, and seems to aim rather at an effect upon the blood and senses than upon the spirit and intellect; it loves hard-hitting rather than persuading. The newspaper, with its party spirit, its thorough-goingness, its resolute avoidance of shades and distinctions, its short, highly-charged, heavy-shotted articles, its style so unlike that style *lenis minimèque pertinax*—easy and not too violently insisting,— which the ancients so much admired, is its true literature; the provincial spirit likes in the newspaper just what makes the newspaper such bad food for it,—just what made Goethe say, when he was pressed hard about the immorality of Byron's poems, that, after all, they were not so immoral as the newspapers. The French talk of the *brutalité des journaux anglais*. What strikes them comes from the necessary inherent tendencies of newspaper-writing not being checked in England by any centre of intelligent and urbane spirit, but rather stimulated by coming in contact with a provincial spirit. Even a newspaper like the *Saturday Review*, that old friend of all of us, a newspaper expressly aiming at an immunity from the common newspaper-spirit, aiming at being a sort of organ of reason,—

and, by thus aiming, it merits great gratitude and has done great good,—even the *Saturday Review*, replying to some foreign criticism on our precautions against invasion, falls into a strain of this kind:—

5   "To do this" (to take these precautions) "seems to us eminently worthy of a great nation, and to talk of it as unworthy of a great nation, seems to us eminently worthy of a great fool."

There is what the French mean when they talk of the *bru-*
10   *talité des journaux anglais;* there is a style certainly as far removed from urbanity as possible,—a style with what I call the note of provinciality. And the same note may not unfrequently be observed even in the ideas of this newspaper, full as it is of thought and cleverness: certain ideas allowed to
15   become fixed ideas, to prevail too absolutely. I will not speak of the immediate present, but, to go a little while back, it had the critic who so disliked the Emperor of the French; it had the critic who so disliked the subject of my present remarks—academies; it had the critic who was so fond of the German
20   element in our nation, and, indeed, everywhere; who ground his teeth if one said *Charlemagne* instead of *Charles the Great*, and, in short, saw all things in Teutonism, as Malebranche saw all things in God. Certainly any one may fairly find faults in the Emperor Napoleon or in academies, and merit in the German
25   element; but it is a note of the provincial spirit not to hold ideas of this kind a little more easily, to be so devoured by them, to suffer them to become crotchets.

In England there needs a miracle of genius like Shakspeare's to produce balance of mind, and a miracle of intellectual del-
30   icacy like Dr. Newman's to produce urbanity of style. How prevalent all round us is the want of balance of mind and urbanity of style! How much, doubtless, it is to be found in ourselves,—in each of us! but, as human nature is constituted, every one can see it clearest in his contemporaries. There, above
35   all, we should consider it, because they and we are exposed to the same influences; and it is in the best of one's contemporaries that it is most worth considering, because one then most feels the harm it does, when one sees what they would be without it.

Think of the difference between Mr. Ruskin exercising his genius, and Mr. Ruskin exercising his intelligence; consider the truth and beauty of this:—

"Go out, in the spring-time, among the meadows that slope from the shores of the Swiss lakes to the roots of their lower mountains. There, mingled with the taller gentians and the white narcissus, the grass grows deep and free; and as you follow the winding mountain paths, beneath arching boughs all veiled and dim with blossom,—paths that for ever droop and rise over the green banks and mounds sweeping down in scented undulation, steep to the blue water, studded here and there with new-mown heaps, filling all the air with fainter sweetness,—look up towards the higher hills, where the waves of everlasting green roll silently into their long inlets among the shadows of the pines......"

There is what the genius, the feeling, the temperament in Mr. Ruskin, the original and incommunicable part, has to do with; and how exquisite it is! All the critic could possibly suggest, in the way of objection, would be, perhaps, that Mr. Ruskin is there trying to make prose do more than it can perfectly do; that what he is there attempting he will never, except in poetry, be able to accomplish to his own entire satisfaction: but he accomplishes so much that the critic may well hesitate to suggest even this. Place beside this charming passage another,—a passage about Shakspeare's names, where the intelligence and judgment of Mr. Ruskin, the acquired, trained, communicable part in him, are brought into play,—and see the difference:—

"Of Shakspeare's names I will afterwards speak at more length; they are curiously—often barbarously—mixed out of various traditions and languages. Three of the clearest in meaning have been already noticed. Desdemona—'δυσδαιμονία,' *miserable fortune*—is also plain enough. Othello is, I believe, 'the careful;' all the calamity of the tragedy arising from the single flaw and error in his magnificently collected strength. Ophelia, 'serviceableness,' the true, lost wife of Hamlet, is marked as having a Greek name by that of her brother, Laertes; and its signification is once exquisitely alluded to in that brother's last

word of her, where her gentle preciousness is opposed to the
uselessness of the churlish clergy:—'A *ministering* angel shall
my sister be, when thou liest howling.' Hamlet is, I believe,
connected in some way with 'homely,' the entire event of the
5 tragedy turning on betrayal of home duty. Hermione (ἕρμα),
'pillar-like' (ἧ εἶδος ἔχε χρυσέης Ἀφροδίτης); Titania (τιτήνη), 'the
queen;' Benedick and Beatrice, 'blessed and blessing;' Valen-
tine and Proteus, 'enduring or strong' (*valens*), and 'changeful.'
Iago and Iachimo have evidently the same root—probably
10 the Spanish Iago, Jacob, 'the supplanter.' "

Now, really, what a piece of extravagance all that is! I will
not say that the meaning of Shakspeare's names (I put aside
the question as to the correctness of Mr. Ruskin's etymologies)
has no effect at all, may be entirely lost sight of; but to give
15 it that degree of prominence is to throw the reins to one's
whim, to forget all moderation and proportion, to lose the
balance of one's mind altogether. It is to show in one's criticism,
to the highest excess, the note of provinciality.

Again, there is Mr. Palgrave, certainly endowed with a
20 very fine critical tact: his *Golden Treasury* abundantly proves
it. The plan of arrangement which he devised for that work, the
mode in which he followed his plan out, nay, one might even
say, merely the juxtaposition, in pursuance of it, of two such
pieces as those of Wordsworth and Shelley which form the
25 285th and 286th in his collection, show a delicacy of feeling in
these matters which is quite indisputable and very rare. And
his notes are full of remarks which show it too. All the more
striking, conjoined with so much justness of perception, are
certain freaks and violences in Mr. Palgrave's criticism, mainly
30 imputable, I think, to the critic's isolated position in this country, to his feeling himself too much left to take his own way,
too much without any central authority representing high
culture and sound judgment, by which he may be, on the one
hand, confirmed as against the ignorant, on the other, held in
35 respect when he himself is inclined to take liberties. I mean
such things as this note on Milton's line,—

"The great Emathian conqueror bade spare" . . .

"When Thebes was destroyed, Alexander ordered the house of Pindar to be spared. *He was as incapable of appreciating the poet as Louis XIV. of appreciating Racine; but even the narrow and barbarian mind of Alexander could understand the advantage of a showy act of homage to poetry.*" A note like that I call a freak or a violence; if this disparaging view of Alexander and Louis XIV., so unlike the current view, is wrong,—if the current view is, after all, the truer one of them,—the note is a freak. But, even if its disparaging view is right, the note is a violence; for, abandoning the true mode of intellectual action—persuasion, the instilment of conviction,—it simply astounds and irritates the hearer by contradicting, without a word of proof or preparation, his fixed and familiar notions; and this is mere violence. In either case, the fitness, the measure, the centrality, which is the soul of all good criticism, is lost, and the note of provinciality shows itself.

Thus, in the famous *Handbook*, marks of a fine power of perception are everywhere discernible, but so, too, are marks of the want of sure balance, of the check and support afforded by knowing one speaks before good and severe judges. When Mr. Palgrave dislikes a thing, he feels no pressure constraining him either to try his dislike closely or to express it moderately; he does not mince matters, he gives his dislike all its own way; both his judgment and his style would gain if he were under more restraint. "The style which has filled London with the dead monotony of Gower or Harley Streets, or the pale commonplace of Belgravia, Tyburnia, and Kensington; which has pierced Paris and Madrid with the feeble frivolities of the Rue Rivoli and the Strada de Toledo." He dislikes the architecture of the Rue Rivoli, and he puts it on a level with the architecture of Belgravia and Gower Street; he lumps them all together in one condemnation, he loses sight of the shade, the distinction, which is everything here; the distinction, namely, that the architecture of the Rue Rivoli expresses show, splendour, pleasure,—unworthy things, perhaps, to express alone and for their own sakes, but it expresses them; whereas the architecture of Gower Street and Belgravia merely expresses the impotence of the architect to express anything. Then, as to style:

"sculpture which stands in a contrast with Woolner hardly more shameful than diverting," ... "passing from Davy or Faraday to the art of the mountebank or the science of the spirit-rapper," ... "it is the old, old story with Marochetti, the frog trying to blow himself out to bull dimensions. He may puff and be puffed, but he will never do it." We all remember that shower of amenities on poor M. Marochetti. Now, here Mr. Palgrave himself enables us to form a contrast which lets us see just what the presence of an academy does for style; for he quotes a criticism by M. Gustave Planche on this very M. Marochetti. M. Gustave Planche was a critic of the very first order, a man of strong opinions, which he expressed with severity; he, too, condemns M. Marochetti's work, and Mr. Palgrave calls him as a witness to back what he has himself said; certainly Mr. Palgrave's translation will not exaggerate M. Planche's urbanity in dealing with M. Marochetti, but, even in this translation, see the difference in sobriety, in measure, between the critic writing in Paris and the critic writing in London:—

"These conditions are so elementary, that I am at a perfect loss to comprehend how M. Marochetti has neglected them. There are soldiers here like the leaden playthings of the nursery: it is almost impossible to guess whether there is a body beneath the dress. We have here no question of style, not even of grammar; it is nothing beyond mere matter of the alphabet of art. To break these conditions is the same as to be ignorant of spelling."

That is really more formidable criticism than Mr. Palgrave's, and yet in how perfectly temperate a style! M. Planche's advantage is, that he feels himself to be speaking before competent judges, that there is a force of cultivated opinion for him to appeal to. Therefore, he must not be extravagant, and he need not storm; he must satisfy the reason and taste,— that is his business. Mr. Palgrave, on the other hand, feels himself to be speaking before a promiscuous multitude, with the few good judges so scattered through it as to be powerless; therefore, he has no calm confidence and no self-control; he relies on the strength of his lungs; he knows that big words impose on the mob, and that, even if he is outrageous, most of his audience are apt to be a great deal more so.[1]

Again, the first two volumes of Mr. Kinglake's *Invasion of the Crimea* were certainly among the most successful and renowned English books of our time. Their style was one of the most renowned things about them, and yet how conspicuous a fault in Mr. Kinglake's style is this over-charge of which I have been speaking! Mr. James Gordon Bennett, of the *New York Herald*, says, I believe, that the highest achievement of the human intellect is what he calls "a good editorial." This is not quite so; but, if it were so, on what a height would these two volumes by Mr. Kinglake stand! I have already spoken of the Attic and the Asiatic styles; besides these, there is the Corinthian style. That is the style for "a good editorial," and Mr. Kinglake has really reached perfection in it. It has not the warm glow, blithe movement, and soft pliancy of life, as the Attic style has; it has not the over-heavy richness and encumbered gait of the Asiatic style; it has glitter without warmth, rapidity without ease, effectiveness without charm. Its characteristic is, that it has no *soul;* all it exists for, is to get its ends, to make its points, to damage its adversaries, to be admired, to triumph. A style so bent on effect at the expense of soul, simplicity, and delicacy; a style so little studious of the charm of the great models; so far from classic truth and grace, must surely be said to have the note of provinciality. Yet Mr. Kinglake's talent is a really eminent one, and so in harmony with our intellectual habits and tendencies, that, to the great bulk of English people, the faults of his style seem its merits; all the more needful that criticism should not be dazzled by them.

We must not compare a man of Mr. Kinglake's literary talent with French writers like M. de Bazancourt. We must compare him with M. Thiers. And what a superiority in style has M. Thiers from being formed in a good school, with severe traditions, wholesome restraining influences! Even in this age of Mr. James Gordon Bennett, his style has nothing

---

[1] When I wrote this I had before me the first edition of Mr. Palgrave's *Handbook.* I am bound to say that in the second edition much strong language has been expunged, and what remains, softened.

Corinthian about it; its lightness and brightness make it almost
Attic. It is not quite Attic, however; it has not the infallible
sureness of Attic taste. Sometimes his head gets a little hot
with the fumes of patriotism, and then he crosses the line, he
5   loses perfect measure, he declaims, he raises a momentary smile.
France condemned "à être l'effroi du monde *dont elle pourrait
être l'amour*,"—Cæsar, whose exquisite simplicity M. Thiers so
much admires, would not have written like that. There is, if
I may be allowed to say so, the slightest possible touch of
10   fatuity in such language,—of that failure in good sense which
comes from too warm a self-satisfaction. But compare this
language with Mr. Kinglake's Marshal St. Arnaud—"dismissed
from the presence" of Lord Raglan or Lord Stratford, "cowed
and pressed down" under their "stern reproofs," or under "the
15   majesty of the great Elchi's Canning brow and tight, merciless
lips!" The failure in good sense and good taste there reaches
far beyond what the French mean by *fatuity;* they would
call it by another word, a word expressing blank defect of
intelligence, a word for which we have no exact equivalent
20   in English,—*bête*. It is the difference between a venial, momentary, good-tempered excess, in a man of the world, of an
amiable and social weakness,—vanity; and a serious, settled,
fierce, narrow, provincial misconception of the whole relative
value of one's own things and the things of others. So baneful
25   to the style of even the cleverest man may be the total want
of checks.

    In all I have said, I do not pretend that the examples given
prove my rule as to the influence of academies; they only illustrate it. Examples in plenty might very likely be found to
30   set against them; the truth of the rule depends, no doubt, on
whether the balance of all the examples is in its favour or not;
but actually to strike this balance is always out of the question.
Here, as everywhere else, the rule, the idea, if true, commends
itself to the judicious, and then the examples make it clearer
35   still to them. This is the real use of examples, and this alone is
the purpose which I have meant mine to serve. There is also
another side to the whole question,—as to the limiting and prej-
udicial operation which academies may have; but this side of

the question it rather behoves the French, not us, to study.

The reader will ask for some practical conclusion about the establishment of an Academy in this country, and perhaps I shall hardly give him the one he expects. But nations have their own modes of acting, and these modes are not easily changed; they are even consecrated, when great things have been done in them. When a literature has produced Shakspeare and Milton, when it has even produced Barrow and Burke, it cannot well abandon its traditions; it can hardly begin, at this late time of day, with an institution like the French Academy. I think academies with a limited, special, scientific scope, in the various lines of intellectual work,—academies like that of Berlin, for instance,—we with time may, and probably shall, establish. And no doubt they will do good; no doubt the presence of such influential centres of correct information will tend to raise the standard amongst us for what I have called the *journeyman-work* of literature, and to free us from the scandal of such biographical dictionaries as Chalmers's, or such translations as a recent one of Spinoza, or perhaps, such philological freaks as Mr. Forster's about the one primeval language. But an academy quite like the French Academy, a sovereign organ of the highest literary opinion, a recognised authority in matters of intellectual tone and taste, we shall hardly have, and perhaps we ought not to wish to have it. But then every one amongst us with any turn for literature will do well to remember to what shortcomings and excesses, which such an academy tends to correct, we are liable; and the more liable, of course, for not having it. He will do well constantly to try himself in respect of these, steadily to widen his culture, severely to check in himself the provincial spirit; and he will do this the better the more he keeps in mind that all mere glorification by ourselves of ourselves or our literature, in the strain of what, at the beginning of these remarks, I quoted from Lord Macaulay, is both vulgar, and, besides being vulgar, retarding.

The Function of Criticism at the Present Time

Many objections have been made to a proposition which, in some remarks of mine on translating Homer, I ventured to put forth; a proposition about criticism, and its importance at the present day. I said: "Of the literature of France and Germany, as of the intellect of Europe in general, the main effort, for now many years, has been a critical effort; the endeavour, in all branches of knowledge, theology, philosophy, history, art, science, to see the object as in itself it really is." I added, that owing to the operation in English literature of certain causes, "almost the last thing for which one would come to English literature is just that very thing which now Europe most desires,—criticism;" and that the power and value of English literature was thereby impaired. More than one rejoinder declared that the importance I here assigned to criticism was excessive, and asserted the inherent superiority of the creative effort of the human spirit over its critical effort. And the other day, having been led by Mr. Shairp's excellent notice of Wordsworth [1] to turn again to his biography, I found, in the words of this great man, whom I, for one, must always listen to with the profoundest respect, a sentence passed on the critic's business,

[1] I cannot help thinking that a practice, common in England during the last century, and still followed in France, of printing a notice of this kind,—a notice by a competent critic,—to serve as an introduction to an eminent author's works, might be revived among us with advantage. To introduce all succeeding editions of Wordsworth, Mr. Shairp's notice might, it seems to me, excellently serve; it is written from the point of view of an admirer, nay, of a disciple, and that is right; but then the disciple must be also, as in this case he is, a critic, a man of letters, not, as too often happens, some relation or friend with no qualification for his task except affection for his author.

258

which seems to justify every possible disparagement of it. Wordsworth says in one of his letters:—

"The writers in these publications" (the Reviews), "while they prosecute their inglorious employment, can not be supposed to be in a state of mind very favourable for being affected by the finer influences of a thing so pure as genuine poetry."

And a trustworthy reporter of his conversation quotes a more elaborate judgment to the same effect:—

"Wordsworth holds the critical power very low, infinitely lower than the inventive; and he said to-day that if the quantity of time consumed in writing critiques on the works of others were given to original composition, of whatever kind it might be, it would be much better employed; it would make a man find out sooner his own level, and it would do infinitely less mischief. A false or malicious criticism may do much injury to the minds of others; a stupid invention, either in prose or verse, is quite harmless."

It is almost too much to expect of poor human nature, that a man capable of producing some effect in one line of literature, should, for the greater good of society, voluntarily doom himself to impotence and obscurity in another. Still less is this to be expected from men addicted to the composition of the "false or malicious criticism" of which Wordsworth speaks. However, everybody would admit that a false or malicious criticism had better never have been written. Everybody, too, would be willing to admit, as a general proposition, that the critical faculty is lower than the inventive. But is it true that criticism is really, in itself, a baneful and injurious employment; is it true that all time given to writing critiques on the works of others would be much better employed if it were given to original composition, of whatever kind this may be? Is it true that Johnson had better have gone on producing more *Irenes* instead of writing his *Lives of the Poets;* nay, is it certain that Wordsworth himself was better employed in making his Ecclesiastical Sonnets than when he made his celebrated Preface, so full of criticism, and criticism of the works of others? Wordsworth was himself a great critic, and it is to be sincerely regretted that he has not left us more criticism; Goethe was one

of the greatest of critics, and we may sincerely congratulate
ourselves that he has left us so much criticism. Without wasting
time over the exaggeration which Wordsworth's judgment on
criticism clearly contains, or over an attempt to trace the causes,
—not difficult, I think, to be traced,—which may have led
Wordsworth to this exaggeration, a critic may with advantage
seize an occasion for trying his own conscience, and for asking
himself of what real service at any given moment the practice
of criticism either is or may be made to his own mind and spirit,
and to the minds and spirits of others.

The critical power is of lower rank than the creative. True;
but in assenting to this proposition, one or two things are to be
kept in mind. It is undeniable that the exercise of a creative
power, that a free creative activity, is the highest function of
man; it is proved to be so by man's finding in it his true happiness. But it is undeniable, also, that men may have the sense of
exercising this free creative activity in other ways than in producing great works of literature or art; if it were not so, all
but a very few men would be shut out from the true happiness
of all men. They may have it in well-doing, they may have it
in learning, they may have it even in criticising. This is one
thing to be kept in mind. Another is, that the exercise of the
creative power in the production of great works of literature
or art, however high this exercise of it may rank, is not at all
epochs and under all conditions possible; and that therefore
labour may be vainly spent in attempting it, which might with
more fruit be used in preparing for it, in rendering it possible.
This creative power works with elements, with materials; what
if it has not those materials, those elements, ready for its use?
In that case it must surely wait till they are ready. Now, in
literature,—I will limit myself to literature, for it is about literature that the question arises,—the elements with which the
creative power works are ideas; the best ideas, on every matter
which literature touches, current at the time. At any rate we
may lay it down as certain that in modern literature no manifestation of the creative power not working with these can
be very important or fruitful. And I say *current* at the time, not
merely accessible at the time; for creative literary genius does

not principally show itself in discovering new ideas, that is rather the business of the philosopher. The grand work of literary genius is a work of synthesis and exposition, not of analysis and discovery; its gift lies in the faculty of being happily inspired by a certain intellectual and spiritual atmosphere, by a certain order of ideas, when it finds itself in them; of dealing divinely with these ideas, presenting them in the most effective and attractive combinations,—making beautiful works with them, in short. But it must have the atmosphere, it must find itself amidst the order of ideas, in order to work freely; and these it is not so easy to command. This is why great creative epochs in literature are so rare, this is why there is so much that is unsatisfactory in the productions of many men of real genius; because for the creation of a master-work of literature two powers must concur, the power of the man and the power of the moment, and the man is not enough without the moment; the creative power has, for its happy exercise, appointed elements, and those elements are not in its own control.

Nay, they are more within the control of the critical power. It is the business of the critical power, as I said in the words already quoted, "in all branches of knowledge, theology, philosophy, history, art, science, to see the object as in itself it really is." Thus it tends, at last, to make an intellectual situation of which the creative power can profitably avail itself. It tends to establish an order of ideas, if not absolutely true, yet true by comparison with that which it displaces; to make the best ideas prevail. Presently these new ideas reach society, the touch of truth is the touch of life, and there is a stir and growth everywhere; out of this stir and growth come the creative epochs of literature.

Or, to narrow our range, and quit these considerations of the general march of genius and of society,—considerations which are apt to become too abstract and impalpable,—every one can see that a poet, for instance, ought to know life and the world before dealing with them in poetry; and life and the world being in modern times very complex things, the creation of a modern poet, to be worth much, implies a great critical effort behind it; else it must be a comparatively poor, barren,

and short-lived affair. This is why Byron's poetry had so little
endurance in it, and Goethe's so much; both Byron and Goethe
had a great productive power, but Goethe's was nourished by
a great critical effort providing the true materials for it, and
5   Byron's was not; Goethe knew life and the world, the poet's
necessary subjects, much more comprehensively and thoroughly than Byron. He knew a great deal more of them, and
he knew them much more as they really are.

It has long seemed to me that the burst of creative activity
10   in our literature, through the first quarter of this century, had
about it in fact something premature; and that from this cause
its productions are doomed, most of them, in spite of the san-
guine hopes which accompanied and do still accompany them, to
prove hardly more lasting than the productions of far less
15   splendid epochs. And this prematureness comes from its having
proceeded without having its proper data, without sufficient
materials to work with. In other words, the English poetry of
the first quarter of this century, with plenty of energy, plenty
of creative force, did not know enough. This makes Byron so
20   empty of matter, Shelley so incoherent, Wordsworth even,
profound as he is, yet so wanting in completeness and variety.
Wordsworth cared little for books, and disparaged Goethe.
I admire Wordsworth, as he is, so much that I cannot wish him
different; and it is vain, no doubt, to imagine such a man dif-
25   ferent from what he is, to suppose that he *could* have been
different. But surely the one thing wanting to make Wordsworth an even greater poet than he is,—his thought richer, and
his influence of wider application,—was that he should have
read more books, among them, no doubt, those of that Goethe
30   whom he disparaged without reading him.

But to speak of books and reading may easily lead to a misunderstanding here. It was not really books and reading that
lacked to our poetry at this epoch; Shelley had plenty of reading, Coleridge had immense reading. Pindar and Sophocles—as
35   we all say so glibly, and often with so little discernment of the
real import of what we are saying—had not many books;
Shakspeare was no deep reader. True; but in the Greece of
Pindar and Sophocles, in the England of Shakspeare, the poet

lived in a current of ideas in the highest degree animating and
nourishing to the creative power; society was, in the fullest
measure, permeated by fresh thought, intelligent and alive. And
this state of things is the true basis for the creative power's
exercise, in this it finds its data, its materials, truly ready for   5
its hand; all the books and reading in the world are only valuable
as they are helps to this. Even when this does not actually exist,
books and reading may enable a man to construct a kind of
semblance of it in his own mind, a world of knowledge and intelligence in which he may live and work. This is by no means   10
an equivalent to the artist for the nationally diffused life and
thought of the epochs of Sophocles or Shakspeare; but, besides
that it may be a means of preparation for such epochs, it does
really constitute, if many share in it, a quickening and sustain-
ing atmosphere of great value. Such an atmosphere the many-   15
sided learning and the long and widely-combined critical effort
of Germany formed for Goethe, when he lived and worked.
There was no national glow of life and thought there as in the
Athens of Pericles or the England of Elizabeth. That was the
poet's weakness. But there was a sort of equivalent for it in the   20
complete culture and unfettered thinking of a large body of
Germans. That was his strength. In the England of the first
quarter of this century there was neither a national glow of life
and thought, such as we had in the age of Elizabeth, nor yet
a culture and a force of learning and criticism such as were to   25
be found in Germany. Therefore the creative power of poetry
wanted, for success in the highest sense, materials and a basis;
a thorough interpretation of the world was necessarily denied
to it.

At first sight it seems strange that out of the immense stir of   30
the French Revolution and its age should not have come a crop
of works of genius equal to that which came out of the stir
of the great productive time of Greece, or out of that of the
Renascence, with its powerful episode the Reformation. But the
truth is that the stir of the French Revolution took a character   35
which essentially distinguished it from such movements as these.
These were, in the main, disinterestedly intellectual and spiritual
movements; movements in which the human spirit looked for

its satisfaction in itself and in the increased play of its own activity. The French Revolution took a political, practical character. The movement which went on in France under the old *régime*, from 1700 to 1789, was far more really akin than

5 that of the Revolution itself to the movement of the Renascence; the France of Voltaire and Rousseau told far more powerfully upon the mind of Europe than the France of the Revolution. Goethe reproached this last expressly with having "thrown quiet culture back." Nay, and the true key to how much in our

10 Byron, even in our Wordsworth, is this!—that they had their source in a great movement of feeling, not in a great movement of mind. The French Revolution, however,—that object of so much blind love and so much blind hatred,—found undoubtedly its motive-power in the intelligence of men, and not in their

15 practical sense; this is what distinguishes it from the English Revolution of Charles the First's time. This is what makes it a more spiritual event than our Revolution, an event of much more powerful and world-wide interest, though practically less successful; it appeals to an order of ideas which are universal,

20 certain, permanent. 1789 asked of a thing, Is it rational? 1642 asked of a thing, Is it legal? or, when it went furthest, Is it according to conscience? This is the English fashion, a fashion to be treated, within its own sphere, with the highest respect; for its success, within its own sphere, has been prodigious. But

25 what is law in one place is not law in another; what is law here to-day is not law even here tomorrow; and as for conscience, what is binding on one man's conscience is not binding on another's. The old woman who threw her stool at the head of the surpliced minister in St. Giles's Church at Edinburgh obeyed

30 an impulse to which millions of the human race may be permitted to remain strangers. But the prescriptions of reason are absolute, unchanging, of universal validity; *to count by tens is the easiest way of counting*—that is a proposition of which every one, from here to the Antipodes, feels the force; at least

35 I should say so if we did not live in a country where it is not impossible that any morning we may find a letter in the *Times* declaring that a decimal coinage is an absurdity. That a whole nation should have been penetrated with an enthusiasm for pure

reason, and with an ardent zeal for making its prescriptions
triumph, is a very remarkable thing, when we consider how
little of mind, or anything so worthy and quickening as mind,
comes into the motives which alone, in general, impel great
masses of men. In spite of the extravagant direction given to this   5
enthusiasm, in spite of the crimes and follies in which it lost
itself, the French Revolution derives from the force, truth, and
universality of the ideas which it took for its law, and from
the passion with which it could inspire a multitude for these
ideas, a unique and still living power; it is—it will probably long   10
remain—the greatest, the most animating event in history. And
as no sincere passion for the things of the mind, even though
it turn out in many respects an unfortunate passion, is ever quite
thrown away and quite barren of good, France has reaped
from hers one fruit—the natural and legitimate fruit, though   15
not precisely the grand fruit she expected: she is the country
in Europe where *the people* is most alive.

But the mania for giving an immediate political and practical
application to all these fine ideas of the reason was fatal. Here
an Englishman is in his element: on this theme we can all go   20
on for hours. And all we are in the habit of saying on it has undoubtedly a great deal of truth. Ideas cannot be too much prized
in and for themselves, cannot be too much lived with; but to
transport them abruptly into the world of politics and practice,
violently to revolutionise this world to their bidding,—that is   25
quite another thing. There is the world of ideas and there is
the world of practice; the French are often for suppressing the
one and the English the other; but neither is to be suppressed.
A member of the House of Commons said to me the other day:
"That a thing is an anomaly, I consider to be no objection to   30
it whatever." I venture to think he was wrong; that a thing
is an anomaly *is* an objection to it, but absolutely and in the
sphere of ideas: it is not necessarily, under such and such circumstances, or at such and such a moment, an objection to it in
the sphere of politics and practice. Joubert has said beautifully: 35
"C'est la force et le droit qui règlent toutes choses dans le
monde; la force en attendant le droit." (Force and right are the
governors of this world; force till right is ready.) *Force till right*

is ready; and till right is ready, force, the existing order of
things, is justified, is the legitimate ruler. But right is something
moral, and implies inward recognition, free assent of the will;
we are not ready for right,—*right,* so far as we are concerned,
is not ready,—until we have attained this sense of seeing it and
willing it. The way in which for us it may change and transform
force, the existing order of things, and become, in its turn, the
legitimate ruler of the world, should depend on the way in
which, when our time comes, we see it and will it. Therefore
for other people enamoured of their own newly discerned right,
to attempt to impose it upon us as ours, and violently to substitute their right for our force, is an act of tyranny, and to be
resisted. It sets at nought the second great half of our maxim,
force till right is ready. This was the grand error of the French
Revolution; and its movement of ideas, by quitting the intellectual sphere and rushing furiously into the political sphere,
ran, indeed, a prodigious and memorable course, but produced
no such intellectual fruit as the movement of ideas of the Renascence, and created, in opposition to itself, what I may call an
epoch of concentration. The great force of that epoch of concentration was England; and the great voice of that epoch of
concentration was Burke. It is the fashion to treat Burke's
writings on the French Revolution as superannuated and conquered by the event; as the eloquent but unphilosophical tirades
of bigotry and prejudice. I will not deny that they are often
disfigured by the violence and passion of the moment, and that
in some directions Burke's view was bounded, and his observation therefore at fault. But on the whole, and for those who can
make the needful corrections, what distinguishes these writings
is their profound, permanent, fruitful, philosophical truth.
They contain the true philosophy of an epoch of concentration,
dissipate the heavy atmosphere which its own nature is apt to
engender round it, and make its resistance rational instead
of mechanical.

But Burke is so great because, almost alone in England, he
brings thought to bear upon politics, he saturates politics with
thought. It is his accident that his ideas were at the service of
an epoch of concentration, not of an epoch of expansion; it is

his characteristic that he so lived by ideas, and had such a
source of them welling up within him, that he could float even
an epoch of concentration and English Tory politics with them.
It does not hurt him that Dr. Price and the Liberals were en-
raged with him; it does not even hurt him that George the 5
Third and the Tories were enchanted with him. His greatness is
that he lived in a world which neither English Liberalism nor
English Toryism is apt to enter;—the world of ideas, not the
world of catchwords and party habits. So far is it from being
really true of him that he "to party gave up what was meant 10
for mankind," that at the very end of his fierce struggle with the
French Revolution, after all his invectives against its false pretensions, hollowness, and madness, with his sincere conviction
of its mischievousness, he can close a memorandum on the best
means of combating it, some of the last pages he ever wrote,— 15
the *Thoughts on French Affairs*, in December 1791,—with these
striking words:—

"The evil is stated, in my opinion, as it exists. The remedy
must be where power, wisdom, and information, I hope, are
more united with good intentions than they can be with me. 20
I have done with this subject, I believe, for ever. It has given
me many anxious moments for the last two years. *If a great
change is to be made in human affairs, the minds of men will
be fitted to it; the general opinions and feelings will draw that
way. Every fear, every hope will forward it; and then they* 25
*who persist in opposing this mighty current in human affairs,
will appear rather to resist the decrees of Providence itself, than
the mere designs of men. They will not be resolute and firm, but
perverse and obstinate.*"

That return of Burke upon himself has always seemed to me 30
one of the finest things in English literature, or indeed in any
literature. That is what I call living by ideas: when one side
of a question has long had your earnest support, when all your
feelings are engaged, when you hear all round you no language
but one, when your party talks this language like a steam- 35
engine and can imagine no other,—still to be able to think, still
to be irresistibly carried, if so it be, by the current of thought
to the opposite side of the question, and, like Balaam, to be un-

able to speak anything *but what the Lord has put in your mouth*. I know nothing more striking, and I must add that I know nothing more un-English.

For the Englishman in general is like my friend the Member of Parliament, and believes, point-blank, that for a thing to be an anomaly is absolutely no objection to it whatever. He is like the Lord Auckland of Burke's day, who, in a memorandum on the French Revolution, talks of "certain miscreants, assuming the name of philosophers, who have presumed themselves capable of establishing a new system of society." The Englishman has been called a political animal, and he values what is political and practical so much that ideas easily become objects of dislike in his eyes, and thinkers "miscreants," because ideas and thinkers have rashly meddled with politics and practice. This would be all very well if the dislike and neglect confined themselves to ideas transported out of their own sphere, and meddling rashly with practice; but they are inevitably extended to ideas as such, and to the whole life of intelligence; practice is everything, a free play of the mind is nothing. The notion of the free play of the mind upon all subjects being a pleasure in itself, being an object of desire, being an essential provider of elements without which a nation's spirit, whatever compensations it may have for them, must, in the long run, die of inanition, hardly enters into an Englishman's thoughts. It is noticeable that the word *curiosity*, which in other languages is used in a good sense, to mean, as a high and fine quality of man's nature, just this disinterested love of a free play of the mind on all subjects, for its own sake,—it is noticeable, I say, that this word has in our language no sense of the kind, no sense but a rather bad and disparaging one. But criticism, real criticism, is essentially the exercise of this very quality. It obeys an instinct prompting it to try to know the best that is known and thought in the world, irrespectively of practice, politics, and everything of the kind; and to value knowledge and thought as they approach this best, without the intrusion of any other considerations whatever. This is an instinct for which there is, I think, little original sympathy in the practical English nature, and what there was of it has undergone a long benumbing period of blight and suppression in the epoch of concentration which followed the French Revolution.

But epochs of concentration cannot well endure for ever; epochs of expansion, in the due course of things, follow them. Such an epoch of expansion seems to be opening in this country. In the first place all danger of a hostile forcible pressure of foreign ideas upon our practice has long disappeared; like the traveller in the fable, therefore, we begin to wear our cloak a little more loosely. Then, with a long peace, the ideas of Europe steal gradually and amicably in, and mingle, though in infinitesimally small quantities at a time, with our own notions. Then, too, in spite of all that is said about the absorbing and brutalising influence of our passionate material progress, it seems to me indisputable that this progress is likely, though not certain, to lead in the end to an apparition of intellectual life; and that man, after he has made himself perfectly comfortable and has now to determine what to do with himself next, may begin to remember that he has a mind, and that the mind may be made the source of great pleasure. I grant it is mainly the privilege of faith, at present, to discern this end to our railways, our business, and our fortune-making; but we shall see if, here as elsewhere, faith is not in the end the true prophet. Our ease, our travelling, and our unbounded liberty to hold just as hard and securely as we please to the practice to which our notions have given birth, all tend to beget an inclination to deal a little more freely with these notions themselves, to canvass them a little, to penetrate a little into their real nature. Flutterings of curiosity, in the foreign sense of the word, appear amongst us, and it is in these that criticism must look to find its account. Criticism first; a time of true creative activity, perhaps,—which, as I have said, must inevitably be preceded amongst us by a time of criticism,—hereafter, when criticism has done its work.

It is of the last importance that English criticism should clearly discern what rule for its course, in order to avail itself of the field now opening to it, and to produce fruit for the future, it ought to take. The rule may be summed up in one

word,—*disinterestedness.* And how is criticism to show disinterestedness? By keeping aloof from what is called "the practical view of things;" by resolutely following the law of its
own nature, which is to be a free play of the mind on all subjects which it touches. By steadily refusing to lend itself to
any of those ulterior, political, practical considerations about
ideas, which plenty of people will be sure to attach to them,
which perhaps ought often to be attached to them, which in
this country at any rate are certain to be attached to them
quite sufficiently, but which criticism has really nothing to do
with. Its business is, as I have said, simply to know the best
that is known and thought in the world, and by in its turn
making this known, to create a current of true and fresh ideas.
Its business is to do this with inflexible honesty, with due ability;
but its business is to do no more, and to leave alone all questions
of practical consequences and applications, questions which
will never fail to have due prominence given to them. Else
criticism, besides being really false to its own nature, merely
continues in the old rut which it has hitherto followed in this
country, and will certainly miss the chance now given to it.
For what is at present the bane of criticism in this country?
It is that practical considerations cling to it and stifle it. It
subserves interests not its own. Our organs of criticism are
organs of men and parties having practical ends to serve, and
with them those practical ends are the first thing and the play
of mind the second; so much play of mind as is compatible
with the prosecution of those practical ends is all that is wanted.
An organ like the *Revue des Deux Mondes,* having for its
main function to understand and utter the best that is known
and thought in the world, existing, it may be said, as just an
organ for a free play of the mind, we have not. But we have the
Edinburgh Review, existing as an organ of the old Whigs, and
for as much play of the mind as may suit its being that; we
have the *Quarterly Review,* existing as an organ of the Tories,
and for as much play of mind as may suit its being that; we have
the *British Quarterly Review,* existing as an organ of the political Dissenters, and for as much play of mind as may suit
its being that; we have the *Times,* existing as an organ of the

common, satisfied, well-to-do Englishman, and for as much
play of mind as may suit its being that. And so on through all
the various fractions, political and religious, of our society;
every fraction has, as such, its organ of criticism, but the
notion of combining all fractions in the common pleasure of a 5
free disinterested play of mind meets with no favour. Directly
this play of mind wants to have more scope, and to forget the
pressure of practical considerations a little, it is checked, it is
made to feel the chain. We saw this the other day in the extinction, so much to be regretted, of the *Home and Foreign Review.* 10
Perhaps in no organ of criticism in this country was there so
much knowledge, so much play of mind; but these could not
save it. The *Dublin Review* subordinates play of mind to the
practical business of English and Irish Catholicism, and lives.
It must needs be that men should act in sects and parties, that 15
each of these sects and parties should have its organ, and should
make this organ subserve the interests of its action; but it would
be well, too, that there should be a criticism, not the minister
of these interests, not their enemy, but absolutely and entirely
independent of them. No other criticism will ever attain any 20
real authority or make any real way towards its end,—the
creating a current of true and fresh ideas.

It is because criticism has so little kept in the pure intellectual
sphere, has so little detached itself from practice, has been so
directly polemical and controversial, that it has so ill accom- 25
plished, in this country, its best spiritual work; which is to
keep man from a self-satisfaction which is retarding and vul-
garising, to lead him towards perfection, by making his mind
dwell upon what is excellent in itself, and the absolute beauty
and fitness of things. A polemical practical criticism makes men 30
blind even to the ideal imperfection of their practice, makes
them willingly assert its ideal perfection, in order the better to
secure it against attack; and clearly this is narrowing and baneful
for them. If they were reassured on the practical side, speculative considerations of ideal perfection they might be brought 35
to entertain, and their spiritual horizon would thus gradually
widen. Sir Charles Adderley says to the Warwickshire
farmers:—

"Talk of the improvement of breed! Why, the race we ourselves represent, the men and women, the old Anglo-Saxon
race, are the best breed in the whole world. . . . The absence
of a too enervating climate, too unclouded skies, and a too luxurious nature, has produced so vigorous a race of people, and
has rendered us so superior to all the world."

Mr. Roebuck says to the Sheffield cutlers:—

"I look around me and ask what is the state of England? Is
not property safe? Is not every man able to say what he likes?
Can you not walk from one end of England to the other in
perfect security? I ask you whether, the world over or in past
history, there is anything like it? Nothing. I pray that our
unrivalled happiness may last."

Now obviously there is a peril for poor human nature in
words and thoughts of such exuberant self-satisfaction, until
we find ourselves safe in the streets of the Celestial City.

> "Das wenige verschwindet leicht dem Blicke
> Der vorwärts sieht, wie viel noch übrig bleibt—"

says Goethe; "the little that is done seems nothing when we
look forward and see how much we have yet to do." Clearly
this is a better line of reflection for weak humanity, so long
as it remains on this earthly field of labour and trial.

But neither Sir Charles Adderley nor Mr. Roebuck is by
nature inaccessible to considerations of this sort. They only
lose sight of them owing to the controversial life we all lead,
and the practical form which all speculation takes with us.
They have in view opponents whose aim is not ideal, but practical; and in their zeal to uphold their own practice against
these innovators, they go so far as even to attribute to this
practice an ideal perfection. Somebody has been wanting to
introduce a six-pound franchise, or to abolish church-rates, or
to collect agricultural statistics by force, or to diminish local
self-government. How natural, in reply to such proposals, very
likely improper or ill-timed, to go a little beyond the mark,
and to say stoutly, "Such a race of people as we stand, so
superior to all the world! The old Anglo-Saxon race, the best
breed in the whole world! I pray that our unrivalled happiness

may last! I ask you whether, the world over or in past history, there is anything like it?" And so long as criticism answers this dithyramb by insisting that the old Anglo-Saxon race would be still more superior to all others if it had no church-rates, or that our unrivalled happiness would last yet longer with a six-pound franchise, so long will the strain, "The best breed in the whole world!" swell louder and louder, everything ideal and refining will be lost out of sight, and both the assailed and their critics will remain in a sphere, to say the truth, perfectly unvital, a sphere in which spiritual progression is impossible. But let criticism leave church-rates and the franchise alone, and in the most candid spirit, without a single lurking thought of practical innovation, confront with our dithyramb this paragraph on which I stumbled in a newspaper immediately after reading Mr. Roebuck:—

"A shocking child murder has just been committed at Nottingham. A girl named Wragg left the workhouse there on Saturday morning with her young illegitimate child. The child was soon afterwards found dead on Mapperly Hills, having been strangled. Wragg is in custody."

Nothing but that; but, in juxtaposition with the absolute eulogies of Sir Charles Adderley and Mr. Roebuck, how eloquent, how suggestive are those few lines! "Our old Anglo-Saxon breed, the best in the whole world!"—how much that is harsh and ill-favoured there is in this best! *Wragg!* If we are to talk of ideal perfection, of "the best in the whole world," has any one reflected what a touch of grossness in our race, what an original shortcoming in the more delicate spiritual perceptions, is shown by the natural growth amongst us of such hideous names,—Higginbottom, Stiggins, Bugg! In Ionia and Attica they were luckier in this respect than "the best race in the world;" by the Ilissus there was no Wragg, poor thing! And "our unrivalled happiness;"—what an element of grimness, bareness, and hideousness mixes with it and blurs it; the workhouse, the dismal Mapperly Hills,—how dismal those who have seen them will remember;—the gloom, the smoke, the cold, the strangled illegitimate child! "I ask you whether, the world over or in past history, there is anything like it?" Perhaps not, one is inclined to answer; but at any rate, in that case, the world is [not] very much to be pitied. And the final touch, —short, bleak, and inhuman: *Wragg is in custody*. The sex lost in the confusion of our unrivalled happiness; or (shall I say?)

5 the superfluous Christian name lopped off by the straight-forward vigour of our old Anglo-Saxon breed! There is profit for the spirit in such contrasts as this; criticism serves the cause of perfection by establishing them. By eluding sterile conflict, by refusing to remain in the sphere where alone narrow and

10 relative conceptions have any worth and validity, criticism may diminish its momentary importance, but only in this way has it a chance of gaining admittance for those wider and more perfect conceptions to which all its duty is really owed. Mr. Roebuck will have a poor opinion of an adversary who replies

15 to his defiant songs of triumph only by murmuring under his breath, *Wragg is in custody;* but in no other way will these songs of triumph be induced gradually to moderate themselves, to get rid of what in them is excessive and offensive, and to fall into a softer and truer key.

20 It will be said that it is a very subtle and indirect action which I am thus prescribing for criticism, and that, by embracing in this manner the Indian virtue of detachment and abandoning the sphere of practical life, it condemns itself to a slow and obscure work. Slow and obscure it may be, but it

25 is the only proper work of criticism. The mass of mankind will never have any ardent zeal for seeing things as they are; very inadequate ideas will always satisfy them. On these inadequate ideas reposes, and must repose, the general practice of the world. That is as much as saying that whoever sets himself to see things

30 as they are will find himself one of a very small circle; but it is only by this small circle resolutely doing its own work that adequate ideas will ever get current at all. The rush and roar of practical life will always have a dizzying and attracting effect upon the most collected spectator, and tend to draw him into

35 its vortex; most of all will this be the case where that life is so powerful as it is in England. But it is only by remaining collected, and refusing to lend himself to the point of view of the practical man, that the critic can do the practical man

any service; and it is only by the greatest sincerity in pursuing his own course, and by at last convincing even the practical man of his sincerity, that he can escape misunderstandings which perpetually threaten him.

For the practical man is not apt for fine distinctions, and yet in these distinctions truth and the highest culture greatly find their account. But it is not easy to lead a practical man,—unless you reassure him as to your practical intentions, you have no chance of leading him,—to see that a thing which he has always been used to look at from one side only, which he greatly values, and which, looked at from that side, quite deserves, perhaps, all the prizing and admiring which he bestows upon it,—that this thing, looked at from another side, may appear much less beneficent and beautiful, and yet retain all its claims to our practical allegiance. Where shall we find language innocent enough, how shall we make the spotless purity of our intentions evident enough, to enable us to say to the political Englishman that the British Constitution itself, which, seen from the practical side, looks such a magnificent organ of progress and virtue, seen from the speculative side,—with its compromises, its love of facts, its horror of theory, its studied avoidance of clear thoughts,— that, seen from this side, our august Constitution sometimes looks,—forgive me, shade of Lord Somers!—a colossal machine for the manufacture of Philistines? How is Cobbett to say this and not be misunderstood, blackened as he is with the smoke of a lifelong conflict in the field of political practice? how is Mr. Carlyle to say it and not be misunderstood, after his furious raid into this field with his *Latter-day Pamphlets?* how is Mr. Ruskin, after his pugnacious political economy? I say, the critic must keep out of the region of immediate practice in the political, social, humanitarian sphere, if he wants to make a beginning for that more free speculative treatment of things, which may perhaps one day make its benefits felt even in this sphere, but in a natural and thence irresistible manner.

Do what he will, however, the critic will still remain exposed to frequent misunderstandings, and nowhere so much as in this country. For here people are particularly indisposed even to comprehend that without this free disinterested treatment of things, truth and the highest culture are out of the question. So immersed are they in practical life, so accustomed to take all their notions from this life and its processes, that they are apt to think that truth and culture themselves can be reached by the processes of this life, and that it is an impertinent singularity to think of reaching them in any other. "We are all *terræ filii*," cries their eloquent advocate; "all Philistines together. Away with the notion of proceeding by any other course than the course dear to the Philistines; let us have a social movement, let us organise and combine a party to pursue truth and new thought, let us call it *the liberal party*, and let us all stick to each other, and back each other up. Let us have no nonsense about independent criticism, and intellectual delicacy, and the few and the many. Don't let us trouble ourselves about foreign thought; we shall invent the whole thing for ourselves as we go along. If one of us speaks well, applaud him; if one of us speaks ill, applaud him too; we are all in the same movement, we are all liberals, we are all in pursuit of truth." In this way the pursuit of truth becomes really a social, practical, pleasurable affair, almost requiring a chairman, a secretary, and advertisements; with the excitement of an occasional scandal, with a little resistance to give the happy sense of difficulty overcome; but, in general, plenty of bustle and very little thought. To act is so easy, as Goethe says; to think is so hard! It is true that the critic has many temptations to go with the stream, to make one of the party movement, one of these *terræ filii*; it seems ungracious to refuse to be a *terræ filius*, when so many excellent people are; but the critic's duty is to refuse, or, if resistance is vain, at least to cry with Obermann: *Périssons en résistant*.

How serious a matter it is to try and resist, I had ample opportunity of experiencing when I ventured some time ago to criticise the celebrated first volume of Bishop Colenso.[1] The

---

[1] So sincere is my dislike to all personal attack and controversy, that I abstain from reprinting, at this distance of time from the occasion which called them forth, the essays in which I criticised Dr. Colenso's book; I feel bound, however, after all that has passed, to make here a final declaration of my sincere impenitence for having published them. Nay, I cannot forbear repeating yet once more, for his benefit and that of his

echoes of the storm which was then raised I still, from time
to time, hear grumbling round me. That storm arose out of a
misunderstanding almost inevitable. It is a result of no little
culture to attain to a clear perception that science and religion
are two wholly different things. The multitude will for ever   5
confuse them; but happily that is of no great real importance,
for while the multitude imagines itself to live by its false science,
it does really live by its true religion. Dr. Colenso, however, in
his first volume did all he could to strengthen the confusion,[1]
and to make it dangerous. He did this with the best intentions,   10
I freely admit, and with the most candid ignorance that this
was the natural effect of what he was doing; but, says Joubert,
"Ignorance, which in matters of morals extenuates the crime, is
itself, in intellectual matters, a crime of the first order." I criticised Bishop Colenso's speculative confusion. Immediately there   15
was a cry raised: "What is this? here is a liberal attacking a
liberal. Do not you belong to the movement? are not you a
friend of truth? Is not Bishop Colenso in pursuit of truth?
then speak with proper respect of his book. Dr. Stanley is another friend of truth, and you speak with proper respect of his   20
book; why make these invidious differences? both books are
excellent, admirable, liberal; Bishop Colenso's perhaps the most
so, because it is the boldest, and will have the best practical consequences for the liberal cause. Do you want to encourage to
the attack of a brother liberal his, and your, and our implacable   25
enemies, the *Church and State Review* or the *Record*,—the
High Church rhinoceros and the Evangelical hyæna? Be silent,
therefore; or rather speak, speak as loud as ever you can! and
go into ecstasies over the eighty and odd pigeons."
But criticism cannot follow this coarse and indiscriminate   30

---

readers, this sentence from my original remarks upon him: *There is truth
of science and truth of religion; truth of science does not become truth
of religion till it is made religious.* And I will add: Let us have all the
science there is from the men of science; from the men of religion let us
have religion.   35
[1] It has been said I make it "a crime against literary criticism and the
higher culture to attempt to inform the ignorant." Need I point out that
the ignorant are not informed by being confirmed in a confusion?

method. It is unfortunately possible for a man in pursuit of
truth to write a book which reposes upon a false conception.
Even the practical consequences of a book are to genuine criticism no recommendation of it, if the book is, in the highest
5   sense, blundering. I see that a lady who herself, too, is in pursuit
of truth, and who writes with great ability, but a little too
much, perhaps, under the influence of the practical spirit of
the English liberal movement, classes Bishop Colenso's book and
M. Renan's together, in her survey of the religious state of
10   Europe, as facts of the same order, works, both of them, of
"great importance;" "great ability, power, and skill;" Bishop
Colenso's, perhaps, the most powerful; at least, Miss Cobbe
gives special expression to her gratitude that to Bishop Colenso
"has been given the strength to grasp, and the courage to teach,
15   truths of such deep import." In the same way, more than one
popular writer has compared him to Luther. Now it is just
this kind of false estimate which the critical spirit is, it seems
to me, bound to resist. It is really the strongest possible proof
of the low ebb at which, in England, the critical spirit is,
20   that while the critical hit in the religious literature of Germany
is Dr. Strauss's book, in that of France M. Renan's book, the
book of Bishop Colenso is the critical hit in the religious literature of England. Bishop Colenso's book reposes on a total misconception of the essential elements of the religious problem,
25   as that problem is now presented for solution. To criticism,
therefore, which seeks to have the best that is known and
thought on this problem, it is, however well meant, of no importance whatever. M. Renan's book attempts a new synthesis
of the elements furnished to us by the Four Gospels. It attempts,
30   in my opinion, a synthesis, perhaps premature, perhaps impossible, certainly not successful. Up to the present time, at any
rate, we must acquiesce in Fleury's sentence on such recastings
of the Gospel-story: *Quiconque s'imagine la pouvoir mieux
écrire, ne l'entend pas.* M. Renan had himself passed by an-
35   ticipation a like sentence on his own work, when he said: "If
a new presentation of the character of Jesus were offered to
me, I would not have it; its very clearness would be, in my
opinion, the best proof of its insufficiency." His friends may

with perfect justice rejoin that at the sight of the Holy Land, and of the actual scene of the Gospel-story, all the current of M. Renan's thoughts may have naturally changed, and a new casting of that story irresistibly suggested itself to him; and that this is just a case for applying Cicero's maxim: Change of mind is not inconsistency—*nemo doctus unquam mutationem consilii inconstantiam dixit esse.* Nevertheless, for criticism, M. Renan's first thought must still be the truer one, as long as his new casting so fails more fully to commend itself, more fully (to use Coleridge's happy phrase about the Bible) to *find* us. Still M. Renan's attempt is, for criticism, of the most real interest and importance, since, with all its difficulty, a fresh synthesis of the New Testament *data*,—not a making war on them, in Voltaire's fashion, not a leaving them out of mind, in the world's fashion, but the putting a new construction upon them, the taking them from under the old, traditional, conventional point of view and placing them under a new one,—is the very essence of the religious problem, as now presented; and only by efforts in this direction can it receive a solution.

Again, in the same spirit in which she judges Bishop Colenso, Miss Cobbe, like so many earnest liberals of our practical race, both here and in America, herself sets vigorously about a positive reconstruction of religion, about making a religion of the future out of hand, or at least setting about making it. We must not rest, she and they are always thinking and saying, in negative criticism, we must be creative and constructive; hence we have such works as her recent *Religious Duty*, and works still more considerable, perhaps, by others, which will be in every one's mind. These works often have much ability; they often spring out of sincere convictions, and a sincere wish to do good; and they sometimes, perhaps, do good. Their fault is (if I may be permitted to say so) one which they have in common with the British College of Health, in the New Road. Every one knows the British College of Health; it is that building with the lion and the statue of the Goddess Hygeia before it; at least I am sure about the lion, though I am not absolutely certain about the Goddess Hygeia. This building does credit, perhaps, to the resources of Dr. Morison and his disciples;

but it falls a good deal short of one's idea of what a British
College of Health ought to be. In England, where we hate
public interference and love individual enterprise, we have a
whole crop of places like the British College of Health; the grand
5   name without the grand thing. Unluckily, creditable to individual enterprise as they are, they tend to impair our taste by
making us forget what more grandiose, noble, or beautiful character properly belongs to a public institution. The same may be
said of the religions of the future of Miss Cobbe and others.
10   Creditable, like the British College of Health, to the resources
of their authors, they yet tend to make us forget what more
grandiose, noble, or beautiful character properly belongs to
religious constructions. The historic religions, with all their
faults, have had this; it certainly belongs to the religious senti-
15   ment, when it truly flowers, to have this; and we impoverish our
spirit if we allow a religion of the future without it. What then
is the duty of criticism here? To take the practical point of
view, to applaud the liberal movement and all its works,—its
New Road religions of the future into the bargain,—for their
20   general utility's sake? By no means; but to be perpetually dissatisfied with these works, while they perpetually fall short
of a high and perfect ideal.

For criticism, these are elementary laws; but they never can
be popular, and in this country they have been very little fol-
25   lowed, and one meets with immense obstacles in following
them. That is a reason for asserting them again and again. Crit-
cism must maintain its independence of the practical spirit and
its aims. Even with well-meant efforts of the practical spirit
it must express dissatisfaction, if in the sphere of the ideal they
30   seem impoverishing and limiting. It must not hurry on to the
goal because of its practical importance. It must be patient,
and know how to wait; and flexible, and know how to attach
itself to things and how to withdraw from them. It must be
apt to study and praise elements that for the fulness of spiritual
35   perfection are wanted, even though they belong to a power
which in the practical sphere may be maleficent. It must be
apt to discern the spiritual shortcomings or illusions of powers
that in the practical sphere may be beneficent. And this without

any notion of favouring or injuring, in the practical sphere, one power or the other; without any notion of playing off, in this sphere, one power against the other. When one looks, for instance, at the English Divorce Court,—an institution which perhaps has its practical conveniences, but which in the ideal sphere is so hideous; an institution which neither makes divorce impossible nor makes it decent, which allows a man to get rid of his wife, or a wife of her husband, but makes them drag one another first, for the public edification, through a mire of un-utterable infamy,—when one looks at this charming institution, I say, with its crowded trials, its newspaper reports, and its money compensations, this institution in which the gross un-regenerate British Philistine has indeed stamped an image of himself,—one may be permitted to find the marriage theory of Catholicism refreshing and elevating. Or when Protestantism, in virtue of its supposed rational and intellectual origin, gives the law to criticism too magisterially, criticism may and must remind it that its pretensions, in this respect, are illusive and do it harm; that the Reformation was a moral rather than an intellectual event; that Luther's theory of grace no more exactly reflects the mind of the spirit than Bossuet's philosophy of history reflects it; and that there is no more antecedent probability of the Bishop of Durham's stock of ideas being agreeable to perfect reason than of Pope Pius the Ninth's. But criticism will not on that account forget the achievements of Protestantism in the practical and moral sphere; nor that, even in the intel-lectual sphere, Protestantism, though in a blind and stumbling manner, carried forward the Renascence, while Catholicism threw itself violently across its path.

I lately heard a man of thought and energy contrasting the want of ardour and movement which he now found amongst young men in this country with what he remembered in his own youth, twenty years ago. "What reformers we were then!" he exclaimed; "what a zeal we had! how we canvassed every institution in Church and State, and were prepared to remodel them all on first principles!" He was inclined to regret, as a spiritual flagging, the lull which he saw. I am disposed rather to regard it as a pause in which the turn to a new mode of

spiritual progress is being accomplished. Everything was long
seen, by the young and ardent amongst us, in inseparable connection with politics and practical life. We have pretty well
exhausted the benefits of seeing things in this connection, we
have got all that can be got by so seeing them. Let us try a
more disinterested mode of seeing them; let us betake ourselves
more to the serener life of the mind and spirit. This life, too,
may have its excesses and dangers; but they are not for us at
present. Let us think of quietly enlarging our stock of true
and fresh ideas, and not, as soon as we get an idea or half an
idea, be running out with it into the street, and trying to make
it rule there. Our ideas will, in the end, shape the world all the
better for maturing a little. Perhaps in fifty years' time it
will in the English House of Commons be an objection to an
institution that it is an anomaly, and my friend the Member of
Parliament will shudder in his grave. But let us in the meanwhile
rather endeavour that in twenty years' time it may, in English
literature, be an objection to a proposition that it is absurd. That
will be a change so vast, that the imagination almost fails to
grasp it. *Ab integro sæclorum nascitur ordo.*

If I have insisted so much on the course which criticism
must take where politics and religion are concerned, it is because, where these burning matters are in question, it is most
likely to go astray. I have wished, above all, to insist on the
attitude which criticism should adopt towards things in general;
on its right tone and temper of mind. But then comes another
question as to the subject-matter which literary criticism
should most seek. Here, in general, its course is determined for
it by the idea which is the law of its being; the idea of a disinterested endeavour to learn and propagate the best that is
known and thought in the world, and thus to establish a current
of fresh and true ideas. By the very nature of things, as England
is not all the world, much of the best that is known and thought
in the world cannot be of English growth, must be foreign; by
the nature of things, again, it is just this that we are least likely
to know, while English thought is streaming in upon us from
all sides, and takes excellent care that we shall not be ignorant
of its existence. The English critic of literature, therefore, must

dwell much on foreign thought, and with particular heed on any part of it, which, while significant and fruitful in itself, is for any reason specially likely to escape him. Again, judging is often spoken of as the critic's one business, and so in some sense it is; but the judgment which almost insensibly forms itself in a fair and clear mind, along with fresh knowledge, is the valuable one; and thus knowledge, and ever fresh knowledge, must be the critic's great concern for himself. And it is by communicating fresh knowledge, and letting his own judgment pass along with it,—but insensibly, and in the second place, not the first, as a sort of companion and clue, not as an abstract lawgiver,—that the critic will generally do most good to his readers. Sometimes, no doubt, for the sake of establishing an author's place in literature, and his relation to a central standard (and if this is not done, how are we to get at our *best in the world?*) criticism may have to deal with a subject-matter so familiar that fresh knowledge is out of the question, and then it must be all judgment; an enunciation and detailed application of principles. Here the great safeguard is never to let oneself become abstract, always to retain an intimate and lively consciousness of the truth of what one is saying, and, the moment this fails us, to be sure that something is wrong. Still, under all circumstances, this mere judgment and application of principles is, in itself, not the most satisfactory work to the critic; like mathematics, it is tautological, and cannot well give us, like fresh learning, the sense of creative activity.

But stop, some one will say; all this talk is of no practical use to us whatever; this criticism of yours is not what we have in our minds when we speak of criticism; when we speak of critics and criticism, we mean critics and criticism of the current English literature of the day; when you offer to tell criticism its function, it is to this criticism that we expect you to address yourself. I am sorry for it, for I am afraid I must disappoint these expectations. I am bound by my own definition of criticism: *a disinterested endeavour to learn and propagate the best that is known and thought in the world.* How much of current English literature comes into this "best that is known and thought in the world?" Not very much, I fear; certainly

less, at this moment, than of the current literature of France
or Germany. Well, then, am I to alter my definition of criticism, in order to meet the requirements of a number of practising English critics, who, after all, are free in their choice of
a business? That would be making criticism lend itself just
to one of those alien practical considerations, which, I have
said, are so fatal to it. One may say, indeed, to those who have
to deal with the mass—so much better disregarded—of current
English literature, that they may at all events endeavour, in
dealing with this, to try it, so far as they can, by the standard
of the best that is known and thought in the world; one may
say, that to get anywhere near this standard, every critic should
try and possess one great literature, at least, besides his own;
and the more unlike his own, the better. But, after all, the criticism I am really concerned with,—the criticism which alone
can much help us for the future, the criticism which, throughout Europe, is at the present day meant, when so much stress
is laid on the importance of criticism and the critical spirit,—
is a criticism which regards Europe as being, for intellectual
and spiritual purposes, one great confederation, bound to a
joint action and working to a common result; and whose members have, for their proper outfit, a knowledge of Greek,
Roman, and Eastern antiquity, and of one another. Special,
local, and temporary advantages being put out of account, that
modern nation will in the intellectual and spiritual sphere make
most progress, which most thoroughly carries out this pro-
gramme. And what is that but saying that we too, all of us,
as individuals, the more thoroughly we carry it out, shall make
the more progress?

There is so much inviting us!—what are we to take? what
will nourish us in growth towards perfection? That is the
question which, with the immense field of life and of literature
lying before him, the critic has to answer; for himself first,
and afterwards for others. In this idea of the critic's business the
essays brought together in the following * pages have had their
origin; in this idea, widely different as are their subjects, they
have, perhaps, their unity.

    * [In this edition, "preceding."—Ed.]

I conclude with what I said at the beginning: to have the sense of creative activity is the great happiness and the great proof of being alive, and it is not denied to criticism to have it; but then criticism must be sincere, simple, flexible, ardent, ever widening its knowledge. Then it may have, in no contemptible measure, a joyful sense of creative activity; a sense which a man of insight and conscience will prefer to what he might derive from a poor, starved, fragmentary, inadequate creation. And at some epochs no other creation is possible.

Still, in full measure, the sense of creative activity belongs only to genuine creation; in literature we must never forget that. But what true man of letters ever can forget it? It is no such common matter for a gifted nature to come into possession of a current of true and living ideas, and to produce amidst the inspiration of them, that we are likely to underrate it. The epochs of Æschylus and Shakspeare make us feel their preeminence. In an epoch like those is, no doubt, the true life of literature; there is the promised land, towards which criticism can only beckon. That promised land it will not be ours to enter, and we shall die in the wilderness: but to have desired to enter it, to have saluted it from afar, is already, perhaps, the best distinction among contemporaries; it will certainly be the best title to esteem with posterity.

Preface to *Essays in Criticism*

Several of the Essays which are here collected and reprinted had the good or the bad fortune to be much criticised at the time of their first appearance. I am not now going to inflict upon the reader a reply to those criticisms; for one or two expla
5 nations which are desirable, I shall elsewhere, perhaps, be able some day to find an opportunity; but, indeed, it is not in my nature,—some of my critics would rather say, not in my power, —to dispute on behalf of any opinion, even my own, very obstinately. To try and approach truth on one side after another,
10 not to strive or cry, nor to persist in pressing forward, on any one side, with violence and self-will,—it is only thus, it seems to me, that mortals may hope to gain any vision of the mysterious Goddess, whom we shall never see except in outline, but only thus even in outline. He who will do nothing but fight
15 impetuously towards her on his own, one, favourite, particular line, is inevitably destined to run his head into the folds of the black robe in which she is wrapped.

So it is not to reply to my critics that I write this preface, but to prevent a misunderstanding, of which certain phrases
20 that some of them use make me apprehensive. Mr. Wright, one of the many translators of Homer, has published a letter to the Dean of Canterbury, complaining of some remarks of mine, uttered now a long while ago, on his version of the *Iliad*. One cannot be always studying one's own works, and I was really
25 under the impression, till I saw Mr. Wright's complaint, that I had spoken of him with all respect. The reader may judge of my astonishment, therefore, at finding, from Mr. Wright's pamphlet, that I had "declared with much solemnity that there is not any proper reason for his existing." That I never said;

but, on looking back at my Lectures on translating Homer, I find that I did say, not that Mr. Wright, but that Mr. Wright's version of the *Iliad*, repeating in the main the merits and defects of Cowper's version, as Mr. Sotheby's repeated those of Pope's version, had, if I might be pardoned for saying so, no proper reason for existing. Elsewhere I expressly spoke of the merit of his version; but I confess that the phrase, qualified as I have shown, about its want of a proper reason for existing, I used. Well, the phrase had, perhaps, too much vivacity; we have all of us a right to exist, we and our works; an unpopular author should be the last person to call in question this right. So I gladly withdraw the offending phrase, and I am sorry for having used it; Mr. Wright, however, would perhaps be more indulgent to my vivacity, if he considered that we are none of us likely to be lively much longer. My vivacity is but the last sparkle of flame before we are all in the dark, the last glimpse of colour before we all go into drab,—the drab of the earnest, prosaic, practical, austerely literal future. Yes, the world will soon be the Philistines'! and then, with every voice, not of thunder, silenced, and the whole earth filled and ennobled every morning by the magnificent roaring of the young lions of the *Daily Telegraph*, we shall all yawn in one another's faces with the dismallest, the most unimpeachable gravity.

But I return to my design in writing this Preface. That design was, after apologising to Mr. Wright for my vivacity of five years ago, to beg him and others to let me bear my own burdens, without saddling the great and famous University to which I have the honour to belong with any portion of them. What I mean to deprecate is such phrases as, "his professorial assault," "his assertions issued *ex cathedrâ*," "the sanction of his name as the representative of poetry," and so on. Proud as I am of my connection with the University of Oxford,[1] I can truly say, that knowing how unpopular a task one is undertaking when one tries to pull out a few more stops in that powerful but at present somewhat narrow-toned organ, the modern Englishman, I have always sought to stand by myself,

[1] When the above was written the author had still the Chair of Poetry at Oxford, which he has since vacated.

and to compromise others as little as possible. Besides this, my native modesty is such, that I have always been shy of assuming the honourable style of Professor, because this is a title I share with so many distinguished men,—Professor Pepper, Professor Anderson, Professor Frickel, and others,—who adorn it, I feel, much more than I do.

However, it is not merely out of modesty that I prefer to stand alone, and to concentrate on myself, as a plain citizen of the republic of letters, and not as an office-bearer in a hierarchy, the whole responsibility for all I write; it is much more out of genuine devotion to the University of Oxford, for which I feel, and always must feel, the fondest, the most reverential attachment. In an epoch of dissolution and transformation, such as that on which we are now entered, habits, ties, and associations are inevitably broken up, the action of individuals becomes more distinct, the shortcomings, errors, heats, disputes, which necessarily attend individual action, are brought into greater prominence. Who would not gladly keep clear, from all these passing clouds, an august institution which was there before they arose, and which will be there when they have blown over?

It is true, the *Saturday Review* maintains that our epoch of transformation is finished; that we have found our philosophy; that the British nation has searched all anchorages for the spirit, and has finally anchored itself, in the fulness of perfected knowledge, on Benthamism. This idea at first made a great impression on me; not only because it is so consoling in itself, but also because it explained a phenomenon which in the summer of last year had, I confess, a good deal troubled me. At that time my avocations led me to travel almost daily on one of the Great Eastern Lines,—the Woodford Branch. Every one knows that the murderer, Müller, perpetrated his detestable act on the North London Railway, close by. The English middle class, of which I am myself a feeble unit, travel on the Woodford Branch in large numbers. Well, the demoralisation of our class, —the class which (the newspapers are constantly saying it, so I may repeat it without vanity) has done all the great things which have ever been done in England,—the demoralisation, I say, of our class, caused by the Bow tragedy, was something bewildering. Myself a transcendentalist (as the *Saturday Review* knows), I escaped the infection; and, day after day, I used to ply my agitated fellow-travellers with all the consolations which my transcendentalism would naturally suggest to me. I reminded them how Cæsar refused to take precautions against assassination, because life was not worth having at the price of an ignoble solicitude for it. I reminded them what insignificant atoms we all are in the life of the world. "Suppose the worst to happen," I said, addressing a portly jeweller from Cheapside; "suppose even yourself to be the victim; *il n'y a pas d'homme nécessaire.* We should miss you for a day or two upon the Woodford Branch; but the great mundane movement would still go on, the gravel walks of your villa would still be rolled, dividends would still be paid at the Bank, omnibuses would still run, there would still be the old crush at the corner of Fenchurch Street." All was of no avail. Nothing could moderate, in the bosom of the great English middle-class, their passionate, absorbing, almost blood-thirsty clinging to life. At the moment I thought this over-concern a little unworthy; but the *Saturday Review* suggests a touching explanation of it. What I took for the ignoble clinging to life of a comfortable worldling, was, perhaps, only the ardent longing of a faithful Benthamite, traversing an age still dimmed by the last mists of transcendentalism, to be spared long enough to see his religion in the full and final blaze of its triumph. This respectable man, whom I imagined to be going up to London to serve his shop, or to buy shares, or to attend an Exeter Hall meeting, or to assist at the deliberations of the Marylebone Vestry, was even, perhaps, in real truth, on a pious pilgrimage, to obtain from Mr. Bentham's executors a sacred bone of his great, dissected master.

And yet, after all, I cannot but think that the *Saturday Review* has here, for once, fallen a victim to an idea,—a beautiful but deluding idea,—and that the British nation has not yet, so entirely as the reviewer seems to imagine, found the last word of its philosophy. No, we are all seekers still! seekers often make mistakes, and I wish mine to redound to my own discredit only, and not to touch Oxford. Beautiful city! so venerable, so lovely, so unravaged by the fierce intellectual life of our century, so serene!

"There are our young barbarians, all at play!"

5   And yet, steeped in sentiment as she lies, spreading her gardens to the moonlight, and whispering from her towers the last enchantments of the Middle Age, who will deny that Oxford, by her ineffable charm, keeps ever calling us nearer to the true goal of all of us, to the ideal, to perfection,—to beauty, in a word, 10 which is only truth seen from another side?—nearer, perhaps, than all the science of Tübingen. Adorable dreamer, whose heart has been so romantic! who hast given thyself so prodigally, given thyself to sides and to heroes not mine, only never to the Philistines! home of lost causes, and forsaken beliefs, and 15 unpopular names, and impossible loyalties! what example could ever so inspire us to keep down the Philistine in ourselves, what teacher could ever so save us from that bondage to which we are all prone, that bondage which Goethe, in his incomparable lines on the death of Schiller, makes it his friend's highest praise 20 (and nobly did Schiller deserve the praise) to have left miles out of sight behind him;—the bondage of *"was uns alle bändigt,* DAS GEMEINE!*"* She will forgive me, even if I have unwittingly drawn upon her a shot or two aimed at her unworthy son; for she is generous, and the cause in which I fight is, after all, hers. 25 Apparitions of a day, what is our puny warfare against the Philistines, compared with the warfare which this queen of romance has been waging against them for centuries, and will wage after we are gone?

On the Study of Celtic Literature

"They went forth to the war, but they always fell."
OSSIAN

The summer before last I spent some weeks at Llandudno, on
the Welsh coast. The best lodging-houses at Llandudno look
eastward, towards Liverpool; and from that Saxon hive swarms
are incessantly issuing, crossing the bay, and taking possession of
the beach and the lodging-houses. Guarded by the Great and   5
Little Orme's Head, and alive with the Saxon invaders from
Liverpool, the eastern bay is an attractive point of interest, and
many visitors to Llandudno never contemplate anything else.
But, putting aside the charm of the Liverpool steamboats, perhaps the view, on this side, a little dissatisfies one after a while;   10
the horizon wants mystery, the sea wants beauty, the coast
wants verdure, and has a too bare austereness and aridity. At
last one turns round and looks westward. Everything is
changed. Over the mouth of the Conway and its sands is the
eternal softness and mild light of the west; the low line of the   15
mystic Anglesey, and the precipitous Penmaenmawr, and the
great group of Carnedd Llewelyn and Carnedd David and their
brethren fading away, hill behind hill, in an aërial haze, make
the horizon; between the foot of Penmaenmawr and the bending coast of Anglesey, the sea, a silver stream, disappears one   20
knows not whither. On this side, Wales,—Wales, where the past
still lives, where every place has its tradition, every name its
poetry, and where the people, the genuine people, still knows
this past, this tradition, this poetry, and lives with it, and clings
to it; while, alas, the prosperous Saxon on the other side,   25
the invader from Liverpool and Birkenhead, has long ago forgotten his. And the promontory where Llandudno stands is
the very centre of this tradition; it is Creuddyn, *the bloody city,*
where every stone has its story; there, opposite its decaying

rival, Conway Castle, is Diganwy, not decaying but long since utterly decayed, some crumbling foundations on a crag-top and nothing more;—Diganwy, where Mael-gwyn shut up Elphin, and where Taliesin came to free him. Below, in a
5   fold of the hill, is Llan-rhos, the church of the marsh, where the same Mael-gwyn, a British prince of real history, a bold and licentious chief, the original, it is said, of Arthur's Lancelot, shut himself up in the church to avoid the Yellow Plague, and peeped out through a hole in the door, and saw the monster
10 and died. Behind among the woods, is Glod-daeth, *the place of feasting*, where the bards were entertained; and farther away, up the valley of the Conway towards Llanrwst, is the Lake of Geirionydd and Taliesin's grave. Or, again, looking seawards and Anglesey-wards, you have Pen-mon, Seiriol's isle and
15 priory, where Mael-gwyn lies buried; you have the *Sands of Lamentation* and Llys Helig, *Helig's Mansion*, a mansion under the waves, a sea-buried palace and realm. *Hac ibat Simois; hic est Sigeia tellus.*

    As I walked up and down, last August year, looking at the
20 waves as they washed this Sigeian land which has never had its Homer, and listening with curiosity to the strange, unfamiliar speech of its old possessors' obscure descendants,— bathing people, vegetable-sellers, and donkey boys,—who were all about me, suddenly I heard, through the stream of unknown
25 Welsh, words, not English, indeed, but still familiar. They came from a French nursery-maid with some children. Profoundly ignorant of her relationship, this Gaulish Celt moved among her British cousins, speaking her polite neo-Latin tongue, and full of compassionate contempt, probably, for the Welsh barbarians
30 and their jargon. What a revolution was here! How had the star of this daughter of Gomer waxed, while the star of these Cymry, his sons, had waned! What a difference of fortune in the two, since the days when, speaking the same language, they left their common dwelling-place in the heart of Asia; since
35 the Cimmerians of the Euxine came in upon their western kinsmen, the sons of the giant Galates; since the sisters, Gaul and Britain, cut the mistletoe in their forests, and saw the coming of Cæsar! *Blanc, rouge, rocher, champ, église, seigneur,*— these words, by which the Gallo-Roman Celt now names white,

and red, and rock, and field, and church, and lord, are no part
of the speech of his true ancestors, they are words he has learnt;
but since he learned them they have had a world-wide success,
and we all teach them to our children, and armies speaking
them have domineered in every city of that Germany by which   5
the British Celt was broken, and in the train of these armies,
Saxon auxiliaries, a humbled contingent, have been fain to
follow;—the poor Welshman still says, in the genuine tongue
of his ancestors,[1] *gwyn, goch, craig, maes, llan, arglwydd;* but
his land is a province, and his history petty, and his Saxon   10
subduers scout his speech as an obstacle to civilisation; and
the echo of all its kindred in other lands is growing every day
fainter and more feeble; gone in Cornwall, going in Brittany
and the Scotch Highlands, going, too, in Ireland;—and there,
above all, the badge of the beaten race, the property of the   15
vanquished.

But the Celtic genius was just then preparing, in Llandudno,

---

[1] Lord Strangford remarks on this passage:—"Your Gomer and your
Cimmerians are of course only lay figures, to be accepted in the rhetorical
and subjective sense. As such I accept them, but I enter a protest against   20
the 'genuine tongue of his ancestors.' Modern Celtic tongues are to the
old Celtic heard by Julius Cæsar, broadly speaking, what the modern Romanic tongues are to Cæsar's own Latin. Welsh, in fact, is a *detritus;* a
language in the category of modern French, or, to speak less roughly and
with a closer approximation, of old Provençal, not in the category of   25
Lithuanian, much less in the category of Basque. By true inductive research, based on an accurate comparison of such forms of Celtic speech,
oral and recorded, as we now possess, modern philology has, in so far
as was possible, succeeded in restoring certain forms of the parent speech,
and in so doing has achieved not the least striking of its many triumphs;   30
for those very forms thus restored have since been verified past all cavil
by their actual discovery in the old Gaulish inscriptions recently come to
light. The *phonesis* of Welsh as it stands is modern, not primitive; its
grammar,—the verbs excepted,—is constructed out of the fragments of its
earlier forms, and its vocabulary is strongly Romanised, two out of the   35
six words here given being Latin of the Empire. Rightly understood, this
enhances the value of modern Celtic instead of depreciating it, because
it serves to rectify it. To me it is a wonder that Welsh should have retained so much of its integrity under the iron pressure of four hundred
years of Roman dominion. Modern Welsh tenacity and cohesive power   40
under English pressure is nothing compared with what that must have
been."

to have its hour of revival. Workmen were busy in putting up
a large tent-like wooden building, which attracted the eye of
every newcomer, and which my little boys believed (their
wish, no doubt, being father to their belief) to be a circus. It
5   turned out, however, to be no circus for Castor and Pollux,
but a temple for Apollo and the Muses. It was the place where
the Eisteddfod, or Bardic Congress of Wales, was about to be
held; a meeting which has for its object (I quote the words of
its promoters) "the diffusion of useful knowledge, the eliciting
10 of native talent, and the cherishing of love of home and honourable fame by the cultivation of poetry, music, and art." My
little boys were disappointed; but I, whose circus days are over,
I, who have a professional interest in poetry, and who, also,
hating all one-sidedness and oppression, wish nothing better
15 than that the Celtic genius should be able to show itself to the
world and to make its voice heard, was delighted. I took my
ticket, and waited impatiently for the day of opening. The
day came, an unfortunate one; storms of wind, clouds of dust,
an angry, dirty sea. The Saxons who arrived by the Liverpool
20 steamers looked miserable; even the Welsh who arrived by land,
—whether they were discomposed by the bad morning, or by
the monstrous and crushing tax which the London and North-
Western Railway Company levies on all whom it transports
across those four miles of marshy peninsula between Conway
25 and Llandudno,—did not look happy. First we went to the
Gorsedd, or preliminary congress for conferring the degree of
bard. The Gorsedd was held in the open air, at the windy corner
of a street, and the morning was not favourable to open-air
solemnities. The Welsh, too, share, it seems to me, with their
30 Saxon invaders, an inaptitude for show and spectacle. Show
and spectacle are better managed by the Latin race, and those
whom it has moulded; the Welsh, like us, are a little awkward
and resourceless in the organisation of a festival. The presiding
genius of the mystic circle, in our hideous nineteenth century
35 costume relieved only by a green scarf, the wind drowning his
voice and the dust powdering his whiskers, looked thoroughly
wretched: so did the aspirants for bardic honours; and I believe, after about an hour of it, we all of us, as we stood

shivering round the sacred stones, began half to wish for the Druid's sacrificial knife to end our sufferings. But the Druid's knife is gone from his hands; so we sought the shelter of the Eisteddfod building.

The sight inside was not lively. The president and his supporters mustered strong on the platform. On the floor the one or two front benches were pretty well filled, but their occupants were for the most part Saxons, who came there from curiosity, not from enthusiasm; and all the middle and back benches, where should have been the true enthusiasts,—the Welsh people,—were nearly empty. The president, I am sure, showed a national spirit which was admirable. He addressed us Saxons in our own language, and called us "the English branch of the descendants of the ancient Britons." We received the compliment with the impassive dulness which is the characteristic of our nature; and the lively Celtic nature, which should have made up for the dulness of ours, was absent. A lady who sat by me, and who was the wife, I found, of a distinguished bard on the platform, told me, with emotion in her look and voice, how dear were these solemnities to the heart of her people, how deep was the interest which is aroused by them. I believe her, but still the whole performance, on that particular morning, was incurably lifeless. The recitation of the prize compositions began: pieces of verse and prose in the Welsh language, an essay on punctuality being, if I remember right, one of them; a poem on the march of Havelock, another. This went on for some time. Then Dr. Vaughan,—the well-known Nonconformist minister, a Welshman, and a good patriot,— addressed us in English. His speech was a powerful one, and he succeeded, I confess, in sending a faint thrill through our front benches; but it was the old familiar thrill which we have all of us felt a thousand times in Saxon chapels and meeting-halls, and had nothing bardic about it. I stepped out, and in the street I came across an acquaintance fresh from London and the parliamentary session. In a moment the spell of the Celtic genius was forgotten, the Philistinism of our Saxon nature made itself felt; and my friend and I walked up and down by the roaring waves, talking not of ovates and bards, and triads and englyns, but of the sewage question, and the glories of our local self-government, and the mysterious perfections of the Metropolitan Board of Works.

I believe it is admitted, even by the admirers of Eisteddfods in general, that this particular Eisteddfod was not a success. Llandudno, it is said, was not the right place for it. Held in Conway Castle, as a few years ago it was, and its spectators,— an enthusiastic multitude,—filling the grand old ruin, I can imagine it a most impressive and interesting sight, even to a stranger labouring under the terrible disadvantage of being ignorant of the Welsh language. But even seen as I saw it at Llandudno, it had the power to set one thinking. An Eisteddfod is, no doubt, a kind of Olympic meeting; and that the common people of Wales should care for such a thing, shows something Greek in them, something spiritual, something humane, something (I am afraid one must add) which in the English common people is not to be found. This line of reflection has been followed by the accomplished Bishop of St. David's, and by the *Saturday Review;* it is just, it is fruitful, and those who pursued it merit our best thanks. But, from peculiar circumstances, the Llandudno meeting was, as I have said, such as not at all to suggest ideas of Olympia, and of a multitude touched by the divine flame, and hanging on the lips of Pindar. It rather suggested the triumph of the prosaic, practical Saxon, and the approaching extinction of an enthusiasm which he derides as factitious, a literature which he disdains as trash, a language which he detests as a nuisance.

I must say I quite share the opinion of my brother Saxons as to the practical inconvenience of perpetuating the speaking of Welsh. It may cause a moment's distress to one's imagination when one hears that the last Cornwall peasant who spoke the old tongue of Cornwall is dead; but, no doubt, Cornwall is the better for adopting English, for becoming more thoroughly one with the rest of the country. The fusion of all the inhabitants of these islands into one homogeneous, English-speaking whole, the breaking down of barriers between us, the swallowing up of separate provincial nationalities, is a consummation to which the natural course of things irresistibly tends; it is a necessity of what is called modern civilisation, and modern civilisation is a real, legitimate force; the change must come, and its accomplishment is a mere affair of time. The sooner the Welsh language disappears as an instrument of the practical, political, social life of Wales, the better; the better for England, the better for Wales itself. Traders and tourists do excellent service by pushing the English wedge farther and farther into the heart of the principality; Ministers of Education, by hammering it harder and harder into the elementary schools. Nor, perhaps, can one have much sympathy with the literary cultivation of Welsh as an instrument of living literature; and in this respect Eisteddfods encourage, I think, a fantastic and mischief-working delusion. For all serious purposes in modern literature (and trifling purposes in it who would care to encourage?) the language of a Welshman is and must be English; if an Eisteddfod author has anything to say about punctuality or about the march of Havelock, he had much better say it in English; or rather, perhaps, what he has to say on these subjects may as well be said in Welsh, but the moment he has anything of real importance to say, anything the world will the least care to hear, he must speak English. Dilettantism might possibly do much harm here, might mislead and waste and bring to nought a genuine talent. For all modern purposes, I repeat, let us all as soon as possible be one people; let the Welshman speak English, and, if he is an author, let him write English.

So far, I go along with the stream of my brother Saxons; but here, I imagine, I part company with them. They will have nothing to do with the Welsh language and literature on any terms; they would gladly make a clean sweep of it from the face of the earth. I, on certain terms, wish to make a great deal more of it than is made now; and I regard the Welsh literature, —or rather, dropping the distinction between Welsh and Irish, Gaels and Cymris, let me say Celtic literature,—as an object of very great interest. My brother Saxons have, as is well known, a terrible way with them of wanting to improve everything but themselves off the face of the earth; I have no such passion for finding nothing but myself everywhere; I like

variety to exist and to show itself to me, and I would not for
the world have the lineaments of the Celtic genius lost. But I
know my brother Saxons, I know their strength, and I know
that the Celtic genius will make nothing of trying to set up
5   barriers against them in the world of fact and brute force, of
trying to hold its own against them as a political and social
counter-power, as the soul of a hostile nationality. To me
there is something mournful (and at this moment, when one
sees what is going on in Ireland, how well may one say so!) in
10 hearing a Welshman or an Irishman make pretensions,—natural
pretensions, I admit, but how hopelessly vain!—to such a rival
self-establishment; there is something mournful in hearing an
Englishman scout them. Strength! alas, it is not strength, strength
in the material world, which is wanting to us Saxons; we have
15 plenty of strength for swallowing up and absorbing as much as
we choose; there is nothing to hinder us from effacing the last
poor material remains of that Celtic power which once was
everywhere, but has long since, in the race of civilisation, fallen
out of sight. We may threaten them with extinction if we
20 will, and may almost say in so threatening them, like Cæsar
in threatening with death the tribune Metellus who closed the
treasury doors against him: "And when I threaten this, young
man, to threaten it is more trouble to me than to do it." It is
not in the outward and visible world of material life that the
25 Celtic genius of Wales or Ireland can at this day hope to count
for much; it is in the inward world of thought and science.
What it *has* been, what it *has* done, let it ask us to attend to
that, as a matter of science and history; not to what it will be
or will do, as a matter of modern politics. It cannot count
30 appreciably now as a material power; but, perhaps, if it can
get itself thoroughly known as an object of science, it may
count for a good deal,—far more than we Saxons, most of us,
imagine,—as a spiritual power.

The bent of our time is towards science, towards knowing
35 things as they are; so the Celt's claims towards having his
genius and its works fairly treated, as objects of scientific
investigation, the Saxon can hardly reject, when these claims
are urged simply on their own merits, and are not mixed up

with extraneous pretensions which jeopardise them. What the French call the *science des origines*, the science of origins,— a science which is at the bottom of all real knowledge of the actual world, and which is every day growing in interest and importance,—is very incomplete without a thorough critical account of the Celts, and their genius, language, and literature. This science has still great progress to make, but its progress, made even within the recollection of those of us who are in middle life, has already affected our common notions about the Celtic race; and this change, too, shows how science, the knowing things as they are, may even have salutary practical consequences. I remember, when I was young, I was taught to think of Celt as separated by an impassable gulf from Teuton; [1]

[1] Here again let me have the pleasure of quoting Lord Strangford:— "When the Celtic tongues were first taken in hand at the dawn of comparative philological inquiry, the tendency was, for all practical results, to separate them from the Indo-European aggregate, rather than to unite them with it. The great gulf once fixed between them was narrowed on the surface, but it was greatly and indefinitely deepened. Their vocabulary and some of their grammar was seen at once to be perfectly Indo-European, but they had no case-endings to their nouns,—none at all in Welsh, none that could be understood in Gaelic; their *phonesis* seemed primeval and inexplicable, and nothing could be made out of their pronouns which could not be equally made out of many wholly un-Aryan languages. They were therefore co-ordinated, not with each single Aryan tongue, but with the general complex of Aryan tongues, and were conceived to be anterior to them and apart from them, as it were the strayed vanguard of European colonisation or conquest from the East. The reason of this misconception was, that their records lay wholly uninvestigated as far as all historical study of the language was concerned, and that nobody troubled himself about the relative age and the development of forms, so that the philologists were fain to take them as they were put into their hands by uncritical or perverse native commentators and writers, whose grammars and dictionaries teemed with blunders and downright forgeries. One thing, and one thing alone, led to the truth: the sheer drudgery of thirteen long years spent by Zeuss in the patient investigation of the most ancient Celtic records, in their actual condition, line by line and letter by letter. Then for the first time the foundation of Celtic research was laid; but the great philologist did not live to see the superstructure which never could have been raised but for him. Prichard was first to indicate the right path, and Bopp, in his monograph of 1839, displayed his incomparable and masterly sagacity as usual, but for want

my father, in particular, was never weary of contrasting them;
he insisted much oftener on the separation between us and
them than on the separation between us and any other race in
the world; in the same way Lord Lyndhurst, in words long
famous, called the Irish, "aliens in speech, in religion, in blood."
This naturally created a profound sense of estrangement; it
doubled the estrangement which political and religious differences already made between us and the Irish: it seemed to make
this estrangement immense, incurable, fatal. It begot a strange
reluctance, as any one may see by reading the preface to the
great textbook for Welsh poetry, the *Myvyrian Archæology*,
published at the beginning of this century, to further,—nay,
allow,—even among quiet, peaceable people like the Welsh,
the publication of the documents of their ancient literature, the
monuments of the Cymric genius; such was the sense of repul-
sion, the sense of incompatibility, of radical antagonism, making
it seem dangerous to us to let such opposites to ourselves have
speech and utterance. Certainly the Jew,—the Jew of ancient
times, at least,—then seemed a thousand degrees nearer than
the Celt to us. Puritanism had so assimilated Bible ideas and
phraseology; names like Ebenezer, and notions like that of hew-
ing Agag in pieces, came so natural to us, that the sense of
affinity between the Teutonic and the Hebrew nature was quite
strong; a steady, middle-class Anglo-Saxon much more imagined himself Ehud's cousin than Ossian's. But meanwhile,
the pregnant and striking ideas of the ethnologists about the
true natural grouping of the human race, the doctrine of a
great Indo-European unity, comprising Hindoos, Persians,

_____

of any trustworthy record of Celtic words and forms to work upon, the
truth remained concealed or obscured until the publication of the *Grammatica Celtica*. Dr. Arnold, a man of the past generation, who made more
use of the then uncertain and unfixed doctrines of comparative philology
in his historical writings than is done by the present generation in the
fullest noonday light of the *Vergleichende Grammatik*, was thus justified
in his view by the philology of the period, to which he merely gave an
enlarged historical expression. The prime fallacy then as now, however,
was that of antedating the distinction between Gaelic and Cymric Celts."

Greeks, Latins, Celts, Teutons, Slavonians, on the one hand, and, on the other hand, of a Semitic unity and of a Mongolian unity, separated by profound distinguishing marks from the Indo-European unity and from one another, was slowly acquiring consistency and popularising itself. So strong and real could the sense of sympathy or antipathy, grounded upon real identity or diversity in race, grow in men of culture, that we read of a genuine Teuton, Wilhelm von Humboldt, finding, even in the sphere of religion, that sphere where the might of Semitism has been so overpowering, the food which most truly suited his spirit in the productions not of the alien Semitic genius, but of the genius of Greece or India, the Teuton's born kinsfolk of the common Indo-European family. "Towards Semitism he felt himself," we read, "far less drawn;" he had the consciousness of a certain antipathy in the depths of his nature to this, and to its "absorbing, tyrannous, terrorist religion," as to the opener, more flexible Indo-European genius, this religion appeared. "The mere workings of the old man in him!" Semitism will readily reply; and though one can hardly admit this short and easy method of settling the matter, it must be owned that Humboldt's is an extreme case of Indo-Europeanism, useful as letting us see what may be the power of race and primitive constitution, but not likely, in the spiritual sphere, to have many companion cases equalling it. Still, even in this sphere, the tendency is in Humboldt's direction; the modern spirit tends more and more to establish a sense of native diversity between our European bent and the Semitic bent, and to eliminate, even in our religion, certain elements as purely and excessively Semitic, and therefore, in right, not combinable with our European nature, not assimilable by it. This tendency is now quite visible even among ourselves, and even, as I have said, within the great sphere of the Semitic genius, the sphere of religion; and for its justification this tendency appeals to science, the science of origins; it appeals to this science as teaching us which way our natural affinities and repulsions lie. It appeals to this science, and in part it comes from it; it is, in considerable part, an indirect practical result from it.

In the sphere of politics, too, there has, in the same way, appeared an indirect practical result from this science; the sense of antipathy to the Irish people, of radical estrangement from them, has visibly abated amongst all the better part of us; the
5   remorse for past ill-treatment of them, the wish to make amends, to do them justice, to fairly unite, if possible, in one people with them, has visibly increased; hardly a book on Ireland is now published, hardly a debate on Ireland now passes in Parliament, without this appearing. Fanciful as the notion may at
10 first seem, I am inclined to think that the march of science,— science insisting that there is no such original chasm between the Celt and the Saxon as we once popularly imagined, that they are not truly, what Lord Lyndhurst called them, *aliens in blood* from us, that they are our brothers in the great Indo-
15 European family,—has had a share, an appreciable share, in producing this changed state of feeling. No doubt, the release from alarm and struggle, the sense of firm possession, solid security, and overwhelming power; no doubt these, allowing and encouraging humane feelings to spring up in us, have done
20 much; no doubt a state of fear and danger, Ireland in hostile conflict with us, our union violently disturbed, might, while it drove back all humane feelings, make also the old sense of utter estrangement revive. Nevertheless, so long as such a malignant revolution of events does not actually come about,
25 so long the new sense of kinship and kindliness lives, works, and gathers strength; and the longer it so lives and works, the more it makes any such malignant revolution improbable. And this new, reconciling sense has, I say, its roots in science.

However, on these indirect benefits of science we must not
30 lay too much stress. Only this must be allowed; it is clear that there are now in operation two influences, both favourable to a more attentive and impartial study of Celtism than it has yet ever received from us. One is the strengthening in us of the feeling of Indo-Europeanism; the other, the strengthening
35 in us of the scientific sense generally. The first breaks down barriers between us and the Celt, relaxes the estrangement between us; the second begets the desire to know his case thoroughly, and to be just to it. This is a very different matter from

the political and social Celtisation of which certain enthusiasts dream; but it is not to be despised by any one to whom the Celtic genius is dear; and it is possible, while the other is not.

[1]

To know the Celtic case thoroughly, one must know the Celtic people; and to know them one must know that by which a people best express themselves,—their literature. Few of us have any notion what a mass of Celtic literature is really yet extant and accessible. One constantly finds even very accomplished people, who fancy that the remains of Welsh and Irish literature are as inconsiderable by their volume, as, in their opinion, they are by their intrinsic merit; that these remains consist of a few prose stories, in great part borrowed from the literature of nations more civilised than the Welsh or Irish nation, and of some unintelligible poetry. As to Welsh literature, they have heard, perhaps, of the *Black Book of Caermarthen*, or of the *Red Book of Hergest*, and they imagine that one or two famous manuscript books like these contain the whole matter. They have no notion that, in real truth, to quote the words of one who is no friend to the high pretensions of Welsh literature, but their most formidable impugner, Mr. Nash:—"The Myvyrian manuscripts alone, now deposited in the British Museum, amount to 47 volumes of poetry, of various sizes, containing about 4700 pieces of poetry, in 16,000 pages, besides about 2000 englynion or epigrammatic stanzas. There are also, in the same collection, 53 volumes of prose, in about 15,300 pages, containing a great many curious documents on various subjects. Besides these, which were purchased of the widow of the celebrated Owen Jones, the editor of the *Myvyrian Archæology*, there are a vast number of collections of Welsh manuscripts in London, and in the libraries of the gentry of the principality." The *Myvyrian Archæology*, here spoken of by Mr. Nash, I have already mentioned; he calls its editor, Owen Jones, celebrated; he is not so celebrated but that he claims a word, in passing, from a professor of poetry. He was

a Denbighshire *statesman*, as we say in the north, born before the middle of last century, in that vale of Myvyr, which
has given its name to his archæology. From his childhood he
had that passion for the old treasures of his country's literature,
5   which to this day, as I have said, in the common people of
Wales is so remarkable; these treasures were unprinted,
scattered, difficult of access, jealously guarded. "More than
once," says Edward Lhuyd, who in his *Archæologia Britannica*,
brought out by him in 1707, would gladly have given them to
10 the world, "more than once I had a promise from the owner,
and the promise was afterwards retracted at the instigation of
certain persons, pseudo-politicians, as I think, rather than men
of letters." So Owen Jones went up, a young man of nineteen, to London, and got employment in a furrier's shop in
15 Thames Street; for forty years, with a single object in view, he
worked at his business; and at the end of that time his object
was won. He had risen in his employment till the business had
become his own, and he was now a man of considerable means;
but those means had been sought by him for one purpose only,
20 the purpose of his life, the dream of his youth,—the giving
permanence and publicity to the treasures of his national literature. Gradually he got manuscript after manuscript transcribed, and at last, in 1801, he jointly with two friends brought
out in three large volumes, printed in double columns, his
25 *Myvyrian Archæology of Wales*. The book is full of imper-
fections; it presented itself to a public which could not judge
of its importance, and it brought upon its author in his lifetime more attack than honour. He died not long afterwards, and
now he lies buried in All-hallows Church, in London, with his
30 tomb turned towards the east, away from the green vale of
Clwyd and the mountains of his native Wales; but his book is
the great repertory of the literature of his nation, the comparative study of languages and literatures gains every day
more followers, and no one of these followers, at home or
35 abroad, touches Welsh literature without paying homage to
the Denbighshire peasant's name; if the bards' glory and his
own are still matter of moment to him,—*si quid mentem
mortalia tangunt*,—he may be satisfied.

Even the printed stock of early Welsh literature is, therefore, considerable, and the manuscript stock of it is very great
indeed. Of Irish literature, the stock, printed and manuscript,
is truly vast; the work of cataloguing and describing this has
been admirably performed by another remarkable man, who   5
died only the other day, Mr. Eugene O'Curry. Obscure Scaliger
of a despised literature, he deserves some weightier voice to
praise him than the voice of an unlearned bellettristic trifler
like me; he belongs to the race of the giants in literary research
and industry,—a race now almost extinct. Without a literary   10
education, and impeded too, it appears, by much trouble of
mind and infirmity of body, he has accomplished such a thorough work of classification and description for the chaotic mass
of Irish literature, that the student has now half his labour
saved, and needs only to use his materials as Eugene O'Curry   15
hands them to him. It was as a professor in the Catholic University in Dublin that O'Curry gave the lectures in which he
has done the student this service; it is touching to find that
these lectures, a splendid tribute of devotion to the Celtic cause,
had no hearer more attentive, more sympathising, than a man,   20
himself, too, the champion of a cause more interesting than
prosperous,—one of those causes which please noble spirits, but
do not please destiny, which have Cato's adherence, but not
Heaven's,—Dr. Newman. Eugene O'Curry, in these lectures
of his, taking as his standard the quarto page of Dr. O'Donovan's   25
edition of the *Annals of the Four Masters* (and this printed
monument of one branch of Irish literature occupies by itself,
let me say in passing, seven large quarto volumes, containing
4215 pages of closely printed matter), Eugene O'Curry says,
that the great vellum manuscript books belonging to Trinity   30
College, Dublin, and to the Royal Irish Academy,—books with
fascinating titles, the *Book of the Dun Cow*, the *Book of
Leinster*, the *Book of Ballymote*, the *Speckled Book*, the *Book
of Lecain*, the *Yellow Book of Lecain*,—have, between them,
matter enough to fill 11,400 of these pages; the other vellum   35
manuscripts in the library of Trinity College, Dublin, have
matter enough to fill 8200 pages more; and the paper manuscripts of Trinity College, and the Royal Irish Academy to-

gether, would fill, he says, 30,000 such pages more. The
ancient laws of Ireland, the so-called Brehon laws, which a commission is now publishing, were not as yet completely transcribed when O'Curry wrote; but what had even then been
transcribed was sufficient, he says, to fill nearly 8000 of Dr.
O'Donovan's pages. Here are, at any rate, materials enough
with a vengeance. These materials fall, of course, into several
divisions. The most literary of these divisions, the *Tales*, consisting of *Historic Tales* and *Imaginative Tales*, distributes the
contents of its *Historic Tales* as follows:—Battles, voyages,
sieges, tragedies, cow-spoils, courtships, adventures, land-ex-
peditions, sea-expeditions, banquets, elopements, loves, lake-
irruptions, colonisations, visions. Of what a treasure-house of
resources for the history of Celtic life and the Celtic genius
does that bare list, even by itself, call up the image! The *Annals
of the Four Masters* give "the years of foundations and de-
structions of churches and castles, the obituaries of remarkable
persons, the inaugurations of kings, the battles of chiefs, the
contests of clans, the ages of bards, abbots, bishops, etc." [1]
Through other divisions of this mass of materials,—the books
of pedigrees and genealogies, the martyrologies and festologies,
such as the *Félire of Angus the Culdee*, the topographical tracts,
such as the *Dinnsenchas*,—we touch "the most ancient traditions of the Irish, traditions which were committed to writing
at a period when the ancient customs of the people were unbroken." We touch "the early history of Ireland, civil and
ecclesiastical." We get "the origin and history of the countless
monuments of Ireland, of the ruined church and tower, the
sculptured cross, the holy well, and the commemorative name
of almost every townland and parish in the whole island." We
get, in short, "the most detailed information upon almost every
part of ancient Gaelic life, a vast quantity of valuable details of
life and manners." [2]

And then, besides, to our knowledge of the Celtic genius,
Mr. Norris has brought us from Cornwall, M. de la Villemarqué
from Brittany, contributions, insignificant indeed in quantity,

[1] Dr. O'Conor in his *Catalogue of the Stowe MSS.* (quoted by O'Curry).
[2] O'Curry.

if one compares them with the mass of the Irish materials extant, but far from insignificant in value.

We want to know what all this mass of documents really tells us about the Celt. But the mode of dealing with these documents, and with the whole question of Celtic antiquity, has hitherto been most unsatisfactory. Those who have dealt with them, have gone to work, in general, either as warm Celt-lovers or as warm Celt-haters, and not as disinterested students of an important matter of science. One party seems to set out with the determination to find everything in Celtism and its remains; the other, with the determination to find nothing in them. A simple seeker for truth has a hard time between the two. An illustration or so will make clear what I mean. First let us take the Celt-lovers, who, though they engage one's sympathies more than the Celt-haters, yet, inasmuch as assertion is more dangerous than denial, show their weaknesses in a more signal way. A very learned man, the Rev. Edward Davies, published in the early part of this century two important books on Celtic antiquity. The second of these books, *The Mythology and Rites of the British Druids,* contains, with much other interesting matter, the charming story of Taliesin. Bryant's book on mythology was then in vogue, and Bryant, in the fantastical manner so common in those days, found in Greek mythology what he called an arkite idolatry, pointing to Noah's deluge and the ark. Davies, wishing to give dignity to his Celtic mythology, determines to find the arkite idolatry there too, and the style in which he proceeds to do this affords a good specimen of the extravagance which has caused Celtic antiquity to be looked upon with so much suspicion. The story of Taliesin begins thus:—

"In former times there was a man of noble descent in Penllyn. His name was Tegid Voel, and his paternal estate was in the middle of the Lake of Tegid, and his wife was called Ceridwen."

Nothing could well be simpler; but what Davies finds in this simple opening of Taliesin's story, is prodigious:—

"Let us take a brief view of the proprietor of this estate. Tegid Voel—*bald serenity*—presents itself at once to our fancy.

The painter would find no embarrassment in sketching the portrait of this sedate venerable personage, whose crown is partly stripped of its hoary honours. But of all the gods of antiquity, none could with propriety sit for this picture except-
5   ing Saturn, the acknowledged representative of Noah, and the husband of Rhea, which was but another name for Ceres, the genius of the ark."

And Ceres, the genius of the ark, is of course found in Ceridwen, "the British Ceres, the arkite goddess who initiates
10   us into the deepest mysteries of the arkite superstition."

Now the story of Taliesin, as it proceeds, exhibits Ceridwen as a sorceress; and a sorceress, like a goddess, belongs to the world of the supernatural; but, beyond this, the story itself does not suggest one particle of relationship between Ceridwen
15   and Ceres. All the rest comes out of Davies's fancy, and is established by reasoning of the force of that about "bald serenity."

It is not difficult for the other side, the Celt-haters, to get a triumph over such adversaries as these. Perhaps I ought to ask
20   pardon of Mr. Nash, whose *Taliesin* it is impossible to read without profit and instruction, for classing him among the Celt-haters: his determined scepticism about Welsh antiquity seems to me, however, to betray a preconceived hostility, a bias taken beforehand, as unmistakable as Mr. Davies's prepossessions. But
25   Mr. Nash is often very happy in demolishing, for really the Celt-lovers seem often to try to lay themselves open, and to invite demolition. Full of his notions about an arkite idolatry and a Helio-dæmonic worship, Edward Davies gives this trans-lation of an old Welsh poem, entitled *The Panegyric of Lludd*
30   *the Great:*—

"A song of dark import was composed by the distinguished Ogdoad, who assembled on the day of the moon, and went in open procession. On the day of Mars they allotted wrath to their adversaries; on the day of Mercury they enjoyed their
35   full pomp; on the day of Jove they were delivered from the detested usurpers; on the day of Venus, the day of the great influx, they swam in the blood of men;[1] on the day of the

---

[1] Here, where Saturday should come, something is wanting in the man-uscript.

Sun there truly assemble five ships and five hundred of those who make supplication: O Brithi, O Brithoi! O son of the compacted wood, the shock overtakes me; we all attend on Adonai, on the area of Pwmpai."

That looks Helio-dæmonic enough, undoubtedly; especially when Davies prints *O Brithi, O Brithoi!* in Hebrew characters, as being "vestiges of sacred hymns in the Phœnician language." But then comes Mr. Nash, and says that the poem is a Middle-Age composition, with nothing Helio-dæmonic about it; that it is meant to ridicule the monks; and that *O Brithi, O Brithoi!* is a mere piece of unintelligible jargon in mockery of the chants used by the monks at prayers; and he gives this counter-translation of the poem:—

"They make harsh songs; they note eight numbers. On Monday they will be prying about. On Tuesday they separate, angry with their adversaries. On Wednesday they drink, enjoying themselves ostentatiously. On Thursday they are in the choir; their poverty is disagreeable. Friday is a day of abundance, the men are swimming in pleasures. On Sunday, certainly, five legions and five hundreds of them, they pray, they make exclamations: O Brithi, Brithoi! Like wood-cuckoos in noise they will be, every one of the idiots banging on the ground."

As one reads Mr. Nash's explanation and translation after Edward Davies's, one feels that a flood of the broad daylight of common-sense has been suddenly shed over the *Panegyric on Lludd the Great,* and one is very grateful to Mr. Nash.

Or, again, when another Celt-lover, Mr. Herbert, has bewildered us with his fancies, as uncritical as Edward Davies's; with his neo-Druidism, his Mithraic heresy, his Crist-celi, or man-god of the mysteries; and, above all, his ape of the sanctuary, "signifying the mercurial principle, that strange and unexplained disgrace of paganism," Mr. Nash comes to our assistance, and is most refreshingly rational. To confine ourselves to the ape of the sanctuary only. Mr. Herbert constructs his monster,—to whom, he says, "great sanctity, together with foul crime, deception, and treachery," is ascribed,—out of four lines of old Welsh poetry, of which he adopts the following translation:—

"Without the ape, without the stall of the cow, without the

mundane rampart, the world will become desolate, not requiring the cuckoos to convene the appointed dance over the
green."

One is not very clear what all this means, but it has, at any
rate, a solemn air about it, which prepares one for the development of its first-named personage, the ape, into the mystical
ape of the sanctuary. The cow, too,—says another famous Celt-
lover, Dr. Owen, the learned author of the *Welsh Dictionary*,
—the cow (*henfon*) is the cow of transmigration; and this also
sounds natural enough. But Mr. Nash, who has a keen eye
for the piecing which frequently happens in these old fragments, has observed that just here, where the ape of the sanctuary and the cow of transmigration make their appearance,
there seems to come a cluster of adages, popular sayings; and
he at once remembers an adage preserved with the word *henfon*
in it, where, as he justly says, "the cow of transmigration cannot very well have place." This adage, rendered literally in
English, is: "Whoso owns the old cow, let him go at her tail;"
and the meaning of it, as a popular saying, is clear and simple
enough. With this clue, Mr. Nash examines the whole passage,
suggests that *heb eppa*, "without the ape," with which Mr.
Herbert begins, in truth belongs to something going before
and is to be translated somewhat differently; and, in short, that
what we really have here is simply these three adages one
after another: "The first share is the full one. Politeness is
natural, says the ape. Without the cow-stall there would be no
dung-heap." And one can hardly doubt that Mr. Nash is quite
right.

Even friends of the Celt who are perfectly incapable of
extravagances of this sort fall too often into a loose mode of
criticism concerning him and the documents of his history,
which is unsatisfactory in itself, and also gives an advantage to
his many enemies. One of the best and most delightful friends
he has ever had,—M. de la Villemarqué,—has seen clearly
enough that often the alleged antiquity of his documents cannot
be proved, that it can be even disproved, and that he must
rely on other supports than this to establish what he wants; yet
one finds him saying: "I open the collection of Welsh bards

from the sixth to the tenth century. Taliesin, one of the oldest of them,"... and so on. But his adversaries deny that we have really any such thing as a "collection of Welsh bards from the sixth to the tenth century," or that a "Taliesin, one of the oldest of them," exists to be quoted in defence of any thesis. Sharon Turner, again, whose *Vindication of the Ancient British Poems* was prompted, it seems to me, by a critical instinct at bottom sound, is weak and uncritical in details like this: "The strange poem of Taliesin, called the *Spoils of Annwn,* implies the existence (in the sixth century, he means) of mythological tales about Arthur; and the frequent allusions of the old Welsh bards to the persons and incidents which we find in the *Mabinogion,* are further proofs that there must have been such stories in circulation amongst the Welsh." But the critic has to show, against his adversaries, that the *Spoils of Annwn* is a real poem of the sixth century, with a real sixth-century poet called Taliesin for its author, before he can use it to prove what Sharon Turner there wishes to prove; and, in like manner, the high antiquity of persons and incidents that are found in the manuscripts of the *Mabinogion,*—manuscripts written, like the famous *Red Book of Hergest,* in the library of Jesus College at Oxford, in the fourteenth and fifteenth centuries,—is not proved by allusions of the old Welsh bards, until (which is just the question at issue) the pieces containing these allusions are proved themselves to possess a very high antiquity. In the present state of the question as to the early Welsh literature, this sort of reasoning is inconclusive and bewildering, and merely carries us round in a circle. Again, it is worse than inconclusive reasoning, it shows so uncritical a spirit that it begets grave mistrust, when Mr. Williams ab Ithel, employed by the Master of the Rolls to edit the *Brut y Tywysogion,* the "Chronicle of the Princes," says in his introduction, in many respects so useful and interesting: "We may add, on the authority of a scrupulously faithful antiquary, and one that was deeply versed in the traditions of his order—the late Iolo Morganwg—that King Arthur in his Institutes of the Round Table introduced the age of the world for events which occurred before Christ, and the year of Christ's nativity for all

subsequent events." Now, putting out of the question Iolo
Morganwg's character as an antiquary, it is obvious that no
one, not Grimm himself, can stand in that way as "authority"
for King Arthur's having thus regulated chronology by his
5   Institutes of the Round Table, or even for there ever having
been any such institutes at all. And finally, greatly as I respect
and admire Mr. Eugene O'Curry, unquestionable as is the
sagacity, the moderation, which he in general unites with his
immense learning, I must say that he, too, like his brother Celt-
10   lovers, sometimes lays himself dangerously open. For instance,
the Royal Irish Academy possesses in its Museum a relic of the
greatest value, the *Domhnach Airgid,* a Latin manuscript of
the four gospels. The outer box containing this manuscript is
of the fourteenth century, but the manuscript itself, says
15   O'Curry (and no man is better able to judge), is certainly of
the sixth. This is all very well. "But," O'Curry then goes on,
"I believe no reasonable doubt can exist that the *Domhnach
Airgid* was actually sanctified by the hand of our great
Apostle." One has a thrill of excitement at receiving this assur-
20   ance from such a man as Eugene O'Curry; one believes that he
is really going to make it clear that St. Patrick did actually
sanctify the *Domhnach Airgid* with his own hands; and one
reads on:—

"As St. Patrick, says an ancient life of St. Mac Carthainn pre-
25   served by Colgan in his *Acta Sanctorum Hiberniæ,* was on his
way from the north, and coming to the place now called
Clogher, he was carried over a stream by his strong man,
Bishop Mac Carthainn, who, while bearing the Saint, groaned
aloud, exclaiming: 'Ugh! Ugh!'

30   " 'Upon my good word,' said the Saint, 'it was not usual
with you to make that noise.'

" 'I am now old and infirm,' said Bishop Mac Carthainn,
'and all my early companions in mission-work you have settled
down in their respective churches, while I am still on my
35   travels.'

" 'Found a church then,' said the Saint, 'that shall not be
too near us (that is to his own Church of Armagh) for familiarity, nor too far from us for intercourse.'

"And the Saint then left Bishop Mac Carthainn there, at Clogher, and bestowed the *Domhnach Airgid* upon him, which had been given to Patrick from heaven, when he was on the sea, coming to Erin."

The legend is full of poetry, full of humour; and one can quite appreciate, after reading it, the tact which gave St. Patrick such a prodigious success in organising the primitive church in Ireland; the new bishop, "not too near us for familiarity, nor too far from us for intercourse," is a masterpiece. But how can Eugene O'Curry have imagined that it takes no more than a legend like that, to prove that the particular manuscript now in the Museum of the Royal Irish Academy was once in St. Patrick's pocket?

I insist upon extravagances like these, not in order to throw ridicule upon the Celt-lovers,—on the contrary, I feel a great deal of sympathy with them,—but rather, to make it clear what an immense advantage the Celt-haters, the negative side, have in the controversy about Celtic antiquity; how much a clear-headed sceptic, like Mr. Nash, may utterly demolish, and, in demolishing, give himself the appearance of having won an entire victory. But an entire victory he has, as I will next proceed to show, by no means won.

[II]

I said that a sceptic like Mr. Nash, by demolishing the rubbish of the Celtic antiquaries, might often give himself the appearance of having won a complete victory, but that a complete victory he had, in truth, by no means won. He has cleared much rubbish away, but this is no such very difficult feat, and requires mainly common-sense; to be sure, Welsh archæologists are apt to lose their common-sense, but at moments when they are in possession of it they can do the indispensable, negative part of criticism, not, indeed, so briskly or cleverly as Mr. Nash, but still well enough. Edward Davies, for instance, has quite clearly seen that the alleged remains of old Welsh literature are not to be taken for genuine just as they stand: "Some paltry and mendicant minstrel, who only chaunted it as an old song, has tacked on" (he says of a poem he is discussing) "three lines, in a style and measure totally different from the preceding verses: 'May the Trinity grant us mercy in the day of judgment: a liberal donation, good gentlemen!' " There, fifty years before Mr. Nash, is a clearance very like one of Mr. Nash's. But the difficult feat in this matter is the feat of construction; to determine when one has cleared away all that is to be cleared away, what is the significance of that which is left; and here, I confess, I think Mr. Nash and his fellow-sceptics, who say that next to nothing is left, and that the significance of whatever is left is next to nothing, dissatisfy the genuine critic even more than Edward Davies and his brother enthusiasts, who have a sense that something primitive, august, and interesting is there, though they fail to extract it, dissatisfy him. There is a very edifying story told by O'Curry of the effect produced on Moore, the poet, who had undertaken to write the history of Ireland (a task for which he was quite unfit), by the contemplation of an old Irish manuscript. Moore had, without knowing anything about them, spoken slightingly of the value to the historian of Ireland of the materials afforded by such manuscripts; but, says O'Curry:—

"In the year 1839, during one of his last visits to the land of his birth, he, in company with his old and attached friend Dr. Petrie, favoured me with an unexpected visit at the Royal Irish Academy. I was at that period employed on the Ordnance Survey of Ireland, and at the time of his visit happened to have before me on my desk the *Books of Ballymote and Lecain, The Speckled Book, The Annals of the Four Masters,* and many other ancient books, for historical research and reference. I had never before seen Moore, and after a brief introduction and explanation of the nature of my occupation by Dr. Petrie, and seeing the formidable array of so many dark and time-worn volumes by which I was surrounded, he looked a little disconcerted, but after a while plucked up courage to open the *Book of Ballymote* and ask what it was. Dr. Petrie and myself then entered into a short explanation of the history and character of the books then present as well as of ancient Gaedhelic documents in general. Moore listened with great attention, alternately scanning the books and myself, and then asked me, in a serious tone, if I understood them, and how I had learned to do so. Having satisfied him upon these points, he turned to Dr. Petrie and said: 'Petrie, these huge tomes could not have been written by fools or for any foolish purpose. I never knew anything about them before, and I had no right to have undertaken the *History of Ireland.*' "

And from that day Moore, it is said, lost all heart for going on with his *History of Ireland,* and it was only the importunity of the publishers which induced him to bring out the remaining volume.

Could not have been written by fools, or for any foolish purpose. That is, I am convinced, a true presentiment to have in one's mind when one looks at Irish documents like the *Book of Ballymote,* or Welsh documents like the *Red Book of Hergest.* In some respects, at any rate, these documents are what they claim to be, they hold what they pretend to hold, they touch that primitive world of which they profess to be the voice. The true critic is he who can detect this precious and genuine part in them, and employ it for the elucidation of the Celt's genius and history, and for any other fruitful purposes to which it can be applied. Merely to point out the mixture of what is late and spurious in them, is to touch but the fringes of the matter. In reliance upon the discovery of this mixture of what is late and spurious in them, to pooh-pooh them altogether, to treat them as a heap of rubbish, a mass of Middle-Age forgeries, is to fall into the greatest possible error. Granted that all the manuscripts of Welsh poetry (to take that branch of Celtic literature which has had, in Mr. Nash, the ablest disparager), granted that all such manuscripts that we possess are, with the most insignificant exception, not older than the twelfth century; granted that the twelfth and thirteenth centuries were a time of great poetical activity in Wales, a time when the mediæval literature flourished there, as it flourished in England, France, and other countries; granted that a great deal of what Welsh enthusiasts have attributed to their great traditional poets of the sixth century belongs to this

later epoch,—what then? Does that get rid of the great traditional poets, the Cynveirdd or old bards, Aneurin, Taliesin,
Llywarch Hen, and their compeers,—does that get rid of the
great poetical tradition of the sixth century altogether; does
5   it merge the whole literary antiquity of Wales in her mediæval
literary antiquity, or, at least, reduce all other than this to insignificance? Mr. Nash says it does; all his efforts are directed
to show how much of the so-called sixth-century pieces may
be resolved into mediæval, twelfth-century work; his grand
10 thesis is that there is nothing primitive and pre-Christian in
the extant Welsh literature, no traces of the Druidism and
Paganism every one associates with Celtic antiquity; all this,
he says, was extinguished by Paulinus in A.D. 59, and never
resuscitated. "At the time the Mabinogion and the Taliesin
15 ballads were composed, no tradition or popular recollection
of the Druids or the Druidical mythology existed in Wales.
The Welsh bards knew of no other mystery, nor of any
mystic creed, unknown to the rest of the Christian world."
And Mr. Nash complains that "the old opinion that the Welsh
20 poems contain notices of Druid or Pagan superstitions of a
remote origin" should still find promulgators; what we find in
them is only, he says, what was circulating in Wales in the
twelfth century, and "one great mistake in these investigations
has been the supposing that the Welsh of the twelfth, or even
25 of the sixth century, were wiser as well as more Pagan than their
neighbours."

    Why, what a wonderful thing is this! We have, in the first
place, the most weighty and explicit testimony,—Strabo's,
Cæsar's, Lucan's,—that this race once possessed a special, pro-
30 found, spiritual discipline, that they were, to use Mr. Nash's
words, "wiser than their neighbours." Lucan's words are
singularly clear and strong, and serve well to stand as a land-
mark in this controversy, in which one is sometimes embarrassed
by hearing authorities quoted on this side or that, when one does
35 not feel sure precisely what they say, how much or how little;
Lucan, addressing those hitherto under the pressure of Rome,
but now left by the Roman civil war to their own devices,
says:—

"Ye too, ye bards, who by your praises perpetuate the
memory of the fallen brave, without hindrance poured forth
your strains. And ye, ye Druids, now that the sword was
removed, began once more your barbaric rites and weird
solemnities. To you only is given knowledge or ignorance
(whichever it be) of the gods and the powers of heaven; your
dwelling is in the lone heart of the forest. From you we learn,
that the bourne of man's ghost is not the senseless grave, not the
pale realm of the monarch below; in another world his spirit
survives still;—death, if your lore be true, is but the passage
to enduring life."

There is the testimony of an educated Roman, fifty years
after Christ, to the Celtic race being then "wiser than their
neighbours;" testimony all the more remarkable because civilized nations, though very prone to ascribe to barbarous people
an ideal purity and simplicity of life and manners are by no
means naturally inclined to ascribe to them high attainment in
intellectual and spiritual things. And now, along with this testimony of Lucan's, one has to carry in mind Cæsar's remark, that
the Druids, partly from a religious scruple, partly from a desire
to discipline the memory of their pupils, committed nothing
to writing. Well, then come the crushing defeat of the Celtic
race in Britain and the Roman conquest; but the Celtic race
subsisted here still, and any one can see that, while the race
subsisted, the traditions of a discipline such as that of which
Lucan has drawn the picture were not likely to be so very
speedily "extinguished." The withdrawal of the Romans, the
recovered independence of the native race here, the Saxon
invasion, the struggle with the Saxons, were just the ground
for one of those bursts of energetic national life and self-con-
sciousness which find a voice in a burst of poets and poetry.
Accordingly, to this time, to the sixth century, the universal
Welsh tradition attaches the great group of British poets,
Taliesin and his fellows. In the twelfth century there began for
Wales, along with another burst of national life, another burst
of poetry; and this burst *literary* in the stricter sense of the
word,—a burst which left, for the first time, written records.
It wrote the records of its predecessors, as well as of itself,

and therefore Mr. Nash wants to make it the real author of the
whole poetry, one may say, of the sixth century as well as its
own. No doubt one cannot produce the texts of the poetry
of the sixth century; no doubt we have this only as the twelfth
5   and succeeding centuries wrote it down; no doubt they mixed
and changed it a great deal in writing it down. But, since a
continuous stream of testimony shows the enduring existence
and influence among the kindred Celts of Wales and Brittany, from the sixth century to the twelfth, of an old national
10 literature, it seems certain that much of this must be traceable
in the documents of the twelfth century, and the interesting
thing is to trace it. It cannot be denied that there is such a
continuous stream of testimony; there is Gildas in the sixth
century, Nennius in the eighth, the laws of Howel in the tenth;
15 in the eleventh, twenty or thirty years before the new literary
epoch began, we hear of Rhys ap Tudor having "brought with
him from Brittany the system of the Round Table, which at
home had become quite forgotten, and he restored it as it is,
with regard to minstrels and bards, as it had been at Caerleon-
20 upon-Usk, under the Emperor Arthur, in the time of the sover-
eignty of the race of the Cymry over the island of Britain and
its adjacent islands." Mr. Nash's own comment on this is:
"We here see the introduction of the Arthurian romance from
Brittany, preceding by nearly one generation the revival of
25 music and poetry in North Wales;" and yet he does not seem
to perceive what a testimony is here to the reality, fulness, and
subsistence of that primitive literature about which he is so
sceptical. Then in the twelfth century testimony to this primitive literature absolutely abounds; one can quote none better
30 than that of Giraldus de Barri, or Giraldus Cambrensis, as he is
usually called. Giraldus is an excellent authority, who knew well
what he was writing about, and he speaks of the Welsh bards
and rhapsodists of his time as having in their possession "ancient
and authentic books" in the Welsh language. The apparatus of
35 technical terms of poetry, again, and the elaborate poetical
organisation which we find both in Wales and Ireland, existing from the very commencement of the mediæval literary
period in each, and to which no other mediæval literature, so

far as I know, shows at its first beginnings anything similar, indicates surely, in these Celtic peoples, the clear and persistent tradition of an older poetical period of great development, and almost irresistibly connects itself in one's mind with the elaborate Druidic discipline which Cæsar mentions. 5

But perhaps the best way to get a full sense of the storied antiquity, forming as it were the background to those mediæval documents which in Mr. Nash's eyes pretty much begin and end with themselves, is to take, almost at random, a passage from such a tale as *Kilhwch and Olwen,* in the *Mabinogion,* 10 —that charming collection, for which we owe such a debt of gratitude to Lady Charlotte Guest (to call her still by the name she bore when she made her happy entry into the world of letters), and which she so unkindly suffers to remain out of print. Almost every page of this tale points to traditions and 15 personages of the most remote antiquity, and is instinct with the very breath of the primitive world. Search is made for Mabon, the son of Modron, who was taken when three nights old from between his mother and the wall. The seekers go first to the Ousel of Cilgwri; the Ousel had lived long enough 20 to peck a smith's anvil down to the size of a nut, but he had never heard of Mabon. "But there is a race of animals who were formed before me, and I will be your guide to them." So the Ousel guides them to the Stag of Redynvre. The Stag has seen an oak sapling, in the wood where he lived, grow up 25 to be an oak with a hundred branches, and then slowly decay down to a withered stump, yet he had never heard of Mabon. "But I will be your guide to the place where there is an animal which was formed before I was;" and he guides them to the Owl of Cwm Cawlwyd. "When first I came hither," 30 says the Owl, "the wide valley you see was a wooded glen. And a race of men came and rooted it up. And there grew a second wood; and this wood is the third. My wings, are they not withered stumps?" Yet the Owl, in spite of his great age, had never heard of Mabon; but he offered to be guide "to where 35 is the oldest animal in this world, and the one that has travelled most, the Eagle of Gwern Abwy." The Eagle was so old, that a rock, from the top of which he pecked at the stars every eve-

ning, was now not so much as a span high. He knew nothing
of Mabon; but there was a monster Salmon, into whom he
once struck his claws in Llyn Llyw, who might, perhaps, tell
them something of him. And at last the Salmon of Llyn Llyw
5   told them of Mabon. "With every tide I go along the river
upwards, until I come near to the walls of Gloucester, and
there have I found such wrong as I never found elsewhere."
And the Salmon took Arthur's messengers on his shoulders up
to the wall of the prison in Gloucester, and they delivered
10 Mabon.

Nothing could better give that sense of primitive and pre-
mediæval antiquity which to the observer with any tact for
these things is, I think, clearly perceptible in these remains,
at whatever time they may have been written; or better serve
15 to check too absolute an acceptance of Mr. Nash's doctrine,—
in some respects very salutary,—"that the common assumption
of such remains of the date of the sixth century, has been made
upon very unsatisfactory grounds." It is true, it has; it is true,
too, that, as he goes on to say, "writers who claim for produc-
20 tions actually existing only in manuscripts of the twelfth, an
origin in the sixth century, are called upon to demonstrate the
links of evidence, either internal or external, which bridge
over this great intervening period of at least five hundred
years." Then Mr. Nash continues: "This external evidence is
25 altogether wanting." Not altogether, as we have seen; that
assertion is a little too strong. But I am content to let it pass,
because it is true, that without internal evidence in this matter
the external evidence would be of no moment. But when Mr.
Nash continues further: "And the internal evidence even of
30 the so-called historical poems themselves, is, in some instances
at least, opposed to their claims to an origin in the sixth
century," and leaves the matter there, and finishes his chapter,
I say that is an unsatisfactory turn to give to the matter, and
a lame and impotent conclusion to his chapter; because the
35 one interesting, fruitful question here is, not in what instances
the internal evidence opposes the claims of these poems to a
sixth-century origin, but in what instances it supports them,
and what these sixth-century remains, thus established, signify.

So again with the question as to the mythological import of these poems. Mr. Nash seems to me to have dealt with this, too, rather in the spirit of a sturdy enemy of the Celts and their pretensions,—often enough chimerical,—than in the spirit of a disinterested man of science. "We find in the oldest compositions in the Welsh language no traces," he says, "of the Druids, or of a pagan mythology." He will not hear of there being, for instance, in these compositions, traces of the doctrine of the transmigration of souls, attributed to the Druids in such clear words by Cæsar. He is very severe upon a German scholar, long and favourably known in this country, who has already furnished several contributions to our knowledge of the Celtic race, and of whose labours the main fruit has, I believe, not yet been given us,—Mr. Meyer. He is very severe upon Mr. Meyer, for finding in one of the poems ascribed to Taliesin, "a sacrificial hymn addressed to the god Pryd, in his character of god of the Sun." It is not for me to pronounce for or against this notion of Mr. Meyer's. I have not the knowledge which is needed in order to make one's suffrage in these matters of any value; speaking merely as one of the unlearned public, I will confess that allegory seems to me to play, in Mr. Meyer's theories, a somewhat excessive part; Arthur and his Twelve (?) Knights of the Round Table signifying solely the year with its twelve months; Percival and the Miller signifying solely steel and the grindstone; Stonehenge and the *Gododin* put to purely calendarial purposes; the *Nibelungen*, the *Mahabharata*, and the *Iliad*, finally following the fate of the *Gododin;* all this appears to me, I will confess, a little prematurely grasped, a little unsubstantial. But that any one who knows the set of modern mythological science towards astronomical and solar myths, a set which has already justified itself in many respects so victoriously, and which is so irresistible that one can hardly now look up at the sun without having the sensations of a moth; —that any one who knows this should find in the Welsh remains no traces of mythology is quite astounding. Why, the heroes and heroines of the old Cymric world are all in the sky as well as in Welsh story; Arthur is the Great Bear, his harp is the constellation Lyra; Cassiopeia's chair is Llys Don,

Don's Court; the daughter of Don was Arianrod, and the
Northern Crown is Caer Arianrod; Gwydion was Don's son,
and the Milky Way is Caer Gwydion. With Gwydion is
Math, the son of Mathonwy, the "man of illusion and phantasy;" and the moment one goes below the surface,—almost
before one goes below the surface,—all is illusion and phantasy,
double-meaning, and far-reaching mythological import, in the
world which all these personages inhabit. What are the three
hundred ravens of Owen, and the nine sorceresses of Peredur,
and the dogs of Annwn the Welsh Hades, and the birds of
Rhiannon, whose song was so sweet that warriors remained
spell-bound for eighty years together listening to them? What
is the Avanc, the water-monster, of whom every lake-side in
Wales, and her proverbial speech, and her music, to this day
preserve the tradition? What is Gwyn the son of Nudd, king
of fairie, the ruler of the Tylwyth Teg, or family of beauty,
who till the day of doom fights on every first day of May,—the
great feast of the sun among the Celtic peoples,—with
Gwythyr, for the fair Cordelia, the daughter of Lear? What
is the wonderful mare of Teirnyon, which on the night of
every first of May foaled, and no one ever knew what became
of the colt? Who is the mystic Arawn, the king of Annwn,
who changed semblance for a year with Pwyll, prince of
Dyved, and reigned in his place? These are no mediæval personages; they belong to an older, pagan, mythological world.
The very first thing that strikes one, in reading the *Mabinogion*,
is how evidently the mediæval story-teller is pillaging an antiquity of which he does not fully possess the secret; he is like
a peasant building his hut on the site of Halicarnassus or
Ephesus; he builds, but what he builds is full of materials of
which he knows not the history, or knows by a glimmering
tradition merely;—stones "not of this building," but of an
older architecture, greater, cunninger, more majestical. In the
mediæval stories of no Latin or Teutonic people does this strike
one as in those of the Welsh. Kilhwch, in the story, already
quoted, of *Kilhwch and Olwen*, asks help at the hand of
Arthur's warriors; a list of these warriors is given, which fills
I know not how many pages of Lady Charlotte Guest's book;
this list is a perfect treasure-house of mysterious ruins:—

"Teithi Hen, the son of Gwynhan—(his dominions were swallowed up by the sea, and he himself hardly escaped, and he came to Arthur, and his knife had this peculiarity, that from the time that he came there no haft would ever remain upon it, and owing to this a sickness came over him, and he pined away during the remainder of his life, and of this he died).

"Drem, the son of Dremidyd—(when the gnat arose in the morning with the sun, Drem could see it from Gelli Wic in Cornwall, as far off as Pen Blathaon in North Britain).

"Kynyr Keinvarvawc—(when he was told he had a son born, he said to his wife: Damsel, if thy son be mine, his heart will be always cold, and there will be no warmth in his hands)."

How evident, again, is the slightness of the narrator's hold upon the Twrch-Trwyth and his strange story! How manifest the mixture of known and unknown, shadowy and clear, of different layers and orders of tradition jumbled together, in the story of Bran the Blessed, a story whose personages touch a comparatively late and historic time. Bran invades Ireland, to avenge one of "the three unhappy blows of this island," the daily striking of Branwen by her husband Matholwch, King of Ireland. Bran is mortally wounded by a poisoned dart, and only seven men of Britain, "the Island of the Mighty," escape, among them Taliesin:—

"And Bran commanded them that they should cut off his head. And take you my head, said he, and bear it even unto the White Mount in London, and bury it there with the face towards France. And a long time will you be upon the road. In Harlech you will be feasting seven years, the birds of Rhiannon singing unto you the while. And all that time the head will be to you as pleasant company as it ever was when on my body. And at Gwales in Penvro you will be fourscore years, and you may remain there, and the head with you uncorrupted, until you open the door that looks towards Aber Henvelen and towards Cornwall. And after you have opened that door, there you may no longer tarry; set forth then to London to bury the head, and go straight forward.

"So they cut off his head, and those seven went forward therewith. And Branwen was the eighth with them, and they came to land at Aber Alaw in Anglesey, and they sate down to rest. And Branwen looked towards Ireland and towards the Island of the Mighty, to see if she could descry them. 'Alas,' said she, 'woe is me that I was ever born; two islands have been destroyed because of me.' Then she uttered a loud groan, and there broke her heart. And they made her a four-sided grave, and buried her upon the banks of the Alaw.

"Then they went on to Harlech, and sate down to feast and to drink there; and there came three birds and began singing, and all the songs they had ever heard were harsh compared thereto; and at this feast they continued seven years. Then they went to Gwales in Penvro, and there they found a fair and regal spot overlooking the ocean, and a spacious hall was therein. And they went into the hall, and two of its doors were open, but the third door was closed, that which looked towards Cornwall. 'See yonder,' said Manawyddan, 'is the door that we may not open.' And that night they regaled themselves, and were joyful. And there they remained fourscore years, nor did they think they had ever spent a time more joyous and mirthful. And they were not more weary than when first they came, neither did they, any of them, know the time they had been there. And it was as pleasant to them having the head with them as if Bran had been with them himself.

"But one day said Heilyn, the son of Gwyn: 'Evil betide me if I do not open the door to know if that is true which is said concerning it.' So he opened the door and looked towards Cornwall and Aber Henvelen. And when they had looked, they were as conscious of all the evils they had ever sustained, and of all the friends and companions they had lost, and of all the misery that had befallen them, as if all had happened in that very spot; and especially of the fate of their lord. And because of their perturbation they could not rest, but journeyed forth with the head towards London. And they buried the head in the White Mount."

Arthur afterwards, in his pride and self-confidence, disinterred the head, and this was one of "the three unhappy disclosures of the island of Britain."

There is evidently mixed here, with the newer legend, a *detritus,* as the geologists would say, of something far older;

and the secret of Wales and its genius is not truly reached until this *detritus,* instead of being called recent because it is found in contact with what is recent, is disengaged, and is made to tell its own story.

But when we show him things of this kind in the Welsh remains, Mr. Nash has an answer for us. "Oh," he says, "all this is merely a machinery of necromancers and magic, such as has probably been possessed by all people in all ages, more or less abundantly. How similar are the creations of the human mind in times and places the most remote! We see in this similarity only an evidence of the existence of a common stock of ideas, variously developed according to the formative pressure of external circumstances. The materials of these tales are not peculiar to the Welsh." And then Mr. Nash points out, with much learning and ingenuity, how certain incidents of these tales have their counterparts in Irish, in Scandinavian, in Oriental romance. He says, fairly enough, that the assertions of Taliesin, in the famous *Hanes Taliesin,* or *History of Taliesin,* that he was present with Noah in the Ark, at the Tower of Babel, and with Alexander of Macedon, "we may ascribe to the poetic fancy of the Christian priest of the thirteenth century, who brought this romance into its present form. We may compare these statements of the universal presence of the wonder-working magician with those of the gleeman who recites the Anglo-Saxon metrical tale called the *Traveller's Song.*" No doubt lands the most distant can be shown to have a common property in many marvellous stories. This is one of the most interesting discoveries of modern science; but modern science is equally interested in knowing how the genius of each people has differentiated, so to speak, this common property of theirs; in tracking out, in each case, that special "variety of development" which, to use Mr. Nash's own words, "the formative pressure of external circumstances" has occasioned; and not the formative pressure from without only, but also the formative pressure from within. It is this which he who deals with the Welsh remains in a philosophic spirit wants to know. Where is the force, for scientific purposes, of telling us that certain incidents by which Welsh poetry

has been supposed to indicate a surviving tradition of the
doctrine of transmigration, are found in Irish poetry also, when
Irish poetry has, like Welsh, its roots in that Celtism which is
said to have held this doctrine of transmigration so strongly?
5   Where is even the great force, for scientific purposes, of
proving, if it were possible to prove, that the extant remains
of Welsh poetry contain not one plain declaration of Druidical,
Pagan, pre-Christian doctrine, if one has in the extant remains
of Breton poetry such texts as this from the prophecy of
10 Gwenchlan: "Three times must we all die, before we come
to our final repose?" or as the cry of the eagles, in the same
poem, of fierce thirst for Christian blood, a cry in which the
poet evidently gives vent to his own hatred? since the solidarity,
to use that convenient French word, of Breton and Welsh
15 poetry is so complete, that the ideas of the one may be almost
certainly assumed not to have been wanting to those of the
other. The question is, when Taliesin says, in the *Battle of the
Trees:* "I have been in many shapes before I attained a congenial form. I have been a narrow blade of a sword, I have
20 been a drop in the air, I have been a shining star, I have been
a word in a book, I have been a book in the beginning, I have
been a light in a lantern a year and a half, I have been a bridge
for passing over three-score rivers; I have journeyed as an
eagle, I have been a boat on the sea, I have been a director in
25 battle, I have been a sword in the hand, I have been a shield
in fight, I have been the string of a harp, I have been enchanted for a year in the foam of water. There is nothing in
which I have not been,"—the question is, have these "statements of the universal presence of the wonder-working
30 magician" nothing which distinguishes them from "similar creations of the human mind in times and places the most remote;"
have they not an inwardness, a severity of form, a solemnity
of tone, which indicates the still reverberating echo of a profound doctrine and discipline, such as was Druidism? Sup-
35 pose we compare Taliesin, as Mr. Nash invites us, with the gleeman of the Anglo-Saxon *Traveller's Song.* Take the specimen of
this song which Mr. Nash himself quotes: "I have been with the
Israelites and with the Essyringi, with the Hebrews and with the

Indians and with the Egyptians; I have been with the Medes
and with the Persians and with the Myrgings." It is very well
to parallel with this extract Taliesin's: "I carried the banner
before Alexander; I was in Canaan when Absalom was slain;
I was on the horse's crupper of Elias and Enoch; I was on the
high cross of the merciful son of God; I was the chief overseer
at the building of the tower of Nimrod; I was with my King
in the manger of the ass; I supported Moses through the waters
of Jordan; I have been in the buttery in the land of the
Trinity; it is not known what is the nature of its meat and
its fish." It is very well to say that these assertions "we may
fairly ascribe to the poetic fancy of a Christian priest of the
thirteenth century." Certainly we may; the last of Taliesin's
assertions more especially; though one must remark at the same
time that the Welshman shows much more fire and imagination
than the Anglo-Saxon. But Taliesin adds, after his: "I was in
Canaan when Absalom was slain," "*I was in the hall of Don before Gwydion was born;*" he adds, after: "I was the chief overseer at the building of the tower of Nimrod," "*I have been
three times resident in the castle of Arianrod;*" he adds, after:
"I was at the cross with Mary Magdalene," "*I obtained my
inspiration from the cauldron of Ceridwen.*" And finally, after
the mediæval touch of the visit to the buttery in the land of
the Trinity, he goes off at score: "I have been instructed in the
whole system of the universe; I shall be till the day of judgment on the face of the earth. I have been in an uneasy chair
above Caer Sidin, and the whirling round without motion between three elements. Is it not the wonder of the world that
cannot be discovered?" And so he ends the poem. But here is
the Celtic, the essential part of the poem: it is here that the
"formative pressure" has been really in operation; and here
surely is paganism and mythology enough, which the Christian
priest of the thirteenth century can have had nothing to do
with. It is unscientific, no doubt, to interpret this part as Edward Davies and Mr. Herbert do; but it is unscientific also to
get rid of it as Mr. Nash does. Wales and the Welsh genius
are not to be known without this part; and the true critic is he
who can best disengage its real significance.

I say, then, what we want is to *know* the Celt and his genius;
not to exalt him or to abase him, but to know him. And for
this a disinterested, positive, and constructive criticism is
needed. Neither his friends nor his enemies have yet given
5   us much of this. His friends have given us materials for criticism, and for these we ought to be grateful; his enemies have
given us negative criticism, and for this, too, up to a certain
point, we may be grateful; but the criticism we really want
neither of them has yet given us.

10   Philology, however, that science which in our time has had
so many successes, has not been abandoned by her good fortune
in touching the Celt; philology has brought, almost for the
first time in their lives, the Celt and sound criticism together.
The Celtic grammar of Zeuss, whose death is so grievous a
15   loss to science, offers a splendid specimen of that patient, disinterested way of treating objects of knowledge, which is
the best and most attractive characteristic of Germany. Zeuss
proceeds neither as a Celt-lover nor as a Celt-hater; not the
slightest trace of a wish to glorify Teutonism or to abase
20   Celtism, appears in his book. The only desire apparent there,
is the desire to know his object, the language of the Celtic
peoples, as it really is. In this he stands as a model to Celtic
students; and it has been given to him, as a reward for his
sound method, to establish certain points which are henceforth
25   cardinal points, landmarks, in all the discussion of Celtic matters,
and which no one had so established before. People talked
at random of Celtic writings of this or that age; Zeuss has
definitely fixed the age of what we actually have of these writings. To take the Cymric group of languages: our earliest
30   Cornish document is a vocabulary of the thirteenth century;
our earliest Breton document is a short description of an estate
in a deed of the ninth century; our earliest Welsh documents
are Welsh glosses of the eighth century to Eutychus, the gram-
marian, and Ovid's *Art of Love,* and the verses found by
35   Edward Lhuyd in the *Juvencus* manuscript at Cambridge. The
mention of this *Juvencus* fragment, by the bye, suggests the
difference there is between an interested and a disinterested
critical habit. Mr. Nash deals with this fragment; but, in spite

of all his great acuteness and learning, because he has a bias, because he does not bring to these matters the disinterested spirit they need, he is capable of getting rid, quite unwarrantably, of a particular word in the fragment which does not suit him; his dealing with the verses is an advocate's dealing, not a critic's. Of this sort of thing Zeuss is incapable.

The test which Zeuss used for establishing the age of these documents is a scientific test, the test of orthography and of declensional and syntactical forms. These matters are far out of my province, but what is clear, sound, and simple, has a natural attraction for us all, and one feels a pleasure in repeating it. It is the grand sign of age, Zeuss says, in Welsh and Irish words, when what the grammarians call the *"destitutio tenuium"* has not yet taken place; when the sharp consonants have not yet been changed into flat, *p* or *t* into *b* or *d;* when, for instance, *map*, a son, has not yet become *mab; coet,* a wood, *coed; ocet,* a harrow, *oged.* This is a clear, scientific test to apply, and a test of which the accuracy can be verified; I do not say that Zeuss was the first person who knew of this test or applied it, but I say that he is the first person who in dealing with Celtic matters has invariably proceeded by means of this and similar scientific tests; the first person, therefore, the body of whose work has a scientific, stable character; and so he stands as a model to all Celtic inquirers.

His influence has already been most happy; and as I have enlarged on a certain failure in criticism of Eugene O'Curry's,—whose business, after all, was the description and classification of materials rather than criticism,—let me show, by another example from Eugene O'Curry, this good influence of Zeuss upon Celtic studies. Eugene O'Curry wants to establish that compositions of an older date than the twelfth century existed in Ireland in the twelfth century, and thus he proceeds. He takes one of the great extant Irish manuscripts, the *Leabhar na h'Uidhre;* or *Book of the Dun Cow.* The compiler of this book was, he says, a certain Maelmuiri, a member of the religious house of Cluainmacnois. This he establishes from a passage in the manuscript itself: "This is a trial of his pen here, by Maelmuiri, son of the son of Conn na m'Bocht." The date of Maelmuiri he

establishes from a passage in the *Annals of the Four Masters,*
under the year 1106: "Maelmuiri, son of the son of Conn na
m'Bocht, was killed in the middle of the great stone church of
Cluainmacnois, by a party of robbers." Thus he gets the date
5 of the *Book of the Dun Cow.* This book contains an elegy on
the death of St. Columb. Now, even before 1106, the language
of this elegy was so old as to require a gloss to make it intelligible, for it is accompanied by a gloss written between
the lines. This gloss quotes, for the explanation of obsolete
10 words, a number of more ancient compositions; and these compositions, therefore, must, at the beginning of the twelfth
century, have been still in existence. Nothing can be sounder;
every step is proved, and fairly proved, as one goes along.
O'Curry thus affords a good specimen of the sane mode of
15 proceeding so much wanted in Celtic researches, and so little
practised by Edward Davies and his brethren; and to found this
sane method, Zeuss, by the example he sets in his own depart-
ment of philology, has mainly contributed.

    Science's reconciling power, too, on which I have already
20 touched, philology, in her Celtic researches, again and again
illustrates. Races and languages have been absurdly joined,
and unity has been often rashly assumed at stages where one
was far, very far, from having yet really reached unity. Science
has and will long have to be a divider and a separatist, break-
25 ing arbitrary and fanciful connections, and dissipating dreams
of a premature and impossible unity. Still, science,—true
science,—recognises in the bottom of her soul a law of ultimate
fusion, of conciliation. To reach this, but to reach it legit-
imately, she tends. She draws, for instance, towards the same
30 idea which fills her elder and diviner sister, poetry,—the idea
of the substantial unity of man; though she draws towards
it by roads of her own. But continually she is showing us
affinity where we imagined there was isolation. What school-
boy of us has not rummaged his Greek dictionary in vain for
35 a satisfactory account of that old name for the Peloponnese,
the *Apian Land?* and within the limits of Greek itself there
is none. But the Scythian name for earth, "apia," *watery,*
water-issued, meaning first *isle* and then *land*—this name, which

we find in "avia," Scandin*avia*, and in "ey," Aldern*ey*, not only explains the *Apian Land* of Sophocles for us, but points the way to a whole world of relationships of which we knew nothing. The Scythians themselves again,—obscure, far-separated Mongolian people as they used to appear to us,—when we find that they are essentially Teutonic and Indo-European, their very name the same word as the common Latin word "scutum," the *shielded* people, what a surprise they give us! And then, before we have recovered from this surprise we learn that the name of their father and god, Targitavus, carries us I know not how much further into familiar company. This divinity, *Shining with the targe,* the Greek Hercules, the Sun, contains in the second half of his name, *tavus*, "shining," a wonderful cement to hold times and nations together. *Tavus*, "shining," from "tava"—in Sanscrit, as well as Scythian, "to burn" or "shine,"—is *Divus, dies, Zeus,* Θεός, *Dêva*, and I know not how much more; and *Taviti*, the bright and burnt, fire, the place of fire, the hearth, the centre of the family, becomes the family itself, just as our word family, the Latin *familia*, is from *thymelé*, the sacred centre of fire. The hearth comes to mean home. Then from home it comes to mean the group of homes, the tribe; from the tribe the entire nation; and in this sense of nation or people, the word appears in Gothic, Norse, Celtic, and Persian, as well as in Scythian; the *Theuthisks*, Deutschen, Tudesques, are the men of one *theuth*, nation, or people; and of this our name *Germans* itself is, perhaps, only the Roman translation, meaning the men of one germ or stock. The Celtic divinity, Teutates, has his name from the Celtic *teuta*, people; *taviti*, fire, appearing here in its secondary and derived sense of *people*, just as it does in its own Scythian language in Targitavus's second name, *Tavit-varus, Teutaros*, the protector of the people. Another Celtic divinity, the Hesus of Lucan, finds his brother in the Gaisos, the sword, symbolising the god of battles of the Teutonic Scythians.[1] And after philology has

---

[1] See *Les Scythes les Ancêtres des Peuples Germaniques et Slaves*, par F. G. Bergmann, professeur à la faculté des Lettres de Strasbourg: Colmar, 1858. But Professor Bergmann's etymologies are often, says Lord Strangford, "false lights, held by an uncertain hand." And Lord Strangford

thus related to each other the Celt and the Teuton, she takes
another branch of the Indo-European family, the Sclaves, and
shows us them as having the same name with the German
Suevi, the *solar* people; the common ground here, too, being
5   that grand point of union, the sun, fire. So, also, we find Mr.

---

continues:—"The Apian land certainly meant the watery land, *Meer-
umschlungen*, among the pre-Hellenic Greeks, just as the same land is
called Morea by the modern post-Hellenic or Romaic Greeks from *more*,
the name for the sea in the Slavonic vernacular of its inhabitants during
10   the heart of the Middle Ages. But it is only connected by a remote and
secondary affinity, if connected at all, with the *avia* of Scandinavia, assuming that to be the true German word for *water*, which, if it had come
down to us in Gothic, would have been *avi*, genitive *aujôs*, and not a mere
Latinised termination. Scythian is surely a negative rather than a positive
15   term, much like our *Indian*, or the *Turanian* of modern ethnologists, used
to comprehend nomads and barbarians of all sorts and races north and
east of the Black and Caspian seas. It is unsafe to connect their name with
anything as yet; it is quite as likely that it refers to the bow and arrow
as to the shield, and is connected with our word to *shoot, scéotan, skiutan,*
20   Lithuanian *szau-ti*. Some of the Scythian peoples may have been Anarian,
Allophylic, Mongolian; some were demonstrably Aryan, and not only
that, but Iranian as well, as is best shown in a memoir read before the
Berlin Academy this last year; the evidence having been first indicated
in the rough by Schaffarik the Slavonic antiquary. Coins, glosses, proper
25   names, and inscriptions prove it. Targitaos (not -tavus) and the rest is
guess-work or wrong. Herodotus's Ταβιτὶ for the goddess Vesta is not
connected with the root *div* whence Dêvas, Deus, etc., but the root
tap, in Latin *tep* (of tepere, tepefacere), Slavonic *tepl, topl* (for *tep* or
top), in modern Persian *tâb*. *Thymele* refers to the hearth as the place
30   of smoke (θύω, *thus, fumus*), but *familia* denotes household from *famulus*
for *fagmulus*, the root *fag* being equated with the Sansk. *bhaj, servira*.
Lucan's Hesus or Esus may fairly be compared with the Welsh *Hu*
Gadarn by legitimate process, but no letter-change can justify his connection with *Gaisos*, the spear, not the sword, Virgil's *gæsum*, A.S. *gár*,
35   our verb to *gore*, retained in its outer form in *gar*-fish. For *Theuthisks*,
lege *Thiudisks*, from *thiuda, populus;* in old high German Diutisk,
Diotisk, *popularis, vulgaris*, the country vernacular as distinguished from
the cultivated Latin; hence the word *Dutch, Deutsch*. With our ancestors *theód* stood for nation generally and *getheóde* for any speech. Our
40   *diet* in the political sense is the same word, but borrowed from our German cousins, not inherited from our fathers. The modern Celtic form is
the Irish *tuath*, in ancient Celtic it must have been *teuta, touta*, of which

Meyer, whose Celtic studies I just now mentioned, harping again and again on the connection even in Europe, if you go back far enough, between Celt and German. So, after all we have heard, and truly heard of the diversity between all things Semitic and all things Indo-European, there is now an Italian   5
philologist at work upon the relationship between Sanscrit and Hebrew.

Both in small and great things, philology, dealing with Celtic matters, has exemplified this tending of science towards unity. Who has not been puzzled by the relation of the Scots with   10
Ireland—that *vetus et major Scotia*, as Colgan calls it? Who does not feel what pleasure Zeuss brings us when he suggests that *Gael*, the name for the Irish Celt, and *Scot*, are at bottom the same word, both having their origin in a word meaning *wind*, and both signifying *the violent stormy people?* [1] Who   15
does not feel his mind agreeably cleared about our friends the Fenians, when he learns that the root of their name, *fen*, "white," appears in the hero Fingal; in Gwynned, the Welsh name for North Wales; in the Roman Venedotia; in Vannes in Brittany; in Venice? The very name of Ireland, some say, comes   20
from the famous Sanscrit word *Arya*, the land of the Aryans, or noble men; although the weight of opinion seems to be in favour of connecting it rather with another Sanscrit word, *avara*, occidental, the western land or isle of the west.[2] But, at any rate, who that has been brought up to think the Celts utter   25

---

we actually have the adjective *toutius* in the Gaulish inscription of Nismes. In Oscan we have it as *turta, tuta*, its adjective being handed down in Livy's *meddix tuticus*, the mayor or chief magistrate of the *tuta*. In the Umbrian inscriptions it is *tota*. In Lithuanian *tauta*, the country opposed to the town, and in old Prussian *tauta*, the country generally, *en*   30
Prusiskan tautan, im Land zu Preussen."

[1] Lord Strangford observes here:—"The original forms of Gael should be mentioned—Gaedil, Goidil: in modern Gaelic orthography Gaoidheal where the *dh* is not realised in pronunciation. There is nothing impossible in the connection of the root of this with that of Scot, *if* the *s* of the   35
latter be merely prosthetic. But the whole thing is *in nubibus*, and given as a guess only." ·

[2] "The name of Erin," says Lord Strangford, "is treated at length in a

aliens from us and our culture, can come without a start of
sympathy upon such words as *heol* (sol), or *buaist* (fuisti)?
or upon such a sentence as this, *"Peris Duw dui funnaun"*
("God prepared two fountains")? Or when Mr. Whitley

5 Stokes, one of the very ablest scholars formed in Zeuss's school,
a born philologist,—he now occupies, alas! a post under the
Government of India, instead of a chair of philology at home,
and makes one think mournfully of Montesquieu's saying, that
had he been an Englishman he should never have produced his

10 great work, but have caught the contagion of practical life,
and devoted himself to what is called "rising in the world,"—
when Mr. Whitley Stokes, in his edition of *Cormac's Glossary*,
holds up the Irish word *tríath*, the sea, and makes us remark
that, though the names *Triton, Amphitrite*, and those of corre-

15 sponding Indian and Zend divinities, point to the meaning *sea*,
yet it is only Irish which actually supplies the vocable, how
delightfully that brings Ireland into the Indo-European con-
cert! What a wholesome buffet it gives to Lord Lyndhurst's
alienation doctrines!

20   To go a little farther. Of the two great Celtic divisions of
language, the Gaelic and the Cymric, the Gaelic, say the
philologists, is more related to the younger, more synthetic,
group of languages, Sanscrit, Greek, Zend, Latin, and Teutonic; the Cymric to the older, more analytic Turanian group.

25 Of the more synthetic Aryan group, again, Zend and Teutonic are, in their turn, looser and more analytic than Sanscrit
and Greek, more in sympathy with the Turanian group and
with Celtic. What possibilities of affinity and influence are
here hinted at; what lines of inquiry, worth exploring, at

30 any rate, suggest themselves to one's mind. By the forms of
its language a nation expresses its very self. Our language
is the loosest, the most analytic, of all European languages.
And we, then, what are we? what is England? I will not answer,
A vast obscure Cymric basis with a vast visible Teutonic

35 superstructure; but I will say that that answer sometimes sug-

---

masterly note by Whitley Stokes in the first series of Max Müller's lectures (4th ed.) p. 255, where its earliest *tangible* form is shown to have
been Iverio. Pictet's connection with Arya is quite baseless."

gests itself, at any rate,—sometimes knocks at our mind's door
for admission; and we begin to cast about and see whether it
is to be let in.

But the forms of its language are not our only key to a
people; what it says in its language, its literature, is the great
key, and we must get back to literature. The literature of the
Celtic peoples has not yet had its Zeuss, and greatly it wants
him. We need a Zeuss to apply to Celtic literature, to all its
vexed questions of dates, authenticity, and significance, the
criticism, the sane method, the disinterested endeavour to get
at the real facts, which Zeuss has shown in dealing with Celtic
language. Science is good in itself, and therefore Celtic literature,—the Celt-haters having failed to prove it a bubble,—
Celtic literature is interesting, merely as an object of knowledge. But it reinforces and redoubles our interest in Celtic
literature if we find that here, too, science exercises the reconciling, the uniting influence of which I have said so much;
if we find here, more than anywhere else, traces of kinship,
and the most essential sort of kinship, spiritual kinship, between
us and the Celt, of which we had never dreamed. I settle nothing, and can settle nothing; I have not the special knowledge
needed for that. I have no pretension to do more than to try
and awaken interest; to seize on hints, to point out indications,
which, to any one with a feeling for literature, suggest themselves; to stimulate other inquirers. I must surely be without
the bias which has so often rendered Welsh and Irish students
extravagant; why, my very name expresses that peculiar
Semitico-Saxon mixture which makes the typical Englishman;
I can have no ends to serve in finding in Celtic literature more
than is there. What *is* there, is for me the only question.

[III]

We have seen how philology carries us towards ideas of
affinity of race which are new to us. But it is evident that this
affinity, even if proved, can be no very potent affair, unless it
goes beyond the stage at which we have hitherto observed it.

Affinity between races still, so to speak, in their mother's womb, counts for something, indeed, but cannot count for very much. So long as Celt and Teuton are in their embryo rudimentary state, or, at least, no such great while out of their cradle, still engaged in their wanderings, changes of place and struggle for development, so long as they have not yet crystallised into solid nations, they may touch and mix in passing, and yet very little come of it. It is when the embryo has grown and solidified into a distinct nation, into the Gaul or German of history, when it has finally acquired the characters which make the Gaul of history what he is, the German of history what he is, that contact and mixture are important, and may leave a long train of effects; for Celt and Teuton by this time have their formed, marked, national, ineffaceable qualities to oppose or to communicate. The contact of the German of the Continent with the Celt was in the prehistoric times, and the definite German type, as we know it, was fixed later, and from the time when it became fixed was not influenced by the Celtic type. But here in our country, in historic times, long after the Celtic embryo had crystallised into the Celt proper, long after the Germanic embryo had crystallised into the German proper, there was an important contact between the two peoples; the Saxons invaded the Britons and settled themselves in the Britons' country. Well, then, here was a contact which one might expect would leave its traces; if the Saxons got the upper hand, as we all know they did, and made our country be England and us be English, there must yet, one would think, be some trace of the Saxon having met the Briton; there must be some Celtic vein or other running through us. Many people say there is nothing at all of the kind, absolutely nothing; the *Saturday Review* treats these matters of ethnology with great power and learning, and the *Saturday Review* says we are "a nation into which a Norman element, like a much smaller Celtic element, was so completely absorbed that it is vain to seek after Norman or Celtic elements in any modern Englishman." And the other day at Zurich I read a long essay on English literature by one of the professors there, in which the writer observed, as a remarkable thing, that while other countries conquered by the Germans,—France, for instance, and Italy, —had ousted all German influence from their genius and literature, there were two countries, not originally Germanic, but conquered by the Germans, England and German Switzerland, of which the genius and the literature were purely and unmixedly German; and this he laid down as a position which nobody would dream of challenging.

I say it is strange that this should be so, and we in particular have reason for inquiring whether it really is so; because though, as I have said, even as a matter of science the Celt has a claim to be known, and we have an interest in knowing him, yet this interest is wonderfully enhanced if we find him to have actually a part in us. The question is to be tried by external and by internal evidence; the language and the physical type of our race afford certain data for trying it, and other data are afforded by our literature, genius, and spiritual production generally. Data of this second kind belong to the province of the literary critic; data of the first kind to the province of the philologist and of the physiologist.

The province of the philologist and of the physiologist is not mine; but this whole question as to the mixture of Celt with Saxon in us has been so little explored, people have been so prone to settle it off-hand according to their prepossessions, that even on the philological and physiological side of it I must say a few words in passing. Surely it must strike with surprise any one who thinks of it, to find that without any immense inpouring of a whole people, that by mere expeditions of invaders having to come over the sea, and in no greater numbers than the Saxons, so far as we can make out, actually came, the old occupants of this island, the Celtic Britons, should have been completely annihilated, or even so completely absorbed that it is vain to seek after Celtic elements in the existing English race. Of deliberate wholesale extermination of the Celtic race, all of them who could not fly to Wales or Scotland, we hear nothing; and without some such extermination one would suppose that a great mass of them must have remained

in the country, their lot the obscure and, so to speak, under-
ground lot of a subject race, but yet insensibly getting mixed
with their conquerors, and their blood entering into the composition of a new people, in which the stock of the conquerors
5   counts for most, but the stock of the conquered, too, counts
for something. How little the triumph of the conquerors' laws,
manners, and language, proves the extinction of the old race,
we may see by looking at France; Gaul was Latinised in language, manners, and laws, and yet her people remained essen-
10 tially Celtic. The Germanisation of Britain went far deeper
than the Latinisation of France, and not only laws, manners,
and language, but the main current of the blood, became
Germanic; but how, without some process of radical extirpa-
tion, of which, as I say, there is no evidence, can there have
15 failed to subsist in Britain, as in Gaul, a Celtic current too?
The indications of this in our language have never yet been
thoroughly searched out; the Celtic names of places prove
nothing, of course, as to the point here in question; they come
from the prehistoric times, the times before the nations, Ger-
20 manic or Celtic, had crystallised, and they are everywhere,
as the impetuous Celt was formerly everywhere,—in the Alps,
the Apennines, the Cévennes, the Rhine, the Po, as well as in
the Thames, the Humber, Cumberland, London. But it is said
that the words of Celtic origin for things having to do with
25 every-day peaceful life,—the life of a settled nation,—words
like *basket* (to take an instance which all the world knows)
form a much larger body in our language than is commonly
supposed; it is said that a number of our raciest, most idiomatic,
popular words—for example, *bam, kick, whop, twaddle, fudge,*
30 *hitch, muggy,*—are Celtic. These assertions require to be carefully examined, and it by no means follows that because an
English word is found in Celtic, therefore we get it from
thence; but they have not yet had the attention which, as
illustrating through language this matter of the subsistence and
35 intermingling in our nation of a Celtic part, they merit.

Nor have the physiological data which illustrate this matter
had much more attention from us in England. But in France,
a physician, half English by blood though a Frenchman by

home and language, Monsieur W. F. Edwards, brother to Monsieur Milne-Edwards, the well-known zoologist, published in 1829 a letter to Monsieur Amédée Thierry with this title: *Des Caractères Physiologiques des Races Humaines considérés dans leurs Rapports avec l'Histoire.* The letter attracted great attention on the Continent; it fills not much more than a hundred pages, and they are a hundred pages which well deserve reading and re-reading. Monsieur Thierry in his *Histoire des Gaulois* had divided the population of Gaul into certain groups, and the object of Monsieur Edwards was to try this division by physiology. Groups of men have, he says, their physical type which distinguishes them, as well as their language; the traces of this physical type endure as the traces of language endure, and physiology is enabled to verify history by them. Accordingly, he determines the physical type of each of the two great Celtic families, the Gaels and the Cymris, who are said to have been distributed in a certain order through Gaul, and then he tracks these types in the population of France at the present day, and so verifies the alleged original order of distribution. In doing this, he makes excursions into neighbouring countries where the Gaels and the Cymris have been, and he declares that in England he finds abundant traces of the physical type which he has established as the Cymric, still subsisting in our population, and having descended from the old British possessors of our soil before the Saxon conquest. But if we are to believe the current English opinion, says Monsieur Edwards, the stock of these old British possessors is clean gone. On this opinion he makes the following comment:—

"In the territory occupied by the Saxons, the Britons were no longer an independent nation, nor even a people with any civil existence at all. For history, therefore, they were dead, above all for history as it was then written; but they had not perished; they still lived on, and undoubtedly in such numbers as the remains of a great nation, in spite of its disasters, might still be expected to keep. That the Britons were destroyed or expelled from England, properly so called, is, as I have said, a popular opinion in that country. It is founded on the exaggeration of the writers of history; but in these very writers, when

we come to look closely at what they say, we find the confession
that the remains of this people were reduced to a state of strict
servitude. Attached to the soil, they will have shared in that
emancipation which during the course of the Middle Ages
gradually restored to political life the mass of the population
in the countries of Western Europe; recovering by slow degrees their rights without resuming their name, and rising
gradually with the rise of industry, they will have got spread
through all ranks of society. The gradualness of this movement, and the obscurity which enwrapped its beginnings, allowed the contempt of the conqueror and the shame of the
conquered to become fixed feelings; and so it turns out, that
an Englishman who now thinks himself sprung from the Saxons
or the Normans, is often in reality the descendant of the
Britons."

So physiology, as well as language, incomplete though the
application of their tests to this matter has hitherto been, may
lead us to hesitate before accepting the round assertion that
it is vain to search for Celtic elements in any modern Englishman. But it is not only by the tests of physiology and language
that we can try this matter. As there are for physiology physical marks, such as the square head of the German, the round
head of the Gael, the oval head of the Cymri, which determine
the type of a people, so for criticism there are spiritual marks
which determine the type, and make us speak of the Greek
genius, the Teutonic genius, the Celtic genius, and so on. Here
is another test at our service; and this test, too, has never yet
been thoroughly employed. Foreign critics have indeed occasionally hazarded the idea that in English poetry there is a
Celtic element traceable; and Mr. Morley, in his very readable
as well as very useful book on the English writers before
Chaucer, has a sentence which struck my attention when I
read it, because it expresses an opinion which I, too, have long
held. Mr. Morley says:—"The main current of English literature cannot be disconnected from the lively Celtic wit in which
it has one of its sources. The Celts do not form an utterly
distinct part of our mixed population. But for early, frequent,
and various contact with the race that in its half-barbarous days

invented Ossian's dialogues with St. Patrick, and that quickened afterwards the Northmen's blood in France, Germanic England would not have produced a Shakspeare." But there Mr. Morley leaves the matter. He indicates this Celtic element and influence, but he does not show us,—it did not come within the scope of his work to show us,—how this influence has declared itself. Unlike the physiological test, or the linguistic test, this literary, spiritual test is one which I may perhaps be allowed to try my hand at applying. I say that there is a Celtic element in the English nature, as well as a Germanic element, and that this element manifests itself in our spirit and literature. But before I try to point out how it manifests itself, it may be as well to get a clear notion of what we mean by a Celtic element, a Germanic element; what characters, that is, determine for us the Celtic genius, the Germanic genius, as we commonly conceive the two.

[IV]

Let me repeat what I have often said of the characteristics which mark the English spirit, the English genius. This spirit, this genius, judged, to be sure, rather from a friend's than an enemy's point of view, yet judged on the whole fairly, is characterised, I have repeatedly said, by *energy with honesty*. Take away some of the energy which comes to us, as I believe, in part from Celtic and Roman sources; instead of energy, say rather *steadiness;* and you have the Germanic genius: *steadiness with honesty*. It is evident how nearly the two characterisations approach one another; and yet they leave, as we shall see, a great deal of room for difference. Steadiness with honesty; the danger for a national spirit thus composed is the humdrum, the plain and ugly, the ignoble: in a word, *das Gemeine, die Gemeinheit,* that curse of Germany, against which Goethe was all his life fighting. The excellence of a national spirit thus composed is freedom from whim, flightiness, perverseness; patient fidelity to Nature,—in a word, *science,*— leading it at last, though slowly, and not by the most brilliant

road, out of the bondage of the humdrum and common, into
the better life. The universal dead-level of plainness and home-
liness, the lack of all beauty and distinction in form and fea-
ture, the slowness and clumsiness of the language, the eternal
beer, sausages, and bad tobacco, the blank commonness everywhere, pressing at last like a weight on the spirits of the traveller
in Northern Germany, and making him impatient to be gone,
—this is the weak side; the industry, the well-doing, the patient
steady elaboration of things, the idea of science governing all
departments of human activity,—this is the strong side; and
through this side of her genius, Germany has already obtained
excellent results, and is destined, we may depend upon it, however her pedantry, her slowness, her fumbling, her ineffective-
ness, her bad government, may at times make us cry out, to
an immense development.[1]

For dulness, the creeping Saxons,—says an old Irish poem,
assigning the characteristics for which different nations are
celebrated:—

> For acuteness and valour, the Greeks,
> For excessive pride, the Romans,
> For dulness, the creeping Saxons;
> For beauty and amorousness, the Gaedhils.

We have seen in what sense, and with what explanation, this
characterisation of the German may be allowed to stand; now
let us come to the beautiful and amorous Gaedhil. Or rather,
let us find a definition which may suit both branches of the
Celtic family, the Cymri as well as the Gael. It is clear that
special circumstances may have developed some one side in
the national character of Cymri or Gael, Welshman or Irishman, so that the observer's notice shall be readily caught by
this side, and yet it may be impossible to adopt it as characteristic of the Celtic nature generally. For instance, in his beautiful
essay on the poetry of the Celtic races, M. Renan, with his
eyes fixed on the Bretons and the Welsh, is struck with the
timidity, the shyness, the delicacy of the Celtic nature, its pref-

[1] It is to be remembered that the above was written before the recent
war between Prussia and Austria.

erence for a retired life, its embarrassment at having to deal
with the great world. He talks of his *douce petite race
naturellement chrétienne*, his *race fière et timide, à l'extérieur
gauche et embarrassée*. But it is evident that this description,
however well it may do for the Cymri, will never do for the
Gael, never do for the typical Irishman of Donnybrook fair.
Again, M. Renan's *infinie délicatesse de sentiment qui caracté-
rise la race Celtique*, how little that accords with the popular
conception of an Irishman who wants to borrow money! *Sentiment* is, however, the word which marks where the Celtic
races really touch and are one; sentimental, if the Celtic nature
is to be characterised by a single term, is the best term to take.
An organisation quick to feel impressions, and feeling them
very strongly; a lively personality therefore, keenly sensitive
to joy and to sorrow; this is the main point. If the downs of
life too much outnumber the ups, this temperament, just because it is so quickly and nearly conscious of all impressions,
may no doubt be seen shy and wounded; it may be seen in wistful regret, it may be seen in passionate, penetrating melancholy;
but its essence is to aspire ardently after life, light, and emotion,
to be expansive, adventurous, and gay. Our word *gay*, it is said,
is itself Celtic. It is not from *gaudium*, but from the Celtic *gair*,
to laugh; [1] and the impressionable Celt, soon up and soon down,
is the more down because it is so his nature to be up—to be
sociable, hospitable, eloquent, admired, figuring away bril-
liantly. He loves bright colours, he easily becomes audacious,
overcrowing, full of fanfaronade. The German, say the physiologists, has the larger volume of intestines (and who that has
ever seen a German at a table-d'hôte will not readily believe
this?), the Frenchman has the more developed organs of
respiration. That is just the expansive, eager Celtic nature; the

[1] The etymology is Monsieur Henri Martin's, but Lord Strangford
says:—"Whatever *gai* may be, it is assuredly not Celtic. Is there any authority for this word *gair*, to laugh, or rather 'laughter,' beyond O'Reilly?
O'Reilly is no authority at all except in so far as tested and passed by the
new school. It is hard to give up *gavisus*. But Diez, chief authority in
Romanic matters, is content to accept Muratori's reference to an old
High-German *gâhi*, modern *jähe*, sharp, quick, sudden, brisk, and so to
the sense of lively, animated, high in spirits."

head in the air, snuffing and snorting; *a proud look and a high
stomach,* as the Psalmist says, but without any such settled
savage temper as the Psalmist seems to impute by those words.
For good and for bad, the Celtic genius is more airy and unsubstantial, goes less near the ground, than the German. The
Celt is often called sensual; but it is not so much the vulgar
satisfactions of sense that attract him as emotion and excitement;
he is truly, as I began by saying, sentimental.

Sentimental,—*always ready to react against the despotism
of fact;* that is the description a great friend [1] of the Celt gives
of him; and it is not a bad description of the sentimental temperament; it lets us into the secret of its dangers and of its
habitual want of success. Balance, measure, and patience, these
are the eternal conditions, even supposing the happiest temperament to start with, of high success; and balance, measure, and
patience are just what the Celt has never had. Even in the world
of spiritual creation, he has never, in spite of his admirable gifts
of quick perception and warm emotion, succeeded perfectly,
because he never has had steadiness, patience, sanity enough to
comply with the conditions under which alone can expression
be perfectly given to the finest perceptions and emotions. The
Greek has the same perceptive, emotional temperament as the
Celt; but he adds to this temperament the sense of *measure;*
hence his admirable success in the plastic arts, in which the
Celtic genius, with its chafing against the despotism of fact, its
perpetual straining after mere emotion, has accomplished nothing. In the comparatively petty art of ornamentation, in rings,
brooches, crosiers, relic-cases, and so on, he has done just
enough to show his delicacy of taste, his happy temperament;
but the grand difficulties of painting and sculpture, the prolonged dealings of spirit with matter, he has never had patience
for. Take the more spiritual arts of music and poetry. All
that emotion alone can do in music the Celt has done; the very
soul of emotion breathes in the Scotch and Irish airs; but with
all this power of musical feeling, what has the Celt, so eager
for emotion that he has not patience for science, effected in

[1] Monsieur Henri Martin, whose chapters on the Celts, in his *Histoire
de France,* are full of information and interest.

music, to be compared with what the less emotional German, steadily developing his musical feeling with the science of a Sebastian Bach or a Beethoven, has effected? In poetry, again, —poetry which the Celt has so passionately, so nobly loved; poetry where emotion counts for so much, but where reason, 5 too, reason, measure, sanity, also count for so much,—the Celt has shown genius, indeed, splendid genius; but even here his faults have clung to him, and hindered him from producing great works, such as other nations with a genius for poetry, —the Greeks, say, or the Italians,—have produced. The Celt 10 has not produced great poetical works, he has only produced poetry with an air of greatness investing it all, and sometimes giving, moreover, to short pieces, or to passages, lines, and snatches of long pieces, singular beauty and power. And yet he loved poetry so much that he grudged no pains to it; but 15 the true art, the *architectonicé* which shapes great works, such as the *Agamemnon* or the *Divine Comedy*, comes only after a steady, deep-searching survey, a firm conception of the facts of human life, which the Celt has not patience for. So he runs off into technic, where he employs the utmost elaboration, 20 and attains astonishing skill; but in the contents of his poetry you have only so much interpretation of the world as the first dash of a quick, strong perception, and then sentiment, infinite sentiment, can bring you. Here, too, his want of sanity and steadfastness has kept the Celt back from the highest success. 25

If his rebellion against fact has thus lamed the Celt even in spiritual work, how much more must it have lamed him in the world of business and politics! The skilful and resolute appliance of means to ends which is needed both to make progress in material civilisation, and also to form powerful states, is just 30 what the Celt has least turn for. He is sensual, as I have said, or at least sensuous; loves bright colours, company, and pleasure; and here he is like the Greek and Latin races; but compare the talent the Greek and Latin (or Latinised) races have shown for gratifying their senses, for procuring an outward life, rich, 35 luxurious, splendid, with the Celt's failure to reach any material civilisation sound and satisfying, and not out at elbows, poor, slovenly, and half-barbarous. The sensuousness of the Greek

made Sybaris and Corinth, the sensuousness of the Latin made
Rome and Baiæ, the sensuousness of the Latinised Frenchman
makes Paris; the sensuousness of the Celt proper has made Ireland. Even in his ideal heroic times, his gay and sensuous nature
cannot carry him, in the appliances of his favourite life of
sociability and pleasure, beyond the gross and creeping Saxon
whom he despises; the regent Breas, we are told in the *Battle*
of Moytura of the Fomorians, became unpopular because
"the knives of his people were not greased at his table, nor
did their breath smell of ale at the banquet." In its grossness
and barbarousness is not that Saxon, as Saxon as it can be? just
what the Latinised Norman, sensuous and sociable like the
Celt, but with the talent to make this bent of his serve to a
practical embellishment of his mode of living, found so dis-
gusting in the Saxon.

And as in material civilisation he has been ineffectual, so has
the Celt been ineffectual in politics. This colossal, impetuous,
adventurous wanderer, the Titan of the early world, who in
primitive times fills so large a place on earth's scene, dwindles
and dwindles as history goes on, and at last is shrunk to what
we now see him. For ages and ages the world has been constantly slipping, ever more and more, out of the Celt's grasp.
"They went forth to the war," Ossian says most truly, "*but*
they always fell."

And yet, if one sets about constituting an ideal genius, what
a great deal of the Celt does one find oneself drawn to put
into it! Of an ideal genius one does not want the elements,
any of them, to be in a state of weakness; on the contrary, one
wants all of them to be in the highest state of power; but with
a law of measure, of harmony, presiding over the whole. So
the sensibility of the Celt, if everything else were not sacrificed
to it, is a beautiful and admirable force. For sensibility, the
power of quick and strong perception and emotion, is one of
the very prime constituents of genius, perhaps its most positive
constituent; it is to the soul what good senses are to the body,
the grand natural condition of successful activity. Sensibility
gives genius its materials; one cannot have too much of it, if
one can but keep its master and not be its slave. Do not let us

wish that the Celt had had less sensibility, but that he had been more master of it. Even as it is, if his sensibility has been a source of weakness to him, it has been a source of power too, and a source of happiness. Some people have found in the Celtic nature and its sensibility the main root out of which chivalry and romance and the glorification of a feminine ideal spring; this is a great question, with which I cannot deal here. Let me notice in passing, however, that there is, in truth, a Celtic air about the extravagance of chivalry, its reaction against the despotism of fact, its straining human nature further than it will stand. But putting all this question of chivalry and its origin on one side, no doubt the sensibility of the Celtic nature, its nervous exaltation, have something feminine in them, and the Celt is thus peculiarly disposed to feel the spell of the feminine idiosyncrasy; he has an affinity to it; he is not far from its secret. Again, his sensibility gives him a peculiarly near and intimate feeling of nature and the life of nature; here, too, he seems in a special way attracted by the secret before him, the secret of natural beauty and natural magic, and to be close to it, to half-divine it. In the productions of the Celtic genius, nothing, perhaps, is so interesting as the evidences of this power: I shall have occasion to give specimens of them by and by. The same sensibility made the Celts full of reverence and enthusiasm for genius, learning, and the things of the mind; *to be a bard, freed a man,*—that is a characteristic stroke of this generous and ennobling ardour of theirs, which no race has ever shown more strongly. Even the extravagance and exaggeration of the sentimental Celtic nature has often something romantic and attractive about it, something which has a sort of smack of misdirected good. The Celt, undisciplinable, anarchical, and turbulent by nature, but out of affection and admiration giving himself body and soul to some leader, that is not a promising political temperament, it is just the opposite of the Anglo-Saxon temperament, disciplinable and steadily obedient within certain limits, but retaining an inalienable part of freedom and self-dependence; but it is a temperament for which one has a kind of sympathy notwithstanding. And very often, for the gay defiant reaction against fact of the lively Celtic nature one

5

10

15

20

25

30

35

has more than sympathy; one feels, in spite of the extravagance, in spite of good sense disapproving, magnetised and exhilarated by it. The Gauls had a rule inflicting a fine on every warrior who, when he appeared on parade, was found to stick out too much in front,—to be corpulent, in short. Such a rule is surely the maddest article of war ever framed, and to people to whom nature has assigned a large volume of intestines, must appear, no doubt, horrible; but yet has it not an audacious, sparkling, immaterial manner with it, which lifts one out of routine, and sets one's spirits in a glow?

All tendencies of human nature are in themselves vital and profitable; when they are blamed, they are only to be blamed relatively, not absolutely. This holds true of the Saxon's phlegm as well as of the Celt's sentiment. Out of the steady humdrum habit of the creeping Saxon, as the Celt calls him,—out of his way of going near the ground,—has come, no doubt, Philistinism, that plant of essentially Germanic growth, flourishing with its genuine marks only in the German fatherland, Great Britain and her colonies, and the United States of America; but what a soul of goodness there is in Philistinism itself! and this soul of goodness I, who am often supposed to be Philistinism's mortal enemy merely because I do not wish it to have things all its own way, cherish as much as anybody. This steady-going habit leads at last, as I have said, up to science, up to the comprehension and interpretation of the world. With us in Great Britain, it is true, it does not seem to lead so far as that; it is in Germany, where the habit is more unmixed, that it can lead to science. Here with us it seems at a certain point to meet with a conflicting force, which checks it and prevents its pushing on to science; but before reaching this point what conquests has it not won! and all the more, per- haps, for stopping short at this point, for spending its exertions within a bounded field, the field of plain sense, of direct prac- tical utility. How it has augmented the comforts and con- veniences of life for us! Doors that open, windows that shut, locks that turn, razors that shave, coats that wear, watches that go, and a thousand more such good things, are the invention of the Philistines.

Here, then, if commingling there is in our race, are two very unlike elements to commingle; the steady-going Saxon temperament and the sentimental Celtic temperament. But before we go on to try and verify, in our life and literature, the alleged fact of this commingling, we have yet another element to take into account, the Norman element. The critic in the *Saturday Review*, whom I have already quoted, says that in looking for traces of Normanism in our national genius, as in looking for traces of Celtism in it, we do but lose our labour; he says, indeed, that there went to the original making of our nation a very great deal more of a Norman element than of a Celtic element, but he asserts that both elements have now so completely disappeared, that it is vain to look for any trace of either of them in the modern Englishman. But this sort of assertion I do not like to admit without trying it a little. I want, therefore, to get some plain notion of the Norman habit and genius, as I have sought to get some plain notion of the Saxon and Celtic. Some people will say that the Normans are Teutonic, and that therefore the distinguishing characters of the German genius must be those of their genius also; but the matter cannot be settled in this speedy fashion. No doubt the basis of the Norman race is Teutonic; but the governing point in the history of the Norman race,—so far, at least, as we English have to do with it,—is not its Teutonic origin, but its Latin civilisation. The French people have, as I have already remarked, an undoubtedly Celtic basis, yet so decisive in its effect upon a nation's habit and character can be the contact with a stronger civilisation, that Gaul, without changing the basis of her blood, became, for all practical intents and purposes, a Latin country, France and not Ireland, through the Roman conquest. Latinism conquered Celtism in her, as it also conquered the Germanism imported by the Frankish and other invasions; Celtism is, however, I need not say, everywhere manifest still in the French nation; even Germanism is distinctly traceable in it, as any one who attentively compares the French with other Latin races will see. No one can look carefully at the French troops in Rome, amongst the Italian population, and not perceive this trace of Germanism; I do not mean in

the Alsatian soldiers only, but in the soldiers of genuine France. But the governing character of France, as a power in the world, is Latin; such was the force of Greek and Roman civilisation upon a race whose whole mass remained Celtic, and where the
5   Celtic language still lingered on, they say, among the common people, for some five or six centuries after the Roman conquest. But the Normans in Neustria lost their old Teutonic language in a wonderfully short time; when they conquered England they were already Latinised; with them were a number of
10 Frenchmen by race, men from Anjou and Poitou, so they brought into England more non-Teutonic blood, besides what they had themselves got by intermarriage, than is commonly supposed; the great point, however, is, that by civilisation this vigorous race, when it took possession of England, was Latin.

15   These Normans, who in Neustria had lost their old Teutonic tongue so rapidly, kept in England their new Latin tongue for some three centuries. It was Edward the Third's reign before English came to be used in law-pleadings and spoken at court. Why this difference? Both in Neustria and in England
20 the Normans were a handful; but in Neustria, as Teutons, they were in contact with a more advanced civilisation than their own; in England, as Latins, with a less advanced. The Latinised Normans in England had the sense for fact, which the Celts had not; and the love of strenuousness, clearness, and rapidity,
25 the high Latin spirit, which the Saxons had not. They hated the slowness and dulness of the creeping Saxon; it offended their clear, strenuous talent for affairs, as it offended the Celt's quick and delicate perception. The Normans had the Roman talent for affairs, the Roman decisiveness in emergencies. They
30 have been called prosaic, but this is not a right word for them; they were neither sentimental, nor, strictly speaking, poetical. They had more sense for rhetoric than for poetry, like the Romans; but, like the Romans, they had too high a spirit not to like a noble intellectual stimulus of some kind, and thus
35 they were carried out of the region of the merely prosaic. Their foible,—the bad excess of their characterising quality of strenuousness,—was not a prosaic flatness, it was hardness and insolence.

I have been obliged to fetch a very wide circuit, but at last I have got what I went to seek. I have got a rough, but, I hope, clear notion of these three forces, the Germanic genius, the Celtic genius, the Norman genius. The Germanic genius has steadiness as its main basis, with commonness and humdrum for its defect, fidelity to nature for its excellence. The Celtic genius, sentiment as its main basis, with love of beauty, charm, and spirituality for its excellence, ineffectualness and self-will for its defect. The Norman genius, talent for affairs as its main basis, with strenuousness and clear rapidity for its excellence, hardness and insolence for its defect. And now to try and trace these in the composite English genius.

[v]

To begin with what is more external. If we are so wholly Anglo-Saxon and Germanic as people say, how comes it that the habits and gait of the German language are so exceedingly unlike ours? Why while the *Times* talks in this fashion: "At noon a long line of carriages extended from Pall Mall to the Peers' entrance of the Palace of Westminster," does the *Cologne Gazette* talk in this other fashion: "Nachdem die Vorbereitungen zu dem auf dem Gürzenich-Saale zu Ehren der Abgeordneten statt finden sollenden Bankette bereits vollständig getroffen worden waren, fand heute vormittag auf polizeiliche Anordnung die Schliessung sämmtlicher Zugänge zum Gürzenich statt?" [1] Surely the mental habit of people who

---

[1] The above is really a sentence taken from the *Cologne Gazette*. Lord Strangford's comment here is as follows:—"Modern Germanism, in a general estimate of Germanism, should not be taken, absolutely and necessarily, as the constant, whereof we are the variant. The Low Dutch of Holland, anyhow, are indisputably as genuine Dutch as the High Dutch of Germany proper. But do they write sentences like this one,—*informe, ingens, cui lumen ademptum?* If not, the question must be asked, not how we have come to deviate, but how the Germans have come to deviate. Our modern English prose in plain matters is often all just the same as the prose of *King Alfred* and the *Chronicle*. Ohthere's *North Sea Voyage* and Wulfstan's *Baltic Voyage* is the sort of thing which is sent in every day,

express their thoughts in so very different a manner, the one rapid, the other slow, the one plain, the other embarrassed, the one trailing, the other striding, cannot be essentially the same. The English language, strange compound as it is, with its want of inflections, and with all the difficulties which this want of inflections brings upon it, has yet made itself capable of being, in good hands, a business instrument as ready, direct, and clear, as French or Latin. Again: perhaps no nation, after the Greeks and Romans, has so clearly felt in what true rhetoric, rhetoric of the best kind, consists, and reached so high a pitch of excellence in this, as the English. Our sense for rhetoric has in some ways done harm to us in our cultivation of literature, harm to us, still more, in our cultivation of science; but in the true sphere of rhetoric, in public speaking, this sense has given us orators whom I do think we may, without fear of being contradicted and accused of blind national vanity, assert to have inherited the great Greek and Roman oratorical tradition more than the orators of any other country. Strafford, Bolingbroke, the two Pitts, Fox,—to cite no other names,—I imagine few will dispute that these call up the notion of an oratory, in kind, in extent, in power, coming nearer than any other body of modern oratory to the oratory of Greece and Rome. And the affinity of spirit in our best public life and greatest public men to those of Rome, has often struck observers, foreign as well as English. Now, not only have the Germans shown no eminent aptitude for rhetoric such as the English have shown,—that was not to be expected, since our public life has done so much to develop an aptitude of this kind, and the public life of the Germans has done so little, —but they seem in a singular degree devoid of any aptitude at all for rhetoric. Take a speech from the throne in Prussia, and compare it with a speech from the throne in England. Assuredly it is not in speeches from the throne that English rhetoric or any rhetoric shows its best side;—they are often

one may say, to the Geographical or Ethnological Society, in the whole style and turn of phrase and thought."

The mass of a stock must supply our data for judging the stock. But see, moreover, what I have said at p. 353.

cavilled at, often justly cavilled at;—no wonder, for this form of composition is beset with very trying difficulties. But what is to be remarked is this;—a speech from the throne falls essentially within the sphere of rhetoric, it is one's sense of rhetoric which has to fix its tone and style, so as to keep a certain note always sounding in it; in an English speech from the throne, whatever its faults, this rhetorical note is always struck and kept to; in a Prussian speech from the throne, never. An English speech from the throne is rhetoric; a Prussian speech is half talk,—heavy talk,—and half effusion. This is one instance, it may be said; true, but in one instance of this kind the presence or the absence of an aptitude for rhetoric is decisively shown. Well, then, why am I not to say that we English get our rhetorical sense from the Norman element in us,—our turn for this strenuous, direct, high-spirited talent of oratory, from the influence of the strenuous, direct, high-spirited Normans? Modes of life, institutions, government, and other such causes, are sufficient, I shall be told, to account for English oratory. Modes of life, institutions, government, climate, and so forth,— let me say it once for all,—will further or hinder the development of an aptitude, but they will not by themselves create the aptitude or explain it. On the other hand, a people's habit and complexion of nature go far to determine its modes of life, institutions, and government, and even to prescribe the limits within which the influences of climate shall tell upon it.

However, it is not my intention, in these remarks, to lay it down for certain that this or that part of our powers, shortcomings, and behaviour, is due to a Celtic, German, or Norman element in us. To establish this I should need much wider limits, and a knowledge, too, far beyond what I possess; all I purpose is to point out certain correspondences, not yet, perhaps, sufficiently observed and attended to, which seem to lead towards certain conclusions. The following up the inquiry till full proof is reached,—or perhaps, full disproof,—is what I want to suggest to more competent persons. Premising this, I now go on to a second matter, somewhat more delicate and inward than that with which I began. Every one knows how well the Greek and Latin races, with their direct sense for the visible,

palpable world, have succeeded in the plastic arts. The sheer
German races, too, with their honest love of fact, and their
steady pursuit of it,—their fidelity to nature, in short,—have
attained a high degree of success in these arts; few people
will deny that Albert Dürer and Rubens, for example, are to
be called masters in painting, and in the high kind of painting.
The Celtic races, on the other hand, have shown a singular
inaptitude for the plastic arts; the abstract, severe character of
the Druidical religion, its dealing with the eye of the mind
rather than the eye of the body, its having no elaborate temples
and beautiful idols, all point this way from the first; its sentiment cannot satisfy itself, cannot even find a resting-place for
itself, in colour and form; it presses on to the impalpable, the
ideal. The forest of trees and the forest of rocks, not hewn
timber and carved stones, suit its aspirations for something not
to be bounded or expressed. With this tendency, the Celtic
races have, as I remarked before, been necessarily almost impotent in the higher branches of the plastic arts. Ireland, that
has produced so many powerful spirits, has produced no great
sculptors or painters. Cross into England. The inaptitude for
the plastic art strikingly diminishes, as soon as the German, not
the Celtic element, preponderates in the race. And yet in England, too, in the English race, there is something which seems
to prevent our reaching real mastership in the plastic arts, as
the more unmixed German races have reached it. Reynolds
and Turner are painters of genius, who can doubt it? but take
a European jury, the only competent jury in these cases, and
see if you can get a verdict giving them the rank of masters,
as this rank is given to Raphael and Correggio, or to Albert
Dürer and Rubens. And observe in what points our English pair
succeed, and in what they fall short. They fall short in
architectonicé, in the highest power of composition, by which
painting accomplishes the very uttermost which it is given to
painting to accomplish; the highest sort of composition, the
highest application of the art of painting, they either do not
attempt, or they fail in it. Their defect, therefore, is on the side
of art, of plastic art. And they succeed in magic, in beauty,
in grace, in expressing almost the inexpressible: here is the

charm of Reynolds's children and Turner's seas; the impulse to
express the inexpressible carries Turner so far, that at last it
carries him away, and even long before he is quite carried away,
even in works that are justly extolled, one can see the stamp-
mark, as the French say, of insanity. The excellence, therefore,
the success, is on the side of spirit. Does not this look as if a
Celtic stream met the main German current in us, and gave it
a somewhat different course from that which it takes naturally?
We have Germanism enough in us, enough patient love for fact
and matter, to be led to attempt the plastic arts, and we make
much more way in them than the pure Celtic races make; but
at a certain point our Celtism comes in, with its love of emotion,
sentiment, the inexpressible, and gives our best painters a bias.
And the point at which it comes in is just that critical point
where the flowering of art into its perfection commences; we
have plenty of painters who never reach this point at all, but
remain always mere journeymen, in bondage to matter; but
those who do reach it, instead of going on to the true consummation of the masters in painting, are a little overbalanced
by soul and feeling, work too directly for these, and so
do not get out of their art all that may be got out of it.

The same modification of our Germanism by another force
which seems Celtic, is visible in our religion. Here, too, we
may trace a gradation between Celt, Englishman, and German,
the difference which distinguishes Englishman from German
appearing attributable to a Celtic element in us. Germany is
the land of exegesis, England is the land of Puritanism. The
religion of Wales is more emotional and sentimental than
English Puritanism; Romanism has indeed given way to Calvinism among the Welsh,—the one superstition has supplanted
the other,—but the Celtic sentiment which made the Welsh
such devout Catholics, remains, and gives unction to their
Methodism; theirs is not the controversial, rationalistic, intellectual side of Protestantism, but the devout, emotional, religious
side. Among the Germans, Protestantism has been carried on
into rationalism and science. The English hold a middle place
between the Germans and the Welsh; their religion has the
exterior forms and apparatus of a rationalism, so far their Ger-

manic nature carries them; but long before they get to science, their feeling, their Celtic element catches them, and turns their religion all towards piety and unction. So English Protestantism has the outside appearance of an intellectual system, and the
5   inside reality of an emotional system: this gives it its tenacity and force, for what is held with the ardent attachment of feeling is believed to have at the same time the scientific proof of reason. The English Puritan, therefore (and Puritanism is the characteristic form of English Protestantism), stands between
10   the German Protestant and the Celtic Methodist; his real affinity indeed, at present, being rather with his Welsh kinsman, if kinsman he may be called, than with his German.

Sometimes one is left in doubt from whence the check and limit to Germanism in us proceeds, whether from a Celtic
15   source or from a Norman source. Of the true steady-going German nature the bane is, as I remarked, flat commonness; there seems no end to its capacity for platitude; it has neither the quick perception of the Celt to save it from platitude, nor the strenuousness of the Norman; it is only raised gradually
20   out of it by science, but it jogs through almost interminable platitudes first. The English nature is not raised to science, but something in us, whether Celtic or Norman, seems to set a bound to our advance in platitude, to make us either shy of platitude or impatient of it. I open an English reading-book for
25   children, and I find these two characteristic stories in it, one of them of English growth, the other of German. Take the English story first:—

"A little boy accompanied his elder sister while she busied herself with the labours of the farm, asking questions at every
30   step, and learning the lessons of life without being aware of it.

" 'Why, dear Jane,' he said, 'do you scatter good grain on the ground; would it not be better to make good bread of it than to throw it to the greedy chickens?'

" 'In time,' replied Jane, 'the chickens will grow big, and
35   each of them will fetch money at the market. One must think on the end to be attained without counting trouble, and learn to wait.'

"Perceiving a colt, which looked eagerly at him, the little

boy cried out: 'Jane, why is the colt not in the fields with the labourers helping to draw the carts?'

" 'The colt is young,' replied Jane, 'and he must lie idle till he gets the necessary strength; one must not sacrifice the future to the present.' "

The reader will say that is most mean and trivial stuff, the vulgar English nature in full force; just such food as the Philistine would naturally provide for his young. He will say he can see the boy fed upon it growing up to be like his father, to be all for business, to despise culture, to go through his dull days, and to die without having ever lived. That may be so; but now take the German story (one of Krummacher's), and see the difference:—

"There lived at the court of King Herod a rich man who was the king's chamberlain. He clothed himself in purple and fine linen, and fared like the king himself.

"Once a friend of his youth, whom he had not seen for many years, came from a distant land to pay him a visit. Then the chamberlain invited all his friends and made a feast in honour of the stranger.

"The tables were covered with choice food placed on dishes of gold and silver, and the finest wines of all kinds. The rich man sate at the head of the table, glad to do the honours to his friend who was seated at his right hand. So they ate and drank, and were merry.

"Then the stranger said to the chamberlain of King Herod: 'Riches and splendour like thine are nowhere to be found in my country.' And he praised his greatness, and called him happy above all men on earth.

"Well, the rich man took an apple from a golden vessel. The apple was large, and red, and pleasant to the eye. Then said he: 'Behold, this apple hath rested on gold, and its form is very beautiful.' And he presented it to the stranger, the friend of his youth. The stranger cut the apple in two; and behold, in the middle of it there was a worm!

"Then the stranger looked at the chamberlain; and the chamberlain bent his eyes on the ground, and sighed."

There it ends. Now I say, one sees there an abyss of platitude

open, and the German nature swimming calmly about in it,
which seems in some way or other to have its entry screened
off for the English nature. The English story leads with a
direct issue into practical life: a narrow and dry practical life,
5   certainly, but yet enough to supply a plain motive for the
story; the German story leads simply nowhere except into
bathos. Shall we say that the Norman talent for affairs saves
us here, or the Celtic perceptive instinct? one of them it must
be, surely. The Norman turn seems most germane to the matter
10 here immediately in hand; on the other hand, the Celtic turn,
or some degree of it, some degree of its quick perceptive instinct, seems necessary to account for the full difference between the German nature and ours. Even in Germans of
genius or talent the want of quick light tact, of instinctive per-
15 ception of the impropriety or impossibility of certain things,
is singularly remarkable. Herr Gervinus's prodigious discovery
about Handel being an Englishman and Shakspeare a German,
the incredible mare's-nest Goethe finds in looking for the
origin of Byron's *Manfred*,—these are things from which no
20 deliberate care or reflection can save a man; only an instinct
can save him from them, an instinct that they are absurd; who
can imagine Charles Lamb making Herr Gervinus's blunder,
or Shakspeare making Goethe's? but from the sheer German
nature this intuitive tact seems something so alien, that even
25 genius fails to give it. And yet just what constitutes special
power and genius in a man seems often to be his blending with
the basis of his national temperament, some additional gift or
grace not proper to that temperament; Shakspeare's greatness
is thus in his blending an openness and flexibility of spirit, not
30 English, with the English basis; Addison's, in his blending a
moderation and delicacy, not English, with the English basis;
Burke's, in his blending a largeness of view and richness of
thought, not English, with the English basis. In Germany itself,
in the same way, the greatness of their great Frederic lies in
35 his blending a rapidity and clearness, not German, with the
German basis; the greatness of Goethe in his blending a love of
form, nobility, and dignity,—the grand style,—with the German basis. But the quick, sure, instinctive perception of the

incongruous and absurd not even genius seems to give in Germany; at least, I can think of only one German of genius, Lessing (for Heine was a Jew, and the Jewish temperament is quite another thing from the German), who shows it in an eminent degree.

If we attend closely to the terms by which foreigners seek to hit off the impression which we and the Germans make upon them, we shall detect in these terms a difference which makes, I think, in favour of the notion I am propounding. Nations in hitting off one another's characters are apt, we all know, to seize the unflattering side rather than the flattering; the mass of mankind always do this, and indeed they really see what is novel, and not their own, in a disfiguring light. Thus we ourselves, for instance, popularly say "the phlegmatic Dutchman" rather than "the sensible Dutchman," or "the grimacing Frenchman" rather than "the polite Frenchman." Therefore neither we nor the Germans should exactly accept the description strangers give of us, but it is enough for my purpose that strangers, in characterising us with a certain shade of difference, do at any rate make it clear that there appears this shade of difference, though the character itself, which they give us both, may be a caricature rather than a faithful picture of us. Now it is to be noticed that those sharp observers, the French,—who have a double turn for sharp observation, for they have both the quick perception of the Celt, and the Latin's gift for coming plump upon the fact,—it is to be noticed, I say, that the French put a curious distinction in their popular, depreciating, we will hope inadequate, way of hitting off us and the Germans. While they talk of the *"bêtise* allemande," they talk of the *"gaucherie* anglaise;" while they talk of the "Allemand *balourd,"* they talk of the "Anglais *empêtré;"* while they call the German *"niais,"* they call the Englishman *"mélancolique."* The difference between the epithets *balourd* and *empêtré* exactly gives the difference in character I wish to seize; *balourd* means heavy and dull, *empêtré* means hampered and embarrassed. This points to a certain mixture and strife of elements in the Englishman; to the clashing of a Celtic quickness of perception with a Germanic instinct for going steadily along close

to the ground. The Celt, as we have seen, has not at all, in
spite of his quick perception, the Latin talent for dealing with
the fact, dexterously managing it, and making himself master
of it; Latin or Latinised people have felt contempt for him on
this account, have treated him as a poor creature, just as the
German, who arrives at fact in a different way from the
Latins, but who arrives at it, has treated him. The couplet of
Chrestien of Troyes about the Welsh:—

> . . . Gallois sont tous, par nature,
> Plus fous que bêtes en pâture—

is well known, and expresses the genuine verdict of the Latin
mind on the Celts. But the perceptive instinct of the Celt feels
and anticipates, though he has that in him which cuts him off
from command of the world of fact; he sees what is wanting
to him well enough; his mere eye is not less sharp, nay, it is
sharper, than the Latin's. He is a quick genius, checkmated
for want of strenuousness or else patience. The German has
not the Latin's sharp precise glance on the world of fact, and
dexterous behaviour in it; he fumbles with it much and long,
but his honesty and patience give him the rule of it in the long
run,—a surer rule, some of us think, than the Latin gets;—still,
his behaviour in it is not quick and dexterous. The Englishman, in so far as he is German,—and he is mainly German,—
proceeds in the steady-going German fashion; if he were all
German he would proceed thus for ever without self-conscious-
ness or embarrassment; but, in so far as he is Celtic, he has
snatches of quick instinct which often make him feel he is
fumbling, show him visions of an easier, more dexterous behaviour, disconcert him and fill him with misgiving. No people,
therefore, are so shy, so self-conscious, so embarrassed as the
English, because two natures are mixed in them, and natures
which pull them such different ways. The Germanic part,
indeed, triumphs in us, we are a Germanic people; but not so
wholly as to exclude hauntings of Celtism, which clash with
our Germanism, producing, as I believe, our *humour*, neither
German nor Celtic, and so affect us that we strike people as
odd and singular, not to be referred to any known type, and

like nothing but ourselves. "Nearly every Englishman," says an excellent and by no means unfriendly observer, George Sand, "nearly every Englishman, however good-looking he may be, has always something singular about him which easily comes to seem comic;—a sort of typical awkwardness (*gau-cherie typique*) in his looks or appearance, which hardly ever wears out." I say this strangeness is accounted for by the English nature being mixed as we have seen, while the Latin nature is all of a piece, and so is the German nature, and the Celtic nature.

It is impossible to go very fast when the matter with which one has to deal, besides being new and little explored, is also by its nature so subtle, eluding one's grasp unless one handles it with all possible delicacy and care. It is in our poetry that the Celtic part in us has left its trace clearest, and in our poetry I must follow it before I have done.

[VI]

If I were asked where English poetry got these three things, its turn for style, its turn for melancholy, and its turn for natural magic, for catching and rendering the charm of nature in a wonderfully near and vivid way,—I should answer, with some doubt, that it got much of its turn for style from a Celtic source; with less doubt, that it got much of its melancholy from a Celtic source; with no doubt at all, that from a Celtic source it got nearly all its natural magic.

Any German with penetration and tact in matters of literary criticism will own that the principal deficiency of German poetry is in style; that for style, in the highest sense, it shows but little feeling. Take the eminent masters of style, the poets who best give the idea of what the peculiar power which lies in style is,—Pindar, Virgil, Dante, Milton. An example of the peculiar effect which these poets produce, you can hardly give from German poetry. Examples enough you can give from German poetry of the effect produced by genius, thought, and feeling expressing themselves in clear language, simple

language, passionate language, eloquent language, with harmony and melody; but not of the peculiar effect exercised by
eminent power of style. Every reader of Dante can at once
call to mind what the peculiar effect I mean is; I spoke of it in
5   my lectures on translating Homer, and there I took an example
of it from Dante, who perhaps manifests it more eminently
than any other poet. But from Milton, too, one may take examples of it abundantly; compare this from Milton:—

> . . . . . nor sometimes forget
10   Those other two equal with me in fate,
> So were I equall'd with them in renown,
> Blind Thamyris and blind Mæonides—

with this from Goethe:—

> Es bildet ein Talent sich in der Stille,
15   Sich ein Character in dem Strom der Welt.

Nothing can be better in its way than the style in which Goethe
there presents his thought, but it is the style of prose as much
as of poetry; it is lucid, harmonious, earnest, eloquent, but it
has not received that peculiar kneading, heightening, and re-
20   casting which is observable in the style of the passage from
Milton,—a style which seems to have for its cause a certain
pressure of emotion, and an ever-surging, yet bridled, excitement in the poet, giving a special intensity to his way of delivering himself. In poetical races and epochs this turn for style
25   is peculiarly observable; and perhaps it is only on condition of
having this somewhat heightened and difficult manner, so different from the plain manner of prose, that poetry gets the privilege of being loosed, at its best moments, into that perfectly
simple, limpid style, which is the supreme style of all, but the
30   simplicity of which is still not the simplicity of prose. The
simplicity of Menander's style is the simplicity of prose, and
is the same kind of simplicity as that which Goethe's style, in
the passage I have quoted, exhibits; but Menander does not
belong to a great poetical moment, he comes too late for it; it
35   is the simple passages in poets like Pindar or Dante which are
perfect, being masterpieces of *poetical* simplicity. One may

say the same of the simple passages in Shakspeare; they are perfect, their simplicity being a *poetical* simplicity. They are the
golden, easeful, crowning moments of a manner which is always pitched in another key from that of prose, a manner
changed and heightened; the Elizabethan style, regnant in most   5
of our dramatic poetry to this day, is mainly the continuation
of this manner of Shakspeare's. It was a manner much more
turbid and strewn with blemishes than the manner of Pindar,
Dante, or Milton; often it was detestable; but it owed its existence to Shakspeare's instinctive impulse towards *style* in   10
poetry, to his native sense of the necessity for it; and without
the basis of style everywhere, faulty though it may in some
places be, we should not have had the beauty of expression,
unsurpassable for effectiveness and charm, which is reached
in Shakspeare's best passages. The turn for style is perceptible   15
all through English poetry, proving, to my mind, the genuine
poetical gift of the race; this turn imparts to our poetry a
stamp of high distinction, and sometimes it doubles the force
of a poet not by nature of the very highest order, such as Gray,
and raises him to a rank beyond what his natural richness and   20
power seem to promise. Goethe, with his fine critical perception, saw clearly enough both the power of style in itself, and
the lack of style in the literature of his own country; and perhaps if we regard him solely as a German, not as a European,
his great work was that he laboured all his life to impart style   25
into German literature, and firmly to establish it there. Hence
the immense importance to him of the world of classical art,
and of the productions of Greek or Latin genius, where style
so eminently manifests its power. Had he found in the German
genius and literature an element of style existing by nature and   30
ready to his hand, half his work, one may say, would have been
saved him, and he might have done much more in poetry. But
as it was, he had to try and create, out of his own powers, a
style for German poetry, as well as to provide contents for
this style to carry; and thus his labour as a poet was doubled.   35
   It is to be observed that power of style, in the sense in which
I am here speaking of style, is something quite different from
the power of idiomatic, simple, nervous, racy expression, such

as the expression of healthy, robust natures so often is, such as
Luther's was in a striking degree. Style, in my sense of the word,
is a peculiar recasting and heightening, under a certain condition of spiritual excitement, of what a man has to say, in such
a manner as to add dignity and distinction to it; and dignity
and distinction are not terms which suit many acts or words
of Luther. Deeply touched with the *Gemeinheit* which is the
bane of his nation, as he is at the same time a grand example of
the honesty which is his nation's excellence, he can seldom
even show himself brave, resolute, and truthful, without showing a strong dash of coarseness and commonness all the while;
the right definition of Luther, as of our own Bunyan, is that he
is a Philistine of genius. So Luther's sincere idiomatic German,
—such language as this: "Hilf lieber Gott, wie manchen Jam-
mer habe ich gesehen, dass der gemeine Mann doch so gar
nichts weiss von der christlichen Lehre!"—no more proves a
power of style in German literature, than Cobbett's sinewy
idiomatic English proves it in English literature. Power of style,
properly so called, as manifested in masters of style like Dante
or Milton in poetry, Cicero, Bossuet or Bolingbroke in prose,
is something quite different, and has, as I have said, for its characteristic effect, this: to add dignity and distinction.

Style, then, the Germans are singularly without, and it is
strange that the power of style should show itself so strongly
as it does in the Icelandic poetry, if the Scandinavians are such
genuine Teutons as is commonly supposed. Fauriel used to talk
of the Scandinavian Teutons and the German Teutons, as if
they were two divisions of the same people, and the common
notion about them, no doubt, is very much this. Since the war
in Schleswig-Holstein, however, all one's German friends are
exceedingly anxious to insist on the difference of nature between themselves and the Scandinavians; when one expresses
surprise that the German sense of nationality should be so
deeply affronted by the rule over Germans, not of Latins or
Celts, but of brother Teutons or next door to it, a German will
give you I know not how long a catalogue of the radical points
of unlikeness, in genius and disposition, between himself and a
Dane. This emboldens me to remark that there is a fire, a sense

of style, a distinction, in Icelandic poetry, which German poetry has not. Icelandic poetry, too, shows a powerful and developed technic; and I wish to throw out, for examination by
those who are competent to sift the matter, the suggestion that
this power of style and development of technic in the Norse
poetry seems to point towards an early Celtic influence or in-
termixture. It is curious that Zeuss, in his grammar, quotes a
text which gives countenance to this notion; as late as the
ninth century, he says, there were Irish Celts in Iceland; and
the text he quotes to show this, is as follows:—"In 870 A.D.,
when the Norwegians came to Iceland, there were Christians
there, who departed, and left behind them Irish books, bells,
and other things; from whence it may be inferred that these
Christians were Irish." I speak, and ought to speak, with the
utmost diffidence on all these questions of ethnology; but I
must say that when I read this text in Zeuss, I caught eagerly
at the clue it seemed to offer; for I had been hearing the
Nibelungen read and commented on in German schools (German schools have the good habit of reading and commenting
on German poetry, as we read and comment on Homer and
Virgil, but do *not* read and comment on Chaucer and Shakspeare), and it struck me how the fatal humdrum and want
of style of the Germans had marred their way of telling this
magnificent tradition of the *Nibelungen*, and taken half its
grandeur and power out of it; while in the Icelandic poems
which deal with this tradition, its grandeur and power are
much more fully visible, and everywhere in the poetry of the
Edda there is a force of style and a distinction as unlike as possible to the want of both in the German *Nibelungen*.[1] At the

[1] Lord Strangford's note on this is:—"The Irish monks whose bells and
books were found in Iceland could not have contributed anything to the
old Norse spirit, for they had perished before the first Norsemen had set
foot on the island. The form of the old Norse poetry known to us as
Icelandic, from the accident of its preservation in that island alone, is
surely Pan-Teutonic from old times; the art and method of its strictly
literary cultivation must have been much influenced by the contemporary
Old-English national poetry, with which the Norsemen were in constant
contact; and its larger, freer, and wilder spirit must have been owing to
their freer and wilder life, to say nothing of their roused and warring

same time the Scandinavians have a realism, as it is called, in their genius, which abundantly proves their relationship with the Germans; any one whom Mr. Dasent's delightful books have made acquainted with the prose tales of the Norsemen,
5   will be struck with the stamp of a Teutonic nature in them; but the Norse poetry seems to have something which from Teutonic sources alone it could not have derived; which the Germans have not, and which the Celts have.

This something is *style*, and the Celts certainly have it in a
10   wonderful measure. Style is the most striking quality of their poetry. Celtic poetry seems to make up to itself for being unable to master the world and give an adequate interpretation of it, by throwing all its force into style, by bending language at any rate to its will, and expressing the ideas it has with un-
15   surpassable intensity, elevation, and effect. It has all through it a sort of intoxication of style,—a *Pindarism*, to use a word formed from the name of the poet, on whom, above all other poets, the power of style seems to have exercised an inspiring and intoxicating effect; and not in its great poets only, in
20   Taliesin, or Llywarch Hen, or Ossian, does the Celtic genius show this Pindarism, but in all its productions:—

"The grave of March is this, and this the grave of Gwythyr;
Here is the grave of Gwgawn Gleddyfrudd;
But unknown is the grave of Arthur."

25   That comes from the Welsh *Memorials of the Graves of the Warriors*, and if we compare it with the familiar memorial inscriptions of an English churchyard (for we English have so much Germanism in us that our productions offer abundant examples of German want of style as well as of its opposite):—

30   "Afflictions sore long time I bore,
Physicians were in vain,
Till God did please Death should me seize
And ease me of my pain"—

─────────────────────────────

paganism. They could never have known any Celts save when living in
35   embryo with other Teutons."
Very likely Lord Strangford is right, but the proposition with which he begins is at variance with what the text quoted by Zeuss alleges.

if, I say, we compare the Welsh memorial lines with the English, which in their *Gemeinheit* of style are truly Germanic, we shall get a clear sense of what that Celtic talent for style I have been speaking of is.

Or take this epitaph of an Irish Celt, Angus the Culdee, whose *Félire*, or festology, I have already mentioned;—a festology in which, at the end of the eighth or beginning of the ninth century, he collected from "the countless hosts of the illuminated books of Erin" (to use his own words) the festivals of the Irish saints, his poem having a stanza for every day in the year. The epitaph on Angus, who died at Cluain Eidhnech, in Queen's County, runs thus:—

> "Angus in the assembly of Heaven,
>   Here are his tomb and his bed;
>   It is from hence he went to death,
>   In the Friday, to holy Heaven.

> "It was in Cluain Eidhnech he was rear'd;
>   It was in Cluain Eidhnech he was buried;
>   In Cluain Eidhnech, of many crosses,
>   He first read his psalms."

That is by no eminent hand; and yet a Greek epitaph could not show a finer perception of what constitutes propriety and felicity of style in compositions of this nature. Take the well-known Welsh prophecy about the fate of the Britons:—

> "Their Lord they will praise,
>   Their speech they will keep,
>   Their land they will lose,
>   Except wild Wales."

To however late an epoch that prophecy belongs, what a feeling for style, at any rate, it manifests! And the same thing may be said of the famous Welsh triads. We may put aside all the vexed questions as to their greater or less antiquity, and still what important witness they bear to the genius for literary style of the people who produced them!

Now we English undoubtedly exhibit very often the want of sense for style of our German kinsmen. The churchyard

lines I just now quoted afford an instance of it; but the whole
branch of our literature,—and a very popular branch it is, our
hymnology,—to which those lines are to be referred, is one
continued instance of it. Our German kinsmen and we are the
great people for hymns. The Germans are very proud of their
hymns, and we are very proud of ours; but it is hard to say
which of the two, the German hymn-book or ours, has least
poetical worth in itself, or does least to prove genuine poetical
power in the people producing it. I have not a word to say
against Sir Roundell Palmer's choice and arrangement of
materials for his *Book of Praise;* I am content to put them on a
level (and that is giving them the highest possible rank) with
Mr. Palgrave's choice and arrangement of materials for his
Golden Treasury; but yet no sound critic can doubt that, so
far as poetry is concerned, while the *Golden Treasury* is a monument of a nation's strength, the *Book of Praise* is a monument
of a nation's weakness. Only the German race, with its want of
quick instinctive tact, of delicate, sure perception, could have
invented the hymn as the Germans and we have it; and our
non-German turn for style,—style, of which the very essence
is a certain happy fineness and truth of poetical perception,—
could not but desert us when our German nature carried us into
a kind of composition which can please only when the perception is somewhat blunt. Scarcely any one of us ever judges
our hymns fairly, because works of this kind have two sides,—
their side for religion and their side for poetry. Everything
which has helped a man in his religious life, everything which
associates itself in his mind with the growth of that life, is
beautiful and venerable to him; in this way, productions of
little or no poetical value, like the German hymns and ours,
may come to be regarded as very precious. Their worth in this
sense, as means by which we have been edified, I do not for a
moment hold cheap; but there is an edification proper to all
our stages of development, the highest as well as the lowest,
and it is for man to press on towards the highest stages of his
development, with the certainty that for those stages, too,
means of edification will not be found wanting. Now certainly
it is a higher state of development when our fineness of per-

ception is keen than when it is blunt. And if,—whereas the Semitic genius placed its highest spiritual life in the religious sentiment, and made that the basis of its poetry,—the Indo-European genius places its highest spiritual life in the imaginative reason, and makes that the basis of its poetry, we are none the better for wanting the perception to discern a natural law, which is, after all, like every natural law, irresistible; we are none the better for trying to make ourselves Semitic, when Nature has made us Indo-European, and to shift the basis of our poetry. We may mean well; all manner of good may happen to us on the road we go; but we are not on our own real right road, the road we must in the end follow.

That is why, when our hymns betray a false tendency by losing a power which accompanies the poetical work of our race on our other more suitable lines, the indication thus given is of great value and instructiveness for us. One of our main gifts for poetry deserts us in our hymns, and so gives us a hint as to the one true basis for the spiritual work of an Indo-European people, which the Germans, who have not this particular gift of ours, do not and cannot get in this way, though they may get it in others. It is worth noticing that the masterpieces of the spiritual work of Indo-Europeans taking the pure religious sentiment, and not the imaginative reason, for their basis, are works like the *Imitation,* the *Dies Iræ*, the *Stabat Mater,*—works clothing themselves in the Middle-Age Latin, the genuine native voice of no Indo-European nation. The perfection of their kind, but that kind not perfectly legitimate, they take a language not perfectly legitimate; as if to show, that when mankind's Semitic age is once passed, the age which produced the great incomparable monuments of the pure religious sentiment, the books of Job and Isaiah, the Psalms,—works truly to be called inspired, because the same divine power which worked in those who produced them works no longer,—as if to show us, that, after this primitive age, we Indo-Europeans must feel these works without attempting to remake them; and that our poetry, if it tries to make itself simply the organ of the religious sentiment, leaves the true course, and must conceal this by not speaking a living language. The moment it speaks a living language, and still makes itself the organ of the religious sentiment only, as in the German and English hymns, it betrays weakness;—the weakness of all false tendency.

But if, by attending to the Germanism in us English and to its works, one has come to doubt whether we, too, are not thorough Germans by genius and with the German deadness to style, one has only to repeat to oneself a line of Milton,—a poet intoxicated with the passion for style as much as Taliesin or Pindar,—to see that we have another side to our genius beside the German one. Whence do we get it? The Normans may have brought in among us the Latin sense for rhetoric and style,—for, indeed, this sense goes naturally with a high spirit and a strenuousness like theirs,—but the sense for style which English poetry shows is something finer than we could well have got from a people so positive and so little poetical as the Normans; and it seems to me we may much more plausibly derive it from a root of the poetical Celtic nature in us.

Its chord of penetrating passion and melancholy, again, its *Titanism* as we see it in Byron,—what other European poetry possesses that like the English, and where do we get it from? The Celts, with their vehement reaction against the despotism of fact, with their sensuous nature, their manifold striving, their adverse destiny, their immense calamities, the Celts are the prime authors of this vein of piercing regret and passion,— of this Titanism in poetry. A famous book, Macpherson's *Ossian*, carried in the last century this vein like a flood of lava through Europe. I am not going to criticise Macpherson's *Ossian* here. Make the part of what is forged, modern, tawdry, spurious, in the book, as large as you please; strip Scotland, if you like, of every feather of borrowed plumes which on the strength of Macpherson's *Ossian* she may have stolen from that *vetus et major Scotia*, the true home of the Ossianic poetry, Ireland; I make no objection. But there will still be left in the book a residue with the very soul of the Celtic genius in it, and which has the proud distinction of having brought this soul of the Celtic genius into contact with the genius of the nations of modern Europe, and enriched all our poetry by it. Woody Morven, and echoing Lora, and Selma with its silent halls!—

we all owe them a debt of gratitude, and when we are unjust
enough to forget it, may the Muse forget us! Choose any one of
the better passages in Macpherson's *Ossian* and you can see even
at this time of day what an apparition of newness and power
such a strain must have been to the eighteenth century:— 5

"I have seen the walls of Balclutha, but they were desolate.
The fox looked out from the windows, the rank grass of the
wall waved round his head. Raise the song of mourning, O
bards, over the land of strangers. They have but fallen before
us, for one day we must fall. Why dost thou build the hall, son 10
of the winged days? Thou lookest from thy towers to-day; yet
a few years, and the blast of the desert comes; it howls in thy
empty court, and whistles round thy half-worn shield. Let the
blast of the desert come! we shall be renowned in our day."

All Europe felt the power of that melancholy; but what I 15
wish to point out is, that no nation of Europe so caught in its
poetry the passionate penetrating accent of the Celtic genius, its
strain of Titanism, as the English. Goethe, like Napoleon, felt
the spell of Ossian very powerfully, and he quotes a long passage from him in his *Werther*. But what is there Celtic, turbu- 20
lent, and Titanic about the German Werther, that amiable,
cultivated, and melancholy young man, having for his sorrow
and suicide the perfectly definite motive that Lotte cannot be
his? Faust, again, has nothing unaccountable, defiant, and Titanic in him; his knowledge does not bring him the satisfaction 25
he expected from it, and meanwhile he finds himself poor and
growing old, and baulked of the palpable enjoyment of life;
and here is the motive for Faust's discontent. In the most energetic and impetuous of Goethe's creations,—his *Prometheus,*
—it is not Celtic self-will and passion, it is rather the Germanic 30
sense of justice and reason, which revolts against the despotism
of Zeus. The German *Sehnsucht* itself is a wistful, soft, tearful
longing, rather than a struggling, fierce, passionate one. But the
Celtic melancholy is struggling, fierce, passionate; to catch its
note, listen to Llywarch Hen in old age, addressing his 35
crutch:—

"O my crutch! is it not autumn, when the fern is red, the water-
flag yellow? Have I not hated that which I love?

"O my crutch! is it not winter-time now, when men talk together after that they have drunken? Is not the side of my bed left desolate?

"O my crutch! is it not spring, when the cuckoo passes through
5   the air, when the foam sparkles on the sea? The young maidens no longer love me.

"O my crutch! is it not the first day of May? The furrows, are they not shining; the young corn, is it not springing? Ah! the sight of thy handle makes me wroth.

10 "O my crutch! stand straight, thou wilt support me the better; it is very long since I was Llywarch.

"Behold old age, which makes sport of me, from the hair of my head to my teeth, to my eyes, which women loved.

"The four things I have all my life most hated fall upon me to-
15 gether,—coughing and old age, sickness and sorrow.

"I am old, I am alone, shapeliness and warmth are gone from me; the couch of honour shall be no more mine; I am miserable, I am bent on my crutch.

"How evil was the lot allotted to Llywarch, the night when he
20 was brought forth! sorrows without end, and no deliverance from his burden."

There is the Titanism of the Celt, his passionate, turbulent, indomitable reaction against the despotism of fact; and of whom does it remind us so much as of Byron?

25   "The fire which on my bosom preys
                    Is lone as some volcanic isle;
                    No torch is kindled at its blaze;
                    A funeral pile!"

Or, again:—

30   "Count o'er the joys thine hours have seen,
                    Count o'er thy days from anguish free,
                    And know, whatever thou hast been,
                    'Tis something better not to be."

One has only to let one's memory begin to fetch passages from
35 Byron striking the same note as that passage from Llywarch Hen, and she will not soon stop. And all Byron's heroes, not so much in collision with outward things, as breaking on some rock of revolt and misery in the depths of their own nature;

Manfred, self-consumed, fighting blindly and passionately with
I know not what, having nothing of the consistent development
and intelligible motive of Faust,—Manfred, Lara, Cain, what
are they but Titanic? Where in European poetry are we to find
this Celtic passion of revolt so warm-breathing, puissant, and   5
sincere; except perhaps in the creation of a yet greater poet
than Byron, but an English poet, too, like Byron,—in the Satan
of Milton?

> · · · · "What though the field be lost?
> All is not lost; the unconquerable will,   10
> And study of revenge, immortal hate,
> And courage never to submit or yield,
> And what is else not to be overcome?"

There, surely, speaks a genius to whose composition the Celtic
fibre was not wholly a stranger!   15
    And as, after noting the Celtic Pindarism or power of style
present in our poetry, we noted the German flatness coming
in in our hymns, and found here a proof of our compositeness
of nature; so, after noting the Celtic Titanism or power of rebellious passion in our poetry, we may also note the Germanic   20
patience and reasonableness in it, and get in this way a second
proof how mixed a spirit we have. After Llywarch Hen's:—

> "How evil was the lot allotted to Llywarch, the night when he
>   was brought forth"—

after Byron's:—   25

> "Count o'er the joys thine hours have seen"—

take this of Southey's, in answer to the question whether he
would like to have his youth over again:—

> "Do I regret the past?
> Would I live o'er again   30
> The morning hours of life?
> Nay, William, nay, not so!
> Praise be to God who made me what I am,
> Other I would not be."

There we have the other side of our being; the Germanic goodness, docility, and fidelity to nature, in place of the Celtic Titanism.

The Celt's quick feeling for what is noble and distinguished
gave his poetry style; his indomitable personality gave it pride
and passion; his sensibility and nervous exaltation gave it a better gift still, the gift of rendering with wonderful felicity the
magical charm of nature. The forest solitude, the bubbling
spring, the wild flowers, are everywhere in romance. They
have a mysterious life and grace there; they are Nature's own
children, and utter her secret in a way which makes them something quite different from the woods, waters, and plants of
Greek and Latin poetry. Now of this delicate magic, Celtic
romance is so pre-eminent a mistress, that it seems impossible
to believe the power did not come into romance from the
Celts.[1] Magic is just the word for it,—the magic of nature;
not merely the beauty of nature,—that the Greeks and Latins
had; not merely an honest smack of the soil, a faithful realism,
—that the Germans had; but the intimate life of Nature, her
weird power and her fairy charm. As the Saxon names of
places, with the pleasant wholesome smack of the soil in them,—
Weathersfield, Thaxted, Shalford,—are to the Celtic names of
places, with their penetrating, lofty beauty,—Velindra, Tyn-
tagel, Caernarvon,—so is the homely realism of German and
Norse nature to the fairy-like loveliness of Celtic nature.
Gwydion wants a wife for his pupil: "Well," says Math, "we
will seek, I and thou, by charms and illusions, to form a wife
for him out of flowers. So they took the blossoms of the
oak, and the blossoms of the broom, and the blossoms of the
meadow-sweet, and produced from them a maiden, the fairest
and most graceful that man ever saw. And they baptized her,
and gave her the name of Flower-Aspect." Celtic romance is
full of exquisite touches like that, showing the delicacy of the

[1] Rhyme,—the most striking characteristic of our modern poetry as
distinguished from that of the ancients, and a main source, to our poetry,
of its magic and charm, of what we call its *romantic element*,—rhyme
itself, all the weight of evidence tends to show, comes into our poetry
from the Celts.

Celt's feeling in these matters, and how deeply Nature lets him come into her secrets. The quick dropping of blood is called "faster than the fall of the dewdrop from the blade of reed-grass upon the earth, when the dew of June is at the heaviest." And thus is Olwen described: "More yellow was her hair than the flower of the broom, and her skin was whiter than the foam of the wave, and fairer were her hands and her fingers than the blossoms of the wood-anemony amidst the spray of the meadow fountain." For loveliness it would be hard to beat that; and for magical clearness and nearness take the following:—

"And in the evening Peredur entered a valley, and at the head of the valley he came to a hermit's cell, and the hermit welcomed him gladly, and there he spent the night. And in the morning he arose, and when he went forth, behold, a shower of snow had fallen the night before, and a hawk had killed a wild-fowl in front of the cell. And the noise of the horse scared the hawk away, and a raven alighted upon the bird. And Peredur stood and compared the blackness of the raven, and the whiteness of the snow, and the redness of the blood, to the hair of the lady whom best he loved, which was blacker than the raven, and to her skin, which was whiter than the snow, and to her two cheeks, which were redder than the blood upon the snow appeared to be."

And this, which is perhaps less striking, is not less beautiful:—

"And early in the day Geraint and Enid left the wood, and they came to an open country, with meadows on one hand and mowers mowing the meadows. And there was a river before them, and the horses bent down and drank the water. And they went up out of the river by a steep bank, and there they met a slender stripling with a satchel about his neck; and he had a small blue pitcher in his hand, and a bowl on the mouth of the pitcher."

And here the landscape, up to this point so Greek in its clear beauty, is suddenly magicalised by the romance touch:—

"And they saw a tall tree by the side of the river, one-half of which was in flames from the root to the top, and the other half was green and in full leaf."

Magic is the word to insist upon,—a magically vivid and near

interpretation of nature; since it is this which constitutes the special charm and power of the effect I am calling attention to, and it is for this that the Celt's sensibility gives him a peculiar aptitude. But the matter needs rather fine handling, and it is
5   easy to make mistakes here in our criticism. In the first place, Europe tends constantly to become more and more one community, and we tend to become Europeans instead of merely Englishmen, Frenchmen, Germans, Italians; so whatever aptitude or felicity one people imparts into spiritual work, gets
10   imitated by the others, and thus tends to become the common property of all. Therefore anything so beautiful and attractive as the natural magic I am speaking of, is sure, nowadays, if it appears in the productions of the Celts, or of the English, or of the French, to appear in the productions of the Germans also,
15   or in the productions of the Italians; but there will be a stamp of perfectness and inimitableness about it in the literatures where it is native, which it will not have in the literatures where it is not native. Novalis or Rückert, for instance, have their eye fixed on nature, and have undoubtedly a feeling for
20   natural magic; a rough-and-ready critic easily credits them and the Germans with the Celtic fineness of tact, the Celtic nearness to Nature and her secret; but the question is whether the strokes in the German's picture of nature [1] have ever the indefinable delicacy, charm, and perfection of the Celt's touch in the pieces
25   I just now quoted, or of Shakspeare's touch in his daffodil, Wordsworth's in his cuckoo, Keats's in his Autumn, Ober-

----

[1] Take the following attempt to render the natural magic supposed to pervade Tieck's poetry:—"In diesen Dichtungen herrscht eine geheimnissvolle Innigkeit, ein sonderbares Einverständniss mit der Natur, beson-
30   ders mit dem Pflanzen- und Steinreich. Der Leser fühlt sich da wie in einem verzauberten Walde; er hört die unterirdischen Quellen melodisch rauschen; wildfremde Wunderblumen schauen ihn an mit ihren bunten sehnsüchtigen Augen; unsichtbare Lippen küssen seine Wangen mit neckender Zärtlichkeit; *hohe Pilze, wie goldne Glocken, wachsen klingend*
35   *empor am Fusse der Bäume;*" and so on. Now that stroke of the *hohe Pilze*, the great funguses, would have been impossible to the tact and delicacy of a born lover of nature like the Celt, and could only have come from a German who has *hineinstudirt* himself into natural magic. It is a crying false note, which carries us at once out of the world of
40   nature-magic and the breath of the woods, into the world of theatre-magic and the smell of gas and orange-peel.

mann's in his mountain birch-tree or his Easter-daisy among the Swiss farms. To decide where the gift for natural magic originally lies, whether it is properly Celtic or Germanic, we must decide this question.

In the second place, there are many ways of handling nature, and we are here only concerned with one of them; but a rough-and-ready critic imagines that it is all the same so long as nature is handled at all, and fails to draw the needful distinction between modes of handling her. But these modes are many; I will mention four of them now: there is the conventional way of handling nature, there is the faithful way of handling nature, there is the Greek way of handling nature, there is the magical way of handling nature. In all these three last the eye is on the object, but with a difference; in the faithful way of handling nature, the eye is on the object, and that is all you can say; in the Greek, the eye is on the object, but lightness and brightness are added; in the magical, the eye is on the object, but charm and magic are added. In the conventional way of handling nature, the eye is not on the object; what that means we all know, we have only to think of our eighteenth-century poetry:—

> "As when the moon, refulgent lamp of night"—

to call up any number of instances. Latin poetry supplies plenty of instances too; if we put this from Propertius's *Hylas:*—

> . . . "manus heroum . . . .
> Mollia composita litora fronde tegit"—

side by side with the line of Theocritus by which it was suggested:—

> "λειμὼν γάρ σφιν ἔκειτο μέγας, στιβάδεσσιν ὄνειαρ"—

we get at the same moment a good specimen both of the conventional and of the Greek way of handling nature. But from our own poetry we may get specimens of the Greek way of handling nature, as well as of the conventional: for instance, Keats's:—

> "What little town, by river or seashore,
>   Or mountain-built with quiet citadel,
>   Is emptied of its folk, this pious morn?"

is Greek, as Greek as a thing from Homer or Theocritus; it is composed with the eye on the object, a radiancy and light clearness being added. German poetry abounds in specimens of the faithful way of handling nature; an excellent example is
5 to be found in the stanzas called *Zueignung,* prefixed to Goethe's poems; the morning walk, the mist, the dew, the sun, are as faithful as they can be, they are given with the eye on the object, but there the merit of the work, as a handling of nature, stops; neither Greek radiance nor Celtic magic is added;
10 the power of these is not what gives the poem in question its merit, but a power of quite another kind, a power of moral and spiritual emotion. But the power of Greek radiance Goethe could give to his handling of nature, and nobly too, as any one who will read his *Wanderer,*—the poem in which a wanderer
15 falls in with a peasant woman and her child by their hut, built out of the ruins of a temple near Cuma,—may see. Only the power of natural magic Goethe does not, I think, give; whereas Keats passes at will from the Greek power to that power which is, as I say, Celtic; from his:—

20   "What little town, by river or seashore"—

to his:—
            "White hawthorn and the pastoral eglantine,
            Fast-fading violets cover'd up in leaves"—

or his:—
25   . . . "magic casements, opening on the foam
            Of perilous seas, in fairy lands forlorn"—

in which the very same note is struck as in those extracts which I quoted from Celtic romance, and struck with authentic and unmistakable power.
30   Shakspeare, in handling nature, touches this Celtic note so exquisitely, that perhaps one is inclined to be always looking for the Celtic note in him, and not to recognise his Greek note when it comes. But if one attends well to the difference between the two notes, and bears in mind, to guide one, such
35 things as Virgil's "moss-grown springs and grass softer than sleep:"—

"Muscosi fontes et somno mollior herba"—

as his charming flower-gatherer, who:—

"Pallentes violas et summa papavera carpens
Narcissum et florem jungit bene olentis anethi"—

as his quinces and chestnuts:— 5

. . . "cana legam tenera lanugine mala
Castaneasque nuces" . . . .

then, I think, we shall be disposed to say that in Shakspeare's:—

"I know a bank where the wild thyme blows,
Where oxlips and the nodding violet grows,
Quite over-canopied with luscious woodbine, 10
With sweet musk-roses and with eglantine"—

it is mainly a Greek note which is struck. Then, again in his:—

. . . . . "look how the floor of heaven
Is thick inlaid with patines of bright gold!" 15

we are at the very point of transition from the Greek note to
the Celtic; there is the Greek clearness and brightness, with the
Celtic aërialness and magic coming in. Then we have the sheer,
inimitable Celtic note in passages like this:—

"Met we on hill, in dale, forest or mead, 20
By paved fountain or by rushy brook,
Or in the beached margent of the sea"—

or this, the last I will quote:—

"The moon shines bright. In such a night as this,
When the sweet wind did gently kiss the trees, 25
And they did make no noise, in such a night
Troilus, methinks, mounted the Trojan walls—

. . . . . . "in such a night
Did Thisbe fearfully o'ertrip the dew—

. . . . . . "in such a night 30
Stood Dido, with a willow in her hand,
Upon the wild sea-banks, and waved her love
To come again to Carthage."

And those last lines of all are so drenched and intoxicated with the fairy-dew of that natural magic which is our theme, that I cannot do better than end with them.

And now, with the pieces of evidence in our hand, let us go
5   to those who say it is vain to look for Celtic elements in any Englishman, and let us ask them, first, if they seize what we mean by the power of natural magic in Celtic poetry; secondly, if English poetry does not eminently exhibit this power; and, thirdly, where they suppose English poetry got it from?

10   I perceive that I shall be accused of having rather the air, in what I have said, of denying this and that gift to the Germans, and of establishing our difference from them a little ungraciously and at their expense. The truth is, few people have any real care to analyse closely in their criticism; they merely
15   employ criticism as a means for heaping all praise on what they like, and all blame on what they dislike. Those of us (and they are many) who owe a great debt of gratitude to the German spirit and to German literature, do not like to be told of any powers being lacking there; we are like the young ladies who
20   think the hero of their novel is only half a hero unless he has all perfections united in him. But nature does not work, either in heroes or races, according to the young ladies' notion. We all are what we are, the hero and the great nation are what they are, by our limitations as well as by our powers, by lacking
25   something as well as by possessing something. It is not always gain to possess this or that gift, or loss to lack this or that gift. Our great, our only first-rate body of contemporary poetry is the German; the grand business of modern poetry,—a moral interpretation, from an independent point of view, of man and
30   the world,—it is only German poetry, Goethe's poetry, that has, since the Greeks, made much way with. Campbell's power of style, and the natural magic of Keats and Wordsworth, and Byron's Titanic personality, may be wanting to this poetry; but see what it has accomplished without them! How much more
35   than Campbell with his power of style, and Keats and Wordsworth with their natural magic, and Byron with his Titanic personality! Why, for the immense serious task it had to per-

form, the steadiness of German poetry, its going near the ground, its patient fidelity to nature, its using great plainness of speech, poetical drawbacks in one point of view, were safeguards and helps in another. The plainness and earnestness of the two lines I have already quoted from Goethe:— 5

> "Es bildet ein Talent sich in der Stille,
> Sich ein Character in dem Strom der Welt"—

compared with the play and power of Shakspeare's style or Dante's, suggest at once the difference between Goethe's task and theirs, and the fitness of the faithful laborious German spirit 10 for its own task. Dante's task was to set forth the lesson of the world from the point of view of mediæval Catholicism; the basis of spiritual life was given, Dante had not to make this anew. Shakspeare's task was to set forth the spectacle of the world when man's spirit re-awoke to the possession of the world at 15 the Renaissance. The spectacle of human life, left to bear its own significance and tell its own story, but shown in all its fulness, variety, and power, is at that moment the great matter; but, if we are to press deeper, the basis of spiritual life is still at that time the traditional religion, reformed or unreformed, of 20 Christendom, and Shakspeare has not to supply a new basis. But when Goethe came, Europe had lost her basis of spiritual life; she had to find it again; Goethe's task was,—the inevitable task for the modern poet henceforth is,—as it was for the Greek poet in the days of Pericles, not to preach a sublime sermon on 25 a given text like Dante, not to exhibit all the kingdoms of human life and the glory of them like Shakspeare, but to interpret human life afresh, and to supply a new spiritual basis to it. This is not only a work for style, eloquence, charm, poetry; it is a work for science; and the scientific, serious German spirit, not 30 carried away by this and that intoxication of ear, and eye, and self-will, has peculiar aptitudes for it.

We, on the other hand, do not necessarily gain by the commixture of elements in us; we have seen how the clashing of natures in us hampers and embarrasses our behaviour; we might 35 very likely be more attractive, we might very likely be more successful, if we were all of a piece. Our want of sureness of

taste, our eccentricity, come in great measure, no doubt, from
our not being all of a piece, from our having no fixed, fatal,
spiritual centre of gravity. The Rue de Rivoli is one thing, and
Nuremberg is another, and Stonehenge is another; but we have
5   a turn for all three, and lump them all up together. Mr. Tom
Taylor's translations from Breton poetry offer a good example
of this mixing; he has a genuine feeling for these Celtic matters,
and often, as in the *Evil Tribute of Nomenoë*, or in *Lord Nann
and the Fairy*, he is, both in movement and expression, true and
10   appropriate; but he has a sort of Teutonism and Latinism in
him too, and so he cannot forbear mixing with his Celtic strain
such disparates as:—

> " 'Twas mirk, mirk night, and the water bright
>   Troubled and drumlie flowed"—

15   which is evidently Lowland-Scotchy; or as:—

> "Foregad, but thou'rt an artful hand!"

which is English-stagey; or as:—

> "To Gradlon's daughter, bright of blee,
>   Her lover he whispered tenderly—
20   *Bethink thee, sweet Dahut! the key!*"

which is Anacreontic in the manner of Tom Moore. Yes, it
is not a sheer advantage to have several strings to one's bow!
if we had been all German, we might have had the science of
Germany; if we had been all Celtic, we might have been pop-
25   ular and agreeable; if we had been all Latinised, we might have
governed Ireland as the French govern Alsace, without getting
ourselves detested. But now we have Germanism enough to
make us Philistines, and Normanism enough to make us im-
perious, and Celtism enough to make us self-conscious and awk-
30   ward; but German fidelity to Nature, and Latin precision and
clear reason, and Celtic quick-wittedness and spirituality, we
fall short of. Nay, perhaps, if we are doomed to perish (Heaven
avert the omen!), we shall perish by our Celtism, by our self-
will and want of patience with ideas, our inability to see the

way the world is going; and yet those very Celts, by our affinity
with whom we are perishing, will be hating and upbraiding us
all the time.

This is a somewhat unpleasant view to take of the matter;
but if it is true, its being unpleasant does not make it any less
true, and we are always the better for seeing the truth. What
we here see is not the whole truth, however. So long as this
mixed constitution of our nature possesses us, we pay it tribute
and serve it; so soon as we possess it, it pays us tribute and
serves us. So long as we are blindly and ignorantly rolled about
by the forces of our nature, their contradiction baffles us and
lames us; so soon as we have clearly discerned what they are,
and begun to apply to them a law of measure, control, and guidance, they may be made to work for our good and to carry us
forward. Then we may have the good of our German part, the
good of our Latin part, the good of our Celtic part; and instead
of one part clashing with the other, we may bring it in to continue and perfect the other, when the other has given us all the
good it can yield, and by being pressed further, could only give
us its faulty excess. Then we may use the German faithfulness
to Nature to give us science, and to free us from insolence and
self-will; we may use the Celtic quickness of perception to give
us delicacy, and to free us from hardness and Philistinism; we
may use the Latin decisiveness to give us strenuous clear
method, and to free us from fumbling and idling. Already, in
their untrained state, these elements give signs, in our life and
literature, of their being present in us, and a kind of prophecy
of what they could do for us if they were properly observed,
trained, and applied. But this they have not yet been; we ride
one force of our nature to death; we will be nothing but Anglo-
Saxons in the Old World or in the New; and when our race has
built Bold Street, Liverpool, and pronounced it very good, it
hurries across the Atlantic, and builds Nashville, and Jackson-
ville, and Milledgeville, and thinks it is fulfilling the designs of
Providence in an incomparable manner. But true Anglo-Saxons,
simply and sincerely rooted in the German nature, we are not
and cannot be; all we have accomplished by our onesidedness

is to blur and confuse the natural basis in ourselves altogether, and to become something eccentric, unattractive, and inharmonious.

A man of exquisite intelligence and charming character, the late Mr. Cobden, used to fancy that a better acquaintance with the United States was the grand panacea for us; and once in a speech he bewailed the inattention of our seats of learning to them, and seemed to think that if our ingenuous youth at Oxford were taught a little less about the Ilissus, and a little more about Chicago, we should all be the better for it. Chicago has its claims upon us, no doubt; but it is evident that from the point of view to which I have been leading, a stimulation of our Anglo-Saxonism, such as is intended by Mr. Cobden's proposal, does not appear the thing most needful for us; seeing our American brothers themselves have rather, like us, to try and moderate the flame of Anglo-Saxonism in their own breasts, than to ask us to clap the bellows to it in ours. So I am inclined to beseech Oxford, instead of expiating her over-addiction to the Ilissus by lectures on Chicago, to give us an expounder for a still more remote-looking object than the Ilissus,—the Celtic languages and literature. And yet why should I call it remote? if, as I have been labouring to show, in the spiritual frame of us English ourselves, a Celtic fibre, little as we may have ever thought of tracing it, lives and works. *Aliens in speech, in religion, in blood!* said Lord Lyndhurst; the philologists have set him right about the speech, the physiologists about the blood; and perhaps, taking religion in the wide but true sense of our whole spiritual activity, those who have followed what I have been saying here will think that the Celt is not so wholly alien to us in religion. But, at any rate, let us consider that of the shrunken and diminished remains of this great primitive race, all, with one insignificant exception, belongs to the English empire; only Brittany is not ours; we have Ireland, the Scotch Highlands, Wales, the Isle of Man, Cornwall. They are a part of ourselves, we are deeply interested in knowing them, they are deeply interested in being known by us; and yet in the great and rich universities of this great and rich country there is no chair of Celtic, there is no study or teaching of Celtic matters;

those who want them must go abroad for them. It is neither
right nor reasonable that this should be so. Ireland has had in
the last half century a band of Celtic students,—a band with
which death, alas! has of late been busy,—from whence Oxford or Cambridge might have taken an admirable professor of 5
Celtic; and with the authority of a university chair, a great
Celtic scholar, on a subject little known, and where all would
have readily deferred to him, might have by this time doubled
our facilities for knowing the Celt, by procuring for this country Celtic documents which were inaccessible here, and pre- 10
venting the dispersion of others which were accessible. It is
not much that the English Government does for science or literature; but if Eugene O'Curry, from a chair of Celtic at Oxford, had appealed to the Government to get him copies or the
originals of the Celtic treasures in the Burgundian Library at 15
Brussels, or in the library of St. Isidore's College at Rome, even
the English Government could not well have refused him. The
invaluable Irish manuscripts in the Stowe Library the late Sir
Robert Peel proposed, in 1849, to buy for the British Museum;
Lord Macaulay, one of the trustees of the Museum, declared, 20
with the confident shallowness which makes him so admired
by public speakers and leading-article writers, and so intolerable to all searchers for truth, that he saw nothing in the whole
collection worth purchasing for the Museum, except the correspondence of Lord Melville on the American war. That is 25
to say, this correspondence of Lord Melville's was the only
thing in the collection about which Lord Macaulay himself
knew or cared. Perhaps an Oxford or Cambridge professor of
Celtic might have been allowed to make his voice heard, on a
matter of Celtic manuscripts, even against Lord Macaulay. The 30
manuscripts were bought by Lord Ashburnham, who keeps
them shut up, and will let no one consult them (at least up to
the date when O'Curry published his *Lectures* he did so) "for
fear an actual acquaintance with their contents should decrease
their value as matters of curiosity at some future transfer or 35
sale." Who knows? Perhaps an Oxford professor of Celtic
might have touched the flinty heart of Lord Ashburnham.

At this moment, when the narrow Philistinism, which has

long had things its own way in England, is showing its natural
fruits, and we are beginning to feel ashamed, and uneasy, and
alarmed at it; now, when we are becoming aware that we have
sacrificed to Philistinism culture, and insight, and dignity, and
acceptance, and weight among the nations, and hold on events
that deeply concern us, and control of the future, and yet that
it cannot even give us the fool's paradise it promised us, but is
apt to break down, and to leave us with Mr. Roebuck's and Mr.
Lowe's laudations of our matchless happiness, and the largest
circulation in the world assured to the *Daily Telegraph,* for our
only comfort; at such a moment it needs some moderation not
to be attacking Philistinism by storm, but to mine it through
such gradual means as the slow approaches of culture, and the
introduction of chairs of Celtic. But the hard unintelligence,
which is just now our bane, cannot be conquered by storm; it
must be suppled and reduced by culture, by a growth in the
variety, fulness, and sweetness of our spiritual life; and this end
can only be reached by studying things that are outside of ourselves, and by studying them disinterestedly. Let us reunite
ourselves with our better mind and with the world through
science; and let it be one of our angelic revenges on the Philistines, who among their other sins are the guilty authors of
Fenianism, to found at Oxford a chair of Celtic, and to send,
through the gentle ministration of science, a message of peace
to Ireland.

Introduction to

On the Study of Celtic Literature

The following * remarks on the study of Celtic Literature
formed the substance of four lectures given by me last year
and the year before in the chair of poetry at Oxford. They
were first published in the *Cornhill Magazine*, and are now reprinted from thence. Again and again, in the course of them, I   5
have marked the very humble scope intended; which is, not to
treat any special branch of scientific Celtic studies (a task for
which I am quite incompetent), but to point out the many directions in which the results of those studies offer matter of
general interest, and to insist on the benefit we may all derive   10
from knowing the Celt and things Celtic more thoroughly. It
was impossible, however, to avoid touching on certain points
of ethnology and philology, which can be securely handled
only by those who have made these sciences the object of
special study. Here the mere literary critic must owe his whole   15
safety to his tact in choosing authorities to follow, and whatever he advances must be understood as advanced with a sense
of the insecurity which, after all, attaches to such a mode of
proceeding, and as put forward provisionally, by way of hypothesis rather than of confident assertion.   20

To mark clearly to the reader both this provisional character
of much which I advance, and my own sense of it, I have inserted, as a check upon some of the positions adopted in the
text, notes and comments with which Lord Strangford has
kindly furnished me. Lord Strangford is hardly less distin-   25
guished for knowing ethnology and languages so scientifically
than for knowing so much of them; and his interest, even from
the vantage-ground of his scientific knowledge, and after mak-

* [In this edition, "preceding."—ED.]

ing all due reserves on points of scientific detail, in my treatment,—with merely the resources and point of view of a literary critic at my command,—of such a subject as the study of
Celtic Literature, is the most encouraging assurance I could have
received that my attempt is not altogether a vain one.

Both Lord Strangford and others whose opinion I respect
have said that I am unjust in calling Mr. Nash, the acute and
learned author of *Taliesin, or the Bards and Druids of Britain,*
a "Celt-hater." "He is a denouncer," says Lord Strangford in a
note on this expression, "of Celtic extravagance, that is all; he is
an anti-Philocelt, a very different thing from an anti-Celt, and
quite indispensable in scientific inquiry. As Philoceltism has
hitherto,—hitherto, remember,—meant nothing but uncritical
acceptance and irrational admiration of the beloved object's
sayings and doings, without reference to truth one way or the
other, it is surely in the interest of science to support him in the
main. In tracing the workings of old Celtic leaven in poems
which embody the Celtic soul of all time in a mediæval form,
I do not see that you come into any necessary opposition with
him, for your concern is with the spirit, his with the substance
only." I entirely agree with almost all which Lord Strangford
here urges, and indeed, so sincere is my respect for Mr. Nash's
critical discernment and learning, and so unhesitating my recognition of the usefulness, in many respects, of the work of demolition performed by him, that in originally designating him as a
Celt-hater, I hastened to add, as the reader will see by referring
to the passage,[1] words of explanation and apology for so calling
him. But I thought then, and I think still, that Mr. Nash, in pursuing his work of demolition, too much puts out of sight the
positive and constructive performance for which this work of
demolition is to clear the ground. I thought then, and I think
still, that in this Celtic controversy, as in other controversies,
it is most desirable both to believe and to profess that the work
of construction is the fruitful and important work, and that we
are demolishing only to prepare for it. Mr. Nash's scepticism
seems to me,—in the aspect in which his work, on the whole,
shows it,—too absolute, too stationary, too much without a fu-

[1] See p. 308 of the following [*i.e.*, preceding] essay.

ture; and this tends to make it, for the non-Celtic part of his readers, less fruitful than it otherwise would be, and for his Celtic readers, harsh and repellent. I have therefore suffered my remarks on Mr. Nash still to stand, though with a little modification; but I hope he will read them by the light of these explanations, and that he will believe my sense of esteem for his work to be a thousand times stronger than my sense of difference from it.

To lead towards solid ground, where the Celt may with legitimate satisfaction point to traces of the gifts and workings of his race, and where the Englishman may find himself induced to sympathise with that satisfaction and to feel an interest in it, is the design of all the considerations urged in the following essay. Kindly taking the will for the deed, a Welshman and an old acquaintance of mine, Mr. Hugh Owen, received my remarks with so much cordiality, that he asked me to come to the Eisteddfod last summer at Chester, and there to read a paper on some topic of Celtic literature or antiquities. In answer to this flattering proposal of Mr. Owen's, I wrote him a letter which appeared at the time in several newspapers, and of which the following extract preserves all that is of any importance: —

"My knowledge of Welsh matters is so utterly insignificant that it would be impertinence in me, under any circumstances, to talk about those matters to an assemblage of persons, many of whom have passed their lives in studying them.

"Your gathering acquires more interest every year. Let me venture to say that you have to avoid two dangers in order to work all the good which your friends could desire. You have to avoid the danger of giving offence to practical men by retarding the spread of the English language in the principality. I believe that to preserve and honour the Welsh language and literature is quite compatible with not thwarting or delaying for a single hour the introduction, so undeniably useful, of a knowledge of English among all classes in Wales. You have to avoid, again, the danger of alienating men of science by a blind, partial, and uncritical treatment of your national antiquities. Mr. Stephens's excellent book, *The Literature of the Cymry*,

shows how perfectly Welshmen can avoid this danger if they
will.

"When I see the enthusiasm these Eisteddfods can awaken in
your whole people, and then think of the tastes, the literature,
the amusements, of our own lower and middle class, I am filled
with admiration for you. It is a consoling thought, and one
which history allows us to entertain, that nations disinherited
of political success may yet leave their mark on the world's
progress, and contribute powerfully to the civilisation of mankind. We in England have come to that point when the continued advance and greatness of our nation is threatened by
one cause, and one cause above all. Far more than by the help-
lessness of an aristocracy whose day is fast coming to an end,
far more than by the rawness of a lower class whose day is only
just beginning, we are imperilled by what I call the 'Philistinism' of our middle class. On the side of beauty and taste, vulgarity; on the side of morals and feeling, coarseness; on the side
of mind and spirit, unintelligence,—this is Philistinism. Now,
then, is the moment for the greater delicacy and spirituality of
the Celtic peoples who are blended with us, if it be but wisely
directed, to make itself prized and honoured. In a certain measure the children of Taliesin and Ossian have now an opportunity for renewing the famous feat of the Greeks, and con-
quering their conquerors. No service England can render the
Celts by giving you a share in her many good qualities, can sur-
pass that which the Celts can at this moment render England,
by communicating to us some of theirs."

Now certainly, in that letter, written to a Welshman and
on the occasion of a Welsh festival, I enlarged on the merits
of the Celtic spirit and of its works, rather than on their de-
merits. It would have been offensive and inhuman to do otherwise. When an acquaintance asks you to write his father's epitaph, you do not generally seize that opportunity for saying
that his father was blind of one eye, and had an unfortunate
habit of not paying his tradesmen's bills. But the weak side of
Celtism and of its Celtic glorifiers, the danger against which
they have to guard, is clearly indicated in that letter; and in
the remarks reprinted in this volume,—remarks which were

the original cause of Mr. Owen's writing to me, and must have been fully present to his mind when he read my letter,—the shortcomings both of the Celtic race, and of the Celtic students of its literature and antiquities, are unreservedly marked, and, so far as is necessary, blamed.[1] It was, indeed, not my purpose to make blame the chief part of what I said; for the Celts, like other people, are to be meliorated rather by developing their gifts than by chastising their defects. The wise man, says Spinoza admirably, "*de humana impotentia non nisi parce loqui curabit, at largiter de humana virtute seu potentia.*" But so far as condemnation of Celtic failure was needful towards preparing the way for the growth of Celtic virtue, I used condemnation.

The *Times*, however, prefers a shorter and sharper method of dealing with the Celts, and in a couple of leading articles, having the Chester Eisteddfod and my letter to Mr. Hugh Owen for their text, it developed with great frankness, and in its usual forcible style, its own views for the amelioration of Wales and its people. *Cease to do evil, learn to do good*, was the upshot of its exhortations to the Welsh; by *evil*, the *Times* understanding all things Celtic, and by *good*, all things English. "The Welsh language is the curse of Wales. Its prevalence, and the ignorance of English have excluded, and even now exclude the Welsh people from the civilisation of their English neighbours. An Eisteddfod is one of the most mischievous and selfish pieces of sentimentalism which could possibly be perpetrated. It is simply a foolish interference with the natural progress of civilisation and prosperity. If it is desirable that the Welsh should talk English, it is monstrous folly to encourage them in a loving fondness for their old language. Not only the energy and power, but the intelligence and music of Europe have come mainly from Teutonic sources, and this glorification of everything Celtic, if it were not pedantry, would be sheer ignorance. The sooner all Welsh specialities disappear from the face of the earth the better."

And I need hardly say that I myself, as so often happens to me at the hands of my own countrymen, was cruelly judged by

[1] See particularly pp. 296–97 of the following [*i.e.*, preceding] essay.

the *Times*, and most severely treated. What I said to Mr. Owen about the spread of the English language in Wales being quite compatible with preserving and honouring the Welsh language and literature, was tersely set down as "arrant nonsense," and I was characterised as "a sentimentalist who talks nonsense about the children of Taliesin and Ossian, and whose dainty taste requires something more flimsy than the strong sense and sturdy morality of his fellow Englishmen."

As I said before, I am unhappily inured to having these harsh interpretations put by my fellow Englishmen upon what I write, and I no longer cry out about it. And then, too, I have made a study of the Corinthian or leading article style, and know its exigences, and that they are no more to be quarrelled with than the law of gravitation. So, for my part, when I read these asperities of the *Times*, my mind did not dwell very much on my own concern in them; but what I said to myself, as I put the newspaper down, was this: "*Behold England's difficulty in governing Ireland!*"

I pass by the dauntless assumption that the agricultural peasant whom we in England, without Eisteddfods, succeed in developing, is so much finer a product of civilisation than the Welsh peasant, retarded by these "pieces of sentimentalism." I will be content to suppose that our "strong sense and sturdy morality" are as admirable and as universal as the *Times* pleases. But even supposing this, I will ask: Did any one ever hear of strong sense and sturdy morality being thrust down other people's throats in this fashion? Might not these divine English gifts, and the English language in which they are preached, have a better chance of making their way among the poor Celtic heathen, if the English apostle delivered his message a little more agreeably? There is nothing like love and admiration for bringing people to a likeness with what they love and admire; but the Englishman seems never to dream of employing these influences upon a race he wants to fuse with himself. He employs simply material interests for his work of fusion; and, beyond these, nothing except scorn and rebuke. Accordingly there is no vital union between him and the races he has annexed; and while France can truly boast of her "magnificent unity," a unity of

spirit no less than of name between all the people who compose her, in England the Englishman proper is in union of
spirit with no one except other Englishmen proper like himself.
His Welsh and Irish fellow-citizens are hardly more amalga-
mated with him now than they were when Wales and Ireland
were first conquered, and the true unity of even these small
islands has yet to be achieved. When these papers of mine on
the Celtic genius and literature first appeared in the *Cornhill
Magazine*, they brought me, as was natural, many communications from Welshmen and Irishmen having an interest in the
subject: and one could not but be painfully struck, in reading
these communications, to see how profound a feeling of aversion and severance from the English they in general manifested.
Who can be surprised at it, when he observes the strain of the
Times in the articles just quoted, and remembers that this is the
characteristic strain of the Englishman in commenting on whatsoever is not himself? And then, with our boundless faith in
machinery, we English expect the Welshman as a matter of
course to grow attached to us, because we invite him to do
business with us, and let him hold any number of public meetings and publish all the newspapers he likes! When shall we
learn that what attaches people to us is the spirit we are of, and
not the machinery we employ?

Last year there was a project of holding a Breton Eisteddfod
at Quimper in Brittany, and the French Home Secretary,
whether wishing to protect the magnificent unity of France
from inroads of Bretonism, or fearing lest the design should be
used in furtherance of Legitimist intrigues, or from whatever
motive, issued an order which prohibited the meeting. If Mr.
Walpole had issued an order prohibiting the Chester Eisteddfod, all the Englishmen from Cornwall to John o' Groat's
House would have rushed to the rescue; and our strong sense
and sturdy morality would never have stopped gnashing their
teeth and rending their garments till the prohibition was re-
scinded. What a pity our strong sense and sturdy morality fail
to perceive that words like those of the *Times* create a far
keener sense of estrangement and dislike than acts like those of
the French Minister! Acts like those of the French Minister are

attributed to reasons of State, and the Government is held
blamable for them, not the French people. Articles like those
of the *Times* are attributed to the want of sympathy and of
sweetness of disposition in the English nature, and the whole
English people gets the blame of them. And deservedly; for
from some such ground of want of sympathy and sweetness in
the English nature, do articles like those of the *Times* come,
and to some such ground do they make appeal. The sympathetic and social virtues of the French nature, on the other
hand, actually repair the breaches made by oppressive deeds
of the Government, and create, among populations joined with
France as the Welsh and Irish are joined with England, a sense
of liking and attachment towards the French people. The
French Government may discourage the German language in
Alsace and prohibit Eisteddfods in Brittany; but the *Journal des
Débats* never treats German music and poetry as mischievous
lumber, nor tells the Bretons that the sooner all Breton specialities disappear from the face of the earth the better. Accordingly, the Bretons and Alsatians have come to feel themselves a
part of France, and to feel pride in bearing the French name;
while the Welsh and Irish obstinately refuse to amalgamate
with us, and will not admire the Englishman as he admires himself, however much the *Times* may scold them and rate them,
and assure them there is nobody on earth so admirable.

And at what a moment does it assure them of this, good heavens! At a moment when the ice is breaking up in England,
and we are all beginning at last to see how much real confusion
and insufficiency it covered; when, whatever may be the merits,—and they are great,—of the Englishman and of his strong
sense and sturdy morality, it is growing more and more evident
that, if he is to endure and advance, he must transform himself,
must add something to his strong sense and sturdy morality, or
at least must give to these excellent gifts of his a new development. My friend, Mr. Goldwin Smith, says, in his eloquent way,
that England is the favourite of Heaven. Far be it from me to
say that England is not the favourite of Heaven; but at this
moment she reminds me more of what the prophet Isaiah calls,
"a bull in a net." She has satisfied herself in all departments with

clap-trap and routine so long, and she is now so astounded at finding they will not serve her turn any longer! And this is the moment, when Englishism pure and simple, which with all its fine qualities managed always to make itself singularly unattractive, is losing that imperturbable faith in its untransformed self which at any rate made it imposing,—this is the moment when our great organ tells the Celts that everything of theirs not English is "simply a foolish interference with the natural progress of civilisation and prosperity;" and poor Talhaiarn, venturing to remonstrate, is commanded "to drop his outlandish title, and to refuse ever to talk Welsh in Wales!"

But let us leave the dead to bury their dead, and let us who are alive go on unto perfection. Let the Celtic members of this empire consider that they too have to transform themselves; and though the summons to transform themselves be often conveyed harshly and brutally, and with the cry to root up their wheat as well as their tares, yet that is no reason why the summons should not be followed so far as their tares are concerned. Let them consider that they are inextricably bound up with us, and that, if the suggestions in the following * pages have any truth, we English, alien and uncongenial to our Celtic partners as we may have hitherto shown ourselves, have notwithstanding, beyond perhaps any other nation, a thousand latent springs of possible sympathy with them. Let them consider that new ideas and forces are stirring in England, that day by day these new ideas and forces gain in power, and that almost every one of them is the friend of the Celt and not his enemy. And, whether our Celtic partners will consider this or no, at any rate let us ourselves, all of us who are proud of being the ministers of these new ideas, work incessantly to procure for them a wider and more fruitful application; and to remove the main ground of the Celt's alienation from the Englishman, by substituting, in place of that type of Englishman with whom alone the Celt has too long been familiar, a new type, more intelligent, more gracious, and more humane.

* [In this edition, "preceding."—Ed.]

APPENDIX

The Crewian Orations

As Professor of Poetry, Arnold was obliged in alternate years
to compose and deliver in Latin at the annual Encænia the
Crewian Oration in commemoration of the founders and bene-
factors of the university. The benefaction of Nathaniel Lord
Crewe added an annual £20 to his stipend. He performed this   5
task on June 16, 1858; June 20, 1860; July 2, 1862; June 8,
1864; and June 13, 1866. (In odd-numbered years the Crewian
Oration was delivered by the Public Orator.) The discourses of
1858 and 1862 were printed as pamphlets and have been published with an English translation by Professor George J. Ryan   10
in Fraser Neiman's edition of *Essays, Letters, and Reviews*
by Matthew Arnold (Cambridge, Massachusetts: Harvard University Press, 1960). The other three apparently survive only in
the very inadequate reports of the newspapers.

Of the 1858 oration *The Times* (June 17, p. 12, col. 4) re-   15
marked that "unfortunately, [Mr. Arnold] was unable to make
himself heard." The oration of 1860 was thus reported by
The Oxford University Herald: City and County Advertiser
(June 23, p. 11, col. 3): "It was listened to without the inter-
ruptions of former years. The Professor's topics were the   20
presence of the Prince of Wales in Oxford, the death of Dr.
Williams, late Warden of New College, and that of the late
Boden Professor of Sanskrit, Dr. H. H. Wilson; the comple-
tion of the New Museum, and the desire of the University of
Oxford for a visit from Her Majesty. The University career   25
of H.R.H. the Prince of Wales was spoken of in the following
terms:—'Non voluit Princeps noster a communi civium vitâ
secerni, in penetralibus aulæ abdi, perniciosâ grege assentatorum
cingi; voluit in eam civitatem ascribi, cujus aditus æquè medi-

397

ocribus et magnis patefactus; palam inter vos vitam agit; eruditissimos homines audit, familiares suos eligit optimum quemque. Felix iste populus, qui principes ab ineunte ætate sic informatos adeptus sit! qui civili conciliatione sociârit sibi illum adolescentem, quem postea habebit dominum! cujus ipsa regum progenies et lumen regni multis gradibus officiorum ad hoc regium nomen ascendat! ut idem Princeps nobilis dicatur, et jucundus condiscipulus; nec magis Reginæ Filius cupiat videri, quam Academicus æquissimo jure ac fœdere.'" The Prince, wearing the nobleman's dress gown, was seated in a chair on the right of the Vice-Chancellor.

The Encænia of 1864 was a noisy one, and Arnold's oration was drowned out by the raucous shouts of the undergraduates who had spied an unpopular Pro-Proctor behind the Vice-Chancellor's chair.—*Oxford Chronicle*, June 11, p. 5, col. 3. The oration for 1866 "was short and to the point, containing a touching eulogy of the late John Keble, a former Poetry Professor, but the impatience of the undergraduates allowed little of it to be heard, except by those in the immediate vicinity of the professor."—*Times*, June 14, p. 14, col. 4. Keble was Arnold's godfather.

Critical and Explanatory Notes

Three books have been used so often that they are referred to in these notes only by short titles: *Matthew Arnold's Books: Toward a Publishing Diary*, ed. William E. Buckler (Geneva: E. Droz, 1958), *The Note-Books of Matthew Arnold*, ed. H. F. Lowry, Karl Young, and W. H. Dunn (London: Oxford University Press, 1952), and *The Letters of Matthew Arnold to Arthur Hugh Clough*, ed. H. F. Lowry (London: Oxford University Press, 1932). G. W. E. Russell's collection of *Letters of Matthew Arnold, 1848–1888* is available in so many editions that page references are little help; nearly all the letters quoted here without other reference may be found by their date in his collection. A very few passages are from unpublished manuscripts.

[ESSAYS IN CRITICISM]

The first edition of *Essays in Criticism* (1865) contained a Preface, "The Function of Criticism at the Present Time," "The Literary Influence of Academies," "Maurice de Guérin," "Eugénie de Guérin," "Heinrich Heine," "Pagan and Mediaeval Religious Sentiment," "Joubert," "Spinoza" (*i.e.*, "A Word More about Spinoza," from *Macmillan's Magazine*), and "Marcus Aurelius."

The second edition (1869) contained the same essays, but the Preface was shortened and the essay on Spinoza, now called "Spinoza and the Bible," was augmented by the engrafting of long passages from "The Bishop and the Philosopher." In the third edition (1875) a new essay, "A Persian Passion Play," was inserted after "Pagan and Mediaeval Religious Sentiment"; this essay will be published in a later volume of the present edition. Thereafter, the contents of *Essays in Criticism* remained fixed. It was not referred to as "First Series" until after Arnold's death, when his publisher gathered a number of his later articles as *Essays in Criticism. Second Series* (1888).

Whether Arnold or Macmillan first proposed the collection of his essays into a book is not clear from the surviving correspondence; one would guess the former, and in a conversation that took place sometime before July 26, 1864. "I have enough already and more than enough to make a volume," he wrote to Macmillan on July 28, "and they have been so carefully revised once that I shall have very little more to do to them; only I must write an introduction, and this I will do sometime in the course of the autumn. About Christmas or the beginning of the new year would do very well, wouldn't it, for the book to appear." Five days later he sent a list of the essays he would include: those on Maurice and Eugénie de Guérin, Heine, Marcus Aurelius, Joubert, "Pagan and Christian Religious Sentiment," and "Literary Influence of Academies." "To these I might perhaps add the short paper on Spinoza which appeared in your Magazine in November or December last, and one on Dante & Beatrice which appeared in 'Fraser' in May or April, 1863—I doubt about this Dante & Beatrice paper, however. Then there will be an introduction of the length of one of the main papers. [I shall not reprint, while Colenso's appeal is pending, my article on him, nor that on Stanley, which was a supplement to it.] . . . I am not at all clear that the papers should be printed in the order in which I have put them down."

"What to call the volume is not easily settled," he wrote in the same letter. "I had thought of 'Essays of Criticism' in the old sense of the word *Essay—attempt—specimen;* but perhaps this would hardly do. What do you think of 'Essays *in* Criticism?' " Doubtless with the French custom in mind, he proposed that the book be issued "in *paper* instead of those odious [cloth] boards . . . , a yellow paper—neatly lettered. The only covering in which a new book can be pleasant reading is a paper wrapper—and it would save price, too, and in the best way. . . . I am the most unpopular of authors, but I think this volume will pay its expenses. If not, I shall retire into a monastery, and try this infernal English public no more."—Buckler, *Matthew Arnold's Books,* pp. 66–67.

The collecting of the essays proceeded in a somewhat leisurely fashion, but on November 19, three weeks after the lecture on "The Functions of Criticism at the Present Time" was delivered, Macmillan reported that the typesetting might begin at any time. He proposed to charge five shillings a copy (in the conventional cloth binding), but Arnold, with an eye on *Enoch Arden*'s six shilling price, urged the same for his book, and prevailed. It was advertised in the *Athenaeum* of February 11, 1865. The enthusiastic note on it in the *Examiner* a week later led Macmillan to advertise it a second time, with excerpts from that paper; Arnold promptly begged him not again to "put the newspaper panegyrics at the bottom. I have an inexpressible dislike to it."—Buckler, pp. 68–70.

The book was a decided success, though not, perhaps, a sensation. Arnold was told somewhat prematurely about May 1 that it had been reprinted in America and that he might hope for some money from that quarter. The Ticknor and Fields edition, which added *A French Eton* and the four lectures *On Translating Homer* to the *Essays in Criticism*, was published in Boston about June 23 at $1.75. It seems to have been done without Arnold's consent or prior knowledge, and payment was slow in coming, so that Arnold suspected he had to do with genuine pirates; at length, perhaps under pressure from Macmillan, the Boston firm contented him with a payment of £50 late in September, 1866 (and this was to pay also for the advance sheets of "Thyrsis," which made its first appearance in *Every Saturday*). His royalties from Macmillan by that time were only £12.6.5; after 1866 they cannot be disentangled in his accounts from the payments he received for his other books on their list. The first edition was out of print by the middle of 1868 and Macmillan proposed a new one. Arnold's alterations had long been planned: as early as April 3, 1865, he told Lady de Rothschild that if he republished the book he would "leave out some of the preface and the notes, as being too much of mere temporary matter." Some last-minute delays held up publication until after Christmas; the new edition was ready (according to the advertisement in the *Times*) on December 28, at the same price as the first. The title page was dated 1869.

The low price meant a proportionately low income for Arnold, so that as the second edition was becoming exhausted early in 1875 he proposed to transfer the work to Smith and Elder, publishers of *Culture and Anarchy* and most of his subsequent prose, in the hope that they would pay him more. Macmillan pleaded that when the initial terms were fixed Arnold had not been so widely known as he was in 1875, and "it was not so apparent then as it is now that your audience was of a kind not to be materially increased by a lower price"—precisely Arnold's argument ten years earlier. The addition of a new essay ("A Persian Passion Play") was to serve as the excuse for raising the price to nine shillings; Macmillan continued as publisher, received the copy for the new edition from Arnold about August 9, 1875, and published the book about December 29. Once again Arnold in revising sought to strike out one or two personal allusions: "As I draw nearer to my bitter end, the desire increases

in me to die at peace with all men."—Buckler, pp. 71–73. Stereotype
plates were made in October, 1883; subsequent Macmillan editions
in England and America were made from these plates until about
1924.

During the last year and a half before the publication of *Essays in
Criticism* Arnold was formulating more and more clearly the aims
of his writing and the means by which he hoped to accomplish them.
"To an eminently *decorous* clerical journal [like the *Guardian*] my
tendency to say exactly what I think about things and people is thoroughly distasteful and disquieting. However, one cannot change
English ideas so much as, if I live, I hope to change them, without
saying imperturbably what one thinks and making a good many
people uncomfortable. The great thing is to speak without a particle
of vice, malice, or rancour," he told his mother on May 19, 1863.
"K. [Mrs. Forster] said to me that I was becoming as dogmatic as
Ruskin. I told her the difference was that Ruskin was 'dogmatic
and *wrong*,' and here is this charming reviewer [in *The Westminster
Review*, October, 1863] who comes to confirm me." "It is very animating to think that one at last has a chance of *getting at* the English
public. Such a public as it is, and such a work as one wants to do
with it! Partly nature, partly time and study, have also by this time
taught me thoroughly the precious truth that everything turns upon
one's exercising the power of *persuasion*, of *charm*; that without
this all fury, energy, reasoning power, acquirement, are thrown
away and only render their owner more miserable. Even in one's
ridicule one must preserve a sweetness and good-humour" (October
29, 1863). "I think in this concluding half of the century the English
spirit is destined to undergo a great transformation; or rather, perhaps I should say, to perform a great evolution.... I shall do what
I can for this movement in literature; freer perhaps in that sphere
than I could be in any other, but with the risk always before me,
if I cannot charm the wild beast of Philistinism while I am trying to
convert him, of being torn to pieces by him; and, even if I succeed
to the utmost and convert him, of dying in a ditch or a workhouse
at the end of it all" (to Mrs. Forster, November 14, 1863). "[The
Saturday Review's] complaint that I do not argue reminds me of
dear old Edward [his brother], who always says when any of his
family do not go his way, that they do not reason. However, my
sinuous, easy, unpolemical mode of proceeding has been adopted by
me, first, because I really think it the best way of proceeding if one
wants to get at, and keep with, truth; secondly, because I am convinced only by a literary form of this kind being given to them can

ideas such as mine ever gain any access in a country such as ours" (December 7, 1864). And, after reading R. H. Hutton's review of the volume in the *Spectator*, February 25, 1865, in which after much praise the reviewer added that Arnold's one limitation was "a deficiency in sympathies lying beyond the intellectual sphere," he wrote, "No one has a stronger and more abiding sense than I have of the 'daemonic' element—as Goethe called it—which underlies and encompasses our life; but I think, as Goethe thought, that the right thing is, while conscious of this element, and of all that there is inexplicable round one, to keep pushing on one's posts into the darkness, and to establish no post that is not perfectly in light and firm. One gains nothing on the darkness by being, like Shelley, as incoherent as the darkness itself." As he reread his essays to prepare them for this collection, he was "struck by the admirable riches of human nature that are brought to light in the group of persons of whom they treat, and the sort of unity that as a book to stimulate the better humanity in us the volume has" (January 21, 1865).

The whole question of the relation of Arnold's style to his purpose, of "disinterestedness" as an ideal and as a stratagem, both in the pivotal volume of *Essays in Criticism* and in his other writings, is illuminatingly discussed in E. K. Brown's *Matthew Arnold: a Study in Conflict* (Chicago: University of Chicago Press, 1948), a book which, despite its insights, is curiously uncertain in its central conception. R. A. Donovan ("The Method of Arnold's *Essays in Criticism*," *PMLA*, LXXI, 922–31 [December, 1956]) demonstrates convincingly that Arnold was right in finding unity in his volume: the essays are bound together by a common source of inspiration (France), a common theme (the attack on British Philistinism, provincialism, complacency), a common method (the comparative, or juxtaposing of opposites to arrive at a position intermediate between the two), and a common aim (in Arnold's words, "to inculcate intelligence, in a high sense of the word, upon the English nation as what they most want"). Most of the essays were conceived at the same time: "Maurice de Guérin," "Eugénie de Guérin," "Marcus Aurelius," and "Academies" were all planned (and the first completed) about the end of November, 1862, and the articles on Heine, Joubert, and Spinoza before the end of January, 1863. The "Dante and Beatrice" paper may well have been omitted simply because it was *not* part of this conception; the Colenso paper, which is the first real "Essay in Criticism," was too topical for the book.

The significance of *Essays in Criticism* was quickly recognized in the most flattering way, through the attention given to it by first-rate reviewers and writers. E. S. Dallas' *The Gay Science*, an "attempt to settle the first principles of Criticism," only a year later has already integrated Arnold into its system of thought. Swinburne devoted to the *Essays* a third of his article on "Mr. Arnold's New Poems" (*Fortnightly Review*, VIII, 414–45 [October, 1867]), an article as enthusiastic in its praise as it was lively and independent in its criticism, especially of Arnold's unhappy taste in French writers. In France, where Sainte-Beuve praised Arnold's "Eugénie de Guérin" as the work of "un étranger qui nous connaît mieux que personne" (*Nouveaux lundis*, IX, 250, from the *Constitutionnel* of January 2, 1865), the *Revue des deux mondes* (seconde période, LXII, 744–67 [April 1, 1866]) devoted a long article on "La Critique contemporaine en Angleterre" to Arnold; "it is by a M. [Louis] Étienne, of whom I know nothing," Arnold told his mother. (Swinburne knew of him and regarded him as a staunch warrior in the army of the Philistines.) "Here in England we know and care very little about any people but ourselves, but on the Continent,—in Germany, Switzerland, Italy,— . . . people will remark [Sainte-Beuve's praise] and set it to one's credit. The 'serious esteem' which one may thus acquire by the testimony of competent judges coming to the ears of competent hearers, and leading them, in their turn, to interest themselves in what one does, is the only thing in the way of literary praise really worth caring for." Arnold sent a copy of the *Essays* to Sainte-Beuve. In America young Henry James commended Arnold's delicate perceptions, his fascinating style, and the intelligent amiability of the Preface, and understood perfectly that the reason criticism keeps aloof from "the region of immediate practice" is that if the high ground of theory is taken the practical consequences are inevitable and need no further attention (*North American Review*, CI, 206–13 [July, 1865]). Herman Melville bought a copy of the American edition on July 10, 1869, and jotted down approving marginal comments.

Modern scholarship and criticism also have been much concerned with the book, as a glance at the head-notes to the individual essays, below, will show. Two editions have usefully faced the problem of scholarly annotation, that by Clement A. Miles and Leonard Smith (Oxford: Clarendon Press, 1918) and that by Sister Thomas Marion Hoctor (Ann Arbor: University Microfilms, 1958); the latter also lists textual variants. The relation of the book to French criticism and French literature, which has caught the eye of its readers from the start, is the subject of Part I of Ruth Zabriskie Temple's *The Critic's Alchemy* (New York: Twayne Publishers, 1953); she finds

Arnold totally inadequate as an interpreter of French poetry because of his bias against the alexandrine and his romantic conviction that poetry may not properly be the product of reason, and he failed altogether to sense what was really valuable in the theory and practice of the French critics he admired: he was inferior to Sainte-Beuve and Renan whenever he treated their subjects. Not everyone will agree with the latter judgment, and Swinburne was on somewhat surer ground than Mrs. Temple in his remarks on Arnold's failure to appreciate French poetry. The personal relations between Arnold and Sainte-Beuve have been treated piecemeal in half a dozen places; the most recent and complete summary is my article, "Documents in the Matthew Arnold–Sainte-Beuve Relationship," *Modern Philology*, LX (1962), and Arnold's letters to Sainte-Beuve are printed in the Appendix to Louis Bonnerot's *Matthew Arnold, Poète* (Paris: Didier, 1947). Paul Furrer, *Der Einfluss Sainte-Beuve's auf die Kritik Matthew Arnold's* (Wetzikon, 1920) shows the similarity in tone and technique between the two writers, as well as Arnold's dependence upon Sainte-Beuve for his leading ideas about French literature. Arnold's essays are dominated, he finds, by a central idea of Culture; Sainte-Beuve is governed by no such central idea, but merely by the wish to see what makes a man noteworthy or celebrated. Furrer does almost nothing with specific borrowings. Arnold Whitridge's brief discussion of the same problem is couched in rather general terms, but is written with truth and gracefulness that his grandfather would have been glad to own: "Matthew Arnold and Sainte-Beuve," *PMLA*, LIII, 303–13 (March, 1938). There have been a few somewhat trifling articles on Arnold's borrowings from Renan, and Furrer's monograph has a brief excursus on Renan, but the most satisfactory examination of this relationship is by S. M. B. Coulling, "Renan's Influence on Arnold's Literary and Social Criticism," *Florida State University Studies*, no. 5, pp. 95–112 (1952): "Arnold's indebtedness to Renan has been given exaggerated importance, just as his obvious similarities to Renan have obscured his essential dissimilarities"; Renan's chief influence, he says, was on Arnold's lectures on Celtic literature.

Of modern critical writing upon *Essays in Criticism* one can hardly do more than list a few of the most distinguished pieces: Stanley T. Williams, "Matthew Arnold as a Critic of Literature," *University of California Chronicle*, XXVI, 183–208 (April, 1924); H. W. Garrod, *Poetry and the Criticism of Life* (Cambridge: Harvard University Press, 1931); F. R. Leavis, "Revaluations, XI: Arnold as Critic," *Scrutiny*, VII, 319–32 (December, 1938); the seventh chapter of Lionel Trilling's *Matthew Arnold* (New York: Norton, 1939), and E. B. Greenwood, "Matthew Arnold: Thoughts on a Centenary," *The Twentieth Century*, CLXII, 469–79 (November, 1957). D. G. James's lectures, *Matthew Arnold and the Decline of English Romanticism* (Oxford, 1961), focus principally upon Arnold's "Preface" of 1853 and "The Function of Criticism at the Present Time"; they are perverse in their definition of romantic theory, provocative in their urging of Arnold's inconsistencies, and illuminating in their insights into his character.

P.2. Epigraph. *Reflections on the Revolution in France*, exactly two-thirds through.

[DANTE AND BEATRICE]

Although almost from the outset Arnold conceived of printing the lectures he gave from the Chair of Poetry at Oxford ("The second lecture will stand well enough when it is printed," he wrote to his mother on May 30, 1858), none were published until he turned to Homer as his subject. Thereafter, however, all but two saw print, at least partially. Returning from Homer to his "course" on the Modern Element in Literature, he lectured on March 29, 1862, on "The Modern Element in Dante." It was nearly a year later that he told his mother (March 5, 1863) that he was getting ready an old lecture which he was giving to Froude for *Fraser's*. As published there in May, the article is only about one-fourth the length of his usual lecture and devotes itself almost entirely to the translation of the *Vita Nuova* by Arnold's friend Theodore Martin, whose wife, Helena Faucit, Arnold had once hoped to see on the stage as Merope. He received £ 3. 7. 6 from *Fraser's* for the article. When he collected his lectures for *Essays in Criticism*, he toyed with the idea of including this one, then rejected the notion.

3:13. *The Vita Nuova* of Dante, translated, with an Introduction and Notes, by Theodore Martin. London: Parker, Son, and Bourn, 1862 (actually mid-December, 1861). The publisher of the book was likewise publisher of *Fraser's Magazine*, in which Arnold's essay first appeared.

3:17–20. "She was a Phantom of delight," last four lines. Arnold quotes the lines as Martin gives them on p. xi. Martin uses Wordsworth's language frequently in this part of his essay and quotes lines 17–18 of the same poem on p. xxxii.

4:22–28. Martin, pp. x, xxxii, xxi.

4:32–5:13. *Vita Nuova*, II, 1–12; III, 1–10; X, 6–10; XXII, 13–35;

XIV, 1–39; XXIX, 3–7; XXXV, 1–7; XL, 1–5; XLI, 1–11. Arnold quotes Martin's translation, pp. 21, 61, 68–69. Martin says that at their first meeting Dante was "a boy of nine" and Beatrice "a girl of eight"; Dante's words are: "sì che quasi dal principio del suo anno nono apparve a me, ed io la vidi quasi alla fine del mio nono."

5:16–17. Martin, p. xlv; *Purgatorio*, XXXII, 5; *Paradiso*, XXX, 26.

6:18–32. Martin, pp. xxxii (the lines from Wordsworth), x, xvi–xix.

6:35–7:13. Martin, pp. xix, xxii, xx, xxi. Martin wrote "return[ed] it in any, and in what degree" and "it startles and jars us."

7:14–35. Martin, pp. xxiii, xxvii–xxviii, xxv, xxii. The verses are from Tennyson's "Love and Duty," 80–81.

7:37–8:12. Martin, pp. xli–xlii.

8:13–15. *Purgatorio*, XXXI, 49–63; Martin, p. xl.

8:17–29. Martin, pp. 114–15, xxxix, xli.

8:35–36. "To [rhetoric] poetry would be made subsequent, or, indeed, rather precedent, as being less subtile and fine, but more simple, sensuous, and passionate."—Milton, Tractate *Of Education*.

9:1–2. Petrarca, *Rerum Memorandarum Libri*, ed. Giuseppe Billanovich (Firenze, 1945), II, 83: "moribus parumper contumacior et oratione liberior quam delicatis ac fastidiosis etatis nostre principum auribus atque oculis acceptum foret."

9:2–6. Perhaps Boccaccio, *Vita di Dante*, ed. Francesco Macrì-Leone (Firenze, 1888), pp. 43–45 (Chapter VIII).

9:19–21. Martin, p. 115; Boccaccio, *Vita di Dante*, pp. 61–62 (Chapter XII).

9:37–10:19. *Purgatorio*, XXX, 101, 121–138, 142–145.

10:21–26. Martin, p. xli.

10:37. *Purgatorio*, XXX, 130.

[MAURICE DE GUÉRIN]

On Saturday, November 15, 1862, Arnold delivered at Oxford his lecture on "A Modern French Poet"; he had already agreed that Froude should have it for *Fraser's Magazine*, where it appeared in January, 1863 (Arnold explained to Sainte-Beuve that he chose *Fraser's* as "almost the only literary journal in England where the writer could sign his article"). He received £11 5s from the publication. The writing was done at the Athenaeum Club after the day's school inspecting was over—from about two until six every afternoon of the week of November 3, and it was not completed by the end of that week. "I think it will be found an interesting piece of criticism," he told his mother, "but I never feel quite sure how far there is really at present, in this country a public for criticism, or indeed for any literary work except novels and religious books." Nevertheless he was full of ideas for further work: he planned to publish an article a month at least through June. "I am making money to take me to Rome, and I have, I am happy to say, written so little that I have at least ten subjects which it has long been in my mind to treat, and which, but for some stimulus, I should never have set about treating." The article brought him "a long and charming letter from Sainte-Beuve" and another from Guérin's editor, G. S. Trebutien, the latter accompanied by the gift of Eugénie de Guérin's printed *Journal* from her surviving sister Marie. As the notes below indicate, Arnold took Sainte-Beuve's *Causeries* on Guérin as a guide and model, and frequently used quotations from Guérin that Sainte-Beuve had already used. Nevertheless, he was especially concerned to fit Guérin into a context that was familiar to his English readers. If in this earliest of the *Essays in Criticism* Arnold makes his closest approach to Sainte-Beuve's method and thought, a comparison of their treatments of Guérin shows how different Arnold's temperament was from that of his French friend. Perhaps because he could take more for granted from his audience, Sainte-Beuve seems a good deal the more superficial, remarkable though he is for his sanity and sympathy.* Arnold sent a copy to Sainte-Beuve, who acknowledged it with pleasure but modestly disclaimed the ambition of being called "the first of living critics."—A. F. Powell, "Sainte-Beuve and Matthew Arnold—an Unpublished Letter," *French Quarterly*, III, 154–55 (September, 1921); and see Arnold's reply in L. Bonnerot, *Matthew Arnold, Poète*, pp. 531–33.

12:13–15. George Sand, "Poètes et romanciers modernes de la France—38. George de Guérin," *Revue des deux mondes*, 4th ser., XXII, 569–91 (May 15, 1840). Sainte-Beuve was also a contributor to this series.

12:15–17. Sand, *La Dernière Aldini* (Paris: Calmann-Lévy), pp. 269–96. The sentence Arnold quotes above is on p. 293; in Trebutien's second edition (below), it is on p. 385.

12:27. Sainte-Beuve reviewed an advance copy of Guérin's *Reli-*

---

* Against this judgment one may set that of young Henry James, who found "Sainte-Beuve's 'Causerie' on Guérin an example of his best manner, and Mr. Matthew Arnold's essay an example of his poorest," except "for the good taste of his selections—always one of Mr. Arnold's great merits."—*Nation* (New York), IV, 188 (March 7, 1867).

quiae, ed. Trebutien, in the *Moniteur universel* on September 24 and October 1, 1860 (*Causeries du lundi,* XV, 1–34). His notice was prefixed to the edition Arnold used: Maurice de Guérin, *Reliquiae,* publié par G. S. Trebutien (Paris: Didier, 1861), 2 vols. In these notes, references are to the more accessible Maurice de Guérin, *Journal, lettres et poèmes,* publiés... par G. S. Trebutien (Nouv. éd.; Paris: Didier, 1862); references to Sainte-Beuve's essay are also to this edition.

13:18–19. Linnaeus (Carl von Linné, 1707–78), botanist and zoologist; Henry Cavendish (1731–1810), chemist and physicist; Baron Cuvier (1769–1832), naturalist and marine biologist.

13:22–24. *Winter's Tale,* IV, iv, 118–20.

13:26–29. "The Solitary Reaper," lines 13–16.

13:31–32. Sonnet, "Bright Star," lines 5–6. Keats wrote "pure ablution." George H. Ford, who remarks that as the essay on Joubert was first entitled "A French Coleridge," so this essay might have been called "A French Keats," gives a perceptive account of Arnold's judgment of Keats here, as well as in the lectures on Celtic literature and elsewhere.—*Keats and the Victorians* (New Haven: Yale University Press, 1944), pp. 51–66. See also Leon A. Gottfried, *Matthew Arnold and the Romantics* (Ann Arbor: University Microfilms, 1958), pp. 199–202.

13:33. *Atala* (Paris: Garnier, 1929), p. 27 ("Les Chasseurs"). Sainte-Beuve singled out this phrase for comment: "Est-il besoin d'indiquer cet effet magique d'harmonie qui rend l'effet de lumière vague et d'ombre [?sombre]: *sur la cime indéterminée des forêts?*— *Chateaubriand et son groupe* (Nouv. éd.; Paris, 1889), I, 236.

13:34–37. Senancour, *Obermann,* Lettre XI. See p. 377:1.

14:4–7. Sainte-Beuve's objection, on the other hand, is that though Guérin attempted to adapt the alexandrine to the conversational tone —an attempt of which the critic heartily approved—he lacked the science of versification.—ed. Trebutien, pp. xix–xx. See Guérin's own statement, p. 321.

14:36. Arnold had been more sweeping and less accurate in the earliest version of the essay: "Gray—does not use that couplet at all."

16:4–28. Like Sainte-Beuve, Arnold begins with a reference to George Sand's publication of "Le Centaure," then turns to a description of Lamennais at La Chênaie. Both draw on the "Impressions et Souvenirs" of F. du Breil de Marzan appended to Trebutien's edition (1864, pp. 426–28).

16:14. Olympe-Philippe Gerbet (1798–1864), an editor (with

Lamennais, Lacordaire, and Montalembert) of *l'Avenir*, later an ultramontanist writer and Bishop of Perpignan after 1853.

16:15. René-François Rohrbacher (1789–1856) became professor of scripture and ecclesiastical history in the seminary at Nancy and was author of a *Universal History of the Catholic Church* in twenty-nine volumes, 1842–53.

16:35. E.g., in *Campagne in Frankreich, 1792:* "Das Studium der Kunst wie das der alten Schriftsteller gibt uns einen gewissen Halt, eine Befriedigung in uns selbst"; in *Wilhelm Meisters Lehrjahre,* VIII, iii: "Eben so nöthig scheint es mir gewisse Gesetze auszu-sprechen und den Kindern einzuschärfen, die dem Leben einen ge-wissen Halt geben."—*Werke* (Weimar, 1898, 1901), XXXIII, 188; XXIII, 178.

16:37–17:13. Ed. Trebutien, pp. 429–30. Arnold somewhat abbre-viates (and thereby improves) the passage he translates. Lamennais journeyed to Rome to appeal to the Holy See against the suppression of his liberal journal, *l'Avenir*. The doctrines of *l'Avenir* were con-demned, and Lamennais' submission, apparently sincere, was never-theless short-lived.

17:14–22. *Ibid.,* pp. 130–31 (Guérin to Abbé Buquet at the Col-lége Stanislas, 1828).

17:22–18:2. *Ibid.,* pp. 423–25 (Eugénie de Guérin's notes).

17:35–36. Wordsworth, "Address to My Infant Daughter, Dora," line 65.

18:2–4. Ed. Trebutien, p. viii ("Eugénie de Guérin, son égale, sinon sa supérieure en talent et en âme").

18:5–14. *Ibid.,* pp. 6, 430–31 (Guérin, Journal, August 13, 1832, and de Marzan, "Impressions").

18:22–37. *Ibid.,* pp. 181–82. Sainte-Beuve also quoted some phrases from this passage (pp. x, xii).

19:1–10. *Ibid.,* p. 9; quoted also by Sainte-Beuve (p. xii).

19:13–20. *Ibid.,* pp. 12–13; quoted also by Sainte-Beuve (p. xiii). Arnold corrected his translation when a blunder was pointed out by a reviewer: "We have often found the translated excerpts unimpres-sive; and this is the effect—in some instances at least—of a negli-gence and inaccuracy that we should not have expected. Here is one of the pretty reflections on natural objects which abound in Guérin's journal:—'I have been to look at our primroses; ... [they] made one think of a group of young girls surprised by a *wave,* and sheltering under a white cloth.' Think of it who can! A fair group getting under a white cloth to keep the salt water from their well-shaped stockings. But this is not what De Guérin wrote and M. de Ste.

Beuve cited. We should have had 'surprised by a shower' (*une ondée*) and sheltering themselves 'under an apron' (*un tablier*). Thus we may realize the image and the comparison in all respects more *correctly*."—*Pall Mall Gazette*, February 24, 1865, p. 7.

19:21–32. *Ibid.*, pp. 25, 36–37; quoted also by Sainte-Beuve (pp. xv, xvii).

19:33–20:3. *Ibid.*, p. 192; partly quoted by Sainte-Beuve (p. xviii).

20:5–11. *Ibid.*, p. 41 (Journal, June 13, 1833); partly quoted by Sainte-Beuve (p. xviii).

20:13–15. *Ibid.*, p. 280.

20:25–26. *Ibid.*, p. xxx (Sainte-Beuve's essay). When he published the essay in his *Causeries*, Sainte-Beuve corrected his erroneous report of the visit to Wordsworth, but La Morvonnais did correspond with "ce grand et pacifique esprit, avec ce patriarche de la muse intime."

20:32–35. *Ibid.*, p. 186 (April 29, 1833).

21:1–20. *Ibid.*, pp. 281–83 (letter to La Morvonnais, February, 1834).

21:24–32. *Ibid.*, pp. 317–18 (August 13, 1834); Sainte-Beuve quotes the second sentence of this passage (p. xix).

22:8–16. *Ibid.*, p. 25 (Journal, April 5, 1833); Sainte-Beuve points out the same conflict in the entry for that day, but he quotes the descriptive portion and summarizes the religious (p. xv).

22:17–20. *Ibid.*, p. 189 (May 8, 1833).

22:24–38. *Ibid.*, pp. 25–26 (Journal, April 10, 1833).

23:1–9. *Ibid.*, pp. 451, 453, 459 (the "Impressions" of de Marzan).

23:14–23. *Ibid.*, p. 39 (Journal, May 9, 1833).

23:25–34. *Ibid.*, pp. 19–20 (Journal, March 24, 1833, altered to make Guérin seem a witness of what a friend had reported); partly quoted by Sainte-Beuve (p. xi).

24:1–3. *Ibid.*, p. 205 (not "to himself" but in a letter to de Marzan).

24:3–28. *Ibid.*, pp. 454–56 (de Marzan's "Impressions").

24:17–18. *Ibid.*, p. 180.

25:1–2. *Ibid.*, p. 457. Guérin was with La Morvonnais only in December and a few days late in January, but Arnold follows de Marzan's "Impressions."

25:6–29. *Ibid.*, pp. 56–58; quoted also by Sainte-Beuve (pp. xxv–xxvi).

25:32–26:38. *Ibid.*, pp. 62–64; quoted also by Sainte-Beuve (pp. xxvii–xxix).

27:4–30. *Ibid.*, pp. 69–70; quoted also by Sainte-Beuve (p. xxx).

27:32–33. *Ibid.*, p. 73; alluded to by Sainte-Beuve (p. xxxi).

27:37–38. Gilbert White, *The Natural History of Selborne*, Letter 43, September 9, 1778 (Everyman's Library ed., p. 205). His phrase is, "The wood-pecker sets up a sort of loud and hearty laugh"; Guérin refers to "le sifflement gai du pivert." Arnold perhaps translated Guérin under the influence of White's phrase, then added his footnote after he had forgotten the language of the original.

28:1–4. Ed. Trebutien, pp. 259–60, 289 (letters to La Morvonnais, February 1 and 28, 1834).

28:6–7. *Ibid.*, p. 269 (letter to his sister Eugénie, February 2, 1834).

28:14–15. For two short periods in 1757 and 1758 Goldsmith was an usher at the Peckham Academy, in South London; it was, to him, the most humiliating experience of his life. Bottles, in Arnold's *Friendship's Garland*, was educated at an academy in Peckham. Hartley Coleridge, eldest son of the poet, was for a time a master at Ambleside School. He continued to reside at Grasmere and Rydal, near the Arnold home at Fox How, until his death in 1849.

28:16–20. Ed. Trebutien, pp. 310–14 (letter to La Morvonnais, July 9, 1834).

28:20–21. *Ibid.*, p. 318 (letter to Eugénie, September 10, 1834).

28:23–31. *Ibid.*, p. 326 (letter to La Morvonnais, October 19, 1834). Arnold probably should have translated "déjeuner" as "lunch," not "breakfast."

28:31–35. *Ibid.*, p. 350 (letter to Eugénie, October 11, 1835).

29:4–7. *Ibid.*, pp. 368, 370 (letter to Paul Quemper, March 15, 1838, and to La Morvonnais, November 8, 1838).

29:9. Milton, "Lycidas," line 75.

29:10–15. Ed. Trebutien, p. 372.

29:15–17. Sainte-Beuve, in *ibid.*, pp. xxxvi, vii.

29:22–26. *Ibid.*, p. 292 (letter to his sister Eugénie, April 9, 1834).

29:26–29. *Ibid.*, p. 357 (letter to his sister Marie, October 30, 1835).

29:33–34. *Ibid.*, p. 283 (letter to La Morvonnais, written for publication in *France catholique*, February 15, 1834).

29:34–30:3. *Reliquiae,* ed. Trebutien (1861), II, xlix–li (a passage not reprinted in 1862).

30:5–10. Ed. Trebutien (1862), pp. 73, 87 (Journal of January 20 and June 26, 1834).

30:10–13. Sainte-Beuve in *ibid.*, p. xxxiii. Sainte-Beuve had known Guérin in Paris.

30:16–20. *Ibid.*, pp. 5–6 (Journal, August 13, 1832).

30:32–33. "Expostulation and Reply," line 24.

30:33. Coleridge speaks of himself in this way in his early poem, "The Eolian Harp," and Joubert says of himself, with somewhat different emphasis, "Je suis comme une harpe éolienne, qui rend quelques beaux sons, mais qui n'exécute aucun air. Aucun vent constant n'a soufflé sur moi."—*Pensées* (7th ed.; Paris, 1880), II, 5.

30:37–38. Arnold, "Obermann," lines 97–98.

31:8–10. "Hyperion. A Fragment," I, 340–42.

31:16–24. Ed. Trebutien, p. 467 (letter of April 11, 1838, in the reprint of George Sand's article). Arnold's "philosopher" translates Guérin's "physicien."

31:26–28. *Ibid.*, p. 86 (June 25, 1834).

31:30–32:4. *Ibid.*, pp. 92–93 (August 20, 1834).

32:5–7. *Ibid.*, p. 320 (letter to his sister Eugénie, September 10, 1834).

32:8–9. *Ibid.*, p. 126 (October 13, 1835). Guérin used the same language in a letter to La Morvonnais about this date (p. 352).

32:15–17. The posthumous volume of poems by the Scottish poet David Gray (1838–61) was published with a prefatory notice by Richard Monckton Milnes (later Lord Houghton) in 1862. Milnes' *Life, Letters, and Literary Remains of John Keats* (1848) had given an important impulse to Keats's reputation.

32:24–25. Ed. Trebutien, p. 79 (Journal, May 7, 1834).

32:26–27. *Ibid.*, p. 80 (Journal, May 18, 1834).

32:29–33:6. *Ibid.*, pp. 116–17 (Journal, April 3, 1835), somewhat condensed by Arnold.

33:21–22. *Choephoroi*, line 313; *Prometheus Bound*, line 90: "Let the doer be done by" and "multitudinous laughter [of the ocean's waves]."

33:24–25. Sonnet 33, lines 1–2.

33:27–28. *Hamlet*, V, ii, 10–11. Shakespeare wrote "how we will."

33:35. "Poetry ... [is] more simple, sensuous, and passionate [than rhetoric]."—Milton, Tractate *Of Education*. See 8:35.

34:6–7. F. T. Palgrave, ed., *The Golden Treasury of the Best Songs and Lyrical Poems in the English Language* (London, 1861); Shelley, with twenty-two poems, is outnumbered only by Wordsworth and Shakespeare.

34:10–11. Genesis 2:19: "Whatsoever Adam called every living creature, that was the name thereof."

34:15–19. The one is warm and fostering, the other great and unapproachable. For "alma parens" see Vergil *Aeneid* x. 252. George

Sand said of Guérin: "Il a dû, avant tout, obéir à son sentiment per-
sonnel, à son entraînement prononcé, et l'on peut dire passionné,
vers les secrets de la nature."—ed. Trebutien, p. 466.

34:23–26. Ed. Trebutien, p. 115 (Journal, March 27, 1835).

34:26–35:2. *Ibid.*, p. 360 (letter of December 5, 1835).

35:7. Houghton remarked on the "overconfidence" of Gray,
which, however, "gave way as soon as he knew he was really appreciated and cared for. His vanity sang forth, as it were, in the night
of his discouragement, to give himself fortitude to bear the solitude
and the gloom."

35:7–13. Ed. Trebutien, pp. 76–77 (Journal, March 23, 1834).

35:13–19. *Ibid.*, p. 79 (Journal, May 7, 1834).

35:20–24. *Ibid.*, pp. 83–84 (Journal, June 10, 1834).

35:31–35. Sainte-Beuve, in *ibid.*, p. xxxiv.

35:37–36:1. Sainte-Beuve, in *ibid.*, p. xxxv.—When Sainte-Beuve
wrote, this fragment had not yet been found; it was published in
Trebutien's second edition and Arnold thereupon dropped the
words "which is lost."

36:12–39:35. "Le Centaure" is printed in Trebutien, pp. 375–86;
Arnold's extracts are from pp. 375–77, 378–79, 381–84, 385, 386.

39:19. "Who stand around" translates "qui l'entourent." In the
first two editions, the clause was not set off by commas; these were
introduced in 1869, presumably to relieve the awkward contradiction between "stand" and "dance."

[THE BISHOP AND THE PHILOSOPHER]

Arnold was so much the debater and controversialist that once he
conceived the idea of "contrasting Colenso and Co.'s jejune and
technical manner of dealing with Biblical controversy with that
of Spinoza in his famous treatise on the *Interpretation of Scripture*,"
he was carried along by greater enthusiasm than he had shown for
any task since his dissection of Newman's *Iliad*. His object would
be, he thought, to show "how, the heresy on both sides being
equal, Spinoza broaches his in that edifying and pious spirit by
which alone the treatment of such matters can be made fruitful,
while Colenso and the English Essayists [of *Essays and Reviews*],
from their narrowness and want of power, more than from any other
cause, do not." "I know Spinoza's works very well, and I shall be
glad of an opportunity of thus dealing with them," he wrote to his
mother on November 19, 1862. By December 3 he had offered his

article to *Macmillan's Magazine;* not a word was yet on paper, but the essay was "getting very ripe in my head." Six days later it was half written. "The tone ... is a little sharper than I could wish, but the man is really such a goose that it is difficult not to say sharp things of him. I get an opportunity of saying a good word of Stanley, Keble, and one or two other friends and of giving a rap over the knuckles to one or two who are not friends. I worked very hard last week, passing some 6 or 7 hours each day in reading over and over the authors I am going to deal with and in settling my mode of treating the subject, and now I am writing away at a great rate." He seems barely to have met the editor's deadline of 11 A.M. on December 15, but Masson was delighted when he read the article. "I don't imagine he would speak so strongly of anything he thought would not go down with the public, and how far anything of mine will go down with this monster I myself never feel sure beforehand," Arnold told his mother on December 17 as he enclosed Masson's letter. "I was pleased with this performance ..., however, and glad of the opportunity of saying what I had to say." The January issue of *Macmillan's* appeared before Christmas. Arnold was paid £16; with the check Alexander Macmillan enclosed a distressed letter from Colenso himself, to whom Macmillan (as publisher of Colenso's more orthodox books) had sent a copy of the article. But for Macmillan as for Masson it was an "admirable paper."

Arnold's earliest reference to Spinoza is in a letter to Clough on October 23, 1850: he speaks of his "positive and vivifying atmosphere" and remarks, "I have been studying [him] lately with profit." But he probably read him earlier: his brother Thomas, writing to Clough from Arnold's London lodgings on the eve of his departure for New Zealand in November, 1847, mentioned that he was taking with him Spinoza, Hegel, Rousseau, and Emerson (see Kenneth Allott in *Victorian Studies*, III, 320 [March, 1960]). The *Tractatus* is quoted in the *Note-Books* for 1856 and was part of his reading for September, 1858. He planned to read in it again in the summer of 1860, and took it with him to Fox How in September, 1862.

The association of Spinoza's name with the authors of *Essays and Reviews* was not original with Arnold; it seems even to have been a commonplace. Charles Forster, whose name was to receive no honorable mention in Arnold's essay on Academies, delivered a sermon in Canterbury Cathedral on May 6, 1861, and then printed it under the title *Spinoza Redivivus: or, the Reappearance of His*

School and Spirit in the Volume Entitled "Essays and Reviews."
That Forster's tone was very unlike Arnold's is clear enough from
a few sentences of his sermon: "In truth, the whole course of false
reasoning and fallacious sophistry, pursued throughout this heretical
volume, and very specially in its treatment of the Holy Scriptures,
is the exact counterpart of that first devised, in the 17th century,
by the atheistical Jew. I state this advisedly, after a close persual of
the Life of Spinoza, and a careful collation, of his modes of treating
Scripture, with the modes adopted in this book. The parallel has
been noticed by others: but I have verified it for myself" (p. 17).
The *Times,* amusing itself at Colenso's expense on February 16,
1863—after Arnold had published—tells how the bishop set to work
translating the Bible with the help of "an intelligent Zulu, a sort of
coloured Spinoza, as it would seem. This *enfant terrible* ... began
to ask impertinent questions, which Dr. Colenso found a difficulty
in answering.... Instead of Dr. Colenso converting the Zulu, the
Zulu converted Dr. Colenso" (p. 8, col. 4).

Arnold's pleasure in his article came not only from his love of
sport, but from his sense that he was continuing his father's work—
though the time had come when the work could no longer be carried on from the pulpits of the Established Church. "[Papa] is the
last free speaker of the Church of England clergy who speaks without being shackled, and without being obviously aware that he is
so, and that he is in a false position in consequence; and the moment
a writer feels this his power is gone. I may add, that if a clergyman
does not feel this now, he ought to feel it. The best of them (Jowett
for example) obviously do feel it, and I am quite sure Papa would
have felt it had he been living now, and thirty years younger. Not
that he would have been less a Christian, or less zealous for a national Church, but his attention would have been painfully awake
to the truth that to profess to see Christianity through the specta-
cles of a number of second or third-rate men who lived in Queen
Elizabeth's time (and this is what office-holders under the Thirty-
Nine Articles do)—men whose works one never dreams of reading
for the purpose of enlightening and edifying oneself—is an intolerable absurdity, and that it is time to put the formularies of the
Church of England on a solider basis. Or a clergyman may abstain
from dealing with speculative matters at all: he may confine himself
to such matters as Stanley does, or to pure edification, and then,
too, he is in a sound position. But the moment he begins to write
for or against Colenso he is inevitably in a false position."—Letter
to his mother, December 17, 1862.

Arnold never republished the essay. When he used some parts

of it to amplify his later essay on Spinoza, he rigorously excluded every allusion to Colenso and to *Essays and Reviews*. Yet he proclaimed his impenitence for having published it at the same time he offered his "dislike to all personal attack and controversy" as the ground for leaving it now buried. Perhaps also he was aware that his game was too easy for a real sportsman: Colenso's book was so patently stupid that all intelligent reviewers had dismissed it, frequently with ridicule.* If "candidates for consecration should be examined in the Holy Scriptures," said the *Times,* there would be no "recurrence of this untoward affair." The essay is an important step in the development of Arnold's idea of the function of criticism.

40:1. "Alle Engländer sind als solche ohne eigentliche Reflexion; die Zerstreuung und der Parteigeist lassen sie zu keiner ruhigen Ausbildung kommen. Aber sie sind gross als praktische Menschen."
—Eckermann, *Gespräche mit Goethe,* February 24, 1825 (in a discussion of Byron).

40:26. The Court of Arches is the ecclesiastical court of appeal of the Archbishop of Canterbury. In 1862 it tried two of the authors of *Essays and Reviews* on charges of heterodoxy.

42:7–8. Ernst Wilhelm Hengstenberg, professor of theology in the University of Berlin, wrote a number of treatises defending the genuineness (in the orthodox sense) of books of the Bible that had been called in question by the higher criticism. As Arnold suggests below, Colenso devoted himself to strenuous refutations of Hengstenberg's commentaries.

42:15–17. The authorship of the *Imitation of Christ* was in dispute in Arnold's day; it is now acknowledged to be by Thomas à Kempis (d. 1471). *The Christian Year* was a collection of devotional poems by Arnold's godfather, John Keble, first published anonymously in 1827.

42:22–23. Mrs. Mary Sewell's *Mother's Last Words. A Ballad for Boys* (London, 1861), issued as a twopenny pamphlet, was a sentimental jusification of God's providence, with warnings against drinking and thieving and assurances that honorable labor would be rewarded—by honorable and threadbare poverty and the hope of an early summons to heaven.

42:34–37; 43:6–8. "Every controversy which is for the [honour of the] Name of Heaven will finally be established, but that which

---

* For Arnold's explanation to Macmillan of the omission of the essay from his book, see p. 400.

is not for the [honour of the] Name of Heaven will not finally be established. Where is a controversy for the [honour of the] Name of Heaven? Such is the controversy between Hillel and Shammai, but that which was not for the [honour of the] Name of Heaven was the controversy of Korah and all his company."—*The Ethics of the Fathers*, translated from the original Hebrew text [by Robert Young] (Edinburgh, 1852), p. 33 (Part V, 18). The treatise is that portion of the Mishnah (Talmud) known as Aboth or Pirḳe Aboth.

43:12. John William Colenso (bishop of Natal), *The Pentateuch and Book of Joshua Critically Examined* (1862–79). Citations in these notes are from the New York edition of Part I (1863), the only part of the work with which Arnold was concerned.

43:36. "Poetic Justice, with her lifted scale, / Where, in nice balance, truth with gold she weighs, / And solid pudding against empty praise."—Pope, *Dunciad*, I, 52–54.

44:14–15. Ecclesiasticus 28:9.

44:15–18. Matthew 13:11.

44:18–19. Pindar *Olympian Odes* II. 83–86.

44:19–21. In Book VII of the *Republic* (522–33, 537), Socrates prescribes a strenuous ten-year course of study in mathematics and physics as preliminary to the study of "dialectic," or philosophy, which is restricted to those who by the age of thirty have shown the most talent and perseverance in these scientific disciplines.

44:21–22. Paraphrase of Spinoza, *Tractatus Theologico-Politicus*, Praefatio, 35: "Multis nec otium nec animus forsan erit, omnia perlegere."—*Opera*, ed. C. H. Bruder (Leipzig, 1846), III, 11.

44:22–24. Sermon XVIII, "Many Called, Few Chosen," *Parochial and Plain Sermons* (New impression; London, 1901), V, 268.

45:6–16. Colenso, *Pentateuch*, Preface, pp. 26, 7, 19 and "Concluding Remarks," ¶176 (italics Arnold's).

45:19–24. F. C. Cook, "Ideology and Subscription," in William Thomson, ed., *Aids to Faith . . . Being a Reply to "Essays and Reviews"* (London, 1861), p. 146, quoted by Colenso, p. 17n.

45:25–28. J. W. Burgon, *Inspiration and Interpretation: Seven Sermons . . . [in] Answer to . . . "Essays and Reviews"* (London, 1861), p. 89, quoted by Colenso, p. 46.

45:29–31. Edward Garbett, *The Pentateuch in Its Relation to Other Scriptures, and to the Scheme of Christianity*. Sermon preached before the University of Oxford, November 16, 1862.

45:36. Colenso's *Arithmetic, Designed for the Use of Schools* (1843) and *The Elements of Algebra, Designed for the Use of Schools* (2nd ed., 1841) went through numerous editions and were widely used.

46:11–23. A. P. Stanley, *Sinai and Palestine, in Connection with Their History* (London, 1856), is quoted and refuted by Colenso, Chapter XII, ¶83–85. Hengstenberg, *Dissertations on the Genuineness of the Pentateuch,* is confuted in Chapter III, ¶27–29, and elsewhere.

46:31–47:8. Colenso, Chapter XXIII, ¶177, 185, 187–89. Arnold's precise references mock Colenso's pedantry.

47:16. See Luke 10:34.

47:34–35. Colenso, p. 26: "I believe that there are not a few among the more highly educated classes of society in England, and multitudes among the more intelligent operatives, who are in danger of drifting into irreligion and practical atheism." "Operatives" means "working men"; Arnold seems to find the word amusing.

48:11–35. Arnold states, in the manner of a textbook in arithmetic, the problem Colenso deals with in his Chapter II (reconciling Genesis 38 with 46:12). Colenso phrases the problem from Exodus (16:16) almost as Arnold does (Chapter VIII, ¶55) and speculates where the Israelites could have acquired and how they could have transported so many tents. The figure of two million is extrapolated from Numbers 1:3 and 2:32 (Colenso, Chapter V, ¶39). The third problem is posed by Leviticus 12:6–8, 10:16–20, and Numbers 18:10 if we assume that 264 children a-day are born to a population of two million (Colenso, Chapter XI, ¶74 and Chapter XX, especially ¶156). The problem posed by Numbers 3:43 occupies Colenso's Chapter XIV. The final problem, dealing with the Passover sacrifice commanded in Deuteronomy 16:6, is expressed by Colenso, Chapter XXI, ¶161, almost in the language Arnold uses.

48:36. Horace *Odes* II. iii. 25.

49:1–3. Colenso deals with the assembly of the congregation at the door of the tabernacle (Leviticus 8:3) in Chapter IV and with the number of descendants of Dan (Genesis 46:23; Numbers 26:42, 2:26, 26:43) in Chapter XVIII, ¶125.

49:5. "And thrice he routed all his foes, and thrice he slew the slain."—Dryden, *Alexander's Feast,* line 68.

49:12–15. Colenso, Chapter II, ¶18 and Preface, p. 12: "In January, 1861, I had not even begun to enter on these enquiries.... I had not the most distant idea of the results to which I have now arrived."

49:37. Benedict de Spinoza, *Tractatus Theologico-Politicus,* tr. from the Latin with an Introduction and Notes by the editor [Robert Willis]. London: Trübner & Co., 1862.

50:16–28. Spinoza, *Tractatus,* ed. Bruder, Praefatio, 33–34. He

expressed his disapproval of a Dutch translation of his work in his
Letter 47, to Jarig Jellis, February 17, 1671.—R. Willis, *Benedict
de Spinoza; His Life, Correspondence, and Ethics* (London, 1870),
p. 335.

50:31–51:4. Colenso, Chapter I, ¶4; Spinoza, *Tractatus*, VIII, 3
and Praefatio, 34.

51:16. Priests of the Church of England, at their ordination,
pledge themselves "to minister the Doctrine and Sacraments, and
the Discipline of Christ, as the Lord hath commanded, and as this
Church and Realm hath received the same."

51:21–22. The Royal Declaration of Charles I, prefixed to the
Thirty-nine Articles in the Prayer Book, expresses the royal intention "to conserve and maintain the Church committed to Our
Charge, in the Unity of true Religion, and in the Bond of Peace;
and not to suffer unnecessary Disputations, Altercations, or Questions to be raised, which may nourish Faction both in the Church
and Commonwealth."

51:29–31. An allusion to Bishop Tait of London: "Stanley ... is
evidently annoyed that I should treat any amount of freedom of
speculation as unorthodox for an English clergyman, and particularly annoyed by my touch at Tait. But when in a conservative
country like this shall we get the Church of England enlarged so
long as her authorities keep crying out uncontradicted that there
is room for all in her at present, and perfect liberty of thought and
speech—which there is *not*. I asked him in my answer why Tait
should be at London House rather than John Mill, except because
he had consented to serve the State as a public instructor in terms
of less ample liberty than John Mill would demand," Arnold wrote
to his mother on December 25, 1862.

51:34–37. Prof. Thomas M. Raysor calls my attention to Chapters
5 and 6 of Coleridge's *On the Constitution of the Church and State*,
and especially: "The Clerisy of the nation, or national Church,
in its primary acceptation and original intention, comprehended
the learned of all denominations, the sages and professors of the law
and jurisprudence, of medicine and physiology, of music, of military and civil architecture, of the physical sciences, with the mathematical as the common organ of the preceding; in short, all the so-
called liberal arts and sciences, the possession and application of
which constitute the civilization of a country, as well as the theological. . . . I do not assert that the proceeds from the Nationalty
can not be rightfully vested, except in what we now mean by
clergymen and the established clergy. I have everywhere implied

the contrary."—*Complete Works*, ed. W. G. T. Shedd (New York, 1853), VI, 53, 56.

52:3–6. The allusion is to the conclusion of the First Part of Bunyan's *Pilgrim's Progress*. Lambeth, a borough of London on the south side of the Thames, contains the palace of the Archbishop of Canterbury.

53:8–9. See note to p. 49:12–15.

53:12–13. Ecclesiasticus 19:10 in the Authorized Version. The Douay Version reads: "Hast thou heard a word against thy neighbour? Let it die within thee, trusting that it will not burst thee."

53:17. *Essays and Reviews* (London, 1860): Essays by Frederick Temple, Rowland Williams, Baden Powell, Henry Bristow Wilson, C. W. Goodwin, Mark Pattison, and Benjamin Jowett. Arnold knew Temple and Jowett when he was an undergraduate at Balliol and had been associated with Pattison in the work of the Newcastle Commission.

53:26–28. *Ethics of the Fathers*, tr. Young, p. 35 (Part V, 20).

53:33. The parallels between Temple's essay and Lessing's *Die Erziehung des Menschengeschlechts* had been pointed out by E. M. Goulburn in *Replies to "Essays and Reviews"* (1862): "We think that the original conception of Lessing ... has materially suffered in clearness and power from Dr. Temple's method of treatment." Goulburn was Temple's predecessor as Headmaster of Rugby and an acquaintance of Arnold's.

53:38. Hebrews 5:12–14.

54:30–31. Horace *Odes* I. iii. 25–26.

54:33. The race of Japhet is the Indo-European.

54:34–35. Edward Garbett; see note to p. 45:29–31.

55:1. Matthew 5:48: "Be ye therefore perfect, even as your Father which is in heaven is perfect."

55:12–13. Perhaps an allusion to the caldron in which Medea brewed the potion that rejuvenated Jason's father Aeson, in Ovid *Metamorphoses* VII. 262–93.

[TRACTATUS THEOLOGICO-POLITICUS]

Arnold's article on "The Bishop and the Philosopher" was in the hands of the printer, but still unpublished, when the first English translation of Spinoza's *Tractatus* appeared—without a translator's name, but done by Robert Willis. Arnold had looked forward to it eagerly; sadly disappointed with the translator's work, he reviewed it at once for the *London Review* (December 27, 1862).

Though the review was anonymous, echoes of it in Arnold's later essay on Spinoza and in "The Literary Influence of Academies" make the authorship unquestionable. He was paid six guineas for this and the article on "Ordnance Maps" published in volume II of the present edition.

58:21–34. Spinoza, *Tractatus Theologico-Politicus*, ed. C. H. Bruder (Leipzig, 1846), "Praefatio," 14; Willis's translation, p. 23. The italics are Arnold's. Willis writes "would indeed be impossible to say."

59:7–20. Spinoza, *Tractatus*, "Praefatio," 18–19; Willis's translation, p. 25. The italics are Arnold's. Willis writes "unfathomable mysteries" (as does Arnold in line 29).

60:9–13. Spinoza, *Tractatus*, I, 19, 20; Willis's translation, pp. 37, 38. Willis writes "in their wickedness."

60:27–61:3. Spinoza, *Tractatus*, IV, 27, 38; Willis's translation, pp. 96, 99. Willis writes "God commanded Adam."

61:6–17. Spinoza, *Tractatus*, XV, 44; Willis's translation, p. 269. Spinoza writes "doceat."

61:29–32. Willis's "Introduction," p. 14.

62:3. Willis's translation, p. 324n.

62:31–63:14. Willis's "Introduction," pp. 4, 10, 11, 17. Willis writes "occasionally been proved."

63:19. The Cato Street Conspiracy was a plot of the radicals, led by Arthur Thistlewood, to assassinate the entire Tory cabinet of the Liverpool-Castlereagh government on February 23, 1820; the plot was betrayed and five of its leaders were hanged and decapitated. The time was that of "Peterloo" and the Six Acts; George III had died only a few days before the conspiracy.

63:21. William Howley (1766–1848), Bishop of London from 1813 to 1828, then Archbishop of Canterbury until his death, was remarkable for nothing except his good temper. The *Times* obituary on February 12, 1848, p. 8, col. 3, makes a delicate attempt to find some positive ground for eulogy: "Generally speaking, he performed the minor duties of his high office with perfect propriety. ... For many years past everyone within the sphere of the Archbishop's influence has been accustomed to regard him with a greater or less degree of veneration, if on no other ground at least on that of age." Sydney Smith, a schoolfellow at Winchester and vigorous opponent in matters of ecclesiastical policy, described Howley's career as "one of gentleness, kindness, and the most amiable and high-principled courtesy to his Clergy."—First Letter to Archdeacon Singleton.

64:10. "These hangman's hands," *Macbeth*, II, ii, 28.

[DR. STANLEY'S LECTURES ON THE
JEWISH CHURCH]

The controversy stirred up by "The Bishop and the Philosopher" led Arnold to resolve upon a reply; he conceived of the *Times* as its medium and (wishing it to be as final and comprehensive as possible) determined not to hasten unduly. Nevertheless, he found the publication of Stanley's *Lectures on the History of the Jewish Church* very opportune, as giving him scope for explaining how a work on religion could edify the populace without being false. "My conscience a little smote me with having been, in my first article, too purely negative and intellectual on such a subject," he explained to his sister on February 3, 1863. Stanley had read the essay on Colenso with some misgivings: he inclined to believe that the Church of England already had room for all shades of speculative opinion, whereas Arnold feared that it was becoming less and less open to freedom of intellect. But Stanley was a warm friend of the Arnold family, the biographer of Thomas Arnold, and the author of a volume attacked by Colenso. The essay on his *Lectures* is more immediately a reply to the criticisms of "The Bishop and the Philosopher" than Arnold at first, perhaps, intended; in any case, like the more topical portions of that essay it was never republished by Arnold. For its appearance in the February number of *Macmillan's* he was paid £10.

65:1. Arthur Penrhyn Stanley, *Lectures on the History of the Jewish Church*. Part I: Abraham to Samuel. London, 1863. Stanley was regius professor of ecclesiastical history in the University of Oxford and his book consists of "Lectures, actually or in substance, addressed to my usual hearers at Oxford, chiefly candidates for Holy Orders."

65:8–10. Letter signed "J. G.," published under the heading "The Bishop and the Professor" in *The Examiner*, January 17, 1863, p. 36; see note to p. 74:9–11.

65:10–13. "The Educated Few," *Saturday Review*, XV, 71–72 (January 17, 1863): "Culture, when it is only the culture of a few, is very superficial, and does the nation very little good. A nation in which a few clever men thought like Spinoza, and all the women and the rest of the men were edified by the liquefaction of the blood of St. Januarius, would not come up to the ideal of a Christian and civilized State." *The Examiner*, January 17, 1863, p. 36, sums up Arnold's argument as "the jesuitical doctrine that truths of religion are for a select circle of *cognoscenti*, and that the vulgar are not to be disturbed in possession of convenient fictions tending to the support of an irrational faith."

65:21. F. D. Maurice, "Spinoza and Professor Arnold," *Spectator*, XXXVI, 1472–74 (January 3, 1863).

65:29. Parmenides was a Greek philosopher of the early fifth century B.C. who denied creation ("Ex nihilo nihil fit") and the reality of change; Hegel developed the contrary idea of Parmenides' predecessor Heraclitus that there is no reality except change or flux (τὰ πάντα ῾ρεῖ). Spinoza defines the *summum bonum* in *Tractatus*, ed. Bruder, IV, 12; much of this and of Arnold's next paragraph depends upon Spinoza's views in *Tractatus*, V, 35–39.

67:35. Most notably in his great *Dialogue on the Two Principal Systems of the World, the Ptolemaic and the Copernican* (1632), for which he was condemned by the Inquisition for holding and believing "the false and anti-scriptural doctrine that the sun is the centre of the world, and that it does not move from east to west, and that the earth does move, and is not the centre of the world." —Philip Kelland, "Galileo," *The Museum*, II, 311 (October, 1862), an article Arnold undoubtedly read.

68:6. Joshua 10:12–13: "And he said in the sight of Israel, Sun, stand thou still upon Gibeon; and thou, Moon, in the valley of Ajalon. And the sun stood still, and the moon stayed, until the people had avenged themselves upon their enemies." Stanley discusses the impact of Galileo and Copernicus upon this passage, *History of the Jewish Church* (New York, 1863), I, 274–77.

68:17–19. The language is Arnold's; see p. 166:14–16. Spinoza's words are, "Et quamvis praeter haec plura in Scriptura contineantur, quae mere historica sunt et ex lumine naturali percepta, nomen [*i.e.*, 'verbum Dei'] tamen a potiore [causa] sumitur."—XII, 22.

68:26. J. W. Colenso, in *The Pentateuch and Book of Joshua Critically Examined* (1862).

68:38–69:1. See p. 45:26–28.

69:9–12. Colenso, *Pentateuch* (New York, 1863), I, 16n.

69:20–21. In the *Odyssey*.

70:16–17. Colenso, *Pentateuch*, Chapter IX: "The Israelites Armed" (a discussion of Exodus 13:18).

70:18–21. Stanley, *Jewish Church* (New York, 1863), I, 131.

70:21–25. *Ibid.*, I, 137.

70:25–35. *Ibid.*, I, 139–40, 143 (quoting Psalms 77:20), 144.

70:35–71:6. *Ibid.*, I, 150–52 (quoting Psalms 18:11).

71:8–16. *Ibid.*, I, 173–74. Stanley himself alludes to William Warburton's *The Divine Legation of Moses Demonstrated.*

71:17–18. Spinoza, *Tractatus*, ed. Bruder, I, 11.

71:19–22. Stanley, *Jewish Church*, I, 451, 456.

71:22–33. *Ibid.*, I, 463, 495–96.

71:34–35. For "enlarged and straitened" see note to p. 121:14.

71:36–72:1. *Ibid.*, I, xxxix–xl ("Introduction").

72:23–26. Colenso, *Pentateuch* (New York, 1863), I, 79, 192. Colenso was a missionary bishop to the Zulus.

72:35. Vergil *Aeneid* iv. 625.

73:14–15. The Statistical Society of London was founded in 1834; the Royal Geographical Society of London in 1830, and the Ethnological Society in 1843. Each published a journal.

73:24–34. The reviewer of Stanley's *History of the Jewish Church* in *The Athenaeum*, January 17, 1863, pp. 83–84.

73:38–74:2. Romans 12:2.

74:2–4, 7–8. The reviewer in *The Athenaeum* regrets Stanley's statement (I, 218) that "we need not here discuss the vexed question...form" and cites as an evasion his comment (I, 54) that "there are doubtless many difficulties which may be raised on the offering of Isaac: but there are few, if any, which will not vanish away before the simple pathos and lofty spirit of the narrative itself, provided that we take it, as in fairness it must be taken, as a whole."

74:9–11. "J. G.," in a letter to the editor of the *Examiner*, wrote, "The Bishop told what he believed to be the truth, using a plain-spoken honesty not according to the Professor's opinion of a Bishop's duty." The Editor himself, in an article on the same page entitled "The Bishop and the Professor," remarked on "the displeasure with which Professor Arnold's article...is spoken of by liberal men of all shades of religious opinion."—January 17, 1863, p. 36.

74:19–20. See p. 53:17.

74:23–31. Colenso, *Pentateuch*, I, 79, 192, 16n.

74:33–35. I Corinthians 9:16: "Woe is unto me, if I preach not the gospel!" Luke 12:50: "I have a baptism to be baptized with; and how am I straitened till it be accomplished!" See also p. 53:13.

75:17–23. See p. 54:5–9.

75:32. Richard Whately.

76:9–10. *Public Opinion* was "a weekly journal, embodying the opinions of the press on all the great topics of the day, political and social, home and foreign," established in 1861. The controversy over Colenso was a great boon to its circulation: its issue of November 15, 1862, with summaries or excerpts from fifteen reviews of the book, had to be reprinted to meet the demand; thereafter until the end of the year every number was devoted largely to that controversy. With "letters on our table which would fill several numbers of *Public Opinion*," the editors on January 3, 1863, declared the correspondence on the subject closed; it reopened when the second part of Colenso's book appeared.

76:13. The first letter of "Eagle Eye" appeared in *Public Opinion* on November 29: "The Old Testament is a cloud of superstition, preventing us finding out the only true and living God of love, benevolence, justice, and mercy.... Let the constantly increasing wickedness of our socal system strike upon the hearts of our rulers with the voice of thunder.... Because our Church is content to contract its teachings within the narrow limits of a dead priesthood instead of buckling on the armour of knowledge, [it will not] meet good men, in kindliness of spirit, who are anxious to spunge from the Bible the errors and contradictions that have made three parts of this nation infidels, or, worse still, a sad spectacle for humanity to gaze upon" (p. 1012). A second letter of "Eagle Eye" (he later complained) was not printed, but a third, most cantankerous, dated from 17 Liverpool Terrace, Islington, appeared on December 27.

76:18. Matthew 5:13: "Ye are the salt of the earth."

76:24. Luke 17:10: "So likewise ye, when ye shall have done all those things which are commanded you, say, we are unprofitable servants: we have done that which was our duty to do."

77:1–6. "Homer noch einmal," a short piece first printed in *Über Kunst und Alterthum*, VI, i, 69–71 (1827); Goethe, *Werke* (Weimar, 1903), XLI (2), 235–36. Arnold used this same statement about the influence of the *Zeitgeist* in a letter to Clough on July 20, 1848 (ed. Lowry, p. 86). For a discussion of Arnold's use of the term see Fraser Neiman, "The Zeitgeist of Matthew Arnold," *PMLA*, LXXII, 977–96 (December, 1957).

77:35. Johann Tauler (c. 1300–61), German mystic whose sermons were first printed at Leipzig in 1498.

78:5. Arnold customarily attributed this definition of the State to Burke, though it is not precisely his. See *Prose Works*, ed. Super, II, 377.

78:9–10. In 1817 Frederick William III of Prussia decreed the Union of Lutheran and Reformed Churches into the "United Evangelical" Church and forbade any body that called itself Lutheran to separate from this Union. The consequence was a considerable exodus of conservative Lutherans to the United

States, where some of them established the Missouri Synod. By 1827 the two confessions had been united also in Nassau, Baden, Saxe-Weimar, and Württemberg.—A. L. Drummond, *German Protestantism since Luther* (London: Epworth Press, 1951), pp. 194–97, 200.

78:14. II Corinthians 3:6.

78:20–21. John Toland's deistical *Christianity Not Mysterious* was published in London in 1696.

79:4–5. Philippians 2:12, explained by Luther in 1533 as "Ihr solt nit willd sein, sicut nunc est mundus."—*Werke: Tischreden* (Weimar, 1912), I, 245, no. 527.

79:9. The dogma of Papal Infallibility was promulgated on July 18, 1870, after definition by the Vatican Council.

79:16–19. See note to p. 65:10–13.

80:9–11. Mark 10:38. "None will marvel that Michelagnolo should be a lover of solitude, devoted as he was to Art, which demands the whole man, with all his thoughts, for herself." —G. Vasari, *Lives of the Most Eminent Painters,* tr. Mrs. Jonathan Foster (London, 1852), V, 335. "The nephews of those who had filled [Michelangelo's] cup with bitterness stood uncovered before him."—"Michael Angelo," *Quarterly Review,* American ed. CIII, 266 (April, 1858).

80:23. See p. 138:12.

81:34–37. Isaiah 63:9.

82:4–5. The *Agnus Dei.*

82:6. John 3:10.

82:15–16. Luke 19:40; Mark 7:37.

[EUGÉNIE DE GUÉRIN]

Even before the appearance of his essay on Maurice de Guérin, Arnold told his mother that he proposed to do one on Eugénie for the May (1863) number of *Macmillan's Magazine.* Doubtless attracted by the higher scale of pay of the *Cornhill,* however, he inquired of the publisher of that journal about the middle of February whether such an article might serve for his April number. —Buckler, *Matthew Arnold's Books,* p. 63. George Smith's delay in replying (though the reply was affirmative) caused Arnold to lay the project aside for two months; he read Eugénie's *Journal* (the gift of her sister Marie) while on holiday with his family at Ramsgate in April, and on the twenty-ninth he promised that Smith should have the manuscript ten days later, for his June number.

May 9 found him still at work on it, and he got an extension until the eleventh. Smith's suggestion that he translate into English whatever he quoted from her book probably accorded with his own intention. As he began to write, he complained to his mother that his article was not "such a labour of love as I imagined before-hand it would be, though she is a truly remarkable person." One might infer something of this attitude both from the number of quotations that fill out the latter part of his essay and from the occasional negligence with which he translated them. In contrast to his practice in "Maurice de Guérin," Arnold used almost no passages that had been quoted by Sainte-Beuve in his *Causeries* upon Eugénie. Arnold was paid £21 for the article by the proprietors of the *Cornhill*.

Eugénie de Guérin attracted a good deal of attention from the English periodicals, partially at least because the French Academy voted a prize to her posthumously published *Journal*. When Arnold proposed his essay for the *Cornhill*, Smith knew that the editors of the *Edinburgh Review* planned an article on her, and there was some fear lest it appear before Arnold's could be written. It did not come out until a year later (CXX, 249–67; July, 1864), a tame and tepid account, somewhat dependent on Arnold (who is not mentioned), and worth reading only to enforce one's conviction of the sparkle and genius of Arnold's work. In particular, there is much to be learned about style by setting Arnold's translations beside those of the anonymous reviewer—the passage on p. 92 beside the following, for example:

"I am furious against the grey cat. That naughty animal has just carried off a little frozen pigeon which I was warming at the corner of the fire. It began to revive, poor creature! I wished to tame it; it would have loved me; and all that crunched by a cat! What mishaps in life! This event, and all those of to-day, have passed in the kitchen; it is there that I stay all the morning and part of the evening since I have been without Mimi. It is necessary to superintend the cook, and papa sometimes comes down, and I read to him near the oven, or at the corner of the fire, some morsels of the antiquities of the Anglo-Saxon Church. This big book astonished Pierril (a servant lad). 'What a lot of words are in it!' he said, in his patois. He is a droll creature."

83:3–8. Eugénie de Guérin, *Journal et fragments*, publiés par G. S. Trebutien (Paris: Didier, 1865), pp. 443–44 (notebook entry dated September 17, 1841). This book first appeared as *Journal et lettres* in 1862, but the passage was quoted from her *Reliquiae* (see below) in an article in *The National Review* for January, 1861.

83:9–10. Orestes was the brother of Electra, Chrysothemis their sister, and Pylades Orestes' bosom friend.

83:15–18. Eugénie de Guérin, *Lettres*, publiées par G. S. Trebutien (Paris: Didier, 1865), p. 418 (letter of March 10, 1841). This edition first appeared late in 1864, but nineteen of the letters in it had been appended to the 1862 edition of her *Journal*.

83:20–25. *Ibid.*, p. 450 (letter of July 2, 1842); also *Journal*, p. 447 (dated "1842, à Rivières").

83:28–84:1. E. de Guérin, *Journal*, p. 383 (June 9, 1840).

84:7–12. See, for example, the letter to La Morvonnais, July 2, 1842.—*Lettres*, pp. 449–50. Eugénie died in 1848; Trebutien's first edition of her brother's *Reliquiae* appeared in 1861. Arnold's account of her death is influenced by the language of Trebutien's "Avertissement" to her *Journal*, p. viii.

84:22–24. At the beginning of 1864 the publishers boasted that eight editions were exhausted in sixteen months. Sainte-Beuve reviewed Trebutien's editions of brother and sister in an article of September 1, 1862, reprinted in *Nouveaux lundis*, III.

84:25–26. Eugénie de Guérin, *Reliquiae*, publié par J. B. d'Aurevilly et G. S. Trebutien (Caen: privately printed by Hardel, 1855). This volume was reviewed by Sainte-Beuve on February 9, 1856, an article reprinted in *Causeries du lundi*, XII, and known to Arnold.

84:26–27. "Eugénie de Guérin," *National Review*, XII (January, 1861), 145–51 (review of the preceding). The writer makes the same contrast between his subject and the usual novel-reading Englishman's impression of the French that Arnold makes in "Maurice de Guérin."

85:5–10. Arnold draws from the memoir Eugénie wrote to accompany her brother's works.—Maurice de Guérin, *Journal, &c.*, ed. Trebutien (1862), pp. 119–20.

85:11–13. E. de Guérin, *Journal*, p. 382 (June 1, 1840).

85:13–86:13. *Ibid.*, pp. v–viii. The brief summary of Maurice's career parallels that given by Sainte-Beuve in *Causeries* (Paris, 1857), XII, 193–98.

85:37–38. E. de Guérin, *Lettres*, p. 300 (letter of July 26, 1839, announcing her brother's death).

86:2–4. Sainte-Beuve, *Causeries*, XII, 203.

86:4–6. E. de Guérin, *Journal*, pp. 317–18 (December 31, 1839).

86:10. *Ibid.*, p. 275 (July 21, 1839): "Encore à lui, à Maurice mort, à Maurice au Ciel." Again, Arnold owes something of his expression to Trebutien's "Avertissement," pp. vi–vii.

86:17–22. See note to p. 18:2–4. Sainte-Beuve commented on Arnold's caveat in his article on "Lettres d'Eugénie de Guérin," January 2, 1865.—*Nouveaux lundis* (new ed.; Paris, 1884), IX, 250–51.

86:34–87:1. E. de Guérin, *Journal*, pp. 262–63 (May 1, 1839).

87:3–14. M. de Guérin, *Journal &c.*, pp. 351–52; see also p. 104 (letter of mid-October, 1835, and Journal, December 10, 1834).

87:21–25. *Ibid.*, p. 345 (letter of March 4, 1835, referring to La Morvonnais).

87:33. St. François de Sales (1567–1622), Bossuet (1627–1704), and La Mothe-Fénelon (1651–1715) were French theologians of great distinction both for piety and style; they are frequently alluded to by Eugénie.

87:36–37. E. de Guérin, *Journal*, p. 89 (August 21, 1835).

88:10–24. *Ibid.*, pp. 155, 201 (February 12 and May 12, 1838).

88:26–27. *Ibid.*, p. 76 (May 22, 1835), quoting Fénelon, "Lettres Spirituelles," xxxvii: *Oeuvres* (Paris, 1882), I, 473.

88:28–36. *Ibid.*, p. 181 (April 2, 1838).

89:6. *E.g.*, Sainte-Beuve, *Causeries*, XII, 203.

89:12–14. In a review published in the *Frankfurter gelehrte Anzeigen* in 1772 or 1773; *Werke* (Weimar, 1896), XXXVII, 256.

89:26–30. E. de Guérin, *Journal*, p. 111 (March 14, 1836).

89:39–90:4. M. de Guérin, *Journal &c.*, pp. 198–99 (letter of June 21, 1833).

90:7–15. *Ibid.*, pp. 270–71 (letter of February 2, 1834).

90:16–17. E. de Guérin, *Journal*, p. 64 (April 24, 1835).

90:28–30. The Albigensians, who took their name from the town of Albi near the Guérins' villa, were a twelfth-century heretical sect finally suppressed in a bloody crusade launched by Pope Innocent III in 1209. The Camisards were Calvinists who rose in revolt in 1702 in consequence of the revocation of the Edict of Nantes. The Cévennes are mountains of Languedoc.

91:24–30. E. de Guérin, *Journal*, pp. 91, 144 (August 24, 1835; January 27, 1838).

92:1–25. *Ibid.*, pp. 6–7 (November 18, 1834). "My gravity as a catechist was gone for that evening" translates "mon sérieux de catéchiste s'en alla pour la soirée" and "his little dog" translates "son petit cochon." St. Brice's day is November 13.

92:28–29. *E.g.*, *ibid.*, p. 114 (March 22, 1836).

92:31–93:2. *Ibid.*, p. 31 (January 3, 1835). The friend was La Morvonnais.

93:6–18. *Ibid.*, pp. 24–25.

93:20. *Ibid.*, pp. 81–82, 430–32. *Old Mortality* became *Les Puritains.*

93:23–25. *Ibid.*, p. 123 (May 7, 1837).

93:31–36. *Ibid.*, pp. 11–14 (November 24–26, 1834).

93:37–94:11. *Ibid.*, pp. 64–65 (April 24, 1835). Arnold omits a sentence he has already quoted on p. 90 and several others that are heavily religious. "That you see what I write" translates "que ce papier c'est toi."

94:18–25. *Ibid.*, pp. 31–32 (January 3, 1835); this passage immediately follows that quoted on pp. 92–93.

94:27–31. *Ibid.*, p. 35 (March 1, 1835).

94:36–95:12. *Ibid.*, pp. 92–93 (August 27, 1835). The friend again was La Morvonnais.

95:20–36. *Ibid.*, pp. 16–17 (November 29, 1834).

96:7–29. *Ibid.*, pp. 28–29 (December 31, 1834). Arnold's footnote approximates one by Eugénie's editor.

97:14–15. Benjamin Gregory, *Memoir of Emma Tatham. With "The Angels' Spell" and Other Pieces Not Published During Her Lifetime.* London, 1859.

97:23. Margate is a seaside resort near the easternmost tip of Kent, on the south side of the Thames Estuary. Arnold took his family for a holiday in nearby Ramsgate in the spring of 1863, while he was meditating this article, and was not fond of the region.

97:28–33. E. de Guérin, *Journal*, pp. 60–61 (April 15, 16, 1835).

97:34–36. *Ibid.*, p. 138 (May 22, 1837). The story is from *De Civitate Dei,* Book XXII, chapter viii, end.

97:38–98:6. The first and third quotations are from Gregory, *Emma Tatham*, pp. 43 and 121 ("Several young female teachers of the Sabbath-school"). The story of her singing, on the morning of her death, "to the tune called 'Hanover,' . . . in a distinct, sweet voice, 'My Jesus to know, . . .' " is told by Mrs. J. Cooke Westbrook, *Etchings and Pearls: or, a Flower for the Grave of Emma Tatham* (2nd ed.; London, 1857). But Arnold seems to have used neither of these sources directly, since in neither does the venerable Mr. Thomas Rowe appear.

98:12–13. Matthew 23:23.

98:31. Exeter Hall, a building in the Strand used for religious and philanthropic assemblies, came to stand for a certain type of fundamental evangelicalism.

98:34–99:2. E. de Guérin, *Journal*, pp. 70, 108, 94, 108 (April 28, 1835; March 12, 1836; August 29, 1835).

99:3–16. *Ibid.*, pp. 15–16 (November 28, 1834).

99:17–35. *Ibid.*, pp. 109, 107–8 (March 12, 1836).

100:1–6. *Ibid.*, p. 259 (April 24, 1839). "Today" translates "demain."

100:8–11. *Ibid.*, p. 38 (March 4, 1835); but she was praying before a picture of Calvary, not an image of the Virgin. Arnold's critics did not miss the blunder. "Mr. Matthew Arnold greatly underrates the quantity of this element of simple belief which exists in this journal, and by-the-bye, in speaking of her 'freedom from superstition' falls into a curious little error. After repeating her child's story of having seen some stains upon her frock vanish when she prayed to a holy image, Mr. Arnold, who has called it an 'image of the Virgin,' adds, 'Even the austerest Protestant will not judge such Mariolatry as this very harshly. But in general . . . it is Jesus not Mary.' Rather remarkably, the apology was not necessary in this very case, for the image was an image of Jesus and not of Mary."—*Pall Mall Gazette*, October 14, 1865, p. 11 (in a review of Trebutien's *Journal of Eugénie de Guérin*).

100:14–22. *Ibid.*, pp. 85, 336 (July 31, 1835; January 26, 1840), quoting Matthew 11:28, Isaiah 53:3, and Luke 24:46 or Acts 17:3.

100:26–101:4. *Ibid.*, p. 118 (n.d.; 1836). Arnold's "may well make us tremble, all of us who have advanced more than a few steps in life" translates "fait trembler l'âme qui s'y livre, pour si peu qu'elle ait vécu." He uses the Prayer Book translation of Psalm 130:3.

101:9–26. *Ibid.*, p. 203 (May 14, 1838).

101:33–102:5. *Ibid.*, p. 394 (July 30, 1840). These reflections, written more than a year after Maurice's death, were set in motion by the news of a suicide not far away.

102:8–15, 21–27. *Ibid.*, pp. 335–36 (January 26, 1840).

103:1–16. *Ibid.*, pp. 264–65.

103:23–26. *Ibid.*, p. 271 (May 21, 1839).

103:33–35. *Ibid.*, p. 332 (January 22, 1840).

103:37–104:11. *Ibid.*, p. 280 (August 4, 1839), quoted also by Sainte-Beuve, *Causeries*, XII, 194.

104:13–24. *Ibid.*, p. 276 (July 21, 1839). This is the first entry addressed "à Maurice au Ciel," and the pronoun throughout is "you," not "he."

104:28–105:8. *Ibid.*, pp. 283–84 (August 20, 1839), also addressed directly to Maurice.

105:11–16. *Ibid.*, pp. 373, 364 (May 1 and April, 1840).

105:17–26. *Ibid.*, p. 375 (May, 1840).

105:29–37. *Ibid.*, p. 401 (August, 1840).

105:34. In Normandy, home of the Reformed Cistercians, one of the strictest monastic orders.

106:4–5. See note to p. 12:13–15.

106:11. E. de Guérin, *Journal*, p. ii.

106:26–27. Horace *Odes* I. iii. 2 (of Castor and Pollux).

[HEINRICH HEINE]

Arnold's Oxford lecture on "The Modern Element in Romanticism," delivered March 26, 1863, was not published. On June 13, he delivered his lecture on "Heinrich Heine"; on the same day he offered it to Smith for the *Cornhill* "because it both pays best and has much the largest circle of readers"; the essay was published there in August and Arnold received £21 for it. *Littell's Living Age* reprinted it in Boston on October 10 and the *Revue britannique* translated it in July, 1864. His correspondence with Smith over the proofs indicates that the lecture had to be trimmed somewhat for publication, and that at least one quotation (130:20–131:3) was dropped because Smith thought it in bad taste and Arnold agreed. He was at work on the lecture by May 6, when he spent three hours at the Taylor Library in Oxford. About a week later, declining the offer of an edition of Heine on loan from M. E. Grant Duff, he explained, "I am even going, for the sake of a restricted cadre, to make my text the *Romancero* only, illustrating my remarks upon it by some quotations from the other works, but of these quotations I have more than I can use already. . . . My object is not so much to give a literary history of Heine's works, as to mark his place in modern European letters, and the special tendency and significance of what he did." Three days after the lecture he told his mother, "I have almost always a very fair attendance; to be sure, it is chiefly composed of ladies, but . . . I am obliged always to think, in composing my lectures, of the public who will read me, not of the dead bones who will hear me, or my spirit would fail. . . . There was, nevertheless, one thing which even a wooden Oxford audience gave way to—Heine's wit. I gave them about two pages of specimens of it, and they positively laughed aloud. I have had two applications for the lecture from magazines." *

* One of these applications was from Emily Faithfull for her *Victoria Magazine*, made apparently through John Llewelyn Davies, to whom Arnold wrote on June 18, 1863: "I have so much interest in Miss Faithfull

Arnold's interest in Heine was not new. In May, 1848, he told his mother he had been reading "a mixture of poems and travelling journal by Heinrich Heine, the most famous of the young German literary set. He has a good deal of power, though more trick; however he has thoroughly disgusted me." It was the "Byronism of a German" that he found offensive, and he brought to bear against Heine Goethe's statement that the Germans could have no real comedy. "I see the French call this Heine a 'Voltaire au clair de lune,' which is very happy." The reading lists in his *Note-Books* frequently name Heine; though it does not always appear that Arnold carried out his intentions, he planned to read Heine's *Gedichte* in September, 1852; *Lutèce* in August, 1855; *Reisebilder*, I, in July, 1858, and again in the summer of 1860; Heine (no work specified) in the summer of 1861. In March of that year he told Clough that Musset and Heine were "far more profitable studies" than Tennyson, "if we are to study contemporaries at all." The reading became more serious as he determined to write his poem on "Heine's Grave" in January, 1862: in March he read "Heine—vol. I"; in September he planned to read *Reisebilder*, vols. I, II and III, and *Romancero;* at another time during the year, *Germania* and *Chant de Lazare.* In January, 1863, he read *Reisebilder*, III; in March, the *Romancero, Reisebilder*, IV, and articles on and by Heine in the *Revue des deux mondes.* His poem appears to have been completed in April. Of the articles in the *Revue des deux mondes* the most influential was that by Saint-René Taillandier, "Henri Heine, sa vie et ses écrits," n.s. XIV, 5–35 (April 1, 1852), though it was in no sense the model for his lecture.

Professor E. M. Butler's essay, "Heine in England and Matthew Arnold," in *German Life and Letters,* n.s. IX, 157–65 (April, 1956), is an excellent study of Arnold's essay and poem on Heine that concentrates more on Arnold's limitations than on his virtues. She regards Arnold as too narrow in his view, almost perverse in his insistence that Heine "wanted love." Arnold's error in applying

---

and her work that I should be really glad to contribute an article to her magazine if I could. I have got a little entangled about the lecture on Heine, which (if it is not too long) would I think be suitable enough for her magazine, and interesting: if I find myself free to dispose of it I will at any rate write to you again. That was a man of genius who could really use his tools! What perfection of clearness he has, as clear as Voltaire he is, and with all the depth of Germany. But he was a precious scamp for all that."—C. L. Davies, ed., *From a Victorian Post-Bag* (London, 1926), p. 76.

Goethe's phrase to Heine was, however, universal when he wrote: Eckermann's text was not corrected until 1868. The third chapter of Sol Liptzin's *The English Legend of Heinrich Heine* (New York, 1954), reprinted from *Journal of English and Germanic Philology*, XLIII, 317–25 (July, 1944), is a more sympathetic account of poem and essay, both of which are placed in the context of current English opinions of Heine. Walther Fischer, lecturing in 1953 in the same building where Arnold had delivered his lecture, found Arnold's translations very competent but uninspired. He pointed out the extent to which Arnold's ideas about Heine developed into ideas about English society in *Culture and Anarchy*.—"Matthew Arnold und Deutschland," *Germanisch-Romanische Monatsschrift*, XXXV, 119–37 (April, 1954).

107:1–7. *Reisebilder*, Part III, i: "Reise von München nach Genua," Chapter XXXI, last paragraph. Professor Butler has criticized Arnold justly for translating *"brav"* as "brave," less justly for italicizing the word *sword*, which gets emphasis from its position in the original.

107:9. "genus irritabile vatum," Horace *Epistles* II. ii. 102.

107:25. Carlyle's *Critical and Miscellaneous Essays* include five on Goethe, two on Jean Paul, one on Tieck's edition of Novalis, and nine others on German literature, all first published in the critical and literary journals of 1827–32.

109:3–17. *Reisebilder*, Part IV: "Englische Fragmente," Schlusswort, paragraphs 5–7.

109:18–20, 110:7–14. "Ein Wort für junge Dichter," published posthumously in 1833; *Werke* (Weimar, 1907), XLII (ii), 106–7.

109:31–32. See Matthew 9:17.

110:16. *Othello*, II, i, 162.

111:11. Heine was born in Düsseldorf on December 13, 1797, but spent his young manhood at Hamburg.

111:13–16. Düsseldorf was governed by the French from 1795 to 1813, except for a short interruption in 1801. Under this rule the Jews had civil and political equality with the Germans; their political rights were withdrawn by Prussia after 1813. But it was not only the Jews who had prospered under Napoleon: the head of the Prussian administration in Coblenz reported to the Prussian chancellor that everyone in the Rhenish provinces would thankfully welcome the return of French domination.—M. J. Wolff, *Heinrich Heine* (Munich, 1922), pp. 7–11.

111:21. See *Paradise Lost*, II, 51.

111:28. Soli was an ancient Greek town on the coast of Cilicia, in Asia Minor, north of Cyprus; its reputation for speaking bad Greek has given us the word "solecism."

111:38–112:1. "What, in the Devil's name, is the use of Respectability, with never so many gigs and silver spoons, if thou inwardly art the pitifulest of all men?"—*Critical and Miscellaneous Essays,* "Count Cagliostro," seventh paragraph. Carlyle explains the origin of his symbol in a footnote halfway through his second essay on Jean Paul Friedrich Richter.

112:10. Heine explains the use of the term in German student slang: "Im allgemeinen werden die Bewohner Göttingens eingeteilt in Studenten, Professoren, Philister und Vieh."—*Reisebilder* I: "Die Harzreise," second paragraph.

112:12. For "children of light" see Luke 16:8, John 12:36, Ephesians 5:8, and I Thessalonians 5:5.

112:23–27. *Reisebilder* IV: "Englische Fragmente," chapter XI, "Die Befreiung," last paragraph. The "new religion" is "die Freiheit,... die Religion unserer Zeit."

112:33–35. *Romanzero,* Book II, the poem "Jetzt wohin?" stanza 4.

112:36–37. Speaking of a supercargo on a vessel in the East India Docks, London.—"Englische Fragmente," Chapter X, "Wellington," third paragraph from end.

113:20, 22. Hebrews 11:9: "By faith [Abraham] sojourned in the land of promise." Leviticus 26:19: "I will make your heaven as iron, and your earth as brass."

113:22–29. Heine uses much this criterion to distinguish himself from Goethe: "Im Grunde aber sind Ich und Göthe zwey Naturen, die sich in ihrer Heterogenität abstossen müssen. *Er* ist von Haus aus ein leichter Lebemensch, dem der Lebensgenuss das Höchste, und der das Leben für und in der Idee wohl zuweilen fühlt und ahnt und in Gedichten ausspricht, aber nie tief begriffen und noch weniger gelebt hat. Ich hingegen bin von Haus aus ein Schwärmer, d.h. bis zur Aufopferung begeistert für die Idee und immer gedrängt, in dieselbe mich zu versenken.... Es ist noch die grosse Frage, ob der Schwärmer, der selbst sein Leben für die Idee hingiebt, nicht in einem Momente mehr und glücklicher lebt als Herr von Göthe während seines ganzen 76jähringen egoistisch behaglichen Lebens."—Heine, *Briefe,* ed. Friedrich Hirth (Mainz, 1948), I, 155 (letter to Moses Moser, July 1, 1825).

113:35–37. I Chronicles 20:5–6: "And there was war again with the Philistines; and Elhanan ... slew Lahmi the brother of Goliath the Gittite, whose spear staff was like a weaver's beam. And yet again there was war at Gath, where was a man of great stature, whose fingers and toes were four and twenty, six on each hand, and six on each foot: and he also was the son of the giant." I Samuel 17:7: "And the staff of [Goliath's] spear was like a weaver's beam."

113:38–114:18. "Englische Fragmente," Chapter VII, conclusion. "His radical laugh" translates "seinem radikalen Lächeln." The Crown and Anchor Tavern was in Arundel Street, Strand.

114:19–38. This paragraph presumably was cut from the *Cornhill* article in proofs, for reasons of space; see Buckler, *Matthew Arnold's Books*, p. 64.

114:19. Genesis 37:25: "A company of Ishmeelites came from Gilead with their camels bearing spicery and balm and myrrh." Jeremiah 8:22: "Is there no balm in Gilead?"

114:25. Bismarck became prime minister and foreign minister of Prussia in 1862.

114:28–29. Wordsworth, "Resolution and Independence," line 77.

115:3–13. Paraphrase of *Ludwig Börne. Eine Denkschrift*, beginning of Book II, dated "Helgoland, den 1. Julius 1830." Arnold's "Hodge" is Heine's "Michel."

115:18–117:2. "Englische Fragmente," Schlusswort, end.

117:12–13, 38. Heinrich Heine's *Sämmtliche Werke* (Philadelphia, 1856–61), 7 vols. A twenty-two volume edition began to appear at Hamburg in 1861, with A. Strodtmann as editor.

117:28–29. "Die Wärterin . . . trug ihn dann, wie man ein Kind trägt, auf den Händen von der niedrigen Couchette, auf welcher ich ihn hingestreckt gefunden, wieder in sein Bett zurück."—Adolf Stahr, *Nach fünf Jahren* (Oldenburg, 1857), I, 208.

117:29–31. "Der Kranke hob die feine fast durchsichtig mager Hand an das rechte Auge, um das Lid emporzuziehen und einen Blick auf uns zu werfen. Nur dies Auge besitzt Lichtschimmer." —Stahr, *Zwei Monate in Paris* (Oldenburg, 1851), II, 308–9.

117:37–118:4. Stahr, *Nach fünf Jahren*, I, 218–19.

118:5–15. Both these anecdotes are related by Adolf Strodtmann, *H. Heine's Leben und Werke* (3rd edition; Hamburg, 1884), II, 360, but since Strodtmann's work first appeared in 1867–69 it cannot have been Arnold's source.

118:30–119:1. *Ibid.*, I, 219.

119:17–20. Josef Görres (1776–1848), a German scholar and aesthetician, his schoolfellow Clemens Brentano (1778–1842), and Brentano's brother-in-law Achim von Arnim (1781–1831) were leaders of the Heidelberg school of romantic medievalism in Germany; the latter two published an influential collection of folk songs called *Des Knaben Wunderhorn* in 1806. Arnold's statement here echoes that of Saint-René Taillandier, "Poètes contemporains de l'Allemagne: Henri Heine, sa vie et ses écrits," *Revue des deux mondes*, n.s. XIV, 16 (April 1, 1852).

119:25–28. *Ibid.*, p. 19.

120:1–13. *Reisebilder* III, ii: "Die Bäder von Lucca," Chapter X, beginning.

120:14. "Ich bin der Sohn der Revolution."—*Ludwig Börne*, Book II, letter dated "Helgoland, den 10. August." Taillandier refers to "son rôle d'*initiateur*," *op. cit.*, p. 22.

120:18–21. "Es war die grosse Aufgabe meines Lebens, an dem herzlichen Einverständnisse zwischen Deutschland und Frankreich zu arbeiten und die Ränke der Feinde der Demokratie zu vereiteln, welche die internationalen Vorurteile und Animositäten zu ihrem Nutzen ausbeuten."—Testament dated November 13, 1851.

121:14. Job 12:23.

122:15. Lucan *Pharsalia* i. 135.

122:34–123:4. *Reisebilder* II: "Ideen. Das Buch Le Grand," Chapter VII, middle.

123:8–12. *Ibid.*, Chapter IX, end.

123:14–28. "Englische Fragmente," Chapter I: "Gespräch auf der Themse," latter part. Perhaps because he was using a French version, Arnold makes some alterations; the German reads: "Der Franzose liebt die Freiheit wie seine erwählte Braut. . . . Der flatterhafte Franzose wird seiner geliebten Braut vielleicht treulos und verlässt sie, und tänzelt singend nach den Hofdamen seines königlichen Palastes." This last alludes with deliberate ambiguity to the courtesans that frequented the gardens of the Palais Royal.

124:3–4. Though I have not identified this couplet, it will perhaps reinforce Arnold's point to quote three lines of Lamartine that use the same clichés:

"Ainsi, quand je partis, tout trembla dans cette âme;
Le rayon s'éteignit; et sa mourante flamme
Remonta dans le Ciel pour n'en plus revenir."
—*Les Harmonies*, IV, x:"Le Premier regret," lines 112–14.

Émile Legouis protests, however, against Arnold's choice of "ce distique médiocre . . . comme type de notre rythme et de notre vers, de tous nos vers," of "deux alexandrins, non point célèbres ni populaires,—j'avoue que je ne les ai jamais entendu citer que par lui et que j'ignore où il les a pris, bien qu'il y ait dans l'antithèse et le balancement artificiel de leurs hémistiches quelque chose qui dénonce Hugo en ces moments les moins heureusement inspirés."—

Défense de la poésie française à l'usage des lecteurs anglais (Paris and London, 1912), p. 21.

124:6–7. Mariana's song, *Measure for Measure*, IV, i, 1–2.

124:9–10. *Romanzero*, Book II: "Lazarus," IV ("Sterbende"), lines 5–6.

124:30–125:25. *Buch der Lieder*: "Aus der Harzreise" ("Berg-Idylle," 2), lines 21– end. Taillandier gives the same lines in French, *op. cit.*, pp. 17–18.

125:30. Heine describes his *Matratzengruft* in the "Nachwort" to *Romanzero*, dated September 30, 1851.

125:36. See p. 109:14.

126:8–127:27. From *Romanzero*, Book II; Arnold translates the last twenty-two quatrains of the poem.

127:35–128:1. "Es war die sogenannte Zeit der Wiederaufersteh-ung oder besser gesagt der Wiedergeburt der antiken Weltan-schauung, wie sie auch ganz richtig mit dem Namen Renaissance bezeichnet wird. In Italien konnte sie leichter zur Blüte und Herr-schaft gelangen als in Deutschland, wo ihr durch die gleich-zeitige neue Bibelübersetzung auch die wiedergeburt des judäischen Geistes, die wir die evangelische Renaissance nennen möchten, so bilderstürmend fanatisch entgegentrat. Sonderbar! die beiden grossen Bücher der Menschheit, die sich vor einem Jahrtausend so feindlich befehdet und wie kampfmüde während dem ganzen Mittelalter vom Schauplatz zurückgezogen hatten, der Homer und die Bibel, treten zu Anfang des sechzehnten Jahrhunderts wieder öffentlich in die Schranken."—*Der Doktor Faust*, "Erläuterungen," midpoint. "L'inspiration juive ou nazaréenne et l'inspiration grecque, il l'a dit souvent, voilà les deux grands systèmes auxquels il faut bien que tout aboutisse; Homère et la Bible contiennent à ses yeux toute la philosophie de l'histoire. Cette fois il n'en parle plus en riant; le monde grec et le monde juif obsèdent son âme inquiète. C'était le poète des Hellènes qu'il préférait jadis quand la jeunesse l'emportait sur son char au bruit des cymbales retentissantes; maintenant la jeunesse a disparu, l'éclat du monde réel s'évanouit: c'est l'heure des pensées graves, et Jehuda ben Halevy a remplacé Homère."—Taillandier, *op. cit.*, p. 33.

128:6. "The Spirit itself maketh intercession for us with groan-ings which cannot be uttered."—Romans 8:26.

128:8–38. *Reisebilder* III: "Die Bäder von Lucca," Chapter IX, one-third through.

129:2–131:3. "Prinzessin Sabbath," "Jehuda ben Halevy," and "Disputation" make up the third book of *Romanzero*, "Hebräische

Melodien." Arnold translates lines 72–80, 17–32 of the first; Part 2, lines 76–96, Part 3, lines 177–200, 205–16 of the second, and lines 261–84, 289–92 of the last.

130:20–131:3. For the cutting of this passage from the proofs of the *Cornhill* version, see Buckler, *Matthew Arnold's Books*, p. 64.

131:7–18. *Romanzero*, Book II: "Lazarus," IV ("Sterbende"). Arnold quoted two lines of the poem in German, p. 124:9–10. The sentence about Germany and her Christmas tree is from the poem "Im Oktober 1849," stanza 1 (*Romanzero*, Book II: "Lazarus," XVI).

131:19–20. Genesis 47:9.

131:20–32. "Nachwort zum 'Romanzero,'" first paragraph.

132:5. On Christmas day, 1825, Goethe and Eckermann conversed about Byron at some length; the conversation then shifted (final paragraph) to "one of our most recent German poets," whose name was represented in print only by three asterisks; of him Goethe remarked, "Er besitzt manche glänzende Eigenschaften; allein ihm fehlt—die *Liebe*." When Eckermann learned that the public generally misapplied the reference to Heine, he inserted Platen's name in the Index to his second edition (with a reference to this point) and provided that Platen should be named in the text of subsequent editions, the first of which did not appear until 1868, five years after Arnold's essay. See J. P. Eckermann, *Gespräche mit Goethe*, ed. Eduard Castle (Berlin, 1916), III, 85 ("Anmerkungen zu Band I"). The reviewer of Eckermann in the *Foreign Quarterly Review* was among those who ventured to apply the remark to Heine.—XVIII, 16 (October, 1836).

132:38. Matthew 22:14.

[MARCUS AURELIUS]

As early as November 27, 1862, Arnold told his mother that he planned to publish an article on Marcus Aurelius in the February number of *Fraser's;* by February 4 the article was still unwritten, but still intended for a spring issue of the same magazine. However, having failed Emily Faithfull with his article on "Heine" for her new *Victoria Magazine*, a journal manufactured entirely by women, he gave her this essay; it appeared in the issue for November, 1863, and brought him £20. "Miss Faithfull's lady compositors have made some detestable misprints, to my great disgust," he told Lady de Rothschild; but she did not neglect to advertise his work: "[I see] myself placarded all over London as having written on

Marcus Aurelius, and . . . walked up Regent Street behind a man with a board on his back announcing the same interesting piece of news," he wrote to his mother.

Though Arnold's early poetry shows a strong Stoic influence, his favorite was Epictetus; Marcus Aurelius is seldom mentioned. Arnold's *Note-Books* show that he planned to read the *Meditations* in April, 1854; then in July, 1863, he indicated his intention to begin writing his essay and to read the pertinent materials, and in September he completed his work. His diary for August 25 records the sentence which he used as thesis for his sonnet, "Worldly Place," composed doubtless at this time.

Kenneth Allott has pointed out that this essay and "On the Modern Element in Literature" suggested to Pater the parallel between Antonine Rome and Victorian England for his *Marius the Epicurean.*—"Pater and Arnold," *Essays in Criticism* II, 219–21 (April, 1952).

133:1–5. Chapter II: "On Liberty of Thought and Discussion," eighth paragraph from end.

133:22–23. Seneca *Epistulae Morales* XV. iii. 46 (or xcv. 46): "Vita sine proposito vaga est."

133:23–29. *De Imitatione Christi*, I, xix, 3–5; xi, 7; xix, 12; xxiv, 5. All these are quoted in the *Note-Books*.

134:19. See Matthew 7:14.

135:3–6. *Encheiridion* 53 (quoting the Hymn of Cleanthes).

135:9–12. Psalms 143:10 (Prayer-Book version); Isaiah 60:19; Malachi 4:2.

135:13–16. John 1:13, 3:3; I John 5:4.

135:20–21. Mark 9:23; II Corinthians 5:17.

135:22–27. *Encheiridion* 43.

135: 29–30. Matthew 18:22.

135:37–38. Matthew 22: 37–39.

136:5. The Utilitarian school.

136:15. *The Thoughts of the Emperor Marcus Aurelius Antoninus*, translated by George Long (London: Bell & Daldy, 1862).

136:28. *The Civil Wars of Rome: Select Lives Translated from Plutarch*, with notes, by G. Long (London, 1844–48), 5 vols.

136:34–35. From the Sixth Article of Religion in the Book of Common Prayer (of the Apocryphal Books).

137:5–6. Prefatory essay, "M. Aurelius Antoninus," third paragraph from end. Jeremy Collier's translation of *The Emperor Marcus Antoninus, His Conversation with Himself* was published in 1701.

138:1–14. III. 14.

138:27. Arnold might have added "physic" and "politic" for "physics" and "politics."

139:3–4. Cicero *Tusculan Disputations* I. xv. 34 (quoting Ennius on his poetry).

139:35–37. Marci Antonini Imperatoris et Philosophi, *De Vita Sua Libri XII* (Lyons, 1626), Preface.

140:22. Matthew 4:8.

140:30. The word "enlightened" is there only by implication. Trajan warns Pliny not to admit anonymous accusations as evidence against Christians, "nam et pessimi exempli nec nostri saeculi est." —Pliny *Epistles* x. 97.

140:37–38. Edward Augustus Freeman, later regius professor of modern history at Oxford. See note to p. 250:19–22.

141:3–19. Arnold summarizes the biographical information in Long's prefatory essay, "M. Aurelius Antoninus."

141:22–26. See *ibid.*, fourth paragraph.

141:28. Coleridge, "Ode to Tranquility," line 31.

141:33–36. I. 3. Arnold uses Long's translation for all quotations except the two samples from Collier's.

141:37. A long abuse of the women of Rome, written about the time of Marcus Aurelius's birth.

142:1–4. I. 5.

142:5. Juvenal iii. 78.

142:11–13. I. 16.

142:16. Horace *Odes* IV. ix. 28.

142:19–22. Long alludes to this story without quoting the Emperor's words, which are recorded in Vulcacius Gallicanus' life of Avidius Cassius viii. 1: "Etiam doluit ereptam sibi esse occasionem misericordiae."—*Scriptores Historiae Augustae.*

142:33–35. "Those who could afford it had his statue or bust, and when Capitolinus wrote, many people still had statues of Antoninus among the Dei Penates or household deities. He was in a manner made a saint."—Long, prefatory essay, "M. Aurelius Antoninus."

143:8–32. Arnold draws on Long's prefatory essay for this discussion, but adds the name of Pothinus (perhaps from Fleury). Like Arnold, Long discusses Roman ignorance of Christian principles and suggests that "many fanatical and ignorant Christians, for there were many such, contributed to excite the fanaticism on the other side and to embitter the quarrel between the Roman government and the new religion."

144:18–19. *Annals* xv. 44.

145:14–16. See Matthew 13:24–30.

145:23–28. Arnold, who began his essay by quoting from the

second chapter of Mill's essay *On Liberty,* clearly had in mind here Mill's eloquent paragraph on Marcus Aurelius' persecutions of Christianity: "It is a bitter thought, how different a thing the Christianity of the world might have been, if the Christian faith had been adopted as the religion of the empire under the auspices of Marcus Aurelius instead of those of Constantine."—*On Liberty,* Chapter II, one-fourth through. Mill's essay may also have suggested the parallel with the Mormons.

145:36. Claude Fleury, *Histoire ecclésiastique* (Paris, 1722), vol. I, book iii, sect. 45: "Marc-Aurele étoit habile & vertueux, & faisoit profession ouverte de philosophie, qui étoit ce que les payens connoissoient de meilleur pour les moeurs: ... mais il n'en étoit pas moins attaché aux superstitions du paganisme.... La secte de philosophie qu'il avoit embrassée, étoit celle des Stoiciens les plus superstitieux de tous: & qui faisoient profession d'être inflexibles dans leurs résolutions, & inexorables envers les coupables. Ainsi Marc-Aurele persecuta les chrétiens, quoiqu'il se piquât de clemence, & qu'il eût accoûtumé de punir au-dessous de la rigueur des loix."

146:20–22. Reported in Dio Cassius LXXIII. iv. 7.

146:28–30. See I Corinthians 13:2.

147:10–148:2. I. 12, 14; IV. 24 (reading "say or do" for Long's "say and do"); III. 4 (reading "thoughts about sensual enjoyments" for "thoughts about pleasure or sensual enjoyments at all"). For "drive at practice," see p. 138:13.

148:4–5. IV. 2 (reading "nothing" for Long's "no act").

148:12–13. Matthew 6:6.

148:18–36. V. 6 (italics Arnold's, and reading "caught" for Long's "tracked," "its honey" for "the honey"); IX. 42 (italics Arnold's).

149:2. Luke 17:21.

149:5–6. A Roman and a Greek Stoic writer of the first century A.D.; see pp. 133–35.

149:9. P. 134:36.

149:16–18. I. 15 (Arnold's italics).

149:25–36. III. 2; Arnold modifies Long's translation somewhat.

150:5–23. V. 5 (reading "art at once able" for Long's "art immediately able," "as to which" for "in which," "mean" for "stingy," "no indeed" for "no by the gods," "neglecting nor" for "neglecting it nor").

150:29–37. VIII. 34 (reading "here is this" for Long's "here there is this," "goodness with which ... privileged" for "benevolence with which ... distinguished," and omitting seventeen words of the last sentence).

151:3–16. IV. 3 (omitting fifteen words before "Constantly").

151:23–152:11. I. 17 (condensed and somewhat modified from Long).

152:19–153:8. IV. 28; V. 11 (reading "weak woman" for Long's "feeble woman," and "of one of the ... of man" for "of a domestic animal"); X. 8 (reading "equal-minded" for Long's "a man of equanimity," "desiring that ... by them" for "desiring to be called by these names by others," "another being" for "another person," "to the Happy Islands" for "to certain islands of the Happy," and omitting a long sentence after "return to them").

153:10. See Marcus Aurelius IV. 50 or IX. 32.

153:19–31. IV. 32 (reading "somebody" for Long's "some," "to be consuls or kings" for "consulship, kingly power," "go to" for "remove to," "All is again" for "Again, all is," and omitting one sentence).

153:33–154:1. V. 33 (reading "and people are like" for "and [like]," "crying, and then straightway laughing" for "laughing, and then straightway weeping"). The verse is Hesiod *Works and Days* 197.

154:3–12. IX. 30 (omitting, after "olden time," the words "and the life of those who will live after thee").

154:13–14. VII. 55.

154:17–20. VI. 48.

154:27–28. IV. 16.

154:33–155:8. IX. 3 (reading "will not be from" for Long's "will be not from," and "distress caused by the difference" for "trouble arising from the discordance").

155:9–10. Matthew 17:17.

155:12–15. X. 15 (omitting a sentence, and reading "as he was meant to live" for "according to nature").

155:23–30. VI. 45; V. 8; VII. 55.

156:2–17. IV. 1 (condensed); X. 31 (with omissions); X. 33 (reading "to be miserable" for "to lament," and "in every matter which presents itself" for "in the matter which is subjected and presented to thee").

156:18–19. Romans 8:28.

157:2. St. Justin Martyr, early Christian apologist living at Rome, addressed his First Apology to Antoninus Pius and his adopted sons Marcus Aurelius and Lucius Verus. His Second Apology was addressed to the Roman Senate shortly after the accession of Marcus Aurelius in 161 A.D. About four years later he and some of his followers were denounced as Christians, scourged, and beheaded.

157:4. The ancient Alogi were heretics in Asia Minor during the reign of Marcus Aurelius who are said to have denied the divinity of the Holy Ghost and of the Logos (the "Word" of John 1:1).

157:7. "Gnosis," or "knowledge" (i.e., revealed knowledge of God and of human destiny, transmitted by secret tradition) was of central importance to certain Christian sects (the "Gnostics") of the second century A.D.

157:12–13. Marcus Aurelius XI. 3.

157:17. Vergil *Aeneid* vi. 314.

[SPINOZA AND THE BIBLE]

Arnold had more to say about Spinoza than he could conveniently fit into his discussion of Colenso. At first he thought of doing an article for the *Times* that would answer the criticisms of his first article (letter to his mother, January 7, 1863); then (presumably because the article on Stanley's *Lectures* served that purpose) his plan for the *Times* became simply an article on Spinoza (letter of February 4); in his *Note-Books* he lists "Spinoza for 'Times'" immediately under "Stanley's Lectures on the Jewish Church" as work to be composed in January. On April 17 he told his mother that he had completed his "Spinoza article for the *Times* (if the *Times* will but print it, now that the Session is going on)." His reason for thinking of the *Times* is not clear: there had been no comment in its pages upon his first article, and its leading article on Colenso did not appear until several weeks after his decision. Arnold was still at the beginning of his career of writing for the periodicals and was only beginning to find the ones most congenial to him. The decision in this case proved unhappy; the article did not appear in the *Times,* and the next we hear of it is in a letter of November 19 to his mother: "I am not quite pleased with my *Times* Spinoza as an article for *Macmillan;* it has too much of the brassiness and smartness of a *Times* article in it. This should be a warning to me not to write for the *Times,* or indeed for any newspaper." For "A Word More about Spinoza" in *Macmillan's Magazine* for December, 1863, Arnold received seven guineas.

In the first edition of *Essays in Criticism* the article was printed in this form, though with the title reduced merely to "Spinoza." An acute critic in a journal to which Arnold himself frequently contributed remarked, " 'The Bishop and the Philosopher'... has not been printed. Its absence is no matter for regret.... But the reprinted essay on Spinoza looks at present very abrupt and incomplete without the tract that was originally its counterpart; it is difficult to imagine the drift of it."—*Pall Mall Gazette*, February 24, 1865, p. 7. For his second edition, then, Arnold expanded the essay by grafting into it the passages about the *Tractatus Theo-logico-Politicus* from the Colenso essay; under its new title of "Spinoza and the Bible" it could claim greater completeness and a better right to a place with the other "Essays in Criticism;" at the same time the discussion of the *Tractatus* had been purged of the outdated controversies that had first called it forth.

"You say, very justly," Arnold wrote to his mother on January 7, 1863, "that one's aim in speaking about such a man [as Spinoza] must be rather to modify opinion about him than to give it a de-cisive turn in his favour; indeed, the latter I have no wish to do, so far as his doctrines are concerned, for, so far as I can understand them, they are not mine. But what the English public cannot un-derstand is that a man is a just and fruitful object of contemplation much more by virtue of what spirit he is of than by virtue of what system of doctrine he elaborates." He was moved by much the same scruples as Renan, who expressed this dilemma about publishing his religious writings: "Je sais que cette foi aux vérités supérieures, dégagée des symboles dont les religions l'ont revêtue, ne contentera jamais la majorité des hommes, habituée à porter dans les choses infinies la grossière précision que réclame la pratique de la vie, et incapable de se dégager, même dans les questions morales, de toute vue intéressée. L'humanité a l'esprit étroit; ses jugements sont toujours partiels; le nombre d'hommes capables de saisir finement les vraies analogies des choses est imperceptible. Comme, d'un côté, il est essentiel que tous croient au devoir, et que, d'un autre côté, il est impossible que tous aient la vue épurée de ce qui fonde le devoir, le penseur honnête éprouve d'abord une sorte de crainte en portant l'analyse sur les jugements étroits qui sont, pour la plupart de ses semblables, la raison de bien faire."–"Préface," *Essais de morale et de critique* (4th ed.; Paris, 1889), pp. v–vi.

158:1–18. Arnold translated this from the Latin of J. van Vlo-ten, ed., *Ad Benedicti de Spinoza Opera...Supplementum* (Am-sterdam, 1862), p. 290. See Robert Willis, *Benedict de Spinoza* (London, 1870), pp. 34–35.

158:21. The date is given as 1660 in Benedicti de Spinoza *Opera Quae Supersunt Omnia*, ed. C. H. Bruder (Leipzig, 1843), I, ix.

159:1. Voltaire, *Dictionnaire philosophique, s.v.* "Dieu, dieux," Sect. III (1771); *Le Philosophe ignorant* (1766); *Lettres à S.A. Monseigneur le Prince de* ***** (1767), and elsewhere.—*Oeuvres* *complètes* (Paris, 1878–79), XVIII, 365–69; XXVI, 65–69, 522–26. But Voltaire can hardly be said to have "disparaged" Spinoza, despite his disagreements.

159:2. Pierre Bayle, *Dictionaire historique et critique* (2nd ed.; Rotterdam, 1702), *s.v.* "Spinoza"—a violent attack on his impiety and atheism.

159:11–13. *Tractatus Theologico-Politicus*, [translated] from the Latin, with an Introduction and Notes by the editor [Robert Willis]. (London, 1862). See Arnold's review on pp. 56–64.

159:19–34. Willis's translation, p. 25; *Tractatus*, ed. Bruder, Praefatio, 18–19. Arnold's italics emphasize the blunders. For Arnold's own translation of part of this passage, see p. 171:5–7.

159:37–38. Common epithets for Heraclitus and Democritus; Arnold is using the terms here in a very general sense.

160:5–10. Willis's "Introduction," p. 15; see also pp. 9–11.

160:28–34. *Tractatus*, ed. Bruder, Praefatio, 14, 19. See Galatians 5:20, 22.

161:9–169:31. Spinoza's treatise is closely reasoned and deliberately repetitive. Moreover, Arnold's masterful synthesis is no mere mechanical précis of the original. Nevertheless, the following passages in Bruder's edition supply the basis of most of his statements, paragraph by paragraph. It will be noted that he is not here concerned with the political theories Spinoza advanced in his final chapters (XVI–XX), though these were undoubtedly the principal substance of the treatise in Spinoza's own eyes.

1. ("The comments of men...."): Praefatio, 14, 19–21; VII, 23; Praefatio, 24.
2. ("In what then...."): I, 1–4, 7–8.
3. ("The prophets...."): I, 9, 22, 25, 46; II, 41.
4. ("Whence, then...."): II, 4, 6, 9–10.
5. ("The power...."): IV, 12–13; II, 34 (XIII, 10–11), 36, 50, 26–27, 24, 16, 19, 52–53.
6. ("To know...."): IV, 12; III, 44, 12–22, 49–51; IV, 5–8, 40–41.
7. ("Christ came when that...."): IV, 14–21, 29–35; XI, 1, 4–7, 15–16, 19–22; XIII, 4.
8. ("What, then,...."): XIII, 6–8; V, 4, 8–9; XIV, 9; XII, 22–24; VII, 35, 7–12; XV, 22, 26–37, 45.
9. ("It follows...."): XIV, 37–38, 4–6, 13, 24, 20, 30–32, 39; VII, 4; XX, 43–46.
10. ("But the multitude...."): VI, 1, 4, 6, 9, 16–19, 30, 67; VII, 13; VI, 40, 44–45, 48, 53–56, 59; VIII, 42, 48; IX, 2; X, 6, 5, 12–13, 23, 28, 3, 43–47 & n.; XII, 28.

162:12–18. Exodus 33:11, 20; 32:10; 20:5. I Kings 22:19. Daniel 7:9. Ezekiel 1:4, 27–28. Matthew 3:16 (Luke 3:22). Acts 2:3.

162:25. For "testimony of conscience" see II Corinthians 1:12.

163:8. *El Sadai* is translated "Almighty God" in the King James Version (Genesis 17:1); see Exodus 6:3.

163:11–16. I Samuel 15:29; Jeremiah 18:8, 10; Joshua 10:11–13.

163:21–23. II Kings 3:14–15.

164:9–10. Deuteronomy 5:33.

165: 2–5. Luke 8:10; I Corinthians 3:1–2.

165:26–30. See Romans 15:20. For the discrepancies, compare the statements on faith in Romans 4 and James 2:20.

165:35–36. Spinoza, *Tractatus*, ed. Bruder, XIII, 4.

166:3–6. Isaiah 1:16–17.

166:10–12. John 15: 8–12; I John 3:11.

166:22–23. John 1:1–17.

166:38–167:1. Matthew 13:35.

167:2–3. I Corinthians 1:27–28.

167:12–16. Spinoza, *Tractatus*, ed. Bruder, XV, 45.

167:24–26. Hebrews 11:6.

168:21–22. Jeremiah 31:35–36.

168:24. *Tractatus*, ed. Bruder, VII, 13.

168:28–31. *Ibid.*, VI, 48 based on Exodus 14:27 and 15:10. Arnold's account is slightly misleading, since the east wind that opened the sea *is* mentioned directly in Exodus (14:21); Spinoza refers to the (?west) wind that closed the sea upon the Egyptians.

170:13–14. Genesis 12:6; Spinoza, *Tractatus*, ed. Bruder, VIII, 9.

170:16–17. Deuteronomy 34:10; Spinoza, VIII, 17.

170:18–21. Genesis 36:31; Spinoza, VIII, 19.

170:21–27. Deuteronomy 3:11; Spinoza, VIII, 11 (citing II Samuel 12:30).

170:27–33. I Samuel 9:9; Spinoza, VIII, 40.

170:35–36. Spinoza, IX, 31 ("Non est, cur circa haec lectorem diu detineam"); IX, 51.

171:1–2. Deuteronomy 34:5–6; Spinoza, VIII, 17.

171:5–7. Spinoza, Praefatio, 19. Arnold adds "Christ and".

171:12–13. Titus 3:3.

171:17–18. W. E. Gladstone, *The State in Its Relations with the Church* (1838; 4th ed., 2 vols., 1841). This is an ardent defense of the Establishment and the Church of England against rationalists and utilitarians. Arnold interprets rather than translates Spinoza's title, *Tractatus Theologico-Politicus.*

171:24–33. *Tractatus,* ed. Bruder, I, 3 & 44.

172:2-8. *Ibid.*, I, 11; VI, 46-48, 43, 39-40.

172:16-18. *Ibid.*, I, 14.

172:30-35. *Ibid.*, VI, 65.

173:3-4. *Ibid.*, VI, 51.

173:8-12. *Ibid.*, XII, 26.

173:21. Exeter Hall, a building in the Strand used for religious and philanthropic assemblies, came to stand for a certain type of fundamental evangelicalism.

173:21-25. *Tractatus*, ed. Bruder, VI, 30-33, or III, 38. For the censorship, see X, 5, 45.

173:30-34. *Ibid.*, VI, 67, citing Jeremiah 31:35-36. Arnold seemed almost to endorse Spinoza's use of the passage in his summary of the *Tractatus* (p. 168:21-22).

173:35. Genesis 9:1.

174:12-18. *Tractatus*, ed. Bruder, XVII, 93-102. Spinoza quotes Ezekiel 20:26 thus: "Eo quod impuravi ipsos muneribus suis remittendo omnem aperturam vulvae [id est primogenitum], ut eos vastarem, ut scirent quod ego sum Iehova," and links it with the appointment of the Levites to the ministry of the temple in Numbers 8:16-17. The English Bible here is a hopeless muddle.

174:19-21. A. P. Stanley, *Lectures on the History of the Jewish Church* (New York, 1863), I, 512 and Lecture 20 *passim*. On pp. 485-87 Stanley quotes the praise of the Prophetical Order in J. S. Mill's *Representative Government*, pp. 41-42 (end of Chapter II).

174:22-23. *Tractatus*, ed. Bruder, XVIII, 13-14.

175:3-4. Robert Willis, whose translation of the *Tractatus* Arnold criticized, in 1870 published a translation of the *Ethics* and *Letters*.

175:32-37. F. D. Maurice, "Spinoza and Professor Arnold," *Spectator*, XXXVI, 1474 (January 3, 1863). Maurice replied briefly to Arnold's remark in a footnote to an article in the next number of *Macmillan's Magazine*, IX, 197 (January, 1864).

176:15-16. "Ambition should be made of sterner stuff."—*Julius Caesar*, III, ii, 98.

176:20-21. See Spinoza, *Ethics*, ed. Bruder, p. 218 (Appendix to Part I): "Ut iam autem ostendam, naturam finem nullum sibi praefixum habere, et omnes causas finales nihil nisi humana esse figmenta, non opus est multis."

176:27-38. *Tractatus*, ed. Bruder, VI, 34. Arnold has reversed the order of the passages, which are part of the same sentence, and has put his second one into the first person ("we") instead of Spinoza's "they" (i.e., philosophers as contrasted with prophets).

177:12–18. *Ethics,* Part 4, propos. 21 (demonstration); propos. 20 (demonstration) combined with definition 8; propos. 18 (scholium); Part 3 (end), Definitions of Emotions, nos. 2 & 3 (ed. Bruder, pp. 346, 345 & 333, 344, 317). See Arnold, *Note-Books,* ed. Lowry, p. 131 (1870).

177:32–34. Exodus 10; Judges 6:39–40.

177:36–37. II Corinthians 7:10.

177:38. *Purgatorio,* XXIII, 81. See Arnold, *Note-Books,* p. 483.

178:1–2. For example, *Ethics,* Part 4, propos. 28 & 37.

178:33. Justus Lipsius (1547–1606), distinguished Flemish classical scholar.

178:37–179:9. Van Vloten, *Supplementum,* Preface, pp. iv–v, somewhat abbreviated and with Arnold's italics.

179:28–30. David Friedrich Strauss, *The Life of Jesus Critically Examined,* translated from the fourth German edition by George Eliot (London, 1846).

180:1–5. Spinoza, *Tractatus,* ed. Bruder, IV, 14, 21.

180:8. The *Masora* is the compilation of early traditional Hebrew learning on the text of the Old Testament. The *Record* was a Church of England weekly, edited at this time by Edward Garbett, to whose sermon at Oxford Arnold alluded on p. 45:29–31.

180:9–19. A paraphrase of Spinoza, *Tractatus,* XII, 15, 25, 1–2, 16.

180:27–31. These anecdotes are related in John Colerus, *Life of Benedict de Spinosa* (London, 1706; facsimile ed., The Hague, 1906), pp. 42–43, 46–48, and repeated in Spinoza, *Opera,* ed. Bruder, I, x–xi.

180:32–35. Spinoza's insistence on anonymity is reported in the Preface of the Editor of the *Opera Posthuma,* Jarig Jellis; see *Ethics,* ed. Bruder, p. 151. For his motive, see *Ethics,* pp. 326, 385 (No. 44 of the "Definitions of the Emotions" at the end of Part III and No. 25 of the "Appendix" at the end of Part IV).

180:35–37. Spinoza, *Tractatus,* ed. Bruder, XII, 4.

181:3–5. Isaiah 63:16.

181:26–27. In the Ethics Spinoza commonly uses the terms *idea adaequata* and *idea inadaequata.* He explains briefly in his letter 64 that an "adequate" idea is essentially the same as a "true" idea.

181:28–30. "Dieser kühne Geist [Heraklit] hat zuerst das tiefe Wort gesagt: 'Das Seyn ist nicht mehr als das Nichtseyn,' es ist ebenso wenig; oder 'Seyn und Nichts sey dasselbe,' das Wesen sey die Veränderung."—G. W. F. Hegel, *Vorlesungen über die*

Geschichte der Philosophie, Sämtliche Werke (Stuttgart, 1928), XVII, 348.

182:2–3. "Es giebt keine andre Philosophie, als die Philosophie des Spinoza."—Lessing in conversation with Friedrich Heinrich Jacobi, reported in Jacobi's *Ueber die Lehre des Spinoza, Werke* (Leipzig, 1819), IV (i), 55.

182:3–5. Goethe, *Dichtung und Wahrheit*, Books 14, 16; *Werke* (Weimar, 1890–91), XXVIII, 287–89; XXIX, 7–14. See Eckermann's summary of these books, *Gespräche mit Goethe*, February 28, 1831.

182:9–15. Heine, *Geständnisse, Gesammelte Werke* (Berlin, 1955), V, 588–89, 590; *Zur Geschichte der Religion und Philosophie in Deutschland, ibid.*, V, 256. Arnold somewhat mistranslates the former and paraphrases the latter.

182:24–31. In San Marco, Florence. Arnold had not seen the original.

182:33. John 14:2.

182:35. Shakespeare, *Antony and Cleopatra*, V, ii, 284.

182:38. "[Solomon] in suis Proverbiis vocat humanum intellectum verae vitae fontem, et infortunium in sola stultitia constituit."—*Tractatus*, ed. Bruder, IV, 41, with reference to Proverbs 16:22.

[NOTES TO CANCELED PASSAGES]

523:23–25. Genesis 38; Spinoza, *Tractatus*, IX, 8–11; Colenso, Chapters II–III.

523:25–28. Ezra 2; Spinoza X, 31–33; Colenso, "Preface," p. 29 ("Should God in His Providence call me to the work, I shall not shrink from the duty ...").

523:30. "Thy land [shall be called] Beulah [i.e., 'married']: for the Lord delighteth in thee."—Isaiah 62:4.

[JOUBERT]

Joseph Joubert was one of half a dozen subjects Arnold proposed to treat in essays in the first part of the year 1863; there was no thought then of using him as the subject of a lecture. But for some reason he abandoned his series on the Modern Element in Literature after giving his lecture on "The Modern Element in Romanticism" on March 26; a projected lecture on "Elizabethanism. Shakspeare" was never written, and the essay on Joubert, entitled merely "A French Coleridge," became the final Oxford lecture for 1863, delivered on November 28. Much as he enjoyed his reading the lecture seems to have given him a good deal of trouble: he reported to his mother on November 4 that he was writing at it, yet more than a fortnight later, with the lecture only nine days away, he told her not a word had yet been written. In the end, he wrote at it on trains and in stations the day before he gave it, and completed it in his bedroom between five and eight in the morning of the lecture. No other of his lectures was so dependent upon a single source as this lecture was on Raynal's edition of Joubert. Though "the Crown Princess of Prussia was being lionised over Oxford" and the necessity of attending upon her kept away many of his ordinary hearers among the senior members of the university, "the room was full, there being many more undergraduates than usual. People seemed much interested, and I am convinced that the novelty of one's subjects acts as a great and useful stimulus."

There is no indication how much revision the essay underwent before publication, but very little time elapsed: it appeared, anonymously, in the *National Review* for January, 1864, with the title "Joubert; or, a French Coleridge," and was reprinted in *Littell's Living Age* (Boston) on March 5. Arnold was paid £22 by the former journal. "I would far rather have it said how delightful and interesting a man was Joubert than how brilliant my article is," he told his mother. "In the long-run one makes enemies by having one's brilliancy and ability praised; one can only get oneself really accepted by men by making oneself forgotten in the people and doctrines one recommends." A week later came the *Spectator*'s comment that the translations had "a spirit and meaning given to them in their English dress which make them not merely equal, but in some respects superior expressions of the same thought;... they are [perhaps now and then] a little too good." The essay was "by far the ablest on the subject we have ever seen."—XXXVII, 131 (January 30, 1864).

184:6–7. *Portraits littéraires* (Nouv. éd.; Paris, 1882), II, 306–26, reprinted from *Revue des deux mondes*, 4th ser., XVI, 666–81 (December 1, 1838). Sainte-Beuve also wrote on Joubert in *Causeries du lundi*, I (article dated December 10, 1849), and, as he says, Joubert appears on nearly every page of his *Chateaubriand et son groupe littéraire sous l'Empire*.

184:12–188:33. Arnold draws his biographical information from the "Notice sur la vie, le caractère et les travaux de M. J. Joubert" which Joubert's nephew Paul de Raynal prefixed to his two-volume edition of Joubert's works in 1842. The edition used in these notes is *Pensées de J. Joubert, précédées de sa correspondance* (Septième éd.; Paris, 1880), 2 vols.; Raynal's "Notice" is on I, i–xciii. In this edition the first volume is devoted to correspondence, the second to *Pensées*, though the latter gives its title to both volumes.

184:12–29. *Pensées*, I, iv–vi, ix–x, xiii. Arnold misread the statement about the management of the school of Toulouse; the "Notice" speaks of "quelques pères de la Doctrine chrétienne chargés de la direction du collége de Toulouse. Habiles comme les jésuites, leurs prédécesseurs, à démêler dans la foule les jeunes gens propres à honorer la congrégation, les bons pères savaient, comme les jésuites, les attirer à eux par de riantes espérances" (p. v).

184:26–29. Denis Diderot (1713–84), a materialist and skeptic, was one of the most influential critics and philosophers of his brilliant century. He was director of the *Encyclopédie*, on which he was assisted by Jean le Rond d'Alembert (1717–83), philosopher and mathematician of European reputation, and Jean-François Marmontel (1723–99), the principal contributor of literary articles. Jean-François de La Harpe (1739–1803) was a literary critic and friend of Voltaire's. Louis de Fontanes (1757–1821) was a critic, a poet in the didactic tradition (he translated Pope's *Essay on Man*), and became, under Napoleon, first *Grand-maître de l'Université impériale*, the head of the state system of secondary and higher education.

184:30–31. *Pensées*, I, xiv.

185:1–2. Raynal, *ibid.*, I, i, quotes the footnote on p. 1 of Chateaubriand's *Voyage en Italie:* "Homme... d'un talent qui lui aurait donné une réputation méritée, s'il n'avait voulu cacher sa vie." Epicurus' "λάθε βιώσας," "Live obscurely," is Usener's fragment 551.

185:6–20. *Pensées*, I, xxvi–xxviii.

185:21–24. The story is told by Diogenes Laertius II. 69: "When Dionysius [tyrant of Syracuse] asked why philosophers go to rich men's houses, while rich men no longer visit philosophers, Aristippus replied that the philosophers know what they are in need of, the rich men do not."

185:28–186:3. *Pensées*, I, lxv–lxvi. Fontanes wrote: "M. Joubert ... est mon ami depuis trente ans. C'est le compagnon de ma vie, le confident de toutes mes pensées." Arnold's reflections on this episode somewhat parallel those of Raynal.

186:12–29. *Ibid.*, I, xxiv, xxxii, xliv–xlvi, xxxvi–xxxvii, xli–xliii.

About the choice of books, Raynal is more emphatic than Arnold represents him: "Il ne fallait chercher là ni Voltaire, ni J.-J. Rousseau, ni les autres écrivains de l'école philosophique." But Arnold may be justified by Joubert's letter to Mme de Beaumont, May, 1797: "Quant à moi, je vous en remercie. Dieu me préserve d'avoir jamais en ma possession un Voltaire tout entier!"—*Ibid.*, I, xlv and 32. The praise of Mme de Beaumont undoubtedly owes something to the warm admiration expressed by Sainte-Beuve, *Causeries du lundi* (3rd ed.; Paris, 1857), I, 164.

186:30–33. For Joubert on Mme de Staël, see *Pensées*, II, 387 (XXIV, v, 35); on Benjamin Constant, *ibid.*, I, 35–36 (letter of June 26, 1797).

186:38–187:35. *Ibid.*, I, lxii–lxiv, lxvii, lvi–lvii, lxix–lxx.

187:35–188:2. The word "aménité" is used of him both by Raynal (*ibid.*, I, lvii) and Sainte-Beuve (*Portraits littéraires*, II, 310), the latter in italics.

188:2–3. *Pensées*, I, lxxvii; Sainte-Beuve, *Portraits littéraires*, II, 324n.

188:3–12. *Journal des Débats*, May 8, 1824; reprinted in *Pensées*, I, lxxxii–lxxxiii.

188:13–23. *Pensées*, I, lxxxviii, lxxviii.

188:23. *Recueil des pensées de M. Joubert*, ed. Chateaubriand (Paris, 1838), printed only for friends; not published or offered for sale.

188:29–31. *Pensées, essais et maximes de J. Joubert*, ed. Paul de Raynal (Paris, 1842), 2 vols.
Pensées, essais, maximes et correspondance de J. Joubert (2nd ed.; Paris, 1850), 2 vols. (another edition, Paris, 1861).
Pensées de J. Joubert, précédées de sa correspondance, ed. Louis de Raynal (Paris, 1862), 2 vols.

188:38. From April 15, 1816, until his death, Coleridge lived in the house of and under the care of James Gillman, a physician in practice in Highgate.

190:14–15. Charles de Rémusat, "Des Controverses religieuses en Angleterre, II: Coleridge—[Thomas] Arnold," *Revue des deux mondes*, seconde période, V, 512 (October 1, 1856). Rémusat characterizes as "jugements assez saugrenus" Coleridge's systematic analysis of the "intellectual character [of] the three great countries of Europe . . . namely, Germany, England, and France," in which he finds that where Germany and England have Genius, France has Cleverness.—*The Friend*, ed. H. N. Coleridge (London, 1837), III, 69–72 (second section, essay I, note).

190:21–24. Sainte-Beuve, *Tableau historique et critique de la poésie française ... au XVIe. siècle* (Nouv. éd.; Paris, n.d.), p. 386, replying to such judgments as Goethe's in his "Notes to *Rameau's Neffe*," *Werke* (Weimar, 1900), XLV, 173. "Die Franzosen haben einen Poeten du Bartas, den sie gar nicht mehr, oder nur mit Verachtung nennen." "En fait de poëtes et d'écrivains, chaque nation est, ce semble, le premier juge des siens; si grand que soit Goethe, cela ne le rend pas un arbitre plus sûr des vers français."

190:36. See below, p. 192:31–33.

191:18–30. The first Preface to *Atala*, quoted by Sainte-Beuve, *Chateaubriand et son groupe littéraire sous l'Empire* (Nouv. éd.; Paris, 1889), I, 199–200. See Arnold, *Note-Books*, ed. Lowry, p. 482.

191:26. *Iliad* xxiv. 505–6. Arnold drew one of his touchstone passages in "The Study of Poetry" from the same scene of the *Iliad*. See also "On Translating Homer," *Prose Works*, ed. Super, I, 212.

191:29–30. Genesis 45:4.

191:35–37. Sainte-Beuve, *Chateaubriand*, II, 399; see Arnold, *Note-Books*, ed. Lowry, p. 475. Chateaubriand died on July 4, 1848.

192:11–13. See note to p. 190:14–15.

192:22–33. Joubert, *Pensées*, I, 143 (letter to Molé, February 18, 1805; see also that of January 9). Louis-Matthieu Molé was to preside over the Cabinet under Louis-Philippe for two years, beginning April 15, 1837. Louis Racine, second son of the dramatist, published a prose translation of *Paradise Lost* in 1755.

193:12. Julien-Louis Geoffroy (1743–1814) was dramatic critic for the *Journal des Débats*, a daily newspaper noted throughout its long career (1789–1939) for its interest in literary matters.

193:17–18. Coleridge, *Biographia Literaria*, Chapter XXI.

193:18–23. Joubert, *Pensées*, I, 58 (letter to Mme de Beaumont, August 1, 1801, enclosing the supplement to the *Journal des Débats* of that date). The *Génie du christianisme* was not published until April, 1802; Joubert's letter does not indicate the subject of Geoffroy's article.

194:14–23. Joubert, *Pensées*, II, 154 (xii, 23, 25).

194:26–195:17. *Ibid.*, I, 100–101 (letter of September 17, 1803).

195:22–196:2. *Ibid.*, II, 293 (xxii, 99).

196:8–13. *Ibid.*, II, 308 (xxiii, 36).

196:14–32. *Ibid.*, II, 62–63 (iv, 63).

196:36. *Hamlet*, V, i, 199.

197:1–7. Joubert, *Pensées*, II, 10, 8, 8, 5 ("Preliminary").

197:22–24. *Ibid.*, II, 26 (i, 91).

197:25–34. *Ibid.*, II, 25 (i, 85).

197:35–36. *Ibid.*, II, 12 (i, 6).

197:37–198:16. *Ibid.*, II, 143 (xi, 37).

198:17–27. *Ibid.*, II, 31 (i, 119, 120).

198:28–30. *Ibid.*, II, 20 (i, 52).

198:35–199:6. *Ibid.*, II, 21–22 (i, 61, 62).

199:10–19. *Ibid.*, II, 22–23 (i, 68).

199:22. Heine too, for Arnold, was a "child of light" (p. 113:32).

199:28–33. *Ibid.*, II, 33 (i, 129).

199:35. Joachim of Flora was a twelfth-century Italian Cistercian abbot and mystic, founder of a monastic order. He was an older contemporary of St. Francis.

200:1–3. Joubert, *Pensées*, II, 23–24 (i, 75).

200:4. The Jansenists were a party in the French and Belgian church of the seventeenth century, followers of Cornelius Jansen, who appealed to the doctrines of St. Augustine against the scholasticism of the Jesuits. In one respect they approached Calvinism in doctrine, though always anti-Protestant. As against the theological reasonings of the Jesuits they advocated appeal to religious and spiritual experience. They were vigorously condemned by the bull *Unigenitus* in 1713.

200:11–31. Joubert, *Pensées*, II, 33–34 (i, 130). See Matthew 22:14; Ephesians 2:3; Galatians 3:26; Mark 2:17.

200:33–201:22. Joubert, *Pensées*, II, 34–36 (i, 135, 132, 131).

201:24. "loosenesses" was Arnold's translation (line 6 above) of Joubert's "inexactitudes."

201:33–34. Joubert, *Pensées*, II, 311 (xxiii, 54).

201:37–202:4. *Ibid.*, II, 325 (xxiii, 128); "mais l'âme dit: 'Vous me faites mal.'"

202:6–12. *Ibid.*, II, 389–90 (xxiv, § vi).

202:20. A sixteen-line poem in blank verse that stands as a preface to Wordsworth's collected poems.

202:23–203:2. Joubert, *Pensées*, II, 339–40 (xxiii, 218). Arnold omits the sentences which may have suggested his comment in the next paragraph: "Il n'y a que les livres sacrés qui obtiennent un empire étendu et durable. Tous les autres ne font qu'occuper plus ou moins sérieusement les moments perdus de quelques désoeuvrés."

203:14–26. *Ibid.*, II, 343–44 (xxiv, § i, 12, 14, 10). One notes in the second of these the germ of Arnold's famous epigram on Shelley; see also p. 146:7–8.

203:29-33. *Ibid.*, II, 351 (xxiv, § ii, 6). Pierre Nicole (1625-95) was a Jansenist moralist and theologian of Port-Royal.

203:36. Macaulay uses the expression "a rhetorician so skillful as Bossuet," but hardly in a pejorative sense.—*History of England*, Chapter III ("Influences of French Literature").

204:1-13. Joubert, *Pensées*, II, 351-52 (xxiv, § ii, 10).

204:17-29, 36-37. *Ibid.*, II, 377-79 (xxiv, § v, 13, 11, 9, 15).

204:38-205:3. *Ibid.*, II, 378 (xxiv, § v, 14-15).

205:14-32. *Ibid.*, II, 364-66 (xxiv, § iv, 22, 26, 29, 32, 33).

205:38-206:1. Presumably, in *Dichtung und Wahrheit*, middle of Book XI, and in Eckermann's *Conversations with Goethe*.

206:3-30. Joubert, *Pensées*, II, 367-70 (xxiv, § iv, 35, 38, 42, 48-50).

206:37-207:17. *Ibid.*, II, 203-4 (xvii, 1, 3).

207:20-29. *Ibid.*, II, 178, 180 (xv, 5, 14, 15).

207:37-208:1. *Ibid.*, II, 95, 96, 58 (vii, 62, 73; iv, 39).

208:11-14. *Ibid.*, I, 96 (letter of September 14, 1803); II, 67, 142-43, 69 (v, 30; xi, 36; v, 46).

208:21-24. Matthew 6:22-23: "The light of the body is the eye: if therefore thine eye be single, thy whole body shall be full of light. But if thine eye be evil, thy whole body shall be full of darkness. If therefore the light that is in thee be darkness, how great is that darkness." Here is the basis of the maxim of Bishop Wilson that Arnold used so effectively in *Culture and Anarchy*.

208:37-38. See II Corinthians 1:12 and p. 162:25-26.

208:38-209:2. *Pensées*, II, 85 (vi, last sentence).

209:7-8. See I Peter 4:11.

209:17. Eugène Scribe (1791-1861), the most successful and one of the most prolific dramatists of the day, was especially admired for plot construction and stagecraft.

210:22. Arnold conceived that he himself had this quality. He wrote to Sainte-Beuve on January 13, 1864: "Lorsqu'on me loue, ici, d'un article de critique, je réponds toujours: 'Si j'ai quelque chose de bon, c'est à M. Sainte Beuve que je le dois.' En effet, si la nature m'a donné un certain goût pour la modération et pour la *vraie vérité*, c'est de vous, uniquement de vous, que j'ai un peu appris la manière de m'en servir et d'en tirer parti."—L. Bonnerot, *Matthew Arnold, Poète*, pp. 536-37.

211:10-18. One catches here echoes of biblical phrases from John 12:36 and Genesis 12:6. Dagon was the god of the Philistines (Judges 16:23).

[PAGAN AND MEDIAEVAL RELIGIOUS SENTIMENT]

The lecture Arnold delivered at Oxford on Saturday, March 5, 1864, upon "Pagan and Christian Religious Sentiment" is hardly mentioned in his letters, which at this time are full of his work on *A French Eton.* There can be little doubt that some of the feeling toward the dissenting clergy which governed his thoughts about education also entered the lecture, only to be dropped before he published it; he told his mother on March 17, "My Oxford lecture will be in this next *Cornhill,* but a good deal about Protestantism is left out, as I think I told you it would be, as it could not be stated fully enough quite to explain and secure itself." For its appearance in the April *Cornhill* he was paid £ 20. When the article was reprinted in *Essays in Criticism,* its title was belatedly changed to conform to the more limited scope indicated in his letter. The greater part of it was translated in the *Revue britannique* for April, 1871.

"The subject is not treated by disquisition, but by examples from Theocritus, Saint Francis, and others," Arnold told the publisher of *The Cornhill* the day after he delivered the lecture.—Buckler, *Matthew Arnold's Books,* p. 65. Theocritus had made an occasional appearance in his lists of projected reading (in April and June, 1861, May, 1862, and again, with Bion and Moschus, at the end of 1863); for St. Francis his principal source was a pair of articles, "François d'Assise," by Charles Berthoud in the *Revue germanique* of July 1 and September 1, 1863 (XXVI, 224–52; XXVII, 69–101), which he read in October. His notebooks for the latter part of that year and for 1864 contain a good many jottings from those articles and from A. F. Ozanam's *Les Poètes franciscains en Italie au treizième siècle* (Paris, 1852). His translation of Theocritus' fifteenth idyl is done with his usual felicity.

212:1–9. "The Catholic Congress of Malines," *Dublin Review,* n.s. I, 488 (October, 1863); quoted by Arnold in *Note-Books,* ed. Lowry, p. 23 (for the year 1863).

212:12. See note to p. 173:21.

213:2. Charles Haddon Spurgeon (1834–92) was a Baptist preacher of strong Calvinist convictions whose oratorical gifts drew such crowds that a new church, the Metropolitan Tabernacle, had to be built for him in Newington Causeway, Southwark. Though he preached at Exeter Hall before the Tabernacle was completed, he was at odds with the Evangelicals of the Church of England for whom Arnold usually uses "Exeter Hall" as symbol.

213:2–3. Gibbon tells the story that when his general, Amrou, asked the Caliph Omar after capturing Alexandria in 640 (or 641) A.D. whether he might spare the famous library, Omar replied, "If these writings of the Greeks agree with the book of God, they are useless and need not be preserved; if they disagree, they are pernicious and ought to be destroyed." "The sentence was executed," Gibbon continues, repeating a legend of which he was rightly skeptical, "with blind obedience: the volumes of paper or parchment were distributed to the four thousand baths of the city; and such was their incredible multitude that six months were barely sufficient for the consumption of this precious fuel."—*Decline and Fall of the Roman Empire*, Chapter LI.

213:4. Jacques-Paul Migne (1800–75), a parish priest who became editor and publisher of the immense series Arnold lists lower down on the page. Arnold spent more than a week in the Museum in January, 1860, preparing his report on French education, and was much impressed with the improvements made three years earlier. The reader today will find the arrangement not very different from the one Arnold describes.

213:9. A series of reprints of 17th-century Church of England divines, published in 83 volumes (1841–63) under Tractarian influence.

213:12. Thomas Chalmers (1780–1847), Scottish evangelical preacher and theologian, founder of the Free Church in Scotland in 1843.

213:14. William Ellery Channing (1780–1842), liberal Congregationalist pastor in Boston and leading American proponent of Unitarian theology.

213:22. A series of lives of the saints, arranged in the order of their feasts in the ecclesiastical year, begun by the Bollandists (Jesuits) in the 17th century. The first volumes were published at Antwerp in 1643. By the date of this essay nearly sixty volumes had appeared, and a new edition of the first fifty-four volumes was published 1863–68.

213:24. A semi-annual London periodical begun in 1846.

213:25–27. Migne's three *Encyclopedias of Theology* run to 168 volumes in all. The *Patrologiae Cursus* comes to another 468 volumes. Four other series published by him total 174 volumes.

213:31. Matthew 13:47–48.

214:7–8. Robert Smith Candlish (1806–73) was, next to Chalmers, the most prominent leader of the Free Church in Scotland. George Douglas Campbell, 8th Duke of Argyll (1823–1900), a Liberal leader and prolific writer on such matters as the reconciliation of scientific progress with religion, had first obtained notice as a writer of pamphlets that attempted to avert the Disruption of the Church of Scotland.

214:14. Juvenal i. 85.

214:19–20. The *Dictionnaire des apocryphes* (1856–58) makes up vols. XXIII–XXIV of the *Troisième et dernière encyclopédie théologique*. Arnold quotes a long passage from its Preface in his *Note-Books* for 1864 (ed. Lowry, p. 27).

214:28–31. The *Dictionnaire des erreurs sociales* (1852) is vol. XIX of the *Nouvelle encyclopédie théologique*. Arnold quotes from the article on "Anglicanisme," column 36; religious persecutions, says the article, were "un moment suspendues par la reine Marie."

215:6–23. The *Dictionnaire des origines du christianisme* (1856) is vol. XV of the *Troisième et dernière encyclopédie théologique*. "Quel tableau de corruption et de décomposition toujours croissantes nous présente le monde païen!" The story of feeding slaves to the lampreys (not oysters) is based on Pliny *Natural History* IX. xxxix; that of killing a slave to see how a man dies on Plutarch's "Life of Flamininus" XVIII (but Plutarch makes the victim a prisoner condemned to death, not a slave). The story of Galen's mother is not in the article at all; its origin is Galen himself, *On the Affections of the Mind*. Arnold quotes passages from columns 1054 and 1055 of the *Dictionnaire*.

215:34. See p. 141:33–36.

216:1. Populous industrial districts of London, east of the (modern) Liverpool St. Station.

216:3. A mountainous agricultural district northeast of Rome.

216:4. Arnold wrote to his mother from the Hertford assize on March 5, 1862: "The culprits in front of me—two Hertford labourers and a straw plaiter (a girl)— are such specimens of barbarism to look at as you seldom saw, the girl more particularly. The state of the peasantry in these metropolitan counties is lamentable."

220:13. Sophron was a Syracusan writer of mimes, or dialogues, in the fifth century B.C. His works have not survived.

222:16. Wordsworth, "Address to My Infant Daughter, Dora," line 65; quoted also p. 17:35–36.

222:29. A member of the company of strolling players to which Wilhelm attached himself in the *Lehrjahre*.

223:12–13. The coming of Antichrist was announced in I John

2:18. Berthoud, "François d'Assise," p. 243, describes the age of St. Francis as "un temps où l'on croyait le monde arrivé à son crépuscule, et où l'approche de Antéchrist se faisait pressentir."

223:24–29. "Avec François d'Assise, le monachisme se transforme. Il rentre dans le monde qu'il avait fui, non pour participer à ses inquiétudes et à ses ambitions, mais pour lui donner des biens éternels en échange de la pauvre offrande qu'il lui mendie chaque jour.... La compassion la plus intime et la plus profonde pour les pauvres, cette compassion si vive, qu'elle était une souffrance réelle, n'empêche pas François de trouver, pour lui-même, sa suprême joie dans la pauvreté."—*Ibid.*, pp. 240–41.

223:29–30. *Ibid.*, p. 232.

223:35–38. *Ibid.*, p. 86: "La vallée de l'Ombrie, avec ses petites villes au flanc des montagnes, était sa Galilée. Souvent, lorsqu'une bourgade apprenait son approche, les confréries, les corps de métiers, les enfants, bannières déployées, avec des rameaux verts, au son des cloches et au chant des cantiques, allaient au-devant de lui; le jour de sa venue était une fête."

224:1–3. "La Pentecôte resta, longtemps encore, l'époque où la grande famille de François se réunissait de toutes parts, et lui-même put assister à l'une de ces fêtes où 5,000 de ses compagnons... faisaient retentir l'air de chants de louanges.... On les appela d'abord les pauvres pénitents d'Assise. François, de retour de Rome, les nomma *Minorites*, c'est-à-dire les plus petits de tous les moines, les petits du royaume de Dieu."—*Ibid.*, p. 245. St. Francis' first two disciples were Bernardo da Quintavalle and Pietro Cattaneo.

224:4–8. *Ibid.*, p. 236.

224:9–19. *Ibid.*, p. 77. The alternate names are given by Ozanam, *Les Poètes franciscains* (6th ed.: 1882), p. 387.

224:24–225:15. The Canticle is given in Italian and French by Berthoud, pp. 77–79; by Ozanam, pp. 387–88 and 82–85.

226:1. Berthoud discusses the versions of the story of St. Francis' receiving the *stigmata* on Monte Alverno in 1224—"le plus grand miracle du moyen âge, le plus grand miracle même de tous les âges croyants" (pp. 92–96).

226:3–8. *Ibid.*, p. 97.

226:21–22. Luther, *Table Talk*, tr. and ed. William Hazlitt (London, 1867), pp. 211, 213.

227:3. "O, dieser Streit wird enden nimmermehr.
      Stets wird die Wahrheit hadern mit dem Schönen,
      Stets wird geschieden sein der Menschheit Heer
      In zwei Partei'n: Barbaren und Hellenen."
        —"Es träumte mir von einer Sommernacht," ll. 129–32.

227:10–29. *Zur Geschichte der Religion und Philosophie in Deutschland*, Book I, 10th paragraph.

228:4. Keats, "Ode on a Grecian Urn," line 10.

228:6. I.e., turtledoves.

228:16–229:22. *Geständnisse* (Winter, 1854), last three paragraphs. Heine dates the story of the poor clerk in 1480, well outside the range of the Limburg Chronicle, which notes it at the end of the account of 1374 as having occurred "five or six years before."

230:7–8. "Doch sehen wir überall die Lehre von den beiden Prinzipien hervortreten; dem guten Christus steht der böse Satan entgegen; die Welt des Geistes wird durch Christus, die Welt der Materie durch Satan repräsentiert."—*Religion . . . in Deutschland*, Book I, 9th paragraph.

231:10–11. Wordsworth, "Tintern Abbey," lines 39–40.

231:25–30. Sophocles *Oedipus Tyrannos* 863–71.

[THE LITERARY INFLUENCE OF ACADEMIES]

One of the greatest satisfactions of Arnold's official visit to France in 1859 was his meeting with the most brilliant of the French intellectuals, Sainte-Beuve, Cousin, Michelet, Villemain, and—perhaps most important to him at this time—Renan, "between whose line of endeavour and my own I imagine there is considerable resemblance," he told his sister Jane Forster soon after his return. "The difference is, perhaps, that he tends to inculcate *morality*, in a high sense of the word, upon the French nation as what they most want, while I tend to inculcate *intelligence*, also in a high sense of the word, upon the English nation as what they most want; but with respect both to morality and intelligence, I think we are singularly at one in our ideas, and also with respect both to the progress and the established religion of the present day." The other scholars and critics Arnold met in France belonged to an older generation; Renan alone was the same age as himself. "The best book of his for you to read, in all ways, is his *Essais de morale et de critique*, lately published." One of the essays in that volume was "L'Académie française," a review of a new edition of a history of the Academy that Sainte-Beuve had also reviewed in the *Moniteur*. At Sainte-Beuve's urging Arnold had prolonged his stay in Paris to attend the public session of the Academy on August 25.

Among the subjects for articles with which his mind was filled, then, Eugénie de Guérin, A French Eton and "Academies (such as the French Institute)" are named together in his letters of November 27, 1862, and (with Joubert) of February 4, 1863 ("Maurice de Guérin" was already completed). There was at first no apparent thought of using any of these as Oxford lectures. By the end of 1863, exhausted by the very considerable production of that year, he announced that for the next twelve months "I mean to do nothing for the magazines except one article on the effect of institutions like the French Academy. But I hope to do some poetry and to ripen."

On Saturday, June 4, 1864, Arnold delivered at Oxford his lecture on "The Influence of Academies on National Spirit and Literature"; one of his hearers was Algernon Swinburne. Nine days earlier he offered the essay to Smith, publisher of *The Cornhill:* "I think the subject may be made interesting, and hope to treat it in a plain common-sense way that people who are not academicians may care to follow."—Buckler, *Matthew Arnold's Books*, p. 65. But the lecture required a little adapting for the magazine, and Smith had a few suggestions to offer. "Two or three pages at the beginning about the limits of criticism" Arnold thought "might as well be left out," and he may have modified his remarks on Ruskin in deference to Smith's personal friendship for him. The article appeared in the August number and was reprinted in Boston by *Littell's Living Age* on September 17; Arnold received £25 for the former "—the most I have yet received." Two evidences of its success gave him pleasure—a letter from Disraeli (to whom Lady de Rothschild had sent a copy) and an article on Provinciality in Miall's *Nonconformist*, "of all papers in the world," which spoke of Arnold as "a writer, who, by the power both of his thoughts and of his style, is beginning to attract great attention" (January 18, 1865). A somewhat abbreviated version appeared in the *Revue britannique* for May, 1871.

Renan's essay on the Academy was an elegant and well-reasoned defense of the "forty" against its French critics; though in a few respects, such as the opening paragraph, the comparison of the French temper with that of other nations ("Le génie français n'est pas de tous ceux qui se partagent le monde le plus philosophique, le plus poétique surtout; mais c'est certainement le plus complet, le plus mesuré, le plus propre à créer une forme de culture intellectuelle qui s'impose à tous"), and the remarks on the relation of genius to restraint, it may have suggested some of the form and matter of Arnold's essay, it was not in any way his model. Renan does not use Arnold's key word, "provincialism," though he has its counterpart virtue of "civilité," "la langue des gens du monde." His two principal points were that it was essential, besides all the learned societies that represent separate branches of scientific knowledge, for one society to represent the nobility of the human spirit itself, whatever its special activity—"il est donc essentiel qu'à côté des Académies qui représentent les branches diverses du savoir positif, il y en ait une qui représente la noblesse même de l'esprit humain dans ses applications les plus diverses"—and that the Academy had provided for each century the very standards needed to balance that century's characteristic excesses: in the nineteenth century, the resistance to materialism, commercialism, vulgarization. "I hardly know how to express the exceedingly complex duties which fall upon it in our century, charged as it is to make up the loss of every other sort of aristocracy; but if one gives the name of 'resistance' to that moral protest which, at certain epochs, is the first duty of those who are unwilling to be accomplices in the abasement of character and spirit, we must say that the Academy has nobly resisted."—Renan, *Essais de morale et de critique* (Paris, 1889), p. 348. Congenial as these ideas are to Arnold, they are only representative of an essay with which he must have been in whole-hearted agreement; an essay which had, moreover, something of the apophthegmatic style of which he was so fond: "Tout le monde doit avoir des préjugés, excepté le critique," and "Les fautes littéraires sont de [la] part [d'un tel corps] de peu de conséquence; quant aux fautes scientifiques, il lui est difficile de les éviter: l'essentiel est qu'il ne commette jamais une faute de tact."

Sainte-Beuve's essay (*Causeries du lundi*, XIV, 195–217; from the *Moniteur* of July 19, 1858) was a more genial and anecdotal sketch upon which Arnold drew for some of his account of the Academy's history; it lacks the profundity of Renan's, but it did supply Arnold with the term "provincialisme"—"quelques habitudes de province, au moins dans le goût"; Sainte-Beuve's term for the opposite quality is "urbanité." Another remark of Sainte-Beuve's, which Arnold jotted down in one of his "general" note-books under the heading "Cultivated Literary Opinion," is central to his position both in this essay and in others he wrote about this time: "Pour qu'une littérature ait de la vie avec ensemble et consistance, if faut une certaine stabilité non stagnante; il faut, pour l'émulation, un cercle de juges compétents et d'élite, quelque chose ou quelqu'un qui organise, qui régularise, qui modère et qui contienne, que l'écrivain ait en vue et qu'il désire de satisfaire; sans quoi il s'émancipe outre mesure, il se disperse et s'abandonne.... Les grands siècles littéraires ont toujours eu ainsi un juge, un tribunal dispensateur, de qui l'écrivain se sentait dépendre, quelque balcon ... duquel descendait la palme et la récompense."—*Chateaubriand et son groupe littéraire* (new ed.; Paris, 1889), I, 52–53; see Arnold, *Note-Books*, ed. Lowry, p. 458. J. C. Major shows Arnold's somewhat wider use of Sainte-Beuve in his article on "Matthew Arnold and Attic Prose Style" (*PMLA*, LIX, 1086–1103 [December, 1944]), an article which discusses the importance Arnold attached to "style" and the characteristic excellences of prose style for him: simplicity, clarity, delicacy, urbanity, and "wholeness." Arnold, he says, "generally follows Sainte-Beuve's use of the words *Attic, Asiatic, provincial* and *urbane.*"

It should be added that the functions of the Academy had been discussed recently in an article in *Macmillan's Magazine*, "Concerning the Organization of Literature" (IX, 426–36 [March, 1864]), and that Lord Stanhope had spoken at a recent dinner of the Literary Fund on the usefulness an Academy would have in England. (The *Macmillan's* article is anonymous, but is attributed to Francis Espinasse by W. D. Templeman, "Arnold's 'The Literary Influence of Academies,'" *Studies in Philology*, XLIII, 91 [January, 1946].)

232:2–3. P. Pellisson et P. J. T. d'Olivet, *Histoire de l'Académie française*, avec une introduction, des éclaircissements et notes par M. Ch.–L. Livet (Paris, 1858). This book was the occasion of Sainte-Beuve's and Renan's essays.

232:10–14. George Otto Trevelyan, "Letters from a Competition Wallah," *Macmillan's Magazine*, X, 3 (May, 1864): minute of Macaulay on education in India, dated February 2, 1835. The third part of Arnold's "A French Eton" appeared in the same number of *Macmillan's*.

232:14–16. "*Segnities* is, as Spinoza says, with *superbia* the great bane of man."—Arnold to Clough, September 29, 1859 (ed. Lowry, p. 151). See also Arnold, *Prose Works*, ed. Super, II, 160.

232:20–233:24. The summary of the Academy's founding comes from Pellisson and d'Olivet, *Académie française*, I, 8–9, 13–16, 34–35, 41–42.

233:24–27. "Vous ne croirez pas, et personne ne s'imaginera sans doute, que [le Parlement de Paris] appréhendât pour le style des procureurs."—*Ibid.*, I, 45; see also I, 23.

233:31–35. *Ibid.*, I, vii and 493.

233:38–234:2. *Ibid.*, I, 22 (pointed out also by Sainte-Beuve, *Causeries*, XIV, 206).

234:10–27. *Ibid.*, I, 33, 23–24, 63–64, 86–93.

234:27–33. Sainte-Beuve, *Causeries*, XIV, 207–8. "Tout cela est bien vague," he comments.

235:4–9. *Ibid.*, XIV, 208, 205.

235:9–20. Renan, *Essais de morale et de critique* (1889), pp. 350, 344, 350–51, 345.

235:28–29. "Epilog zu Schillers Glocke," line 32.

235:34–236:7. *De Officiis* I. iv–v.

236:16–21. Sainte-Beuve, *Causeries*, XIV, 209.

240:25–26. Chemists like Joseph Priestley (1733–1804) and Joseph Black (1728–99).

240:28–29. Jean Bernouilli (or Bernoulli) (1667–1748), a Basle mathematician regarded by his contemporaries as in the same rank as Newton and Leibniz, was the teacher of Leonard Euler (1707–83), a native of Basle and one of the most distinguished geometricians of modern times. It was with Euler's support that Joseph-Louis Lagrange (1736–1813), mathematician and astronomer, became president of the Academy of Berlin. Pierre-Simon Laplace (1749–1827) was also a mathematician and astronomer.

242:4–5. "A French Dictionnaire des Contemporaines has just been published, which ... contains a biography of me, correct in its facts, and flattering in its judgments.... The Dictionary on the whole seems excellent—and is a most useful & much wanted reference book: our only English book of the kind 'Men of the Time' is a trumpery affair, compiled by a clique who have seen nothing and who know nobody."—Arnold to his mother, December 1, 1858.

242:6–7. Henry George Bohn (1796–1884) published over six hundred volumes of inexpensive classics in various series. The translations in Bohn's Classical Library and Bohn's Philosophical Library are frequently pedestrian, but they sometimes (as with Spinoza) remain the best ones available in English and the venture was most commendable and most profitable to the publisher. Désiré Nisard, author of a *Histoire de la littérature française* (1844–61) and an academician supervised the publication of a twenty-eight volume *Collection des auteurs latins* (1837–47), with texts in Latin and French.

242:29. " 'Diocess' was the classical English type from the sixteenth to the end of the eighteenth century; it was the only form recognized by Dr. Johnson and the other eighteenth-century lexicographers and was retained by some (notably by the *Times* newspaper) in the nineteenth century, in which, however, *diocese* (as in

French) has become the established spelling."—*N.E.D.* Δίς, Διός was a synonym for Zeus, whose Latin name, Jupiter, was a common nickname of the *Times*.

242:32. The *Journal des Débats* was a Paris daily newspaper.

243:7–8. J. W. Donaldson's *Jashar* (London and Berlin, 1854) was a scholarly treatise in Latin that attempted to reconstruct from fragments scattered throughout the Old Testament the Book of Jasher alluded to in Joshua 10:13 and II Samuel 1:18. Arnold's argument would seem to suffer somewhat from the fact that the book was found unsatisfactory even by the more enlightened English critics (the less enlightened ones were offended by the scholarly tampering with Scripture). A second edition was published in 1860.

243:10–16. Renan, "L'Histoire du peuple d'Israël," *Études d'histoire religieuse* (7th ed.; Paris, 1880), p. 83n. Renan's point is merely that this book has nothing in common with the "higher criticism" of Ewald and its truly significant discoveries, yet has been mistaken as a representative of that school.

243:35. Arnold refers to the anonymous article (which he attributed to Goldwin Smith), "On a Citation from M. Renan in the 'Cornhill Magazine' for August," *Daily News*, August 4, 1864, p. 2. It was in this article, as Arnold told his mother three days later, that "Goldwin Smith has attacked me as 'a jaunty gentleman' in the *Daily News*."

243:24–244:7. Renan, "Mahomet et les origines de l'islamisme," *ibid.*, p. 222. Washington Irving's *Mahomet and His Successors* (2 vols., 1849–50) is described by Stanley T. Williams in the *D.A.B.* as "a feeble repercussion of standard biographies of the prophet." Charles Forster describes his own *Mahometanism Unveiled* (2 vols., London, 1829) as "an inquiry . . . on a new principle, tending to confirm the evidences, and aid the propagation, of the Christian faith." Renan alludes to Forster's discussion of prophecy, especially I, 166–70.

244:14. Charles Forster, *The One Primeval Language, Traced Experimentally Through Ancient Inscriptions in Alphabetic Characters of Lost Powers from the Four Continents* (London, 1851–54), 3 vols.

244:22. Newman's *Apologia* first appeared in seven weekly pamphlets from April 21 to June 2, 1864.

244:25. Sainte-Beuve discusses the quality of "élégance et urbanité" at the beginning of his essay on the "Histoire de l'Académie française" (*Causeries*, XIV, 195), and two paragraphs later (p. 197) introduces the word Arnold sets in opposition to it, "provincial-isme," "quelques habitudes de province." A longer discussion of "urbanité" occurs in an essay on Mme de Caylus, *Causeries*, III.

244:32–33. Arnold justified his use of the word in a letter to his mother on November 9, 1866: "As to 'note,' it is used in the sense of the Latin word *nota* to mean a *mark*. It has long been used in theology, and from thence I took it."

245:32–246:3. Delivered in October, 1650. Jeremy Taylor, *Whole Works*, ed. R. Heber and C. P. Eden (London, 1861), VIII, 447.

246:14–19. Preached at Paris about 1659. Bossuet, *Oeuvres choisies*, ed. J. Calvet (14th ed.; Paris: A. Hatier, 1947), p. 53.

246:24–28. *Works* (London, 1852), IV, 348 ("Reflections on the Revolution in France," 13th paragraph from the end).

246:30–34. *Ibid.*, IV, 370 ("Letter to a Member of the National Assembly," 26th paragraph).

246:36–38. *Ibid.*, IV, 374 ("Letter to a Member . . ." 35th paragraph).

247:2–7. *Ibid.*, IV, 202 ("Reflections on the Revolution in France," one-fourth through).

247:12–14. Quintilian, when he discusses the kinds of style, remarks: "In fact that distinction between Attic and Asiatic was very ancient. The former were regarded as concise and well balanced, the latter inflated and empty; in the former there was no super-fluity; the latter lacked judgment above all, and measure (modus)." —XII. x. 16. Sainte-Beuve quotes this passage in *Chateaubriand et son groupe* (new ed.; 1889), I, 253n.

247:27–39. "Even the largest indulgence for paradoxes, again, will scarcely pardon a writer [like Arnold] who is acquainted with the astonishing platitudes of French Academicians of the second order, and who yet attempts to persuade himself that Addison put commonplaces into good English because there was no Academy to reveal to him the poverty of his thoughts."—*Saturday Review*, XVIII, 175 (August 6, 1864).

248:14–21. *Spectator*, no. 465 (August 23, 1712), beginning; quoted in Arnold, *Note-Books*, ed. Lowry, pp. 29–30 (1864).

248:31–33. Joubert, *Pensées*, ed. Raynal (7th ed.; Paris, 1877), II, 188 (Titre xvi, 17); quoted in Arnold, *Note-Books*, ed. Lowry, p. 543.

249:23–24. Cicero *De Officiis* I. xxxvii. 134.

249:27–30. "Dichter und Schriftsteller sich wunderlich gebärden müssten, um sittenverderberischer zu sein als die Zeitungen des Tags."—"Byrons Don Juan," *Über Kunst und Alterthum,* III, 82 (1821); *Werke* (Weimar, 1902), XLI (i), 249.

250:19–22. For example, "By identifying itself with Teutonic 'Francia,' [modern Parisian France] contrives to degrade Charles the Great into a Frenchman."—"Savoy," *Saturday Review,* IX, 175 (February 11, 1860). See also XII, 348 (October 5, 1861), and XVI, 435 (September 26, 1863). For probable attribution of these articles to E. A. Freeman, see F. E. Faverty, *Matthew Arnold, the Ethnologist* (Evanston, Illinois: Northwestern University Press, 1951), p. 197, n.27.

250:22–23. Nicolas Malebranche (1638–1715), French theologian, scientist, and philosopher, "advanced an original solution of the Cartesian dualism of spirit and matter: denying the action of matter on spirit and spirit on matter, he found in God the source of our notions of the material world and the sole and universal cause, operating the movements of external objects and of our ideas so as to produce correspondence between the two."—*Oxford Companion to French Literature.*

251:4–15. *Modern Painters,* Part IV, chapter xiv, § 51.—*Works,* ed. Cook and Wedderburn, V, 289.

251:29–252:10. *Munera Pulveris,* Chapter V, § 134n. (quoting *Odyssey* iv. 14). Ruskin makes further suggestions of the same sort in *Val d'Arno,* Lecture VIII, § 213.—*Works,* XVII, 257–58; XXIII, 125.

252:20. When the *Golden Treasury* appeared at the end of 1861, Arnold sent a copy to Sainte-Beuve, much to Palgrave's delight.— L. Bonnerot, *Matthew Arnold, Poète,* p. 529; T. B. Smart, "Matthew Arnold and Sainte-Beuve," *Athenaeum,* September 3, 1898, p. 325, and Charles L. Graves, *Life and Letters of Alexander Macmillan* (London, 1910), p. 184. And his enterprise was rewarded. He had called Sainte Beuve's attention to Marvell's "Horatian Ode upon Cromwell's Return from Ireland," an excellent poem long neglected by English readers but now recalled to their notice by Palgrave. In an article on Taine's *History of English Literature* in the *Constitutionnel* of June 6, 1864 (two days after Arnold delivered his lecture, two months before it was published), Sainte-Beuve called attention to Marvell's poem in the same terms and referred to that "charmant petit livre," the *Golden Treasury,* as "tout un trésor, en effet, de forte ou suave poésie."—*Nouveaux lundis* (4th ed.; Paris, 1885), VIII, 100n. This praise must have mitigated whatever offence Arnold's criticism could have given to his friend Palgrave (to whom Arnold sent a copy of the first edition of *Essays in Criticism*).

252:25. Shelley's "A Lament" ("O World! O Life! O Time!") and Wordsworth's "My heart leaps up when I behold."

253:1–5. Note (on p. 314) to No. 70, Milton's Sonnet "When the Assault was Intended to the City," line 10. Palgrave (a contributor to the *Saturday Review*) was more provincial than Arnold indicates: he used the form "Lewis XIV."

253:25–29, 254:1–6. Palgrave, *Handbook to the Fine Art Collection in the International Exhibition of 1862* (London and Cambridge, 1862). The second edition, "revised and completed" under the title *Descriptive Handbook to the Fine Art Collections in the International Exhibition of 1862* appeared in the same year. Arnold was not alone in criticising the *Handbook*'s disrespect to Marochetti. In defending himself in a new edition, Palgrave modified his language without withdrawing his judgment. He retained the quotation from Planche; the other passages cited by Arnold were removed. His condemnation of the architectural style of parts of London, Paris, and Madrid (*Descriptive Handbook*, p. 161) is based on the conviction that "Gothic is simply the one style which, by the circumstances of its development, has united in itself all the best constructive and the best ornamental forms of the world's inventions in Architecture" (p. 163).

254:20–27. "Les conditions dont je parle sont tellement élémentaires, que j'ai peine à m'expliquer comment M. Marochetti les a méconnues. Il ne s'agit pas ici en effet d'une question de style, pas même d'une question de grammaire, mais tout simplement d'une question d'alphabet, ou, si l'on veut, de syllabaire. Violer les conditions dont je parle équivaut à ne pas savoir épeler." "Il y a des fantassins qui rappellent les soldats de plomb si chers aux écoliers. Il est presque impossible de deviner le corps sous le vêtement."— Gustave Planche, "Statue équestre de M. le duc d'Orléans de M. Marochetti," *Revue des deux mondes*, n.s. XI, 738, 739 (August 15, 1845); quoted by Palgrave, *Descriptive Handbook*, p. 116.

255:3–4. A. W. Kinglake, *The Invasion of the Crimea: Its Origin, and an Account of Its Progress down to the Death of Lord Raglan*, Vols. 1–2 (London, 1863). These volumes reached a fourth edition in the year of publication. The work was completed in eight volumes by 1887.

255:8–10. In his novel *Marion* (3 vols., London, 1864), Joseph A. Scoville, writing under the pseudonym of "Manhattan," quotes

James Gordon Bennett (to whom the novel is dedicated) as saying to the hero: "One day you will be able to write a clever editorial, which is the highest style of composition known." The passage is cited in a review of the novel in the *Saturday Review*, XVII, 600 (May 14, 1864), and alluded to in a review in the *Spectator*, XXXVII, 539–40 (May 7, 1864).

255:13–14. Quintilian (VIII. iii. 28) quotes Vergil's *Catalepton* II for its epigrammatic mockery of affectation: "That great lover of Corinthian words, Britain's Thucydides (who in his madness thinks he's the Attic one), how badly he has ground up his Gallic 'tau,' 'min,' and 'spin' and stirred up all those words into a brew for his brother." De Quincey referred to Jeremy Taylor's style as the "florid or Corinthian order of rhetoric."—"Rhetoric," *Collected Writings*, ed. David Masson (Edinburgh, 1890), X, 106.

255:31. César de Bazancourt (1810–65), author of *L'Expédition de Crimée jusqu'à la prise de Sébastopol* (Paris, 1856).

256:12–16. "Imagination may see the process—may see the light, agile Frenchman coming gaily into the room, content with himself, content with all the world, and charmed at first with the sea-blue depth of the eyes that lightened upon him from under the shadow of the Canning brow, but presently beginning to understand the thin, tight, merciless lips of his host, and then finding himself cowed and pressed down by the majesty and the graciousness of the welcome; for the welcome was such as the great Eltchi would be sure to give to one who (for imperative reasons of State) was to be treated as his honoured guest, but who was also a vain mortal, pretending to the command of the Ottoman army, and daring to come with his plot avowed into the very presence of an English Ambassador" (3rd ed.; II, 33–34). "Lord Raglan's answer was stern. He removed the grounds which the Marshal had assigned for his departure, and then pointed gravely to the true line of duty for the future.... Coming from Lord Raglan, this language was a reproof" (II, 148–49).

257:11–13. "L'investigation, en effet, dans le champ des études historiques comme dans celui de la nature, suppose des précautions dont les hommes du monde, d'ordinaire trop peu en garde contre l'erreur ou la fraude, sont peu capables. Constater un fait n'est pas si facile qu'ils le pensent, et quand les personnes peu au courant des méthodes veulent se former un jugement dans les choses qui sont du domaine des savants de profession, il y a infiniment à parier qu'elles tomberont dans quelque grosse erreur. Mais les spécialités ne sont pas tout: une Académie des sciences, divisée, comme celle de Berlin par exemple, en deux sections, l'une pour les sciences physiques et mathématiques, l'autre pour les sciences historiques et philologiques, est loin de correspondre à l'ensemble de l'esprit humain.—Renan, *Essais de morale et de critique,* pp. 346–47.

257:18. Alexander Chalmers, ed., *The General Biographical Dictionary* (1812–17). 32 vols.

257:19. See pp. 56–64, 159.

[NOTES TO CANCELED PASSAGES]

529:22. "I have been able to stand fast to the tenor of the narrative as given in the first and second editions, . . . by merely inserting a few footnotes, . . . without resorting to the plan of withdrawing any words from the text."—Kinglake, *Crimea,* "Advertisement to the Third Edition," p. iv. See John 19:22: "Pilate answered, What I have written I have written."

[THE FUNCTION OF CRITICISM AT THE PRESENT TIME]

Arnold's decision to collect his *Essays in Criticism* was taken about the time he was revising his Oxford lecture on Academies for *The Cornhill.* After listing for Macmillan the articles he planned to include in the book, he added (August 2, 1864), "Then there will be an introduction of the length of one of the main papers." The entry in his reading list for October, "Renan's Introduction on Criticism" (i.e., the Preface to *Essais de morale et de critique*), shows something of the turn his mind was taking as he wrote it. On October 12 he told Macmillan: "The introduction for this present volume I am now busy with: it will be on criticism—the functions of criticism at the present time. I have promised it to [Walter] Bagehot for his new National and shall also give it as a lecture at Oxford—so the poor creature will be turned to account." —Buckler, *Matthew Arnold's Books,* p. 68. He delivered it from the chair of Poetry on October 29 and published it in *The National Review* for November; he received 21 guineas for the article. The title was changed from "The *Functions*" to "The *Function* of Criticism" when the essays were collected into a book.

Though Arnold in his letters made the distinction between Renan's purpose of inculcating morality and his own of inculcating intelligence, he was entirely at one with him concerning the function of criticism: "En envisageant la critique et le libre développement de l'esprit comme des forces ennemies, les personnes préoccupées d'une manière un peu superficielle du bonheur de l'espèce humaine ne s'aperçoivent pas qu'elles vont directement contre le but qu'elles veulent atteindre. L'extinction de l'esprit critique, en effet, amène nécessairement le béotisme ou la frivolité, qui marquent la fin de toute moralité sérieuse, et amènent plus de maux pour une nation que le libre examen avec ses conséquences légitimes ou supposées."—*Essais de morale et de critique* (Paris, 1889), p. vii. Like Arnold, though with far more reservations about the felicity of the result, Renan regarded the French Revolution as the beginning of an epoch (pp. x–xi), and both were well aware of the spirit of middle-class materialism which it liberated.

Placed at the beginning of Arnold's book, the essay was intended to state the general purpose which the other essays seemed to him to serve; it attracted the principal attention of the reviewers and has been the best-known of his essays ever since. Its keynote, "disinterestedness," which Arnold adopted from Sainte-Beuve, has seemed paradoxical to critics like Professor Geoffrey Tillotson (in his witty and perceptive lecture, "Matthew Arnold: the Critic and the Advocate," *Essays by Divers Hands*, n.s. XX, 29–41 [1943]) and E. K. Brown (see p. 403), and long before either to William Crary Brownell in a superb essay in his *Victorian Prose Masters*: if the "endeavour to learn . . . the best that is known and thought in the world" may indeed be "disinterested," the endeavour to "propagate" it, "and thus to establish a current of fresh and true ideas" requires quite another frame of mind, and in this very essay Arnold uses all the devices of the reformer and propagandist. Perhaps there is a little wilful misunderstanding of Arnold's use of "disinterestedness," especially on Brown's part; as Arnold himself told his mother when the *Saturday Review* replied to this essay in December, 1864: "Indeed, I cannot do what I want without, now and then, a little explosion which fidgets people." Nevertheless, the apparently divided current of the essay has led such very opposed schools as the "Art for art's sake" critics and the social reformers to claim it as an ancestor. What Pater made of Arnold's doctrine is the subject of Geoffrey Tillotson's "Arnold and Pater: Critics Historical, Aesthetic and Unlabelled," in his *Criticism and the Nineteenth Century* (London: Athlone Press, 1951). William A. Madden's "The Divided Tradition of English Criticism," *PMLA*, LXXIII, 69–80 (March, 1958), finds the clue to the critical ideas of Arnold

and his successors in the currents of religious faith of the past hundred years. T. S. Eliot sees the same division as do Brownell, Tillotson, and Brown: "Where Sir Charles Adderley and Mr. Roebuck appear, there is more life than in the more literary criticism. Arnold is in the end, I believe, at his best in satire and in apologetics for literature, in his defence and enunciation of a needed attitude."
—"Arnold and Pater," *Selected Essays* (New York: Harcourt, Brace, 1950), p. 384. Eliot takes Arnold's thesis as the text for one of his early essays, "The Second-Order Mind" (*The Dial*, LXIX, 586–89 [December, 1920]) and uses the title for another of his essays ("The Function of Criticism"); his constant concern with the problem is apparent from the title of his Charles Eliot Norton Lectures at Harvard University in 1932–33: *The Use of Poetry and the Use of Criticism.* F. W. Bateson's essay, "The Function of Criticism at the Present Time," in a journal that also owes its title to Arnold, *Essays in Criticism*, III, 1–27 (January, 1953), surveys mid-twentieth century criticism with more than one plea for Arnold's three chief virtues of intellectual clarity, spiritual integrity, and social conscience.

258:4–16. *On Translating Homer*, Lecture II, last paragraph. Arnold may not have been upon oath in describing the reception of his proposition. Only one reviewer of the Homeric lectures seems to have quoted his sentence, and that with approbation: the author of "Recent Homeric Critics and Translators," *North British Review*, XXXVI, 348 (May, 1862). Arnold had been much pleased with this article, as he told his mother on May 3.

258:17–18. "Wordsworth: the Man and the Poet," *North British Review*, XLI, 1–54 (August, 1864). The article was anonymous, but the author, John Campbell Shairp, had been a friend of Arnold since they were undergraduates together at Balliol. Shairp makes a complimentary reference to Arnold in the essay (p. 32).

259:3–17. Christopher Wordsworth, *Memoirs of William Wordsworth* (London, 1851), II, 53, 439 (letter to Bernard Barton, January 12, 1816, and notes of Lady Richardson, November, 1843).

262:9–17. Arnold's view of the romantic movement reflects a passage from Sainte-Beuve that he copied into one of his "general note-books" under the heading "Second-rate Epochs": "L'inconvénient . . . d'avoir à chercher ces beautés simples ou grandioses en y remontant avec effort, plutôt que de les rencontrer directement et de première venue, . . . devient un des caractères inhérents à toutes les secondes et troisièmes époques; et c'est pour cela que nous ne sommes pas en 1800 à l'aurore d'un grand siècle, mais seulement au début de la plus brillante des périodes de déclin."—*Chateaubriand et son groupe littéraire* (new ed.; Paris, 1889), I, 200; see Arnold, *Note-Books*, ed. Lowry, pp. 458–59.

262:22. *Ibid.*, II, 437–38 (Lady Richardson, August 26, 1841), and II, 478.

264:8–9. "Franzthum drängt in diesen verworrenen Tagen, wie ehmals

Lutherthum es gethan, ruhige Bildung zurück."

—"Vier Jahreszeiten: Herbst," no. 62; *Werke* (Weimar, 1887), I, 354.

264:28–29. Jenny Geddes, on July 23, 1637; see *D.N.B.*

264:32–37. Decimal coinage and the metric system were established in France in 1799–1803. The Decimal Association was formed in London on June 12, 1854. A bill for changing weights and measures to the decimal system passed a second reading in Commons on July 1, 1863, but was later withdrawn. The communication Arnold envisioned had indeed already appeared when he wrote—three columns entitled "The Decimal and Metric Systems in Practice," signed "B," and proclaiming (in answer to the Parliamentary proponents of the decimal system, Ewart and Cobden) that the duodecimal system was more rational, the English system more practical.—*Times*, July 9, 1863, p. 5, cols. 1–3. A long discussion of the problem, all in favor of the English system, appeared in the *Times* of September 15 and 17, 1863, p. 7, cols. 1–4, and p. 6, cols. 1–3.

265:16–17. See *England and the Italian Question*, section IV, end, in Arnold, *Prose Works*, ed. Super, I, 78–79.

265:29–31. Whether Arnold's member of the House of Commons existed in fact or not, the idea had become axiomatic. The *Times*, in a leading article that Arnold certainly read (since it was on John Walter's motion to exempt schools from the requirement of hiring certificated teachers), remarked: "Englishmen are so accustomed to anomaly that they attach a constitutional virtue to it, call it 'English,' and would not for the world see it mended.... But there is a point beyond which our zeal for anomalies must yield to common sense and common justice."—May 6, 1863, p. 9, col. 3.

265:35–37. J. Joubert, *Pensées*, ed. Paul de Raynal (7th ed.; Paris, 1877), II, 178 (Titre xv, no. 2).

266:35–37. Arnold here echoes a letter he wrote in January, 1864, to his sister Mrs. W. E. Forster: "What makes Burke stand out so splendidly among politicians is that he treats politics with his thought and imagination; therefore, whether one agrees with him or not, he always interests you, stimulates you, and does you good. I have been attentively reading lately his *Reflections on the French Revolution*, and have felt this most strongly, much as there is in his view of France and her destinies which is narrow and erroneous. But I advise ... you ... indeed to read something of Burke's every year."

267:4. Richard Price (1723–91), Nonconformist minister whose sermon of November 4, 1789, in praise of the French Revolution stirred Burke to the writing of his *Reflections on the Revolution in France.*

267:10–11. Goldsmith, "Retaliation," line 32.

267:18–29. *Works* (London, 1852), IV, 591 ("Thoughts on French Affairs," concluding paragraph). Burke lived nearly six years longer and continued to write as formerly against the French Revolution. When Arnold called these "some of the last pages [Burke] ever wrote," he may have been misled by his recollection of a passage in a letter Burke wrote to his son in September, 1791, respecting this book—a passage Arnold had copied into one of his "general" note-books: "I shall make one effort more, and that shall be my last. Wisdom and religion dictate that we should follow events, and not attempt to lead, much less to force them."— R. C. Tobias, "On Dating Matthew Arnold's 'General Note-books,'" *Philological Quarterly*, XXXIX, 431–32 (October, 1960); see Arnold, *Note-Books*, ed. Lowry, p. 442.

268:1–2. Numbers 22:38.

268:7–10. William Eden, first Baron Auckland (1744–1814), a warm supporter and close personal friend of Pitt's, was ambassador extraordinary at The Hague throughout 1791–93, the early period of the wars that followed the French Revolution. I do not find precisely the words Arnold quotes. In his pamphlet, *Some Remarks on the Apparent Circumstances of the War in the Fourth Week of October, 1795*, which drew a pained remonstrance from Burke, Auckland says of the French government (pp. 22–23): "One set of miscreants rapidly succeeded another by a sort of hereditary succession, and every new administration murdered its predecessors." In a letter to Lord Loughborough from The Hague, January 6, 1793, he wrote: "The coxcombs of the Assemblée Constituente, who called themselves philosophers and legislators, were bad enough in every point of view. They were irreligious, immoral, mischievous by action, presumptuous and hard-hearted; ... but they were angels in comparison of either of the leading factions of the present Assembly."—*Journal and Correspondence of William, Lord Auckland* (London, 1861), II, 484.

268:11. The πολιτικὸν ζῷον of Aristotle's *Politics* I. i. 9.

269:8–10. The Aesopic fable of the wind and the sun.

270:1. One sees in Arnold's use of the word "disinterestedness" and the concept it represents his principal debt to Sainte-Beuve. "Dégagé de tout rôle et presque de tout lien, observant de près depuis bientôt vingt-cinq ans les choses et les personnages littéraires, n'ayant aucun intérêt à ne pas les voir tels qu'ils sont, je puis dire que je regorge de vérités. J'en dirai au moins quelques-unes. C'est la seule satisfaction de l'écrivain sérieux dans la dernière moitié de la vie."—*Chateaubriand et son groupe*, conclusion of the 1849 Preface (new ed.; Paris, 1889, I, 19). On January 6, 1854, Arnold wrote to Sainte-Beuve: "Depuis la mort de Goethe vous êtes resté, selon moi, le seule guide et la seule espérance de ceux qui aiment surtout la vérité dans les arts et dans la littérature, et qui pourtant désirent trouver une critique vraie, naturelle et sérieuse— une critique possédant à fond la connaissance des choses littéraires et imbue d'un esprit essentiellement philosophique et européen. Pour moi, Monsieur, toutes les fois que le chagrin me prend en regardant la littérature de nos jours—avec ses productions hâtives et à peine ébauchées, avec son peu de savoir, avec son manque total de convenance et de mesure, avec son esprit de secte étroit et inintelligent—je me rejette plus que jamais vers vous; et bien que vous ne parliez en général que de la littérature française, cependant, comme vous regardez toute chose d'un point de vue universel, tout le monde peut toujours trouver de l'instruction en vous lisant."— L. Bonnerot, *Matthew Arnold, Poète* (Paris: Didier, 1947), pp. 518– 19. Arnold quotes in his *Note-Books* for 1864 (p. 29) a sentence from Renan on the duty of a professor in the University: to teach "sans aucune vue d'application immédiate, sans autre but que la culture désintéressée de l'esprit."—"L'Instruction supérieure en France," *Revue des deux mondes*, seconde période, LI, 81 (May 1, 1864). The word "disinterestedness" was also generally used to translate Goethe's *uneigennützigkeit*, the characteristic he found pre-eminent in Spinoza (*Dichtung und Wahrheit*, Book XIV, beginning).

270:21–27. On July 26, 1861, Arnold wrote in the same vein to Sainte-Beuve: "Je me suis convaincu depuis longtemps, que, pour presque tout le monde, la vérité, dans la critique, a quelque chose de fort déplaisant; elle leur paraît ironique et désobligeante; on veut une vérité accommodée aux vues et aux passions des partis et des coteries. Ceci est encore plus vrai en Angleterre qu'en France, où l'amour des choses de l'esprit est plus vif que chez nous, et fait pardonner plus de témérités à un penseur fin et neuf." Sainte-Beuve quoted this letter in an article on "Chateaubriand jugé par un ami intime en 1803" in the *Constitutionnel* of July 21, 1862.—L. Bonnerot, *Matthew Arnold, Poète*, p. 527, and Sainte-Beuve, *Nouveaux lundis* (4th ed.; Paris, 1884), III, 3.

271:10. A liberal Catholic quarterly published in continuation of the earlier monthly *Rambler* from 1862 to 1864 under the editorship of Lord Acton and dissolved by him in the face of threatened censure from the ecclesiastical authorities. Arnold's brother Thomas was a contributor to the *Review*.

272:1–6. Charles Adderley (later Sir Charles and Baron Norton), Conservative M.P. for N. Staffordshire, speaking to the Warwickshire Agricultural Association at Leamington on September 16, 1863; reported in the *Times*, September 17, p. 5, col. 6, and copied by Arnold in his *Note-Books*, ed. Lowry, pp. 21–22.

272:8–13. John Arthur Roebuck, Benthamite M.P. for Sheffield, speaking at a dinner at Cutlers' Hall, Sheffield, on August 18, 1864; reported in the *Times*, August 19, p. 4, cols. 4–5, and subject of a leading article August 20, p. 8, cols. 4–5. See *Note-Books*, ed. Lowry, pp. 25–26.

272:17–18. Goethe, *Iphigenie auf Tauris*, I, ii, 91–92; see *Note-Books*, ed. Lowry, pp. 3, 5.

272:30–33. Liberal and Utilitarian proposals. The Reform Act of 1832 provided a uniform franchise for householders rated at ten pounds or over. In 1860 Palmerston's government introduced a bill (later withdrawn) for a six-pound borough franchise. Church rates were taxes upon the assessed property in the parish, levied by the vestry for the maintenance of the church. The Whigs failed in an attempt to abolish them in 1834; other Church-Rates Abolition Bills were defeated by the Lords in 1858, 1860, and 1867, and only in 1868 did Gladstone succeed in abolishing them. The difficulty of collecting agricultural statistics was the subject of Parliamentary debate on June 7, 1864, and the use of compulsion was repudiated at that time. Almost the whole of Arnold's lifetime saw the gradual diminution of the power of local government, from the Poor Laws Amendment Act of 1834 through loss of highway duties, weakening of local control over the police, and compulsory provision of sanitary inspectors.

273:16–20. Elizabeth Wragg committed this deed on Saturday,

September 10, 1864; "I should never have done it if I had had a home for him," she said. She was found guilty of manslaughter and sentenced to twenty years penal servitude on March 13, 1865; the *Times* reported the trial March 15, p. 12, col. 3. The Mapperley Hills are to the north of the industrial city of Nottingham, the center of English lace and hosiery manufacture.

273:30. These three names, like "Wragg," are of great antiquity: see Henry Harrison, *Surnames of the United Kingdom. A Concise Etymological Dictionary* (London, 1912–18).

274:22. Arnold's letters to Clough show an early interest in the *Bhagavad-Gita;* he speaks of its doctrine of "abandoning practice, and abandoning the fruits of action" on March 4, 1848.—*Letters to Clough,* ed. Lowry, p. 71.

274:27–32. Arnold borrows the terms "adequate" and "inadequate ideas" from Spinoza; see p. 181:26–28.

275:23. John, Lord Somers (1651–1716) presided over the drafting of the Declaration of Rights after the abdication of James II. He was a distinguished statesman and constitutional lawyer.

276:6. For "terrae filius" see Persius vi. 59. "We are all alike *terrae filii*" is one of the closing sentences of a sprightly article entitled "The Few and the Many" (*London Review,* V, 111 [January 31, 1863]), attacking Arnold's doctrine (in "The Bishop and the Philosopher") that "the highly instructed few, and not the scantily instructed many, will ever be the organ to the human race of knowledge and truth." Arnold was himself at that time a contributor to the *London Review.*

276:12–15. Arnold here alludes to criticisms of his remarks on Colenso, which he discusses more specifically below.

276:23–24. *Wilhelm Meisters Lehrjahre,* Book VII, Chapter IX, "Lehrbrief."—*Werke* (Weimar, 1901), XXIII, 124 ("Handeln ist leicht, Denken schwer; nach dem Gedanken handeln unbequem.")

276:29. Senancour, *Obermann,* Letter XC, ninth paragraph.

276:35, 277:31–33. "The Bishop and the Philosopher" and "Dr. Stanley's Lectures," pp. 40–55, 65–82; see especially p. 74:16–18.

277:13–14. *Pensées,* ed. Raynal, II, 311 (Titre xxiii, no. 54); quoted also on p. 201:33–34.

277:14–16. See, for example, the reviews and correspondence in *Popular Opinion* late in 1862 (described in note to p. 76:9–10, 13).

277:26. The rather short-lived *Church and State Review,* edited "Pro Ecclesia Dei" by Archdeacon George Anthony Denison, was founded in June, 1862, partly to counteract the venom of *Essays and Reviews.* It was an implacable enemy of Stanley's, and in one number attacked his *Jewish Church* and Colenso's *Pentateuch* in consecutive articles (April 1, 1863). It returned to the attack on the former a month later: "This is the poison which is now permitted to be distilled from the chair of Ecclesiastical History at Oxford into the ears of ardent and impulsive young men" (II, 210).

277:29. See p. 48:23–26, dealing with Colenso, *Pentateuch*, Part I, Chapter XX, 156.

277:36–37. [Fitzjames Stephen], "Mr. Matthew Arnold and His Countrymen," *Saturday Review*, XVIII, 685 (December 3, 1864).

278:5–15. Frances Power Cobbe, *Broken Lights: an Inquiry into the Present Condition and Future Prospects of Religious Faith* (London, 1864). Appendix I of Part I (pp. 101–15) is devoted to Colenso, Appendix II (pp. 115–36) to Renan. The phrases Arnold quotes appear on pp. 116 and 104.

278:33–34. Claude Fleury, *Histoire ecclésiastique* (Paris, 1722), I, [xxii] (Preface); see Arnold, *Note-Books*, ed. Lowry, p. 22.

278:35–38. *Études d'histoire religieuse* (7th ed.; Paris, 1880), pp. 199–200 (in a review of "Les Historiens critiques de Jésus"). Renan's *Vie de Jésus* was the fruit of a subsequent visit to the Holy Land in 1860–61.

279:6–7. *Ad Atticum* XVI. vii. 3.

279:10. *Confessions of an Inquiring Spirit*, end of Letter I and beginning of Letter II: "In the Bible there is more that *finds* me than I have experienced in all other books put together."

279:14. See Joubert, *Pensées*, II, 365 (Titre xxiv, § iv, 25): "Voltaire aurait lu avec patience trente ou quarante volumes in-folio pour y trouver une petite plaisanterie irréligieuse. C'était là sa passion, son ambition, sa manie."

279:27. *Religious Duty* (London, 1864) had as its "vast Object" "the development of Theism as a Religion for Life no less than a Philosophy for the Intellect" (p. v).

279:33. Founded by James Morison (1770–1840), self-styled "the Hygeist," in 1828 for the dispensing of his vegetable pills. The College was in Hamilton Place, New Road—the modern King's Cross Road at the end near Pentonville Road. "Morison's Pill" gives its name to a chapter in Carlyle's *Past and Present* (I, iv).

281:4. The Court for Divorce and Matrimonial Causes was established by the Divorce Law of 1857. Arnold's reading list for October, 1864 (*Note-Books*, ed. Lowry, p. 575), included an article on "The Laws of Marriage and Divorce," *Westminster Review*, LXXXII, 442–69 (October, 1864). As this article points out (and as many a report in the journals of the day bears witness), "Contemplating the process [of divorce] in the mistaken light of a vindictive means of redress, [the law] requires the dismissal of a petition where the petitioner has connived at or condoned the guilt of the respondent, and it permits, on the same principle, counterallegations of delinquency or recrimination."

281:20. Grace, for Luther, is the "free, unmerited favour of God to sinners, in opening His fatherly heart to them in the forgiving love of Christ.... 'The soul, through faith alone, without works, is, from the Word of God, justified, sanctified, endued with truth, peace, and liberty, and filled full with every good thing, and is truly made the child of God.' "—R. H. Coats in *Encyclopaedia of Religion and Ethics*, XI, s.v. "Sanctification," quoting Luther "On Christian Liberty."

281:21. Jacques-Bénigne Bossuet (1627–1704), in his *Discourse on Universal History* (1681) conceives of all human affairs as expressing the purpose of God regarding humanity; the idea of Providence is the law of history. An article entitled "Bossuet's Education of the Dauphin," *Saturday Review*, XVIII, 272–74 (August 27, 1864), may well have suggested this allusion to Arnold.

281:23. Charles Thomas Baring (1807–79), a strong evangelical.

281:24. Pius IX, Pope 1846–78, re-established a Roman Catholic hierarchy in England in 1850 and in 1869 was to convoke the Vatican Council that made papal infallibility a dogma of the Church (1870).

282:20. Vergil *Eclogues* iv. 5.

284:19–23. "La culture intellectuelle de l'Europe est un vaste échange où chacun donne et reçoit à son tour, où l'écolier d'hier devient le maître d'aujourd'hui. C'est un arbre où chaque branche participe à la vie des autres, où les seuls rameaux inféconds sont ceux qui s'isolent et se privent de la communion avec le tout."— E. Renan, "L'Instruction supérieure en France," *Revue des deux mondes*, seconde période, LI, 95 (May 1, 1864).

285:19–21. Like Moses: Deuteronomy 32:48–52; 34:1–6.

[NOTES TO CANCELED PASSAGES]

530:39–531:3, 27–29. [Fitzjames Stephen,] "Mr. Matthew Arnold and His Countrymen," *Saturday Review* XVIII, 685 (the former passage somewhat unfairly misrepresented).

531:29. Alexander Bain (1818–1903), professor of logic and English in Aberdeen University from 1860, was a follower of Hobbes,

Locke, and James Mill in psychology, a materialist in his philosophy, and utilitarian in his ethics.

533:38–534:2. [Fitzjames Stephen,] "Mr. Matthew Arnold and His Countrymen," p. 685.

534:36. Milton, "On the Morning of Christ's Nativity," line 199.

[PREFACE TO "ESSAYS IN CRITICISM"]

With the introductory essay on "The Functions of Criticism" completed, Arnold turned to his Preface, which proved more troublesome to him than he had expected. Proofs of the book were nearly finished and sheets nearly all printed by January 21, 1865, but still Arnold had not got his Preface as he wanted it. It turned out to be a brilliant piece of topical satire, for the explanation of which one must turn frequently to the newspapers that were appearing as he wrote—the *Saturday Review* and the *Examiner* for December 3, 1864, for example. As the *Pall Mall Gazette* remarked, it added a *Dunciad* to Arnold's *Essay on Criticism*. "[It] will make you laugh," he told his mother.

Renan's Preface to *Essais de morale et de critique*, while not Arnold's model, was clearly in his mind as he wrote, with its description of the many shapes of truth at the beginning and the eloquent tribute to his native Brittany at the end (like Arnold's praise of Oxford), and with this defense of his writing a Preface at all: "J'ai cru ces observations nécessaires afin d'expliquer pourquoi je me suis interdit de répondre ici à des critiques qui ont été adressées à mes précédentes études. Ce n'est point là l'effet du dédain; c'est la conséquence de cette idée, fort arrêtée chez moi, que chacun se fait une foi selon sa mesure. Défendre un dogme, c'est prouver qu'on y tient et par conséquent qu'on en a besoin. La vivacité de ces attaques m'a même parfois inspiré de l'estime pour ceux qui en étaient les auteurs, et j'ai songé avec plaisir qu'elles détourneraient de me lire ceux pour qui une telle lecture serait en effet mauvaise."—1889 ed., p. viii.

Neither the public nor the private reception of the Preface was indifferent. Arnold's mother did not laugh, nor did his sister Frances; he began to suspect that no members of his own family, "from their training and their habits of thinking and feeling," would find it to their taste, not even Mrs. Forster, the closest of all to him. On the other hand, Lady de Rothschild and J. D. Coleridge were greatly taken with it—"but then they again were just the people to be taken with it." The *Examiner* found it bright and effervescent, better than a glass of champagne; the *London Review*, to which Arnold occasionally contributed, thought it a pity he ever wrote "such a piece of idle and incoherent chatter." *The North British Review*, in a serious and significant discussion of the book (XLII, 158–82 [March, 1865]) objected to the "vivacities"— "but then it is a Scotchman who writes," Arnold told his mother.* "The best justification of the Preface is the altered tone of the *Saturday*." The Scotchman prevailed: after two weeks' reflection upon the matter, Arnold surrendered. "Perhaps I shall leave out some of the lighter parts of the preface and notes, if the book comes to a second edition; for the Essays are of too grave a character to tack much matter of an ephemeral kind permanently to them: but, meanwhile, I am convinced the preface has produced a good effect on the whole."

286:3–6. "From anything like a direct answer, or direct controversy, I shall religiously abstain," Arnold told his mother on December 7, 1864; "but here and there I shall take an opportunity of putting back this and that matter into its true light, if I think [Fitzjames Stephen] has pulled them out of it."

286:7. "Like his French models, Mr. Arnold has quick sympathies and a great gift of making telling remarks; but, also like them, he has hardly any power of argument. At least, if he has, he rarely shows it."—[Fitzjames Stephen,] "Mr. Matthew Arnold and His Countrymen," *Saturday Review*, XVIII, 683 (December 3, 1864).

286:9–14. "Des voiles impénétrables nous dérobent le secret de ce monde étrange dont la réalité à la fois s'impose à nous et nous accable; la philosophie et la science poursuivront à jamais, sans jamais l'atteindre, la formule de ce Protée qu'aucune raison ne limite, qu'aucun langage n'exprime."—Renan, "Préface," *Essais de morale et de critique*, pp. i–ii.

286:20–22. *A Letter to the Dean of Canterbury* [Henry Alford] *on the Homeric Lectures of Matthew Arnold, Esq.* (London, 1864).

286:28–29. "This redoubted opponent... has declared with so much solemnity, that there is not 'any proper reason for my existing'" (p. 6).

287:2–7. *On Translating Homer*, Lecture I: Arnold, *Prose Works*, ed. Super, I, 103.

287:10. "You see before you, gentlemen, what you have often

* Professor W. E. Houghton, using the editor's list of contributors, identifies the author of the review as Henry Hill Lancaster.

heard of, *an unpopular author,*" Arnold told the income tax commissioners late in 1870, and they reduced the assessment of his royalties from £1000 a year to £200.—*Letters,* ed. Russell, II, 47 (December 4, 1870).

287:22. Professor S. M. B. Coulling has traced Arnold's skirmishes with the young lions in "Matthew Arnold and the *Daily Telegraph,*" *Review of English Studies,* XII, n.s., 173–79 (May, 1961).

287:29–31. Wright, pp. 6, 12.

288:4–5. John Henry Pepper (1821–1900), John Henry Anderson (1814–74), and Wiljalba Frikell (1818–1903) were thaumaturgists and prestidigitators who in 1865 were or had recently been performing in London. See H. R. Evans, *The Old and the New Magic* (Chicago, 1906). It was the custom of the trade for these gentlemen to call themselves "Professor," a title Arnold disliked: "The article in the *Westminister* ... contains so much praise that you must have thought I wrote it myself, except that I should hardly have called myself by the hideous title of 'Professor.' "—Arnold to Lady de Rothschild, October 13, 1863.

288:22–26. "Once get [the English nation] well convinced of the truth of a general principle, ... and it will do anything. For instance, the English nation believes in political economy, and the consequence is that it is the only nation in the world which has established free trade.... Bentham persuaded the English nation that the greatest happiness of the greatest number was the true rule for legislation, and every part of the law has been reformed by degrees by the application, more or less skilful and complete, of that abstract principle."—[Fitzjames Stephen,] "Mr. Matthew Arnold and His Countrymen," *Saturday Review,* XVIII, 684 (December 3, 1864).

288:31. Arnold and his family spent the summer of 1864 at The Rectory, Woodford, Essex. The Great Eastern Railway from Woodford joined the North London Railway near the spot where the murder (below) was committed, and proceeded to the same terminus in Fenchurch Street.

288:31–33. On July 9, 1864, Franz Müller murdered and robbed Thomas Briggs in a first-class railway carriage on a train traveling between Bow Station and Hackney Wick on the North London Railway, threw the body from the train, and made good his escape at the next stop before the fact of the murder was discovered by a boarding passenger's laying his hand "on a cushion steeped in gore." By the time the identity of the murderer was established, he was aboard ship and sailing for America. After extradition he was tried and hanged. The *Saturday Review* on July 16 (p. 72) had a leading article entitled "Railway Imprisonment" that pointed out the impossibility of emergency communication with the outside world once the compartment door was closed.

289:2–3. "Mr. Arnold's whole essay ['The Functions of Criticism at the Present Time'] assumes the truth of the transcendental theory of philosophy."—[Fitzjames Stephen,] "Mr. Arnold and His Countrymen," p. 684.

289:6–8. Plutarch *Life of Caesar* lvii. 4; Velleius Paterculus *Roman History* ii.57.

289:28. See note to p. 173:21.

289:29–30. The St. Marylebone Vestry was the popularly elected governing body of the Parish (now Borough) of St. Marylebone, in Arnold's day decidedly bourgeois in composition and one of the most outspoken of the local governing bodies in London.

289:31–32. The skeleton of Jeremy Bentham, surmounted with a waxen head, is preserved, clad in his clothes, at University College, London; the mummified head is also there, separated from the skeleton.

290:4. "*There* were his young barbarians all at play."—Byron, *Childe Harold's Pilgrimage*, IV, cxli, 5.

290:11. The Tübingen school of theology, headed by Ferdinand Christian Baur and for a time the seat of David Friedrich Strauss, was, to the English, "terrible for its powerful scientific development of Rationalism.... The great aim of [its] critical labours [has been] ... to explain the natural origin not merely of the Gospels (the special task of Strauss), but of the Christian Scriptures as a whole."—"Tübingen in 1864," *Macmillan's Magazine*, X, 433, 441 (October, 1864).

290:21–22. See p. 235:28–29.

[NOTES TO CANCELED PASSAGES]

535:31–32. "In fact, no nation in the world is so logical as the English nation."—[Fitzjames Stephen,] "Mr. Arnold and His Countrymen," p. 684.

536:17–27. Wright's *Letter* is headed "Mapperley Hall, Nottingham, 1864." Arnold quotes pp. 12 ("condemned ... umpire"), 16 ("rebutted" and "extinguisher ... upon me"), 14 ("condemned ... myself" and "somewhat crestfallen"); the parodies are on pp. 7 and 15. Tennyson's epigram, "Translations of Homer" (of which Arnold quotes line 4), was published in *The Cornhill Magazine*, VIII, 707 (December, 1863), along with Tennyson's own attempt at a few lines of Homer in blank verse prefaced by this note: "Some, and among these one at least of our best and greatest, have endeavoured to give us the *Iliad* in English hexameters, and by what appears to me their failure, have gone far to prove the impossibility of the task. I have long held by our blank verse in this matter, and now after having spoken so disrespectfully here of these hexameters, I . . . feel bound to subjoin a specimen . . . of a blank-verse translation." Arnold was somewhat disingenuous to protest his ignorance that the line was aimed at himself, since he had supposed the prose compliment was for him. "Tennyson's allusion was meant for me," he told his mother when the *Cornhill* verses first appeared (December 29, 1863); "the only compliment of the kind he has ever paid—and Palgrave says he always declares there is no one whose judgment he values so much." Hallam Tennyson, however, believed the words "best and greatest" referred to Sir John Herschel. See R. H. Super, "Matthew Arnold and Tennyson," *Times Literary Supplement*, October 28, 1960, p. 693.

536:34–35. See p. 273:16–20. The *Saturday Review* carried on the skirmish with Arnold by replying to his Preface in "Mr. Matthew Arnold amongst the Philistines," XIX, 235–36 (February 25, 1865), in which article it answered his question: "She is still in custody in Nottingham Gaol, and will be tried at the assizes to be held there sometime between the 9th and 13th of next month."

537:1. The *Guardian* was an Anglican weekly newspaper, owned by W. E. Gladstone and frequently contributed to by Arnold's friend Coleridge. Professor S. M. B. Coulling points out that the *Guardian* on May 13, 1863, had rebuked Arnold for his ridicule of Francis Newman in the lectures on Homer.—"Matthew Arnold and the *Daily Telegraph*," *Review of English Studies*, XII, n.s., 173 (May, 1961).

537:12. "Presbyter Anglicanus" was the pseudonym of Joseph Hemington Harris, author of several books on theological questions of the day and of frequent letters to the editor of the *Examiner*. Disraeli, speaking in the Sheldonian Theatre at a meeting in aid of the Oxford Diocesan Society on November 25, 1864, disparaged the liberal party of the church and made fun of its leaders; the remark quoted by Arnold was, according to the *Times* (November 26, p. 8, col. 2), received with "much laughter" and "continued laughter." F. D. Maurice, leader of the liberals, from the time he was forced to resign his professorship of theology at King's College, London, in

1853, was identified with the theological doctrine that caused his dismissal: that the popular belief in the endlessness of future punishment was superstitious, not sanctioned by the strictest interpretation of the Articles. "Presbyter Anglicanus," in a long letter on "Mr. Disraeli at Oxford," *Examiner*, December 3, 1864, pp. 772–73, used the language Arnold quotes. In a later reply to Arnold's remarks here, "Presbyter Anglicanus" denied that he had written on the subject "in half a dozen of the daily newspapers," denied that he failed to see Disraeli's joke, but repeated that he thought the joke contemptible.—"The Philistines of the Nineteenth Century," *Examiner*, March 11, 1865, pp. 147–48. It was not "Presbyter Anglicanus" but "Anti-Esotericus" who wrote against Arnold's Colenso paper in the *Examiner* two years earlier, though "Presbyter Anglicanus" did write on Colenso's side in the matter of the hare's stomach (April 11, 1863, p. 228). [Disraeli's speech at Oxford is best known for his famous pronouncement upon the theory of evolution: "The question is, is man an ape or an angel? Now, I am on the side of the angels."]

537:40–41. Wordsworth's sonnet "1801" ("I grieved for Buonaparté"); Wordsworth wrote "tenderest mood."

538:9. The *Saturday Review* pointed out that though Arnold insisted on Criticism's keeping aloof from the practical, he himself "constantly objects to practical measures on theoretical grounds. . . . By his own rule he cannot inquire into, and has no right to notice, the hideousness of the Divorce Court. . . . When Mr. Arnold has got a theory which will fully explain all the duties of the legislator on the matter of marriage, he will have a right to abuse the Divorce Court."—XVIII, 685. See pp. 533:38–534:37.

538:13. The Palatine Library in Heidelberg was the richest in Europe at the end of the sixteenth century. Its more than 3500 manuscripts were transferred to the Vatican during the Thirty Years' War, and there most of them remain.

538:14. See note to p. 279:33.

538:15–16. Dagon was the god of the Philistines (Judges 16:23; I Samuel 5:2–7). The Caabah is "the sacred edifice at Mecca, which contains the venerated 'Black Stone,' and is the 'Holy of Holies' of Islam."—*N.E.D.* The Palladium was the image of the goddess Pallas in the citadel of Troy, upon which the safety of the city depended.

538:17. The hare is named in the dietary laws of Leviticus 11:6 as an animal that chews its cud; Colenso, by way of controverting the doctrine of the scientific trustworthiness of the Scriptures, quoted in a letter to the *Times* of April 2, 1863 (p. 10, col. 6), Professor

Richard Owen's statement that "the hare does *not* chew the cud; it has *not* the stomach of a ruminant animal."

538:18. Goliath was the great champion of the Philistines (I Samuel 17). Swinburne picked up this allusion to coin a memorable epigram: "From the son of his father and the pupil of his teacher [Wordsworth] none would have looked for such efficient assault and battery of the Philistine outworks; none but those who can appreciate the certain and natural force, in a strong and well-tempered spirit, of loyal and unconscious reaction.... A profane alien in my hearing once defined [Matthew Arnold] as 'David, the son of Goliath.' "—"Mr. Arnold's New Poems," *Fortnightly Review*, VIII, 425 (October, 1867).

538:20. James Clay, M.P., addressed his constituents in Hull early in November, 1864, on the subject of English middle-class education; his thesis was that far too much attention was given to Latin and Greek, for which he would substitute the study of science and other modern disciplines. See note to p. 538:31. Clay was best known as an authority on whist. For Arnold's more serious use of "intellectual deliverance," see *Prose Works*, ed. Super, I, 19.

538:28–30. "Let me remind you ... that in the study of Greek and Latin we are not following classical examples. Words could not express the indignation with which an ancient Greek would have received a request that he would learn Persian, and the Greek language does not contain a word equivalent in sense to our word 'grammar.' Yet these people carried human intelligence further than any people who ever lived! They were educated to understand things about them, and allowing other countries to speak their own language they classed them all with sovereign contempt under the name of barbarians."—Robert Lowe at the distribution of certificates for the Oxford Local Examinations, Nottingham, October 28, 1864; reported in the *Times* next day, p. 5, col. 5. In the same speech (col. 4) Lowe argued against the recommendations of Arnold's *A French Eton*.

538:31. Professor Fraser Neiman has pointed out the sentence in Clay's speech at Hull (note to p. 538:20): "I confess, though I am no follower of Mr. Spurgeon, that there is something about him, in the rapid and natural movements of his thoughts, and the practical fervour of his address, which reminds me of Demosthenes."—"Mr. Clay on the Classics," *Saturday Review*, XVIII, 593 (November 12, 1864). The article ridicules Clay brutally. For Spurgeon, see p. 213:2.

538:33. Jeremiah Joyce, *Scientific Dialogues: Intended for the In-*

struction and Entertainment of Young People; in Which the First Principles of Natural and Experimental Philosophy Are Fully Explained, first published in 1807 and current through revised editions for more than sixty years. The most recent revision had been by Professor Pepper (1861).

538:34. "Old Humphrey" was the pseudonym of George Mogridge (1787–1854), author of nearly two hundred works, "principally tales and religious books for children, religious tracts, and ballads."—*D.N.B.* There was a revival of publication of his works by the Religious Tract Society in the late 1860's; in the United States they were published by the American Sunday-School Union.

538:34. *Deontology; or the Science of Morality. In Which the Harmony and Coincidence of Duty and Self-Interest, Virtue and Felicity, Prudence and Benevolence Are Explained* was put together from Bentham's notes and published after his death by Sir John Bowring (2 vols.; London, 1834).

538:35. Dickens' *Little Dorrit*, an attack on imprisonment for debt and on administrative confusion in government, was issued in parts from December, 1855, to June, 1857.

538:35. Miss Richmal Mangnall's *Historical and Miscellaneous Questions for the Use of Young People*, a sort of popular instructor by the catechetical method, was published in 1800 and went through countless editions and adaptations for two-thirds of a century.

538:35. *The Wide, Wide World* was the first novel of Susan Bogert Warner (1819–85), "New York author of juvenile novels, distinguished by sentimental piety, who wrote under the pseudonym Elizabeth Wetherell. [It] recounts the moral development of a young orphan."—*Oxford Companion to American Literature.* The British Museum Catalogue lists eight London editions in 1852–53.

538:36. For Henry Ward Beecher, see *A French Eton*, Part III: Arnold, *Prose Works*, ed. Super, II, 319. English editions of his sermons were published in 1860 and 1864.

538:39. It was Inspector Richard Tanner who crossed the Atlantic to bring back Müller, the Bow murderer.

539:8–9. "All [metres] have had their partisans, even to that 'pestilent heresy' of the so-called English Hexameter; a metre wholly repugnant to the genius of our language; which can only be pressed into service by a violation of every rule of prosody; and of which, notwithstanding my respect for the eminent men who have attempted to naturalize it, I could never read ten lines without being irresistibly reminded of Canning's 'Dactylics call'st thou them? God help thee, silly one!' "—*The Iliad of Homer Rendered into English Blank Verse,* by Edward Earl of Derby (London, 1864), I, vi–vii. The fourteenth Earl of Derby succeeded Wellington as chancellor of the University of Oxford in 1852. "Lord Derby's Homer [is] a very creditable performance, I think, but where is the soul of poetry in it?" Arnold wrote to his mother on December 20, 1864.

539:13. Pepper's principal illusion was a ghost produced by an effect of lighting.

539:20. Arnold "is so warm upon this subject [of the English inferiority to the French in intellectual and artistic matters] that he has taught himself to write a dialect as like French as pure English can be. Indeed, it is a painful duty to admit that his turn for French is so strong that the undefiled well is sometimes very near defilement."—[Fitzjames Stephen,] "Mr. Arnold and His Countrymen," p. 683.

539:22–24. Charles Haddon Spurgeon's sermon on "Baptismal Regeneration" (1864) brought a reply from William Goode, dean of Ripon, and nearly sixty other pamphleteering critics in the same year; the sermon was deliberately provocative toward the Evangelical party in the Church of England, of which Goode was the recognized champion. Spurgeon might well use the Old Testament phrase, "Thus saith the Lord," to introduce Christ's words: "I say unto you, That ye resist not evil: but whosoever shall smite thee on thy right cheek, turn to him the other also" (Matthew 5:39); but he was by temper very unlikely to heed that admonition.

[ON THE STUDY OF CELTIC LITERATURE]

Arnold's journey to France in 1859 had a by-product less striking, but perhaps only less important than his meeting with the principal academicians; his journey into Brittany to visit the schools there seems to have reminded him not only that he was, on his mother's side, pure Cornish, but that the Cornish were part of a race with many ramifications. "I could not but think of you in Brittany," he told his mother on May 8, 1859, "with Cranics and Trevenecs all about me, and the peasantry with their expressive, rather mournful faces, long noses, and dark eyes, reminding me perpetually of dear Tom [his brother] and Uncle Trevenen, and utterly unlike the French. And I had the climate of England, gray skies and cool air, and the gray rock of the north too, and the clear rushing water." When, therefore, he wrote to his sister at the end of the year that he had five of his Oxford lectures "entirely taken shape in my head, and which I hope to publish at the end of 1860," this conception was not unrelated to his discussion of Renan's *Essais* in the same letter. "I have read few things for a long time with more pleasure than [his] 'Sur la poésie des races celtiques.' I have long felt that we owed far more, spiritually and artistically, to the Celtic races than the somewhat coarse Germanic intelligence readily perceived, and been increasingly satisfied at our own semi-Celtic origin, which, as I fancy, gives us the power, if we will use it, of comprehending the nature of both races. Renan pushes the glorification of the Celts too far; but there is a great deal of truth in what he says, and being on the same ground in my next lecture, in which I have to examine the origin of what is called the 'romantic' sentiment about women, which the Germans quite falsely are fond of giving themselves the credit of originating, I read him with the more interest." We know nothing more of this next lecture, which he delivered on May 19, 1860, as part of his "introductory course ... upon the Modern Element in Literature." Then the Homeric problem intruded itself rather unexpectedly, so that it was not until June 8, 1861, that he resumed his series on "The Modern Element in Literature" with "The Claim of the Celtic Race, and the Claim of the Christian Religion, to Have Originated Chivalrous Sentiment." And then, for a time, the matter dropped.

In the summer of 1864, however, Arnold was somewhat restlessly making the daily journey to London from the Essex town of Woodford, where he had established his household for a season in the country, when he was invited to give the *viva voce* part of the India Examinations in English literature and history; tedious as it was, the week's work brought him £35, with which he instantly determined to give himself and his family a real holiday. "To Llandudno I think we shall go," he wrote to his mother on July 22. "I ... long —quite long—for Wales—that is a country which has always touched my imagination—and I have been there from time to time, at long intervals, and have recollections connected with it." Less than a fortnight later he was in Llandudno, and tramping about the countryside or making rail excursions with his brother Thomas, or with his wife and children, guidebook in hand. "The charm of Wales is the extent of the country, which gives you untouched masses which the tourists do not reach; and then the new race, language, and literature give it a charm and novelty which the Lake country can never have. Wales is as full of traditions and associations as Cumberland and Westmorland are devoid of them." "The poetry of the Celtic race and its names of places quite overpowers me, and it will be long before Tom forgets the line, 'Hear from thy grave, great Taliessin, hear!'—from Gray's Bard, of which I gave him the benefit some hundred times a day on our excursions. . . . All interests are here—Celts, Romans, Saxons, Druidism, Middle Age, Caer, Castle, Cromlech, Abbey,—and this glorious sea and mountains with it all." From Llandudno he went to Fox How, and then made an expedition to the Highlands: "I have a great *penchant* for the Celtic races, with their melancholy and unprogressiveness."

His stay at Llandudno coincided with the Eisteddfod held there that year; though his letters do not allude to the event it became for a moment the focal point of his interest in the Welsh, and by October 12 he had resolved to write upon it. On November 7 he proposed an article on Eisteddfodau to the publisher of *The Cornhill Magazine* for his Christmas number—"a mixture of description and reflexion—[in part from personal observation]—I think I could make it readable. Not above 12 pages."—Buckler, *Matthew Arnold's Books*, p. 92. A month later he could only promise it "in excellent time" for the February number—"Let me say Monday the 9th of January . . . , and I will not fail you." But we hear no more of the "Eisteddfod paper," at least in its original conception.

Two things intervened: his appointment to go abroad for the Schools Inquiry Commission and his increasing awareness of the difficulties of his subject. He decided to lecture upon Celtic literature at Oxford in March. "I hate all over-preponderance of single elements, and all my efforts are directed to enlarge and complete us by bringing in as much as possible of Greek, Latin, Celtic culture. More and more I see hopes of fruit by steadily working in this direction," he told his mother on January 21, 1865, while he was still oppressed by the task of completing his Preface to *Essays in Criticism*. About three weeks later he proposed to the publisher of *The Cornhill* that he send him the lecture about March 10, so that he could read it to his audience from proofs rather than manuscript.—Buckler, *Matthew Arnold's Books*, p. 81. "My lecture is coming near, and the mass I have been led into reading for it oppresses me and still keeps swelling," he told his mother on March 3. "However tomorrow I hope to fairly begin and write." He took to getting up at half past six in the morning to work on it. But a curious fate intervened: the day he had fixed for his lecture was "the day of the United University Sports, and all Oxford will have gone to Cambridge to see them." And so the lecture had to be postponed until after his continental tour. A momentary thought of coming back from Paris to deliver it in the summer term came to nothing, since he was unable to write it abroad.

He returned to England on the last day of October. A month earlier he had learned that he was to be fined for falling behind in the delivery of his Oxford lectures (a threat that seems not to have been carried out), and so he contracted to do two lectures on successive days in December (6th and 7th), naming as his subject "The Study of Celtic Literature." He was hard at work on them by November 25, somewhat anxious because a two-day interruption made him "a little [lose] the exact clue I was following" and because "my subject is one on which controversies are so hot that one has to be careful." On December 4 he told his mother that the two lectures were finished, "and I have all the materials for the third which I shall give next term. So congratulate me." He was less pleased when he set to work on the next lecture early in February, and still less when he completed it on February 23: "I . . . am not satisfied with it, and feel bilious and good for nothing. Happily it is often the case that what I am dissatisfied with at the time of writing, turns out afterwards to be better than I expected; and when one has to treat a subtle matter such as I have been treating now, the marks of a Celtic leaven subsisting in the English spirit and its productions, it is very difficult to satisfy oneself. However, I shall see how it looks to-morrow." He was in fact so dissatisfied with it that it may have undergone considerable revision between delivery at Oxford and publication. Only the first lecture, he feared, would have "much that is light and popularly readable in it"; the second he thought "might be too much sheer disquisition for the *Cornhill* readers."

The "third and last lecture" on February 24, 1866, still did not complete what he had to say on the subject, and so there was a fourth, called "The Celtic Element in English Poetry," delivered on May 26. "It is the best of the four, I think, and the most interesting." The Principal (Charles Williams) of Jesus College, Oxford's Welsh foundation, attended, "brought a flock of younger Celts to hear my lectures," and—beyond the compliment of his mere presence—said audibly after the last one was concluded (quoting *Paradise Lost*), "The Angel ended . . ." One of his flock was John Rhys, who was to be the first incumbent of the chair of Celtic literature when it was established at Jesus College in 1877.

Meanwhile, *The Cornhill* was bringing the lectures out as part of Arnold's scheme to give "for one year at least, an article of literary criticism to each number, . . . a sort of series" (a scheme that never went beyond these four, and the satiric article "My Country-

men"); they appeared in March, April, May, and July, and brought
Arnold £91. 5s. They were reprinted in New York in *The Eclectic
Magazine* for June, August, September, and October. Plans for publication as a book were made by the middle of September, when Arnold told Lady de Rothschild that he would write a preface in
reply to the "inhuman attacks" of the *Times* and the *Daily Telegraph*. Lord Strangford, a friend of Arnold's and a linguistic scholar
of distinction who had reviewed the first *Cornhill* article (*Pall Mall
Gazette*, March 19, 1866), offered "to suggest one or two alterations
on points of etymology—points where I have no doubt I am fearfully shaky" (Arnold told the publisher); these he received about
March 1, 1867, and resolved to include in the book, arranged as
notes.—Buckler, *Matthew Arnold's Books*, pp. 82–83. As so often
happened, his preface gave him trouble; the rest of the book was in
type long before the end of April, but the Introduction was not
done until the middle of May. It shows its kinship with the lecture
on "Culture and Its Enemies," on which he was working at the
same time. The book was published on June 4 (according to the
Times advertisement) at 8s. 6d; it was, Arnold thought (with some
justice), a beautiful book: "I cannot tell you how much I like it."
He hoped it would pay its way (the publishers brought it out at
their own risk), though he did not look for any profit: "As George
Smith well said to me, it is hardly the sort of book a British
parent buys at a railway bookstall for his Jemima." It did not
reach a second edition in England during Arnold's lifetime, though
it was somewhat fortuitously linked with the lectures on Homer
as volume II of Macmillan's uniform edition of Arnold's works for
the American market in 1883.

  Whatever the influence of Renan on Arnold's first (unpublished)
lecture or lectures at Oxford about Celtic matters—and the suggestion of their subject is that the influence was great*—his published
lectures, after several years of reflection, go far beyond Renan's
essay. Renan, himself a Breton, begins with a nostalgic description
of his country, points to the reduced remnant of the once great
Celtic race, and pays lip service to what he calls the "scientific"
study of the Celtic literatures, by which he means the *Myvyrian
Archaiology of Wales*, Lady Charlotte Guest's *Mabinogion*, and the

---

* They seem to derive from a thesis of Renan's: "Comparez Genièvre
et Iseult à ces furies scandinaves de Gudruna et de Chrimhilde, et vous
avouerez que la femme telle que l'a conçue la chevalerie,—cet idéal de
douceur et de beauté posé comme but suprême de la vie,—n'est une
création ni classique, ni chrétienne, ni germanique, mais bien réellement
celtique."—*Essais*, p. 385.

writings of La Villemarqué. After a sentimental characterization of the Celtic race, in which he is far from a scientific basis, Renan turns to an appreciative criticism of the *Mabinogion,* long passages of which he translates (and Arnold quotes at length some of these same passages). This leads him to some observations on the Celtic feeling for nature, a prolonged discussion of the influence of the Arthurian chivalric ideal upon European poetry, and some remarks on the revolution in the feeling of the marvelous brought about by the impact of the Celtic. He then turns to La Villemarqué, explains his theory of the Celtic origin even of those elements of the Arthurian legend that have no clear counterpart in the Welsh books, and writes admiringly of his *Songs of the Breton People* and his *Breton Bards of the Sixth Century,* a century in which the history of the Celts seemed to Renan almost as certainly known to us as the history of the Greeks and Romans. "In this case, by a rare exception, the skeptical view turns out to be quite wrong" (p. 428). Finally, he deals with the peculiar nature of Celtic Christianity and its literature. The statement has been too often made that Arnold merely served up Renan somewhat warmed over: this summary of Renan's essay will at least make clear how wrong such a notion is. None the less, Arnold acknowledged what debts he did owe to Renan, and when his book was printed he sent Renan a copy; the note of acknowledgment in mid-December gave him great pleasure. One further debt to Renan disappeared when the articles were revised for the book: F. E. Faverty has pointed out (pp. 216–18) that Arnold's concept of the professorial function, with which he supported his recommendation of the establishment of a chair of Celtic at Oxford, is close to Renan's statement in "L'Instruction supérieure en France," *Revue des deux mondes,* seconde période, LI, 81, 92–95 (May 1, 1864); see note to p. 270:1.

As we have seen, when Arnold plunged into his subject he discovered there was far more than he had supposed; that in fact the scientific study of language, of palaeography, of anthropology, and of another discipline that promised to be just as scientific, ethnology, was giving Celtic scholars a much firmer basis than they had had or than Renan seemed to understand. How much of this awareness, if any, is due to conversations with his friend Professor Max Müller we have now no way of knowing. Certain it is that Arnold looked in the right places for his materials, and to follow him to his sources is to see his real genius for getting at the heart of his matter, for seizing upon the one point in a book that would be useful to him. The first paragraph of his Introduction states modestly and fairly the relationship of his lectures to the researches of others; but to his grasp of the scholarly problems he added the literary tact which carried him into the area of creative criticism. Scientific research has naturally made much progress in the century since Arnold wrote; his subject may not have a wide interest; but his book is a spectacular achievement in the combination of scholarship and taste.

The lectures had, of course, a practical purpose, both educational and political (Arnold's interest in the Irish question continued very great for the rest of his life). After the third article had been published in *The Cornhill,* he wrote to his mother (May 25, 1866): "The Celtic papers are certainly producing an effect far beyond what I had ventured to hope. This is a great pleasure to me, and a proof how much there is in the way of presenting a subject, for certainly a more hopeless subject in itself to approach the British public with one could hardly imagine." And when he had given the final lecture, he commented: "I have done all, and more than all, I hoped to do by these lectures, whether a professorship of Celtic is immediately founded or not." (It was founded eleven years later, and the Principal of Jesus College was a moving force in its establishment.) But as time went on he found himself a somewhat unwilling champion in a cause for which he preferred that someone else do the fighting. An invitation to speak at the Eisteddfod at Carmarthen in the summer of 1867 tempted him at first; then he turned it down. "[The letter of invitation] gives me great pleasure," he told his mother. "To have one's attempt at fusion and conciliation felt all through Wales is just what I could have wished, and what is so far more desirable than being thought by some hundred or two literary and well-to-do people to have written cleverly and interestingly. It was in my mind to go to Carmarthen and make an address on Progress through Puritanism and Progress through Culture, with reference to Welsh dissent, the Liberation Society's working there, etc., in connexion with these Eisteddfods and their popularity. I think I could have done it successfully, but my desire is always for keeping quiet, and I took advantage of the possibility that my appearance at Carmarthen might be ascribed to popularity-hunting, and the attacks on me do a harm to the Eisteddfod." Again, "My great wish is to do neither less nor more than I am really inclined and fitted to do; neither less, from laziness—nor more, from the temptation of money making, answering attacks, &c. &c." Eight years later (May 20, 1875), he wrote to congratulate Professor J. S. Blackie upon his efforts to establish a chair of Celtic at Edinburgh, but declined an invitation to a meeting Blackie was arranging in London: "The presence of such a dilettante as I am would do you harm rather than good;—any little service I could render, in the way of stirring up, I have rendered." And in reply to a request of the same sort from Norman MacColl he wrote: "I am sure that by my lectures on Celtic Literature I did the very outside of what is permitted to a man ignorant of the Celtic Languages; and that by taking part in the promotion of Celtic Societies, and so forth, I should rather do harm to the cause and expose myself to the charge of a restless dilettantism." He could not always hold by his resolution: less than three years before his death he attended the Eisteddfod at Aberdare as the guest of Lord Aberdare, who had been Vice-President of the Committee of Council on Education from 1864 to 1866, and he twice addressed the assembly (see *Times*, August 28, 1885, p. 6, col. 2).

The Study of Celtic Literature was edited by Alfred Nutt in 1910; his footnotes, chiefly concerned with bringing Arnold up-to-date or with carrying on a debate with his author, have no longer any value. John V. Kelleher's "Matthew Arnold and the Celtic Revival," in *Perspectives of Criticism*, edited by Harry Levin (Cambridge: Harvard University Press, 1950), makes the interesting point that the movement of 1890–1916 reproduced, especially in its minor writers, "element for element, Arnold's picture of Celtic literature, with the difference that every weakness Arnold deplored in the Celt and his works has now become a strange characteristic strength" (pp. 204–5); but Kelleher stands in a glass house when he impugns Arnold's scholarship. A. L. Rowse gives an account of Arnold's Celtic ancestry and temperament in "Matthew Arnold as Cornishman," *Welsh Review*, IV, 39–49 (March, 1945). His doctrines of race were challenged quite early by Henry Stuart Fagan (*Contemporary Review*, VI, 257–61 [October, 1867]), who insisted that there was no such thing as an Irish national character and no logical basis for Arnold's attempt to trace certain characteristics of English poetry to its Celtic elements. Andrew Lang at the end of the century asserted that "what [Arnold and others] called 'Celtic' in poetry or in superstition is really early human, and may become recrudescent anywhere, for good or for evil" ("The Celtic Renascence," *Blackwood's Edinburgh Magazine*, CLXI, 188–89 [February, 1897]), and Yeats in the same year made the same correction of Arnold's view, except that for him, "of all the fountains of the passions and beliefs of ancient times in Europe, ... the Celtic alone has been for centuries close to the main river of European literature" ("The Celtic Element in Literature," *Ideas of Good and Evil* [London, 1914], pp. 201–2). F. E. Faverty's *Matthew Arnold, the Ethnologist* (Evanston, Illinois: Northwestern University Press, 1951), is a very illuminating study of the sources of Arnold's notions; one wishes studies equally good might be made also of Arnold's other books. Faverty's statement is modified with respect to Thomas Arnold by R. K. Barksdale, "Thomas Arnold's Attitude Toward Race," *Phylon Quarterly,* XVIII, 174–80 (April, 1957).

Motto: "His race came forth, in their years; they came forth to war, but they always fell."—"Cath-loda: A Poem," Duan II, *The Poems of Ossian,* translated by James Macpherson, ed. William Sharp (Edinburgh, 1896), p. 14. See Arnold, *Note-Books,* ed. Lowry, p. 34 (1865).

291:1–2. Arnold and his family spent August 4–24, 1864, at 10, St. George's Crescent, Llandudno.

291:28–292:17. All these names and their legends are identified for the modern reader in H. L. V. Fletcher, *The Queen's Wales: North Wales* (London: Hodder and Stoughton, 1955). The story of Mael-gwyn and Elphin is told in Lady Charlotte Guest, tr. *The Mabinogion* (Everyman's Library ed.; London: Dent, 1906), pp. 268–78; of Mael-gwyn and the Yellow Plague in a note on p. 431. The identification of Mael and Lancelot is made (after La Villemarqué) in Ernest Renan, "La Poésie des races celtiques," *Essais de morale et de critique* (4th ed.; Paris, 1889), p. 421.

292:17–18. Ovid *Heroides* I, 33.

292:31–38. According to the mythological ethnology (outdated in Arnold's day, but still familiar for his fanciful use) the Celts were descended from Gomer, son of Japheth, son of Noah (Genesis 10:2); the branch of them known as the Cimmerians, or Cimri, inhabiting lands north of the Black Sea, was the people referred to by Ezekiel (38:6) as "Gomer and all his bands." The giant Galates (Appian *Illyrice* 2) is the mythological eponymous ancestor of the Gauls, that branch of the Celtic race who before the dawn of history inhabited western Europe. The accepted scientific notion was that the Cimmerian migration from their Black Sea home took place in the seventh century B.C.; by the sixth century they had reached western Europe and occupied the north and west of Gaul (including, later, Wales and Cornwall). The older, Gallic branch remained in the south and east of Gaul and the north and west of the British Isles (Scotland and Ireland). See Amédée Thierry, *Histoire des Gaulois* (7th ed.; Paris, 1866), I, 74, and "Introduction," passim.

294:9–11. The "Old Rugbeian" (see note to 294:26) thus quoted the Eisteddfod Committee, and Arnold copied the expressions into his *Note-Books* for 1864 (ed. Lowry, p. 26).

294:22–25. Llandudno, a tiny village until the opening of the Chester-Holyhead railway in 1848, is reached by a branch from the main line two and a half miles long, constructed about a decade later. The town is not even mentioned in *Black's ... Road and Railway Guide Book* for 1859, yet by the time the Arnolds visited it, it was already becoming an elegant watering place.

294:26–295:2. An unfriendly hand (which signed his letter "An Old Rugbeian") described the "Gorsedd" as "the placing in an open street of a circle of limestones and an artificial cromlech, and ... the enacting there certain ceremonies professedly in imitation of the mythical Druids. The ceremony of chairing the principal prizeman and holding a drawn sword over his head was strange, but the game of Druids played outside is a theme I hardly dare approach."— *Times*, August 31, 1864, p. 10, col. 5. Another correspondent three days later regarded the ceremony as blasphemous. The "gorsedd," or throne, gives its name to any sort of tribunal; here it is a "session of the bards."

295:26. Presumably the march of General Sir Henry Havelock to relieve Lucknow in the summer of 1857, during the Indian mutiny.

295:27. Robert Vaughan (1795–1868), Congregationalist divine, founder (in 1845) and for twenty years editor of the *British Quarterly Review*.

295:35–296:3. The parliamentary session ended on July 29. The principal problem of the [London] Metropolitan Board of Works while Arnold was at Llandudno was "the present state of the Thames, which [was] emitting unpleasant odours." About two-thirds of the London sewage flowed into the river at the metropolis; steps were being taken to divert a greater amount downriver.— *Times* August 6, 1864, p. 11, col. 1.

295:38–296:1. Ovates and bards were two of the orders of the Druidic institution; the special qualification of the former was scientific knowledge. (This conception owes much to modern imagination, but the Eisteddfod adopted the terms and symbolism.) Triads were epigrammatic prose statements of laws, chronology, etc., which for mnemonic purposes grouped names, events, and the like in threes; the englyn was a sententious quatrain or epigram. The Eisteddfod provided competition in both forms.

296:18. Connop Thirlwall.

296:19. "The English labourer['s] ... habits of thought are not romantic or intellectual. It would be difficult to induce a set of Dorsetshire or Sussex villagers to compose odes and epigrams, or to listen to the poetical lucubrations of their neighbours. The Llandudno compositions were probably not of a high order, but a literary competition of any kind could only interest a spirited and susceptible community."—"Eisteddfods," *Saturday Review*, XVIII, 325 (September 10, 1864).

296:22–23. The Greek poet Pindar's (518–438 B.C.) surviving odes celebrate the victors in the Greek games at Olympia and elsewhere.

296:31–32. "Dicitur tamen huius populi ultima cornicae linguae gnara *Dolly Pentreath*, Dorothea P., quae obiit a. 1778 nata annos 102."—Kaspar Zeuss, *Grammatica Celtica* (Leipzig, 1853), p. ix, n.

297:3–6. When Arnold began his career as inspector, his territory included nearly the whole of Wales; in the first report he submitted, he said (January 1, 1853): "There can, I think, be no question but that the acquirement of the English language should be more and more insisted upon by your Lordships in your relations with [the elementary schools of Wales], as the one main object for which your aid is granted. Whatever encouragement individuals may think it desirable to give to the preservation of the Welsh language on grounds of philological or antiquarian interest, it must always be the desire of a Government to render its dominions, as far as possible, homogeneous, and to break down barriers to the freest intercourse between the different parts of them. Sooner or later, the difference of language between Wales and England will probably be effaced, as has happened with the difference of language between Cornwall and the rest of England; as is now happening with the difference of language between Brittany and the rest of France; and they are not the true friends of the Welsh people, who, from a romantic interest in their manners and traditions, would impede an event which is socially and politically so desirable for them."—House of Commons, *Sessional Papers*, 1852–53, LXXX, 675.

297:8–10. The *Reports of the Commissioners of Inquiry into the State of Education in Wales*, 1847, were regarded in Wales as part of a conspiracy to stamp out the language, religion, and nationality of the Welsh. One of the commissioners was Ralph Lingen, who as secretary to the Committee of Council on Education, 1849–69, was Arnold's superior and the chief executive officer for education in the nation. England had no minister of education.

298:20–23. Plutarch *Life of Caesar* xxxv.

299:12–300:4. See, for example, Thomas Arnold, *Introductory Lectures on Modern History*, ed. Henry Reed (New York, 1845), pp. 44–46 (Inaugural Lecture), and *History of Rome*, conclusion of Chapter XXII. Arnold discussed his recollection of his father's anti-Celticism in a letter to his mother on March 10, 1866. Faverty (*Matthew Arnold, the Ethnologist*, p. 118) points out that a reviewer of Arnold's *Study of Celtic Literature* remarks, "Never surely did

Nemesis play a merrier trick than when she made the son of that Teuton of Teutons, the Celt-hating Dr. Arnold, indulge in this expansive if not somewhat exaggerated praise of the literature of the older race."—"Folk-lore: Myths and Tales of Various Peoples," *London Quarterly Review*, XXXI, 48 (October, 1868).

299:36, 40–41. Zeuss died in 1856. James Cowles Prichard, M.D., published his *Eastern Origin of the Celtic Nations* in 1831, Franz Bopp his *Celtischen Sprachen in ihrem Verhältnisse zum Sanskrit, Zend, Griechischen, Lateinischen, Germanischen, Littauischen und Slavischen* in 1839. Bopp's great work was in Sanskrit grammar and lexicography, and his *Comparative Grammar of the Sanskrit, Zend, Greek, Latin, Lithuanian, Gothic, German and Slavonic Languages* was first published in German in 1833–52 and in English in 1845–50.

300:4–5. These words were attributed to Lord Lyndhurst by his Liberal and Irish opponents in the Parliamentary debates of 1836, but he denied having used them. See Theodore Martin, *A Life of Lord Lyndhurst* (London, 1883), pp. 346–48.

300:10–18. Owen Jones, Edward Williams, and William Owen Pughe, *The Myvyrian Archaiology of Wales: Collected out of Ancient Manuscripts* (New ed.; Denbigh, 1870), pp. ix–xi *bis*. The "General Advertisement" (pp. v–vii) is dated January 1, 1801.

300:21–22. "And Samuel hewed Agag in pieces before the Lord in Gilgal."—I Samuel 15:33.

300:25. See Judges 3:15–30.

301:8–18. P. A. Challemel-Lacour, *La Philosophie individualiste: étude sur Guillaume de Humboldt* (Paris, 1864), pp. 190–92; first printed as "Guillaume de Humboldt," *Revue germanique et française*, XXVII, 650–79 (December, 1863); XXVIII, 346–74 (February, 1864); XXIX, 65–107 (April, 1864); the relevant passage is on p. 102.

303:15–16. The Black Book of Caermarthen, in the Hengwrt Library, and the Red Book of Hergest, in the Library of Jesus College, Oxford, are mentioned as the chief ancient manuscript sources of Welsh romance literature in Lady Charlotte Guest's Introduction to her *Mabinogion* (Everyman's Library ed., p. 8), which translates eleven tales from the latter.

303:21–31. David William Nash, *Taliesin; or, the Bards and Druids of Britain. A Translation of the Remains of the Earliest Welsh Bards, and an Examination of the Bardic Mysteries* (London, 1858), p. 23.

304:1–31. Arnold depends for his account of Jones upon Théodore Hersart, Vicomte de La Villemarqué, *Les Bardes bretons. Poèmes du VIᵉ. siècle* (New ed.; Paris, 1860), pp. ii–iii, xv.

304:7–13. "Haud semel quidem pollicitus est ... Possessor. At postea à quibusdam magìs pseudopoliticis opinor, quàm literatis dissuasus, promissum revocavit."—Edward Lhuyd, *Archaeologia Britannica* (Oxford, 1707), I, 261, col. 2; quoted both by La Ville-marqué and by Jones (*Myvyrian Archaiology*, p. xi *bis*).

304:31. The River Clwyd flows northward through Denbigh-shire.

304:37–38. Adapted from Vergil *Aeneid* i. 462.

305:6. Joseph Justus Scaliger (1540–1609), French born but of Italian descent, was the greatest classical scholar of his day, a pioneer in the scientific study of textual criticism and ancient chronology.

305:15–18. Eugene O'Curry, *Lectures on the Manuscript Mate-rials of Ancient Irish History, Delivered at the Catholic University of Ireland, During the Sessions of 1855 and 1856* (Dublin, 1861). O'Curry died in 1862.

305:23–24. "Victrix causa deis placuit, sed victa Catoni."—Lu-can *Pharsalia* i. 128. Newman applied this line to himself in the *Apologia*.

305:24. In the Preface to his Lectures O'Curry pays affectionate tribute to Newman, who as rector of the University was respon-sible for establishing his Chair of Irish History and Archaeology, who expressed warm admiration for the lectures, which he con-stantly attended, and who provided for their publication at the ex-pense of the University (pp. vi–viii).

305:25–26. John O'Donovan, ed., *Annals of the Kingdom of Ire-land, by the Four Masters, from the Earliest Period to the Year 1616* (Dublin, 1851), 7 vols. Arnold's phrase, "seven large quarto volumes, [containing] 4,215 pages of closely printed matter" comes from O'Curry, *Lectures*, p. 160.

305:29–306:6. O'Curry, *Lectures*, pp. 182–95, 200–01.

306:10–13. Arnold selects from the classifications at the head of O'Curry's Lectures XI–XIII and at the end of Lecture XIII.

306:15–19. O'Curry, *Lectures*, p. 152. Arnold draws his descrip-tion of "this mass of materials" from pp. 167–68, 174, 188.

306:26–33. O'Curry, *Lectures*, pp. 370, 354, 455–56.

306:35. Edwin Norris, ed. and tr., *The Ancient Cornish Drama* (Oxford, 1859), including a sketch of Cornish grammar and a glos-sary.

306:35–36. See note to p. 304:1; also: *Barzaz-Breiz. Chants popu-laires de la Bretagne* (4th ed.; Paris, 1846), 2 vols. *Myrdhinn, ou l'enchanteur Merlin* (New ed.; Paris, 1862). *La Légende celtique et la poésie des cloîtres en Irlande, en Cambrie et en Bretagne* (Paris, 1864). *Les Romans de la Table-ronde, et les contes des anciens Bretons* (3rd ed.; Paris, 1860).

307:17–20. Edward Davies, *Celtic Researches, on the Origin, Traditions & Language, of the Ancient Britons* (London, 1804), and *The Mythology and Rites of the British Druids* (London, 1809).

307:21–25. Jacob Bryant, *A New System, or, an Analysis of Ancient Mythology* (London, 1774–76; 3rd ed., 1807).

307:31–34. Davies, *Mythology*, p. 189.

307:37–308:10. *Ibid.*, p. 195 (reading "presents itself" for Davies' "presents himself"), and phrases apparently gathered passim from the beginning of Section III, pp. 183–86.

308:11–15. See Nash, *Taliesin*, p. 186: "She is a creation of the fancy, a sorceress, or enchantress, and nothing more."

308:31–309:7. Davies, *Mythology*, pp. 564–65 (reading "*O Brithi Brith oi*, &c."). In his footnote, Davies says, "As it may serve to determine the important question, whether the Druids possessed sacred hymns in the *Phoenician* language, I shall attempt to write the lines in Hebrew characters, with the hope, that some good Orientalist may think them worthy of attention; and if they present the vestiges of Phoenician antiquity, do me the favour of correcting them." Arnold probably quotes indirectly, from Nash, whose phrase is "under the impression that they may be vestiges of sacred hymns in the Phoenician language" (p. 257).

309:8–22. Nash, pp. 255–58.

309:27–310:27. Nash, pp. 240–43, 251, 259–60, demolishing Algernon Herbert, *Britannia after the Romans* (London, 1836–41) and William Owen (Pughe), *Dictionary of the Welsh Language* (1st ed., London, 1803; 2nd ed., Denbigh, 1832). The passage "Without the ape . . . green" is Edward Davies' translation, which Arnold, following Nash, says Herbert "adopts"; he does so essentially, but not literally (II, 6).

310:34–37. For La Villemarqué's conservative and skeptical view, see *Les Bardes bretons*, pp. v–vi, xiii–xiv.

311:8–14. Turner, *Vindication*, 4th ed., in his *History of England* (London, 1839), III, 575.

311:30–312:1. John Williams ab Ithel, ed., *Brut y Tywysogion; or, the Chronicle of the Princes* (London, 1860), p. xii. This volume is in the series of *Chronicles and Memorials of Great Britain and Ireland during the Middle Ages*, published by the authority of Her Majesty's Treasury under the direction of the Master of the Rolls, Sir John Romilly, who selected the editors.

312:1–2. Edward Williams the Bard (1747–1826), better known

as Iolo Morganwg, was one of the editors (with Owen Jones) of the *Myvyrian Archaiology*. The collection of mss. he formed for a continuation of that work was published as *Iolo Manuscripts. A Selection of Ancient Welsh Manuscripts* (Llandovery, 1848).

312:3. Jacob Grimm (1785–1863), German philologist and one of the greatest names in the history of scientific study of language, is referred to by La Villemarqué as "mon illustre ami et maître."— *Les Bardes bretons*, p. [5].

312:10–313:4. O'Curry, *Lectures*, pp. 321–27. Arnold slightly improves the language of O'Curry's translation of the tale.

313:32–314:6. Davies, *Mythology and Rites*, p. 269.

314:16–315:12. O'Curry, *Lectures*, p. 154.

316:7–26. Nash, *Taliesin*, pp. 333, 330–31, 340, 6, 278. Gaius Suetonius Paulinus, Roman commander in Britain under Nero, 59–62 A.D., campaigned in Anglesey and North Wales, but is best known for his defeat of the great British revolt under Boadicea (61 A.D.).

316:28–317:11. These classic texts are cited in every discussion of Celtic antiquities: Strabo *Geography* IV. iv. 4–5; Caesar *Gallic War* vi. 13–20; Lucan *Pharsalia* i. 447–58 (translated by Arnold).

317:19–22. Caesar *Gallic War* vi, 14.

318:13. St. Gildas was a sixth-century Celtic monk, born in Scotland, educated in Wales, and inhabitant of Ireland and later of Brittany. He is author of the quasi-historical *De Excidio Britanniae*.

318:14. Nennius is the traditional author of a late eighth-century Latin compilation, more legendary than historical, the *Historia Britonum*.

318:14. For the Laws of Howel the Good, see *Ancient Laws and Institutes of Wales* (1841), with an English translation of the Welsh text. The date of circa 950 is accepted by Zeuss, *Grammatica Celtica* (1871 ed., p. xxix), and listed, after Zeuss, by Henry Morley, *English Writers I. The Writers Before Chaucer* (London, 1864), p. 217.

318:15–25. Nash, *Taliesin*, p. 29, quoting a Welsh source printed in Williams, *Iolo Manuscripts*, pp. 215, 630.

318:32–34. Quoted by Thomas Stephens, *The Literature of the Kymry* (2nd ed.; London, 1876), p. 102. (The first edition appeared in 1849.)

319:11–320:10. Lady Charlotte, daughter of the Earl of Lindsey and wife of Sir John Guest, was widowed in 1852 and married Charles Schreiber three years later. Her translation of eleven tales from the Red Book of Hergest, together with the later tale of Taliesin, appeared in three volumes in 1849, but not until 1877 in a second edition. "Kilhwch and Olwen" is the seventh of these tales; Arnold's quotations will be found on pp. 123–25 of the Everyman's Library edition. Renan translates this passage from Lady Charlotte's book in "La Poésie des races celtiques," pp. 398–401.

320:15–32. Nash, *Taliesin*, p. 121.

320:34. *Othello*, II, i, 162.

321:5–17. Nash, *Taliesin*, pp. 339, 134, 123, the last quoting Charles Meyer, "On the Importance of the Study of the Celtic Language," *Report of the Seventeenth Meeting of the British Association for the Advancement of Science*, June, 1847, p. 304. No other work of Meyer's is recorded in the British Museum Catalogue, and there is nothing in this paper about an allegorical or calendarial interpretation of folk epics.

321:37. "Arthur ... réside dans la constellation qui porte son nom, (le *chariot d'Arthur;* la Grande-Ourse)."—Henri Martin, *Histoire de France* (4th ed.; Paris, 1865), III, 358.

321:38–322:24. These allusions are drawn from Lady Charlotte Guest's *Mabinogion*, especially from her notes; in Everyman's Library ed., see pp. 300, 298, 349, 191, 289, 397–98, 309–10, (127–28), 28, 14.

322:29–30. The Mausoleum at Halicarnassus and the Temple of Diana at Ephesus were two of the Seven Wonders of the World; like nearly all ancient edifices they were pillaged by later generations for building materials.

322:32. Hebrews 9:11.

322:37–323:12. The list takes up six and a half of the rather crowded pages of the Everyman's Library ed.; Arnold quotes from pp. 102–3.

323:14. The story of the Twrch Trwyth (a boar) is part of "Kilhwch and Olwen," pp. 116–20, 128–34.

323:17–324:36. Guest, *Mabinogion*, pp. 47, 44–47 (the third paragraph much condensed), 292 (note on "Bendigeid Vran").

325:6–26. Nash, *Taliesin*, pp. 180, 183–84, 185. "The materials ... Welsh" seems to be Arnold's summary, not Nash's sentence.

326:9–13. "Prédiction de Gwenc'hlan," in La Villemarqué, *Barzaz-Breiz*, I, 31, 35.

326:17–28. Nash, *Taliesin*, pp. 227–28.

326:35–327:29. *Ibid.*, pp. 185, 162–63.

328:14–329:17. Kaspar Zeuss (1806–56) published his *Grammatica Celtica* in 1853; a second ed. appeared in 1871. For the matters Arnold discusses, see, in the first ed., "Praefatio Auctoris," pp. xxxvii–xxxviii (946) and 87–88, 183–86 (2nd ed., pp. xxvi–xxvii [963], and 75–76, 159–61). The "tenues" are *p, t, c*, which by "destitutio" become *b, d, g*. The only one of his examples Arnold can have taken from Zeuss is *Mab* (p. 184/159).

328:38–329:6. Nash, *Taliesin*, pp. 20, 77–80.

329:30–330:12. O'Curry, *Lectures*, pp. 182–85.

330:33–332:5. Arnold here depends upon F. G. Bergmann, *Les Scythes les ancêtres des peuples germaniques et slaves* (Colmar, 1858). In Bergmann's second ed. (Halle, 1860), Arnold's references may be traced as follows: for "Apian Land" (Sophocles *Oedipus at Colonus* 1303), see p. 35; for "shielded people" (which Bergmann in his second ed. admitted to be a false etymology invented by the early Greeks), p. 3; for Targitavus, pp. 36, 39, 32–33; for "Taviti," etc., pp. 46–48; for "Suevi," pp. 50, 40. Hesus (Lucan *Pharsalia* i, 445) is not discussed here.

333:1–3. Meyer, "Study of Celtic," pp. 307–8.

333:11. John Colgan, *Acta Sanctorum Veteris et Maioris Scotiae, seu Hiberniae Sanctorum Insulae* (Louvain, 1645).

333:12–20. Zeuss, *Grammatica Celtica*, 2nd ed., p. viii n.

333:20–24. Max Müller, *Lectures on the Science of Language* (New York, 1862), I, 237, 244–45, with footnote by Whitley Stokes on the latter.

334:8–11. Perhaps "Je ne me consolerois point de n'avoir pas fait fortune, si j'étois né en Angleterre; je ne suis point fâché de ne l'avoir pas faite en France."—"Pensées diverses," *Oeuvres complètes*, ed. Édouard Laboulaye (Paris, 1879), VII, 155.

334:12–16. Whitley Stokes, *Three Irish Glossaries* (London, 1862), p. xix n.

336:32–35. Review of the third volume of Hook's *Lives of the Archbishops of Canterbury*, *Saturday Review*, XIX, 259 (March 4, 1865).

336:36. Arnold was in Zurich in October, 1865, on his tour for the Schools Inquiry Commission.

338:23–30. H. Morley, *English Writers*, I, 164–66.

339:2. Henri Milne-Edwards (1800–85), born at Bruges of English parents, became one of the most distinguished French zoologists and anatomists of his day, whose *Eléments de zoologie* was long the standard textbook in its field.

339:8–9. Amédée Thierry, *Histoire des Gaulois* (Paris, 1828), "Introduction" (in the 7th ed., 1866, I, 73–74).

339:10–340:15. William Frédéric Edwards, *Des Caractères physiologiques des races humaines* (Paris, 1829), pp. 62–67, 69–71; Arnold quotes from pp. 70–71. The pamphlet runs to 129 pages. It is commended by Thierry in his later editions (e.g., 7th ed., I, 117).

340:21–24. For these types of head, see Henri Martin, *Histoire de France depuis les temps les plus reculés jusqu'en 1789* (4th ed.; Paris, 1865), I, 206, n. 3.

340:34–341:3. H. Morley, *English Writers*, I, 188. Morley uses the spelling "Oisin."

341:21. See, for example, "The Literary Influence of Academies," p. 237:13.

341:30. See pp. 235, 290.

342:19–22. O'Curry, *Lectures*, p. 224, quoting a poem cited in MacFirbis' *Book of Genealogies*.

343:2–4, 7–8. Renan, "Poésie des races celtiques," pp. 436, 381, 384.

343:6. The fair held at Donnybrook, a suburb of Dublin, from 1204 to 1855, became proverbial for disorganized riot and bloodshed.

343:21–23, 32. *Histoire de France*, III, 379n.

343:27–31. After discussing the characteristic head-shapes of various peoples, Henri Martin continues: "Ajoutons à ces traits extérieurs que, dans ses savantes études d'anthropologie comparée, M. Serres constate chez les Français un plus grand développement de l'appareil respiratoire et un moindre volume d'intestins que chez l'Allemand, caractère qu'il faut certainement reporter aux Gaulois et aux Germains."—*Histoire de France*, I, 13, n. 1.

344:1–2. Psalms 101:7 (Prayer-Book version).

344:6–8. "Le défaut essentiel des peuples bretons, le penchant à l'ivresse, ... tient à cet invincible besoin d'illusion. Ne dites pas que c'est appétit de jouissance grossière, car jamais peuple ne fut d'ailleurs plus sobre et plus détaché de toute sensualité; non, les Bretons cherchaient dans l'hydromel ... la vision du monde invisible. Aujourd'hui encore, en Irlande, l'ivresse fait partie de toutes les fêtes patronales, c'est-à-dire des fêtes qui ont le mieux conservé leur physionomie nationale et populaire."—Renan, "Poésie des races celtiques," pp. 386–87.

344:9–10. "Leur mobilité singulière en ce qui concerne les personnes et les choses extérieures ne tient pas seulement à la vivacité de leur imagination, mais aussi à leur indomptable personnalité, toujours prête à réagir contre le despotisme du fait; cette mobilité cache une persistance opiniâtre dans les sentiments intimes et dans les directions essentielles de la vie."—Martin, *Histoire de France*, I, 36. As Arnold suggests, he draws much of his characterization of the Celts from this and neighboring pages of Martin, and from Martin's Book XX.

346:1–2. Sybaris was a Greek city on the Gulf of Tarentum in southern Italy; "her wealthy luxuriousness was proverbial" (*Oxford Classical Dictionary*). Corinth, just south of the isthmus between central Greece and the Peloponnesus, "in the Hellenistic period ... became a centre of industry, commerce, and commercialized pleasure" (*ibid.*). Baiae, on the Bay of Naples near Cumae, became for late Republican and early Imperial Rome "a fashionable, even licentious resort" (*ibid.*), with imposing villas of senators and emperors.

346:7–10. O'Curry, *Lectures*, p. 248.

346:16–22. "Ainsi la race celtique s'est usée à résister au temps et à défendre les causes désespérées. Il ne semble pas qu'à aucune époque elle ait eu d'aptitude pour la vie politique: l'esprit de la famille a étouffé chez elle toute tentative d'organisation plus étendue. Il ne semble pas aussi que les peuples qui la composent soient par eux-mêmes susceptibles de progrès. La vie leur apparaît comme une condition fixe qu'il n'est pas au pouvoir de l'homme de changer. Doués de peu d'initiative, trop portés à s'envisager comme mineurs et en tutelle, ils croient vite à la fatalité et s'y résignent.... De là vient sa tristesse. Prenez les chants de ses bardes du sixième siècle; ils pleurent plus de défaites qu'ils ne chantent de victoires."— Renan, "Poésie des races celtiques," p. 383.

346:23–24. See p. 291.

347:4–16. "S'il était permis d'assigner un sexe aux nations comme aux individus, il faudrait dire sans hésiter que la race celtique, surtout envisagée dans sa branche kymrique ou bretonne, est une race essentiellement féminine. Aucune famille humaine, je crois, n'a porté dans l'amour autant de mystère. Nulle autre n'a conçu avec plus de délicatesse l'idéal de la femme et n'en a été plus dominée. ... La femme telle que l'a conçue la chevalerie,—cet idéal de douceur et de beauté posé comme but suprême de la vie,—n'est une création ni classique, ni chrétienne, ni germanique, mais bien réellement celtique."—Renan, "Poésie des races celtiques," p. 385. See introductory note to these lectures, pp. 491, 494.

347:16–20. "Aucune race ne conversa aussi intimement que la race celtique avec les êtres inférieurs, et ne leur accorda une aussi large part de vie morale.... Cette touchante sympathie tenait elle-même à la vivacité toute particulière que les races celtiques ont portée dans le sentiment de la nature. Leur mythologie ... [est] un naturalisme réaliste en quelque sorte, l'amour de la nature pour elle-même, l'impression vive de sa magie, accompagnée du mouvement de tristesse que l'homme éprouve quand, face à face avec elle, il croit l'entendre lui parler de son origine et de sa destinée."—*Ibid.*, pp. 402–3. S. M. B. Coulling has pointed out that Arnold uses the term "natural magic" some six times in "Maurice de Guérin" and thrice more in these Celtic lectures.—"Renan's Influence on Arnold's Literary and Social Criticism," *Florida State University Studies*, No. 5 (1952), pp. 102–3. A more detailed discussion of the implications of this expression is in Leon A. Gottfried's excellent dissertation, *Matthew Arnold and the Romantics* (Ann Arbor: University Microfilms, 1958), pp. 195–99.

350:7. Neustria, a name of varied significance in the early history of France, here refers to Normandy, the territory ceded to Rollo and his followers in 911 A.D.

351:4–11. Arnold's method foreshadows that of *Culture and Anarchy*, Chapt. III.

351:16–18. "The Opening of Parliament," *Times*, February 7, 1866, p. 5, col. 1.

351:19–24. *Kölnische Zeitung*, July 23, 1865, p. 5, recorded in Arnold's *Note-Books* for 1865 (p. 31). On that very day Arnold wrote to his mother from Rolandseck and mentioned the *Kölnische Zeitung* as one of the two papers available at his hotel.

356:28–357:5. Arnold jotted down this story in his *Note-Books* for 1865 (ed. Lowry, p. 33).

357:14–37. Friedrich Adolf Krummacher, *The Parables*, translated from the seventh German edition (London, 1858), pp. 128–29 ("The Apple"). Arnold's reading-book version slightly modifies the language of this translation.

358:16–17. Gervinus paralleled Händel and Shakespeare, "who maintained in these later centuries the old germanic kindred and fellowship, the possession of whom the two nations share, and for the higher appreciation of whom they mutually strive." Arnold juxtaposes two rather widely separated sentences that seem innocent enough in context: "England has naturalized our Handel and reckoned him as her own," and "Shakespeare, from his diffusion and influence, has become a German poet, almost more than any of our native ones."—G. G. Gervinus, *Shakespeare*, translated by F. E. Bunnett (London, 1863), I, xi, xv.

358:18–19. Review of "Manfred, a Dramatic Poem by Lord Byron," *Über Kunst und Alterthum*, II, 186–92 (1820); *Werke* (Weimar, 1902), XLI (1), 189–93. Goethe associates the women of Manfred with a Florentine woman murdered by her husband for her inclination toward Byron (who in turn may have murdered the husband) and with the beloved of the Spartan general Pausanias, killed inadvertently by him when she entered his bedroom in the dark.

360:9–10. Arnold is not, as has sometimes been said, misquoting this couplet from Renan, "La Poésie des races celtiques," p. 453, but is quoting it accurately as given by Henri Martin, *Histoire de France*, III, 367n.

362:4–7. "Last Words," *Prose Works*, ed. Super, I, 189–90.

362:9–12. *Paradise Lost*, III, 32–35.

362:14–15. *Torquato Tasso*, I, ii, 66–67.

364:14–16. The second sentence of the Preface to Luther's *Catechismus für die gemeine Pfarrherr und Prediger*.

364:26–27. "La branche scandinave . . . [et] la branche germanique des Teutons."—C. C. Fauriel, *Histoire de la poésie provençale* (Paris, 1846), I, 271. Arnold undoubtedly used this work when he prepared his lecture of June 8, 1861 (see p. 491).

364:29–30. The war between Prussia and Denmark in 1864.

365:10–14. Zeuss, *Grammatica Celtica*, 1st ed., p. xii n; 2nd ed., p. x n.

366:3. George Webbe Dasent had translated *Popular Tales from the Norse* (1859), *The Prose Edda* (1842), *The Story of Burnt Njal* (1861), and *The Story of Gisli the Outlaw* (1866).

366:22–24. Guest, *Mabinogion* (Everyman's Library ed.), p. 354.

366:30–33. A. J. C. Hare complained that though "epitaphs on churchyard gravestones have been one of the means by which God is pleased to warn, and rouse, and teach His people," this could not be done "when the epitaph only conveys all that is offensive to the mind; when bad grammar, bad diction, and worse thoughts unite to render it rather ludicrous than instructive. On three several adjoining gravestones I have often noticed variations of that miserable doggrel which tells of—

> 'Affliction sore long time I bore,
>   Physicians were in vain,
> Till death gave ease, as God was please,
>   To ease me of my pain.'

This is only one of many Epitaphs of the same kind, which are among the chief favourites in our country villages, and are often repeated over and over again in the same churchyard."—*Epitaphs for Country Churchyards* (Oxford, 1856), p. iii.

367:5–11. O'Curry, *Lectures*, pp. 367–68.

367:13–20. These are couplets 3 and 4 of a poem that immediately follows the epilogue to the *Félire* in the Speckled Book; see Whitley Stokes, ed., *The Martyrology of Oengus the Culdee* (London, 1905), pp. xxiv–xxv, with a footnote reference to this passage in Arnold.

367:25–28. From "Yr Awdyl Vraith," stanza 32, translated in Guest, *Mabinogion*, p. 284. W. F. Skene comments, "It is generally considered that the history of Wales cannot be referred to with any propriety without quoting these lines."—*The Four Ancient Books of Wales* (Edinburgh, 1868), I, 194–95.

367:30–32. For a brief summary of the debate on the age and historical value of the triads, see Stephens, *Literature of the Kymry*, Chapter III, sect. v, and the recantation (first published in *Archaeologia Cambrensis* for 1862) in his second ed., pp. 493–94.

368:10–11. Roundell Palmer, ed., *The Book of Praise from the Best English Hymn Writers* (London, 1863). This volume was published in the same series as Palgrave's *Golden Treasury*.

371:6–14. "Carthon: a Poem," *The Poems of Ossian*, translated by James Macpherson, ed. William Sharp (Edinburgh, 1896), pp. 175–76.

371:18. Sainte-Beuve, in his essay on the "Mémoires de Napoléon," says "Il prêtait de son génie à Ossian et l'aurait mis volontiers dans sa cassette, comme Alexandre faisait pour Homère."—*Causeries du lundi* (3rd ed.; Paris, 1857), I, 180. See P. van Tieghem, *Ossian en France* (Paris, 1917), II, 3–13.

371:19–20. A passage some ten pages long; *Werke* (Weimar, 1899), XIX, 165–76.

371:37–372:21. La Villemarqué, *Les Bardes bretons* (1860), pp. 131–37 ("Chant de Llwarc'h-Henn sur sa vieillesse").

372:25–28. "On This Day I Complete My Thirty-Sixth Year," lines 9–12.

372:30–33. "Euthanasia," lines 33–36.

373:9–13. *Paradise Lost*, I, 105–9; one of the "touchstone" passages of Arnold's later essay on "The Study of Poetry."

373:29–34. "To a Friend, Inquiring If I Would Live Over My Youth Again" (1799), lines 1–4, 12–13; Southey wrote "again live o'er" and "Praise be to Him."

374:22. Wethersfield, Thaxted, and Shalford in Essex derive their names from Old English roots ("Wihthere's field," "the place where thatch is obtained" and "shallow ford").

374:23–24. Velindre is the name of several Welsh villages and hamlets; Caernarvon is in northwest Wales, opposite Anglesey, and Tintagel, the legendary birthplace of King Arthur, is in Cornwall.

374:26–32. "Math the Son of Mathonwy," *Mabinogion*, tr. Guest, pp. 73–74.

374:34–38. See Edwin Guest, *A History of English Rhythms* (London, 1838), I, 120: "[The Latinist got his rhime] in all probability from the Celtic races; . . . the earliest poems of the Irish have final rhime, and we know that the Welsh used it, at least as early as the sixth century."

375:2–9. "Kilhwch and Olwen," *ibid.*, pp. 97, 110.

375:11–23. "Peredur the Son of Evrawc," *ibid.*, p. 192 (slightly modified).

375:25–32. "Geraint the Son of Erbin," *ibid.*, pp. 245–46 (slightly modified).

375:35–37. "Peredur the Son of Evrawc," *ibid.*, p. 203—despite what Arnold implies, a passage from quite another tale. Arnold reads "they" for Guest's "he."

376:25–377:2. Allusions to Shakespeare, *Winter's Tale*, IV, iv, 118–20; Wordsworth, "The Solitary Reaper," lines 13–16; Keats, "To Autumn," and Senancour, *Obermann*, Letters XI, XCI. See "Maurice de Guérin," p. 13.

376:28–35. Heine, *Die romantische Schule*, Book II, part ii, middle.

377:21. Pope, *Iliad*, VIII, 687.

377:24–25. *Elegies*, I, xx, 21–22.

377:28. *Idyls*, XIII, 34.

377:34–36. "Ode on a Grecian Urn," lines 35–38; for "quiet" read "peaceful."

378:5. The poem beginning "Der Morgen kam; es scheuchten seine Tritte."

378:14. The verse dialogue beginning "Gott segne dich, junge Frau."

378:22–26. "Ode to a Nightingale," lines 46–47, 69–70.

379:1–7. *Eclogues* VII. 45; II. 47–48, 51–52.

379:9–33. *Midsummer Night's Dream*, II, i, 249–52; *Merchant of Venice*, V, i, 58–59; *MND*, II, i, 83–85; *MV*, V, i, 1–4, 6–7, 9–12.

381:26–27. See Matthew 4:8.

382:13–20. Tom Taylor, tr., *Ballads and Songs of Brittany* (London, 1865), pp. 111, 171, 33.

383:32. Bold Street, near the Central Station, contains some of the finest shops in the commercial city of Liverpool; there are still memories of the fine equipages of the rich tradesmen's wives driving here in the last century. See Genesis 1:4, etc.

383:33–34. There are ten Nashvilles (including the capital of Tennessee), fourteen Jacksonvilles, and four Milledgevilles (including the former capital of Georgia) in the United States.

384:6–10. The speech at Rochdale, November 23, 1864, some four months before his death.—Richard Cobden, *Speeches on Questions of Public Policy*, ed. John Bright and James E. Thorold Rogers (London, 1880), p. 491.

385:4. John O'Donovan, editor of the *Annals of the Four Masters*, died in 1861, the year before Eugene O'Curry's death.

385:13–16. O'Curry describes the collections in these libraries and mentions the problem of transcription, *Lectures,* pp. 26–27, 156–57, 174–75.

385:18–36. O'Curry, *Lectures,* p. 155. The fourth Earl of Ashburnham (1797–1878) was Swinburne's uncle. His Stowe Collection was purchased by the British Government in July, 1883, for £45,-000, and the Irish manuscripts were deposited in the Library of the Royal Irish Academy.

386:8–9. See p. 272:8–13. Robert Lowe, a Liberal politician, was especially disliked by Arnold for his wrongheadedness in matters of education and (later) of Ireland. He was Vice-President of the Committee of Council on Education, 1859–64, and Chancellor of the Exchequer, 1868–73.

386:9–10. The liberal *Daily Telegraph,* the first of the penny daily newspapers, was founded in 1855 and within a year had a sale of nearly 30,000 daily. Three years later it claimed a circulation greater than all the other morning papers put together. At some time after its incorporation of the morning *Chronicle* in 1860, it took to printing daily the boast, "Largest circulation in the world."—William, Viscount Camrose, *British Newspapers and Their Controllers* (London: Cassell, 1947), pp. 26–27.

387:25. Percy Ellen Frederick Smythe, eighth Viscount Strangford (1826–69), a distinguished philologist and ethnologist somewhat better known for his mastery of Near Eastern languages and Sanskrit but also competent in Celtic. He was a frequent contributor to the *Pall Mall Gazette* (as was Arnold) and to the *Saturday Review;* he reviewed Arnold's first article on *The Study of Celtic Literature* in the former on March 19, 1866, pp. 3–4.

389:15. Hugh Owen (later Sir Hugh; 1804–81) was an important figure in the promotion of education in Wales; he was the leader in the movement to establish the University College of Wales at Aberystwyth.

389:38. Thomas Stephens, *The Literature of the Kymry* (Llandovery, 1849). Arnold had consulted this volume in the preparation of his lectures but had not named it; a Welsh admirer, Edward Hamer, having called his attention to the omission, Arnold made this amends.

390:23–24. Horace *Epistles* II. i. 156.

391:14–392:8. On Thursday, September 6, 1866, the *Times* (p. 5, col. 6) announced the opening two days earlier of the National Eisteddfod at Chester under the presidency of Sir Watkin Williams Wynn, M.P., and quoted Arnold's letter to Hugh Owen from the *Pall Mall Gazette.* On Saturday, September 8 (p. 8, cols. 4–5) the third leading article used Arnold's letter as provocation to attack the institution of the Eisteddfod. On Friday, September 14 (p. 9, col. 3) appeared a letter in defense signed by "Talhaiarn," who as a modern Welsh bard had opened the ceremonials at Chester, and in the same issue the fourth leading article (p. 6, cols. 5–6) again assailed the Welsh language and culture. Arnold puts together phrases and sentences from both leading articles: the last three sentences of his first paragraph come from the article of September 14, the rest of that paragraph and the attack upon himself from the article of September 8.

391:19. Isaiah 1:16–17; see p. 166:3–6.

392:12. See p. 255.

393:30. Spencer Walpole was Home Secretary in the Derby cabinet from July 6, 1866, until his resignation on May 9, 1867.

394:38. Isaiah 51:20.

395:9. "Talhaiarn" is the Bardic name of the architect and poet John Jones (1810–69) of Llanfair Talhaiarn, Denbighshire. Arnold quotes the *Times* of September 14, 1866, p. 6, col. 6.

395:12, 16–17. Matthew 8:22, 13:29.

Textual Notes

[ESSAYS IN CRITICISM]

65.* Essays in Criticism. | By | Matthew Arnold, | Professor of Poetry in the University of Oxford. | London and Cambridge: | Macmillan and Co. | 1865.

65a. Essays in Criticism. | By | Matthew Arnold, | Professor of Poetry in the University of Oxford. | Boston: | Ticknor and Fields. | 1865.

An identical "Second Edition" and "Third Edition," 1866. These American editions have no textual authority and are not collated.

69. Essays in Criticism. | By | Matthew Arnold. | *Second Edition.* | London: | Macmillan and Co. | 1869. | [*The Right of Translation is reserved.*]

75. Essays in Criticism | By | Matthew Arnold | Formerly Professor of Poetry in the University of Oxford | and Fellow of Oriel College | Third Edition | *Revised and Enlarged* | London | Macmillan and Co | 1875 | [*All rights reserved*]

80. Passages from | the Prose Writings | of | Matthew Arnold | London | Smith, Elder, & Co., 15 Waterloo Place | 1880 | [*All rights reserved*]

Also issued with the imprint: New York | Macmillan and Co., | 1880

83e. Essays in Criticism | By | Matthew Arnold | New York | Macmillan and Co. | 1883

84. Essays in Criticism | By | Matthew Arnold | New Edition | London | Macmillan and Co. | 1884.

From the stereotyped plates of 83e; not collated. Subsequent editions from the same plates were issued with varying dates and imprints in both London and New York. After 1888 the words "First Series" were added to the title.

* For 65 read 1865, etc.

87. Essays in Criticism | By | Matthew Arnold. | *Copyright Edition.* | In two volumes. | Vol. I. [Vol. II.] | Leipzig | Bernhard Tauchnitz | 1887. | *The Right of Translation is reserved*
    This edition has no textual authority and is not collated.

P.2, Epigraph. 65, 65a *only, facing p. 1,* "*The Function of Criticism at the Present Time.*"

[DANTE AND BEATRICE]

Fras. Fraser's Magazine LXVII, 665–69 (May, 1863). Not reprinted by Arnold.

8:3. depth of sincerity of   *Fras.; corrected from Martin.*

[MAURICE DE GUÉRIN]

Fras. Fraser's Magazine LXVII, 47–61 (January, 1863).
Reprinted 65, 65a (not collated), 69, 75, 83e (=84), 87 (not collated).

The following passage appears in 80:   33:13–32 (pp. 32–33, headed "How Poetry Interprets").

14:30. *no* ¶   *Fras.,* 65, 69
14:36. does not use   *Fras.,* 65
15:1. production   *Fras.*
15:20. Addison: the   *Fras.,* 65
15:34. sense.   Brief notices of him the reader may have seen here and there in English or in foreign periodicals; but it is not likely that the two volumes of his remains will have met the eye of more than a very few of those who read this, or that they will ever be
25   widely circulated in this country. To all   *Fras.*
15:37. make my English   *Fras.,* 65, 69
17:33. or to any   *de luxe ed. (1903) and later reprints of* 83e
18:4. brother's *   [*footnote*] * The letters of Eugénie de Guérin, printed seven years ago for private circulation, have just been
30   made public.   *Fras.*
18:19. having then been   *Fras.,* 65
19:14. had its   *Fras.,* 65, 69, *French text;*   has its   75, 83e
19:20. by a wave, and sheltering under a white cloth.   *Fras.,* 65; *jeunes filles surprises par une ondée et se mettant à l'abri sous un tablier blanc.   French text*
20:20. standards.   *Fras.*

20:23. —Hippolyte la Morvonnais, *all; corrected by Ed.*
21:36. dates from *Fras.*
24:21. 7th *all; corrected from French text*
24:34. M. la Morvonnais, *all; corrected by Ed.*
28:1. his acquaintances of Brittany *Fras.*
29:23. to the East, *Fras., French text, erroneously*
29:25. Féli sets out *Fras.*
32:15–16. unheard of, is henceforth written in *Fras.*
33:12. an unique *Fras.*, 65, 69, 75
35:28. memorable in *Fras.*
35:38. 'Bacchante,' which is lost, and which was meant *Fras.*
36:11. with a few *Fras.*
36:12. *title not in Fras.*
37:38–38:1. How ... labour! *not in Fras.*
38:4. Wandering at my *Fras.*
38:8. slope *Fras.; le penchant des monts French text*

[THE BISHOP AND THE PHILOSOPHER]

*Macm.*⁷ *Macmillan's Magazine* VII, 241–56 (January, 1863).
Not reprinted entire by Arnold. Parts of the essay were incorporated into "Spinoza and the Bible," where they will be found in the present edition.

47:8. 487, 750, 756 *Macm.*⁷; *corrected from Colenso*
53:13. behold, it *Macm.*⁷; *corrected from Ecclesiasticus*

[TRACTATUS THEOLOGICO-POLITICUS]

Lond. London Review V, 565–67 (December 27, 1862). Anonymous. Not reprinted by Arnold.

[DR. STANLEY'S LECTURES ON THE JEWISH CHURCH]

Macm. Macmillan's Magazine VII, 327–36 (February, 1863).
Not reprinted by Arnold.

[EUGÉNIE DE GUÉRIN]

Cornh. The Cornhill Magazine VII, 784–800 (June, 1863).

Reprinted 65, 65a (not collated), 69, 75, 83e (=84), 87 (not collated).

The following passage appears in 80:   106:17–23 (p. 11, headed "Distinction").

83:5. pretty bows of   *Cornh.*, 65, 69;   *jolis noeuds de rubans. French text*

83:9. So she speaks   *Cornh.*

83:26. with less of   *Cornh.*, 65, 69

83:26–27. abundance, and facility   *Cornh.*, 65, 69

84:14. to accomplish for   *Cornh.*

84:19–20. And now M. Trébutien has done for   *Cornh.*

84:21. He has published   *Cornh.*

84:37–38. *not in Cornh.*

84:36–85:1. lose an occasion like the present, when Mdlle. de Guérin's journal is for the first   *Cornh.*

85:22. of a religious   *Cornh.*

85:38. one forehead."   *Cornh.;   du même front.   French text*

87:9. From these   *all; corrected from French text*

87:38. and repulse   *Cornh.*

88:6. revolts; somewhere   *Cornh.*, 65, 69

89:14. him; but   *Cornh.*, 65, 69

89:21. repose: the   *Cornh.;*   repose; the   65, 69

90:15. not to follow   *erroneously Cornh.;   On t'a fait un cas de conscience de suivre cet entraînement [of repression], et moi je t'en fais un de ne pas le suivre.   French text*

95:15. from its natural   *Cornh.*, 65, *de luxe ed. (1903) and later reprints of* 83e;   from his natural   69, 75, 83e

99:7. my whole soul   *Cornh.;   faire la revue de toute mon âme devant Dieu.   French text*

99:13. sense of brightness;   *mispr. all;   de nous laisser plus légers, French text*

100:34. place   *Cornh.*, 65, 69, *French text;*   placed   75, 83e

101:12. power upon one's   *Cornh.*

102:18. and its character   *Cornh.*, 65, 69

102:35. 1839; zealously   *Cornh.*, 65, 69

102:39. 4th of   *all; corrected from French text*

103:26. and that then   *Cornh.*, 65, *French text;*   die." Then she went   *Cornh.*, 65, 69

104:5. with me for him a frock   *Cornh.*, 65, 69

104:15. stablish my   *Cornh.*, 65, 69

104:34. wistfully in the   *Cornh.,* 65; wistfully into the   69;   *aux délices, French text*

105:32. into a cloister   *Cornh.,* 65, 69, *French text*

106:16. soul has the   *Cornh.,* 65

[HEINRICH HEINE]

Cornh. The Cornhill Magazine VIII, 233–49 (August, 1863).

Lit.   *Littell's Living Age* LXXIX, 51–62 (October 10, 1863). Reprinted from *Cornh.* Not collated.

Reprinted 65, 65a (not collated), 69, 75, 83e (=84), 87 (not collated).

The following passages appear in 80:   109:21–110:3 (pp. 3–4, headed "The Modern Spirit");   110:19–35 (pp. 38–39, headed "Goethe's Naturalism");   111:26–113:22 (pp. 4–7, headed "Philistinism");   120:32–122:15 (pp. 42–44, headed "Our 1800–1830");   132:17–38 (pp. 44–45, headed "Prodigality of Nature").

107:6–7, 17. the war of liberation of   *Cornh.,* 65, 69

107:19–20. is the critic's highest function;   *Cornh.*

110:20. thinking. He   80

110:22. him. When Goethe is told   80

111:22. With that terrible   *Cornh.,* 65, 69

112:19. to the light;   *Cornh.*

114:19–38. *not in Cornh.*

114:25. to the ministry of   65, 69

117:8. thenceforward,   *Cornh.*; henceforward,   65, 69, 75, 83e

117:32. and suffering, besides this, at short   *Cornh.,* 65, 69

117:35. all this suffering,   *Cornh.,* 65

117:38. *not in Cornh.*

119:14. group all its ideas.   *Cornh.*

119:38. this practical   *Cornh.,* 65

120:30. a critic in the *Cornhill Magazine* will   *Cornh.*

121:7. contemporaries; they   *Cornh.,* 65, 69

121:16. *no* ¶   *Cornh.,* 65, 69

121:34. greatest of them,   *Cornh.,* 65, 69, 80; gravest of them, 75, 83e

122:11. will be long remembered,   *Cornh.,* 65, 69

122:16. was greater than that   *Cornh.,* 65

122:38. infuriated examiner screamed   *Cornh.*

123:20. may fall out   *Cornh.*
126:2. give you a notion   *Cornh.*
128:20. Israel harm,   *Cornh.*, 65
130:20–131:3. *not in Cornh.*
130:20. he shows it us in a   65
131:7. wander to Germany   *Cornh.*
131:36. attacks upon his friends,   *Cornh.*
132:12–13. the war of liberation of   *Cornh.*, 65, 69
132:14. the European literature   *Cornh.*, 65
132:31. English nobleman,   *Cornh.*

[MARCUS AURELIUS]

Vict. The Victoria Magazine II, 1–19 (November, 1863).
  Reprinted 65, 65a (not collated), 69, 75, 83e (=84), 87 (not collated).
  The following passages appear in 80: 134:13–135:3 (pp. 292–94, headed "Morality and Religion"); 140:12–143:3 (pp. 297–302, headed "Marcus Aurelius"); 144:1–146:8 (pp. 294–97, headed "Christianity and the Antonines"); 156:23–157:17 (pp. 302–3, headed "Marcus Aurelius and Christianity").

133:5. ancients." The object   *Vict.*
133:16. than most of its   *Vict.*
133:17–18. of all that the Christian   *Vict.*, 65
134:13. Moral rules,   80
134:29. a living emotion,   *Vict.*, 65;   perfect. An   80
135:3. Zeus and Providence,"   *Vict.*
135:28. Jesus, asked whether   *Vict.*, 65, 69
137:4. his best known predecessor,   *Vict.*, 65, 69
138:19. it renders   *Vict.*, 65, 69
139:13–14. of his rendering are (I cannot but think) as conspicuous   *Vict.*; of his rendering are (I will venture,   65
139:16. work like Marcus Aurelius's,   *Vict.*, 65, 69
139:31. this Greek of   *Vict.*, 65
139:32. is not one of   *Vict.*, 65
139:38. without any charm of   *Vict.*, 65
140:7. be perfectly content   *Vict.*, 65
140:12–13. Marcus Aurelius is perhaps . . . beautiful character in   80
140:24. one or two other sovereigns   *Vict.*, 65, 69, 75, 80;   one or two sovereigns   83e

140:36. inhabit; Alfred   *Vict.*, 65;   inhabit: Alfred   69

141:13. long; we   *Vict.*, 65;   long: we   69

141:22–23. ¶Of the records of his outward life perhaps the most interesting is   80

141:29. the whole that history has   *Vict.*

141:38. March, 180.   *Vict.*, 65

142:10. Again, the vague   80

142:17. *no* ¶   *Vict.*, 65

142:28. sincerity, purity, justice, and   80

142:34. throughout the wide   80

142:35. empire; it   *Vict.*, 65;   empire: it   69

143:1. Britain, Spain, and   80;   bore witness,   *Vict.*, 65, 69

144:1. because they loved   *Vict.*, 65

144:1–2. The Christianity which the Antonines aimed   80

144:21–22. that of Christ can   *Vict.*, 65, 69

144:36 theism; for   *Vict.*;   theism: for   65;   theism;—for   69

144:37. statesman, the character of secret   *Vict.*, 65, 69

145:2. associations as the Code Napoleon.   *Vict.*;   associations as the State-system   65, 69

145:29. be; the   *Vict.*;   be;—the   65, 69

145:31. Palatine. Marcus   *Vict.*, 65, 69;   no grave moral   80

146:23. to evil; for such   *Vict.*;   to evil;—for such   65, 69

146:27. son; one   *Vict.*, 65, 69

146:30. Commodus; the   *Vict.*, 65;   Commodus: the   69

147:7. also; how   *Vict.*, 65

148:11. motives of self-interest, or   *Vict.*

148:30. acts thus   *all; corrected from Long*

149:1. offer of   *Vict.*

149:23. following seems to me to have no parallel in   *Vict.*

149:33. a feeling and deeper   *Vict.*

151:3. retreat   *all; corrected from Long*

154:23. all is it   *Vict.*, 65

155:20–156:19. *printed as footnote attached to* valid.* (156:23) *Vict.*, 65

155:20–21. *Perhaps there is one exception. He is fond   *Vict.*, 65

155:33. *advantage;* even to a sound   *Vict.*, 65;   *advantage.* Even to a sound   69

156:7. made all things   *all; corrected from Long*

156:17. sense it is most   *Vict.*, 65

156:20. [*no* ¶] In general the action he prescribes   *Vict.*, 65

156:23. Marcus Aurelius remains   80

156:24–25. of all scrupulous and difficult, yet pure and upward-striving souls, in those *Vict.*, 65

156:26. faith, that have no open vision; he *Vict.*, 65; faith, and yet have no open vision: he 69; faith, but have, nevertheless, no open vision. He 80

156:29. not on this account that such *Vict.*, 65

156:30. which gives to *Vict.*, 65

156:35. his spirit longed; *Vict.*

156:36. near him, he touched *Vict.*, 65

156:38. one knows must *Vict.*, 65

156:38–157:1. remained, even had they presented themselves to him, in a great *Vict.*, 65

157:2–3. how would they have ... measure would they have *Vict.*, 65

157:4. *Alogi* in ancient and modern times, *Vict.*, 65, 69

[SPINOZA AND THE BIBLE]

Macm.[9] "A Word More about Spinoza," *Macmillan's Magazine* IX, 136–42 (December, 1863).

   Reprinted as "Spinoza," 65, 65a (not collated); expanded with long passages from "The Bishop and the Philosopher" and entitled "Spinoza and the Bible," 69, 75, 83e (=84), 87 (not collated).

Macm.[7] "The Bishop and the Philosopher," *Macmillan's Magazine* VII, 241–56 (January, 1863).

   For 161:9–171:18, 179:17–182:15.

   The following passage appears in 80: 181:8–182:15 (pp. 305–7, headed "Spinoza").

Title. "A Word More about Spinoza" *Macm.*[9]; "Spinoza" 65

159:8. his works *Macm.*[9]

159:11–13. one of his works at last makes its appearance in English —his "Tractatus Theologico-Politicus," of which I spoke here some months ago, just before the English translation of it appeared. It is *Macm.*[9]

159:12. *Politicus,*—at last makes its 65

160:17. again return, *Macm.*[9]

160:23–24. Now I wish to observe—what it was irrelevant to my purpose to observe when I before spoke of the "Tractatus Theologico-Politicus"—that just on *Macm.*[9]

161:9–169:36. *not in Macm.⁹, 65; interpolated from Macm.⁷ in 69, 75, 83e*

161:9. of men had been   *Macm.⁷*

161:11. He had determined to go   *Macm.⁷*

161:17. impossible: for   *Macm.⁷*

161:25. he had   *Macm.⁷*

162:31. This, the testimony   *Macm.⁷*

164:27. *no* ¶   *Macm.⁷*

166:15. history, is sometimes   *Macm.⁷*

166:17. reasoning, is sometimes   *Macm.⁷*

168:5. seems venerable   *Macm.⁷*

169:36–170:5. By the … then? *not in Macm.⁹, 65; interpolated from Macm.⁷ in 69, 75, 83e; see 52:18–24*

169:36. But, by the   *Macm.⁷*

170:1. undeniably becomes interesting   *Macm.⁷*

170:2. are alleged contradictions in   *Macm.⁷, 69*

170:4. of Europe, informed of this, asks   *Macm.⁷, 69;*   is, as I have said,—*What   Macm.⁷*

170:5–11. What follows … Christianity? *not in Macm.⁹, 65, 69; interpolated from Macm.⁷ in 75, 83e; see 49:18–24*

170:11–13. Spinoza … brevity. *not in Macm.⁹, 65; see 52:24–31*

170:11–12. to this question.   69

170:13–171:18. *not in Macm.⁹, 65; interpolated from Macm.⁷ in 69, 75, 83e*

170:34–35. necessary. He, too, like the Bishop of Natal, touches on the family of Judah; but he devotes one page to this topic, and the Bishop of Natal devotes thirteen. To the sums in Ezra—with which the Bishop of Natal, "should God, in His providence, call him to continue the work," will assuredly fill folios—Spinoza devotes barely a page. He is anxious to escape from the region of these verbal matters, which to the Bishop of Natal are a sort of intellectual land of Beulah, into a higher region; he apologises for lingering over them so long: *Macm.⁷*

171:20. ability; but   *Macm.⁹, 65, 69*

171:21. he does not give us his own   *Macm.⁹, 65, 69*

172:9. the Voice which   *Macm.⁹, 65;*   the voice which   69

172:10. a *vera vox.*   *Macm.⁹, 65, 69, 75*

172:14. the voice to have been   *Macm.⁹, 65, 69*

173:20–21. thus voluntarily becomes   *Macm.⁹, 65*

173:34. an ordinary   *Macm.⁹*

174:16–18. rejection cast priesthood of   *mispr.* 75;   rejection cast upon the priesthood of   *wrongly emended* 83e

174:29. this base and supports are,   *Macm.*[9]

175:16. power, I wish, before concluding these remarks, to say **a** few words.   *Macm.*[9]

175:38. to me fanciful.   *Macm.*[9]

177:21. *maintain man's being.... Happiness*   *Macm.*[9], 65

178:1. *no* ¶   *Macm.*[9], 65

178:4–5. same thing as the   *Macm.*[9]

178:8. laws of nature,   *Macm.*[9], 65

178:12–13. two states there   *Macm.*[9]

178:15. comprehension, a demonstration of Euclid.   *Macm.*[9], 65

178:24. *Macm.*[9], 65 *insert here* "It is true . . . had them,   (182:20–36 *and textual note*)

178:24. ¶ One of these admirers,   *Macm.*[9], 65

178:35. his reader   *Macm.*[9], 65

179:2. himself injustice   *Macm.*[9], 65

179:17–182:15. *not in Macm.*[9], 65; *interpolated from Macm.*[7] *in* 69, 75, 83e

179:17–18. ¶ Unction Spinoza's work has not;   *Macm.*[7]

179:19. which it exhibits. But he is instructive and suggestive even to the most instructed thinker; and to give him full right of citizenship in the Republic of Letters this is enough. And yet, so *Macm.*[7]

179:24. he can never write   *Macm.*[7]

179:25–26. because, with all his wit and clear sense, he handles religious ideas wholly without   *Macm.*[7], 69

179:28. Strauss treated   *Macm.*[7];   Dr. Strauss has treated   69

179:30. he treated it wholly   *Macm.*[7];   he treats it wholly   69

179:33. for mere mockery . . . for mere demolition.   *Macm.*[7]

180:20. [*no* ¶] And his life   *Macm.*[7]

180:28. them: the same   *Macm.*[7]

181:9. Spinoza still shines, while the light   80

182:16. [*no* ¶] Nay, when M. Van Vloten   *Macm.*[9], 65

182:20–36. "It is true . . . had them, he horrifies a certain school of his admirers by talking of "God" where they talk of "forces," and by talking of "the love of God" where they talk of "a rational curiosity." *follows* indestructible interest (178:24) *in Macm.*[9], 65

182:34. mansions, are needed   *Macm.*[9], 65

182:36. His own language   *Macm.*[9], 65

[JOUBERT]

Nat. The National Review XVIII, 168–90 (January, 1864). Anonymous.

Lit. Littell's Living Age LXXX, 462–75 (March 5, 1864). Anonymous. Reprinted from *Nat.* Not collated.

Reprinted 65, 65a (not collated), 69, 75, 83e (=84), 87 (not collated).

The following passages appear in 80: 189:21–190:13 (pp. 60–61, headed "Coleridge"); 209:3–211:18 (pp. 61–65, headed "Joubert and Jeffrey").

In Nat., which is unsigned, all first-person pronouns are plural (except in quotations).

Title: "Joubert; or, a French Coleridge." *Nat.*
183:22. genuine organ for *Nat.*
185:20. seems to us a *Nat.*, 65, 69
186:8. system had long *Nat.*
186:31. Constant; neither *Nat.*, 65, 69
186:34. *no* ¶ *Nat.*, 65, 69
187:1. sufferings, *Nat.*, 65
187:7. in such need. *Nat.*
187:10. works; but *Nat.*, 65, 69
187:25. *no* ¶ *Nat.*, 65, 69
187:29-30. mind, he was religious; he was a religious philosopher. *Nat.*, 65, 69; mind, he was a religious philosopher. 75, 83e
187:36. which we have *Nat.*, 65
187:38. alas, I have *mispr.* 69
188:38. Gilman's *all; corrected by Ed.*
189:14. an organ for finding *Nat.*
189:16. seeking it is *Nat.*, 65
189:17. the organ for finding *Nat.*
190:4. great action lay *Nat.*, 65, 69
190:6-8. minds, in the generation which grew up round him, capable of profiting by it; his action *Nat.;* minds, in ... by it. His action 65, 69
190:9. continues; when *Nat.*, 65, 69
190:21. *saugrenus;* it *Nat.*, 65, 69
191:9. that the English *Nat.*, 65
191:17. only let us consider *Nat.*

192:3. and the English are   *Nat.*

192:4. if they knew   *Nat.*

192:18. remarkable organ for   *Nat.*

192:19. of that organ,   *Nat.*

193:17. with much the same want of deference   *Nat.*

194:26. is best,   *Nat.*

195:18. We know not whether   *Nat.*

196:36. is "to consider ... consider" as   *Nat.*, 65, 69

197:13. by setting ideals,   *Nat.*, 65, 69

197:20–21. Let ... does.   *not in Nat.*, 65, 69

197:26. Mahomet or Luther,   *Nat.*, *French text;* Mahomet and Luther,   65, 69, 75, 83e

197:31. the devotion and government   *mispr. Nat.*

199:7. Who has ever   *Nat.*

200:36. done the whole mischief.   *Nat.*, 65

201:31. We begin with   *Nat.*

204:27. of the ancients,   *Nat.*, *French text;* of his ancients,   65, 69, 75, 83e

206:33. his affinity   *Nat.*

207:13. word *dominium.*   *Nat.*, 65, *French text.*

207:14. of an ancient,   *Nat.*

208:31. case of Joubert's English parallel, it   *Nat.*

209:11. at bottom   *Nat.*, 80

209:18. Why then, we repeat,   *Nat.*

210:11. no organ for   *Nat.*, 65

210:12–13. intelligent out-post of   *Nat.*, 65

210:18. have somewhere said,   80

210:32–33. make him safe?   *Nat.*, 65, 69

211:7. from generation to generation in   *Nat.*

211:9. upon a thousand   80

211:10. Philistines'   *Nat.*, 65

211:12. mark of Bel and Dagon upon   *Nat.*

[PAGAN AND MEDIAEVAL RELIGIOUS SENTIMENT]

Cornh. The Cornhill Magazine IX, 422–35 (April, 1864).
  Reprinted 65, 65a (not collated), 69, 75, 83e (=84), 87 (not collated).
  The following passages appear in 80: 212:19–214:11 (pp.

181–84, headed "Catholicism"); 226:17–35 (p. 173, headed "Renascence and Reformation").

Title: "Pagan and Christian Religious Sentiment." *Cornh.*
212:19–21. In spite of all the shocks which the feelings of a good Catholic have in this 80
213:7. represented; indeed, Mr. Panizzi knows *Cornh.;* represented, indeed; Mr. Panizzi knows 65
213:8. otherwise. All 80
213:9. there. There 80
213:35. not, I think, the *Cornh.,* 65
215:33. the noble of pagan *Cornh.,* 65
216:6. are not for *Cornh.,* 65
218:1. as you've got *Cornh.,* 65, 69
218:10. like. I'm *Cornh.*
220:35. Syrian spikenard; *Cornh.;* Syrian unguent; 65
221:14. the waves plash *Cornh.*
223:7. sense of tightness, of oppression, *Cornh.,* 65
223:29. popular interest of *Cornh.*
224:4. Minorites. He found *Cornh.,* 65
224:18. Adonis; *Canticle Cornh.,* 65, 69
225:16–17. senses. It is *Cornh.,* 65
225:18. misery. When *Cornh.,* 65
225:32–33. of supernatural love *Cornh.*
225:35. words are an *Cornh.,* 65
226:5–6. find him doubting "whether *Cornh.,* 65
226:17. in great part, 80
226:24–28. Voltaire. The real Reformation, Luther's Reformation, the German Reformation, was a *Cornh.*
226:29. sense. It 80
226:33. representative. The grand *Cornh.,* 65; representative. And the grand reaction, once more, against 80
226:37. already spoken here; *Cornh.*
227:13. all round us, *Cornh.*
228:18. in the most *Cornh.,* 65, 69, *German text;* in most 75, 83e
228:32. year 1840, *mispr.* 65; 1480 *German text*
229:18. and from under *Cornh.,* 65, *German text;* and then from under 69, 75, 83e
229:19. upon one in *mispr. Cornh.*
230:13–14. of mediæval Christianity— *Cornh.*
230:25. value; an epoch which alone goes *Cornh.,* 65, 69

230:34. year 530 B.C. to about the year 430,— *Cornh.*, 65, 69
231:12. affords to the poet *Cornh.*, 65, 69
231:17–19. dispute. But no other *Cornh.*, 65
231:31. Let Theocritus or St. Francis beat *Cornh.*, 65

[THE LITERARY INFLUENCE OF ACADEMIES]

Cornh. The *Cornhill Magazine* X, 154–72 (August, 1864).
Lit.   *Littell's Living Age* LXXXII, 560–72 (September 17, 1864).
Reprinted from *Cornh.* Not collated.
Reprinted 65, 65a (not collated), 69, 75, 83e (=84), 87 (not collated).

The following passages appear in 80: 236:16–237:4 (pp. 10–11, headed "Literary Conscience"); 241:35–242:24 (pp. 14–15, headed "The Journeyman-work of Literature"); 244:22–245:15 (pp. 15–16, headed "The Note of Provinciality"); 257:4–28 (pp. 16–17, headed "An English Academy").

232:5. of that absence, *Cornh.*
235:16. same advantages *Cornh.*, 65
236:11. Now, certainly, *Cornh.*
236:31. sphere. The 80
237:28. *no* ¶ *Cornh.*
239:7. a wide scale, *Cornh.*
239:20–21. No doubt his verse suffers from the same defects
    Cornh., 65, 69
239:22–23. with real success in it; but *Cornh.*, 65, 69
240:2. and the great *Cornh.*
240:27. master; the *Cornh.*, 65, 69
242:37–38. *not in Cornh.*, 65
243:35–38. *not in Cornh.*
244:24–25. in this country,—*urbanity;* 80
245:7. can be fairly said to 80
247:27–39. *not in Cornh.*
247:28–29. possible. I detest paradox, and I agree 65
248:10. Marmontel; therefore, *Cornh.*, 65, 69
255:3–5. Again, the most successful English book of last season was certainly Mr. Kinglake's *Invasion of the Crimea.* Its style *Cornh.*, 65
255:6. about it, *Cornh.*, 65
255:11–12. would Mr. Kinglake stand! *Cornh.*, 65

255:22. triumph. "His features put on that glow which, seen in
men of his race—race known by the kindling gray eye, and the
light, stubborn, crisping hair—discloses the rapture of instant
fight." How glittering that is, but how perfectly frosty! "There
was a salient point of difference between the boulevards and the 5
hill-sides of the Alma. The Russians were armed." How trenchant
that is, but how perfectly unscrupulous! This is the Corinthian
style; the glitter of the East with the hardness of the West; "the
passion for tinsel,"—some one, himself a Corinthian, said of Mr.
Kinglake's style,—"of a sensuous Jew, with the savage spleen of 10
a dyspeptic Englishman." I do not say this of Mr. Kinglake's style
—I am very far from saying it. To say it is to fall into just that
cold, brassy, [that hard, brassy, 65] over-stretched style which
Mr. Kinglake himself employs so far too much, and which I,
for my part, reprobate. But when a brother Corinthian of Mr. 15
Kinglake's says it, I feel what he means.
 A style so *Cornh.*, 65
255:29. by them, but should try closely this, the form of his work.
The matter of the work is a separate thing; and, indeed, this has
been, I believe, withdrawn from discussion, Mr. Kinglake de- 20
claring that this must and shall stay as it is, and that he is
resolved, like Pontius Pilate, to stand by what he has written.
And here, I must say, he seems to me to be quite right. On the
breast of that huge [the huge 65, 69] Mississippi of falsehood
called *history*, a foam-bell more or less is of no consequence. 25
But he may, at any rate, ease and soften his style. *Cornh.*, 65,
69
255:31. with writers like *Cornh.*, 65
255:36–38. *not in Cornh.*
256:7–8. Thiers so admires, *Cornh.*, 65
257:4. Nations have 80
257:8. produced Swift and Burke, 80

[THE FUNCTION OF CRITICISM
AT THE PRESENT TIME]

Nat. The National Review I (n.s.), 230–51 (November, 1864).
Reprinted 65, 65a (not collated), 69, 75, 83e (=84), 87 (not
collated).
 The following passages appear in 80: 261:2–18 (p. 19, headed
"Creative Epochs"); 262:34–263:29 (pp. 40–42, headed "Goethe's

Foundation"); 264:37–265:17 (pp. 130–31, headed "French Revolution"); 266:22–268:3 (pp. 58–60, headed "Burke"); 268:19–
269:3 (pp. 11–12, headed "Curiosity"); 275:15–24 (pp. 81–82,
headed "British Constitution"); 279:20–280:13 (pp. 222–23,
headed "Religious Reconstruction"); 284:16–29 (p. 4, headed
"Range of Modern Criticism").

Title: "The Functions of Criticism at the Present Time." *Nat.*
258:4. I said that "of   *Nat.*
258:6. had been   *Nat.*
258:11. was just   *Nat.*
258:17–18. led by an excellent notice of Wordsworth published
   in the *North British Review,* to turn   *Nat.,* 65, 69; by a Mr.
   Shairp's   75, 83e; *corrected by Ed.*
258:21–30. *not in Nat.*
258:25–26. notice (it is permitted, I hope, to mention his name)
   might,   65, 69
260:14. the true function   *Nat.,* 65, 69
260:15. by his finding   *Nat.*
260:20. men; they   *Nat.,* 65, 69
260:26. attempting it, and may with more   *Nat.*
260:34. time; at   *Nat.,* 65, 69
261:2. philosopher; the   *Nat.,* 65; philosopher: the   69
261:38. it would be   *Nat.*
262:2–3. both had   *Nat.*
262:19–20. Byron so one-toned,   *Nat.*
262:26. different; but   *Nat.,* 65, 69
262:31. no ¶   *Nat.*
263:3. alive; and   *Nat.,* 65, 69
263:10. work; this   *Nat.,* 65; work: this   69
264:2. activity: the   *Nat.,* 65, 69
264:3–12. character. This Revolution—the object of   *Nat.*
264:13. found, indeed, its   *Nat.*
264:16. time; this   *Nat.,* 65, 69
264:28. another's; the   *Nat.,* 65, 69
264:29. surpliced clergyman in the Tron Church at   *Nat.*
264:33. *the simplest way   Nat.,* 65
264:33. *counting,** [*footnote*] * A writer in the *Saturday Review,*
   who has offered me some counsels about style for which I am
   truly grateful, suggests that this should stand as follows:—*To*
40 *take as your unit an established base of notation, ten being given*

*as the base of notation, is, except for numbers under twenty, the
simplest way of counting.* I tried it so, but I assure him, without
jealousy, that the more I looked at his improved way of putting
the thing, the less I liked it. It seems to me that the maxim, in
this shape, would never make the tour of a world, where most 5
of us are plain easy-spoken people. He forgets that he is a rea-
soner, a member of a school, a disciple of the great Bentham, and
that he naturally talks in the scientific way of his school, with
exact accuracy, philosophic propriety; I am a mere solitary wanderer in search of the light, and I talk an artless, unstudied, every- 10
day, familiar language. But, after all, this is the language of the
mass of the world.

The mass of Frenchmen who felt the force of that prescription
of the reason which my reviewer, in his purified language, states
thus:—*to count by tens has the advantage of taking as your unit* 15
the base of an established system of notation, certainly rendered
this, for themselves, in some such loose language as mine. My
point is that they felt the force of a prescription of the reason
so strongly that they legislated in accordance with it. They may
have been wrong in so doing; they may have foolishly omitted to 20
take other prescriptions of reason into account;—the non-English
world does not seem to think so, but let that pass;—what I say
is, that by legislating as they did they showed a keen susceptibility
to purely rational, intellectual considerations. On the other hand,
does my reviewer say that we keep our monetary system un- 25
changed because our nation has grasped the intellectual proposition which he puts, in his masterly way, thus: *to count by twelves*
has the advantage of taking as your unit a number in itself far
more convenient than ten for that purpose?" Surely not; but
because our system is there, and we are too practical a people to 30
trouble ourselves about its intellectual aspect.

To take a second case. The French Revolutionists abolished
the sale of offices, because they thought (my reviewer will kindly
allow me to put the thing in my imperfect, popular language)
the sale of offices a gross anomaly. We still sell commissions in 35
the army. I have no doubt my reviewer, with his scientific powers,
can easily invent some beautiful formula to make us appear to be
doing this on the purest philosophical principles; the principles
of Hobbes, Locke, Bentham, Mr. Mill, Mr. Bain, and himself, their
worthy disciple. But surely the plain unscientific account of the 40
matter is, that we have the anomalous practice (he will allow it

is, in itself, an anomalous practice?) established, and that (in the words of senatorial wisdom already quoted) "for a thing to be an anomaly we consider to be no objection to it whatever."   65

265:27–28. suppressing one and   *Nat.*

266:8. world, will depend   *Nat.*, 65, 69

266:23–24. superannuated and proved wrong by   80

266:28. fault; but   *Nat.*, 65, 69

266:30–31. truth; they   *Nat.*, 65, 69

266:37. thought; it   *Nat.*, 65, 69

267:4–5. were displeased with   *Nat.*

267:16. in 1791,—   *Nat.*

267:35. talks this like   *Nat.*

268:32. quality; it   *Nat.*, 65, 69

269:1. of check and suppression   *Nat.*

269:36. what rules for   *Nat.*

269:38–270:1. The rules may be given in one word; by being *dis-interested*. And how is it to be disinterested?   *Nat.*

270:2–3. aloof from practice; by resolutely   *Nat.*, 65, 69

270:5. touches; by   *Nat.*, 65, 69

270:22. stifle it; it   *Nat.*, 65, 69

270:23. own; our   *Nat.*, 65, 69

270:31. not; but   *Nat.*, 65, 69

271:9. its chain; we   *Nat.;*   the chain; we   65, 69

271:10–11. *Review;* perhaps   *Nat.*, 65, 69

271:13. it; the   *Nat.*, 65;   it: the   69

271:14. business of Roman Catholicism,   *Nat.*

271:26. its true spiritual   *Nat.*

271:37. Mr. Adderley says   *Nat.*, 65, 69

272:22. labour and effort.   *Nat.*

272:23. [*no* ¶] But neither Mr. Adderley … are by   *Nat.*, 65, 69; Sir Charles Adderley … are by   75

273:9–10. perfectly unintelligent,   *Nat.*

273:14. soon after   *Nat.*, 65, 69

273:21. *no* ¶   *Nat.*, 65, 69, 75

273:22. Mr. Adderley   *Nat.*, 65, 69

273:28. the most delicate   *Nat.*

273:38–274:1. it?" It may be so, one is inclined   *Nat.*

274:2. is very much   *all; corrected by Ed.*

275:11. side more than deserves,   *Nat.*, 65, 69

275:36. nowhere more than in   *Nat.*

276:8–9. other way than the way dear   *Nat.*

276:14. many; don't *Nat.,* 65, 69

276:16. along; if *Nat.,* 65; along: if 69

276:21-22. excitement of a little resistance, an occasional scandal to give *Nat.*

276:26. party of movement, *Nat.,* 65, 69

276:33-38, 277:31-35. *not in Nat.*

276:35. criticised the Bishop of Natal's book; 65

276:37-38. them. The Bishop of Natal's subsequent volumes are in great measure free from the crying fault of his first; he has at length succeeded in more clearly separating, in his own   10 thoughts, the idea of science from the idea of religion; his mind appears to be opening as he goes along, and he may perhaps end by becoming a useful biblical critic, though never, I think, of the first order.

Still, in here taking leave of him at the moment when he is   15 publishing, for popular use, a cheap edition of his work, I cannot forbear 65

277:5. things; the *Nat.,* 65, 69

277:6. confound them, *Nat.*

277:7. while it imagines itself *Nat.*

277:22-23. perhaps the most, because *Nat.*

277:25. a fellow liberal *Nat.*

277:29. the 800 and odd *mispr. Nat.*

277:30. *no* ¶ *Nat.,* 65

278:31-32. Perhaps we shall always have to acquiesce *Nat.*

279:1. perfect truth rejoin *Nat.*

279:6-7. *nemo unquam voluit mutationem consilii inconstantiam esse habendam. Nat.*

279:13-18. *data* is the very essence of *Nat.*

279:16-17. the old, adoptive, traditional, unspiritual point 65, 69

279:20. In the same 80

279:24. it; we *Nat.,* 65, 69

279:38. Morrison *all; corrected by Ed.*

280:22. high and noble ideal. *Nat.*

280:23. In criticism these *Nat.*

280:25. meets immense *Nat.*

281:5. which no doubt has *Nat.*

281:6. hideous; * [*footnote*] * A critic, already quoted, says that I have no right, on my own principles, to "object to practical measures on theoretical grounds," and that only "when a man has   40 got a theory which will fully explain all the duties of the legislator on the matter of marriage, will he have a right to abuse the Divorce Court." In short, he wants me to produce a plan for a new and improved Divorce Court, before I call the present one hideous. But God forbid that I should thus enter into competition with the Lord Chancellor! It is just this invasion of the practical sphere which is really against my principles; the taking a practical measure into the world of ideas, and seeing how it looks there, is, on the other hand, just what I am recommending. It is because we have not been conversant enough with ideas that our practice now falls so short; it is only by becoming more conversant with them that we shall make it better. Our present Divorce Court is not the result of any legislator's meditations on the subject of marriage; rich people had an anomalous privilege of getting divorced; privileges are odious, and we said everybody should have the same chance. There was no meditation about marriage here; that was just the mischief.

If my practical critic will but himself accompany me, for a little while, into the despised world of ideas;—if, renouncing any attempt to patch hastily up, with a noble disdain for transcendentalists, our present Divorce law, he will but allow his mind to dwell a little, first on the Catholic idea of marriage, which exhibits marriage as indissoluble, and then upon that Protestant idea of marriage, which exhibits it as a union terminable by mutual consent,—if he will meditate well on these, and afterwards on the thought of what married life, according to its idea, really is, of what family life really is, of what social life really is, and national life, and public morals,—he will find, after a while, I do assure him, the whole state of his spirit quite changed; the Divorce Court will then seem to him, if he looks at it, strangely hideous; and he will at the same time discover in himself, as the fruit of his inward discipline, lights and resources for making it better, of which now he does not dream.

He must make haste, though, for the condition of his "practical measure" is getting awkward; even the British Philistine begins to have qualms as he looks at his offspring; even his "thrice-battered God of Palestine" is beginning to roll its eyes convulsively. 65

281:6. makes separation impossible   *Nat.*
281:11. with its crowded benches,   *Nat.*, 65, 69
281:28. continued the Renaissance,   *Nat.*
282:3. life; we   *Nat.*, 65, 69

282:4. of seeing them in *Nat.*
282:24–28. astray. In general its course *Nat., 65*
282:25. adopt towards everything; 69
282:26–28. mind. Then comes the question ... which criticism should 69
282:36. streaming upon us *Nat.* .
282:38. existence; the English critic, therefore, *Nat., 65, 69*
283:3. reason likely to ... him. Judging *Nat.*
283:8. be his great ... himself, and it *Nat.;* be the critic's great ... himself; and it 65, 69
283:12. that he will *Nat., 65, 69*
283:20–21. consciousness of what one *Nat.*
283:22. wrong. But under *Nat.*
283:27–285:1. But ... beginning: *not in Nat.*
284:16. The criticism which, 80
284:22. their common outfit, 80
285:1–2. To have this sense, is as I said at the beginning, the great happiness *Nat.*
285:12. true men of *Nat.*
285:17–18. life of a literature; *Nat., 65, 69, 75*

[PREFACE TO *Essays in Criticism*]

Texts: 65, 65a (not collated), 69, 75, 83e (=84), 87 (not collated)
   The following passages appear in 80: 287:13–23 (p. 81, headed "The Young Lions"); 290:1–28 (pp. 74–75, headed "Oxford").

Title: Preface. 65; Preface (1865) 69, 75, 83e
286:2. have had 65
286:10. not to persist 65
286:18. ¶ I am very sensible that this way of thinking leaves me under great disadvantages in addressing a public composed from a people "the most logical," says the *Saturday Review*, "in the 30 whole world." But the truth is, I have never been able to hit it off happily with the logicians, and it would be mere affectation in me to give myself the airs of doing so. They imagine truth something to be proved, I something to be seen; they something to be manufactured, I as something to be found. I have a pro- 35 found respect for intuitions, and a very lukewarm respect for the elaborate machine-work of my friends the logicians. I have always thought that all which was worth much in this elaborate

machine-work of theirs came from an intuition, to which they
gave a grand name of their own. How did they come by this
intuition? Ah! if they could tell us that. But no; they set their
machine in motion, and build up a fine showy edifice, glittering
5   and unsubstantial like a pyramid of eggs; and then they say:
"Come and look at our pyramid." And what does one find it?
Of all that heap of eggs, the one poor little fresh egg, the original
intuition, has got hidden away far out of sight and forgotten.
And all the other eggs are addled.

10   So it is not to build rival pyramids against my logical enemies
that I write   65

286:21. has just published   65

287:9. vivacity: alas! vivacity is one of those faults which advancing
years will only too certainly cure; that, however, is no real ex-
15 cuse; we have all   65

287:13–15. used it; Mr. Wright, however, will allow me to observe
that he has taken an ample revenge. He has held me up before
the public as "condemned by my own umpire;" as "rebutted,"
and "with an extinguisher put upon me" by Mr. Tennyson's re-
20 markable pentameter,
        "When did a frog coarser croak upon our Helicon?"
(till I read Mr. Wright I had no notion, I protest, that this exquisite stroke of pleasantry was aimed at me); he has exhibited
me as "condemned by myself, refuted by myself," and, finally,
25 my hexameters having been rejected by all the world, "somewhat
crest-fallen." And he has himself made game of me, in this
forlorn condition, by parodying those unlucky hexameters. So
that now, I should think, he must be quite happy.

        Partly, no doubt, from being crest-fallen, but partly, too, from
30 sincere contrition for that fault of over-vivacity which I have
acknowledged, I will not raise a finger in self-defence against Mr.
Wright's blows. I will not even ask him,—what it almost irresistibly rises to my lips to ask him when I see he writes from
Mapperly,—if he can tell me what has become of that poor
35 girl, Wragg? She has been tried, I suppose: I know how merciful
a view judges and juries are apt to take of these cases, so I cannot
but hope she has got off. But what I should so like to ask is,
whether the impression the poor thing made was, in general,
satisfactory: did she come up to the right standard as a member
40 of "the best breed in the whole world?" were her life-experiences
an edifying testimony to "our unrivalled happiness?" did she find
Mr. Roebuck's speech a comfort to her in her prison? But I

must stop; or my kind monitor, the *Guardian*, whose own
gravity is so profound that the frivolous are sometimes apt to give
it a heavier name, will be putting a harsh construction upon my
innocent thirst for knowledge, and again taxing me with the
unpardonable crime of being amusing.   5
    Amusing—good heavens! we shall none of us be amusing much
longer. Mr. Wright would perhaps be more indulgent to my
vivacity if he considered this. It is but the last   65
287:13. Mr. Wright would perhaps   80
287:17. drab. Who that reads the *Examiner* does not know that   10
representative man, that Ajax of liberalism, one of our modern
leaders of thought, who signs himself "Presbyter Anglicanus?"
For my part, I have good cause to know him; terribly severe he
was with me two years ago, when he thought I had spoken with
levity of that favourite pontiff of the Philistines, the Bishop of   15
Natal. But his masterpiece was the other day. Mr. Disraeli, in the
course of his lively speech at Oxford, talked of "nebulous professors, who, if they could only succeed in obtaining a perpetual
study of their writings, would go far to realise that eternity of
punishment which they object to." Presbyter Anglicanus says   20
"it would be childish to affect ignorance" that this was aimed at
Mr. Maurice. If it was, who can doubt that Mr. Maurice himself,
full of culture and urbanity as he is, would be the first to pronounce it a very smart saying, and to laugh at it good-humour-
edly? But only listen to Mr. Maurice's champion:—   25
    "This passage must fill all sober-minded men with astonishment
and dismay; they will regard it as one of the most ominous signs
of the time. This contemptible joke, which betrays a spirit of
ribald profanity not easily surpassed, excited from the Bishop, the
clergy, and laity present, not an indignant rebuke, but 'continued   30
laughter.' Such was the assembly of Englishmen and Christians,
who could listen in uproarious merriment to a Parliamentary
leader while he asserted that the vilest iniquity would be well
compensated by a forced perusal of the writings of Frederick
Denison Maurice!"   35
    And, for fear this trumpet-blast should not be carried far
enough by the *Examiner*, its author, if I am not greatly mistaken,
blew it also, under a different name, in half a dozen of the daily
newspapers. As Wordsworth asks:—

            "........ the happiest mood   40
        Of that man's mind, what can it be? ..."

was he really born of human parents, or of Hyrcanian tigers?
if the former, surely to some of his remote ancestors, at any
rate,—in far distant ages, I mean, long before the birth of Puritanism,—some conception of a joke must, at one moment or other
of their lives, have been conveyed. But there is the coming east
wind! there is the tone of the future!—I hope it is grave enough
for even the *Guardian;*—the earnest, prosaic   65

287:23-24. gravity. No more vivacity then! my hexameters, and
dogmatism, and scoffs at the Divorce Court, will all have been
put down; I shall be quite crest-fallen. But does Mr. Wright
imagine that there will be any more place, in that world, for
his heroic blank verse Homer than for my paradoxes? If he does,
he deceives himself, and knows little of the Palatine Library of
the future. A plain edifice, like the British College of Health
enlarged: inside, a light, bleak room, with a few statues; Dagon
in the centre, with our English Caabah, or Palladium of enlightenment, the hare's stomach; around, a few leading friends of
humanity or fathers of British philosophy;—Goliath, the great
Bentham, Presbyter Anglicanus, our intellectual deliverer Mr.
James Clay, and . . . yes! with the embarrassed air of a late convert, the editor of the *Saturday Review.* Many a shrewd nip
has he in old days given to the Philistines, this editor; many a
bad half-hour has he made them pass; but in his old age he has
mended his courses, and declares that his heart has always been
in the right place, and that he is at bottom, however appearances
may have been against him, staunch for Goliath and "the most
logical nation in the whole world." Then, for the book-shelves.
There will be found on them a monograph by Mr. Lowe on the
literature of the ancient Scythians, to revenge them for the in-
iquitous neglect with which the Greeks treated them; there will
be Demosthenes, because he was like Mr. Spurgeon: but, else,
from all the lumber of antiquity they will be free. Everything
they contain will be modern, intelligible, improving; *Joyce's
Scientific Dialogues, Old Humphrey, Bentham's Deontology,
Little Dorrit, Mangnall's Questions, The Wide Wide World,
D'Iffanger's Speeches, Beecher's Sermons;*—a library, in short,
the fruit of a happy marriage between the profound philosophic
reflection of Mr. Clay, and the healthy natural taste of Inspector
Tanner. ¶ But I return   65

287:29. professional assault," *mispr.* 65
287:37-38. *not in* 65; still had the   69

288:6–7. than I do. These eminent men, however, belonging to a hierarchy of which Urania, the Goddess of Science herself, is the sole head, cannot well by any vivacity or unpopularity of theirs compromise themselves with their superiors; because with their Goddess they are not likely, until they are translated to the 5 stars, to come into contact. I, on the other hand, have my humble place in a hierarchy whose seat is on earth; and I serve under an illustrious Chancellor who translates Homer, and calls his Professor's leaning towards hexameters "a pestilent heresy." Nevertheless, that cannot keep me from admiring the performance of 10 my severe chief; I admire its freshness, its manliness, its simplicity; although, perhaps, if one looks for the charm of Homer, for his play of a divine light..... Professor Pepper must go on, I cannot.

My position is, therefore, one of great delicacy; but it is not 15 from any selfish motives that I prefer 65

288:26. to Benthamism. 65

288:31–32. that Müller perpetrated 65

288:35–36. our class,—which 65

289:5. transcendentalism, and my turn for the French, would 65 20

289:27–30. to London to buy shares, or to attend an Exeter Hall meeting, or to hear Mr. D'Iffanger speak, or to see Mr. Spurgeon, with his well-known reverence for every authentic *Thus saith the Lord*, turn his other cheek to the amiable Dean of Ripon,— was, perhaps, in real truth 65 25

289:30. was, perhaps, in 69

289:31. sacred 65, 69, 75; secret 83e

290:8. us near to 65

290:18. in those incomparable 65, 69

290:22. Oxford will forgive 80

[ON THE STUDY OF CELTIC LITERATURE]

Cornh. The *Cornhill Magazine* XIII, 282–96 (March, 1866) [pp. 291–313 in this edition]; XIII, 469–83 (April, 1866) [pp. 313–35]; XIII, 538–55 (May, 1866) [pp. 335–61]; XIV, 110–28 (July, 1866) [pp. 361–86].

Does not include the Introduction. The four articles are called "Part I," "Part II," etc., and are not further divided.

Ecl. The *Eclectic Magazine* III (n.s.), 728–39 (June, 1866);

IV (n.s.), 201–212, 274–87, 443–56 (August, September, October, 1866). Reprinted from *Cornh*. Not collated.

PMG   "The Eisteddfod," *Pall Mall Gazette*, September 5, 1866, p. 6. Copied in *The Times*, September 6, 1866, p. 5, col. 6. Prints much of Arnold's letter to Hugh Owen, pp. 389:23–390:27 in this edition.

67.*   On | *the Study* | of | Celtic Literature. | By | Matthew Arnold, | Professor of Poetry in the University of Oxford. | *London*: | *Smith, Elder and Co.,* *65, Cornhill.* | *1867.*

80.   Passages from | the Prose Writings | of | Matthew Arnold | London | Smith, Elder, & Co., 15 Waterloo Place | 1880 | [*All rights reserved*]
    Also issued with the imprint: New York | Macmillan and Co., | 1880

830.   On the Study | of | Celtic Literature | and on | Translating Homer | By | Matthew Arnold | New York | Macmillan and Co. | 1883

91.   The Study | of | Celtic Literature | By | Matthew Arnold | Popular Edition | London | Smith, Elder, & Co., 15 Waterloo Place | 1891 | [*All rights reserved*]
    This edition has no textual authority and is not collated.

The following passages appear in 80: 344:9–346:24 (pp. 27–30, headed "The Celtic Genius"); 348:11–38 (pp. 157–58, headed "Good of Philistinism"); 358:25–359:5 (pp. 52–53, headed "Blending of Temperaments"); 368:4–369:1 (pp. 48–49, headed "Hymns, English and German"); 369:21–370:3 (pp. 50–51, headed "Latin Hymns and the 'Imitation'"); 374:4–375:2 (pp. 31–32, headed "Natural Magic"); 380:32–381:32 (pp. 37–38, headed "Dante, Shakspeare, Goethe"); 382:21–383:3 (pp. 53–54, headed "Our English Mixture"); 384:4–30, 385:38–386:25 (pp. 75–77, headed "A Chair of Celtic at Oxford"); 392:31–393:23 (pp. 131–32, headed "England and the Celts"); 395:13–35 (pp. 158–59, headed "A Word to Ireland").

Title: "The Study of Celtic Literature." *Cornh*.
Motto: *not in Cornh*.
292:13. Ceirionydd *Cornh*., 67, 830; *corrected by Ed.*
293:18–42. *not in Cornh*.
295:21. was aroused *Cornh*.
297:8–9. principality; government, by hammering *Cornh*.

* For 67 read 1867, etc.

299:14–42, 300:29–37. *not in Cornh.*

302:1. *no* ¶ *Cornh.*

304:1. Denbighshire peasant, born *Cornh.*

304:2. of the last *Cornh.*

306:3. were not yet *Cornh.*

307:12. time of it between *Cornh.*

309:2,6,10. O Brithi, Brithoi! *Cornh.*

311:11. frequent allusion *Cornh.*, 67, 830; *corrected from Turner*

312:1. out of question *Cornh.*

312:16. That is all *Cornh.*

314:1. petty and mendicant *Cornh.*, 67, 830; *corrected from Davies*

314:3. these lines, *Cornh.*, 67, 830; *corrected from Davies*

315:35. when a mediæval *Cornh.*, 67

316:17. no older mystery, *Cornh.*, 67, 830; *corrected from Nash*

317:22. then comes *Cornh.;* crushing defeat *Cornh.*, 67; crashing defeat 830

319:36. in the world, *Cornh.*, 67, 830; *corrected from Guest*

320:30. historic poems *Cornh.*, 67, 830; *corrected from Nash*

323:1. his domains were *Cornh.*, 67, 830; *corrected from Guest*

324:7. went on to *Cornh.*, *Guest;* went to 67, 830

326:18. ¶ "I have *Cornh.*

327:18. was the chief *Cornh.*, *Nash;* was chief 67, 830

328:10. [*no* ¶] Philology, that science *Cornh.*

328:37–38. between a sound and an unsound critical habit. *Cornh.*

329:19. knew of this *Cornh.;* knew this 67, 830

331:1. "ey" for island, Alderney, *Cornh.;* "ey" for Alderney, 67, 830; *emended by Ed.*

331:35–38, 332:6–42, 333:26–31. *not in Cornh.*

333:10. the relations of *Cornh.*, 67

333:32–38, 334:36–38. *not in Cornh.*

334:5. of the ablest *Cornh.*

334:20. [*no* ¶] To...further: of *Cornh.*

335:13. literature—Mr. Nash and the Celt-haters *Cornh.*

335:30. question. But this question must be for another time. *Cornh.*

339:3. in 1839 *Cornh.*, 67, 830; *corrected by Ed.*

340:22. square head *Cornh.;* square heads *mispr.* 67, 830

342:36–37. *not in Cornh.*

343:2. of his *douce Cornh.*, 67; of the *douce* 830

343:32–39. *not in Cornh.*

344:10. description which a 80

344:11. of him. And 80

344:32–33. All which 80

344:37–38. *not in Cornh.;* M. Henri Martin. [*the rest omitted*]
80

345:8. and have hindered 80

345:31–32. sensual, or at least 80

348:11. in themselves, then, vital *Cornh.*

348:18–19. in Great ... and in the United 80

348:24. last, as we see, up 80

348:28. that it leads to 80

348:37. more of such 80

350:5. language lingered on, *Cornh.*

350:15. *no* ¶ *Cornh.*

350:17. It is said to have been Edward *Cornh.*

350:18–19. English came to be spoken at court. *Cornh.*

351:25–35, 352:35–39. *not in Cornh.*

352:20. few would dispute *Cornh.*

355:4–5. see the corner, as the French *Cornh.*

358:7. bathos. *Cornh.*, 67; pathos. *mispr.* 83o

358:25. Just what 80

358:28. temperament. Shakspeare's 80

360:7. him; the couplet *Cornh.*

361:16. have done. So much has had to be said by way of preparation, and of enabling ourselves to lay the finger, with some cer-
25   tainty, upon what is Celtic and what is not, that I have reached
my limits without accomplishing all I intended, and shall have to
return to the subject yet once more, in order at last to finish with
it. *Cornh.*

361:24. got all its *Cornh.*

362:15. Ein Charakter sich in dem *Cornh.*

364:9–10. cannot even show *Cornh.*

364:18. literature; power *Cornh.*

365:30–39, 366:34–37. *not in Cornh.*

366:23. Gleddyfreidd; *Cornh.*, 67, 83o; *corrected from* Guest

368:20. turn for style, of which *Cornh.*

368:38–369:1. when our poetical perception is 80

369:11. our own real *Cornh.*, 67; our real 83o

369:13. *no* ¶ *Cornh.*

369:21–24. noticing that in our Indo-European Christendom the
best productions of the pure religious sentiment have been works
like 80

369:26. voice of none of us. 80
370:11. brought in the Latin   *Cornh.*
370:28. here; make   *Cornh.*
370:38. echoing Sora,   *Cornh.*, 67, 830; *corrected from Macpherson*
371:8. round her head.   *Cornh.*, 67, 830; *corrected from Macpherson*
374:5. gave to his poetry   80
374:13. delicate natural magic   80
374:34–38. *not in Cornh.*
375:1. how deep nature lets   *Cornh.*
375:9. fountains."   *Cornh.*, 67, 830; *corrected from Guest*
376:27–41. *not in Cornh.*
378:9. magic are added;   *Cornh.*, 67
379:9. bank whereon the wild   *Cornh.*
380:32–33. The natural ... Wordsworth, Byron's vigour of style and Titanic ... to Goethe's poetry;   80
380:34–37. How much more than Byron with his style and personality, and Keats and Wordsworth with their natural magic! 80
381:5. these two lines from Goethe: 80
381:7. Ein Charakter sich in dem   *Cornh.*
381:26. a traditional text   80
382:21–22. It is not   80
382:28. and Latinised Normanism enough   80
384:28–29. activity, of poetry as well as of creed, those who follow the matter out will find that the Celt   80
384:29. saying to-day will think   *Cornh.*
385:19. Peel wished to buy ... Museum, in 1849;   *Cornh.*
385:35. as matter of   *Cornh.*, 67, 830; *corrected from O'Curry*
385:37. Ashburnham. ¶ It is clear that the system of professorships in our universities is at the present moment based on no intelligent principle, and does not by any means correspond with the requirements of knowledge. I do not say any one is to blame for this. Sometimes the actual state of things is due to the wants of   35
another age,—as, for instance, in the overwhelming preponderance of theological chairs; all the arts and sciences, it is well known, were formerly made to centre in theology. Sometimes it is due to mere haphazard, to the accident of a founder having appeared for one study, and no founder having appeared for an-   40
other. Clearly it was not deliberate design which provided Anglo-

Saxon with a chair at Oxford, while the Teutonic languages, as
a group, have none, and the Celtic languages have none. It is as
if we had a chair of Oscan, or of Æolic Greek, before we had
a chair of Greek or Latin. The whole system of our university
chairs evidently wants recasting, and adapting to the needs of
modern science.

I say, *of modern science;* and it is important to insist on these
words. Circumstances at Oxford and Cambridge give special
prominence to their function as finishing schools to carry young
men of the upper classes of society through a certain limited
course of study. But a university is something more and higher
than a great finishing school for young gentlemen, however distinguished. A university is a member of a European confraternity
for continually enlarging the domain of human knowledge and
pushing back in all directions its boundaries. The statutes of the
College of France, drawn up at the best moment of the Renaissance and informed with the true spirit of that generous time,
admirably fix, for a university professor or representative of the
higher studies of Europe, his aim and duty. The *Lecteur Royal*
is left with the amplest possible liberty; only one obligation is
imposed on him,—to promote and develope, to the highest possible pitch, the branch of knowledge with which he is charged.
In this spirit a university should organize its professorships; in
this spirit a professor should use his chair. So that if the Celtic
languages are an important object of science, it is no objection
to giving them a chair at Oxford or Cambridge, that young men
preparing for their degree have no call to study them. The relation of a university chair is with the higher studies of Europe,
and not with the young men preparing for their degree. If its
occupant has had but five young men at his lectures, or but one
young man, or no young man at all, he has done his duty if he
has served the higher studies of Europe; or, not to leave out
America, let us say, the higher studies of the world. If he has not
served these, he has not done his duty though he had at his lectures five hundred young men. But undoubtedly the most fruitful action of a university chair, even upon the young college
student, is produced not by bringing down the university chair
to his level, but by beckoning him up to its level. Only in this
way can that love for the things of the mind, which is the soul
of true culture, be generated,—by showing the things of the mind
in their reality and power. Where there is fire, people will come

to be warmed at it; and every notable spread of mental activity
has been due, not to the arrangement of an elaborate machinery
for schooling, but to the electric wind of a glowing, disinterested play of mind. "Evidences of Christianity," Coleridge used
to say, "I am weary of the word! make a man feel the want of   5
Christianity." "The young men's education," one may in like
manner cry, "I am sick of seeing it organized! make the young
men feel the want, the worth, the power of education." *Cornh.*

386:3–11. alarmed at it; at such a moment   80

386:9. happiness, and the bank-rate of discount at 10 per cent, and   10
the largest   *Cornh.*

389:23–26. *not in PMG*

389:27. A representation to the University of Oxford from the
Eisteddfod, urging the importance of establishing a Chair of
Celtic at Oxford, could not, I think, but have weight with the   15
university. Your gathering acquires   *PMG*

390:3. *no* ¶ *PMG*

390:7. that races disinherited   *PMG*

390:12. above all: far   *PMG*

390:21. make itself felt, prized, and   *PMG*

390:26. moment do for England   *PMG*

393:2. her, in our country the Englishman   80

393:7. When my lucubrations on   80

393:15. 'Times' in commenting on a Welsh Eisteddfod, and remembers   80

395:11. refuse even to   67, 830; *corrected from Times*

395:20–21. and that besides, if we look into the thing closely, we
English   80

395:31. application; work to remove   80

Index

A reference to a page of text should be taken to include the notes to that page.